The history and philosophy of social science

A landmark in its field, this book attains the most exacting scholarly standards whilst making the history of the social sciences enjoyable to read. Scott Gordon provides a magisterial review of the historical development of the social sciences. He examines the problems which confronted the great thinkers in their attempts to construct systematic theories of social phenomena. At the same time, he presents an authoritative survey of the major writers in the fields of economics, sociology and political science. Separate chapters are devoted to particular topics of special significance such as the nature of sociality, the idea of harmonious order, the conflict between progress and perfection, the methodology of history and the relation between biology and the social sciences. In the concluding chapter, the author examines the main lines of thought that have developed in the philosophy of science since the breakdown of logical empiricism, and he shows how the scientific investigation of social phenomena differs from the methodologies of the physical and biological sciences.

This bold new synthesis of the different traditions in the social sciences is at once a major contribution and a superb overview.

Scott Gordon is a Distinguished Professor at the Department of Economics and a Professor at the History and Philosophy of Science Department, Indiana University. He is also Professor of Economics at Queens University, Canada. He is the author of *Welfare, Justice and Freedom* (1980) and of numerous journal articles and has spent a lifetime researching questions in the history and methodology of the social sciences.

The history and philosophy of social science

Scott Gordon

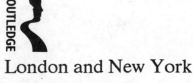

London and New York

First published 1991
by Routledge
11 New Fetter Lane, London EC4P 4EE

Simultaneously published in the USA and Canada
by Routledge
29 West 35th Street, New York, NY 10001

Reprinted 1993

New in paperback 1993

© 1991 H. S. Gordon

Typeset from the author's wordprocessing disks by
NWL Editorial Services, Langport, Somerset

Printed and bound in Great Britain
by Mackays of Chatham plc, Chatham, Kent

British Library Cataloguing in Publication Data
Gordon, Scott
The history and philosophy of social science.
  1. Social science, history
  I. Title
  300.9

Library of Congress Cataloging in Publication Data
Gordon, Scott.
    The history and philosophy of social science/Scott Gordon.
      p.   cm.
    Includes bibliographical references and index.
    ISBN 0–415–05682–9   0–415–09670–7 (pbk)
      1. Social sciences – History.   2. Social sciences – Philosophy.
    I. Title.
    H51.G67   1991   90–45920
    300 – dc20   CIP

ISBN 0–415–05682–9
      0–415–09670–7 (pbk)

Contents

Preface   viii

1 Sociality and social science   1
   A. The concept of 'society'
   B. Types of sociality
   C. Altriciality and enculturation

2 The rise of the Age of Science   16
   A. Leonardo, Vesalius, and Galileo
   B. The scientific attitude
   Appendix: *The sociology of science*

3 Social laws   33
   A. Nomological propositions
   B. Nomological levels
   C. Social and natural science: some preliminary remarks
   D. Positive and normative propositions

4 Political theory and political philosophy   57
   A. Plato, Aristotle, and Polybius
   B. The Venetian constitution
   C. Seventeenth-century England
   D. Montesquieu's interpretation of the English constitution

5 Physiocracy: the first economic model   88
   A. Eighteenth-century France and the Physiocratic school
   B. The Physiocratic model
   C. The significance of Physiocracy in the history of social science

6 The methodology of modelling   100
   A. Examples of models
   B. Some features of models

7 The Scottish Enlightenment of the eighteenth century   111
   A. Scottish moral philosophy

B. *David Hume*
C. *Adam Smith*

8   Progress and perfection   148
A. *The idea of progress*
B. *The idea of a perfect social order*

9   Classical political economy   168
A. *Value*
B. *Rent*
C. *Population*
D. *The model of economic development*
E. *International trade*
F. *Methodology*

10   The idea of harmonious order   211
A. *The metaphysics of harmony*
B. *The ideology of* laissez-faire

11   Utilitarianism   248
A. *Bentham and the Mills*
B. *Henry Sidgwick*
C. *Utilitarianism and economics*
Appendix: *Romanticism*

12   French positivism and the beginnings of sociology   271
A. *Henri Saint-Simon*
B. *Auguste Comte*
C. *The influence of positivism*
D. *French positivism and the philosophy of science*

13   The Marxian theory of society   305
A. *Karl Marx and Friedrich Engels*
B. *History*
C. *Sociology and social psychology*
D. *Economics*
E. *Philosophy*

14   The methodology of history   390
A. *Historical explanation and the natural science model*
B. *Metaphysical history*
C. *Historical explanation as art*
D. *Historical events and social laws*

15   The development of sociological theory   411
A. *Herbert Spencer*
B. *Emile Durkheim*
C. *Max Weber*

16 Biology, social science, and social policy   494
    A. Evolution
    B. The reduction of sociology to biology
    C. Biology and the social sciences

17 The development of economic theory   546
    A. The neoclassical theory of economic organization
    B. Neoclassical economics and the role of the state
    C. The distribution of income
    D. Keynesian macroeconomics

18 The foundations of science   589
    A. The philosophy of science
    B. The study of social phenomena

    Name index   669
    Subject index   680

Preface

Alfred North Whitehead once remarked that 'A science which hesitates to forget its founders is lost.' Daniel J. Boorstin tells us that 'An ample account of the rise of the social sciences would be nothing less than a survey of modern European history.' If I shared these views without reserve, this book would not have been written, for, according to Boorstin, it would be well beyond my capacities and, according to Whitehead, it would constitute academic malpractice.

But perhaps Whitehead may be interpreted as meaning to say that 'a science which *worships* its founders is lost'. With this I can wholly agree. A large part of the history of social science (and, for that matter, natural science as well) is a record of theories and inferences that we now believe to be wrong. To admire John Locke and Adam Smith, or Aristotle and Newton, for what they succeeded in doing in their time is warranted; to worship them uncritically as promulgators of eternal truths is not. This book has been written with the conviction that something of contemporary value can be gained from a study of the efforts of our forefathers to understand the nature of social life, even when they failed; and, indeed, we can learn more from their successes if we are aware of the weaknesses and limitations of theories that we regard, for the nonce, as true.

Daniel Boorstin's remark is more difficult for me to cope with, for this book does not even approach being 'a survey of modern European history'. Though I emphasize the strong orientation of social scientists to the economic, social, and political problems of their own times and places, I do not devote more space than is minimally necessary to considering the historical context of their work. Nor do I discuss the empirical work of social scientists, despite its prominence in the modern practice of these disciplines. My principal objective has been to maintain a strong focus on the flow of *theoretical ideas* in the history of social science, and to connect that history with issues in the philosophy of science. This book, long as it is, is only meant to be an introduction to a very large subject on which there are already many books and articles, and room for more.

Some readers who accept the pragmatic necessity of concentrating on theoretical ideas may nevertheless be surprised to find some things missing that they would consider important. For example, there is no extended discussion here of the ideas of Jean-Jacques Rousseau, or Vilfredo Pareto, or Thorstein Veblen, all of whom deserve study by the serious student. John Stuart Mill, unquestionably one of the most important social scientists and philosophers of the modern era, comes into the discussion here and there but is not given a chapter or section of his own. Some important topics are neglected as well, most conspicuously perhaps the history of socialism. In outlining this book I had originally planned to devote a chapter to a survey of the political, sociological, and economic theories of socialism, and the critiques of them, but have had to abandon this upon realization that it would necessarily constitute a sizeable book in itself. The constraints of space, and time, have forced me to be severely selective, since I believe it is more useful, as an introduction to the history and philosophy of social science, to discuss a limited number of thinkers and topics at some length than to devote a few pages each to a more comprehensive list. The selection has been guided by the aim of presenting the *history* and *philosophy* of social science as distinct, but none the less conjunctive, subjects which illuminate each other. As Immanuel Kant put it, according to Imre Lakatos's felicitous paraphrase: 'philosophy of science without history of science is empty; history of science without philosophy of science is blind'.

What is the point of doing this? Does it have any 'practical' value? Some philosophers of science take the stance that the object of their discipline is to delineate a methodology of investigation that guarantees the discovery of truth, and to prescribe that methodology as canonical imperatives which practising scientists are obligated to follow. If this were possible, our subject would indeed have great practical import; studying the philosophy of social science would be an important part of the training of a modern social scientist. But in fact courses in philosophy (or history) are not typically, or even frequently, part of the prescribed curriculum for graduate study in the social science disciplines. Nor are they prescribed for students in the natural sciences. Professors of research disciplines teach 'scientific method' and note the history of their subject, but they do so without much explicit reference to what philosophers, or historians, talk about. If historians and philosophers of science have something of value to contribute to the work of scientific research, they have not yet been able to convince practising scientists that this is so.

My object in writing this book is not to remedy this. Though I would not go so far as Whitehead does, I am not convinced that knowledge of the history of a science improves one's ability to practise it, and I am even more sceptical of the claim that current research would be facilitated if scientists were to pay close attention to the issues that are the philosophers' stock in trade. Study of the history and philosophy of science can be strongly recommended, but for a different reason: because of the contributions they can make to one's understanding of modern Western civilization. Science is one of the most distinctive, and perhaps the most significant, feature of our contemporary culture. This is so not only because of the substantive findings of scientists and their practical applications but, more importantly, because of the development of the 'scientific way of thinking', which has spread, though not without continuing resistance, beyond the domain of science into all aspects of our lives. This transition from older ways of thinking is very recent, even in the history of the West; in many other areas of the world it has hardly yet even begun. The role of the social sciences in this is no less important than developments in the natural sciences. In brief, my contention is that the study of the history and philosophy of social science stands on its own. It is not a handmaiden to science or a servant of public policy; it enables us to understand and appreciate, in a critical fashion, the intellectual development of our civilization.

During the course of writing this book I have benefited from discussions with colleagues too numerous to mention. But, for reading the whole manuscript, or parts of it, I would like especially to thank Mark Blaug, Patrick Brantlinger, Chung-Ching Chen, Paul Eisenberg, Bruce Fletcher, George von Furstenberg, Roy J. Gardner, Ronald N. Giere, William D. Grampp, D. Wade Hands, Herbert J. Kiesling, Bernard S. Morris, Joel Smith, Nicholas Spulber, Sheldon Stryker, George M. Wilson, and George W. Wilson.

H. S. Gordon
Bloomington, Indiana

Know then thyself, presume not God to scan;
The proper study of mankind is man.

Created half to rise and half to fall;
Great Lord of all things, yet a prey to all;
Sole judge of Truth, in endless Error hurled;
The glory, jest, and riddle of the world!

Alexander Pope, *Essay on Man*

Chapter 1

Sociality and social science

In the modern university the field of study is typically divided into various 'departments' such as Mathematics, Astronomy, Philosophy, Economics, Biology, English, History, and so on. In many universities one finds that some of these departments are grouped together as a 'division' or 'faculty' called 'Social Sciences' or 'Social and Behavioural Sciences'. If our world were very neat, and static, we would have little difficulty in determining what is 'social science', or its various branches; we would only have to examine the curricula and research programmes of the social science departments. But our world is not neat. If an extraterrestrial being were preparing a report on our scholarly and scientific activities, he might start by looking at our university organization, but he would very quickly run into difficulties. He would find, for example, that the study of crime is carried on, not only in the School of Law, but also in departments of Criminology or Forensic Studies, Sociology, Economics, Philosophy, Political Science, and Psychology, some of which are classified as social sciences and some not. He would find that in some universities History is classified as a social science and in others it is in another division, usually called 'Humanities'. If the visitor attempted to obtain some assistance from study of our languages, he would find that the word 'economics', in the classical Greek, meant 'the management of a household' but then he would note that the modern study of this is called 'Home Economics', which is not classified as a social science, while there is another subject, called 'Economics', which is, and there is also another division or school called 'Business' or 'Business Management', which resembles Home Economics in the original Greek meaning in its objectives, but is closer to Economics in the kinds of things studied and the methods employed. What this signifies is that dividing the field of scholarship and science into various departments or faculties or schools is largely a matter of convenience in organization rather than a reflection of intrinsic differences in subject matter. Astronomy *is* different from sociology, to be sure, but a great deal of our classifying is rather arbitrary and may be mainly due to the historical development of the various areas of study.

There is not much point in arguing over what is 'social science' and what is not. If we take the broad view that the social sciences study the social behaviour of the mammalian species *Homo sapiens*, we immediately discover that this is hardly confined to the social science departments of a modern university. Most of the professors in the literature departments are students of human behaviour and, outside the university, what are the novelists, playwrights and poets doing if not this? We could emphasize the word 'science' and say that social science is the study of human behaviour by *scientific methods*. This is a useful distinction. The poet does not go at the problem the same way as the sociologist does. But the distinction can be overdone, especially if the main object in making it is to infer that sociology is meaningful because it is scientific and poetry is meaningless because it is not.

Our object is to study the ways in which people have tried to develop a scientific approach to the investigation of human social behaviour. But we cannot begin by definitively stating what this means. As we shall see, the history of social science shows a great variety of approaches, and we shall have to note that there are many difficult philosophical problems here that are as yet unresolved. By the end of this book the reader should have a deeper appreciation of what the 'science' part of the term 'social science' involves but, even then, it will not be possible to arrive at a definitive statement. In the final chapter I shall survey the main issues that have emerged in the literature on the philosophy of social science and make an effort to identify the philosophical principles that appear to be broadly embraced by the modern practitioners of the social science disciplines.

A. THE CONCEPT OF 'SOCIETY'

Webster's New World Dictionary of the American Language (1978) defines 'social science' as 'the study of people living together in groups, as families, tribes, communities, etc.'. The focus of this definition is upon 'people', that is, humans, but we should note at the outset that 'living together in groups' is not an exclusive characteristic of the species *Homo sapiens*. Most animals, and indeed plants, live in 'groups' in some sense. Sumac bushes are not distributed randomly over the countryside; they clump together in particular locations. A botanist would say, though, that this is because different environments are not equally favourable for the growth of sumac and it is found concentrated in certain locations because the environment there provides a favourable 'niche' for that species. Similarly, if you turn on the porch light on a summer evening, moths will gather around it. This is because some species of moths, as individuals, are 'phototaxic' in their behaviour and will locate themselves close to the limited number of light sources that exist when the sun is not shining. We might find it useful to say that a clump of sumac bushes, or a group of moths around a light, are 'aggregations' but they do not constitute 'societies'.

The words used to make this distinction are somewhat arbitrary but the distinction itself is important, whatever words we use for it. The concept of a 'society' involves the notion that the members of it are interacting with one another. So far as I know, moths are not interacting with one another when they gather around the light; they aggregate because each individual is responding independently to a common external factor. The notion of interaction is, however, only a necessary feature of the concept of society; it is not sufficient, by itself, to indicate what we have in mind when we use the concept. For example, lions interact with gazelles and bees interact with flowering plants, but we do not consider such relationships as *social*. Biologists use the term 'ecological system' to refer to the interactions among different species. The concept of 'society' usually refers to interactions among the members of a single species. We could go a bit further and say that in a society the members of a species *co-operate with one another to achieve objectives collectively that they could not achieve as individuals*.

The traditional social sciences focus their attention upon the behaviour of the species *Homo sapiens*, examining how people interact with one another and how they organize themselves for co-operative activities. But such a statement, if we left it at that, would be seriously deficient because some of the interactions among people are characterized by *conflict* rather than co-operation, and some of the things that people do weaken or damage the system of social organization and work against the achievement of collective objectives. Moreover, the system of social organization may itself be deficient in certain respects that make it difficult, or even impossible, for people to co-operate effectively. So we have to amplify our statement about what the social sciences do in order to take note of the fact that they devote a great deal of attention to *dysfunctional* behaviour, such as crime and war, and *malfunctional* phenomena, such as unemployment and pollution.

Some social scientists (including the writer) would say that the main object of social science is the study of such dysfunctions and malfunctions, just as the medical scientist is mainly concerned with disease. But disease cannot be studied without understanding what constitutes good health. The counterpart of this in social science is that it is necessary to employ some notion of the criteria of a healthy system of social organization. This means that the social sciences are closely connected with that branch of philosophy called 'ethics' – the study of what should be regarded as 'good' and 'bad' in the moral sense of these terms. As we shall see, a great deal of the history of social science has been concerned with ethical issues. We cannot disregard such matters but the discussion of the philosophy of social science in this book will focus mainly on the branch of philosophy called 'philosophy of science' or 'epistemology' – the study of how we are able to know whether our notions or theories about empirical phenomena are 'true' or 'false'.

Humans are not the only animals that form societies, as I am here using that term. As soon as one moves above the level of the single-celled organisms, like the amoeba, some degree of socialness or 'sociality' is evident, since, in most species, reproduction is possible only if two organisms interact co-operatively so as to combine their genetic material. (In fact, biologists have discovered that even single-celled organisms that multiply by division occasionally exchange genetic material in a process that resembles sexual reproduction.) Above this bare minimum we find many species that form family groups in which the two parents continue their co-operation in the rearing of their progeny. Further up the scale we find many species that form larger groups which co-operate in food-gathering, provision of shelter, and defence. And so on, up the scale of sociality to its most elaborate forms in the social insects (ants, termites, bees, etc.), and man.

It seems rather arbitrary to compartmentalize the study of social behaviour, with man in one department and all other animals in another, since sociality is a phenomenon that runs across species differences. Some biologists argue that economics, sociology, political science, and the other social sciences would be more productive if they were reorganized as branches of biology. Throughout this book the reader will find many references to biological factors and biological theories in our study of the history and philosophy of social science. An important feature of modern social science is that it views man as an animal species, different from other animals in important ways to be sure, but not separated from them in the categorical fashion that is implied in theology and was universally believed by thinkers prior to the modern era and the development of empirical science.

B. TYPES OF SOCIALITY

We could try to make a classification of sociality by arranging the various animal species on a scale that would indicate the degree to which their members interact. This might be worth doing, but it would be very difficult because we do not have any satisfactory way of measuring the 'degree of interaction'. One of the persistent problems in science is that often we can make quantitative distinctions conceptually but cannot measure them. Even if we could measure sociality, and locate the species *Homo sapiens* on a general scale, it would not tell us a great deal about human behaviour. More useful, I think, is to recognize that there are different *types* of sociality, which we can distinguish as empirical phenomena even though it is impossible to make specific quantitative measurements of these characteristics.

For our purposes it is useful to distinguish five types of sociality, which are based upon (1) the apparent preference of members of some species for physical closeness: 'gregariousness'; (2) the practice of establishing 'hierarchy'; (3) the existence of 'biological differentiation'; (4) the practice of 'functional specialization'; and (5) 'altruism'.

1. Gregariousness

If a farmer puts ten sheep into a field, they do not distribute themselves evenly or randomly over the area. During the day they crop most parts of the field but they move around it together as a group. A flock of sheep seems to be a social entity of some kind, not merely an 'aggregation'. Without being a sheep it is difficult to say what the object of this behaviour is. The quantity of food available to the sheep is not increased by foraging as a flock rather than individually. The behaviour does not help to protect the members against predators. So far as one can tell, the sheep are not achieving anything collectively that they could not achieve individually, except satisfying an apparent preference for physical closeness. If a flock of sheep is a 'society', its organization is minimal and the utility of the organization is not apparent to an outside observer.

Humans are clearly gregarious, but they do not associate with one another in ways that embrace all the members of the species in a particular area. Smaller groups are formed which include some members and exclude others. People like to be close to those who are similar to themselves in certain respects, but they prefer to be distant from those who are different; human gregariousness is quite severely limited in its scope. In a word, humans *discriminate*. They prefer association with others of the same occupation, socioeconomic class or status, religion, language, nationality, race, colour, and so on. This is the source of some of the most serious problems facing human societies. Some limited associations are much more important in this respect than others. If the tool-and-die makers of a city form an exclusive recreational association it creates few, if any, social problems, but if white residents form white-only residential areas or school districts that is a different matter. Man's limited gregariousness is not, in itself, a social problem, but certain kinds of discrimination are sources of conflict and hostility that are dysfunctional for the collectivity. The study of discrimination, its kinds, its consequences, and its remedies when the consequences are dysfunctional, is a major interest of social scientists.

2. Hierarchy

If a farmer puts twenty hens, previously unassociated with one another, into a barnyard, a great deal of fighting takes place, which continues until a 'pecking order' is established. The hen at the top of the hierarchy may, without fear of retaliation, peck all the other nineteen; the second in rank may peck the eighteen below but not the one above; and so on down to the poor creature at the bottom who may peck no one and may be pecked by all.

In this case we have a highly ordered social structure, so hens form 'societies' rather than mere 'aggregations'. But it is difficult to see what purpose the hierarchical organization serves. It has no utility in providing food, shelter, or defence. The flock of hens are not able to achieve anything collectively that they could not achieve individually, unless we ascribe to them sado- masochistic desires. A biologist would probably point out that hens (and sheep) are domesticated animals and suggest that their social behaviour may be a vestigial remnant of practices that did serve collective purposes for their wild ancestors: the explanation of their behaviour is 'historical' rather than 'functional'.

Hierarchy is characteristic of virtually all human organizations. But the degree of hierarchical order differs very greatly. In an organization like the United States Army all members are ranked in distinct status categories that represent clear relationships of superiority and subordination; generals at the top, then colonels, and so on, down to privates at the bottom. But an organization like the American Economic Association has only a small governing body, all other members not being ranked at all. Organizations also differ greatly in the comprehensiveness of their hierarchical order. The Catholic Church is organized on a hierarchical scheme that embraces the entire communion of Catholic believers throughout the world, whereas many Protestant Churches have very little hierarchical organization that extends beyond the individual local congregation.

A social organization that functions to achieve collective purposes requires some method by which the actions of its individual members are co-ordinated. Hierarchical order is one method of achieving this co-ordination but there does not seem to be any general principle that governs the degree and extent of hierarchy that is necessary to the achievement of collective ends. The interest of social scientists in hierarchy is magnified by the fact that many serious social problems are closely connected with this method of social organization. Hierarchical ordering means that persons in superior positions have power to direct the actions of those in subordinate positions, which raises the issue of freedom and authority. Hierarchical status is often associated with income and wealth, either as cause or consequence, which raises the issue of economic inequality. The hierarchical status of parents may be a very important factor in determining the status of their children, which raises the issues of social mobility, equality of opportunity, and the fairness of the social system.

3. Biological differentiation

In the higher animals such as the vertebrates, which includes man, each species has two forms, male and female. They are characterized by the possession of different anatomical structures for reproduction and, in numerous cases, there are also other differences, such as overall body size. In many species that live in groups it has been observed that males and females engage in a division of labour, some tasks being typically performed by males and others by females. Such groups have a greater degree of sociality than mere gregariousness or hierarchy, since division of labour tends to make the individuals of a group dependent on one another for food, protection, etc. Moreover, there are advantages in the division of labour, whether or not it is based upon biological differentiation, so a group that practises it can indeed achieve something that its members could not achieve as individuals.

Biological differentiation and division of labour based upon it have been developed to the highest degree among the social insects. In the various species of ants, for example, there are the usual morphological differences between males and females but, in addition, there are striking differences among the females. The 'queen' is a specialized egg-producing entity, incapable of performing any other task. The 'soldiers' are sometimes so specialized for their role that they cannot even feed themselves. Among the 'workers' there are often a number of subcategories, biologically differentiated so as to perform the different tasks involved in food-gathering, nest-making, and housekeeping.

An ant colony is a highly organized social system in which the members interact with one another in complex ways, co-operating in a collective enterprise through an extraordinary degree of division of labour. The individual ant is helpless without the services provided by other members of the colony. Even the worker, who can forage for herself, could not survive for any appreciable time on her own. On account of this high degree of individual differentiation and collective integration, some biologists suggest that the ant *colony* should be regarded as the basic biological entity, not the individual ant. Some social scientists and social philosophers take a similar view of humans and their societies. This raises issues that we will repeatedly encounter in the following pages. What is the nature of the relationship of the human individual to his society? Should individual persons be regarded as the primary entities or should we focus instead upon interactions among collective entities such as nations, classes, religions, or civilizations? Is the proper methodology for a scientific study of society 'individualistic' or 'holistic'?

The sociality of the social insects is especially notable in the extent to which it is based upon biological differentiation. But even these species do not have a distinct morphological form for every different task. There is a good deal of division of labour in an ant colony among workers of the same body type. Some biologists believe that they are evolving in the direction of greater morphological differentiation and eventually will become completely differentiated, with as many different types as there are distinct functions.

Prior to the middle of the eighteenth century the view was widely held that groups of humans are biologically different. Orientals, Negroes, and Caucasians were thought to be differentiated, not merely in skin pigmentation and facial appearance but in more 'fundamental' ways as well. Moreover, it was widely believed that such biological differences exist even within the population of a particular geographic area. The caste system of India is perhaps the most extreme example. When Adam Smith remarked, in 1776, that 'the difference between the most dissimilar characters, between a philosopher and a common street porter, for example, seems to arise not so much from nature, as from habit, custom, and education' (*Wealth of Nations*, p. 15), he was expressing a view that was just beginning to become accepted even among so-called 'enlightened' people. Modern biology and physiology have shown that there *are* some racial differences, such as blood-type frequencies, but none of these is of much greater significance than, say, skin pigmentation so far as the functional capacities of the individual person are concerned. The belief that important biological differences exist is not as widespread as it used to be but it is far from uncommon. Many social scientists take the view that biological differences are negligible in fact, but that the persistent *belief* in their existence is a phenomenon that requires a great deal of study, since it leads to much conflict and animosity that is dysfunctional to human social organization.

One type of biological differentiation among humans, however, is more factually significant: gender differences. The biology of reproduction being what it is, the function of nurturing the young during the period of embryological development can be performed only by females. In many human societies, however, role differentiation between men and women is extended much further than this. There is no biological reason why airline pilots and office managers should be male but flight attendants and typists female. Differentiating occupational roles in this way is economically inefficient, since it does not make the best use of the human resources of the society. It may also be viewed as unjust discrimination and an invalid basis for hierarchical ordering, leading to conflicts, animosities, and tensions that threaten the ability of human collectivities to engage in co-operation.

Males and females of the human species, like most other animals, differ in certain secondary characteristics as well as in the primary ones of reproductive anatomy and physiology. Men are, generally speaking, larger and stronger than women and have lower-pitched voices. These characteristics are relevant to the performance of certain occupational roles, but not many, and the number of tasks where these factors are important is decreasing. Role differentiation between men and women in modern societies may be, in part, a remnant of differences that served some functional purpose in earlier times. Unlike other social animals, human societies undergo rapid change. But change does not proceed evenly, so it is possible for some aspects of human sociality to get badly out of step with others. This problem, of great interest to social scientists, is not, of course, confined to role differentiation by gender.

Before we leave this matter, an important technical point must be noted: *categorical* differences should not be confused with *statistical* differences. In the social insects, the biological differentiation upon which the primary division of labour is based is categorical; *all* soldier ants have larger heads and mandibles than *all* workers. In humans, *all* females have wombs and *no* males do. But secondary sex characteristics such as size are statistical; on average, males are larger than females, but some females are larger than some males. If, for a particular task, largeness of size were advantageous, a society in which that task was reserved for males would not be efficient. The same is true for other secondary male–female differences, and for other differences between groups of humans. Where role differentiation is based upon biological differences that are statistical, recruitment into these roles is more efficient if people are treated as individuals rather than as members of gender, racial, economic, or other classes. Interpreting statistical differences as if they were categorical differences is the source of a great many social problems, as well as being a simple scientific error. The contention that there are racial differences in something called 'general intelligence' is probably not true even statistically, but the error is greatly compounded when it is asserted, on the basis of statistical evidence, that there are categorical differences in intelligence among racial groups.

4. Functional specialization

Division of labour not based upon, or associated with, biological differentiation is practised by numerous species of animals, but on the whole it is not very common. Where it occurs, the degree of specialization is very limited, since there are only a small number of distinct tasks. The striking exception to this is man. Some humans, such as the Australian aborigines, practise very little division of labour, but most humans live in societies characterized by functional specialization of a very high order, the distinct 'occupations' or 'roles' being very numerous. A notable feature of human societies is the rapid increase in specialization that has been occurring in modern times. Two centuries ago a farmer's task was the production of 'food'; now the individual farmer often specializes in the production of corn, or lettuce, or potatoes, or some other specific commodity. Biologists may be correct in contending that the degree of biological differentiation among the social insects is increasing by evolution but, if so, it is a very slow development, and very limited, compared to what has been occurring by means of increasing functional specialization in human societies.

The farmer who spends his time producing only corn consumes little, or none, of his own product. His occupation consists of providing something for use by other persons. Meanwhile, the corn farmer is consuming thousands of other goods produced by similarly specialized persons, most of whom are completely unknown to him and may be living far away. Obviously, this is sociality of a very high order. Man lives in a social system that is very elaborate, and virtually worldwide in certain respects. It is a co-operative system in the sense that the individuals serve one another's wants and needs. We sometimes forget this essential fact, because we are more interested in the problems to which this system is subject than in its basic organization. We devote more attention to oil production when the oil stops flowing, just as we begin to take notice of the stomach when we have a stomach ache. The fundamental task of social science is to analyse how this very extensive and complex system works, mainly in order to understand its defects and deficiencies so that it can be made to work better.

To perform this task, the construction of rather abstract *theoretical models* is required. If human society were composed of a small number of institutions, each with a clearly defined and unchanging role, and if all individuals performed specific, unchanging tasks, it might be possible to explain how the system works by simply describing its structure. Some social scientists indeed regard such empirical description as the primary objective of their study, but others feel that it is necessary to go beyond description and try to discover general 'laws' that govern the specific social phenomena, as the physicist tries to discover the laws of matter and motion. An example: the automobile worker spends forty hours a week installing transmissions. He is paid a wage, which is a portion of the value of the automobile. We could simply describe this. Widening the focus, we could record how the value of the automobile is distributed among the various workers, management personnel, share-holders, suppliers of raw materials, and so on. Alternatively, we could try to discover the 'laws' that *determine* the value of the automobile, the levels of wages and salaries, the rate of profit, and so on.

In the following chapters we will devote our attention almost exclusively to social *theory*, that is, the abstract analytical models that social scientists have constructed in their search for general laws. Some social scientists would say that this neglects the largest and most important part of the subject, the descriptive empirical work that social scientists do. Others would go further and say that in this book I am merely recording the history of illusions, since (in their view) there are no social laws at all. My own stance on this matter is that theories are instruments that we employ in order to understand complex empirical phenomena. Abstract model-building and empirical description are *both* essential to the scientific enterprise. When theories are pure works of imagination, losing contact with the real world, they are, indeed, illusions. But description without theory is empty. The scientist who attempts it usually suffers from a different illusion: the belief that he uses no theory, because he is unaware of the theory he is implicitly using.

5. Altruism

Our discussion up to this point seems to be aimed towards the thesis that a high degree of sociality involves extensive division of labour, based upon biological differentiation, functional specialization, or both. So far as non-human species are concerned, social organization based solely upon gregariousness or hierarchy is rather minimal and it is doubtful that a collectivity such as a flock of sheep or hens achieves much that could not be achieved by the members individually. But the thesis that a high degree of sociality always involves division of labour is empirically incorrect. There are many species of animals that live in social groups where co-operation is not based upon biological differentiation or functional specialization of the members.

An example of this is the African elephant. The adult males of this species live as solitary individuals, but the females (and their young) form small groups of ten to twenty members who forage together, defend themselves collectively, and raise their young collectively. The members of these groups of elephants are not biologically differentiated except by age. There is not even any sex differentiation, since adult males are excluded from such groups. There is hierarchy, but only to the extent that one member is the leader (generally the oldest); all other adult members appear to be equal in rank. The role of the leader is very important in the elephant group. If the leader is killed or dies suddenly the organization of the group breaks down and the elephants mill around in disorder until another individual takes command as the new leader. To the extent that there is one leader and numerous followers there is some division of labour in the elephant group, but it is minimal, hardly comparable to the division of labour described in section 4 above.

Nevertheless, the elephant group is highly social. The members assist one another in foraging, the young are cared for by all adults without discrimination as to biological parentage, conflict among members of the groups is unknown or, at least, too rare or too mild to be observed. If a member of the group is injured the others rush to her aid. When danger threatens all adults participate equally in an organized defence strategy, except for the leader, who directs the group's tactics and regularly assumes the most exposed position or engages in the most dangerous action. The basis of this highly effective social organization seems to be the propensity of the female African elephant to engage in *altruistic behaviour* toward other members of her group. The biologist defines 'altruism' as behaviour that benefits others at some cost, or risk of cost, to oneself. This opens a subject that has been of major importance in the history of social science and also looms large in other disciplines such as theology, ethics, and biology.

That man is an altruistic animal is obvious from even the most casual observation. Americans contribute funds for the relief of earthquake victims in Armenia; French doctors devote themselves to combating disease in Chad; firemen risk their lives, at low pay, trying to get the occupants out of a burning building. All human societies (with rare exceptions like the Ik of Uganda) look after the elderly, the maimed, and the needy. All modern societies have systems of *organized* altruism, taxing some members in order to support others who cannot pay for food, housing, education, or medical services. Altruism is an important feature of sociality in human societies, but it is far from general. An old adage says that 'charity begins at home' and, in some societies, it extends little further than the family group. One of the notable features of modern societies is the extension of the scope of altruistic activity, particularly that which is organized through government.

The role of altruism in human sociality, what it *is* and what it *should* be, is a major theme in the literature of social thought. Social scientists find altruism a very difficult phenomenon to analyse, however, and so far they have not had much success in attempting to incorporate altruism in a general analytical model of social behaviour. In the following pages we will from time to time take note of the consideration of altruism as a form of sociality by social scientists, as, for example, in Adam Smith's *Theory of Moral Sentiments* (1759), discussed in Chapter 7, section C. In Chapter 16 C we will examine the recent attempts by biologists to give an explanation of altruistic behaviour as part of a general theory of social organization based upon the operation of the genetic code as a system of behaviour co-ordination.

Classification is very useful in scientific investigation but it may be seriously misleading if one overemphasizes the degree to which the classes correspond to distinct differences in the real world. The classification of five types of sociality outlined above is a case in point. Obviously, we cannot use these categories to differentiate animal species in a rigid way, saying such-and-such species are 'gregarious', others form 'hierarchies', others are 'biologically differentiated', and so on. Most animals fit into more than one category, which means that they do *not* 'fit' if the categories are regarded as exclusive compartments.

This is an important point to keep in mind in our examination of the social sciences. When people say things like 'Man is a gregarious animal,' or 'Man is an altruistic animal,' such statements are perfectly acceptable, unless they imply that man has *no* desire for individual solitude and is *never* egoistic. No sensible person would say that, but one often encounters the contention that man is 'inherently' gregarious, or altruistic, and that the evident desire for solitude, or egoistic behaviour, represents an abberation from, or corruption of, his 'essential' nature. One can argue for a long time about the 'essential nature of man' without getting anywhere. Such fruitless efforts can be avoided if we regard classifications like the 'types of sociality' noted as analytical constructs that are devised by the social scientist to assist him in his studies. They are not purely imaginary, though; they have some reference to the empirical world.

The types of sociality were illustrated above by reference to the behaviour of non-human animals wherever this was possible, but the main object of the classification is to throw some light on sociality in *Homo sapiens*. One of the insights this provides is recognition of the fact that not only is man a highly social species but his sociality is exceedingly varied since his behaviour displays all five types: man is gregarious, forms hierarchies, is biologically differentiated, practises functional specialization, and is altruistic towards his fellows. Before going further we should observe that our typological classification fails to take note of the most important way in which human sociality is unique. All individual social animals, except humans, are members of only one social organization. The individual ant is a member of one particular ant colony; individual hens belong to the flock in one particular barnyard, and so on. In some species the individual may move from membership of one collectivity to another, but at any particular time he is a member of only one, which has a definite spatial location. The individual human, however, is a member of many collectivities. He may simultaneously belong to a nation, a church, a firm, a labour union, a book club, an alumni association, a political party, a conservation society – the list is almost limitless, and changing. Human sociality is 'multisocial' while that of all other species is 'monosocial'.

Many of the social organizations to which humans belong do not have any delimited location in space and time. Moreover, some social activities are carried out in 'organizations' only in a rather abstract sense of that term. When an Indiana corn farmer sells his produce and uses the money to buy California oranges, Maine codfish, Japanese electronic goods, Italian shoes, and so on, he is engaged in a co-operative activity with these other producers but his interaction with them is not personal. The 'markets' through which trading in goods and services takes place are social organizations according to the definition put forward at the beginning of this chapter: markets enable people to achieve ends that they could not attain as isolated individuals. But people are associated in markets through their buying and selling activities, which is quite different from the form of association that one finds, say, in a church, or a political party, or a nation. Human society in general is a complex network or ensemble of different modes of organization, some of which are local while others are virtually worldwide in their scope. The central task of the social sciences is to investigate how these various modes of social organization work and to identify the problems that result from the fact that they do not work perfectly.

C. ALTRICIALITY AND ENCULTURATION

The purpose of this chapter is to introduce our examination of the history and philosophy of social science by describing the basic subject matter of social science and indicating the kinds of problems with which it is concerned. In the preceding sections I discussed the concept of 'society' and surveyed the various types of socialness or 'sociality' that exist in the animal kingdom. This takes us some considerable distance towards explaining, in a general way, what it is that social scientists try to do, but there is a feature of human sociality, not noted as yet, that is vital to any understanding of the social sciences: man is an 'altricial' animal, and a great deal of his behaviour is the consequence of a process of 'enculturation', or 'socialization'.

The term 'altriciality' is borrowed from ornithology (the study of birds), where it is used by biologists to refer to the fact that in many species of birds the newly hatched young are unable to fend for themselves and must be nurtured by adults for some time, and taught many things before they are able to function on their own. This is characteristic not only of birds but of many other animals, including man.

The length of the dependent period in humans is very long. Biological maturity in the sense of ability to reproduce is not reached until the age of twelve or thirteen; full physical maturity requires another five years or more. The young human may begin contributing to the activities of the social group by performing tasks within the family, or outside it, before maturity is attained, but he remains dependent upon his parental family until he reaches physical maturity, marries and forms a family of his own, and/or begins to earn his own living. Economic dependence may last to the age of thirty, or longer, if the individual aims at a professional career that requires many years of schooling and training. During the long period of dependence the main task of the individual is to acquire knowledge and habits that will fit him for independent functioning and will integrate him into the society to which he belongs. The institutions that function in this process (families, churches, schools, etc.) are major objects of study by social scientists. Special note must be taken of the fact that the period of dependence is employed not only to train the young in economic skills but also to inculcate mores, customs, world-views, and values. This is what is meant by 'enculturation': the process by which the individual young are moulded into participating members of a continuing 'culture', following the established customs of that culture and preserving its beliefs. Two important points must be noted about this process, 'multiculturality' and 'imperfect enculturation'.

By 'multiculturality' I mean to refer to the fact that there are *many* human cultures. The young of the species are not enculturated into the general 'family of man' but into much more restricted groups. A surgeon in Dublin may have the same technical skills and perform the same practical tasks as a surgeon in Tokyo, but their beliefs, values, and social behaviour are very different, owing to the different processes of enculturation that have functioned during their periods of dependence. The cultural plasticity of the human species is notable. If a German family moves to the United States, within a generation or two the members become much more American than German in their cultural characteristics, even if there is no intermarriage. There may be a long-run tendency for culture to become homogeneous within a geographic area, but at the present time, multiculturality is characteristic of most modern societies, especially those which, like the United States, continue to receive a steady flow of immigrants from the rest of the world. Multiculturality creates great artistic and intellectual richness, but it also is a potent source of conflict and animosity. Both these aspects of multiculturality are of great importance to social scientists.

By 'imperfect enculturation' I mean to refer to the fact that most societies are not able to mould the young into complete adoption of traditional values, beliefs, and codes of conduct. Some individuals are 'deviants' and there are more in some societies than in others. Deviation, such as criminal behaviour, may be dysfunctional for the society, but other forms of deviation are constructive sources of cultural change. If Copernicus and Galileo had not been deviants we might still believe that the earth is the centre of the universe. If Leonardo, Descartes, Bentham, Beethoven, Darwin, Einstein, and others had been moulded in youth by an enculturating process that was completely effective, the history of the Western world over the past few centuries would have been very different. Great social changes are produced by wars, natural calamities, and the migrations of people, but they are also produced by the artistic and intellectual innovators, great and small, who are able to deviate from the standard path of enculturated beliefs and pursue novel lines of perception and thought.

A very important issue that arises from the imperfection of enculturation in humans and the nature of complex societies is the matter of *loyalty*. An ant is a member of only one social group, its colony, but a human is a member of many, and the claims they make upon his loyalty may conflict. All social institutions depend upon the loyal support of their members, but an individual's nation may demand one thing, his religion another, and his code of professional ethics something else. Since humans are imperfectly enculturated, their loyalties are not fixed and immutable, so institutions vie with one another to attract new members and sustain the loyalty of those they have. In a multisocial society the individual may be pulled in different directions by conflicting interests and moral claims. In addition, some institutions may be able to impose sanctions for disloyalty, such as expulsion, ostracism, imprisonment, or even death. The hierarchical structure of social institutions means that loyalty is defined and interpreted by those who occupy high positions in the hierarchy and sanctions are imposed upon lower members, so the phenomenon of social power is closely connected with the matter of loyalty. The question of loyalty covers many issues, both ethical and scientific, that have been of great interest to students of human behaviour.

At the beginning of this chapter I noted that the study of human sociality is divided into a number of disciplines: sociology, political science, and so on. The division of the field among them is not very definite, partly because they overlap to a considerable extent. Moreover, the research interests of the various social sciences are constantly changing, so any description of them is likely to become out of date before much time has passed. In the following chapters I shall discuss the historical development of the various social sciences as distinct disciplines, such as one finds in the social science 'departments' of a university, but one should keep in mind that the central object of all of them is the same – the investigation of the processes through which individuals are able to form social organizations and reap the benefits of co-operation. In order to place the history of the social sciences within the general context of Western intellectual history we must begin, not with the social sciences themselves, but with the development during the Renaissance of the natural sciences, which profoundly changed not only man's view of the physical world, but also his view of himself and his society.

Chapter 2

The rise of the Age of Science

During the fourteenth and fifteenth centuries in Europe a profound change began to take place in man's conception of the world and his place in it. This change had many aspects – artistic, cultural, economic, political, literary, and intellectual – which historians have vainly tried to capture by the single term 'Renaissance'. In this chapter we will study the changes in intellectual or philosophic outlook of this period that laid the foundations for the development of modern science. This aspect of the Renaissance was undoubtedly its most important contribution to the shaping of modern Western civilization. It led to the age of science and high technology in which we now live. For the history of our own subject, the social sciences, the rise of natural science was of crucial importance. When social sciences began to develop, they were inspired by the achievements of the natural sciences; they attempted to apply to human sociality the new conceptions that the natural sciences had been successfully using in the investigation of natural phenomena. In order to study the history of social science, and appreciate its philosophic problems, we have to devote some attention to the conceptual revolution that was begun, and progressively continued, by natural science.

Ideas and theories are mental phenomena, so they are necessarily associated with individual persons. But they are also social phenomena: when a set of ideas or theories are widely shared, they form part of the culture of the community. In this chapter I will be concerned with the social aspect of the rise of science, but in order to be reasonably concrete in explaining what this involved, I will first discuss as examples three specific persons whose work was important in initiating and developing the scientific approach to knowledge. In section B I will go on to consider the implications of this in a more general way.

A. LEONARDO, VESALIUS, AND GALILEO

1. Leonardo da Vinci (1452–1519)

It may seem strange to begin a discussion of the rise of the Age of Science with consideration of the work of an artist. Leonardo, in fact, was not only a painter; he was also a mechanical engineer and inventor, a mathematician, and a scientist. But it was not his scientific ideas as such that are significant so much as the application of a scientific outlook to his artistic work. As an artist Leonardo continued and developed a new approach to the pictorial arts that had been begun more than a century earlier by Giotto (c. 1267 – c. 1337). Prior to Giotto, painting was ornamental and formal, designed to decorate a space or to depict one of the biblical stories in a conventional or symbolic way. Faces were expressionless, bodies were wooden. Giotto began to paint figures that were human: faces showing emotion, bodies shaped and proportioned like real people – even when they were supposed to be saints or angels. In Leonardo's painting this conception of pictorial art was developed to a high point by works which, whether they were religious or secular, depicted the figures as living individuals that the viewer could understand because they were like the people he knew in everyday life.

In itself this represents an outlook that was to become an essential feature of science. Leonardo carefully observed his subjects and painted his understanding of what he had observed in a straightforward, yet interpretive, way. His object was to depict what his eyes showed him rather than what the ancient authorities told him he ought to see. But Leonardo went further. He made anatomical studies of the human body by dissection. In his notebooks we find many sketches of the human skeleton, the structure of muscles, tendons, and so on. This is the main reason why Leonardo deserves a prominent place in the history of science. He realized that effective observation requires investigation of what is beneath the surface so that one can understand *why* things appear as they do and how they *function*. In order to paint a face showing fear, or anger, or even serenity, one must know the facial musculature that is at work beneath the skin. Leonardo pursued anatomical studies in order to assist his art, but what he was doing is essentially what science has been doing: studying the hidden mechanics of nature.

2. Andreas Vesalius (1514–64)

Vesalius was born in what is now Belgium, but he spent his most productive years in Italy, where he taught at the University of Padua, one of the outstanding centres (if not *the* outstanding centre) of scientific research in the sixteenth century. Like Leonardo, Vesalius was a student of anatomy, but his investigations of the human body aimed at improving the practice of medicine rather than the work of the artist. The significance of Vesalius's work in the history of science is that his discoveries were made by laying aside the traditional anatomical conceptions of his time, which were contained in 'authoritative' texts, and making careful and objective direct observations of his own. Before Vesalius, the established authority on the science of medicine was Galen, a Greek physician of the second century A.D., who wrote an enormous amount on virtually all aspects of the subject. His works were copied and recopied over the succeeding centuries and studied by physicians as the authoritative source of all medical knowledge. Little new work was done, since there did not seem to be any need for physicians to do more than learn from Galen. The study of anatomy by dissection of the human body was not generally considered to be a necessary part of a physician's training. The professors of medicine who did offer their students a direct view of the interior of the human body usually had the messy work of dissection done by assistants, and their main object was to illustrate the Galenic texts in an uncritical way.

Vesalius was originally a follower of Galen, but he did dissection with his own hands and observed with care and objectivity. He became increasingly convinced that Galen was wrong on many points. In fact Galen had probably never dissected a human body; a great deal of his anatomical description was a synthesis of the structures found in a variety of animals, mainly the Barbary Ape. In 1543 Vesalius published his pathbreaking book on human anatomy, *De Humani Corporis Fabrica*, written in Latin, as were all scholarly and scientific works at the time.

As a professor of medicine at the University of Padua Vesalius taught his students that human anatomy can be learned only by direct observation, not from books. In the *Fabrica* he warned against accepting even his own work as definitive and urged the student to dissect and observe in a critical and objective fashion. In this he showed the true outlook of the scientist, for whom nature, not authoritative texts, is the source of knowledge. Moreover, he urged the student of anatomy to stick to scientific matters and not get involved in such subjects as the location of the soul in the human body, a question much discussed in his day. He thereby contributed to the demarcation of science from theology, a matter that was vital to the later development of modern science.

Vesalius's criticisms of Galen were objectively undeniable, but that does not mean that his work on human anatomy was immediately accepted. The *Fabrica* was fiercely attacked by the Galenists, who regarded ancient authority as necessarily superior to new conceptions, no matter how strongly the latter were supported by empirical evidence. For example, John Caius, president of the English College of Physicians from 1555 to 1571, insisted that any physician who disagreed with Galen should be disciplined. Even a half-century or more after the publication of the *Fabrica*, some medical schools (such as that of the University of Paris) were still teaching anatomy from the Galenic texts. This illustrates an important point about intellectual history: new knowledge, especially when it requires a basic change in one's conception of the world, takes a long time to win acceptance and, moreover, its victory is never complete. Even today there are still those who believe that the earth is flat, or that St. Augustine (354–430) was right in ascribing all diseases (of Christians) to demons, or that the universe was literally constructed in six days about five thousand years ago. We live in the Age of Science, but it did not begin suddenly in the sixteenth century, or the fifteenth, and it is not (or not yet) an age in which more than a small proportion of mankind has adopted the scientific approach to knowledge. This is more notable in respect to the study of social phenomena than in the study of natural phenomena. Even sophisticated modern scientists, when confronted with social questions, are prone to think about them in ways that recall St. Augustine more than Vesalius.

3. Galileo Galilei (1564–1642)

Galileo was one of the most important figures in the early history of modern science. He made highly significant contributions in physics and astronomy; he was the first person to make use of the telescope for astronomical observation; he was firmly convinced of the value of experimentation in physics; he recognized the power of mathematics in the formulation of physical laws. His work conspicuously represented the combination of objective observation and rational theoretical analysis that is now characteristic of the scientific approach to knowledge. It opened the way to the systematic formulation of the basic laws of physical mechanics which was later achieved by Isaac Newton (1642–1727).

In this section I want to discuss Galileo's conflict with the Catholic Church authorities, who condemned his views as heretical and placed his writings on the list of prohibited books. Long before, the Church had asserted its authority in matters of natural science. In the thirteenth century, when Aristotle's scientific writings began to attract the interest of European scholars, theologians perceived that many of the propositions they contained were inconsistent with Christian doctrine, and urged the Church authorities to condemn them as heretical. The most celebrated of these condemnations was that of the Bishop of Paris, who, in 1277, issued a list of 219 Aristotelian propositions that Christians were forbidden to believe, on pain of excommunication. By Galileo's time the authority of the Church in such matters was generally accepted, but he held a different view. Galileo was not an atheist or even a Protestant; his struggle with the Church was over the question of the proper scope of religious authority. Like Vesalius, who did not concern himself with the location of the soul in the human body, Galileo acknowledged that there are questions that do not lie within the province of science but, he insisted, there are other questions that are matters of science and do not lie within the province of theology.

The issue that led to Galileo's conflict with the Church was the Copernican theory that the sun, not the earth, is the centre of our planetary system; the sun stands still while the earth revolves around it and rotates upon its axis. When Nicolas Copernicus published his *De Revolutionibus Orbium Coelestium* in 1543 it was accepted by the Church authorities. In fact the book was dedicated to Pope Paul III. For many years it was read freely by Catholics, but towards the end of the sixteenth century, perhaps as part of their reaction to the Protestant Reformation, Catholic theologians began to question whether Copernican theory was heresy, inconsistent with sacred scripture. In some places in the Old Testament the stationary nature of the earth and the mobility of the sun are stated or implied. In the Book of Joshua, for example, it is told how Joshua prayed to God, asking that the sun be stopped in its normal daily movement from east to west in order to provide light for the continuation of a battle in which his forces were engaged. Galileo was convinced that Copernicus was correct but, given the hostility of the Church authorities, he found it prudent not to say so. However, his own discoveries seemed to him to offer definite proof that the sun is stationary, and when he published his *Letters on Sunspots* (1613), he openly adopted the Copernican view of the planetary system. The Church declared this to be heretical in 1616 and Galileo was summoned to defend himself before the court of the Holy Inquisition. He escaped with no more than a warning, but later, when he published his *Dialogue on the Two Chief Systems of the World* (1632), he was tried once again, forced to 'abjure' Copernican theory, and sentenced to live in seclusion.

When, after the publication of his *Letters on Sunspots*, it became known to Galileo that a movement was afoot in Rome to charge him with heresy, he wrote a defence of his views in the form of a long letter addressed formally to the Grand Duchess Christina. It was not published until 1636 but it circulated widely in manuscript copies during the previous twenty years. In this famous letter, which the Church attempted to suppress, Galileo stated with great clarity and elegance his view of the proper relation between science and religion. It is impossible, he argued, that two truths should contradict one another. Holy scripture is unquestionably true, and Copernican theory cannot be in contradiction with it if it also is true. Those who view the theory as heretical are therefore obligated to demonstrate that it is false. By this reasoning Galileo attempted to persuade theologians that even the religious acceptability of a scientific theory must depend upon the empirical inves- tigation of nature, not scripture. 'The Bible,' he wrote, 'was not written to teach us astronomy' but to instruct us in matters which 'surpassing all human reasoning, could not be made credible by science, or by any means than through the very mouth of the Holy Spirit.' No one, he said, doubts the authority of the Pope 'but it is not in the power of any created being to make things true or false, for this belongs to their own natures and to the fact'.

There is a legend that when Galileo was forced to abjure the Copernican theory that the earth is in motion he tapped the ground and muttered, out of hearing of his inquisitors, 'E pur si muove' (And, yet, it moves). Galileo was attempting to claim not that science is superior to religion but that it is independent, resting upon the powers of reason and observation that God himself has given man to use in the study of nature. In effect, he argued forcefully for the secularization of science and a demarcation of the sphere of science from that of religious faith. The attempt of theologians to retain authority in matters of science, Galileo claimed, could only bring discredit upon the Church. In this he was more clearheaded about religion than the theologians, but his *Dialogue* and other works remained on the Catholic Church's list of prohibited books until 1832.

The relation between science and religion in the modern history of the West is a complex one, not merely a matter of conflict and confrontation. We shall have to refer to it from time to time in the course of this book but the subject, as such, is beyond our scope. For a good survey the reader is referred to David C. Lindberg and Ronald L. Numbers, eds., *God and Nature* (1986).

Note: Some qualifications

The period we have been discussing in this section is usually referred to by historians of Western civilization as the 'Renaissance'. The classic study of this era is Jacob C. Burckhardt's *The Civilization of the Renaissance in Italy* (1860), which is mainly an examination of the political and cultural aspects of the period, with little attention to developments in the field of science. Burckhardt noted that the Renaissance, as the name implies, witnessed a 'rebirth' of interest in the writings and art of ancient Greece and Rome, but he emphasized the extent to which the Renaissance also represented something new and different, especially in contrast to the era of the 'Middle Ages' that preceded it. Modern scholars have shown that it is rather misleading to draw a hard distinction between the Renaissance and the Middle Ages. The Renaissance was not so enlightened, and the Middle Ages were not so backward, as has been represented in popular histories. In other words, the impression the reader may receive from section A above requires a bit of qualification.

Stressing the significance of people like Leonardo, Vesalius, and Galileo is useful in tracing the history of the attitude towards knowledge that is the foundation of modern science, but the Renaissance was not an era that can be characterized as intellectually homogeneous. In fact, in addition to developments in science, the period witnessed a rebirth of interest in mysticism, magic, astrology, and the occult. The 'Hermetic' writings of the early Christian era, which embodied such views of the nature of the world, were translated from the original Greek in the sixteenth century, numerous editions were published, and they were eagerly and widely read. The Holy Inquisition was originally established to deal with religious heresy in the thirteenth century, and during the sixteenth century and after it played an important role in the Church's struggle against Protestantism. These activities, and its opposition to Copernican theory, were the Church's effort to combat *ideas* that were viewed as dangerous. But much attention was also devoted to combating the influence of the devil, interpreted literally as a being who could influence worldly events. Many persons were tortured and burnt by Church order, not because they espoused heresy, but because it was believed that they were witches or had made a pact with the devil to further his aim of controlling the world. As we know from the celebrated witch trials at Salem,

Massachusetts, in 1692, this view of reality was not confined to Catholics. Witchcraft remained on the statute books of England as a capital offence until 1736 and there were many protests when it was removed. Moreover, it would be a mistake to regard belief in such things as absent in our enlightened time, with science more powerful than ever. Interest in the occult still flourishes and mysticism enjoys wide currency in popular, and even in academic, attitudes to social phenomena.

The era of the Middle Ages, similarly, was mixed in its intellectual attitudes, far from the uniform backwardness that the term 'medieval' is often used to denote. There was, most notably, an efflorescence of science, both pure and applied, from the eleventh to the thirteenth centuries. In this period the great Gothic cathedrals were built, representing a high development of architectural science and engineering; the clock, a remarkable mechanical achievement, was invented and developed into a very sophisticated instrument; astronomical knowledge was effectively applied to the needs of navigation; metallurgy was significantly improved and better understood; water power and heat were more scientifically utilized as sources of energy for industrial processes; there were important advances in agriculture; and so on. Along with these practical arts came philosophical views foreshadowing the scientific attitudes of the Renaissance. Roger Bacon (c. 1215 – c. 1292), for example, emphasized in his writings the importance of empirical data derived by observation and experimentation, and the use of mathematics, in the search for knowledge about the world, just as Galileo did four centuries later.

This flowering of science and technology in the eleventh, twelfth and thirteenth centuries was seriously stunted by the multiple disasters that struck Western Europe in the fourteenth century: almost continuous warfare; a change in climate that led to repeated crop failures; and major epidemics such as the Black Death, which, during the twenty years after its appearance in 1334, killed off more than half the population of Europe. These events, as great disasters invariably do, stimulated the growth of mysticism, occultism, and the more credulous forms of religious faith, to the detriment of rationalism and science.

Long before the Renaissance, or the high Middle Ages, there were thinkers who exemplified the scientific attitude to a striking degree. For example, Titus Lucretius Carus (c. 99–c. 55 B.C.), a Roman of the time of Julius Caesar, wrote a long poem, De Rerum Natura (On the Nature of Things), which a modern student of intellectual history can only read with astonishment. In it one will find such specific things as the atomic conception of matter; the proposition that the speed of fall of a body in a vacuum is independent of its mass (which Galileo later rediscovered); the theory that the sensation of colour is due to reflected light hitting the eye; the assertion that light travels faster than sound; and the suggestion that the biological inheritance of physical characteristics is governed by a genetic system in which the characteristics are particulate (the view of modern genetics). But more important was Lucretius' general attitude towards nature and how to obtain knowledge of it. He rejected all explanations that relied on gods or spiritual forces; he insisted that all natural phenomena consist of matter and motion; he argued that all true knowledge is derived by sense experience and rational analysis of the implications of empirical observations; he advocated the reduction of complex phenomena to their simpler constituents as the method of scientific investigation. All of these are characteristics of the modern philosophy of science. Lucretius's *De Rerum Natura* was read widely initially but apparently more for its poetic qualities than for its philosophical views. It was considered as rank paganism by early Christian theologians and fell out of view entirely until the sixteenth century, when new editions of it began to be printed.

Another example is Ptolemy (A.D. 90–168) a Greek-Egyptian astronomer and mathematician who constructed the first model of the universe. He is often treated with disrespect in the history of science because he made the error of placing the earth at the centre of the system and assumed that the planets moved in circular orbits, and because he took astrology seriously and wrote the most famous book on it. But the astronomical system delineated in his *Almagest* lasted for fifteen centuries and was of great practical use. He also made important contributions to geography, optics, and other branches of science. His scientific work was based upon the combination of empirical observation and theoretical modelling that we now recognize as the central characteristic of the scientific method.

Nevertheless, modern science 'began' with the Renaissance in the important sense that it started then to have a *continuous* development. A few great men do not create a science; they must be followed by others who carry the work forward, and the followers must be critical of the achievements of the masters, otherwise knowledge degenerates into dogma and progress ends. The test of a true science is not whether men of genius have revealed some of nature's mysteries but whether men of lesser talent can learn to use their methods and reveal more.

B. THE SCIENTIFIC ATTITUDE

In section A we considered the scientific attitude as exemplified in the works and thought of three outstanding figures of the Renaissance. Now I want to discuss the main characteristics and implications of that attitude in a more general way and make some reference to its impact on the social sciences. The discussion will be organized under five headings: (1) the source of scientific knowledge; (2) the demarcation of science; (3) Platonic idealism and Aristotelian essentialism; (4) the Homeric view of events; and (5) the idea of progress.

1. The sources of scientific knowledge

The discussion of Galileo's *Letter to the Grand Duchess Christina* above noted the extent to which he defended himself against the charge of heresy by contending that the only source of knowledge about natural phenomena is the direct examination of the phenomena themselves. This ran counter to the view, widely held at the time, that established religious authority has a great deal to say about what is true and what is false, in respect of natural phenomena as well as in matters of theology, morals, and politics.

An important implication of the view expressed by Galileo is that it rejected the necessity of hierarchical order in the social organization of science. If scientific truth is determinable by authority it is necessary to establish hierarchical order so that differences of view can be resolved by superior authoritative judgement. Differences among laymen are resolved by appeal to priests, differences among priests by bishops, up the ladder of hierarchy, with the Pope at the top. Once a proposition is declared to be true or false by authority at one level in the hierarchy, the judgement is binding on those at lower levels and dispute on the matter ceases. Galileo's view was that differences of view about natural phenomena are resolvable by observation and experiment, not by appeal to authority. Such a process requires no hierarchical social organization. Nature is not influenced by the status of the investigator. Bodies will fall from a height in the same way regardless of who drops them, or who observes their fall. Before the evidence of nature the lowliest person is equal to the highest. Hierarchical order is an effective way of creating intellectual peace, but it is too easy and too perfect. People often complain that scientists (especially social scientists) disagree among themselves. One must, however, expect disagreement, since it is not easy to settle differences by empirical investigation. Authority can settle differences very neatly, but it is a questionable way of assuring that what all persons are required to believe is in fact true. Doubt is more valuable than certainty when one may be quite wrong in what one is certain about.

Neither Galileo nor any other sophisticated scientist would contend that empirical data derived from the observation of nature speak for themselves. Data must always be interpreted. The role of authority in science would not be displaced by empiricism as such if one took the view that the persons who occupy high positions in the hierarchical order possess superior intellectual powers. The central issue here is whether the ability to reason is widely found among human beings or is confined to the few who have high social status. The idea that all persons have rational capacity and that differences in their ability to use it are more a matter of education and training than innate qualities is a view that did not become common until the eighteenth century, but its roots are to be found in the views of earlier scientists who, like Galileo, claimed that the secrets of nature are open to investigation by every man who goes about it properly. It is a question of *method*, not of *status*. The successes of the early scientists did not demonstrate that men are equally endowed with the capacity to reason, but they did show that when men are free to use what reason they possess, without subservience to authority, knowledge will increase progressively.

This view of science has been of profound importance in the modern history of Western civilization. It helped to establish the principle of intellectual freedom, which was extended to areas of human thought and experience well beyond the domain of natural phenomena – to politics, economics, ethics, and even to religion. Once the power of authority had been broken in the field of science, it became possible to release its grip in other areas of human life and thought. So far as the social sciences are concerned, it is doubtful whether they could have come into existence in their modern form without the achievements of the natural sciences that preceded them.

2. The demarcation of science

The scientists of the Renaissance did not contend that the scientific method was applicable to all areas of thought and experience. On the contrary, their view was that the method was limited to the investigation of natural phenomena. This notion that scientific matters are demarcated from others is still held by modern science. I want now to illustrate the non-demarcational view by discussing briefly the Thomistic concept of 'natural law', and then try to clarify what is meant by 'science' by examining the principles upon which it is demarcated from other areas of study.

Christian theology experienced diverse lines of development through the writings of many different theologians, especially during the first few centuries of the Christian era. A systematic statement of Christian theology was not achieved until the thirteenth century by the work of St. Thomas Aquinas (1225–74). His writings, especially the *Summa Theologica*, have exerted enormous influence on theology, and philosophy more generally, down to the present day. In 1879 Pope Leo XIII declared his work to embody the authoritative doctrine of the Catholic Church. It was through Aquinas that the ideas of Aristotle became an important component of Catholic philosophy.

In Aquinas's view there is no fundamental distinction between matters of fact and matters of morals. God has ordained 'natural laws' which govern both. An immoral act is immoral because it is 'unnatural'. The actions of the civil authorities are illegitimate, and do not merit the support of the citizen, if they are contrary to natural law. Moral laws have the same status as the laws of physics: they are absolute, and unalterable by man. However, since it is not obvious what the natural law is, it is the responsibility of the properly constituted religious authorities to determine it. Thus the authority of the Church in the field of morals and politics is derived from its role as the established interpreter of natural law, and since natural law also governs the material world, the Church's authority also extends to views concerning natural phenomena. It is easy to see why the Church could not abandon its authority in matters of science. To have done so would have been to break the monistic conception of natural law and open the door to questioning of clerical authority in matters of politics and ethics. Indeed, this is what in fact occurred. When the Renaissance scientists helped to demarcate the field of science as independent of religion they added weight to a wider movement that led to the separation of Church and state and to the development of ethical philosophies not based upon religious beliefs.

In practice it is fairly easy to distinguish scientific matters from non-scientific ones but it is not easy to state precisely what the *principle* of demarcation is. In fact there is still much dispute among philosophers of science about this. Obviously, it would be a mistake to identify science with 'truth' and non-science with 'falsehood'. Scientists are continually showing that what was previously thought to be true in their own fields is false. Statements about ethical and religious matters may be non-scientific, but this does not imply that they are necessarily false, or meaningless. The principle of demarcation most widely accepted by scientists themselves is *empirical testability*. A statement is 'scientific' if it is of such a nature that it can be tested by observation or experiment. The statement 'Bodies fall at a constant speed in a vacuum' is scientific (even though it is false) because one can test it. The statement 'A person will be punished for immoral acts in the after-life' may be true, but there is no conceivable procedure by which one can test it empirically. The reason why we call physics and chemistry 'sciences' is that they contain a large number of testable propositions and theories. Theology and ethics contain very few, if any.

In the study of social phenomena it is very difficult to apply clear empirical tests, for a variety of reasons. Some would say that sociology, economics, and the other social disciplines are not sciences at all. Some social scientists themselves are strongly opposed to the view that the social disciplines should be judged by the same criteria that are applied to the scientific study of material phenomena. Later in this book we will examine this issue more fully. At the present point, since we are considering the history of social science rather than its philosophy, it is sufficient to note that, whether or not the social disciplines may be called 'sciences', their historical development took place in an era that was profoundly influenced by the specific achievements of the natural sciences and by their success in demarcating the field of science from that of theology. The modern social sciences developed as *secular* disciplines, whether or not they met the criteria of 'science'.

One more point remains to be made in this connection. I am not arguing here that there is an inherent conflict between science and religion. There will indeed be conflict if officials of a Church regard their religious position as giving them authority in scientific matters. But churchmen are not necessarily bound to take this view. One can, for example, argue that any work that reveals truths of nature gives testament to the glory of God, and scientists therefore serve him in their way just as surely as priests do in theirs. Reasoning of this sort was not adopted by Catholic churchmen but, in England in the seventeenth century, many Puritans viewed science in this way, and religion served as an important source of encouragement to science in a society that witnessed the work of William Harvey, Robert Boyle, Isaac Newton, and other outstanding figures in the history of science. More generally, one can say that Protestantism, by denying the necessity of a priest mediating between the ordinary man and Holy Writ, encouraged the idea that ordinary men could also study God's work as manifested in nature. The theology of 'deism' which was prominent, especially in England from the late seventeenth century until the mid-nineteenth, promoted scientific investigation of natural phenomena as a more secure means of proving the existence of God than relying on 'revelation' (see below, Chapter 16 B).

3. Platonic idealism and Aristotelian essentialism

The most important of the thinkers of ancient Greece were Plato (c. 427–c. 347 B.C.) and his pupil, Aristotle (384–322 B.C.). Their ideas have continued to exercise profound influence upon Western thought down to the present day. There are significant respects, however, in which the modern scientific attitude is contrary to the Platonic and Aristotelian outlooks and, to an important extent, the rise of modern science represents a breaking away from these ancient thinkers.

Plato advanced the view that sense experience is, to a considerable degree, misleading or even illusory. The true world is abstract, consisting of the universal 'ideas' of things rather than concrete specific items. Knowledge consists of understanding the 'pure form' of things, which is perfect, not the worldly examples, which are not. Obviously, such a view does not encourage one to search for knowledge of nature by empirical methods, since these serve only to provide sense data, which are regarded as inherently unreliable. The proper route to knowledge is by using the powers of rational thought in a purely abstract way, such as in mathematics, dissociated from the world of sense experience, to grasp the pure form or idea.

It is evident from our discussion so far in this chapter that the basic outlook of modern science is not Platonic idealism. The emphasis of Vesalius, for example, upon the examination of specific anatomical structures in great detail, and his dissatisfaction with Galen's more general and synthetic descriptions, are antagonistic to Platonic philosophy. Galileo was a mathematician and was convinced that mathematics was very useful in physics, but not because he believed that ideal reality is abstract, like mathematics. Mathematics was, for Galileo, simply an instrument that is useful in the empirical investigation of nature. While Platonic idealism has not been without influence on the natural sciences, I think it is fair to say that the main tradition of modern science has been opposed to it.

The same general statement can be made about Aristotle's view that phenomena are explicable in terms of the 'essential nature' of things: stones fall from a height, for example, because it is in their nature to fall, or to move until they rest in their proper place, the surface of the earth. Aristotelian essentialism is obviously not the philosophy of modern science, which focuses upon the structure of matter and the forces operating upon masses, rather than their essential natures. Scientists spend very little time talking about essential properties and, when they do, they are usually making definitions, not offering explanations. Aristotelian essentialism considers that explanations in terms of essential properties are final, since one can carry investigation no further than the discovery of such properties. By contrast, modern scientists regard currently accepted explanations and theories as tentative, open to improvement or displacement by further work.

The modern social sciences are not devoid of Platonic and Aristotelian influences. Some branches of mathematical economics, for example, seem to be sufficiently motivated by the quest for the abstract pure form of an economy to qualify as Platonic idealism. Searching for the 'essential nature of capitalism', an academic activity popular among both conservative and radical social scientists, frequently appears to be an exercise in Aristotelian essentialism. But the main body of modern social science is empirical and, like the natural sciences, seems to have escaped from the influence of the ancient Greek philosophers.

4. The Homeric view

Homer was a Greek poet (or group of poets) who lived in the eighth century B.C., four centuries before Plato and Aristotle. The great epic poems the *Iliad* and the *Odyssey* are still read and form part of the culture of Western civilization. The feature of Homer that I want to note here is the view projected in these poems of the determinants of human and social events: whatever happens is due to the will of the gods. In the field of natural phenomena the counterpart of this is the belief in witchcraft, occult powers, and the like.

It is obvious that no science could be constructed if the Homeric view of the world were correct. We could not discover any laws of nature because there would be none that could not be broken or altered by the desires, or whims, of the gods. The best we could do would be to psychoanalyse the gods in order to understand how *they* behaved; which is in fact what the Homeric poems concern themselves with when the narrative seeks to provide some explanation of events. The natural sciences have extracted themselves altogether from the Homeric view. The modern physicist, or chemist, or biologist, regards phenomena as explicable in terms of laws of nature, which are not subject to alteration by either human or 'supernatural' powers. The laws of nature furnish the explanation of why a cannonball will fall if dropped from a height, and why a bird will not. The flight of the bird is not contrary to the laws of nature, but in accordance with them.

In the field of social phenomena the Homeric view, or an analogue of it, is considerably more tenacious. Few people regard economic and political events as governed by supernatural powers but many consider that they are under the control of powerful real persons who manipulate the world for their own purposes and according to their own wishes. This is known as the 'conspiracy theory' of social phenomena: events are due to the secret machinations of the powerful. Common observation tells us that social phenomena are indeed frequently due to the actions of powerful persons or groups. If this were all that were involved in the Homeric view there could be no quarrel with it, but it implies that this is a *sufficient* explanation of social events; that, in effect, there are no general social laws. If this were so there could be no social science. Instead of using sociology, economics, etc., to explain social phenomena, we would instead rely upon detectives to pull aside the curtain that hides the manipulating conspirators from view. This is an untenable position. Even if events are determined by individual actions we have to explain why the actions have the results they do. If a powerful financier wishes to raise the price of silver, he does not accomplish this end simply by *willing* it, but by doing certain things that cause the price to rise. The connection between action and consequence is discoverable only because the phenomena are governed by general laws. To explain *how* the financier was able to raise the price of silver, or *why* he failed to do so despite his intention, requires something more than the Homeric view of social phenomena. We have to employ a scientific theory to achieve such explanation. One could not regard the statement 'The castle wall fell down because the general willed its destruction' as a complete explanation of an event. Why should one regard a statement like 'The price went up because the financier wanted it to' as a complete explanation?

One of the reasons why it is more difficult to get away from the Homeric view with regard to social than with regard to natural phenomena is that the issue of moral judgement is much more involved in the former than in the latter. If a stone breaks loose from the cornice of a tall building and falls, killing a pedestrian, we do not make moral judgements about the behaviour of the stone. But if someone throws the stone from the top of the building we make moral judgements about the behaviour of the person. There is a strong strain in the literature of social thought that regards the main object of social science as the making of moral judgements. This frequently focuses attention upon the persons or groups who may be construed as victims and victimizers more than upon a detached study of the mechanics of social phenomena.

5. The idea of progress

The idea of progress is so prominent in the culture of modern Western civilization that it is difficult to believe intellectual historians when they tell us that its appearance in Western thought can be dated back no further than the seventeenth century. But the burden of historical evidence seems, broadly speaking, to support the view that the modern era differs from the earlier ones in this very important aspect.

The view of history held by most of the thinkers of the classical age of Greece was that it is characterized by cyclical movements, endlessly repeated, without any long-run change. Plato, who lived during a period of political disturbance, held the ultra-conservative view that all change constitutes decline from, or deterioration of, a former state that was ideal. The same view, in a different context, was embodied in the Old Testament story of man's fall; life outside the gates of Eden could never approach the idyllic perfection that had been irrevocably lost. The New Testament held out the prospect of redemption, but it was a spiritual redemption of the soul, not material progress for the body in worldly existence. St. Augustine's (354–430) *City of God*, written to combat the idea of worldly progress as an objective of Christian effort, exerted a great deal of influence on Western thinking up to and during the Middle Ages. The fall of Rome and the barbarian invasions, with their resulting decline in social stability and loss of technical skills, undoubtedly did much also to keep the idea of progress from arising in Western culture. The cultural and economic developments of the eleventh to the thirteenth centuries gave some stimulus to it, but whatever nascent development of the concept that was present in this era was killed in embryo by the disasters of the fourteenth century.

The idea of progress is, basically, the conception of the present as superior to the past and the belief that the future will be, or can be, better still. This contention was the subject of a long debate during the seventeenth and eighteenth centuries, sometimes called 'the ancients versus moderns controversy' or 'the battle of the books'. It ended in victory for the 'moderns', though, of course, victories in such matters are never complete. There are many people today who view what we call 'progress' as illusory, regarding past ages as superior to the present and others who are convinced that we are in an era of irremediable decline.

The concept of progress is an evaluative one, involving judgements as to what is good and bad, or better and worse. The issue of judgement does not arise if the world is static, or history is cyclical as the Greeks thought. So far as the natural world is concerned, until the nineteenth century it was regarded as static, preserving intact the features that God had decreed during the six days of creation as told in the Book of Genesis. This view was profoundly shaken by Charles Lyell's *Principles of Geology* (1830–3) which demonstrated that a different view of the origin, and evolution, of the planet was necessary. Charles Darwin's *Origin of Species* (1859) contended that modern organic species had evolved from earlier forms, and suggested that even man himself was the result of a process of progressive development rather than fixed and final creation.

It is difficult to say whether the nineteenth-century belief in social progress was derived from discoveries in science or the other way round. But, in one respect, science has to be regarded as antecedent in that, during the Renaissance period, scientists were demonstrating that there could be, and had in fact been, progress in at least one area: human knowledge. Many Renaissance thinkers were passionate admirers of the Greek and Roman literatures, but the Renaissance scientists spoke for the possibility of improving upon them. If this was possible in the domain of knowledge, why not in other areas too, especially since knowledge gives man power to bend nature to his service?

The social sciences developed concurrently with the growth of the idea of progress in Western culture. Undoubtedly they were both a cause and a consequence of that idea. Given the orientation of social science to the pragmatic analysis of social problems, it is unlikely that it could flourish in a static society or one in which people believe that knowledge has no influence upon events. In these respects the way for the development of the social sciences was prepared by the earlier successes of the natural sciences in demonstrating the possibility of secure progress in knowledge. The question of the development of the idea of human progress and its relation to the early beginnings of the social sciences will be discussed further in Chapter 8.

APPENDIX: THE SOCIOLOGY OF SCIENCE

In this chapter I have emphasized the empirical nature of modern science and the objectivity of the knowledge that it furnishes. This is a defensible view of the main characteristics of science, but it would be foolish to claim that scientists are totally detached from their particular cultural environments. Galileo was, no doubt, a cultural deviant in some ways but, in most, he was a Renaissance Italian and shared a common culture even with the officers of the Holy Inquisition. Some historians of science have laid great stress upon the cultural conditioning of the scientist and the connection of his theories with the socioeconomic environment. Numerous scholars, for example, have expressed the view that the Darwinian theory of natural selection reflects the competitive capitalism of the nineteenth-century English economy. Others have argued that while the scientist himself may be objective, the acceptance of his theories depends upon their serviceability to powerful political or economic interests or ideologies. For example, Margaret C. Jacob (*The Newtonians and the English Revolution, 1689–1720*, 1976) contends that Newtonian physics was embraced by leading Anglican theologians (in contrast to Galileo's rejection by Catholic ones) because they regarded it as supporting their view that a capitalistic economy organized through markets and based on self-interested individual action was a stable, harmonious order, ordained by God.

Concerning such questions it is necessary to make two points. First, investigating the social background of scientists and the cultural environment of their times has nothing to do with the validity of their theories. Newton's physics and Darwin's biology are not any less, or more, true as statements *about physical and biological phenomena* because their development and acceptance may have been influenced by social, political, or economic factors. Second, studies of the cultural environment of science, historically or currently, are worthy in themselves. They explore a part of our history and contemporary culture of great importance, and indeed growing importance as the role of science in Western, and other, cultures widens and deepens. This area of research is called the 'sociology of science'. I shall not be able to say much on this topic in the following survey of the social sciences, but in the final chapter we shall have to examine a thesis that has, recently, received considerable attention. This thesis, in its boldest form, claims that the attempts of philosophers to establish the epistemological foundations of science are misguided and doomed to failure. Science is a social phenomenon that should be studied by sociological methods just as other social phenomena such as religion, customs, and *mores* are. According to the so-called 'strong programme in the sociology of science' what we describe as 'scientific' beliefs are no different from any other beliefs, and what we call scientific 'truth' has no more solid foundation than conventional acceptance. As the reader will see, I do not accept this view.

Chapter 3

Social laws

In Chapter 2 we considered the historical importance of the development of the natural sciences in preparing the way for the later emergence of the social sciences. The emphasis there was on features of the 'scientific attitude' that are characteristic of the whole field of science, not unique to any one science or group of sciences. I did not mean to imply, however, that disciplines like economics and sociology are sciences *because* they are like physics and chemistry. The object of Chapter 2 was to examine an important aspect of the intellectual history of the West, not to evaluate the social disciplines by comparison with the natural sciences or by reference to general criteria of scientific philosophy.

The relation of the social to the natural sciences philosophically has been a matter of continuing controversy. Peter Winch, for example, in his *The Idea of a Social Science* (1958) argues that the concepts appropriate to the analysis of social phenomena are demonstrably incompatible with those used in natural science, and F. A. Hayek, a Nobel prizewinner in economics, in his *The Counter-revolution of Science* (1955) complains of the great harm that has been done by modelling the study of social phenomena after the natural sciences. On the other hand, Alexander Rosenberg, a philosopher of science, in his *Microeconomic Laws: a Philosophical Analysis* (1976), takes it for granted that the scientific status of a field of study can be assessed by comparing it to physics. The American Association for the Advancement of Science officially endorses a similar view. Since 1952 it has awarded an annual prize of $1,000 'for a meritorious paper that furthers understanding of human psychological–social–cultural behavior' in order 'to encourage in social inquiry the development and application of the kind of dependable methodology that has proved so fruitful in the natural sciences'.

In this chapter I do not intend to resolve this methodological controversy or even to survey it. A comparison of 'social science' with 'natural science' in a general way is not likely to be very informative, since the various social sciences differ greatly among themselves, and so do the natural sciences. In certain respects, economics resembles physics more than biology does. It would be easy to draw analogies between some parts of sociology and biology, but comparison with chemistry would be very difficult. And so on. Our main examination of the question will be deferred until the final chapter but, at this stage, it will be useful to examine some matters of philosophical importance that are connected with the idea of 'laws' of social phenomena.

All disciplines that describe themselves as 'sciences' have one thing at least in common: they aim at discovering general laws that cover a wide range of specific phenomena. The prototypical example of a general law is Newton's law of gravitational attraction, which says that, given certain conditions (all laws are limited in this way), the force between two bodies is proportional to the product of their masses and inversely proportional to the square of the distance between them. This law embraces all masses – apples, stones, planets, gall bladders, clouds, etc. – and it covers phenomena at all places and times, including the future that has yet to be. Because of its generality we refer to Newton's law as a 'nomological proposition' (classical Greek *nomos*, law).

In the social sciences there are many propositions that are called 'laws', such as, for example, the law of increasing specialization (sociology), the iron law of oligarchy (political science), the laws of motion of capitalism (Marxian economics), Pareto's law of income distribution (economics), the law of diminishing returns (economics), etc. When we examine such statements we discover that, while they all represent generalizations, they involve very different *kinds* of generalizations. The first thing I want to do in this chapter is to draw some distinctions between types of nomological propositions. A great deal of confusion is sometimes created in discussion of 'laws of social behaviour' by the supposition that people always mean the same thing when they use the word 'law'.

A. NOMOLOGICAL PROPOSITIONS

The main distinctions I want to make here are between laws that are purely *empirical*, laws that are *analytical*, and laws that involve the concept of *cause*.

1. Empirical laws

In his *System of Logic* (Book VI, chapter V) John Stuart Mill defines an 'empirical law' as 'an uniformity, whether of succession or of coexistence, which holds true of all instances within our limits of observation, but is not of a nature to afford any assurance that it would hold beyond those limits . . . '. Let us look at two of the laws in the list above that are clearly empirical in nature: 'Pareto's law of income distribution' and 'the iron law of oligarchy' enunciated by Robert Michels. Vilfredo Pareto, Italian engineer–economist– sociologist, put forward the striking law of income distribution in his lectures at the University of Lausanne, published as *Cours d'économie politique* (Course in Political Economy, 1896–7). He examined the data on incomes in all countries for which statistics were then available and became convinced that the pattern of income distribution was substantially the same in all countries and could be represented by the formula:

$$\log N = \log A - \alpha \log X$$

where N is the number of people whose income exceeds X, and A and α are constants. If we plot the (cumulative) income distribution on double-log graph paper it will be a straight line with slope equal to α. The coefficient of α is a measurement of the degree of inequality in the income distribution. Pareto's empirical studies showed not only that the above formula fitted the data well but that, when calculated, α turned out to have substantially the same magnitude in all countries, indicating that the degree of inequality in the distribution of income was uniform. This suggests that α in Pareto's formula is similar to Newton's coefficient of gravitational attraction: a 'natural constant'.

Pareto himself warned against exaggerating the significance of his empirical findings. Generally speaking, professional economists were even more cautious than Pareto and subsequent work made little effort to utilize Pareto's law as a basic proposition in economics. But some economists have taken the view that the discovery of empirical constants like Pareto's α was what would give economics the proper foundations upon which to build a true science. The distinguished economist Joseph A. Schumpeter, commenting on Pareto's law a half-century after it had been published ('Vilfredo Pareto', *Quarterly Journal of Economics*, 1949), chided the profession for failing to appreciate the scientific significance of the discovery of empirical regularities such as the constancy of Pareto's α.

Robert Michels was a German political scientist whose *Political Parties* (1911) is important as an early empirical study of a very basic question: the tendency of social organizations to form hierarchical orders. If democracy is regarded as a political system in which everyone has approximately equal power, then it is unattainable if there is a natural tendency (that is, a 'law') for organizations to become hierarchic, with most power being in the hands of a small number of people (the 'oligarchy') at the top. Michels was an ardent democrat and a socialist. He reasoned that there was no point in looking at conservative institutions to see if they were oligarchic because conservatives do not value democracy anyway. The crucial test would be whether institutions strongly committed to democracy as a political creed were able to organize themselves and operate on a sustained basis of power equality. Accordingly, Michels studied labour unions, and socialist political parties, which he believed to be strongly committed to democracy. Finding that these institutions, however they might have started, invariably became oligarchic in organization, Michels advanced the 'iron law of oligarchy' as an empirical generalization about the political organization of man's social institutions.

Propositions like Pareto's about income distribution and Michels's about political organization are impressive as empirical generalizations, but their

status as 'laws' is clearly contingent, since one contrary instance in each case
would be sufficient to destroy their claims to generality. This is not true of
Newton's law of gravitation. If observations were made which did not agree
with the formula, scientists would not regard them as an indisputable
demonstration that the law was wrong but would try to find out why the data
failed to agree. A striking instance of this was the discovery of the planet
Neptune in 1846. Observation of the orbit of Uranus had shown certain
irregularities, that is, deviations from the orbit that would fit Newton's
formula. Astronomers did not view them as necessarily demolishing
Newtonian theory, since the irregularities could be due to the existence of a
hitherto unknown planet. Using the Newtonian formula, they calculated
where this planet would be if it existed, pointed their telescopes at the
predicted spot in the sky, and lo! Neptune. Newtonian theory, and its
successors in physics, show that robust nomological propositions are not
merely empirical generalizations about specific things, they are comprehensive models covering a wide range of phenomena. In fact they are often as
useful in explaining cases where the data deviate from the theory as cases that
fit. The most robust theories are never destroyed by empirical evidence but
only by the development of a better theory that is even more general in
coverage.

Empirical generalizations like Pareto's and Michels's laws are rather
unsatisfactory as nomological propositions. They have to be abandoned when
one contrary instance is discovered. They cannot be used to investigate
contrary instances, since they are purely empirical. That is, they do not
pretend to explain why the data are what they are. They *are*, and that's that.
J. S. Mill contended that 'an empirical law is a generalization of which, not
content with finding it true, we are obliged to ask, why is it true?'. But
numerous people have treated Pareto's and Michels's laws as if they represent
essential characteristics of the social order, which goes far beyond the recognition of an empirical regularity. One takes a very large leap in going from the
statement 'So far as we know at present, A is characterized by X' to the
statement 'Empirical observation proves that an essential feature of A is X'.

A notable case illustrating the hazards of generating a purely empirical law
and projecting it into the future is a famous paper by Raymond Pearl and
Lowell J. Reed on population growth in the United States (*Proceedings of the
National Academy of Sciences*, 1920). The authors pointed out that they did
not intend to argue that they had discovered the 'underlying organic laws' of
population growth, but they demonstrated that a mathematical equation
could be devised to fit the census data remarkably well. Reasoning that no
population in a limited area can grow indefinitely, they chose an equation
having the characteristic that, when projected beyond the data into the future,
would necessarily generate a series of numbers gradually approaching a
ceiling. From this they concluded that the absolute upper limit of the U.S.
population was 197 million. Making some additional calculations, they stated

that, when that limit was reached, twice as many persons as in 1920 would be engaged in agriculture and, even so, half the nation's food requirements would have to be met by importation.

The Pearl–Reed predictions failed to correspond to events. The population of the United States is now well over 200 million and still growing; the proportion of the labour force engaged in agriculture is less than 5 per cent, and still falling; and the U.S. is a major exporter of food. In order to predict human population accurately, and to arrive at reliable conclusions concerning food production, Pearl and Reed would have had to use a much more comprehensive model, embracing all the social and economic factors that are important determinants of the birth rate, technological change, the prices of food and other commodities, etc. Equations like the one constructed by Pearl and Reed are used effectively by modern population biologists, but only with respect to much simpler cases of non-human organisms where such factors are not operative.

We noted above that a difficulty with purely empirical statements construed as general 'laws' is that one counter-instance is sufficient to destroy the contention. One might respond to the demonstration of such a counter-instance by claiming that it does not truly belong to the class of things covered by the law. Take the empirical generalization 'All swans are white'. If now a bird is observed that is like swans in all respects except colour, one can respond by saying that it is not really a swan. This saves the proposition 'All swans are white' but it is no longer an empirical statement. Since no bird will be called a 'swan' unless it is white, whiteness is not, in this case, an independently observable characteristic of physical objects, but a definitional criterion for the use of the word 'swan'. Obviously it is essential, if one wishes to think clearly, not to confuse empirical propositions with definitions. This is not always as easy as in the above example. In statistical studies, for example, one often finds that the data form a neat pattern except for a few cases, which generates the temptation to eliminate these 'outlyers' as not being true instances of the phenomenon under study.

The principal epistemic message conveyed by this brief discussion of empirical laws is not that empirical evidence is unreliable but that factual information, by itself, cannot provide us with much knowledge of complex phenomena. Modern science is empirical, and to appreciate its methodology it is necessary to understand how empirical evidence articulates with *theoretical* reasoning in providing explanations of phenomena. Francis Bacon, in his *Novum Organum* (1620), attempted to sustain the proposition that absolutely certain knowledge of reality can be obtained purely by collecting and processing factual data. His book played an important role in establishing the empirical orientation of science, but its central epistemic thesis was erroneous.

2. Analytical laws

This term refers to the kinds of laws one finds in the disciplines of logic and mathematics. For example, the 'law of contradiction' states that:

A thing cannot be both X and not-X

and the 'law of the excluded middle' states that:

Everything must be classifiable as an X or a not-X.

The 'law of transitivity' states that quantitative relationships are such that:

If A is greater than B and B is greater than C, then A is greater than C.

A concrete example of the first two of these laws would be the statement:

A thing is either a swan or it is not; it can't be both

and of the transitivity law:

If Albert is taller than Bertha, and Bertha is taller than Clarence, then Albert is taller than Clarence.

It is important to note that examples of this sort merely illustrate the relevant analytic laws; they play no role in proving them. Analytic laws are laws of reason or laws of rational thought, not laws of nature in any empirical sense. When we state the transitivity law we are not asserting anything empirical, such as, for example, that people behave as if they believe that when $A > B$ and $B > C$, then $A > C$; we are saying that any other behaviour would be irrational. We are not required to assert that people *do* always behave rationally; that would be an empirical statement, not an analytic one.

The 'syllogism' of formal deductive logic can be regarded as a prototypical analytical law. Consider the following argument:

1. If all A is B, and
2. If X is A,
3. Then X is B.

This is a valid argument, which does not depend on any proposition about something being true or false empirically. That is why I have written it in terms of purely abstract entities, A, B, and X. If now we substitute the more familiar example:

1. All men are mortal.
2. Socrates is a man.
3. Therefore, Socrates is mortal.

it is evident that the form of the argument has not changed, but it has acquired a significantly different orientation, since, in addition to substituting real-world entities for A, B, and X, the conditional word 'if' has been dropped.

We may construe such a syllogism in three ways: (a) We could say that the word 'men' involves the property 'mortal' *by definition* and that the particular entity 'Socrates' is, similarly, *defined* as belonging to the class 'men'. (b) We could say that (1) and (2) are 'axioms', that is, propositions that are 'self-evidently true'. (c) Or we could regard (1) and (2) as stating empirically true facts. If (c) is adopted, the syllogism no longer presents a purely analytic argument, since we are relying upon the empirical truth of the premises to justify the belief that the conclusion is true, but, to repeat, the form of the argument is analytic or 'deductive'. We should also note that the syllogism:

1. All snodluts are made of jikler.
2. Yakmar is a snodlut.
3. Therefore, yakmar is made of jikler.

is perfectly valid even though 'snodluts', 'jikler', and 'yakmar' are words I have just made up and do not mean anything or refer to anything in the real world. As they say in computer programming, GIGO: garbage in, garbage out. Whatever its terms might be, a syllogism is, in itself, a purely formal argument without empirical content. The concept of an *analytic statement* or an *analytic law* refers to arguments of this sort, as, for example, in pure mathematics.

Analytic statements, in themselves, have nothing to say about the real world. Mathematics is very useful to physicists, but mathematics is not physics. The great mathematician G. H. Hardy once said that 'a mathematician is someone who does not know *what* he is talking about, and does not care'. Practically everyone except unregenerate Platonists and Pythagoreans recognizes this, but the idea that we can learn about social phenomena solely by using deductive logic continues to have considerable appeal, and sometimes it is pushed to extremes. Most economists regard mathematics, and deductive reasoning generally, as indispensable, but insist upon empirical investigation and testing as well. However, there are some who claim that economics is not, or ought not to be, empirical. The proper way to proceed, in studying economic phenomena, in this view, is to lay down certain basic propositions as representing the 'essential properties' of an economy and then deduce the logical implications that follow from them.

This view is, for example, strongly advanced by Martin Hollis, a philosopher, and E. J. Nell, an economist, in their *Rational Economic Man: a Philosophical Critique of Neo-classical Economics* (1975). The same point of view is contained in Ludwig von Mises' works such as his *Human Action* (1949) and in the writings of his disciples who now call themselves the 'Austrian school' of economists. I mention these two examples not merely as illustrations of the view that the social sciences should be practised as analytic, rather than empirical, disciplines, but to demonstrate a difficulty with this approach. Proceeding on the same epistemic principles, Hollis and Nell arrive at conclusions that are very different from those of Mises and the Austrians. Hollis and Nell contend that a market economy is necessarily inefficient and unjust, while the Austrians assert that only a market economy can be efficient and just. If both parties have done their logic properly, this difference must be due to different assumptions about the 'essential properties' of an economy. But those assumptions are not regarded as testable by the parties, because that would turn economics into an empirical science. It comes down to a contest in which each party is claiming that his assumption about 'essential properties' is true *by intuition*, a dispute which is unresolvable by any known method.

This point deserves a bit of further amplification. Let us take the case of the death of Socrates. Historians tell us that he committed suicide by drinking hemlock after he had been condemned by the political authorities of Athens for his heretical teachings. The syllogism used above to account for Socrates' death makes no reference to such things as heresy or hemlock. It tells us that Socrates shared the property of mortality with all other men and, therefore, was destined to die *some* time of *some* thing. Such a syllogism, though containing empirically true premises and using impeccable logic, is cognitively useless. It does not focus upon what we want to know, which is the particular circumstances that led to Socrates' death. A syllogism such as

1. Drinking hemlock causes death.
2. Socrates drank hemlock in 399 B.C.
3. Therefore Socrates died in 399 B.C.

is very little better, though, again, it has factually true premises and a validly deduced conclusion. It might satisfy a physiologist, but not an historian of Athenian society. The point is, the facts employed in a scientific investigation must be relevant to the question that is being addressed. That an argument uses true facts and valid logic does not guarantee that it supplies the explanation we are seeking.

Analytic laws are very useful in science but no discipline that studies phenomena can be satisfactory unless contact is made between the theory and the real world. If we examine the syllogism of deductive logic we can see that one can apply empirical tests either to the *premises* of the syllogism or to its *conclusion*. There is an important difference between these two test locations. Let us take as our example the specific syllogism:

1. All insects have five legs.
2. Mosquitoes are insects.
3. Therefore mosquitoes have five legs.

We could make an empirical investigation of (1) and (2), knowing that, logically, if (1) and (2) are true, (3) must be true. This is known in formal logic as *modus ponens*: the truth of the premises is transmitted to the conclusion. The other way is to make an empirical investigation of (3). If (3) is false, then logic tells us that (1), or (2), or both, must be false. This procedure is known as *modus tollens*. In fact (3) is false, since (normal) mosquitoes have six legs. Therefore (1) or (2), or both, must be false. In this case (1) is false.

Note that there is a logical asymmetry between the *modus ponens* (MP) and *modus tollens* (MT) forms of argument. The MP procedure focuses upon the truth of the premises; the MT procedure upon the falsity of the conclusion. In MP truth is carried forward from the premises to the conclusion, but falsity is not; in MT falsity is carried back from the conclusion to the premises, but truth is not. Let us consider a concrete illustration:

1. All economists are male.
2. Albert Einstein was an economist.
3. Therefore Albert Einstein was male.

In this case the formal logic is impeccable but premises (1) and (2) are both factually false while the conclusion is factually true. This shows that when premises are demonstrated to be false the truth or falsity of the conclusion is still an open question.

Now let us look at the MT procedure. As we have seen, if the conclusion is empirically false then one or more of the premises must be false. But this does not mean that if the conclusion is true the premises must necessarily be true. This is shown by the above syllogism about Einstein. Showing that (3) is true does nothing to certify that (1) and (2) are true. Falsity carries back from conclusion to premises, but truth does not.

This is of some importance in the social sciences, since many of the assumptions that are employed in theoretical models are, at best, simplifications of reality, if not grossly unrealistic. Some students of the methodology of social sciences are very critical of the assumptions that social theories use. Defenders sometimes reply that the real test of a theory is not whether its assumptions are true but whether its conclusions are. This was argued very forcefully by the prominent economist Milton Friedman in a paper on 'The Methodology of Positive Economics' (*Essays in Positive Economics*, 1953) which has been widely, and sometimes hotly, discussed by both philosophers and social scientists. With the aid of our examination of *modus ponens* and *modus tollens*, we can see our way through to an understanding of this matter. If Friedman was claiming that a theory is validated when its conclusions or 'predictions' are true he was claiming too much. Testing conclusions empirically (the MT procedure) cannot carry truth back to the premises, as our Einstein syllogism makes plain. The MT procedure can carry only falsity back. If the conclusion or prediction is wrong the theory must be faulty, but if the prediction is correct the theory is not necessarily true.

Let us now have a look at an important social science law and try to determine what kind of law it is: the 'law of diminishing returns' in the economic theory of production. This law asserts that if production is carried out with a combination of different factors of production, and if some of these factors are constant in amount, then an increase in the other factors will increase production, but not proportionately. This can be shown in a simple diagram (Figure 3-1). Suppose we have in mind a farm with a fixed area of

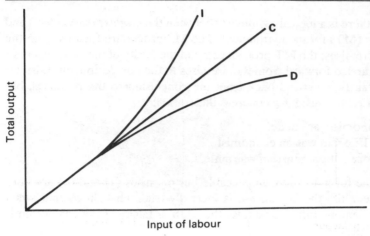

Figure 3-1

arable land and, for the purpose of this illustration, we assume that the only other factor of production is labour, which can be varied in amount. How will output change in response to a change in labour input? If the relationship were a straight line, such as C in Figure 3-1, this would mean that, as labour input increases, total production would increase *proportionately*. This would be a case of 'constant returns'. If production increased less than proportionately, this would be 'diminishing returns', D, and if it increased more than proportionately it would be 'increasing returns', I. The law of diminishing returns says that D is the proper curve to draw, the others being incorrect or impermissible for some reason. Why is this so?

The law of diminishing returns could be treated as an empirical generalization based upon actual data derived from practical or experimental farming. As pointed out in section 1 above, such a law would be rather weak and contingent; it could not bear the heavy weight that modern economic theory loads on it. In standard texts in economic theory the law of diminishing returns is usually presented not as an empirical but as an analytic law. The proof of this is a good example of the *modus tollens* procedure, which focuses on the truth or falsity of a conclusion rather than on the premises that generate it. Let us imagine that we have a 100 acre farm, divided into two fifty-acre fields as shown in Figure 3-2, and that additional input of labour brings constant incremental returns, as drawn. If we allocated labour equally to both fields (L_A to field A and L_B to field B) we would produce a total output of $O_A + O_B$. But if we abandoned field B and put the labour effort formerly used there on field A, we would obtain the same output from fifty acres as we formerly did from 100. (If the distance between L_A and L_A^* equals L_B, simple geometry tells us that O_A^* must be equal to $O_A + O_B$ if the C curve is linear.) But why stop there? Why not put all the labour on twenty-five acres, ten, two,

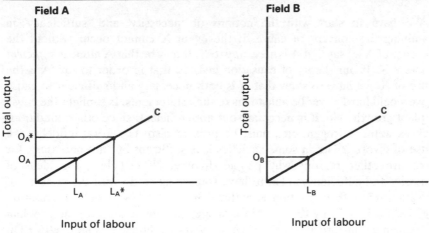

Figure 3-2

one? There would be no reduction in output as one reduced the area farmed, without limit. This conclusion is clearly false empirically, so something must be false in the assumptions. There is only one empirical assumption involved in this reasoning: that the output curve is linear. This must therefore be wrong.

We could go through this again, using the assumption that the output curve is as shown by I in Figure 3-1, that is, increasing returns. We would arrive at the even less acceptable conclusion that when less land is used more output is produced, without limit.

We can now see that it is not altogether correct to say that the *modus tollens* procedure cannot demonstrate the truth of an assumption. If I, C, and D are the only possible alternatives, and we can show that C and I must be false, then D must be true by elimination. We have to be careful, though, to restrict such a method to cases where all alternatives can be specified.

3. Causal laws

What most people would find unsatisfactory about empirical laws and analytic laws is that they do not connect events together in a *causal* fashion. If a 'law' is expected to furnish an *explanation* of why the phenomena are as they are and not otherwise, then empirical laws and analytic laws are not laws at all. Many philosophers, and most scientists, emphasize the importance of causal laws in science but, unfortunately, there is little agreement as to what is meant by the concept of 'cause'. In this section I want to focus on a 'model' of causation which, though unsatisfactory in some ways, helps one to understand how the concept of cause is typically used in common speech, and by scientists in their professional work.

We have to start with the notions of 'necessity' and 'sufficiency' in examining the concept of cause. If the event X cannot occur without the presence of A we say that A is *necessary* to X. It may be that A alone is *sufficient* to cause X. If our theory of causation insisted that in order to say 'A is the cause of X' we have to show that A is both necessary and sufficient to cause X, we would hardly ever be able to make such statements. Is sunlight the cause of plant growth? No; it is necessary but not sufficient, since other conditions such as water, nitrogen, etc., must be present also. Is marital infidelity the cause of divorce? No; in some societies it is sufficient but not necessary, for there are other reasons why people divorce. Nevertheless, the ideas of necessity and sufficiency seem to have something to do with the concept of causation. How they function is outlined in the 'INUS model' of causation suggested originally by Konrad Marc-Wogau in connection with the problem of explaining historical events such as wars, political changes, etc. ('On Historical Explanation', *Theoria*, 1962), and developed more generally by J. L. Mackie ('Causes and Conditions', *American Philosophical Quarterly*, 1965).

Let us consider what is involved in making a statement like 'The forest fire was caused by lightning'. Obviously lightning (L) was not *sufficient* to cause the fire (F), since the forest had to be dry (D) for it to have had the effect it did. But (L) was not *necessary* either, since, given D, F could have resulted from, say, a discarded cigarette (C). To sort this out we have to see how the elements C, L, D, and F fit together. First, we note that in this case there are two *sets* of sufficient conditions:

Sufficient to cause F: (1) L and D.
                            (2) C and D.

In set (1) L and D and in set (2) C and D are 'conjunctive' factors; but the sets (1) and (2) are 'disjunctive'. Now, if we examine the status of lightning, it is clear that this factor is necessary to complete set (1) but it is not sufficient in itself. So we can say:

L is *I*nsufficient to complete causal set (1).
L is *N*ecessary to complete causal set (1).

Now concerning set (1), to which L belongs, we know that it is unnecessary to cause F, since set (2) could also do so, but set (1) is sufficient. So:

Set (1) is *U*nnecessary to F.
Set (1) is *S*ufficient to cause F.

Therefore, when we say that 'lightning caused the forest fire', we mean that L was an *I*nsufficient but *N*ecessary member of a set of factors, and this set was *U*nnecessary but *S*ufficient to cause F. The italicized capitals put on the key words in this sentence form the acronym INUS.

The status of lightning in this model is that it can be causally linked to some forest fires but not all. What about dryness? Sets (1) and (2) both contain D and if we wrote down *all* sets of conditions that are sufficient to cause F, it may be that D would appear in every one. This brings us to an important point that is not embraced by the INUS model in itself: it would not make sense to say 'dryness causes forest fires' if we meant to imply that D was sufficient to F, but it would be perfectly acceptable if we meant by this statement that D increased the *incidence* of F or that it created a greater *probability* of F. This is vitally important to the understanding of 'laws' of social behaviour. For example, the 'law of demand' in economics says: 'Other things held constant, when the price of a commodity goes up, people buy less of it.' It is not necessary that *everyone* buy less, however; the law merely says that the *aggregate* purchase will be less. We can predict the effect of a rise in price on consumers in the aggregate, but not on the individual consumer, in the same way that we can predict that dryness will cause more forest fires to occur but we cannot predict specifically where and when one will occur. A great deal of the controversy over whether the social sciences regard human behaviour as 'determined' is due to misunderstanding of how the concept of cause is employed. We will return to this issue at the end of this chapter.

Another point about causal laws is that they have very broad coverage: they cover events that *have* actually occurred; events that *will* occur (either certainly or probably); and even events that have *not* occurred in the past and will *not* occur in the future. This last looks rather strange, but it becomes quite clear if we consider an example. If I say, 'If conditions of dryness, etc., were present, then lightning *would* cause a forest fire,' this is a legitimate scientific statement even if no forest fire had ever occurred in the past and were never to occur in the future. Statements of the form 'if . . . then . . .' are very important in science.

Going back now to the 'law of demand', we realize that the phrase 'other things held constant . . .' really amounts to saying, more broadly, 'if certain conditions are fulfilled   . . .'. So we can restate the law of demand as a conditional 'if . . . then . . .' statement. Suppose we observe that when the price of steak goes up people buy more. This does not necessarily demonstrate that the law of demand is untrue. If people's incomes go up faster than steak prices do they may well buy more steak. One of the 'if' conditions of the law of demand (unchanged income) has not been met. We can now appreciate that it may be very difficult to test a causal law empirically, especially when it is not possible to make properly controlled experiments. An experiment enables us to take a conditional statement like 'If A, B, and C conditions are met, X will occur', then proceed by deliberately arranging things so that A, B, and C conditions are met in fact and observing whether X occurs. With respect to social phenomena it is virtually never possible to make a deliberate arrangement of the conditions prescribed in a 'law', so we have to make do with weaker empirical tests than are available to the natural sciences.

Because causal laws are conditional 'if . . . then . . .' statements, which with respect to social phenomena are very difficult to test, the door is open to unrestrained speculation about the future and the understanding of the past. One can say something like 'If there were a universally understood language there would be no war' and then proceed to describe the perfect international order that would arise if we all learned Esperanto. Or one could say, 'If Hitler had invaded England right after Dunkirk . . .' and then go on to rewrite the history of the past half-century in hypothetical form, thus 'proving' that Hitler's decision to delay the invasion was the 'key factor' in subsequent historical events. A serious problem in social science is how to determine which conditional statements are scientifically interesting and which are pure speculations that are based on little more than the private intuitions of the persons making the assertions. Unfortunately there are no firm criteria available for making this distinction. In the natural sciences, pure speculation is frankly labelled 'science fiction', while in the social sciences it is often described as 'the real truth' that orthodox social scientists are incapable of appreciating or are suppressing for nefarious reasons.

Untestable speculations about causal factors are sometimes cast in terms of some predestined end that is construed as governing events. The notion that there are general 'historical laws' is sometimes a 'teleological' argument; that is, an argument in which the result of a process is construed to be, as Aristotle would say, its 'final cause'. Let us take the syllogism:

1. The destination of all Eastern 357 flights from Atlanta is St. Louis.
2. This particular flight from Atlanta was an Eastern 357.
3. Therefore it landed at St. Louis.

It does no harm, in common speech, to say that Eastern 357 landed in St. Louis 'because' that was its destination, but this can be seriously misleading in scientific analysis. The destination was not the cause of the aircraft's behaviour; it was guided to St. Louis by a pilot who desired to get there. The doctrine of teleology is a primitive error in reasoning but, unfortunately, it frequently creeps into social analysis. In the particular illustration used, causal efficacy was attributed to the pilot of the aircraft rather than the attracting force of St. Louis. This raises an additional issue of prime importance in the social sciences: can mental states such as 'motives' and 'beliefs' operate as causal factors? I will assume, in the following chapters, that they can, deferring direct discussion of the epistemic status of mental states to Chapter 18.

There is another element in causal laws that we must note. In any statement such as 'The forest fire was due to lightning' or 'If Hitler had ordered the invasion of England right after Dunkirk, Germany would have won the second World War' it is implied that the cause and effect factors are linked together by the existence of certain general 'covering laws'. These laws are empirical statements of what happens under certain conditions *universally*, and therefore serve to explain why an event occurred (or failed to occur) in a specific instance. Thus, in the INUS model, all the sufficient sets explaining forest fires imply unstated propositions of a general sort about the conditions under which combustion will take place. Some philosophers contend that all explanations of empirical phenomena rely upon (or should rely upon) such general covering laws. Some, indeed, argue that the discovery of such laws is the main object of science. In recent years there has been a continuing controversy over these contentions, and especially their applicability to history and the other social sciences. The paper that initiated this controversy is Carl G. Hempel, 'The Function of General Laws in History', *Journal of Philosophy*, 1942. Discussion of this is contained below, in Chapter 14.

B. NOMOLOGICAL LEVELS

If we were to jot down every time we encounter a nomological proposition in our reading and then looked over the list when we had, say, twenty items, we would be struck by differences in the level of organization that is represented by them. Suppose you are a student of biology. You read, for example, about (1) the constancy of the 'Chargaff ratios' in the nucleotides that are part of the DNA molecule inside the cell; (2) the principles that govern cell division in mitosis; (3) the mechanism of cell differentiation in embryonic development; (4) the processes of reproduction; (5) the ecological interaction among the species of plants and animals in an area. These represent very different levels of organization: (1) is at the chemical level; (2) is at the level of the cell; (3) is concerned with tissues and organs; (4) deals with the functions of a whole organism; and (5) focuses upon a community composed of different species of organisms.

When scientists try to establish the 'laws of nature' they are dealing with a reality that is law-governed but one in which different laws operate at different levels of organization. The Chargaff ratios and the principles of predator–prey equilibrium are both biological laws, but the ecologist has very little interest in the former and the latter is not of much relevance to the work of a geneticist. So it serves no purpose to refer in general to 'the laws of biology'. A list of such laws would be so exceedingly heterogeneous that it would have little significance. Biologists stick to specialities such as molecular genetics, cell physiology, embryology, and so on, because the laws that relate to such restricted domains of phenomena form a coherent set, and one can see how new research fits into the body of already established knowledge in the restricted domain of interest.

A philosopher of science who is a strict reductionist would say that this state of affairs merely shows that biology is not yet a highly developed science. In time, all biological phenomena will be explainable in terms of laws that operate at the chemical level. The argument against this view rests mainly on the notion of 'emergent properties', which contends that different levels of organization have properties that cannot be fully explained in terms of knowledge about the constituent elements. For example, take two gases, hydrogen and oxygen; join them in the proper proportion and the result is a liquid, water. With the creation of H_2O new properties emerge that are not characteristic of either H or O but apply only to the combination of the two elements in the ratio of two atoms of H attached to every O. If we now take water and add some carbon and nitrogen in the proper way, amino acids are formed, with yet new and different properties. Joining a number of amino acids makes a protein; combining proteins makes cells; cells make tissues; tissues make organs; organs make organisms; and, sometimes, organisms living together make societies. At each level new properties emerge that scientists study for the purposes of formulating nomological propositions or laws.

There is a bit of mystery, perhaps even mysticism, about the idea of emergent properties. Nature is supposed, according to this, to have rather magical powers, and the true scientist is rather loath to accept this. When we see a magician at a theatre turn a lady into a pigeon we 'know' that there must be some trick to it even if we do not know how the trick is done. Why not take the same attitude to nature's performance in turning gases into liquids, chemicals into tissues, and so on? The fact is, however, that there would be little effective biological research done if every biologist felt compelled to explain the physical chemistry of the phenomena he studies. So biologists take a pragmatic view and restrict themselves to the search for laws of nature at a definite level of organization, the cell, the tissue, or whatever. A bit of mysticism does no harm if it assists empirical work in science. After all, the concept of 'gravity' in physics is rather mystical, since it postulates force or action between bodies without any contact or intermediary between them. When Newton first put forward his theory of gravitational attraction it was roundly criticized by the Cartesians, who felt that it was an essential principle of science that laws of nature refer to strictly mechanical forces and connections; no 'action at a distance', such as Newton's law postulates, was considered by them to be permissible. Despite this defect, Newton's law became the foundation of celestial mechanics and the basis for the accumulation of much knowledge. The bit of mysticism in the concept of gravitation did no harm because scientists did not rest content with it; they used it as the basis of empirical work. The same can be said confidently about the notion of emergent properties, at least in the natural sciences.

In the social sciences, the main interest centres upon what happens when individual persons form social organizations and these organizations or institutions play roles in a larger society such as a nation or, indeed, the world community. New properties emerge at the level of social organization just as they do in chemical and biological organization. Take twenty hermits, put them together in a monastery organized as a communal enterprise; *social* phenomena will emerge that could not have been predicted from the most complete psychological studies of the hermits as individuals. This touches upon a matter that has been a subject of great controversy among social scientists: 'methodological individualism' versus 'methodological holism'. The doctrine of methodological individualism states that the scientific explanation of social phenomena must be based upon laws that refer to the actions of *individual persons*. The doctrine of methodological holism is that the important entities for most social phenomena are more comprehensive, such as socioeconomic classes, or the two sex groups, or nations; and the laws of social phenomena must be stated in terms of such larger entities or 'wholes'.

To some degree, the various social sciences can be differentiated in terms of the levels at which they operate. Historical writing of the older conventional sort is very holistic, focusing upon nations as entities. A. J. Toynbee in his multi-volume *Study of History* (1934–54) contended that even the nation is too small, that history should be written in terms of the problems of, and interaction between, 'civilizations'. Generally speaking, though, historiography has become considerably less holistic than it was, say, in the nineteenth century. Economics is the most individualistic of the social sciences, or at least the branch of orthodox economics called 'microeconomics' is. Keynesian macroeconomics is more holistic and Marxian economics much more. Sociology is holistic but not so much as history is. There is a group of sociologists, however, known as 'exchange theorists', who are as individualistic as any economists.

The controversy between methodological individualists and methodological holists sometimes seem to imply that the laws of social phenomena are, by nature, located at a certain organizational level and not at any other. This seems to me to be mistaken. There are different sets of laws at different levels. The phenomenon of emergent properties is sufficient (though it may not be necessary) to guarantee that this is the case. The question as to what level we should be looking at and what laws we should be using can be answered only in terms of the problem that we are attempting to study. Suppose, for example, one wishes to predict the effect of an increase in the price of gasoline on the quantity of gasoline consumed. For this purpose the microeconomic 'law of demand', which is constructed on individualistic foundations, is very useful, but Karl Marx's holistic 'laws of capitalistic development' are not. On the other hand, if one is interested in predicting the long-run future of Western civilization, the 'law of demand' will provide no help, while Marx's 'laws of capitalist development' are at least conceivably germane. Unfortunately, the issue of methodological individualism and methodological holism has become part of an ideological squabble. Some Marxists feel they must be holists even when it is patently foolish; some libertarians regard the slightest deviation from individualism as undermining the foundations of Western civilization. This does not help to promote the scientific study of social phenomena.

The main difficulty with the doctrine of emergent properties when applied to human social phenomena results from the fact that the individuals who compose a society are, in important respects, the products of a process of social enculturation. That is, they not only make up the society but are made by it. At this point the analogy between social and physical phenomena fails. It is true that new properties emerge when hydrogen and oxygen come together to form water, but no one would claim that the properties of oxygen and hydrogen, considered by themselves, depend upon the properties of water. In a human society the relations between whole and part are reciprocal, the properties of one being affected by those of the other. If twenty adult hermits are put together in a monastery, the individuals would change to some degree; if the same twenty individuals were raised from childhood in the monastery, their personalities would, in large part, be created by the monastery's cultural norms and ambience, a much more profound influence of the whole on the part.

The existence of different levels of organization invites the possibility that the laws that operate at one level might be discovered by referring to another level as a metaphor or analogy. This is especially tempting when one of the sciences is more developed than another. One might, for example, take the view that the laws governing social phenomena are analogous to the (better understood) laws of physiology that operate within an organism. Herbert Spencer (see below, Chapter 15 A) was the most prominent social scientist to use such an analogy extensively, but in fact it has been one of the most common tactics in the history of social science. Other analogies have also been, from time to time, pressed into service, such as the entropy law of modern physics.

The methodology of analogical argument is too complex a subject to be examined here but it is worth noting that analogical reasoning is as dangerous as it is tempting. A common fallacy in reasoning is called by philosophers *ignoratio elenchi*. This refers to the fallacy of setting out to prove one proposition, proceeding to prove a different one, and then claiming that the original objective has been achieved. A metaphor or analogy can effectively illustrate an argument for didactic purposes but it cannot serve as a valid demonstration unless the analogy is very close. To use an illustrative analogy of my own here, the argument by analogy must touch four bases, as in baseball, before a run is scored. Let us symbolize the proposition to be proved as P and the analogy of it as A. To get on first base, it is necessary to show that P and A are indeed similar in certain respects, while recognizing also that they are different in other respects which, for the purpose of the exercise, are construed to be irrelevant. To move to second, A must of course be explicable. If it is not, then the process of explaining P by reference to A merely replaces one mystery by another. In order to be safe on third, the explanation of A must be *true*; otherwise P is being explained by a second-hand argument that is itself false. Finally, to cross home plate, the causal mechanism known to be at work in A must be explicitly shown to parallel the mechanism at work in P. That is to say, one must be able to demonstrate how P works, since that is the object of the exercise. The history of the social sciences is replete with analogical argument but these requirements frequently remain unfulfilled.

C. SOCIAL AND NATURAL SCIENCE: SOME PRELIMINARY REMARKS

The comparison of the social and the natural sciences will occupy our attention frequently in the following pages, as it has done already. At this point it may be useful to draw upon what has been discussed in sections A and B of this chapter to make some remarks on the differences between the social and natural sciences. In previous sections and chapters their similarities have been stressed; but a recognition of their differences is also important. Six major points of difference should be noted.

1. Nomological propositions are possible only with respect to phenomena that have some reasonable degree of uniformity. The number of chromosomes in organic cells varies from species to species, but all (normal) members of the same species are uniform. If one fruitfly had one chromosome number and another were different, or if the number changed randomly from one day to the next, it would not be possible to state any kind of general 'law' about the number of chromosomes in the fruitfly. Some social phenomena may be so diverse that no nomological proposition can be made. A clear case in point perhaps is war. We have many instances of war in recorded history and they have been fairly intensively studied, but no one has yet been able to formulate any general law about war that is even minimally satisfactory. It is likely that some social phenomena will permanently defy nomological generalization, no matter how advanced the social sciences become. In addition, even those social phenomena that *can* be covered by nomological propositions seldom have a degree of uniformity and precision comparable to those of the natural sciences. The 'law of demand' in economics embraces phenomena that are uniform enough to permit a nomological statement to be made, but it does not have the degree of precision and assurance of permanent uniformity of, say, the Chargaff nucleotide ratios or the Boyle–Charles law of gases, or the Mendelian laws of inheritance. In short, it would be a mistake to contend that no social laws can be formulated but it would be unwise, at least at present, to treat social laws as if they were as reliable as natural ones.

2. The social sciences are able to make very little use of controlled experiments. During the past half-century the amount of empirical data available on social phenomena has enormously increased; the modern computer permits the processing of large quantities of data; the theory of statistical methods and their mathematical foundations have been improved and the applications greatly enlarged. Yet many social scientists would cheerfully trade the whole of modern data processing for a few good closed-system experiments. In the search for laws nothing can really compare with the properly designed experiment.

3. Perhaps because of the limited ability to experiment, research in social science cannot be conducted on the basis of pure curiosity to the degree that is possible in the natural sciences. The physicist can wake up in the morning wondering what would happen if he did so-and-so and then go to the laboratory and do it. The economist or anthropologist or historian can wonder as well as the physicist, but all he can do about it in many cases is write a speculative paper so that others can wonder along with him. In view of how much of the nomological content of the natural sciences has resulted from the pure curiosity of the scientist, it is not surprising that, in this respect, progress in the social sciences is slower.

4. Closely connected with the practical or applied aspects of the social sciences is the fact that they are more involved with value judgements than the natural sciences. All applications of science are based on value judgements and there can be as much dispute over physics as over sociology when it comes to public policy concerning the use of knowledge. But a much larger part of social science deals with practical problems, so a much larger part is involved with values. When the natural sciences freed themselves from the grip of theology in the seventeenth century, they also succeeded in creating a high degree of detachment for their work from moral and other valuational criteria. Hardly anyone today believes that moral issues are involved in the geological theory of plate tectonics, or the proposition that there are 'black holes' in outer space, but there are very few subjects in social science that are disconnected from values. Some people indeed regard the whole of social science as disguised value judgement or secret ideology. This is a warped view, to be sure, but it is somewhat easier for a rational person to hold it than to believe that floods are due to immoral behaviour.

5. The social sciences deal with the behaviour of humans, and many (but by no means all) social scientists would claim that this makes them fundamentally different from the natural sciences. In addition to the above four points, the main ground for this view is the contention that humans do not behave in the same sense that rocks, or planets, or even lower organisms can be said to behave. Behind what we observe as human behaviour there are phenomena of *consciousness*. So when we say something like 'If the price of gasoline goes up some people will decide to buy less of it,' the word 'decide' implies the existence of something that is not present in a statement like 'If the wind velocity exceeds 50 m.p.h., some of these bridges will fall.' When we use words such as 'decide', 'choose', 'expect', and so on we are referring to mental *inner states* in human individuals for which there is no counterpart in the material world. This raises some very profound and difficult issues which have been debated intensively since René Descartes, in his *Discourse on Method* (1637), argued that the nature of the world is fundamentally dualistic in that mental phenomena and material phenomena are categorically distinct. The 'mind–body' problem will have to engage our attention from time to time in this book as we survey the history of social science and the arguments that

have been made concerning the methodology that is appropriate for the investigation of social phenomena.

Some social scientists have taken the view that the study of social phenomena is greatly assisted by the fact that the scientist, being human himself, can achieve an empathetic understanding of human behaviour, which penetrates through to the inner consciousness of the behaving entities, thus going beyond simply observing what people do, to a comprehension of why they do it. Social laws, it is claimed, lie at a deeper level than the nomological propositions advanced by natural scientists, who are, necessarily, on less intimate terms with entities such as masses, atoms, cells, etc. Other social scientists, however, regard the attempt to explain social phenomena with the aid of mental concepts as an impermissible resort to elements that are unobservable and inexplicable.

The most far-reaching attempt to eliminate such elements in the methodology of social science is in psychology, where the philosophy of 'behaviourism', represented by the work of B. F. Skinner, has been prominent since the second World War. The contention of behaviourists is not that inner states of consciousness do not exist, but that reference to them is unnecessary in any scientific explanation of behaviour. An illustration: consider the statement 'Henry drank water because the heat had made him thirsty.' There are three elements in this statement with causal connections, as indicated by the arrows:

heat   →   thirst   →   drinking behaviour

The behaviourist argues that 'thirst' is a mental state, not an objectively observable phenomenon. It can be eliminated from the scientific account of the phenomenon and should be. So we have:

heat   →   drinking behaviour

and our explanation of a human phenomenon is methodologically similar to our explanation of the connection between wind velocity and bridge failure.

Many social scientists and philosophers, not to speak of students of the humanities, are more troubled by behaviourism than by the problem it sets out to solve. Anthropologists report that many primitive cultures have animistic beliefs; they regard stones, trees, rivers, mountains and what-not as containing 'spirit' similar to human consciousness. Scientific progress, the discovery of laws of nature, is hardly possible in a culture where animism is the predominant view of the nature of things. But it seems to be going too far when consciousness is banished from consideration altogether. One social scientist (Frank Knight) remarked that, having waged a long struggle to escape from the idea that stones are like men, we now seem to be intent on showing that men are like stones.

The crux of the debate on this question has to do with the nature of causal laws. Is it legitimate to insert references to mental states such as 'thirst' in causal propositions? Is it legitimate to say that human actions resulted from 'desires', 'motives', 'beliefs', and so on; that is, may these be legitimately construed as causal factors? If we say, 'The reason John drank is that he was thirsty,' does this have no more content than the statement 'Heat caused John to drink'? In short, if we give the 'reason' for a human act (i.e. a statement of the motive or intentions of the actor) are we explaining the 'causes' of the observed phenomenon? Many social scientists, and at least some philosophers of science, have no objection to attributing causal status to 'reasons' but there is another problem here: move back a step and ask, what is the cause of the reasons that led to the action? If all reasons can be traced to antecedent material causes, then the world is fully deterministic, whether or not one embraces the specific version of determinism advanced by B. F. Skinner. This can be escaped only by asserting that the mental states of human consciousness are not fully determined; that they have some autonomy or independence of outside factors. This is equivalent to arguing that mental states generate reasons, which act in a causal fashion, but they themselves are uncaused. This may appear to be rather mystical, but it is through this tiny opening in the edifice of modern scientific philosophy that the issue of human freedom to act (and therefore the moral issue of responsibility for one's acts) comes in. Science has laboured hard to eliminate the idea of autonomous causal factors, but this is obviously much more difficult to do with social than with natural phenomena.

6. Finally, we should note once again that whole–part relationships in social phenomena are not like those of the natural world. The characteristics of chemical elements are not dependent upon the compounds and other higher-level entities of which they are parts. Oxygen is oxygen, whether it is in a water molecule or a protein, a tree or a crocodile. But the human individual is different, in some important ways at least, in different social environments. To the degree that scientific explanation requires reduction of wholes to component parts, it poses difficulties in the domain of social phenomena which are much greater than those confronting the natural sciences.

I note these points here in order to assist the reader in grasping the philosophical import of the history of social science that will occupy our main attention in the following pages. These issues will engage our attention again in Chapter 18, where the main issues in the philosophy of science are directly addressed.

D. POSITIVE AND NORMATIVE PROPOSITIONS

The terms 'positive' and 'normative' are frequently used in the literature of social science to differentiate between propositions about empirical facts and propositions that are value judgements. Distinguishing between these two types of propositions is essential if one is to think or speak clearly on any matter, but especially so in dealing with social questions.

The adjectives 'positive' and 'normative' are not particularly satisfactory as labels for the investigation of objective phenomena on the one hand and value judgements on the other. The term 'positive' is intended to refer to knowledge derived by detached empirical investigation, not contaminated by the personal values of the investigator. As an epistemological description, 'positivism' originated in the writings of Henri Saint-Simon and Auguste Comte in the early nineteenth century. But, as we shall see when we come to examine their views (Chapter 12), though these writers intended to endow the term with the kind of objectivity characteristic of the natural sciences, their own work was so infused with value judgements and untestable speculation that they cannot be seriously named as exemplars of positivist methodology, as social scientists now understand it.

The origin of the term 'normative' is even more peculiar. It derives from the Latin word *norma*, which is the name for a carpenter's tool, a square for setting right-angles. From this clearly 'positive' activity, the term came to be used to mean a standard of good conduct, or 'norm', perhaps derived from the notion that a carpenter conducts himself properly when he gets his angles truly ninety degrees when they should be. By the mysterious processes of language evolution 'normative' is now used in English to refer to those aspects of social science where value judgements enter the picture.

Is it valid to make a distinction of this sort? After all, the proposition that the earth is round is, in some sense, a 'belief' (and the members of the Flat Earth Society do not believe it). Why call one belief 'positive' and another 'normative'? All beliefs are indeed subjective, but there are objective ways of testing positive beliefs that cannot be applied to normative beliefs. Let us consider two statements:

Smith believes that the earth is round.
Jones believes that taking another person's property is wrong.

Both of these are positive statements in that they record facts about Smith and Jones. The crucial question is not whether these beliefs are in fact held but whether they can be supported by empirical evidence.

If Smith were challenged by a member of the Flat Earth Society he might put forward arguments such as the following. (a) If the earth is round one would logically expect to observe that a ship sailing away from an observer would disappear bit by bit (the hull first and the flag mast last), and one does in fact observe this. (b) If the earth is not round, one would logically expect that by travelling consistently in one direction, say due west, one would not return to the starting point, but in fact one does return. The state of the world supports Smith's belief by showing that it can account for certain facts (a) and by showing that certain facts cannot be accounted for without it (b). These are powerful (though not totally compelling) arguments for Smith's belief that the world is round. There may also be powerful arguments for Jones's belief that stealing is immoral, but they are not arguments that rest on a comparison between the logical consequences of his hypothesis and the state of the world. So Jones's belief may be as valid as Smith's, and each person may be convinced that he is correct, but they do not have, and cannot have, the same kind of supporting argument.

The essential difference between positive and normative propositions can be put this way: when a positive proposition fails to be supported by empirical evidence, the proposition is called into question; but when a normative proposition is at odds with the state of the world, the state of the world is called into question. Put somewhat differently, when a person's positive beliefs do not agree with the facts, he is rationally obliged to change his beliefs; but when the facts do not agree with a person's normative beliefs he is morally obliged to change the facts if he can. The member of the Flat Earth Society should change his geographical *theory*; the thief should change his *conduct*. Positive and normative propositions are both vital to social science in its efforts to understand and to deal with social problems, but it is essential to clear thinking that they should not be confused.

In this discussion I have treated normative propositions as propositions that have moral content. But we should note that this is not characteristic of all normative propositions. When a mechanic says to a car owner, 'The spark plugs should be changed,' he is referring to an alteration in the state of the world that would improve the mechanical efficiency of an automobile. This is not a moral judgement. But if he were to say, 'The fender should be repaired because a pedestrian might be injured by the sharp projection,' he is implicitly advancing the moral judgement that it is wrong to drive a car that exposes other persons to unnecessary hazards. On the other hand, if the mechanic says, 'The fender should be repaired because it looks ugly,' he is making an aesthetic, not a moral, evaluation. Unfortunately, the term 'normative' is used in a variety of ways, and it is not always easy to tell whether the reference is to a standard of technical efficiency, or an aesthetic criterion, an ethical principle, or some other valuational norm.

Chapter 4

Political theory and political philosophy

The primary aim of all the social sciences is the examination of the ways in which individuals are organized into a collective social system. Political science, as an academic discipline, focuses upon how this is achieved by the agency of 'government'. In the most basic terms, political science is a study of the exercise of coercion. The 'state' is construed to be the ultimate or 'sovereign' repository of coercive power within a defined geographic domain, and political science studies the institutions and practices by which this power is exercised. Even in small tribal societies, anthropologists tell us, the structure of authority is sometimes very complex. It is certainly so in larger and more developed societies where the exercise of state power involves an elaborate process by which that power is translated into specific policies and laws which are then applied to even more specific cases. Like the other social sciences, political science is interested not merely in describing the structure of particular political systems but also in constructing abstract models of types of political systems, and in using such models, together with empirical data, to arrive at evaluative judgements concerning the merits of different systems by reference to some general normative criteria.

As we shall see, some of the most important literature in the history of political science has been written in the form of what should perhaps be called 'hypothetical anthropology', which undertakes to describe how governmental organization might have developed in an imagined 'state of nature', where the degree of sociality is minimal. The main purpose of such scenarios is not to provide a positive model of the state but to arrive at normative principles that can be applied to real political systems as general evaluative criteria. The exercise of coercive power by some persons over others, which is implicit in all forms of social organization by means of government, requires philosophical justification, since, in itself, it is not morally defensible. The hypothetical notion that the origin of governmental power lies in a 'social contract' that was entered into by men in the 'state of nature' became prominent in seventeenth-century English political thought as a way of developing a normative theory of politics. This still has considerable appeal, if we judge by the great interest engendered by similar arguments recently advanced by, for example, the American ethical philosophers John Rawls in *A Theory of Justice* (1971) and Robert Nozick in *Anarchy, State, and Utopia* (1974).

Most of the political science literature proceeds more directly, simply assuming that the state exists as a method of social organization and devoting the main effort to an investigation of how it functions in this regard, without paying much attention to either its possible origins or its actual history. The criterion of normative judgement that one finds in much of this literature is utilitarian: the state is viewed as a social artefact whose main purpose is to serve the welfare of the members of the community. The great exception to this is the European literature of the early Christian and medieval period. St. Augustine (354–430) wrote his *City of God* in order to divert the attention of Christians from their worldly condition to the much more important objective, in his view, of preparing for the after-life. With only a few except-ions, the political literature of the next thousand years was theological in its orientation. But before this period, and since the Renaissance, a secular and utilitarian outlook has characterized the main writings in political philo-sophy. An instruction to the Roman consuls, which dates back as far as the law of the 'Twelve Tables' (*c.* fifth century B.C.) – 'The welfare of the people should be the supreme law' (*Salus populi suprema lex esto*) – captures the essence of secular utilitarianism as a political philosophy. The political science literature we shall be examining in this chapter is dominated by that outlook.

We should note, though, that a theory of the functions of government as a set of social institutions is not the same thing as an empirical account of the historical origins of the state. The social contract theory, in its attempt to extract normative principles from a hypothetical history of what might have occurred in a 'state of nature', confounds these two distinct matters and, in effect, construes the state as a utilitarian artefact created to serve man's communal needs. As history this will not survive examination. The prepond-erant evidence is that governments have arisen, much as gangs of robbers do, to exploit the less well organized rather than to provide services for the collective good (see Robert L. Carneiro, 'A Theory of the Origin of the State', *Science*, 1970, pp. 733–8). But no matter; we are addressing here not the historical question of how governments came originally to be but the theoretical analysis of their role, once established, in social organization. As with many other social institutions, their modern functions may differ greatly from their original ones. Some political theorists adopt the view that govern-ments not only arose as a means by which the few might exploit the many, but that they still have this essential character. We will not examine that view in this chapter, but it will come to our attention from time to time as we proceed with the history of social science.

A. PLATO, ARISTOTLE, AND POLYBIUS

Plato's *Republic* is not a description or analysis of the government of Athens in his time, or an account of its historical development. Its purpose is to describe, in general terms, the main characteristics of a perfect system of government, one that would serve the welfare of the citizens, create civic unity and suppress conflict, provide a just social order, and, once established, require no future alteration. Unlike most other works of the utopian genre, the *Republic* continues to be discussed by political scientists and philosophers 2,400 hundred years after it was written, because it raises issues of profound importance and advances a view of the foundations of good government that is still reflected, in various ways, in modern political thought and practice.

Plato's plan for perfect government rests upon a notion that occupied our attention in Chapter 1, the merits of division of labour. The *Republic* contains a discussion of the division of labour that anticipates many of the economic and sociological arguments that were later made on its behalf by the two great modern-era writers on the topic, Adam Smith and Émile Durkheim (see Chapters 7 C and 15 B). But Plato's main object in discussing this in the *Republic* is to argue that governing is, necessarily, a specialized activity which must be performed by the persons who have both the special natural talents and the rigorous training it requires. In this respect Plato anticipated Henri Saint-Simon and August Comte (Chapter 12) and the numerous others since who have argued that the secret of good government is the selection of good governors, men who have the personal qualities and skills appropriate for the performance of this specialized social function. This contrasts with another view which, as we shall see, stems from Polybius: the contention that good government is primarily a matter of institutional structure, the constitutional arrangement of the mechanisms through which the coercive power of the state is exercised. A great deal of the history of Western political thought could be written in terms of these two conceptions, both of which remain prominent in the political science literature of the present day.

In Plato's ideal society, the rights and responsibilities of political power belong to a special class of 'guardians' consisting of a very small number of persons who have been selected in youth and subjected to many years of rigorous training. Their selection and training are not designed to create a class of persons who are skilled in the arts of public administration. Youths are selected who display those mental qualities that are necessary if one is to become a 'philosopher' and the long training is necessary to realize this potentiality. In order to understand Plato's political theory, therefore, we must note what he had in mind when he argued that, in the ideal society, the guardians must be philosophers.

The knowledge that the ordinary person possesses, says Plato, is limited to what he can infer from the empirical information he obtains by sense perception. This is a severe limitation since the senses of vision, hearing, etc., only reflect the specific properties of particular things; they do not capture the universal or fundamental properties that lie at a deeper level, beyond the reach of the senses. In a famous illustration, Plato compares the ordinary person to a man who lives imprisoned in a cave, chained facing a wall on which appear the flickering shadows cast by the light of a fire behind him. The philosopher is the rare person who is capable of transcending the limitations imposed by sense perception, like a man who has escaped from his imprisonment in the cave and, having emerged into the light of day, perceives the true nature of reality. Plato was not arguing that the deficiencies of sense perceptions are to be overcome by refining and extending their capacities (as the modern scientist does); they must be replaced by the exercise of reason, which, alone, can reveal the transcendental 'pure form' of reality. The few persons who have the requisite mental powers, and have been rigorously trained to use them to arrive at metaphysical truth, must be the guardians of the state, for only they can apprehend the 'pure form of the good', the understanding of which is essential in the governance of a perfect social order.

In Plato's ideal state, the guardians are to have unlimited power. Plato specifies that they must share their property, wives, and children in common in order to eliminate personal ambitions and conflicts among themselves but, beyond this, no restraints are necessary. Since they are philosophers, their understanding of the needs of the society is flawless, and the decrees they issue will, necessarily, serve the general welfare. 'It is absurd,' says Plato, 'that the guardians should need to be guarded,' if they are properly selected and trained. Since Plato's day an immense literature on political theory and political philosophy has been generated, but the *Republic* still remains a classic statement of the view that the key to good government is the selection of the right persons to act as governors. The alternative view, that the key to good government rests upon a constitutional structure that subjects those who wield the authority of the state to supervision and control, rests upon the idea that even 'philosophers' should not be allowed to exercise unlimited power.

Plato's ideal polity is not a one-man dictatorship, but he makes it quite plain that the number of guardians will be very small. The welfare of the people is best served by such an arrangement, but Plato recognizes that the other citizens, not being philosophers, cannot be expected to welcome exclusion from the governance of the state. An ideal state, if it were established, would not be maintained unless the mass of the people were persuaded to allow themselves to be ruled by the few. The stability and permanence of the political order therefore require something more than the selection of those who understand the 'pure form of the good'. It requires, as Plato frankly puts it, the creation of a myth or 'falsehood' to justify the power of the guardians. Though the guardians are in fact ordinary humans, the people must view them as belonging to a categorically different species of beings, who have been fashioned and trained 'under the earth' which is their 'mother' by a special process of creation that has given them 'souls of gold'. This myth, says Plato, must be promoted so assiduously that the citizens will believe it without question, and perhaps the guardians themselves will believe it as well.

The *Republic* deserves the attention that it still receives today because it raises many of the important issues of political theory: the organization of power, the qualities of those who should wield it, the justification of authority, the role of ideology, the political use of falsehood and propaganda. Moreover, ideas similar to Plato's are to be found not only in abstract treatises on library shelves but in the politics of the real world. There are few philosophers among the guardians of present-day states, but the other elements of Plato's prescription are facts of common political experience.

Plato's most famous student, Aristotle, disagreed with his teacher on many points. In his *Politics* (the second part of a general treatise on ethics) Aristotle severely criticizes both the method and the substance of Plato's political theory. The method, complains Aristotle, is too abstract; and the conception of the ideal state reduces to a political system in which the authority of the rulers is really sustained by their ability to command 'heavily armed soldiers'. The study of politics can be scientific, says Aristotle, but it must be based on the empirical examination of real systems of government. No detailed description of actual states is presented in the *Politics*, but Aristotle's argument is guided by what he conceives to be the lessons that have been supplied by political experience. The chief of these, in his view, is that no system of government is perfect. All systems have essential properties which include defects as well as virtues, and even the best system of government is only comparatively better than others. Moreover, even in comparative terms, one cannot say that one particular system of government is best, for, though it may be argued to be so in the abstract, another system might be better in the particular circumstances of a specific society. 'It is evident,' says Aristotle, 'that the form of government is best in which every man, whoever he is, can act for the best and live happily,' but, unlike Plato, he does not undertake to present a design for a government that will, always and perfectly, serve these objectives.

On one point Aristotle agreed with Plato: the great importance of the division of labour, and the application of this to political organization. Nature, says Aristotle, 'makes each thing for a single use, and every instrument is best made when intended for one and not for many uses'. This principle applies also to the members of a community. Like an organism (Aristotle was greatly interested in biology), a state is composed of functionally differentiated elements – farmers, mechanics, warriors, traders, etc. – who must keep to their task if the whole is to be healthy. Magistrates, law-makers, and other state officials are similarly specialized, and the welfare of the whole requires that they, like the others, should continue in their roles and not move from one occupation to another. Moreover, he says, this differentiation of the governing class is ordained by nature: 'that some should rule and others be ruled is a thing, not only necessary, but expedient; from the hour of their birth, some are marked out for subjection, and others for rule'. A state is not merely an aggregation of individual persons; 'man is by nature a political animal . . . [and] thus the state is . . . prior to the family and to the individual, since the whole is necessarily prior to the part', as it is in organisms. Aristotle was one of the great originators of the holistic view of society and its application to political theory. A good polity, in his view, is one in which everyone participates, in various ways, in the formation of public policy, but this does not mean that farmers may become magistrates and traders become legislators. Everyone should keep his place in an established constitutional order. Those who wield the power of the state should be the guardians and administrators of the laws, not ruling the citizens arbitrarily as a master does his slaves or a parent does his children. Some commentators on the *Politics* view it as advancing the notion of 'the rule of law' and the concept of a government that is bound by a constitutional order, but Aristotle does not say enough about these matters to warrant crediting him with more than suggesting these important ideas in passing remarks.

Aristotle was an ardent, not to say compulsive, classifier. His favoured mode of analysis was to arrange empirical phenomena into what he took to be homogeneous categories and describe the 'essential properties' of each category. A great deal of the *Politics* is devoted to the essential properties of three types of states: monarchies, aristocracies, and democracies, or states in which political power resides in the hands of the 'one', the 'few', or the 'many'. This mode of analysis, and Aristotle's specific categories, were the most influential feature of the *Politics*. From the time it began to be studied intensively in the thirteenth century, down almost to the present day, the notion that there are three basic 'forms' of government dominated a great deal of the literature of political science, many writers devoting their efforts to arguing that one form is superior to the others, others contending that the best government is a 'mixture' of the three, and more empirically oriented ones trying to classify real states as belonging to one or other of the classes in the triad. The eighteenth-century English poet, Alexander Pope, expressed his impatience with this mode of analysis in a famous couplet:

> For forms of government let fools contest;
> Whate'er is best administered is best.

but the Aristotelian forms did not disappear from political theory until well into the twentieth century.

The notion that the best kind of government is a mixture of the three pure forms deserves special attention because it was commonly, but mistakenly, associated with two other ideas that will occupy our attention: 'separation of powers' and 'checks and balances'. In the interest of historical accuracy we should also note that though the concept of 'mixed government' is frequently described as 'Aristotelian', it did not originate with Aristotle, nor did he necessarily advocate it as the best form of political organization. The idea that monarchy, aristocracy, and democracy are the three basic forms of government and the argument that the best government is a mixture of them was a commonplace in Aristotle's day, as he himself notes. He does accept the triadic classification, and uses it, but he does not argue that a mixed government is best. 'Some . . . say,' he observes, 'that the best constitution is a combination of all existing forms and they praise the Lacedaemonian [Sparta] because it is made up of oligarchy, monarchy, and democracy,' but he does not indicate that he agrees with this view. Nevertheless, it is common even today to find historians referring to the 'Aristotelian theory of mixed government'. That theory was prominent for a long time, but it was not 'Aristotelian'. For the student of the history of ideas this misnomer is of more than casual interest, because it is indicative of a practice that can sometimes be grossly misleading. One might assume that, when an idea is labelled as 'Aristotelian' or 'Marxian' or 'Keynesian' or some other eponymous term, it originated with or, at least, was prominent in the writings of the person whose name is used in the label. Unfortunately this is frequently incorrect and, in some cases, examination of the original texts reveals that the eponym of the label held very different, even diametrically opposed, views. Karl Marx, after reading an account of his theories by a French 'Marxist' writer, is reported to have said, 'I am *not* a "Marxist".' The same disclaimer might well be made by many of the prominent figures in the history of social thought.

In another of his books, the *Laws*, Plato puts forward an interesting proposition concerning international relations. He argues that a treaty arrangement between sovereign states is more stable if three states are involved rather than a bilateral agreement between any two of them. A bilateral agreement is likely to be broken whenever one of the parties considers itself to be more powerful than the other; but when there are three states involved, any one of them would be faced by the combined power of the other two if it should break the treaty. The 'balance of power' doctrine in international relations, which was widely held by modern political scientists until quite recently, and adopted in practice by many states as the way to prevent war, can be traced back to this Platonic argument. But there is no evidence that he held the view that a similar arrangement could be used in the internal government of a state. As we have seen, the guardians of Plato's ideal state are to possess unlimited power and, in his view, it would be 'absurd' to constrain them.

The idea that the best form of government is one in which there is a constitutional system that constrains the powers of the various organs of the state by setting them in opposition to one another finds no expression in Plato's *Republic* or Aristotle's *Politics*. The first clear statement of this notion, which we now call the theory of 'checks and balances', was made by the Greek-Roman historian, Polybius, who lived in the second century B.C. Not all of Polybius' writings have survived, but apparently he did not undertake to write extensively on political theory as Plato and Aristotle had. He dismisses the *Republic* rather contemptuously as an imaginary state that had never been tested in practice. However, in the course of giving an account of three centuries of Roman history, he offers a theoretical explanation of why Rome, like Sparta earlier, had succeeded in achieving internal political stability and civic liberty, as well as the military capacity for which they were much celebrated. (The relevant passages from Polybius are contained in Appendix 1 of Kurt von Fritz, *The Theory of the Mixed Constitution in Antiquity*, 1975.)

Polybius talks about the 'Aristotelian' three forms of government and he appears to say that the success of Sparta and Rome was due to the fact that they had developed a governmental system which was a mixture of the three forms. He believes that each of the forms has characteristic virtues, as Aristotle contended, and that a mixed government is superior because it need not sacrifice any of these virtues, as an unmixed monarchy, aristocracy, or democracy must. But, if we attend carefully to his language in describing how a mixed government functions, we find a different argument. Speaking of Sparta, he says:

> Lycurgus . . . tried to unite all the characteristics and features of the best governments so that none of the elements can grow unduly powerful . . . since the power of each would be counteracted by that of the others. In this way, he thought, no element could outbalance the others and the political system would for a long time remain in a state of equilibrium.

The idea that Polybius attributes to Lycurgus and which, in his account of Roman history, he describes as having evolved through practice is clearly the concept of a system of checks and balances. He approves of such a system and especially so because it preserves the liberty of the citizens. As he puts it, because of their constitution, 'the Lacedaemonians retained their liberty for a much longer time than any other people that we know of'. He is speaking here not only of the independence that Sparta enjoyed as a state, but the personal freedom of the Spartan citizen from the exercise of arbitrary power by his own government.

As an historian Polybius is not completely reliable, but he introduces in his appraisal of Sparta and Rome the important notion of a governmental system that is organized, not as a hierarchy of command, but as an equilibrium of counterpoised elements. This idea does not prominently appear again in the political literature until the sixteenth century, when commentators, particularly Gasparo Contarini, used it as a frame of analysis for the study of the constitution of the republic of Venice. From the sixteenth century onward, the notion of a checks and balances constitution received more or less continuous attention, most prominently by Italian Renaissance period writers, by English writers during the political disturbances of the seventeenth century, and then, in the eighteenth century, by the Baron de Montesquieu in his famous interpretation of the English constitution, and by the framers of the American constitution.

B. THE VENETIAN CONSTITUTION

Venice lies at the northern end of the Adriatic Sea, on the east side of the Italian peninsula. According to legend, it was founded by people who, endeavoring to escape from the Lombard invaders of Italy in the sixth century, took refuge on the low-lying islands of a lagoon, where they were safe from marauders who were not skilled in water navigation, and commenced to build there the city that we can still see today. The magnificent brick and stone palaces, churches, and other large buildings standing on wooden piles driven into the mudflats of the lagoon bespeak a past era of great opulence and, indeed, in her prime, Venice was probably the wealthiest city in the world. Her population was never much larger than a hundred thousand but, by taking advantage of her strategic geographic position, Venice dominated the lucrative trade between Europe and the East, which she supported by a strong navy and an extensive network of naval and trading stations in the eastern Mediterranean. The important role of Venice in the economic development of Europe during the late Middle Ages and the Renaissance has been amply described by economic historians, but we are concerned here with another topic that has, unfortunately, been little recognized: the city's system of government and the influence of this upon European political thought.

In the Renaissance era, the republic of Venice was greatly admired, and envied, for its wealth and military power, but also on account of its extraordinary political stability, administrative efficiency, and the high degree of personal freedom enjoyed by those who lived under the jurisdiction of the Venetian state. While other Italian cities of the Renaissance oscillated violently from one tyrannous regime to another, Venice was perceived as a model of ideal government. This came to be called the 'myth of Venice' in the later political literature, but it was not a utopian myth, since it was founded upon a functioning political system. Gaetano Cozzi, the leading modern historian of Venice, who has done much to rediscover the reality of Venetian politics, speaks of the foreigners who flocked to Venice during the Reformation period as finding there:

> a unique ambience; a wide circulation of ideas and books which, though often clandestine, was not on that account less stimulating and fruitful; an open style of life, free and easy, with a sense of toleration that was truly exceptional in a Europe still convulsed with religious disputes and enclosed within the defenses of rigid doctrinal beliefs.

Cozzi quotes the great sixteenth-century political writer Jean Bodin, not an admirer of the Venetian government, as nevertheless observing that the city attracted 'those who aspired to live in the greatest freedom and tranquillity; people who wished to engage in trade or industry, or to pursue studies worthy of free men' (Cozzi's introductory commentaries to Paolo Sarpi, *Opere*, 1969).

The Venetian constitution was not a written document but a set of institutional arrangements that were created in the early fourteenth century. During the next 500 years, until Napoleon invaded the city in 1797, this constitutional order survived without a break. Not only did no foreign power succeed in attacking the city successfully, but no attempts to subvert the government from within seriously interrupted its political stability. Venice called itself *La Serenissima* (the Most Serene) in proud, but largely deserved, self-congratulation as an exceptional polity in a Europe that was racked almost everywhere by incessant political upheavals and the suppression of personal freedoms.

Political power in the Venetian republic resided in the hands of an aristocracy that comprised about 5 per cent of the population. All adult males of noble families (some 2,000 persons) had the right to attend the weekly meetings of the Great Council and to stand for election to the various smaller councils through which the policies of state were executed. The most significant feature of the system was that its structure was designed to prevent concentration of power. The Doge, who was elected for life, was so hedged about by restrictions that he could do practically nothing without the know-ledge, and approval, of various other officials. Membership of the other official bodies (elected by the Great Council) was very short-term, usually less than a year, and in most cases not renewable. The powers of the various councils overlapped in complex ways. In essence, the Venetian constitution was a system of checks and balances. Unlike Plato, who felt that men of superior virtue, the guardians, should have absolute power, the Venetians distrusted political authority and feared its concentration in any hands. The system was structured to select able men to fill the offices of state but even more so was it designed to control their power. The essential theory underlying the Venetian constitution is that power can be controlled only by power, a proposition that can be translated into practice by means of a political system composed of separated official bodies arranged in a system of mutual counterpoise. The founding fathers of the American constitution held the same views of power and arrived at a similar solution.

The Venetians, apparently, did not derive this idea from Polybius' discussion of the Spartan and Roman republics. The constitutional system that was constructed in the early fourteenth century was built piecemeal by practical politicians who did not consult the classical Greek or Latin political literature or, for that matter, the political literature that was inspired by Christian theology. Later, the government of Venice was commented upon by many writers, including even the authors of English travel books, who apparently felt that their readers would be interested in this unusual, and highly successful, governmental system.

The most important of the Italian political writers of the Renaissance period was Gasparo Contarini. His *De Magistratibus et Republica Venetorum*, published in 1543 (the same year as Copernicus' *Revolutionibus* and Vesalius' *Fabrica*) was one of the most widely read books on politics of the age. It went through at least eight editions in the original Latin, seven Italian, and two French editions. Only one translation of it was made into English (by Lewes Lewkinor in 1599, entitled *The Commonwealth and Government of Venice*) but it was widely read and discussed in England during the period of political upheaval of the seventeenth century. John Milton, the great poet and political essayist, portrayed the republic of Venice described by Contarini as an ideal system that England, in her time of trouble, should seek to emulate. James Harrington modelled his highly popular utopian account of the mythical *Commonwealth of Oceana* (1656) directly upon Contarini's *Magistratibus*. Many less well known political writers of the period used the 'myth of Venice' to argue the case for a 'republican' form of government in England. (See Zera S. Fink, *The Classical Republicans*, 1945, for a discussion of the role of the Venetian example in the English political literature of the seventeenth century.)

Contarini's *Magistratibus* deserves more recognition than it has received from historians, and not only because of its great influence at a crucial time in the early development of constitutionalism in European politics. It was the first substantial treatise in political *science*, if we hold to the notion that science consists of the examination of empirical phenomena and the attempt to explain them by coherent theoretical argument. Although he was a churchman (later becoming a cardinal) Contarini makes no more than perfunctory references to the deity in the *Magistratibus*. He takes the view that the Venetian constitution had no transcendental origin or purpose but was constructed by practical politicians for secular and utilitarian objectives. He examines the details of the system, and he explains why it functions as it does. In the opening pages of the *Magistratibus* Contarini states his utilitarian orientation to politics without disguise. Men form civil societies and accept the restraints of government he says, 'so that they may live happily and commodiously'. He rejects the notion that the main object of the state is to glorify itself by increased power and victorious warfare.

> There have been many commonwealths [he says] which have far exceeded Venice as well in empire and in greatness of estate, as in military discipline and glory of the wars: yet have there not been any, that may be paragoned with this of ours, for institutions and laws prudently decreed to establish unto the inhabitants a happy and prosperous felicity.

These objectives, he observes, cannot be achieved without political stability, and Venice has succeeded because it has a system of government that provides stability without tyranny. In describing this system, Contarini makes no use at all of the concept of hierarchy. The Venetian political system is depicted not as a power pyramid, but as a complex of intersecting councils that have overlapping responsibilities and act to oversee and control one another. He sometimes speaks of 'mixed government' but he does not use it as an analytical model. In everything except the explicit use of the term, Contarini's conception of the Venetian state is the checks and balances model.

The Venetian republic was not a democracy in the modern sense. Contarini regards the reservation of power to the noble class as wise, though he includes the other citizens as beneficiaries of it. The last chapter of the *Magistratibus* undertakes to explain the fact, which he considered remarkable, that the general body of Venetians had been willing to accept the government of a small aristocracy with such equanimity. Plato, the reader will recall, argued that the citizenry can be persuaded to accept the rule of the guardians only by means of propaganda that promotes a 'noble lie'. Contarini makes no such argument. He gives detailed practical reasons for the willingness of the citizenry to be ruled by the nobles, stressing that not only had the 'seditions and tumults' that plagued other states been avoided, and the government had performed its duties efficiently, but that the ordinary citizen was free from arbitrary and unnecessary interference, that his property was secure, that the same laws applied to all without discrimination, that the ordinary citizens retained control of their own institutions such as occupational guilds, and that their voices were heard, in various ways, by their governors. A 'just and temperate manner of ruling', Contarini declares, not 'violent force, armed garrisons, or fortified towers', is what justifies Venice's description of herself as the Most Serene Republic.

Contarini's empirical account and theoretical analysis of the Venetian political system are somewhat idealized but, in the estimate of historians, they are substantially accurate. Clearly, the *Magistratibus* was an important contribution to political science; because of its empirical orientation, coupled with the use of the checks and balances model, it stands well above all previous political literature in significance. Unfortunately, it did not generate a continuous tradition of political analysis. The decline of Venice as a naval and commercial power, due to the development of maritime technology and the discovery of America and the Cape route to the Orient, suppressed interest in her political system. By the eighteenth century the 'myth of Venice' as the ideal state had been replaced by the image of her as decadent, corrupt, and sinister. The travel books referred to such things as the 'bridge of sighs' over which prisoners were said to be taken from secret tribunals to torture chambers and dungeons, rather than to her remarkable system of government. Contarini's book was no longer read and the checks and balances theory survived only in a vague and disguised form in English political thought until it was revived by the American 'federalist' writers of the constitution era.

C. SEVENTEENTH-CENTURY ENGLAND

The seventeenth century deserves some special attention from the student of the history of Western civilization. Many of the elements that we are now able to recognize clearly as factors contributing to the modern development of that civilization originated in or were firmly established during the seventeenth century. In the field of science, it was during the seventeenth century that the modern approach to knowledge was established by solid achievements. Galileo made his major discoveries in physics, and compiled empirical evidence in support of the Copernican theory. Johannes Kepler announced his discovery of the laws of planetary motion. Isaac Newton's *Mathematical Principles of Natural Philosophy* appeared in 1687, probably the most important book on science ever published, which established the basic laws of motion and constructed a system of celestial mechanics that moulded the discoveries of Copernicus and Kepler into a model that replaced the Ptolemaic system which had dominated astronomical thinking since the second century of the Christian era. Robert Boyle, by his extensive experimental and theoretical work, established the modern science of chemistry, detaching it from the long influence of alchemists and magic-mongers. William Harvey's *On the Movement of the Heart and Blood in Animals* (1628) not only announced the discovery of the circulation of the blood in the animal body but, by viewing the body as a mechanism, laid the foundations of the modern sciences of physiology and medicine. René Descartes, in his *Discourse on Method* (1637), established the mechanistic conception of the world as a fundamental philosophical principle of science. In the same book, he announced the invention of analytical geometry, important in itself, but especially so since it led to the creation of the powerful analytical tool, the calculus, by Isaac Newton and G. W. Leibniz later in the century. Francis Bacon's *Novum Organum* (1620) aimed at constructing principles of inductive reasoning that would serve the needs of empirical science and permit it to escape from the shackles of Aristotelianism. Official recognition of the importance of science in England was given by the creation of the Royal Society in 1662.

In any discussion of seventeenth-century intellectual development, however brief, it is notable that English names begin to appear with much greater frequency than before. The foundations of England's greatness as a military and economic power were laid in the sixteenth century during the long reigns of Henry VIII and Elizabeth I. The island was strategically located to take advantage of the shift of the centre of maritime commerce from the Mediterranean to the Atlantic with the discovery of the Americas and the sea route to the Far East around the Cape of Good Hope. Henry VIII detached England from the religious authority of Rome; Elizabeth successfully prevented European dynastic entanglements. When the Spanish Armada was defeated in 1588, England's national security was assured for a long time to come. The flourishing of science in England during the seventeenth century was probably connected with the nation's emergence as a world power but not in ways that are easy to explain. In fact this period was so disturbed politically that it is hard to believe that it furnished an environment conducive to scientific research and scholarly pursuits. James I succeeded Elizabeth as monarch in 1603 and his reign was, from the first, marked by political conflict. Things got worse when his son, Charles I, ascended the throne in 1625. Full-scale civil war broke out in 1642; Charles was beheaded in 1649; Oliver

Cromwell ruled as dictator until 1660; the monarchy was then restored but Charles II and James II were unpopular, despotic kings and another revolution, in 1688, finally brought an end to the most bitter period of internal conflict in England's history. It was not a happy time; nevertheless, English science flourished.

While it is rather surprising that the natural sciences developed during this disturbed period, the fact that it was an era of intense and fundamental thinking about politics is not surprising at all. One does not depose monarchs (either by execution as in 1649 or by exile as in 1688) without generating controversy concerning political principles. England was not so accustomed to revolutionary change in political authority as to accept it without profound questioning. So it is not to be wondered at that seventeenth-century England, with its revolutionary and dramatic events, provided fertile ground for the growth of political thought. This period generated a vast political literature, which it would not be an exaggeration to describe as the foundation material of modern political philosophy.

I use the term 'political philosophy' in describing this literature because it deals mainly with issues in political science that belong to the domain of ethics. Gasparo Contarini, writing in the calm and opulent world of a sixteenth-century Venetian patrician, could take a great deal for granted in examining his republic's system of government. The English writers of the stormy seventeenth century had to address more fundamental, or 'philosophical', questions, such as 'What makes political power legitimate?' 'What is the nature of law?' 'Why are citizens obligated to obey the law?' 'Is this obligation unlimited, or do people have the right (or the duty) to disobey certain laws?' 'What does it mean to be "free" when one is constrained by law?' 'Do individuals have rights that no law can legitimately take away?' Fundamental questions of this sort captured the attention of seventeenth-century English political writers. We cannot survey this literature *in toto*. The standard practice in the history of political philosophy is to focus mainly upon the thought of the two greatest figures of this period, Thomas Hobbes and John Locke, and I will, likewise, restrict the following discussion to them.

1. Thomas Hobbes (1588–1679)

The keynote of Hobbes's political philosophy is the supreme importance of social order and the justifiable fear that all rational persons have of anything that threatens order. Hobbes referred to himself as having been born with fear of disorder as his 'twin', since his birth was brought on prematurely by his mother's fright at the news of the impending invasion of the Spanish Armada. But, fortunately for Hobbes, not all disturbances of orderly existence are misfortunes. Not long after Thomas's birth his father, a country vicar ill-suited to his profession, was involved in an altercation at the door of his church during which he assaulted a man who had provoked him. Thinking it prudent to place himself beyond the reach of the local magistrates, the vicar abandoned his wife and three young children and departed. That was the last heard of the paterfamilias. Fortunately, he also left behind a brother, Francis Hobbes, who undertook to care for the family and saw to it that young Thomas received an excellent education, culminating in graduation from Oxford at the age of twenty. Hobbes then became tutor to the son of the Duke of Devonshire, which brought him into the circle of the most wealthy and powerful members of English society.

Hobbes turned his attention to political matters when the conflict between the King and Parliament was beginning to tear apart the political structure of English society. His most important book, *Leviathan*, was published in 1651, at one of the crucial points in the political history of the period: after the execution of Charles I and the declaration of Britain as a 'Commonwealth' but before Oliver Cromwell assumed despotic power as 'Lord Protector'. Hobbes subtitled the book 'The Matter, Forme, and Power of a Common-wealth Ecclesiasticall and Civill'. There is no doubt that he wrote it to influence the course of contemporary political events. Whether it did so is debatable, even though Cromwell's behaviour as Protector and the role of the monarchy later, after the Stuart restoration in 1660, can be regarded as in line with Hobbes's analysis and advice. But *Leviathan* most certainly influenced the history and philosophy of social science, being one of the major works that form the transition of thought on social questions from medieval scholasticism to modern science. The author of the article on Hobbes for the *International Encyclopedia of the Social Sciences* concludes his assessment thus:

> By virtue both of his positive doctrines and of the scope and rigor of his philosophical inquiries, Hobbes was one of the foremost agents in the dissemination of the rationalism that altered the moral and mental climate of Europe in the course of the seventeenth century.

The term 'rationalism', when it is used to refer to the intellectual characteristics of the modern era, does not merely mean the use of rigorous reasoning. Medieval philosophy was based upon such reasoning and scholastic theologians were masters of Aristotelian logic. What distinguishes the modern era is the linkage of rational thought to empirical data on concrete phenomena. Hobbes clearly grasped this point and saw its significance. Science, he says in *Leviathan*, is not merely a collection of empirical facts but the knowledge of how they are causally connected. Knowledge of facts is knowledge of 'things past' but science is knowledge of 'the dependence of one fact upon another' and enables us to predict the future. Hobbes believed that this kind of rationalism, which was becoming the philosophy of natural science in his day, was universally applicable. He made a special trip to Italy in 1636 to talk with Galileo and returned to England resolved to do for politics what Galileo had been doing for physics. Government would then cease to be merely a craft, depending upon skill acquired through personal practice and experience; it would become an applied science based upon propositions as certain as the theorems of geometry.

The metaphysical foundation of Hobbes's political theory is that which was given its classic formulation by René Descartes: the conception of reality as consisting of mechanistically linked phenomena. Galileo and the other founders of modern science had at least implicitly adopted the mechanistic view of reality as their fundamental world-view. Hobbes undoubtedly held this view himself before his visit to Galileo. Galileo reinforced his mechanistic belief but, more important for Hobbes's subsequent work in politics, Galileo introduced him to the specific methodology of scientific investigation he had employed in the study of physical phenomena: the 'resolutive–compositive method.'

This method is easily understood by considering Galileo's famous application of it to the study of ballistics. A projectile, when fired from a gun, describes a curve. This curve, argued Galileo, can be decomposed or 'resolved' into two linear motions: the motion in the direction in which the gun barrel points, caused by the force of the explosive charge, and the vertical downward motion towards the earth. Galileo was able to unite or 'compose' these two forces by means of a specific equation which accurately describes the trajectory of a projectile. So the 'resolutive–compositive method' consists of analysing a phenomenon by resolving it into its simple components and then reassembling them by some kind of aggregation. In *Leviathan* Hobbes argues that all proper reasoning consists of applying arithmetic (sometimes in complex forms such as geometry and algebra) to basic entities: 'In what matter soever there is place for *addition* or *subtraction*, there also is place for *Reason*; and where these have no place, there *Reason* has nothing at all to do . . . for *Reason* is nothing but *Reckoning* . . . .'

How does this apply to social phenomena? In Hobbes's view, social phenomena can be resolved into the behaviour of individual persons. The composite phenomenon is nothing more than the sum of the individual behaviours. Thus Hobbes is one of the originators of the principle of 'methodological individualism' in social science. The 'resolutive–compositive' method of scientific investigation can be traced back to Aristotle and is especially prominent in the commentaries on Aristotle by the thirteenth-century English philosopher Robert Grosseteste. By way of Galileo it gave rise to Hobbes's view that social phenomena must be analysed in terms of the motives that govern the actions of individual persons. The principle of methodological individualism has played an important role in the modern social sciences, not so much in the branch of it that Hobbes investigated, but in economics, on which he had little to say. Ironically, also, the doctrine of individualism became, after Hobbes, the foundation of the political theory of pluralist democracy, which, as we shall see, was contrary to his own view of the necessities of social order.

Since the resolutive–compositive method requires one to begin the study of a social phenomenon by reducing it to its components, Hobbes begins his analysis of politics by studying individual psychology. Part I of *Leviathan* is an examination of the nature of man, the necessary 'resolutive' preliminary to the 'compositive' Part II, which deals with the origin, foundations, and characteristics of civil society or 'common-wealth'. In considering Part I of *Leviathan* we have to note, to begin with, that while Hobbes regards human beings as very different from other animals, they are not very different from one another. Because of this it is possible for a social scientist to obtain knowledge of human nature by means of introspection. By examining one's own nature one can know human nature in general. Introspection, in Hobbes's view, reveals that man is endowed with the capacity to reason and a thirst for knowledge that is driven by one paramount motive, the desire to be secure in one's person and property. The similarity of humans to one another means that all men have the same objective and adopt the same means of obtaining it. In Hobbes's view, each man's reason tells him that security can be achieved only by means of an all-powerful state, which is what Hobbes refers to by the term *Leviathan*. Hobbes's political theory consists essentially of an argument in support of this contention.

Men have never lived without government but, says Hobbes, reason tells us what life would be like under such conditions even though direct experience is lacking. Each person, in order to increase his security, would strive to improve his capacity to control the future. This can be achieved to some small degree by amassing wealth, but since the greatest dangers to which one is exposed come not from nature but from other men, security cannot be attained except by having power over others. Thus each man's main effort will be devoted to acquiring and holding such power.

Whatever one may think of Hobbes's political theory, he must be given credit for one thing at least: the first sustained analysis of what modern social scientists call the problem of the 'zero-sum game'. In a zero-sum game, whatever one party wins another party loses; it is impossible for all parties to gain. If everyone's objective is to increase his power relative to others, not everyone can gain, since in order that there be some whose power is increased, there must be others whose power is correspondingly diminished. Later in this book, when we come to discussing economics, we will see that this branch of social science focuses mainly upon situations that are 'positive-sum games'; that is, situations in which it is possible for everyone to gain or, at least, for some to gain without others losing. This is clearly possible if people want material goods and services, since we can increase the *aggregate* production of such things. But if what people want is social power, or social status, or social distinction, there is no way for all to have more. One of the differences among the social sciences is that some branches, like economics, focus mainly upon social phenomena that are positive-sum, or potentially so, while others, like political science, have to deal with various phenomena that are inherently zero-sum.

Actually, it is not quite true to say that Hobbes analysed a zero-sum social situation. His picture of what life would be like without government can more accurately be called a 'negative-sum game', since it would be even worse than a situation in which people lived as solitary individuals or families with no contact among them at all. In the 'state of nature', as Hobbes's hypothetical condition of no-government is called, people would not only be unable to co-operate for any collective purpose but contact among them would actually produce harm to everyone individually through incessant violent conflict.

Human societies, says Hobbes, cannot be organized into co-operative 'commonwealths' in a natural way as is the case with bees and ants because humans strive constantly for relative superiority over one another. To create an orderly social system among humans, it is necessary to create an *artificial* means of attaining and preserving co-operative order. This is achieved by the establishment of government. All rational persons know this, says Hobbes. They know what life would be like in a state of nature. Every man would have whatever he could obtain by whatever means. Property would be one's own only as long as one could keep it. There would be no sense of justice or of right and wrong. These concepts would be as meaningless as they are among the beasts. Unrestrained by morals or law (the former depend on the latter, in Hobbes's view), men in a state of nature are engaged in an unremitting war 'of every man against every man'. No man's possessions, or even his person, are secure. There can be no commerce or industry, building, or the arts, or progress in knowledge, 'and which is worst of all, continual fear, and danger of violent death; and the life of man, solitary, poor, nasty, brutish, and short'.

Since man's reason tells him what the state of nature is like, it is sufficient to enable him to realize that it is the greatest of all possible evils and must be avoided at all cost. The means that have enabled humans to transcend the state of nature and form an orderly society must never be jeopardized. Men need not live in constant fear of one another, but they should fear the breakdown of civil order above all else. So, in order to achieve security and promote the various aspects of 'commodious living', the essential function of government must be recognized. Hobbes's main object, in writing *Leviathan*, was to bring this fundamental truth (as he believed it to be) to the attention of his fellow citizens in an era of great political disorder.

If men were ever in a state of nature, says Hobbes, their reason would tell them what they must do to establish a government. They must enter into a 'covenant' or contract with one another to give up their freedom to engage in violence and other features of the war 'of every man against every man' in order to create a general authority that will have the exclusive right and power to apply coercive force. Fear provides the motive, but reason provides the means, suggesting 'articles of peace, upon which men may be drawn to agreement'. Hobbes is the first important modern writer to argue that the basis of social order is a contract. As we shall see, this idea of social contract has had a large and continuing influence on Western social thought, particularly in the fields of political philosophy and social ethics.

The origins of the idea of contract go back at least to the Old Testament account of God making a covenant with Abraham, but Hobbes's conception of the covenant is thoroughly secular. The covenant is an agreement made among *men*. It is not an agreement between men and God or, indeed, between men and the state; it does not have any prior existence from creation by God; it is like any other contract in which individuals bind themselves in their future actions. But it is absolute; once made it cannot be legitimately broken and the government it establishes has an authority as great as one that has been granted power by God. The notion that the foundation of government is an agreement arrived at by the people justifies Hobbes in claiming that the idea of an unjust government is logically nonsensical. Because of the covenant, the people themselves are the true authors of everything done by government, and to say that the government can act unjustly is equivalent to saying that a man can be unjust to himself. There are some difficulties with this idea. Even if the contract were arrived at by democratic methods, there is the question of the minority who do not agree. And what about future generations: are they bound by a covenant made by their ancestors in which they themselves had no say? What about governments established by military conquest? Hobbes recognizes these difficulties but sweeps them aside, claiming that, despite such problems, governments always act in the name of the people.

Hobbes's political theory is an attempt to destroy the idea that the state and the people can be disjunct entities. Throughout the history of modern political thought we find two ideas contending: one arguing that the state is a comprehensive and transcendent embodiment of the people's will; the other that it is a specific social institution with a specialized function and may even represent the interests of no more than a small minority of the population. Hobbes's concept of the covenant is an effort to legitimize state power on a sort of legalistic ground, similar to that which justifies the enforcement of contracts in commercial relations. He argues that unlimited state power is *necessary* to the maintenance of social order; this is his utilitarian argument. But he also contends that such power is *legitimate* because it is founded upon covenant.

What rights does the individual citizen possess in Hobbes's theory? With respect to other citizens the individual has many rights, all those that are embodied in law; but with respect to the state, the individual has no rights whatever. In the state of nature a man's property or his life can legitimately be taken from him by another man because there is no law. In civil society, life and property are protected by law from other men, but not from the state. It would be utterly illogical, says Hobbes, for the state to be bound by law, for the state itself is the law-maker. Hobbes would not have approved of the establishment of constitutional restrictions on the state such as were embodied in the American Bill of Rights a century and a half later. In his own day Hobbes may have been directing his argument against those who contended that the British citizen had rights embodied in custom and precedent that could not be arbitrarily taken away by the state. The notion of such rights, in Hobbes's view, is logically invalid because of the covenant that established the state; and insistence on them is very dangerous because it weakens the state, leading to civil disorder and threatening a return of the state of nature.

In making a general evaluation of Hobbes, emphasis should be placed on his approach to the study of political matters and the penetrating questions he raised rather than the conclusions he arrived at. Presenting a secular theory of politics was significant in itself and Hobbes's efforts to apply scientific method, despite the unconvincing results, were important in the development of modern social science. However, the specific content of his political theory does not warrant great notice either for its historical influence or for its philosophical merits. His contention that absolute government is both necessary and legitimate may have been influential for a brief period during the seventeenth century, but it did not become the main theme of Western political thought. Totalitarian political theory, in its Western forms such as Mussolini's Italy or Hitler's Germany, owes very little to Hobbes's *Leviathan*, and similar concepts of government elsewhere in the world, such as Stalin's Russia or Pol Pot's Cambodia, are even less traceable to Hobbes as an intellectual influence. The Western political tradition of democracy, limited government, and pluralism is due mainly to eighteenth-century thinkers, but it had its modern beginnings a century earlier in the writings of John Locke, whose political theory we go on now to examine.

2. John Locke (1632–1704)

John Locke was born into a middle-class Somerset family whose standard of living was made comfortable by the inheritance of some property from John's grandfather, who had been in the clothing trade. John's father was an attorney whose earnings were insufficient to enable him to add to the property, but he did not dissipate it, so John inherited sufficient wealth when his father died in 1661 to assure him a modest financial independence.

He was educated at good schools and went on to Oxford University. He found the curriculum rather boring, with its emphasis on scholastic philosophy, but he was attracted to the academic environment and in order to stay on at Oxford without becoming an ordained cleric (as was then required of all faculty members in the philosophic disciplines) he enrolled in the Faculty of Medicine. He was much interested in science and became well acquainted with many of the leading scientific figures of the period, including Robert Boyle and Isaac Newton. Locke made no specific contributions to science but he was elected to the Royal Society in 1688, testifying to the esteem in which he was held by scientists.

Locke never practised medicine as a profession but it was his medical training that brought him into contact with Lord Shaftesbury, head of one of the most powerful and influential families of the English aristocracy. Lord Shaftesbury suffered from a liver disease that Locke was able to cure, but more important than Shaftesbury's gratitude for this was that he was very impressed with Locke's intellectual capacity and retained him as an assistant in his various political and diplomatic activities. Practically all Locke's writings, even his purely philosophical works, are traceable to materials that he prepared at various times for Shaftesbury's use.

Locke's association with Shaftesbury meant that he was unquestionably identified as a member of the political faction opposing the Stuarts, since Shaftesbury was one of the leaders of this group. Shaftesbury was tried for treason in 1681 and, though acquitted, he thought it best to take up residence outside England. Locke followed him to Holland in 1683, where both remained until the 'Glorious Revolution' of 1688. Shaftesbury and Locke were much involved in the plot to replace James II with William of Orange (as they had probably also been involved in the unsuccessful Monmouth rebellion of 1685 and other anti-Stuart movements and intrigues of the period), so they returned to England as part of the victorious party and the new political establishment in 1688.

A feature of these events that should be noted is that the revolution of 1688 definitely assured that England would remain a Protestant country, which had been uncertain under the Stuarts. So John Locke played a role in determining the religious future of England, a matter not dissociated from its intellectual and political future, over which his influence, by his writings, was enormous. However, it would be incorrect to interpret those religious developments as representing the establishment of a dogmatic, repressive Puritan Protestantism in place of an equally dogmatic and repressive Catholicism. The significant intellectual trend in England during the seventeenth century was the growth of secular thinking, which, after 1688, greatly accelerated and became a prominent feature of the eighteenth-century 'enlightenment'. Locke was one of the powerful intellects contributing to this trend. Though he was a sincere Christian, he did far more than any sceptic or atheist to detach philosophy and political theory from theology and religious authority. Locke's opposition to the Stuarts was fundamentally due to the fear not that they would return England to Catholicism, but that they were political despots. His own strong opposition to Catholicism was not theological, but political; he viewed Catholicism as intractably opposed to intellectual freedom and political liberty, which he placed above all other things as properties of a good social order.

Locke was widely known and highly regarded in intellectual circles before the Revolution of 1688 but he had published very little. Then, in 1689, he sent to press three manuscripts: *A Letter Concerning Toleration*, *Two Treatises of Government*, and *Essay Concerning Human Understanding*. The *Two Treatises*, published anonymously but widely believed to have been written by Locke, became the foundation book of modern Western political philosophy; the

Human Understanding became the foundation book of the modern philosophy of science. Peter Laslett, the editor of the definitive edition of the *Two Treatises*, says of Locke's *Human Understanding* that it turned him from a minor intellectual figure 'into a national institution and international influence'. John Maynard Keynes, the great economist, called Locke's *Human Understanding*, 'the first modern English book'.

Our concern is with the history of social science, so we cannot give Locke's *Human Understanding* the attention it would require in a more general study of Western intellectual history. Suffice it to say that it was a book on the fundamental issue of how we acquire knowledge which argued for the dominant role of empirical experience, and emphasized common sense and the ordinary ability of every man to perceive, reason, and understand. Locke detached the study of philosophy from religion by downgrading the reliability of revelation and authority as sources of knowledge and by contending that, as a psychological act, man learns about the real world by means of the perceptions obtained through his five senses. To this Locke added the power of the mind to reason about the information provided by the senses, along lines marked out by René Descartes, whose *Discourse on Method* (1637) he greatly admired. This is what is meant, fundamentally, by the philosophy of 'empiricism.' Modern philosophers are far from satisfied with Locke's theory of knowledge but empiricism continues to be the dominant tradition of Western philosophy and Western science.

It is difficult to trace a direct connection between Locke's epistemological theory in the *Human Understanding* and his political theory in the *Two Treatises of Government*. In fact there are some considerable inconsistencies between them. In a general way they are similar in emphasizing that all men have the capacity to reason and that we learn from experience, but Locke's view that he had discovered a specific method of knowing that could be applied to all subjects is not supported by any convincing demonstration that the *Two Treatises* represents an application of the epistemology of the *Human Understanding*. The *Two Treatises* was more influential because it was known that the work came from the pen of the famous author of the *Human Understanding*, but its long-run impact on Western thinking was really due to its own merits as a book that examined and offered answers to many of the most fundamental and most contentious questions in political science and practical politics.

We shall focus here on the second of Locke's *Two Treatises*, this being by far the more important for the history of social theory, but a brief word on the first is in order. It was a critique of a book by Sir Robert Filmer called *Patriarcha; or the Natural Power of Kings*. Filmer's argument was that the relation between a king and his subjects is like that of a father towards his young children. Monarch and parent have unquestionable authority for the good of those over whom they rule because it is 'natural' that they have such power. Thus the *Patriarcha* was an attempt to support the Tory political doctrine of the absolute power of kings, by appealing not to revelation or scripture but, by analogy, to the biological nature of man as an altricial animal. Filmer died in 1653 but the *Patriarcha* was not published until 1680, obviously as part of the propaganda war of the period. Locke's *Two Treatises of Government* was written probably very shortly thereafter. The fact that it was published in 1690 led historians for many years to think that it had been composed after the Revolution of 1688 as a justification of that change in political authority, but recent scholarship has revealed that it was written much earlier and that its immediate purpose was to refute Filmer and oppose the Tory doctrine of absolute monarchy. In the process Locke advanced a political theory of his own which has had enormous influence on the political thought of the West and must be regarded as one of the intellectual pillars of the modern theory of political democracy.

Like Hobbes, Locke thought of political society as based upon a compact that people make with one another for the purpose of avoiding the difficulties that inevitably attend a 'state of nature'. Hobbes, as we saw above, argued for absolute political power on the ground that nothing can be as bad as the constant warfare of the state of nature; but Locke contended that political despotism is worse than the state of nature and that men act rationally, and within their legitimate rights, if they overthrow a despot. Locke's view of man was that he differs from the beasts in possessing the power of reason. The state of nature is not totally lawless, because each man's reason 'is able to instruct him in the law he is to govern himself by'. He is not free to do anything he pleases because, though there is no government, there is a 'law of nature' governing human conduct:

> The state of nature has a law of nature to govern it, which obliges every one: and reason, which is that law, teaches all mankind, who will but consult it, that being all equal and independent, no one ought to harm another in his life, health, liberty, or possessions.

Any man, says Locke, who behaves violently towards another has abandoned reason, discarding the gift of God that makes him human, so he may be treated by other men as a wild and dangerous animal. A monarch who seeks to establish a despotism and place other men under his absolute power has abandoned reason and rejects the law of nature (which does not cease to rule in political society); he may be legitimately destroyed, and should be, in the interests of the people's welfare.

But if natural law exists in the state of nature, why is there any need for government in the first place? Locke's argument is that there are certain inconveniences in the state of nature. The law of nature exists but every man has authority to execute it. This is not an effective mode of administration. Even if all men wished to obey the law of nature there would be differences of interpretation, with no institutional instruments to arbitrate or resolve them. In addition, some people may abandon their human reason and do violence to others. It is legitimate for any rational man to prevent them or to punish them, but this is not an efficient way of policing the natural law. The result is that a person's actual ability to enjoy his right to 'life, health, liberty, and possessions' is uncertain. For this reason, free and rational men will agree with one another to form a political society for the purpose of securing the rights that each one morally has, but cannot practically count upon, in the state of nature. Thus Locke's fundamental conception of political society is that it is an association which rational men form for utilitarian purposes. The state does not have a divine origin, nor is it the product of metaphysical forces of a secular sort. It is simply a human artefact, invented by intelligent individuals, as a wheelbarrow or a weaving loom is invented, to serve a certain purpose; it has no religious, mystical, metaphysical, or transcendental meaning or significance. This view of the nature of political society was developed further by the philosophy of utilitarianism during the nineteenth century, at a time when the metaphysical theory of the state (nationalism and romanticism) was undergoing its own most important revival and development (see below, Chapter 11).

Like Hobbes's then, Locke's conception of government is that, theoretically speaking, it originates from a social contract made by men with one another in order to eliminate the evils of the state of nature. But whereas Hobbes considered that it was necessary for the state to have absolute power and that the exercise of such power is legitimized by the social contract, Locke maintained that absolute power in the hands of government could never result from a contract among men in a state of nature. No rational man would agree to place himself under the rule of an absolute authority, for that would expose his welfare to even greater hazards than exist in the state of nature. Moreover, even if everyone wished to establish an absolute government, Locke argued, they could not legitimately contract with one another to do so: the freedom that every man has in the state of nature does not include freedom to establish a permanent despotism. Locke perceived that the doctrine of political freedom cannot be extended to the point where it includes freedom to establish a despotism, any more than personal liberty includes the freedom to enslave oneself henceforth to another.

So we see that Locke's conception of government is that its existence derives from the people, who decide to give up their individual right to act as executors of the law of nature and vest this power in a collective institution. But no absolute government can be traced to such a contract. From this an important conclusion follows. If a government attempts to establish absolute power over the people, or if it acts in other ways against the people's interests, then it forfeits its legitimacy, since no social contract would, or could, establish such an authority. If the citizens of a society find themselves faced with such a government they have the right to do away with it and establish a new one. The relevance of Locke's reasoning to the controversy over the legitimacy of the Stuart monarchy was plain enough to the late seventeenth-century reader of the *Two Treatises*; it was equally plain to American readers a century later when the legitimacy of British policy towards the American colonies came into question. (The first American edition of the *Two Treatises* was published in Boston in 1773.) It would not be going too far to say that the philosophical principles underlying the American Revolution were those laid down by John Locke.

Before leaving our sketch of Locke we should pay some attention to an aspect of his political theory that we have not yet specifically discussed: his theory of the right of property ownership. The importance of this in Locke's theory has been greatly exaggerated by some commentators, but it is of considerable interest for the history of social science none the less. The source of the misinterpretation of Locke is that he often says in the *Two Treatises* that the main function of government is the protection of private property. This would appear to be a very conservative political theory; indeed, the property-less man who lives by selling his labour would seem to have very little reason to believe that the state should be concerned for *his* welfare. Many writers prior to the end of the eighteenth century seem to use the term 'the people' in such a way as to exclude the lowest class of unpropertied labour, but there is no passage in Locke's *Two Treatises* that suggests such a restriction and, indeed, he specifically points out that when he uses the term 'property' he means 'that property which men have in their persons as well as their goods' and that when he says that men unite to form a society for the preservation of their 'property' this term must be taken to include 'their lives, liberties, and estates'. So Locke's emphasis upon property in the *Two Treatises* is nothing other than an emphasis on the things that all men hold dear.

So far as 'property' in the restricted sense is concerned, Locke makes two arguments in justification of private ownership, one moral and the other pragmatic. The moral argument is that a person has a right to consider something his own if he has invested his labour in it. All land, for example, is originally utilized in common but when a person works upon the land, and cultivates and improves it, he makes it his private property because he has mixed part of his own person (which he unquestionably owns) with the land. This is a rather mystical theory with many difficulties, some of which Locke recognized. Locke goes on to argue, however, that the main reason for private property in productive resources such as land is that they cannot be efficiently used when held in common. This issue has been debated since Plato (who favoured communal ownership) and Aristotle (who favoured private property for pragmatic reasons) and it continues to be a main point of contention today between supporters of capitalism and supporters of communism. As we shall see later in this book the pragmatic and the ethical aspects of property ownership have been major focal points of social science and social philosophy.

Locke's moral theory of the right of property was based upon labour. This was undoubtedly connected in his thinking with another proposition which he was one of the earliest writers to expound: the contention that the value of anything is solely (or almost solely) due to the labour that has been undertaken to produce it. This is the 'labour theory of value' which we will have to examine quite closely when we come to discussing the writings of Adam Smith, the classical school of economists, and Karl Marx.

D. MONTESQUIEU'S INTERPRETATION OF THE ENGLISH CONSTITUTION

After the 'Glorious Revolution' of 1688, England entered a period of development which made her the most powerful and most influential nation in Europe. Many observers of the shift of the European centre of political gravity towards a previously negligible island on the western edge of the continent credited the emergence there of a superior system of government with playing a leading role in this remarkable turn of history. By the mid-eighteenth century, England was widely viewed by political commentators, as Venice had been earlier, as a working exemplification of an ideal system of government.

Like Venice, too, England did not have a foundational document in which the structure of the state was specified; one could only discover the 'constitution' of England by considering the laws and practices through which the political mechanism operated, and the traditions that acted as general guides for and restraints upon changes in law and practice. Many of the most important features of the English system had historical roots that went back to medieval times: Magna Carta, the institution of Parliament, the common law, etc. The revolution of 1688 was viewed not so much as creating a new political order as restoring one that the Stuarts had attempted to subvert. After 1688 England remained a monarchy, and virtually all political power was in the hands of the same small governing class that had held it previously. Those who sat in the 'House of Commons' were 'commoners' only in the sense that they did not have hereditary titles. The officials in charge of the organs of local government were also members of the untitled upper class, as were most of the people who were empowered to vote in elections. England was an aristocracy, as Aristotle had defined it, that is, a society governed by the 'few'. Indeed, the proportion of the governing class (including all enfranchised persons) to the population was smaller in eighteenth-century England than the proportion of the membership of the Great Council of sixteenth-century Venice had been to the city's population. Participation in the government of England remained a privilege of such a small class for a long time after 1688, until the Reform Act of 1867 initiated the movement towards the modern conception of a generally enfranchised citizenry.

In terms of the distribution of power the English political system differed little from that of other European states. Nevertheless, it was regarded as significantly different, and was widely admired as superior to others. The literature of the eighteenth century indicates that the main reason for this high regard was that the English people, even those who had no political power at all, were less exposed to the hazards of arbitrary state action than the citizens of other nations. The power of the state, though highly concentrated, had been subjected to 'constitutional' control. How this had been achieved was not obvious to casual observation. The underlying principles that controlled the exercise of power had to be sought beneath the surface of political practice; that is to say, a *theory* of the English constitution was required. Of the various eighteenth-century attempts to provide such a general appraisal of the English constitution, by far the most important in terms of its influence on subsequent political thought was the work of a Frenchman, the Baron de Montesquieu. This occupies only some ten pages in Montesquieu's *De l'esprit des lois* (1748), a book of more than 600 pages, but it is hardly an exaggeration to say that those ten pages have had as much influence upon modern Western political thought as any other document, of any length, so Montesquieu's interpretation of the English constitution warrants close examination.

The *Spirit of the Laws*, as it is entitled in English, was not written as a treatise on constitutional theory. Montesquieu's main interest in political organization was, in a sense, 'sociological', since he believed that the political organization of a society must be examined in the context of the society's cultural ambience and values. He did not intend to present the English constitution as a model that should be copied by all societies, since he firmly believed that societies differ in their cultural characteristics and that a system of government that fitted the 'spirit' of one society might not be suitable for another. His discussion of the English system of government was introduced as empirical support of this general thesis. It was an admirable system because it harmonized with the cultural values that animated the English people. 'The government most conformable to nature,' he says, 'is that whose particular disposition best agrees with the humour and disposition of the people in whose favour it is established.' In a later section of the *Laws* Montesquieu enlarges on this theme under the heading 'Of Laws in Relation to the Principles which form the General Spirit, the Morals, and Customs of a Nation'. 'Mankind,' he says, 'are influenced by various causes: by the climate, by the religion, by the laws, by the maxims of government, by precedents, morals, and customs; whence is formed a general spirit of nations.' Even in a despotism, where there are no laws ('that is, none that can properly be called so'), there are 'manners and customs; and if you overturn these you overturn all', for people 'are in general very tenacious of their customs' and are unhappy if they are violently altered.

Montesquieu considers the English constitution to be admirable for two reasons: because it conforms to the fundamental spirit of English society and (now going beyond his basic criterion) because that spirit is itself admirable. Some nations, he says, have been animated by religion, or by desire for conquest, or tranquillity, but 'one nation there is also in the world that has for the direct end of its constitution political liberty'. That nation is England; there liberty has attained 'its highest perfection.' Montesquieu notes that the word 'liberty' has various meanings, denoting different conceptions of freedom, in different cultures. In order to understand the English con- stitution, one must recognize that what the English desire is not the anarchistic 'natural liberty . . . of the Savages', each person being free to do whatever he pleases, but a system of 'political liberty', a regime in which the citizen is constrained by laws, but the authorities who make and administer the laws are also constrained. The genius of the English constitution lies in its having solved the problem of power. The power of the state, necessary to protect the members of society from one another, and from foreign enemies, is strong in England; the citizens are protected *by* the state; but they are also protected *from* the state: they have *political* liberty.

How has this remarkable result been achieved? Montesquieu does not claim that the culture of England endows its governmental authorities with a high sense of civic virtue, or that they are constrained in their exercise of power by their religious beliefs. Plato's 'republic' would be governed by guardians of such merit that they need not themselves be guarded. The absolute sovereign of Hobbes's 'commonwealth' would rule justly because he feared God's wrath if he did not do so. In Montesquieu's analysis of the English political system, arguments of this sort make no appearance. Good government, suitable to the English spirit of liberty, is provided by a con- trivance, a constitutional mechanism, which functions with governors who are ordinary men, each motivated by the desire to promote his own interests.

In describing this constitutional machinery and explaining how it functions, Montesquieu makes no use of the doctrine of 'mixed government'. He mentions the combination of monarchy, aristocracy, and democracy only as an early and transitory form of 'Gothic government'; for general political analysis he classifies governments as being 'monarchies', 'republics', or 'despotisms', and describes the characteristics and tendencies of each of these as pure types, but he does not consider a combination of them to be a realistic practical possibility (see, for example, his discussion of China in Book VII, chapter 21). England, in his view, 'may be justly called a republic, disguised under the form of monarchy'. A modern editor of the *Laws*, D. W. Carrithers, speaks of Montesquieu as representing the English political system as 'a mechanical model well suited to the Newtonian age, . . . a carefully structured equipoise of competing powers'.

Occupying a prominent place in Montesquieu's general political theory and in his analysis and interpretation of the English constitution is the notion that there are three primary activities of the state, and that efficient government requires that these be made the responsibilities of differentiated state institutions. This is the doctrine of 'separation of powers' with its triadic classification of government as composed of 'legislative', 'executive', and 'judicial' branches. Montesquieu did not originate this doctrine, but the *Laws*, more than any other document, was responsible for the importance it attained in the constitutional theory, and practice, of modern democracy. Through the development of the separation of powers doctrine in later eighteenth and early nineteenth-century political thought, and the simultaneous construction by the English classical economists of the economic theory of a competitive market economy, the long-standing belief that social order requires a hierarchical form of organization was effectively contested, by the empirical and analytical demonstration of alternative models. The role of separation of powers theory in this is not obvious, however, since the idea that the different functions of the state should be performed by different institutional organs is not, in itself, inconsistent with the notion that these organs should be related to one another in a hierarchical fashion. The alternative model of political organization, the doctrine of an equilibrium of plural powers, requires their 'separation' from one another, but only in order to make them mutually dependent, in a non-hierarchical manner. This is the notion of separation that one finds in Montesquieu's interpretation of the English constitution and in his analysis of what is necessary for any state, republican or monarchical, whose animating 'spirit' is political liberty.

The main focus of Montesquieu's analysis of the English political system is upon its legislative and executive institutions. Not having in mind a written constitution containing an entrenched statement of civic rights, he does not consider the role of the courts in guarding them. The judiciary is, in Montesquieu's view, a part of the executive branch. As for the other two functions of the state, they must be embodied in different institutions so that they may constrain one another. Even in a republic, where there is no monarch, such constraints are necessary. If legislative and executive functions were performed by the same persons, 'there would be an end then of liberty'. The English constitution does even more to protect it by dividing the legislative branch into two bodies, which 'check one another by the mutual privilege of rejecting' the proposals of each. Anticipating an argument that was later to be brought against the notion of political equilibrium, Montesquieu here adds that this arrangement does not result in stalemate; it requires only that the legislative and executive bodies of the state must move 'in concert'. Obviously, Montesquieu's concept of 'separation' is not meant to denote an arrangement of independent powers but, indeed, the opposite; he explicitly notes that the preservation of liberty requires the executive and legislative organs of the state to be dependent on each another. It is not separation that protects political liberty, but the arrangement of the separated powers in an equilibrium mechanism of mutual dependence.

One need not stretch the text of the *Laws*, or contrive to stitch together selected phrases from it, in order to interpret Montesquieu as advancing the theory of checks and balances. This only requires a recognition that, in discussing the separation of powers, Montesquieu has firmly in mind that its purpose is liberty. Nations whose spirit is animated by different objectives have no need of separation of powers. Montesquieu himself makes the matter plain early in Book XI of the *Laws* in laying down general foundations for his discussion of the English constitution:

> Democratic and aristocratic states are not in their own nature free. Political liberty is to be found only in moderate governments; and even in these it is not always found. It is there only when there is no abuse of power. But constant experience shows us that every man invested with power is apt to abuse it, and to carry his authority as far as it will go. Is it not strange, though true, to say that virtue itself has need of limits?
>
> To prevent this abuse, it is necessary from the very nature of things that power should be a check to power.

Earlier, in Book V of the *Laws*, noting that most nations are despotisms despite the fact that the love of liberty is natural to all mankind, Montesquieu ascribes this to the lack of the necessary political machinery:

> To form a moderate government, it is necessary to combine the several powers; to regulate, temper, and set them in motion; to give as it were ballast to one, in order to enable it to counterpoise the other. This is a masterpiece of legislation, rarely produced by hazard, and seldom attained by prudence.

As noted above, Montesquieu regarded England as essentially a republic, despite having a monarch. Of the three types of government he distinguishes – monarchy, republic, and despotism – it goes almost without saying that he saw little merit in despotism, and it is clear that he favoured the republic over monarchy. But he did not construe England as a republic merely in order to rationalize his admiration of the English constitution with his republican preference. In his view, a monarchy *can* be a 'moderate government' – if the monarch is constrained in the exercise of his prerogative powers. How can such constraints be exercised, if not by the construction of constitutional machinery which, as in England, produces 'a republic under the form of monarchy'? The necessary constraints can be effected through non-governmental institutions such as Churches, by the existence of a powerful nobility, and by long-standing customs that induce the monarch to respect established practice. Montesquieu's appreciation of such factors anticipates the modern theory of pluralist democracy, which extends the notion of mutual counterpoise beyond the checks and balances that exist between the various organs of government, to recognition of the role of non-governmental institutions and established practices in controlling the exercise of state power.

One of the main reasons why Montesquieu's analysis of the English constitution was such an important document in the history of modern political thought is the influence it had upon American opinion during the crucial six years between the conclusion of the Revolutionary War and the adoption of a constitution to bind the thirteen former colonies into a nation. In the political literature of the period that led up to the outbreak of the war, and during it, John Locke was the authority to whom American writers appealed, to justify the assertion of political independence by the British colonies in America. But after the war had been won, Montesquieu was the most frequently quoted writer in the American political literature. The newly independent Americans, despite the passions that had erupted into revolution, looked upon the English constitution as the best that existed, or had ever existed in man's historical experience. The constitution that was adopted in 1789 for the United States of America did not reproduce the details of the English system of government, but it was built upon the principle of checks and balances which, in Montesquieu's appraisal, was the genius of the English constitution.

Chapter 5

Physiocracy: the first economic model

The branch of social science called 'economics' is commonly described as the study of how humans make use of available productive resources (including their own labour and skills) to produce goods and services for human use. This is partly a technical question of the relationship between 'inputs' and 'outputs' but it becomes a matter of *social* science, rather than physics or engineering, because humans practise a high degree of functional specialization. This raises the questions of how the specialized economic activities of individuals are co-ordinated into an orderly system; how different systems of co-ordination work; and what defects or deficiencies a particular system has and how they may be corrected.

The study of such questions is as ancient as any of man's intellectual interests but effective systematic investigation of them is quite recent. Most historians of economics would date it no earlier than the latter half of the eighteenth century. Adam Smith is sometimes described as the father of economics, but shortly before his great *Inquiry into the Nature and Causes of the Wealth of Nations* (1776) was published in England, there flourished in France, at the court of Louis XV, a group of writers to whom must be given the credit for attempting to construct the first systematic and comprehensive theoretical 'model' of economic processes. These were the 'Physiocrats'.

The term 'model' is widely used today in both the natural and the social sciences. In Chapter 6 we will examine some of the various ways in which this word is used and try to clarify its meaning. At present it will be sufficient for our purposes to consider the Physiocrats as attempting to describe, in highly simplified and abstract terms, how the economic system as a whole functions. Though they lived in an era in which economic activities were extensively regulated by governmental laws and administrative orders, they did not investigate these aspects of economic co-ordination but attempted to show that there were natural laws of economics (as in, for example, physics or physiology), not like laws promulgated by kings and legislatures and administered by bureaucrats. Though their success in this was very limited, the work of the Physiocrats did bring to notice the idea that a system of markets, in which voluntary exchanges take place, functions as a mechanism of economic co-ordination. Economists have been studying the market mechanism, its characteristics, conditions, and defects, ever since the Physiocrats, and more incisively Adam Smith, identified it as the process that enables a complex economy to function. The Physiocrats were criticized in their own time for being 'systematic' but this is precisely what makes them significant for the history and philosophy of social science. The fact that abstract models of social processes may be wrong, misleading, or even foolish, does not mean that science is better done in a haphazard fashion.

A. EIGHTEENTH-CENTURY FRANCE AND THE PHYSIOCRATIC SCHOOL

The long reign of Louis XIV, which ended in 1715, left France with a magnificent court and a nearly ruined economy. Louis engaged in a series of wars and built the lavish palace of Versailles, activities that cost much and produced little. In addition he expelled the Protestants from France, which lost some of its most skilled and talented human resources. He proclaimed himself absolute and tolerated no criticism, thus stifling another source of productivity. His Finance Minister, Colbert, embarked on a policy of encouraging industry which emphasized economic activities for which France was not particularly suited and hampered agriculture, in which the country had rich natural resources. The result of this reign of folly was that the economy of France was overburdened by regulations and twisted by policies that stunted its productivity, and, despite the crushing burden of taxes, the flow of revenues into the national exchequer was insufficient to match expenditures. The state sank ever more deeply into debt.

Economic conditions did not improve much under Louis XV, but there was some liberalization in the intellectual atmosphere, especially after the Peace of Aix-la-Chapelle in 1748. An efflorescence of political and social writing took place. Montesquieu's *Spirit of the Laws* appeared in 1748; Diderot and d'Alembert began their great *Encyclopaedia* in 1751; Voltaire, one of the great social commentators of all time, was writing – his immortal satire *Candide* was published in 1759; Jean-Jacques Rousseau's *Social Contract*, one of the most influential books on political thought of modern times, was published in 1762. In addition, French intellectuals became greatly interested in English philosophy, especially the writings of John Locke and David Hume. In this environment of intellectual liberalization and economic difficulty there was much diverse writing on economic matters, but this part of the scene became dominated in the 1760s by François Quesnay and a group of disciples who gathered around him calling themselves 'the economists'. Later they used the term 'Physiocracy' to describe their doctrine, and it is by this name that they are now referred to in the historiography of social thought.

During the height of the Physiocrats' influence, France was only twenty years away from the great social explosion, the French Revolution. One cannot say that if the message of the Physiocrats had been heeded the Revolution would not have occurred but it is possible that, if their suggestions had been used as an initial basis on which to build a progressive policy of economic reform, France would have had its revolution peacefully, as the English had theirs in 1688, and the modern history of Europe, and of the world as a whole, would have been different. The final nail in the scaffold of the feudal system in France was driven by the expense of supporting the Americans in their revolutionary war against England; the policies of the Physiocrats, even if they had been greatly successful, could probably not have enabled the French treasury to undertake such large expenditures without disastrous consequences. The history of what 'might have been' is, however, only speculation. Whatever role the Physiocrats *might* have played in the history of France, they *did* play an important part in the initial development of economics as a scientific discipline.

The originator of the Physiocratic doctrine, François Quesnay (1694–1774), was brought up in peasant surroundings, despite the fact that his father was a lawyer. He had little formal education and was taught to read by a friendly gardener at the age of twelve. He acquired some medical training and commenced to practise when he was twenty-four but then he began to study medical science seriously and published five books on medical topics between 1730 and 1753. These earned him an international reputation as an important medical scientist and a leader of the profession. The British Royal Society elected him to membership in 1752. Because of his high repute Madame de Pompadour, mistress of Louis XV, invited him to Versailles as her personal physician in 1749. From that date onward Quesnay lived within the inner circle of political power in France. He became interested in economic questions and in 1756, at the age of sixty-two, began to publish on that subject, writing some articles for the *Encyclopaedia*. In 1758 he published the first version of the celebrated *Tableau Oeconomique*, in which his model of the economic system was delineated in a geometrical diagram.

The most important of Quesnay's disciples was Victor Riqueti, Marquis de Mirabeau (1715–89), who, before meeting Quesnay, had achieved great popular fame as the author of a book called *The Friend of Mankind, or Treatise on Population* (1756). In this book Mirabeau argued that population growth was the main factor in economic progress and the main object of state policy should be to encourage procreation. Two years later Mirabeau met Quesnay and was persuaded that land, not labour, was the true source of economic wealth. Thenceforth he became an ardent disciple of Quesnay's and a tireless promoter of his ideas. Some historians date the beginning of the Physiocratic school from the first meeting of Quesnay and Mirabeau in the summer of 1758.

Another disciple of Quesnay worth passing mention is Pierre Samuel du Pont de Nemours (1739–1817). He negotiated the treaty with England that recognized American independence. He corresponded extensively with

Thomas Jefferson, who was the American minister to France in 1785–9. It is possible that Jefferson's agrarian economic philosophy was due to the Physiocratic writings, which he admired. Disappointed with the course of the French Revolution, Du Pont moved to the United States in 1793, where his son, E. I. Du Pont (1771–1834), who had studied chemistry under the great Lavoisier, built a gunpowder factory near Wilmington, Delaware, which grew into one of the largest American industrial enterprises.

B. THE PHYSIOCRATIC MODEL

The term 'Physiocracy' suggests to the English ear something like 'physiology', which is an especially tempting interpretation when one knows that Quesnay was a physician. But in fact the term connotes in French the more general concept of law of nature. The Physiocratic model was built on the idea that social phenomena are governed, as are physical phenomena, by laws of nature that are independent of human will and intention. The title of one of the major Physiocratic writings, *L'Ordre naturel et essentiel des sociétés politiques* (The Natural and Essential Order of Political Societies, 1767) by Mercier de la Rivière, captures the idea succinctly. The task of the physicist is to discover the natural laws of physical phenomena so that the engineer may design machines in accordance with them. The task of the economist, correspondingly, is to discover the natural laws governing economic phenomena so that governmental policies can be constructed in accordance with them; otherwise, economic policies cannot be any more successful than engineering that disregards the laws of matter and motion. Quesnay's *Tableau*, which he and his disciples regarded as the central pillar of Physiocratic theory, was an attempt to depict how an economy operates so that the underlying laws are revealed. (There are numerous versions of the *Tableau* and, despite the voluminous explanations accompanying them, historians of economics are still not certain what its fundamental paradigm was, so the interpretation offered here differs in certain respects from some that are contained in the literature on Physiocracy.)

The basic idea underlying the Physiocratic model is that goods and services are produced not for the direct use of their producers but for sale to others. The economy is viewed from the standpoint of markets, as a system of money transactions. In these transactions people receive income through the sale of their products and use this income to buy the products of others. Thus the economic system consists of production activity and market exchanges and the market process is modelled as a circular flow of income received and expenditure made. In order to simplify the market process and to highlight the features of it that reveal the laws governing production, Quesnay conceived of the idea of classifying the participants under three broad headings: those engaged in primary production (which Quesnay usually referred to as 'agriculture', though it also includes other primary industries such as mining

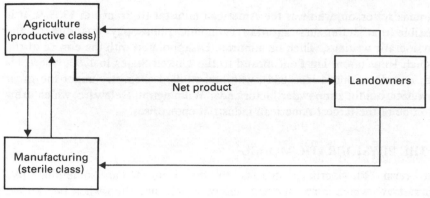

Figure 5-1

and fishing); those engaged in secondary industries or 'manufacturing'; and 'landowners' who receive rental income because of land ownership or fees due them as feudal rights (this category also includes government tax revenue and Church revenue from tithes or contributions).

In Figure 5-1 a simplified diagram of the Physiocratic model is shown, the three boxes representing the three classes of Quesnay's *Tableau*. The light arrows show the flow of expenditure. Those engaged in manufacturing, for example, spend their income on food and raw materials produced in agriculture (the arrow running from manufacturing to agriculture). Of course they also buy manufactured goods but it is not necessary to show this. Similarly, landowners spend their income on agricultural goods and manufactures, and agriculturalists buy manufactures. The circle of income and expenditure is closed.

In this model, those engaged in agriculture and manufacturing obtain income by selling their production. But where does the income of the 'landowners' come from? They do not produce anything. In the diagram the heavy arrow indicates that landowner income is derived from agriculture and, as labelled, represents the 'net product' of that sector of the economy. This is what the Physiocrats regarded as their greatest discovery: that one sector of the economy, and one sector only, produces a net product. Manufacturing only produces a value equal to what it consumes by using up raw materials in production, and food and other things in the maintenance of its work force. This is why agriculture is labeled as containing the 'productive class' and manufacturing the 'sterile class'. The Physiocrats did not mean to imply that manufacturing is a worthless activity but they wanted to point out that, unlike agriculture, it produces no more than it consumes.

In the language of modern economics, the Physiocrats contended that there are two factors of production, labour and land. The difference between them is that labour (including agricultural labour) must be maintained; that is, its services cannot be obtained without cost (food, clothing, shelter, etc.). But land renders its services without cost, and the sunshine and rain that fall upon it are free also. Thus agriculture yields a net product or surplus which, as shown in the diagram, becomes the income of landowners. This, the Physiocrats felt, provides the key to economic development and progress: agriculture is the main strategic sector of the economy, since it alone produces a net product which can be used for capital investment.

From this sketch of the Physiocratic model it is easy to see that the policy prescriptions of Quesnay and his disciples were very different from those that Colbert had assiduously promoted during the reign of Louis XIV. Instead of furthering the growth of 'sterile' industry, they proposed to encourage 'productive' agriculture. Their theory of net product was rather far-fetched, but in terms of the problems of the French economy in their time their policy prescriptions were reasonably sound. Despite its having some of the largest areas of fertile land in Europe, French agriculture was very inefficient, and the lot of the peasantry was miserable. The aristocracy and clergy were content to be absentee landlords receiving rents and tithes that were sufficient to enable them to lead easy and carefree lives; they were not much interested in the burdensome activity of estate management, and less so in innovation.

The Physiocrats had various ideas for the active promotion of agriculture and for its reorganization along more efficient lines, but their basic view of governmental economic regulation was that it usually did more harm than good and they advocated a general dismantling of the restrictive laws and regulations governing trade and industry as well as those governing agriculture. The term *laissez-faire* (initially *laissez-nous faire*, or 'leave us alone') originated in the seventeenth century as a criticism of Colbert's policies of state intervention, but in the 1760s it became a maxim or slogan associated with the ideas of the Physiocrats. Later it became identified with the economic theories of Adam Smith. Neither the Physiocrats nor Adam Smith held the view that the economy would work perfectly if left alone, but they both regarded many of the governmental policies of their time as misguided and advocated that they should be abandoned. (In Chapter 10 below we will examine the more extreme doctrine that a system of markets, without government at all, would co-ordinate the economic activities of functionally specialized individuals into a perfectly harmonious co-operative social order.)

The Physiocrats applied their theory most specifically to the problem of taxation, then as now one of the most vexatious and sensitive issues of governmental policy. The tax system of eighteenth-century France was not only very burdensome; it was also complex, arbitrary, inequitable, and costly to administer. The Physiocrats proposed that the elaborate multi-tax system be replaced by a single tax levied on the net product produced by the agricultural sector. This hardly seems to be in accord with their aim of promoting agriculture but the Physiocrats reasoned from their theoretical model that all taxes are ultimately paid out of the net product of the agricultural sector anyway, regardless of their immediate incidence or specific form. All government revenue must necessarily be derived from the surplus of value produced over cost of production, and agriculture is the only source of such a surplus. (A century earlier John Locke had asserted that all taxation ultimately falls on land but he provided no analytical model in support of his contention.) Thus substantial economies in collection and administration could be achieved by basing the tax system on correct economic laws, and this would therefore redound to the benefit of the agricultural sector. The argument failed to persuade the land-owning aristocracy. Mirabeau's *Theory of Taxation*, published in 1760, was regarded by them as a clear threat and, despite the liberalization of thought under Louis XV, he was arrested and imprisoned (only briefly, because of the intercession of Madame de Pompadour). The Abbé Galiani (1728–87), noted in French court circles for his short stature and long wit, once defined eloquence as 'the art of saying everything without going to the Bastille'. Mirabeau discovered that the skill of even the most eloquent reformer is severely tried when it comes to the question of who is to pay the taxes, and widespread popularity does not serve one in such circumstances nearly as well as having a friend who is close to the centre of power.

C. THE SIGNIFICANCE OF PHYSIOCRACY IN THE HISTORY OF SOCIAL SCIENCE

In a certain sense Physiocracy was little more than an intellectual fad, one of the many of the court of Versailles, and, like all fads, its life was brief. It rose to prominence in the early 1760s but by the later years of that decade it was already in decline and its influence was virtually over by 1770. Quesnay himself ceased to be interested in economics in 1768 and devoted his restless mind to mathematics for the remainder of his life. The appointment of A. R. J. Turgot as Comptroller-General of Finance in 1774 revived hopes of economic reform along Physiocratic lines, but his fall from power two years later permanently ended the Physiocratic movement in France.

One of the main weaknesses of the Physiocratic school was that they failed to develop Quesnay's model. They seem to have had the idea that the essential laws of economics had been revealed at one stroke and that all that was needed was to disseminate these truths. Of the voluminous literature published by the Physiocrats in the 1760s, most was simply promotional. Thus, in this respect, Physiocracy failed one of the crucial tests of a scientific theory: the capacity to generate problems for further research. This weakness alone would have made its life short, since, by the eighteenth century, scientifically-minded persons were far more interested in participating in the discovery of new truth than in propagandizing for truths already known. Adam Smith visited France in the mid-1760's and met the Physiocrats. His own economic ideas may have been influenced by them but he spoke slightingly of them in the *Wealth of Nations*. At any rate, it was Smith's book, published in 1776, that proved to be the main source of inspiration for the development of what is now known as 'classical economics.' The work of Quesnay and his followers virtually disappeared from sight until the mid-nineteenth century, when some economists, most notably Karl Marx, began to retrieve them from the discard box of intellectual history.

It is questionable whether the specific model of economic processes diagrammed in Quesnay's *Tableau* should be regarded as a significant contribution to the development of economic theory, but the conception of a model of the economy as a whole, whatever its specifics, is in itself a notable step in the evolution of scientific economics. Beyond this general point, there are certain features of Physiocratic theory, and its application, that are significant as foreshadowing later developments in economics. These will now be briefly noted.

1. The concept of spontaneous order

The most important idea of the Physiocrats was that economic processes are governed by laws of nature in such a way that the economic world, like the natural world, is, or can be, a system of *spontaneous* order: not man-made or man-governed. This ran counter to much of the economic thinking of the eighteenth century, which viewed the economy as something that required constant management and extensive regulation by the state. As noted above, the Physiocrats did not argue that the institution of the state could be dispensed with; in fact, they favoured despotic government, but they contended that its economic role could be greatly reduced because of the existence of a mechanism of spontaneous order operating through market processes.

This is regarded by historians of economics as the main contribution of Adam Smith. Why are the Physiocrats not credited with it? The reason is that they did not follow their broad insight up by an analysis of the market mechanism. It is one thing to assert that markets co-ordinate the specialized activities of individuals; it is another thing to show *how* this process works. Assertion alone does not make science. Adam Smith began the examination of how the market mechanism functions by focusing upon how it determines market *values*, the prices (of final products and of the services of factors of production) that regulate production and determine the distribution of income. No analysis of this sort was carried out by the Physiocrats. Their model was a schematic representation of the economy in terms of flows of aggregate expenditures between very broadly defined entities: landowners, farmers, and the 'artisans' engaged in manufacturing. They did not explain how the production of specific commodities is determined or how the various participants in their production share their market values. In modern jargon, the Physiocrats were very severely *macro*economic in their approach; *micro*economic analysis, which is fundamental to any satisfactory theory of a market-governed economy, was begun by Adam Smith.

2. Economic classes

The idea that human society is a hierarchical structure and that this structure is composed of distinct and discrete social classes is so old that it can hardly be traced. But the Physiocratic model involved an important innovation in how the class structure of society is conceived by the social scientist. Instead of using the traditional status categories (such as the 'nobles', 'clergy', and 'third estate' of French politics) the *Tableau* contains categories or classes that are *economic* in nature. This is undoubtedly one of the main reasons why Karl Marx admired the Physiocrats: he felt that recognition of the economic basis of class structure was absolutely necessary to the development of social science.

The orthodox classical economists, Adam Smith, David Ricardo, John Stuart Mill, and others, employed economic class categories in their analysis (landowners, labourers, capitalists), so the idea of defining social structure in terms of economic classes was not exclusive to Marx, but Marxian social theory is much more dependent upon it, not only in its economic analysis but in its sociology, ethics, philosophy, political science, and its theory of historical evolution. Modern orthodox economics, which has developed from the initial models of the classical school, no longer makes important analytical use of economic-based social class categories, which is one of the main points of difference today between Marxist and neoclassical economics.

3. Circular flow

The modelling of the economy as a circular flow of expenditure is familiar today to any student who has taken an introductory college course in economics. This cannot, however, be traced directly to the Physiocrats. The classical economists did not pick up the Physiocratic concept of circular flow as an analytic tool. Karl Marx used it to some extent in his theory of capitalist economic development but he did not build his own basic economic model around it. Its revival as an analytical paradigm was mainly due to the work of John Maynard Keynes, whose *General Theory of Employment, Interest, and Money* (1936) has been the most influential book in economics of the twentieth century, responsible for establishing macroeconomics as a major branch of modern economic theory, and for changing the views of economists, and others, on the economic role of the state. Prior to Keynes the historian of economics would have had to regard the circular flow idea of the Physiocrats as a discarded curiosity; now it is a basic analytical concept of scientific economics. Keynes was very knowledgeable about the history of economics, but there is no evidence that he got the idea from reading the Physiocrats.

Where did the Physiocrats themselves get the idea? Numerous historians trace it to William Harvey, who discovered the circulation of blood in the animal organism (*De Motu Cordis*, 1628). This discovery undoubtedly did a great deal to extend the use of the concept of *mechanism* in scientific work to living matter. Quesnay's *Tableau* was an effort to extend it further, to the realm of social phenomena. The fact that Quesnay was a serious student of medicine as well as a competent practitioner means that he was familiar with Harvey's discovery, but this does not prove that it was the specific inspiration of his *Tableau*. In fact the idea of *circulation* as a general paradigmatic concept was very common in eighteenth-century literature. David Hume, writing in 1752, complained that 'circulation' had become a tedious intellectual cliché which 'serves as an account of everything'. So Quesnay did not have to be acquainted with Harvey's work to encounter the idea of circular flow.

4. Surplus

The idea of a 'net product' or surplus plays a large role in Physiocratic theory. Indeed, the main object of the *Tableau* was to contend that there is such a surplus and to locate its origin in land. The concept of surplus occupies an important place in the history of economic theory, playing a central role (after the Physiocrats) in classical economics, Marx's economics, and the model of efficient resource use developed by the neoclassical school in the late nineteenth century. This aspect of economics is the main point of contact between scientific analysis and ethical judgements in economics, as we shall see later in this book when we examine Ricardo's theory of rent, Marx's theory of exploitation, and Alfred Marshall's theory of maximum welfare.

There is no doubt as to the importance of the idea of surplus in the history of economics, but it is not clear how much is due to the Physiocrats. Marx's theory of 'surplus value' resembles Quesnay's 'net product' in singling out one factor of production (though a different one) as the source of surplus. Ricardo's theory of rent is quite different, however, based not on the existence of cost-free productive services and the bounty of nature, as in the Physiocratic model, but on the niggardliness of nature, reflected in the law of diminishing returns. Marshallian welfare economics is based on the law of diminishing utility as well as (and more fundamentally than) the law of diminishing returns. All we can really say is that, in focusing their model on 'net product', the Physiocrats foreshadowed, if only vaguely, a great deal of subsequent economic theory.

5. The single tax

As we shall see later, the idea of land rent as the proper object of taxation and the concept of a single tax reappeared more than a century after the Physiocrats in a book by Henry George called *Progress and Poverty* (1879).

This became a popular best-seller in both America and England and was important in developing the line of reformist political thought represented by non-Marxist, democratic socialist movements. Henry George himself was not a socialist; he felt that he had discovered the one great defect of a capitalist system, which could be corrected by a single tax on land values or rent. In *Progress and Poverty* the foundation of George's argument was Ricardo's theory of rent, but he dedicated his later *Protection or Free Trade* (1891) to the Physiocrats.

From the standpoint of economic analysis, the importance of the Physiocratic theory of taxation was that it was based on the perception that taxes are not necessarily paid by those on whom they are levied; they may be shifted, through the market mechanism, on to the shoulders of others. Obviously the economic effects of a certain type of tax cannot be ascertained without analysis of this shifting phenomenon. This has been a major pre-occupation of taxation economics ever since the Physiocrats. No one believes that all taxes are ultimately paid by landowners, as the Physiocrats claimed, but they did demonstrate the need for an economic model in ascertaining the ultimate incidence of a tax and making an assessment of its economic effects. More generally, one might say that Physiocratic taxation theory demonstrated the need for a way of examining the hidden or unintended consequences of governmental policy, which has occupied a large part of the attention of economists ever since the beginning of the discipline.

6. 'Advances'

In classical economics three categories of factors of production are employed for analytical purposes: land, labour, and capital. The third of these has posed problems of special difficulty for economic theory, many of which are associated with the fact that capital-using methods of production involve *time*. If, say, instead of gathering fruit as best one can with one's bare hands, labour is first devoted to making a fruit-picking tool, the total production of fruit may be increased, but its availability is postponed. There are many economic activities that have this essential nature: increasing, but delaying, production.

The Physiocrats considered only land and labour as factors of production, but they did recognize the central problem of the theory of capital by arguing that funds must be 'advanced' for productive purposes some time before any yield would be forthcoming. In accordance with their theory, they contended that these advances could only come out of the net product. As a consequence of such advances, the total output of the economy would be increased and the circular flow, instead of remaining constant in magnitude from one year to the next, would be enlarged. In this way economic growth occurs.

Though they did little to clarify the role of capital in an economy, the Physiocrats did identify the main problems that this branch of economics must grapple with: the role of capital investment in economic development, the time-consuming nature of capital-using methods of production, and the source of the wealth that is used to make capital investments. The theory of capital is one of the least satisfactory areas of modern economic theory, in large part because economists have not been able to find satisfactory answers to problems that were initially posed by the Physiocrats.

7. Ideology

The Physiocrats, as noted above, were a group of disciples gathered around a master, convinced that they possessed the truth on essential issues of economics. Most of them would have acknowledged that there were still some unsolved scientific problems, but these were regarded as minor; the main task was to convey the truth to others, especially those with political power. Put this way, Physiocracy resembles the ideology of a sect more than the views of a community of scientists. The line between what is a scientific theory and what is a sectarian ideology is difficult to draw, and frequently depends much on who is doing the drawing; one man's 'science' may be another's 'ideology'. Sectarianism and an ideological attitude towards knowledge is not completely absent in natural science but a notable feature of that area of human knowledge is its development, in modern times, of objective criteria by which the validity of empirical propositions may be tested. The social sciences have not been able to develop the same degree of objectivity, for reasons outlined in Chapter 3 C, but, in addition, there has emerged, in the social sciences, the sociological phenomenon of the formation of 'schools'. Economists and other social scientists often identify themselves, and are more frequently identified by others, as 'Marxists' or 'Keynesians' or 'Parsonians' or 'Jungians' or 'monetarists' and so on. Given the strong emotional feelings that are attached to social phenomena and the intense partisanship of social policy, it may well be that social science would have inevitably developed strong sectarian characteristics, but whether that is so or not, the Physiocrats must be credited (or debited) with the historical priority of not only constructing the first analytical model in social science but also wrapping it in a thick blanket of ideology.

Chapter 6

The methodology of modelling

In the previous chapter we examined the economic ideas of the Physiocrats, stressing the fact that in carrying out their investigation of the French economy they constructed and employed an explicit 'model' of economic processes. Since then the practice of constructing analytical models has steadily developed and, although models are more common in economics than in the other social sciences, no branch of the subject is today without its models, and the attempt to construct new models of social processes is one of the most flourishing branches of social science. The term 'model' is, however, rather vague. It is used in a variety of different ways by social scientists and, in addition, it is a common-speech term with a variety of different meanings. The object of this chapter is to clarify the concept of 'model' by noting some of the main common features and differences in the types of models used by social scientists.

This discussion, I should say at once, will serve only to introduce the topic. A full examination of the methodology of modelling in the social sciences would amount to a complete study of the methodological foundations of social science and, indeed, of natural science as well. Needless to say, such a study is beyond the scope of this chapter and of this book as a whole. It will serve our purposes best, I think, if we first examine some specific examples of models before attempting to discuss the methodology of modelling in general.

A. EXAMPLES OF MODELS

1. The circular flow of expenditure

Having had a look in the previous chapter at the 'Tableau Economique' of the Physiocrats it would seem appropriate to use as our first example the modern counterpart of it. This is the model of the economy as a circular flow of expenditure, which is the foundation of the branch of economics called 'macroeconomics'. Modern macroeconomic theory stems historically so much from a single book, J. M. Keynes's *A General Theory of Employment, Interest,*

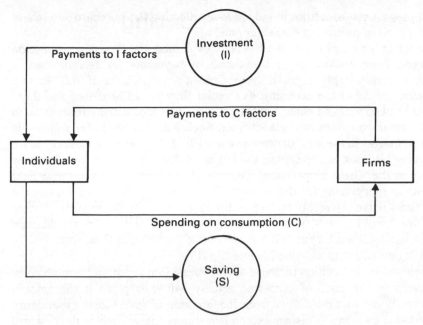

Figure 6-1

and Money (1936), that one often finds it referred to by the eponymous term 'Keynesian economics'. The theories of modern macroeconomics are too complex to be stated without using mathematics, but their central concept of a circular flow of expenditure can be modelled in a simple diagram: Figure 6-1.

In this diagram the economy is depicted as a flow of expenditures between two entities called 'individuals' and 'firms'. All production is presumed to take place inside firms. The firms buy 'factors of production' (labour, the use of capital equipment, raw materials) in order to carry on their production processes, and the expenditures they make for these factors are received by individuals who (as workers and property owners) are pictured as selling these services to firms. Individuals, in turn, make expenditures, buying finished commodities from firms. So money is flowing from individuals to firms for consumer goods and from firms to individuals in payment for the services of production factors needed to produce consumer goods.

This is depicted in the diagram by lines with arrows showing the direction of the money flow. (Consumer goods and factors could be shown as flowing in the opposite direction, but this would only complicate the diagram without adding anything that is not obvious.) The line 'Spending on consumption (C)' shows the movement of money payments from individuals to firms, reflecting the purchase by the former and sale by the latter of consumption goods (food, housing, transport, etc.). The line called 'Payments to C factors' shows the money payments from firms to individuals, reflecting the purchase and sale of factors used in producing consumer goods.

So far only part of Figure 6-1 has been explained: the flow of consumption spending from individuals to firms, and of payments for factors used in producing consumption goods from firms to individuals. If this were a complete model of the economy, its circular flow would be closed and there would be absolutely no change in the pace of economic activity from week to week, month to month, and year to year. Such a model would fail to provide for any *changes* in the level of economic activity. J. M. Keynes's main objective in writing his book was to explain the fall in the level of economic activity now known as the 'Great Depression'. The model can be extended to throw light on this by recognizing (a) that individuals *save* part of their income, and (b) that firms make payments to factors for *investment* (building plant, buying machinery, etc.) as well as consumption goods production. So, as the diagram shows, saving is equivalent to a leakage out of the circular flow, while investment is equivalent to an injection into the flow.

Now we are in position to arrive at something important and non-obvious: a change in the pace of economic activity will take place if the amount individuals try to save differs from the amount of investment expenditure undertaken by firms. If savings exceed investment the volume of the flow will decline – there will be an economic recession; if investment exceeds saving, the flow will increase – there will be an economic boom. Even with this simple model we can carry the analysis a step further: if saving tends to exceed investment the level of economic activity will fall and it will *keep on falling* until saving equals investment. Similarly, if investment tends to exceed saving, economic activity will *keep on increasing* until they become equal. Thus we can say that an economy will be in 'equilibrium' (i.e. no tendency to change) when saving equals investment. The concept of equilibrium is a very important feature of many models used in the social sciences. This model thus enables us to recognize that the magnitudes of saving and investment are crucial to any analysis of booms and depressions. We can then proceed to focus attention on the factors that govern these magnitudes. In this way, the circular flow model of the economy focuses the work of empirical research in a systematic fashion.

The role of government in all this can be analysed by considering it as a third entity in addition to our individuals and firms. (It is not shown in Figure 6-1 because it would complicate the diagram and it is not really necessary, since we now understand how the model works.) Part of the incomes of individuals goes to government as taxes, which act, like savings, as a leakage from the circular flow. The expenditures made by government, on the other hand, act like investment, as an injection into the circular flow. Consequently, when government taxes more than it spends, this tends to slow down the pace of economic activity, and vice versa. This is the logic of what is called 'Keynesian fiscal policy'. The role of the model in generating the prescription that government should have a fiscal deficit when there is recession and a surplus when the economy is too active (inflation) is quite clear. This illustrates how a model of a social process can be used to direct attention to the instruments that may be used to deal with a social problem.

We could extend the model still further by adding the international sector as a fourth entity. When American individuals spend part of their income on imported goods this acts as a leakage from the U.S. circular flow. When foreigners buy from the U.S., on the other hand, this acts as an injection. So the impact of the international sector on the level of American economic activity depends on the difference between imports and exports.

This model of the economy could be elaborated much further, and it is in the modern literature of economics. What we have done here, however, is sufficient to demonstrate the main characteristics of such a model and to indicate how it is used as an analytical tool and a social policy instrument.

2. The market model

In Chapter 1 B 4 above we noted that the high degree of 'functional specialization' characteristic of economically developed human societies requires some mechanism that will integrate the separate activities of many individuals into an orderly system. The study of how this is accomplished by 'markets' is the main focus of the branch of economics called 'microeconomic theory'. Its principal objective is to analyse how market processes determine the quantities of specific goods that will be produced (and used) and the prices at which they will be sold.

The basic idea of microeconomic theory is that markets are two-sided: the purchasers (or users) of commodities on one side of the counter, so to speak, and the producers (or sellers) on the other. What ensues – the quantities of goods produced and used, and their prices – is the result of the interaction of 'the forces of supply and demand'. In a general way this conception of market processes goes back to the eighteenth century and earlier; but it is doing little more than stating the obvious to say that price is 'determined' by 'supply and demand'. A specific model of market processes that goes further than such rather vague and platitudinous statements was not constructed until the nineteenth century, and it did not become an established instrument of economic analysis until the early twentieth century, mainly owing to the geometrical modelling of supply and demand used by Alfred Marshall in his *Principles of Economics* (1890), which became the foundation book of modern microeconomics.

The market model is pictured diagrammatically in Figure 6-2. Here, instead of drawing a metaphorical picture of the economy as we did in section 1 to describe the circular flow model, we make use of a very powerful general analytical instrument that was invented by René Descartes in the early seventeenth century. The axes labelled 'Price' and 'Quantity' in Figure 6-2

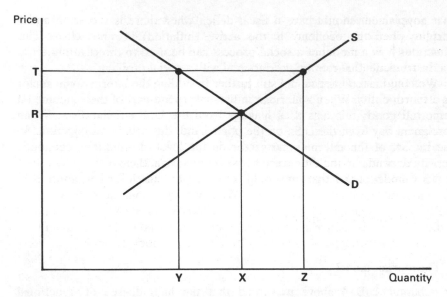

Figure 6-2

compose a system of 'Cartesian co-ordinates' which enable one to plot the
relationship between these two variable magnitudes. The curve labelled D is
the relationship between the quantity of a specific commodity that buyers will
wish to buy and the price of that commodity. The fact that the D curve slopes
down to the right represents the plausible assumption that, *other factors held
constant*, people will want to buy more of this commodity at a lower price than
they would at a higher price. This is the demand curve. The curve labelled S
depicts the quantities the producers are willing to produce at different prices.
Its upward slope to the right embodies the plausible assumption that producers are willing to supply more of a particular commodity at a high price
than at a low price (again subject to the *ceteris paribus* condition: that other
factors are held constant). The S curve is the supply curve for the commodity
in question.

Now that we have demand and supply graphed on the same set of
price–quantity co-ordinates we can state that, in this particular case, the price
of the commodity will be R (measured, say, in cents per pound) and the
quantity of the commodity produced and consumed will be X (say pounds per
week). The reasoning behind this contention is as follows: if the price were
above R at, for the sake of illustration, T, the S curve says that producers will
want to produce Z but, according to the D curve, consumers are only willing
to buy Y. This excess of supply over demand will make a price like T
unsustainable; it will tend to fall. By similar reasoning we would conclude that
any price *below* R (not drawn in the figure) would create an excess of demand

over supply and the price would tend to rise. If any price above R tends to fall and any price below R tends to rise, then R is the 'equilibrium price' of this commodity. For the same reason, X is called the 'equilibrium quantity'.

Every student of elementary economics knows that this is only the beginning of the market model. We can proceed next to relax some of the *ceteris paribus* conditions in order to find out what will happen to price and quantity if wage rates change, prices of competing commodities change, and so on. The model can, in this way, be applied to a large number of specific cases. Of course, as we make the model more complicated we tax the capacity of geometry to depict the situation and eventually we have to resort to algebra, which does not suffer from the restrictions imposed by the limited dimensions of real space.

3. The prisoners' dilemma model

For a third illustration of model construction let us look at one that focuses on the important fact that when a person engages in an action the outcome may depend in part on what other people do. This is obviously the case when one is engaged in a game like, say, bridge or chess, which has to be played with a strategy that takes into account the potential actions of the other players. Realization that many social situations are similar has led to the construction of social models built upon the theory of games. John von Neumann and Oskar Morgenstern, *The Theory of Games and Economic Behaviour* (1944), was the pathbreaking work in this. (Note again how recent this is.) The particular game model known as the 'prisoners' dilemma' has been widely used in virtually all the disciplines of social science.

Suppose that two men, Albert and Benjamin, have committed a burglary and have been arrested. The evidence against them, however, is only circumstantial, and there is no possibility of a conviction unless at least one of them confesses. Obviously the interests of Al and Ben are best served if both keep quiet. The police have separated them, however, so they cannot engage in a co-ordinated strategy. The police tell Al that if he confesses and helps to convict Ben he will get special consideration. They give the same promise to Ben. What is the smart thing for Al and Ben to do *individually*? The data recorded in Figure 6-3 show the alternatives. The numbers in the cells of the diagram show the prison sentence that is expected and will in fact result from each strategy. Al's sentence is recorded in the south-west corner of each cell and Ben's in the north-east corner. Looking at this matrix, we find that if both keep quiet the sentences are zero. But if Al keeps quiet and Ben confesses, Al gets six years in prison and Ben only one. The reverse happens if Ben confesses. What will Al do? The strategy that minimizes his maximum potential sentence is to confess (four compared to six). The same for Ben. So both confess and go off to prison for four years!

The significance of the prisoners' dilemma model is that it provides an explanation of cases where people are unable to obtain what they jointly wish

	BEN	
	Confess	Not confess
AL Confess	4 4	6 1
Not confess	1 6	0 0

Figure 6-3

unless some form of organized co-operation exists. There are many situations in which there is a disagreement between the optimum action for private benefit and the optimum action for collective benefit, and they don't all have to do with benefiting criminals. The model also offers an explanation of behaviour that might otherwise seem peculiar. For example, why do prisoners beat up new arrivals who are 'squealers'? One could say that prisoners are 'morally outraged' by such behaviour and operate their own system of 'justice'. Or one could suggest that it is designed to raise the cost of confessing so that criminals can have more confidence in their accomplices. If the data in the north-west cell of Figure 6-3 read 'four years *plus* a beating' the six years in the south-west and north-east cells might seem superior. The policy of 'honour among thieves' may have more to do with strategy than with 'honour'.

B. SOME FEATURES OF MODELS

The models outlined in section A are examples of analytical procedures that have come into widespread use in the social sciences. In one respect, however, they may present a misleading picture of contemporary social science research, since they were discussed purely as *theoretical* models. If one looks at the current literature of the social sciences it is immediately evident that most research is *quantitative* and *empirical*, making use of data from surveys, reports, censuses, etc., and processing such data by complex statistical methods that have been developed (by physicists, biologists, and mathematicians as well as social scientists), especially during the past half-century or so. Empirical research, however, cannot be conducted without an underlying framework of theory, so our focus here upon theoretical models is not misleading if one keeps in mind that the object of any theory is to enable one to understand empirical phenomena, and the object of quantitative empirical procedures such as statistical methods is to make our understanding more precise by measurement. It is not true that if something cannot be measured it is not worth talking about but, none the less, it is true that when we can measure we can talk more precisely. The scope of this book does not permit much discussion of quantitative empirical methods, but one should keep this aspect of social science research in mind, remembering that theoretical questions, while vitally important, are not the whole of modern social science. Let us now look at some features of theoretical modelling, using the models described above as illustrations.

In some of the general discussion of models by philosophers of science much emphasis is placed upon a quality called 'isomorphism'. This term is extensively used in biology and the other natural sciences, as well as mathematics, to refer to a structural correspondence between two or more things. Thus, for example, all species of mammals can be described as isomorphic in having bodies that are bilaterally symmetrical (two limbs on the left side and two on the right; one ear on one side and one on the other, and so on). When a *model* is described as 'isomorphic' what is usually meant is that there is a high degree of correspondence between the model and the 'real thing'. A clear example is the relationship between a small plastic model of, say, a Boeing 747 and a real Boeing 747: they are isomorphic in their external shapes. Such a model could be merely an ornament or a toy, but it could also be used for research purposes. For example, engineers can learn a great deal about the aerodynamics of an aircraft by placing an isomorphic model of it in a wind tunnel.

If isomorphism were a necessary characteristic of models, the social sciences would not do much modelling, because constructing a model that corresponds to a real society in any direct way is not possible. Of the three models outlined in section A only the first, the circular flow model, has some isomorphic qualities. To some extent the real economy *is* a circular flow process and modelling it in ways that are analogous to a hydraulic system meets the criterion of isomorphism, but the degree of isomorphism here is rather limited, very much less than that achieved by a model of a Boeing 747, or Neils Bohr's model of the atom, or the model of the DNA molecule constructed by Watson and Crick, or Newton's model of the planetary system, or Krebs's model of the process of organic oxidation, or. . . . The fact is, in the natural sciences there are many isomorphic models; in the social sciences, few. This is perhaps one of the great differences between the natural and social sciences. The chemist can construct a diagram of an organic compound that not only shows what atoms it contains but how they are linked together in real three-dimensional space. Compared to this, the market model could be called isomorphic only by violently stretching the meaning of that term. Unable to construct isomorphic models, the social sciences must rely more heavily on other types of models and on other analytical techniques.

In studying the aerodynamics of a wing structure it is not absolutely necessary to build a replica of the wing and test it empirically in a wind tunnel. In principle one could get equally reliable results by using a purely mathematical model and simulating the wind tunnel experiment on a computer. The market model outlined above is more like such a mathematical model than a wind tunnel model. It works as an effective tool for examining a range of economic phenomena, but not because it is isomorphic to the real economy in any literal sense. Similarly, the prisoners' dilemma model is not isomorphic to the actual procedures of a police investigation. It simply consists of systematically recording all the alternatives that decision-makers are faced with in a certain type of situation so that it becomes possible to predict with some confidence the decisions they are likely to make.

The main point I am trying to emphasize here is that the purpose of any model is to serve as a tool or instrument of scientific investigation. For some purposes isomorphic models are very useful but they are not always available, and they are not the only models that are useful. I have laboured this issue somewhat because it is a common complaint that social science models are invalid because they are 'unrealistic'. What underlies this criticism is the assumption that all good models replicate the 'real world' in an isomorphic way. The real test of a model, however, is whether it works effectively as a scientific instrument, not the degree to which it replicates the real world.

Before leaving this point one should note that the existence of isomorphism between a model and the real thing does not guarantee that an analysis of the model will yield true propositions about the real thing. If we place a plastic model of a Boeing 747 in a wind tunnel, some of the results obtained may be valid for the model but not for the real aeroplane. Treating the two things uncritically as if they were the same would be an example of the logical fallacy called *ignoratio elenchi*: assuming that one has demonstrated something to be true of X when the argument or evidence really applies to Y, which is not the same as X in some respect. Awareness of the danger of slipping into this fallacy is necessary if the scientist is to avoid the trap of devoting himself exclusively to the analysis of his model instead of using the model as an instrument for studying the real world. This trap does not catch many natural scientists, because of the established place of experimentation in their disciplines, but it has been an important snare of social scientists. The social scientist who immerses himself in a model may begin to perceive the real world so exclusively in terms of the model that the distinction between them disappears. This is one of the characteristics of 'ideology', not unknown in the natural sciences but much more common in the social sciences.

From what has already been said about isomorphism it is evident that models are simpler than the real-world things or processes they represent. If this were not so, models would be as complex as the real-world phenomena themselves, and just as incomprehensible. The whole point in building an analytical model is to construct a representation that is simpler than the real thing. It is not a valid criticism of a model to say that it is necessarily wrong because it is simpler than the reality it purports to represent.

There is no trick at all in constructing a theoretical model; you simply leave out a lot of the features of the real world. To construct a scientifically useful model, however, one has to be very careful about what one leaves out. In general terms one can say that *irrelevant* features should be left out. So, for example, in constructing a model of a Boeing 747 for the purpose of studying wind turbulence on the upper surface of the wing, the electronic equipment in the real aeroplane's cockpit is irrelevant. Unfortunately, there are few cases that are quite so clear and, moreover, science is often showing that what was previously thought to be irrelevant is relevant after all. The important thing, though, is to recognize that what is relevant depends on the purpose of the model. The navigational instruments of an aircraft are not irrelevant to the general performance of the aircraft in flight; they are irrelevant to the more limited question of wind turbulence on the wing.

If we look at the three social science models outlined in section A, it is clear that they are gross simplifications of the real world. Let us consider one of the factors that they omit: the religion of the people whose activities are modelled. One's first reaction is that this would have little or no effect upon the circular flow of expenditures, or the mechanism of price formation in markets, or on the behaviour of prisoners under interrogation. But this might be too hasty a judgement. A number of years ago the Catholic Church rescinded its rule that the faithful must not eat meat on Fridays. This was clearly not irrelevant to the process of price formation in the markets for meat and fish and it may have affected the circular flow of income in a region like Newfoundland where the export of fish is very important to the economy. The religion of the two prisoners might also have relevance in the model of their behaviour: if they were both Mormons, for example, they might have had more confidence in each other's resolve to keep quiet than if one were a Christian Scientist and the other an Episcopalian. There may be more 'honour among thieves' when they have the same Church affiliation.

These considerations show us something important about the characteristics of a good analytical model: a good model is one that can be used for some purposes even in its simplest form, but can be expanded to include additional factors when their relevance to the problem in hand is suspected. Models differ greatly in their expansion capabilities. One of the main reasons why economists are so fond of the market model of microeconomic theory is that it has shown remarkable capacity for elaboration and modification, and for application to the study of a very wide range of social phenomena.

A feature of models that has not yet been noted is that it is difficult to build models with components that are not conceptually quantitative. By *conceptually* quantitative I do not mean that magnitudes have actually been measured but that one can think about the elements of the model in quantitative terms. The three models outlined in section A are composed of elements that are conceptually quantitative: savings, investment, taxes, government expenditures, exports and imports in the circular flow model are all quantitative in nature. In the market model, the amount of a commodity produced and its price are quantities. In the prisoners' dilemma model, simple conceptual quantification is achieved by supposing the prisoners to be concerned only with number of years in prison.

Some arguments in social science cannot be represented as models (unless one uses that term very loosely) because the constituents of the theory are not conceptually quantitative. Where would our prisoners' dilemma model take us if imprisonment were described, as Hobbes described the state of nature, as a life that is 'solitary, poor, nasty, brutish, and short'? We can turn 'short' (or 'long') into quantitative terms, but the other elements are not conceptually quantitative. This is why we could draw a schematic model to represent the theories of the Physiocrats in Chapter 5 but could not do likewise for the theories of Hobbes and Locke in Chapter 4.

One of the main differences between economics and the other social sciences is that economics is able to make use of a much higher degree of conceptual quantification. Take, for example, two 'functions' or statements of relationship, one from economics and the other from political science:

1. Output of commodity $X = f$ (labour, capital, materials ...).
2. Power of the President $= f$ (his election majority, party representation in Congress ...).

In these two illustrations I have deliberately chosen factors in (2) that appear to be as quantitative as those in (1): votes and party members can be counted. But let us see whether conceptual quantification can be pushed equally far in both cases. A well known proposition in economics says that as one factor of production is increased relative to the others, the incremental output attributable to that factor (its 'marginal product') will decrease. This is the 'law of diminishing returns'. Expressed in mathematical terms, it asserts that the second partial derivatives of the function (1) above are negative. Such a proposition is meaningful only because the factors on both sides of the equation sign in (1) are capable of a high degree of conceptual quantification. An equivalent statement about (2) is not possible. What would it mean to say, for example, that the second partial derivative of presidential power with respect to the incumbent's election majority is negative, or positive, or zero? Propositions of such a sort would not be intelligible.

The import of this is that the reason why economics is more highly developed as an analytical discipline than the other social sciences is that it can work to a greater extent with conceptually quantitative elements. It is not true, as some have contended, that economic relationships are inherently less complicated than political or sociological relationships; but economic relationships are more easily modelled than other social phenomena.

Chapter 7

The Scottish Enlightenment of the eighteenth century

The examination of Physiocracy in Chapter 5 was chiefly aimed at delineating the economic model that was embodied in Quesnay's famous 'Tableau Economique'. It is not a comprehensive study of the Physiocratic school, and it serves even less as an indicator of social thought in France during the latter part of the eighteenth century prior to the Revolution. Physiocracy itself had only a brief popularity in intellectual circles, but there were numerous other important French social thinkers of the period, including Montesquieu, whose influential analysis of the English constitution we examined in Chapter 4. France before the Revolution was, indeed, a place of exceptional intellectual vigour: Rousseau, Voltaire, Laplace, Lavoisier, Turgot, Condillac, Condorcet, Diderot, and d'Alembert being some of the other names still remembered today. In mathematics, natural science, and the social sciences, France gave every indication during the later eighteenth century of becoming the intellectual leader of the Western world. There was only one serious competitor for France's supremacy – Scotland.

One can imagine that if an unbiased observer of the period were to consider these two contestants he would have regarded the outcome as beyond doubt: France, a country of 25 million (twice the population of the United Kingdom as a whole), attracting its own talent and that of the rest of Europe to Paris and the brilliant court of Versailles; Scotland, with 1.5 million, and no comparable social and political centre. Yet Scotland it was that became the seedbed of modern social science, which developed there as part of a remarkable efflorescence that embraced all areas of intellectual activity. From the vantage point of the early eighteenth century, Scotland would appear to be one of the most unlikely places in Europe to become a centre of intellectual innovation. The hold of the Catholic Church had been broken in the sixteenth century but only to be replaced by one of the most narrow and bigoted forms of Protestantism. John Knox (1514?–72), the creator of Scottish Presbyterianism, was a strong believer in formal schooling, but its function was conceived to be the inculcation of fixed doctrine, not the stimulation of inquiring minds. The Scottish Kirk absorbed whatever intellectual talent came to the surface in society and bent it to the service of stamping out all novelty as heresy. And then, quite suddenly, in the mid-eighteenth century, the mists of ignorance cleared and Scotland vaulted from being one of the most backward countries of Europe to one of its most civilized – indeed, the leader, for a period, in the developments that have led historians to call the eighteenth century the Age of Enlightenment. These developments were perhaps due in part to the closer ties with England that followed the Act of Union in 1707, made final by the failure of the Jacobite Rebellion of 1745; and, undoubtedly, the economic changes that invigorated Scottish industry in the latter half of the eighteenth century had some influence. But historians will not hesitate to admit that it is impossible, as yet, to give a convincing account of the reasons for Scotland's rise to eminence.

Whatever its causes, it was a most remarkable development. A modern historian of Scotland describes it thus:

> Scotland forged ahead in the realms of scholarship and learning, of imaginative writing and creative art. Her universities were everywhere admired, her poets, novelists and artists were lauded, her philosophers and historians gained the respectful attention of civilised peoples, and the books and magazines that issued from her presses influenced opinion and judgment throughout the world. (George S. Pryde, *Scotland from 1603 to the Present Day*, 1962, p. 162)

David Hume, himself one of the main creators of this development, and its most outstanding figure of permanent importance, wrote as early as 1757:

> Really, it is admirable how many men of genius this country [Scotland] produces at present. Is it not strange that, at a time when we have lost our princes, our parliaments, our independent government, even the presence of our chief nobility, are unhappy in our accent and pronunciation, speak a very corrupt dialect of the tongue which we make use of; is it not strange, I say, that, in these circumstances, we should be the people most distinguished for literature in Europe. (Quoted by E. C. Mossner, *Life of David Hume*, 1980, p. 370)

By 'literature' Hume meant intellectual productions of all kinds; Scotland was distinguished in the sciences as well as in philosophy and the arts. The University of Edinburgh's medical school was so renowned that students flocked to it from all over, including America. Joseph Black, a physician and chemist at the University of Glasgow and later at Edinburgh, contributed much to the progress of chemistry by developing his theories of latent heat and specific heat. His discovery of carbon dioxide led scientists to recognize that there is more than one kind of gas ('air'). Two of his students discovered nitrogen and strontium. Black befriended and encouraged James Watt in his efforts to develop the steam engine, the practical consequences of which were momentous. James Hutton, another Scottish physician, in a paper read to the Royal Society of Edinburgh in 1785, initiated a revolution in the science of geology by arguing that the history of the earth can be explained by extrapolating backward the processes (such as erosion) now observed to be at work on the planet. In the arts, the outstanding Scottish contribution was in architecture: the Adam brothers and other Scots dominated innovative architecture throughout the United Kingdom during the period. As publishers the Scots deserve special mention for initiating the *Encyclopaedia Britannica* in 1771, which remained for more than a century the most important publication of its kind in English; and for the *Edinburgh Review*, founded in 1802, which led the way in establishing the high-quality periodical as a feature of modern intellectual life. In 1762 Voltaire remarked that 'It is from Scotland that we receive rules of taste in all the arts – from the epic poem to gardening' (Pryde, p. 176). The remark was undoubtedly meant as a caustic comment on the presumptuousness of the Scots, but by the end of the century it could have been made as a matter-of-fact statement.

The Scottish thinkers in whom we are especially interested are those who contributed to the social sciences. The leading figures were Francis Hutcheson, Adam Ferguson, Thomas Reid, Dugald Stewart, Lord Kames (Henry Home), Lord Monboddo (James Burnet), David Hume, and Adam Smith. The last two are the ones of outstanding permanent significance. We cannot here examine the ideas of all of these thinkers. I shall proceed by first discussing the most important general features of the group as a whole in section A, then giving some special attention to the ideas and influences of David Hume and Adam Smith in sections B and C respectively.

A. SCOTTISH MORAL PHILOSOPHY

To the modern reader the term 'moral philosophy' denotes the branch of philosophy that deals with ethics: a relatively small part of only one of the many departmental units in the modern university's curriculum. In the eighteenth century the term was very much broader, embracing not only the whole of what we today classify as 'philosophy' but most of the subjects now included in a modern university's divisions of social sciences and humanities. Historians have often drawn attention to the fact that the social sciences developed from subjects that were previously included in moral philosophy, and it is sometimes inferred from this that the fountainhead of modern social science was ethics. This is historically incorrect, an error due to reading the twentieth-century meaning into an eighteenth-century term. The subject matter of moral philosophy that later developed into the several social sciences was not totally divorced from ethics, but it had no particularly strong connection with it.

In fact the main source of inspiration for the eighteenth-century thinkers was the accomplishments of the natural sciences. The Newtonian system was especially admired as a model of what scholars should aspire to achieve. Alexander Pope, the eighteenth-century poet, was only moderately exaggerating the view of the Enlightenment thinkers when he wrote the famous couplet in his *Essay on Man* (1733–4):

> Nature, and nature's laws lay hid in night;
> God said 'Let Newton be' and all was light.

Newton called his great work *Mathematical Principles of Natural Philosophy* (1687), which shows at once that the term 'philosophy' should not be interpreted in its twentieth-century sense. To call a book on physics 'philosophy' would today seem an abuse of language, but in Newton's time and throughout the ensuing century it was normal terminology. Samuel Johnson once remarked that a book on cooking should be founded on 'philosophical principles', by which he meant a knowledge of the general laws governing the phenomena rather than a mere set of recipes followed without understanding. When an eighteenth-century writer describes a proposition as 'unphilosophical' he means that it lacks what we today would call 'scientific' foundations. The modern usage of the term 'science' stems from the early nineteenth century. When it was used in the eighteenth century, as it was, for example, by Alexander Pope, it meant knowledge in general. H. L. Mencken in his book on *The American Language* noted that, as late as 1890, the word 'scientist' was denounced in England as an 'ignoble Americanism'.

There was much talk during the eighteenth century of extending the application of 'philosophical principles' to the field of human behaviour. This, roughly speaking, is what the term 'moral philosophy' came to denote. Newton himself had suggested, in concluding his book on *Optics* (1704), that if natural philosophy was perfected by the use of scientific method, benefits could be expected to follow for moral philosophy as well. This is probably what David Hume had in mind when he wrote the greatest philosophical work since Aristotle and called it *A Treatise of Human Nature: Being an Attempt to Introduce the Experimental Method of Reasoning into Moral Subjects* (1739–40). By 'experimental method' Hume did not mean laboratory experiments but, more broadly, the general approach of the sciences, which contrasted sharply with the arid *a priori* methods of scholastic philosophy. In Hume's view, the counterpart of the laboratory experiment in social phenomena is history, which furnishes empirical data. Scientific method, using the evidence of experience applied to moral subjects, would lead to the creation of moral philosophy, a general body of knowledge based upon the principles of human nature, just as that method had, in the hands of men such as Newton, created natural philosophy, knowledge based upon discovery of the fundamental laws governing natural phenomena.

How did the Scottish moral philosophers regard 'human nature'? The first point that should be noted is that they did not view man in religious or theological terms. Man was not regarded as a child of God, partaking of divine qualities, with rights and duties derived from his special status in the cosmos of divine creation. He was one among the many species of animals that live upon the planet; different from the others in important ways to be sure, but not having the kind of categorical distinction emphasized by religions that separate him from the rest of the natural world. The important word in the term 'human nature' was 'nature', construed the way the 'natural philosophers' (i.e. the physicists, chemists, biologists, and other scientists) regarded nature. Moral philosophy was viewed as that branch of the general study of natural phenomena which deals with man.

This view of man does not surprise anyone familiar with Hume's thinking, because Hume was a 'sceptic', that is to say, a doubter, about many things in which others firmly believed, including, in this connection, the articles of faith of Christianity and, indeed, all religion. But the same view of human nature was adopted by the other Scottish moral philosophers, most of whom did not share Hume's religious scepticism and were inclined to speak freely of 'Providence' or the 'Deity' as if they had no doubt of the existence of a transcendent being who first created and continues to oversee the universe. How men of religious faith were able to adopt the view that human existence and behaviour were natural phenomena becomes easier to understand when one notes the important change that took place during the eighteenth century in the theology embraced by progressive intellectuals.

The most fundamental philosophical question of theology is the *foundation* of one's belief – in particular points of doctrine or, indeed, in the very existence of a supreme being. The great controversy over this, starting in the seventeenth century and extending throughout the eighteenth, was between those who believed that the evidence for religious belief was provided by *revelation*, that is, for example, the work of God directly shown to man through the holy scriptures, miracles, etc.; and those who believed that the evidence existed in natural phenomena whose arrangement offered proof of having been ordered by a transcendent being. Just as the existence of a clock is evidence that there must have been a clockmaker, so the existence of the natural world, so intricately designed, is evidence for the existence of a cosmic designer. Isaac Newton, in the second edition of his great *Principia*, noted that 'This most beautiful system of the Sun, planets, and comets, could only proceed from the counsel and dominion of an intelligent and powerful Being'. To study nature was, for Newton, equivalent to the study of God; in the next century it became a defence of the most basic proposition in theology.

This approach to theology, which was called 'Natural Religion' or 'Deism', became very popular among intellectuals who prided themselves on being modern, though conservative religionists regarded it as little different from outright atheism. Its effect was to shift attention from the sacred texts and the endless commentaries upon them by generations of theologians and scholastic philosophers to the empirical study of God's work in nature. So the Christian did not have to become a sceptic in order to adopt the view that the way to advance 'moral philosophy' was to study the characteristics of man as a natural phenomenon. It was through this means that religion found its first accommodation to science. That accommodation remains tenuous even today, wherever the foundations of faith are construed otherwise, as based upon the unquestionable evidence of the truth as embodied in a literal fashion in sacred texts.

Regarding man as a natural phenomenon is, however, not sufficient to provide foundations for social science. If one hopes to construct general laws, as the other sciences do, there must be sufficient uniformity of human nature to sustain the validity of general propositions. In certain respects the most notable feature of the thinking of the Scottish philosophers was their insistence upon the similarity of human beings. This was a remarkable departure from contemporary common opinion, even among (or perhaps especially among) the educated. When, in an eighteenth-century book, one encounters the term 'the people' the probability is very high that the author means to refer to much less than half the population, excluding the 'lower orders', who were regarded as closer to 'beasts' than 'people' in their inherent natures, and in their proper status in the social order. The idea that men differ greatly was being supported during this time by a steady stream of accounts by voyagers to hitherto unknown lands that emphasized, and exaggerated, the strange and sometimes bizarre practices they had observed, evidencing the existence of beings who, though members of the biological species *Homo sapiens*, could not be regarded as sharing a commonality with Europeans or, at least, those of them who wrote, and read, books.

The Scottish moral philosophers, by contrast, emphasized the uniformity of human nature. The tales of exotic lands they took as evidence of the diversity of human culture, not of differences in basic human nature. Francis Hutcheson warned against the tendency to regard the practices of other cultures with astonishment, as one might stare with fascination at the behaviour of strange animals. Kames and Monboddo, the members of the group with the greatest interest in what we today call anthropology, took this to heart and strove to sift the sensationalized accounts of exotic cultures for the real gold: the common features of humankind. David Hume, who, as historian, was one of the creators of modern historiography, took the view that 'Mankind are so much the same, in all times and places, that history informs us of nothing new or strange in this particular. Its chief use is only to discover the constant and universal principles of human nature.'

Adam Smith's adoption of this view became the foundation of economic theory, as we shall see. It is worth noting here that it also became the basis of normative economics in that when Smith investigated 'The Nature and Causes of the Wealth of Nations', he meant to include all inhabitants within the term 'nation', which led him immediately to the judgement (which some of his contemporaries found surprising) that a nation cannot be considered rich if its lower classes (who compose the greatest number) are poor. Prior to

Adam Smith the common fashion was to regard the working class as necessary providers of labour in an enterprise whose main purpose was to increase the power and magnificence of the 'nation' as represented by its 'higher orders of men'. By construing the working class as an integral part of the nation whose wealth and culture they studied, Smith and the other Scots laid the groundwork for the development of utilitarianism, which became the social philosophy most influential in the nineteenth century. It was Francis Hutcheson who coined the motto 'the greatest happiness of the greatest number', the phrase that Jeremy Bentham and his disciples used as the utilitarian credo.

The Scottish moral philosophers were primarily interested in the *social* behaviour of man. But this was not so much a restriction of the field as a sharpening of the focus, since, in their view, man is by nature a social animal. In this respect, as in others, man is not unique. Lord Kames held the view that some light might be thrown on human sociality by studying the behaviour of other mammalian species who live in groups and he made some attempts to compile information on this. What distinguishes man from other animals is that his social life is carried on through a structure of social institutions, very elaborate in advanced societies, which performs essential functions in enculturating the young and organizing the activities of individuals into a co-ordinated collective enterprise. Thus the great interest of the Scots in social institutions reflected their view that man is unavoidably a social being, and his ability to lead a good life and improve on it is dependent on the quality of his political, social, and economic organization. The Scottish philosophers gave a respectful hearing to Rousseau's contention that social institutions are detrimental, warping man's character from its idyllic natural state, but the Frenchman they most agreed with was Montesquieu, who argued that it was simply nonsensical to view man as anything but a social creature. 'Man is born in society, and there he remains,' was a remark of Montesquieu's often quoted by the Scottish moralists.

For the Scottish philosophers, and some other writers of the period, the dual nature of man posed a problem that is close to the heart of social science. As individuals we are egocentric, but as members of society we entertain sentiments of benevolence towards others and sometimes act in ways that reflect altruism rather than self-interest. How are these apparently opposed characteristics made congruent? As we saw, Hobbes construed the problem of social order solely in terms of self-interest; egocentric individuals subscribe to a social contract and submit themselves to a sovereign, not for the good of others or for something that may be described vaguely as the 'public good', but each for his own benefit. Such pristine individualism did not appeal to the Scottish philosophers, either as psychology or as social theory. Adam Smith's great contribution was to show that the power of an absolute sovereign is not the only means by which social order may be achieved in a world of self-interested individuals, but his first book, *The Theory of Moral Sentiments*

(1759), was devoted to a study of *social* psychology in terms of man's propensity to desire the welfare of others.

Smith did not offer any resolution of the apparent conflict between egoism and benevolence, thus generating a debate, which has lasted down to the present, on whether his *Moral Sentiments* and his *Wealth of Nations* are inconsistent in their conceptions of man's psychological nature. But some of Smith's Scottish contemporaries addressed themselves to the problem. David Hume, in the *Treatise of Human Nature*, suggested that everyone considers the welfare of other persons but does not give it as much weight as his own. The weight may be very high when the other person is a member of one's family, but diminishes with respect to others less close, and may become very small when one is considering the welfare of persons who belong to very different cultures. Hume had in mind the notion which modern sociologists call 'social distance'. In effect, he argued that while one does not set the welfare of others at naught, one discounts it increasingly as their social distance becomes greater. Before Hume, some writers (including Francis Hutcheson, Smith's teacher) drew a parallel between social distance discounting and Newton's law of gravitational attraction, even suggesting that this psychological tendency conformed to Newton's specific formula, which expresses the force between two masses as inversely proportional to the square of the distance between them. The problem of how benevolence and egoism can be made congruent as properties of human nature was shunted aside in early nineteenth-century social science by the dominance of utilitarian psychology, which focused exclusively on self-interest, but it resurfaced in modern sociology and, recently, in economics, following the line of approach that Hume had suggested two centuries ago.

Concerning the one area of social science that had undergone significant development prior to the era of the Scottish Enlightenment – political theory – the Scottish moralists strongly rejected the accepted methodology. As we saw in Chapter 4, the approach to political analysis established by Hobbes and Locke was to conceive of the institution of government as an artefact created by a definite action, a contract or covenant entered into by individuals in the 'state of nature'. The Scots were aware, I think, that Hobbes and Locke did not mean this to be treated literally as an historical account of actual events, but even as a metaphorical or hypothetical construct they found it seriously misleading. The concept of society founded upon a contract was strongly attacked by David Hume, Adam Smith, Adam Ferguson, and others. The concept of the 'state of nature' was regarded as irrelevant, since man had always lived within a framework of social institutions and particular ones, such as government, had developed naturally and gradually. To regard government as having been established by a discrete contract or even to regard it as representing an implied contract or a hypothetical contract was, in their view, an unprofitable way of approaching the study of government.

This view of the contract theory of society and government became general during the nineteenth century. Though Locke was still regarded with respect, because of his empirical philosophy of knowledge and the liberal thrust of his political theory, the contract approach fell out of favour. As political science developed, its emphasis was upon the evolution of political institutions and their functional roles in social organization. In recent years has there been a revival of contract theory, in the area of ethical philosophy by John Rawls's *A Theory of Justice* (1971), and in the analysis of collective institutions initiated by J. M. Buchanan and Gordon Tullock's *The Calculus of Consent* (1962).

As we noted when the political theory of the seventeenth century was discussed in Chapter 4, Hobbes took the view that a government of unrestricted power is necessary to the maintenance of social order, to prevent the outbreak of the anarchic conflict of every man against every man. The Scottish moralists rejected not only Hobbes's conception of society as based upon a covenant or contract among its members, but also his view of the role of government in social order. In their view a society functions as a co-ordinated enterprise in large part because it is self-governing in the same way as the natural world is self-governing. It is perfectly open to any Newtonian to argue that God made the laws of nature but, once established, it is those laws, not God's intervention, that control the orbit of a planet or the fall of a stone. In a similar fashion the Scottish philosophers conceived of the realm of human behaviour as governed by laws akin to laws of nature, not laws made by sovereigns or legislators and enforced by the police and the courts.

The view of the social system as resting upon a natural mechanism of *spontaneous* order is often attributed to Adam Smith because of the prominent role it plays in the *Wealth of Nations*, but it was a commonly held conception of society among the Scottish moralists and there is no real reason for crediting Smith specifically with its origination, which he himself never claimed. As we saw in Chapter 5, the Physiocrats in France had the same idea. This concept of spontaneous order – social order without anyone giving orders; order without hierarchical structure – was of enormous importance to the later development of the social sciences, especially economics. In a sense, all of economics since the eighteenth century (including Marxian economics) can be regarded as an examination of how this spontaneous order works, as a necessary foundation for the evaluation of its functions in terms of proposed ends or objectives, and as a foundation for proposals to alter its functioning, or to replace it with other methods of co-ordination in order to attain these objectives, or other ones, more effectively. The question of how social order is achieved and maintained is also, of course, a major interest of other social sciences, and an issue of great importance in political philosophy. The notion of spontaneous order will be discussed more fully later in this chapter and in Chapter 10, where we will find that some versions of it are derived from the metaphysical concept of 'natural harmony', an idea which is *not* attributable to Adam Smith or the other Scottish philosophers. For now, however, we shall have to suspend our examination of the matter.

One point must be noted before we close this review of the eighteenth-century Scottish writers. I have refrained from calling them by a collective term such as 'the Scottish school', much less an eponymous one like 'Hutchesonians' or 'Smithians' or some such. The reason for this is that, though this group shared the general views described above, they disagreed in numerous ways and were content to disagree; none of them felt any need to accommodate his views to those of another in order to reach a common doctrine. They did not have a 'leader', they did not form a sect, they did not propagandize for a set of ideas regarded as a doctrinal core. They knew one another well, met and discussed, but did so without attempting to found an institution of any kind. This contrasts sharply with the Physiocrats and, as we shall see, numerous strains of social science in the nineteenth century. One of the strong themes that runs through the history of social science is the tendency of social scientists to form factions dedicated to the support of a doctrine and to engage in propaganda instead of (and sometimes in the guise of) scientific investigation. From this widespread characteristic of human nature the Scottish moralists were singularly free.

B. DAVID HUME (1711–76)

David Hume was the youngest of the three children of Joseph Hume, who lived a comfortable life combining the activities of a lawyer in Edinburgh and a gentleman-farmer of a modest estate that had come down to him from his ancestors. Hume's modern biographer says of the family that 'though unremarkable for their wealth, David Hume's forebears were of moderate affluence and sufficiently distinguished to warrant some pride of race in their most distinguished son' (E. C. Mossner, *The Life of David Hume*, 1980, p. 7). Joseph Hume died when David was only two years old, so the influences of early nurture that played their role in the creation of the great philosopher must be credited to his mother, who remained a widow and devoted herself to the management of the estate and the upbringing of her children. Their initial education was provided by tutors until David and his brother were considered suitably well prepared to enter Edinburgh University. This was in the year 1722, when David was just eleven and his brother John thirteen; the young matured earlier in the eighteenth century than today. David remained at Edinburgh for three years and it was apparently during this period that he began to develop the ideas that were to make such an impact on Western philosophy.

Being the younger of two sons, David knew from youth that he would have to earn his own living, since, according to the established custom of primogeniture, the family estate would go to his elder brother. He had a small inheritance of his own, enough to exist on but no more than that. He resolved to make his fortune, and fame as well, by writing, and he began seriously, about the age of eighteen, to work out the arguments of the book that was published ten years later as the *Treatise of Human Nature* (Vols I and II, 1739; Vol. III, 1740). As it turned out, Hume did win fame and fortune, but not as he had hoped. Very little attention was paid to the *Treatise* and it did not sell even well enough to warrant a second edition during the author's own lifetime. Hume tried to repair the unpopularity of the *Treatise* by publishing a simpler and amended version of his ideas called *Enquiry Concerning Human Understanding* (1748) and *Enquiry Concerning the Principles of Morals* (1751). These did not have the desired effect on Hume's popularity as a writer, but meanwhile he had begun to publish brief essays on political and social questions which were very well received and established his reputation as a thinker, and as a masterful writer of English prose. In the 1750's he began to write and publish, in successive volumes, his *History of Great Britain* (6 vols, 1754–62), which consolidated his reputation in the literary world. As an important philosopher Hume was not recognized during his lifetime: not really until Immanuel Kant perceived that Hume had raised the most important problem in philosophy and devoted his own powerful intellect to devising an answer to what became known as 'the problem of induction'. Much of the important philosophical thinking of the past two centuries has revolved around this, and other issues raised by Hume. Today, Hume's importance in the history of Western philosophy is beyond question.

Hume's neglect as a philosopher during his lifetime does not mean that his views went unnoticed. His philosophy was sceptical, inducing one to doubt many things previously taken for granted. With regard to religion, it was clear to any reader that Hume was not a Christian, that he doubted the validity of arguments purporting to demonstrate the existence of God and, indeed, whether such a proposition was demonstrable by any rational method. Moreover, he obviously had a low opinion of organized religious institutions. The Catholic Church put his name on the Index of prohibited books in 1761, citing simply *opera omnia* (all works), thus dealing with the great heretic's writings, past and future, in a simple and undiscriminating way. The Church of Scotland tried to excommunicate him in 1755–7. The effort failed, mainly because it was recognized to rest on the anachronistic assumption that Hume was subject to the Church's jurisdiction. In another era, or another country, Hume would have been burnt and his books with him, but in eighteenth-century Scotland the General Assembly of the Kirk succeeded only in making itself look foolish. However, opposition to Hume on account of his general scepticism and his view of religion was sufficient to prevent him from being appointed to a university post, which he would have liked. Hume's strongest attack on religion was published only after his death, though it was written twenty-five years earlier (*Dialogues Concerning Natural Religion*, 1779).

Within the scope of this study we must confine ourselves to Hume's significance for the history and philosophy of social science. Hume's general philosophy, dealing as it does with the nature of knowledge and with the status of such crucial concepts as causation, is clearly not detachable from fundamental issues in the philosophy of social science, but to embark on a study of his philosophy of knowledge in relation to social science would be too large an undertaking. So in the main text that follows I will restrict attention to Hume's more direct contributions to social science. An appended 'Note' will give a brief outline of Hume's general philosophy of science, and try to indicate its relation to issues such as those raised in Chapter 3 on 'Social laws'.

In section A above we noted the tension in Scottish Enlightenment thought between the recognition of man as a social creature and insistence on his individuality. This tension of ideas is prominent in the thought of David Hume. Let us look at how he attempted to resolve it.

The problem focuses upon the issue of egoism versus benevolence in man's nature. Thomas Hobbes had argued that man is entirely a self-interested creature, both in 'the state of nature' and, after the contract, in civil society. Hume rejected Hobbes's view as failing to recognize that society is part of man's nature. Does that mean that man is by nature benevolent towards his fellows? As we noted above, Hume followed other Scottish philosophers in arguing that man is egoistic in the sense that he values his own welfare *above* that of others, but not to the degree that he values the welfare of others at zero. A self-interested person may sacrifice his own welfare for that of others if the loss to him is small and the gain to others large. Moreover, a person would evaluate the welfare of others differently depending on their social closeness to himself, a line of thinking that touches upon an important proposition in social psychology: the tendency of most individuals to discount the welfare of others in proportion to the degree of their 'social distance' from themselves. On the basis of this reasoning it is easy to see what Hume had in mind in claiming that the problem of justice arises only in a world of economic scarcity and one in which the inhabitants have a 'confined generosity' towards their fellows. Scarcity means that everyone's welfare cannot be increased without limit, so the issue of how scarce goods ought to be distributed among persons arises; 'confined generosity' is simply Hume's way of expressing what modern sociologists call 'social distance discounting'.

Hume sometimes spoke as though moral issues are no more than matters of custom and convention, which would seem to lead to a degree of moral relativism that few persons would be prepared to accept. His main objective in this connection, however, was not to undermine our moral judgements but to question the arguments made for them; just as in his examination of religion he did not attack the specific doctrines of Christianity, or any other religion, but the 'demonstrations' that religionists offer in claiming the doctrines to be true. Hume contended that is not possible to demonstrate the truth (or falsity) of statements about moral good and evil (or any other value judgements). The first section of Book III of the *Treatise of Human Nature*, which contains his argument on this point, ends by castigating those who slip from making statements involving the verb *is* to ones involving the verb *ought* without recognizing that they belong to categorically different realms of discourse. This argument of Hume's opened a discussion that has persisted down to the present day, known in the philosophical literature as the 'is–ought' or the 'fact–value' dichotomy. Hope continues to be strong that the worlds of 'is' and 'ought' can be rigorously connected, that morality can be made 'scientific', derived from empirical knowledge about the material world; or 'logical', derived by deductive reasoning from axiomatic premises. So far, no one has succeeded in showing convincingly how such connections can be made, so it seems likely that Hume's contention is correct that, however uncomfortable it may make us, we cannot consider moral and other value judgements as derivable from empirical evidence and/or *a priori* reasoning.

This does not mean that moral issues cannot be rationally discussed or that empirical knowledge has no bearing upon them, and Hume went on in the remainder of Book III of the *Treatise* to write trenchantly about justice and other such matters. He proceeded by contending that observation of behaviour excites in us certain feelings of approval or disapproval, just as other sense data give us 'impressions' concerning the physical properties of objects. Limitations of scope do not allow us to examine Hume's moral theory further here but we should note two things about it in anticipation of future discussion. First, Hume's connection of moral sense with feelings of 'pleasure' and 'pain' associated with the observation of good and bad behaviour respectively was part of a line of thinking leading to the philosophy of utilitarianism, which became a powerful influence on social theory and social practice in the nineteenth century. Secondly, Hume's theory invites further exploration of how man develops a 'moral sense'. The investigation of this was the subject of Adam Smith's first book, *The Theory of Moral Sentiments* (1759).

Let us now give some attention to Hume's political theory. In Chapter 4 we saw how Hobbes traced the emergence of governmental power to the incomparable deficiencies of the state of nature and how Locke saw government as an institutional invention whose object was to make each man secure in the possession of his natural rights. Hume had a low opinion of all versions of the contract theory of the state, preferring to regard the state as a necessary element of a larger institution – society – which had developed much more spontaneously and naturally than contract theory implies. To understand Hume's views on this we have to go back to the concept of scarcity again. Here is a passage from the *Treatise* (Book III, Part II, section II):

> Of all the animals with which this globe is peopled, there is none towards whom nature seems, at first sight, to have exercised more cruelty than towards man, in the numberless wants and necessities, with which she has loaded him, and in the slender means, which she affords to the relieving of these necessities.

But man, though inferior to other animals as an individual, is able to increase his power by social association:

> 'Tis by society alone he is able to supply his defects, and raise himself up to an equality with his fellow-creatures, and even acquire a superiority over them. By society all his infirmities are compensated; and tho' in that situation his wants multiply every moment upon him, yet his abilities are still more augmented, and leave him in every respect more satisfied and happy, than 'tis possible for him, in his savage and solitary condition, ever to become.

Thus, in Hume's view, man was not *given* dominion over the earth by God, nor was he endowed by nature with the physical capacity to contest it with other animals, but he had acquired dominion nevertheless, through social organization. Hume anticipated Adam Smith in recognizing that functional specialization ('division of labour') is the source of man's great productive power, in seeing that specialization requires trade, and in appreciating that a system of markets cannot function without a basic framework of common rules of conduct established and enforced by the authority of the state. The real task of political science, then, is to study the various forms of governmental organization so that generalizations may be arrived at that are independent of the personal characteristics of those who occupy official positions (see Hume's essay 'That Politics may be Reduced to a Science'). From Plato's day down to ours the study of politics has been a mixed discipline, some political scientists focusing upon personalities and treating each political event as more or less unique, while others analyse the structure of political organizations and attempt to arrive at general principles applicable to many political events and conditions. Hume obviously had the latter in mind when he referred to the possibility of making politics a 'science'. He would probably conclude that this is much more difficult than he anticipated if he were able to survey the work in political science over the two centuries since his death.

Hume's view of economics would perhaps be different, since the study of economic phenomena has proved to be much more amenable to being 'reduced to a science'. Hume did not write any comprehensive work on economics but some of his short essays on economic subjects are highly interesting from the standpoint of the history and philosophy of social science. I will discuss here only the most famous one, 'Of the Balance of Trade'. This foreshadowed Adam Smith's *Wealth of Nations* (1776) as an argument against tariffs and other state interferences with international commerce but its main interest lies in the way in which Hume pursued the argument, which anticipated perfectly the methodology of modern economics.

The question of international trade and governmental policy related thereto was one of the dominant issues of continuous debate over the role of government during the eighteenth century. International relations generally had long been a primary object of political discussion and of scholarly interest, but prior to the seventeenth century, in countries like England, the chief focus of this was upon such matters as dynastic succession, alliances by treaty or marriage, and, of course, war. During the seventeenth century the expansion of trade brought about a shift of interest from the political to the economic aspects of international relations, not only because trade was becoming more important in itself but because of its recognizable relevance to non-economic matters such as military power, diplomatic influence, etc.

The new interest in international trade as 'an affair of state' as Hume put it, was part of a more general trend in economic policy to which historians have given the name 'mercantilism'. This term does not refer to a coherent system of economic ideas and theories but to the heterogeneous collection of policies that were developed piecemeal during the seventeenth and eighteenth centuries and which, by Hume's day, amounted to an extensive complex of regulations that left hardly any aspect of economic activity untouched. The regulation of international commerce by tariffs, embargoes, and other devices was part of this elaborate complex of economic regulation. Its main object was to produce a 'favourable balance of trade', an excess of exports over imports. The merit of this was argued on various grounds, one of which was that such a favourable trade balance would mean an inflow into the country of monetary coin and bullion (gold and silver), which was regarded in some sense as highly desirable.

Hume tackled this argument in a way that has characterized economics ever since in three important respects (1) Instead of quarrelling over whether a larger stock of precious metals is desirable or not, he asked whether it was in fact *achievable*. (2) In answering the first question he examined the *secondary and tertiary effects* of an increase in precious metals. (3) In bringing this tracing of effects to a conclusion (instead of going on indefinitely) he employed a concept from physical mechanics: *equilibrium*. Hume's argument can be set out as follows:

England	*Other countries*
Increase in money	
Rise in prices	
Increase in imports	Increase in exports
Decrease in exports	Decrease in imports
Outflow of money	Inflow of money

What would happen if there were a sudden increase in the nation's money stock, asks Hume? There would ensue a rise in English prices. This would encourage Englishmen to consume more foreign goods, since they would now be relatively cheap, and foreigners would consume fewer English goods, since they would now be relatively expensive. The effect would be to cause England to import more and export less, and monetary metal would be sent in payment to other countries, who would be importing less and exporting more. Thus prices would now commence to fall in England and rise in other countries. This process would continue until enough metal had moved from England to other countries to restore prices to their previous relationship. It is obvious from Hume's discussion that he regards the same analysis as showing why a policy of restricting international trade by tariffs and prohibitions would be similarly self-defeating. If England restricted imports, the excess of her exports would mean an inflow of monetary metals which would raise prices, which would . . . and so on.

This is a prototypical equilibrium model: assume an equilibrium state of affairs; introduce a disturbance; follow the chain of consequences until equilibrium is restored; compare the new equilibrium with the old to see what the permanent effects of the disturbance are, if any. (In other essays Hume also showed that important events may occur during the transition from one equilibrium to another, a matter that economists have only recently begun to examine analytically.) All the individual elements in Hume's model were well known in his day, but Hume was the first, or one of the first, and certainly the most prominent, writer to put them together in an equilibrium model. It is on this ground that, despite the smallness of his writings on economics, Hume has a firm place in intellectual history as one of the earliest analytical economists. The Physiocrats were more comprehensive in their approach, but Hume was methodologically far more incisive.

Note 1: Hume's epistemology

In Chapter 4 we noted that although John Locke exercised great influence on Western politics through his *Second Treatise of Government*, his role in the philosophy of science is due to his efforts to establish the empirical foundations of knowledge in the *Essay Concerning Human Understanding*. Similarly, one must note that Hume occupies a position in the philosophy of science that is inadequately indicated by a restricted examination of his political, economic, and historical writings. In Chapter 4 we passed over Locke's theory of knowledge with no further comment. It is not possible to survey the history and philosophy of social science without paying more attention to Hume's contribution to fundamental philosophy than we did with Locke. In this note I will give a brief résumé of Hume's epistemology, his theory of how man acquires knowledge, which stirred Western philosophy so profoundly that it agitates still. Hume followed Locke in arguing that knowledge is based upon empirical experience but, instead of giving us assurance, Hume saw that this leads us to have fundamental doubts about the foundations of our knowledge. As Bertrand Russell expressed it, 'In Hume, the empiricist philosophy culminated in a scepticism which none could refute and none could accept.' Since Hume, the only philosophy that has been open to the rational person is not one that is correct, for there is none, but one that possesses only the negative virtue of avoiding being totally wrong, ridiculous, or irrelevant to human concerns.

Hume's epistemology is 'empirical' in two ways: first, it stresses that all our knowledge is based upon the impressions we receive through our senses, and secondly, it recognizes that the theory of knowledge is itself an empirical science, one which investigates the workings of the human mind. Hume's view of the mind is that it is a reasoning apparatus but it has nothing to reason about until it is furnished with sense data. In modern parlance, it is, at birth, like a computer that emerges from the factory and has yet to be loaded with information and supplied with programs. Hume rejected altogether, as Locke had, the doctrine that the mind is furnished, by its very nature, with 'innate ideas'. Even such fundamental conceptions as space, time, and the cause–effect relationship are derived from experience, according to Hume.

In pursuing his analysis of the mind, Hume divided all mental phenomena into two categories: 'impressions', which are immediate sense experiences; and 'ideas', which are memories of or reflections upon the impressions that one has experienced. It is clear, Hume felt, that sense experience is the primary matter of all knowledge; ideas, general concepts, theories, universals, and all such things are secondary or derivative. This contention, that all knowledge is derivative from sense experience, leads directly to the 'problem of induction'. No matter how many swans I have seen, nor how many have been seen by others, there is no justification for asserting the general proposition that 'all swans are white'. If all the swans that have been observed have been white I can say so, but to assert that whiteness is a property of *all* swans is unwarranted, since *all* swans (past, present, and future) have not been observed, and *it is not possible to observe them*. Since making general empirical assertions is what science attempts to do, Hume's argument means that scientists are embarked upon an enterprise that cannot possibly succeed. This is not only true of trivial cases such as propositions about the colour of swans but true of all universal statements, including what scientists call 'laws of nature'. Instead of describing Hume's philosophy as 'empirical' it might be more accurate to describe it as showing the *limits* of empiricism, which fall far short of permitting scientists to do what they most want, that is, discover universal laws of nature.

Hume's theory of knowledge has some special significance in connection with the concept of causality. We noted in Chapter 3 that most scientists are not content with simple empirical generalizations or with purely analytical propositions such as those of deductive logic. They look for connections between empirical phenomena that fit the particular relationship of cause and effect. Scientists want to say more than 'There was a lightning storm over the Monroe forest between two and four in the afternoon on 16 July, 1960, and the following day a forest fire was observed there.' They would like to say, 'The forest fire was *caused by* the lightning storm.' Such an assertion, in Hume's view, rests upon the presumption of the existence in the real world of a type of relationship, causality, which our senses cannot perceive.

Hume himself freely used the terms 'cause' and 'effect'. He did not wish to extirpate them from our language; his object was to clarify their meaning. His contention was that the relationship of causality is not a property of the real world (or, more correctly, cannot be *shown* to be such a property) but a psychological phenomenon, having to do with how the mind, not the material world, functions. If, says Hume, we repeatedly see two events together, with one regularly occurring after the other, we form the 'habit' of expecting that they will always occur in that order, and this expectation is all we mean when we assert that the events are causally linked. If by 'cause' we infer that there is a necessary connection between the two events, we infer too much. We cannot know that there are necessary connections in the real world, so the concept of causality refers only to the psychological tendency to extrapolate past experience into the future: 'all our reasonings concerning causes and effects are derived from nothing but custom'. So, Hume concluded, to the great discomfort of philosophers ever since,

> 'Tis not, therefore, reason which is the guide of life, but custom. That alone determines the mind, in all instances, to suppose the future conformable to the past. However easy this step may seem, reason would never to all eternity, be able to make it.

(Hume's argument is reflected today in the epistemological theory of 'conventionalism', which will be examined below in Chapter 18 A 2.)

It may now be more apparent to the reader why, in Chapter 3, 'causal laws' were not presented as expressing a tight, necessary connection between events. The INUS model there outlined employs the concept of necessity, but in a much looser way. Hume's attack on causality is valid if we think of 'laws of nature' as being of the same kind as the analytical propositions of formal logic. Hume forced philosophers and scientists to give up the idea of a 'logic of induction', but that does not mean that the concept of causation must be totally abandoned. (For a brief account of Hume's epistemology, written by himself, see his *Abstract of a Treatise of Human Nature*, 1740.)

Note 2: Association psychology

It is clear from the short distance we have come so far in tracing the history of social science that a crucial element in its development was the idea of a uniform human nature. Hume not only assumed this in his political, ethical, and economic writings but even construed epistemology as a psychological study, an investigation of that part of human nature having to do with the functioning of the mind. Hume's emphasis upon the mental process of 'association' formed the foundation of an influential line of psychological theory which persists down to the present.

As we have seen in Note 1, the central proposition in Hume's theory of knowledge is that it is impossible to go beyond the data provided by sense impressions. When we speak of the existence of necessary relations (such as that between lightning and forest fire) we are simply indicating our psychological disposition to associate sense impressions that are contiguous in space and time. Also, in Hume's view, universal categories (such as 'all swans') are mental constructs reflecting the disposition of the mind to associate similar particular impressions with one another. Hume made a great deal of use of this psychological theory of association and, indeed, he regarded it as the most distinctive feature of his *Treatise*. On more than one occasion he refers to the principle of association as occupying the same role in the study of human nature as the principle of 'attraction' (Newton's 'gravity') has in the natural sciences, and he undoubtedly has this in mind when he refers to the *Treatise* as 'an attempt to introduce the experimental method of reasoning into moral subjects'. Hume's idea is very similar to that of modern experimental behavioural psychology. His discussion of 'the reason of animals' in the *Treatise* (I, III, XVI) is especially striking in noting the similarity of animal reasoning and human reasoning in their use of association and the development of behaviour by what we would today call the process of 'conditioning'.

To trace this story further we have to note the work of a contemporary of Hume's, the English physician David Hartley (1705–57). There is no evidence that Hartley and Hume influenced one another, or even that they met or corresponded, but their use of the principle of association was so similar that this line of thinking in the history of psychology is sometimes called the 'Hume–Hartley theory'. Hartley read Locke and was impressed, as Hume was, by the conception of the mind as building up its understanding of the world through its reception of sense impressions. Newton, in his book on *Optics* (1704), had suggested that visual data are transmitted from the eye to the brain by 'vibrations' carried along the optic nerves. Hartley generalized this and arrived at the proposition that all mental phenomena are derived from such 'vibrations' and that our thinking process consists of the associations of the mental phenomena so derived. He published his views in a book entitled *Observations on Man: his Frame, his Duty, and his Expectations* (1749). 'Associationism', as it was called, became for a time the dominant school of psychology, exercising strong influence on the social sciences, especially in the early nineteenth century through the adoption of it by the early utilitarians. James Mill's *Analysis of the Phenomena of the Human Mind* (1829), for example, was a straightforward statement and elaboration of the association psychology of Hume and Hartley.

One of the reasons for the influence of Hartley was that he was able to state his psychological views in ways that were appealing to both scientists and religionists. His use of Newton's theory of 'vibrations' appealed to scientists by connecting psychological phenomena to physiological function in man's 'frame', as Hartley called the human body. Joseph Priestley, the famous chemist, was a great enthusiast of associationism and published an abridged version of Hartley's *Observations* in 1775 that had a great deal of influence on Jeremy Bentham, the founder of utilitarianism. At the same time, Hartley recognized man's 'duty' and his religious 'expectation' and used his psychology to throw light on religious experience and to justify the Christian doctrine of a better world to come. Associationism would probably have made its way into modern psychology without Hartley, since Hume's influence as a philosopher was sufficient, when it became powerful, to guarantee it important consideration but, as a result of Hartley's *Observations*, it spread much faster, and perhaps further, than otherwise.

C. ADAM SMITH (1723–90)

Adam Smith was born in the town of Kirkcaldy, near Edinburgh. His father, who was the chief customs officer at Kirkcaldy, died before the child's birth, so, like David Hume, Adam Smith was brought up by a young widowed mother who remained his friend and companion into his own old age. Like Hume also, Smith never married. After schooling in Kirkcaldy, Smith enrolled at the age of fourteen in the University of Glasgow, where he came under the influence of a great teacher and thinker, Francis Hutcheson, who, if anyone can be so singled out, was the first outstanding figure of the Scottish Enlightenment. After graduation from Glasgow, Smith went to Oxford on a scholarship and remained there for six years. Oxford was in the doldrums at the time and it seems that what Smith learned during this period, which was a great deal, was due almost entirely to his own reading. He returned to Scotland in 1746. In 1751 he was appointed to the faculty of the University of Glasgow, originally as Professor of Logic; a year later he became Professor of Moral Philosophy, and it was in this capacity that he developed the ideas that led to the publication in 1759 of his first book, *The Theory of Moral Sentiments*.

Adam Smith's reputation had begun to spread as a result of his lectures before 1759 but the publication of the *Moral Sentiments* established him in the first rank of Europe's thinkers. It led direct to the next phase in his career: he became tutor to the young Duke of Buccleugh in 1764 and, as was customary, took his pupil on a European tour, especially to France. He was in Paris during the zenith of the Physiocrats and met the leading figures of that school as well as most of the other outstanding French intellectuals of the time.

His duties as tutor being ended after his return to Britain in 1766, Smith commenced to write a book which he had had in mind since he was a youth in his twenties. In 1776 this monumental work appeared, *An Inquiry into the Nature and Causes of the Wealth of Nations*. It was a great and immediate success, and continues to be read and discussed down to the present day. The nineteenth-century English historian H. T. Buckle called it 'probably the most important book ever written', considered in terms of its influence. That is clearly an exaggeration, but the more modest claim can be made that the *Wealth of Nations* gave the first effective beginning to the study of a central problem of social science: how the market mechanism works as a mode of organization. There has been much discussion of the influence of the Physiocrats on Smith's economics, stimulated by the knowledge that Smith met them in Paris before he had begun to work seriously on the *Wealth of Nations*. But it is only necessary to compare Physiocratic theory with Smith's to realize that such influence was minor at best and that Smith was way ahead of the Physiocrats in identifying the central problems of economic theory.

The most important general intellectual influence upon Adam Smith was undoubtedly his great friend, David Hume. Smith was not inclined to push an argument quite as far as Hume, but he recognized the importance of Hume's philosophy and, most important, Hume's secular approach to knowledge in the area of 'moral philosophy', and the merit of his insistence that students of social phenomena should employ the method of 'experimental reasoning' that scientists, working in the spirit of empiricism, had established as the correct way to discover the laws of nature.

Adam Smith is best known today as the father of economics, but he made wider contributions to social science that we cannot neglect. The *Moral Sentiments* (and, indeed, the *Wealth of Nations* too) occupies an important place in the history of sociology and social psychology. The founder of American sociology, Albion W. Small, regarded Adam Smith as the precursor of the subject (*Adam Smith and Modern Sociology*, 1907). But in these matters Smith is not quite as unique a figure as he is in economics, since the whole group of Scottish eighteenth-century thinkers must be credited with the development of the ideas that formed the foundations of sociology. The *Moral Sentiments* was an important book in the history of social science, whether one views it generally, or specifically in terms of the development of sociology and social psychology. It was neglected for a while by historians mainly because of the greater significance of the same author's *Wealth of Nations*.

1. Philosophy of science

Adam Smith did not write a comprehensive work on epistemology but as a young man he was very interested in mathematics and the natural sciences, not only because of their substantive contributions to our knowledge of the laws of nature but also because he regarded them as demonstrating the proper method by which knowledge, in all fields, is attained. Throughout our study of the history of social science so far I have stressed the extent to which the early social scientists were impressed by the achievements of the natural scientists and their desire to emulate them in examining man as a social creature. Adam Smith was no exception to this conception of social science; indeed, he was one of its important promoters. As a young man, perhaps when he was a student at Oxford, Smith wrote an essay entitled 'The Principles which Lead and Direct Philosophical Enquiries, Illustrated by the History of Astronomy'. He never published it, but he thought it was worth preserving, since he once wrote to Hume about publishing it if he (Smith) should die, and when in fact his death was near, and he decided to destroy his unfinished work, this essay was one of the few things he preserved from the flames.

From this essay we can see that Smith's view of the methodology of science was that it should, in all fields, apply the combination of empirical evidence and theoretical modelling that Isaac Newton had established in his statement of the laws that govern the motions of the planets. Newton's system was, in Smith's words, 'the greatest discovery that was ever made by man', not only because it stated the laws of celestial mechanics but because it revealed the aim and method of all 'philosophical enquiries'. An inquiry is truly 'philosophical' when it aims at the statement of general laws that govern a wide range of phenomena. The superiority of Newton was that he constructed such general laws instead of contenting himself, as others did, with particular laws for particular cases. The law of gravitational attraction applies to all masses, not just planets. In the same way, when Smith began to study social phenomena, he aimed at arriving at general laws of human behaviour. Humans differ as individuals, and societies differ in their cultures, but it is still possible to state propositions about behaviour that are universally valid if human beings are similar to one another in their basic natures. Smith adopted the views that Hobbes had advanced a century earlier: that there is a common human nature; that it is ascertainable by introspection; and that a scientific study of social phenomena can be built upon this empirical base.

Drawing upon his knowledge of the natural sciences, Adam Smith formulated the method of science as consisting of a compound of theoretical analysis and empirical evidence. He rejected the Cartesians, who wished to deduce what nature was like, and the Baconians, who wanted only to describe its appearances. He embraced Galileo and Newton, who had shown how to theorize with mathematics and test with observation in a complementary fashion. Especially striking is Smith's understanding of the role of theoretical modelling or, in his words, the construction of 'systems' in science. Here is a passage from his essay on astronomy:

> Systems in many respects resemble machines. A machine is a little system, created to perform, as well as to connect together, in reality, those different movements and effects which the artist has occasion for. A system is an imaginary machine invented to connect together in the fancy those different movements and effects which are already in reality performed.

With a bit of modernization of the language it would be difficult to improve on this today as a statement of what a theoretical model is. Adam Smith was to discover, however, as social scientists have repeatedly since, that modelling a society is not as easy as modelling a solar system. Fortunately for the history of social science, Smith did not make the mistake of *reification*, that is, interpreting a model as if it were the real thing, or, worse, the mistake of *Platonism*, viewing a model or theory as if it were more true or more real, in some metaphysical sense, then the world of sense experience. One does not find in the *Wealth of Nations* a tightly drawn model of economic processes such as the Physiocrats' 'Tableau Economique' or the modern economists' model of general equilibrium. Some readers of Smith find him 'unsystematic' but that is mainly due to his unwillingness to push models far beyond the bounds of usefulness. In this Smith reflected another feature of the Scottish Enlightenment: the recognition that good theories can become foolish when pushed too far, reified, or Platonized.

2. The nature of man

The counterpart of Newton's principle of gravitational attraction in the modelling of social phenomena, so Adam Smith would appear to believe, is some universal property of human nature. Here we encounter a difficulty that has been the object of much attention by historians of social science. In the *Moral Sentiments* the Newtonian property, so to speak, is what Smith calls 'sympathy': man's capacity for, and disposition to, the exercise of 'fellow feeling' towards other persons. In the *Wealth of Nations*, however, the Newtonian property is man's self-interest. There appears to be an inconsistency here: 'the Adam Smith problem', it is sometimes called.

Numerous suggestions have been made for resolving this problem, including the view (not at all implausible) that Adam Smith was indeed inconsistent, using one conception of human nature in his analysis of moral psychology and another in his analysis of economic processes. A full discussion of this issue would take us too far afield, so let me simply state what seems to me to be the conception of human nature that applies to both of his books. This is the notion that man is, most significantly, a *rational* creature whose behaviour is deliberate and goal-directed. This conception lies at the root of Hobbes's and Locke's theories of the social contract by which a government is established as a means of social organization, and it also serves Adam Smith in his attempt to describe the more automatic mode of organization through voluntary exchange. Other social scientists, as we shall see, have stressed different, more sociological, factors: the customs and traditions that control behaviour by means of enculturation, peer pressure, etc. In some of the modern literature, under the influence of psychologists such as Sigmund Freud and Karl Jung, other writers have emphasized the influence on human behaviour of deeper factors such as antenatal and infantile experience. The determinants of human behaviour, we now realize, are very complex. Adam Smith simplified, as all scientists do, for heuristic purposes; that is to say, he adopted the notion that man is a rational animal for methodological reasons: it enabled him to proceed with the analysis of social phenomena by construing them as springing from the purposive behaviour of rational individuals that one observes by introspection and by regarding others as homologous to oneself.

According to Adam Smith, man's main goal is to 'better his condition'. The wish to do so, he says, is:

> a desire which, though generally calm and dispassionate, comes with us from the womb, and never leaves us until we go into the grave. In the whole interval which separates those two moments, there is scarce perhaps a single instant in which any man is so completely satisfied with his situation, as to be without any wish of alteration or improvement of any kind.

Though this passage in the *Wealth of Nations* refers specifically to man's propensity to save in order to accumulate wealth, it can be read more generally as expressing Smith's view that man is the dissatisfied animal, always desiring improvement. This articulates with another important aspect of eighteenth-century thought which we shall discuss in Chapter 8: the idea of progress.

The above-quoted passage, and others, have often been noted as demonstrating that Smith's conception of man is that he is interested only in *economic* welfare and that he is concerned only with his *own*. Both are erroneous interpretations. That man desires economic progress does not mean that he does not desire progress in other dimensions as well and, further, the fact that the individual desires improvement in his own condition does not mean that he places no value on improvement in the condition of others. As we noted in our discussion of Hume, it is part of human nature to discount the welfare of others compared to our own, but this does not mean that one discounts others' completely. So the common characterization of Adam Smith's concept of man as a totally self-interested being is inadequate at best; it fails to recognize that Smith's view of human nature is not so severely limited. Let us now go on to study the aspect of it that he examines under the title of 'moral sentiments'.

3. Moral sentiments

In section A of this chapter I noted the hostility of the Scottish philosophers to the concept of a 'state of nature' and the theory that society rests upon a covenant or contract. They viewed man as always having lived in a social state and as being by nature a social animal. Adam Smith's two books can be regarded as studies of the basis of sociality, the *Moral Sentiments* dealing with the ways in which man achieves the degree of behavioural conformity that is necessary for social existence, and the *Wealth of Nations* dealing with the means by which men engaged in specialized functions are able to co-operate with many others, including those with whom they have no personal contact.

The *Moral Sentiments* is not, or it is not *mainly*, a book about ethics, though it had an important influence upon that subject. The main problem Smith sets out to tackle is to explain how it is possible for man to entertain 'fellow feelings' towards others. In short, it is a psychological study, an examination of a particular aspect of human mental processes; it is a *social* psychological study because it deals with mental processes that fundamentally concern interpersonal relations. Once one understands the psychology of this matter, Smith believed, one might be able to go on to consider the ethical problem of what constitutes morally good sentiments and their practical implications in concrete cases. The determination of what *ought* to be cannot be derived from the investigation of what *is*, but the philosophy of empirical science tells us that the study of what is so in fact is the proper place to begin.

The problem, Adam Smith notes, is not to speculate how a perfect being – God – would formulate moral judgements but how a very imperfect being – man – is able to do so. He rejects the idea that man is furnished with an innate moral sense which tells him what is right and what is wrong. Man is unique among the animals in making moral judgements but one finds no reference in Smith's discussion to the Old Testament story that when man ate the apple in the Garden of Eden he acquired knowledge of good and evil that was transmitted down through the ages from generation to generation. All that man possesses, or needs to possess, as the basis of moral judgements, is the simple recognition that other human beings are similar to himself. The key concept in Smith's moral psychology is man's capacity to sympathize with others in a rational fashion. This, he felt, could play the same role in the study of the moral world as gravity does in the study of the physical one.

Adam Smith's concept of 'sympathy' is much the same as what modern psychologists call 'empathy': the capacity to put oneself in another's place, mentally, and thereby experience a kind of surrogate sensation which reflects or parallels the other's direct experience. By this means we take the wants and desires, pleasures and pains, hopes and fears, of others into our own minds. We 'change places with them in fancy', says Smith. This capacity is not restricted to things we approve of but embraces also things we find reprehensible, so it enables us to take the whole range of actions and thoughts into account in forming 'moral sentiments'. This may look as though Smith is saying that moral judgements are matters of personal intuition but, on the contrary, he is attempting to provide such judgements with a factual basis. We can understand this only if we realize that Smith, along with other thinkers of the time, regarded *introspection* as a reliable empirical process enabling one to discover general factual truths by looking inward into one's own thoughts and feelings.

In the discussion of Hume, we noted his theory of social distance discounting (to use modern terminology): the tendency to discount the welfare of others in proportion to their remoteness from us in time, space, or culture. Smith held the same view; in fact he regarded it as an obvious feature of human psychology. In evaluating conflicting claims in terms of their moral merits, however, this creates no problem, since, in Smith's view, man has the capacity to imagine himself as an 'impartial observer' who, being equally detached from the contending parties, is able to arrive at judgements not affected by different degrees of social distance discounting. Smith was optimistic enough (or naive enough) to believe that every person has the capacity to consider what the judgement of an impartial observer would be in cases where he himself is an interested party.

There is another argument, more sociological, in the *Moral Sentiments* that deserves some attention. Smith contends that a person acts morally because he values the approbation of others. Purely self-interested motives will therefore be constrained by the commonly accepted morality of one's society. In Chapter 15 B below, we shall see that this notion was central in Émile Durkheim's analysis of the social role of moral beliefs and his interpretation of religion as a sociological phenomenon. As an argument concerning the sociology of morals, Smith's view has a great deal to commend it, but it does very little to satisfy the ethical philosopher, who is concerned not with the moral rules that people *do* follow, but with the ones they *should* follow. If we were to accept, without reserve, the proposition that a person is behaving morally when he acts in accordance with socially sanctioned norms, we would be adopting a degree of ethical relativism that few philosophers, or other folk, would be willing to embrace. No act could be condemned as immoral if it were condoned by the person's own society and culture. Some 'meta-ethical' principle is required to permit a transcending value judgement.

Smith did not discuss this problem, but it is possible to construe his proposition that all persons are similar as the basis of such a principle. Since this is a proposition about human nature in general, it is not culture-relative. The import of this, though, is that social distance discounting, regardless of its validity as a proposition in psychology or its necessity in practical life, is ethically impermissible. I cannot discuss this problem any further here, but we shall encounter it again when we come to consider Henry Sidgwick's celebrated attempt to construct a meta-ethical utilitarian philosophy (see below, Chapter 11 B). The main significance of Smith's *Moral Sentiments* in the history of ethics lies not in the strength of it particular arguments, but in its extension of the secular orientation of the Scottish Enlightenment to questions that had previously been universally regarded as belonging to the domain of religion.

4. Division of labour

The opening sentence of *An Inquiry into the Nature and Causes of the Wealth of Nations* discloses what the author considers to be the chief cause of that wealth:

> The great improvement in the productive powers of labour, and the greater part of the skill, dexterity, and judgement with which it is anywhere directed, or applied, seem to have been the effects of the division of labour.

Then, after illustrating his point, Smith says that this increase in productivity

> is owing to three different circumstances; first to the increase of dexterity in every particular workman; secondly, to the saving of the time which is commonly lost in passing from one species of work to another; and lastly, to the invention of a great number of machines which facilitate and abridge labour, and enable one man to do the work of many.

He concludes that:

> It is the great multiplication of the productions of all the different arts, in consequence of the division of labour, which occasions, in a well-governed society, that universal opulence which extends itself to the lowest ranks of the people.

Thus, in studying the wealth of a nation, including its 'lowest ranks', Smith does not focus on its endowment of fertile land or other natural resources, the merits of its climate, or the character of its people; he emphasizes a *social* characteristic, the degree to which it practises that type of sociality described in Chapter 1 as based upon 'functional specialization'.

Adam Smith was not the first to point out this feature of human sociality and to note its economic effects. Functional specialization, as we have seen (Chapter 4 A), was an important element in the political theories of Plato and Aristotle. Xenophon, living at the same time (the fourth century B.C.), clearly noted the benefits of division of labour in increasing productivity. In Smith's own century, the idea was expressed before 1776 by Diderot in France, Beccaria in Italy, and Mandeville in England. Among Smith's close acquaintances, the idea was stated clearly by Francis Hutcheson, his teacher at Glasgow College, David Hume, his most intimate friend, and Adam Ferguson, another of the leading figures in the Scottish Enlightenment. In fact some of Adam Smith's famous discussion is virtually copied from earlier writings. But one does not have to be original in order to be creative. Adam Smith took this old idea and used it as the launching pad for a general theory of social organization.

The *Wealth of Nations* opens with three chapters on the division of labour. After describing it as the source of productivity Smith points out that functional specialization cannot be carried on without exchange. Man is, according to Smith, endowed with a 'propensity to truck and barter', so he has the requisite natural characteristics for the development of *markets*. Smith clearly appreciated that this raises a very basic scientific question: how do markets function as a means by which the differentiated activities of many individual producers are co-ordinated? This has been the main question that has concerned economists ever since. The central problem in the theory of markets has to do with explaining the determinants of market values, or prices, and showing how these function in a system of market co-ordination. This will be discussed in subsection 5.

A feature of Adam Smith's discussion of the division of labour that deserves to be noted and emphasized is that it is not based upon biological differentiation among persons. Many of the writers on the division of labour, from Plato on, had stressed its role in taking advantage of innate differences by allocating individuals to roles and tasks for which they were fitted 'by nature'. Like the other members of the Scottish Enlightenment, Smith gave little weight to innate differences:

> The difference in natural talents in different men is, in reality, much less than we are aware of; and the very different genius which appears to distinguish men of different professions, when grown up to maturity, is not upon many occasions so much the cause as the effect of the division of labour. The difference between the most dissimilar characters, between a philosopher and a street porter, for example, seems to arise not so much from nature as from habit, custom, and education.

Thus, in Adam Smith's view, specialization is primarily a cultural, not a biological, phenomenon and the great issues it creates (class status, inequalities in wealth, prestige, power, etc.) are to be located mainly in man's social institutions that perform enculturating functions rather than in his innate constitution. This opens the door to social reform much wider than would be permitted by social philosophers following Plato but, we should note, not as wide as some utopians pushed it in claiming that human nature is so plastic that *any* kind of individual character can be created by appropriate educational regimes (see below, Chapter 8).

In the opening chapters in the *Wealth of Nations* on the division of labour, Smith says nothing of a negative nature concerning it. But elsewhere in the book he makes some very strong remarks about its deleterious consequences:

> In the progress of the division of labour, the employment of the greater part of those who live by labour, that is, of the great body of the people, comes to be confined to a few very simple operations, frequently to one or two. But the understandings of the greater part of men are necessarily formed by their ordinary employments. The man whose whole life is spent in performing a few simple operations, of which the effects too are, perhaps, always the same, or very nearly the same, has no occasion to exert his understanding, or to exercise his invention in finding out expedients for removing difficulties which never occur. He naturally loses, therefore, the habit of such exertion, and generally becomes as stupid and ignorant as it is possible for a human creature to become. The torpor of his mind renders him, not only incapable of relishing or bearing a part in any rational conversation, but of conceiving any generous, noble, or tender sentiment, and consequently of forming any just judgement concerning many even of the ordinary duties of private life. Of the great and extensive interests of his country he is altogether incapable of judging. . . . It corrupts even the

activity of his body, and renders him incapable of exerting his strength with vigour and perseverance, in any other employment than that to which he has been bred . . . . But in every improved and civilized society, this is the state into which the labouring poor, that is, the great body of the people, must necessarily fall, unless government takes some pains to prevent it. (Book V, chapter I, Part III)

No stronger indictment of the division of labour has ever been written, before or since, and this in the same book that has, justly, been regarded as containing the classic espousal of its merits. What is even more striking is that, in this passage, Smith is intent upon arguing that the division of labour can destroy the very qualities of humankind that, elsewhere, he celebrates as fundamental and unique: the capacity for reason, and the exercise of sympathetic concern for others. Smith made no attempt to resolve these different views, separated by 700 pages in the text of the *Wealth of Nations*. He was not alone in his ambivalence. Doubts concerning the division of labour were expressed by his fellow Scots and, as the degree of specialization continued to increase with the march of industrialism, many more writers on social questions were inclined to view it as an evil. One of the few things that Karl Marx makes explicit about the forthcoming ideal state of communism is that occupational specialization will cease to exist. Most of the utopian literature of the nineteenth century takes a similar stance and, in our own day, the evil of the division of labour still provides a standard theme of social criticism and finds expression in films, novels, and other genres of popular commentary on the alienation of man and the degradation of the human condition in modern society.

Despite its central importance in human sociality and the ambivalence of views concerning it, the division of labour has not been the direct object of a great deal of social analysis. In the history of this subject three writers stand out: Plato, who related it to the political organization of society; Adam Smith, whose attribution to it of increased productivity set the stage for an examination of economic organization; and Émile Durkheim, who contended that the division of labour is the essential foundation of the solidarity that binds men together in communities. We have already considered the first two of these; Durkheim's views will be discussed below in Chapter 15 B.

5. Value

In a private enterprise economy, individual production enterprises are not co-ordinated by any central authority; each acts on its own. This does not mean, however, that business firms behave capriciously or arbitrarily. In order to operate successfully a firm must consider what it can obtain in revenue by selling a product and what it will have to pay to obtain the labour, raw materials, and other factors necessary to produce it. These revenues and costs are determined in part by the prices of products and the prices of production factors. The general theory of economic organization through markets explains how movements in these prices adjust the production of commodities and the demands for them to one another. The distribution of income in a specialized economy is also bound up with prices, since what each person receives as income depends not only on the quantity of factors he sells but also on the per-unit price received for them. The income that a labourer receives, for example, depends not only on the number of hours he works but on the wage rate per hour.

The explicit analysis of how a market functions as a co-ordinating mechanism (and its defects) is fairly recent. Adam Smith had an intuitive grasp of it, and he saw clearly the direction in which the analysis had to proceed, but he did not succeed in constructing a complete model in his own work. His greatest specific contribution was, ironically, also his most signal failure in economic analysis: on the one hand he succeeded in pointing out the crucial significance of *value* in the investigation of market co-ordination; on the other hand he advanced a faulty theory of value and also confused the issue considerably by using the term 'value' to denote more than one thing, without sufficiently clarifying the different usages.

The issue that is of central importance for the analysis of the market mechanism is the explanation of the determinants of prices as empirically observable phenomena. If, in an economy using the 'dollar' as a medium of exchange, we find that at a particular time and place the following money prices pertain:

    100 apples (A)   = $20
    1 lb of beans (B)   = $1
    25 yards of cotton (C) = $50

then five apples, a pound of beans, and half a yard of cotton are each severally valued at $1, and we can write the equation:

$$5A = 1B = 0.5C$$

Why are these magnitudes observed to be 5, 1, and 0.5, and not some other numbers? In an elementary course in modern economics it is explained that 'supply and demand' determine these relative values (or their individual prices in the money unit) as sketched in the 'market model' presented above in Chapter 6 A 2. A common explanation of market value in the eighteenth century, including some of Smith's early lectures, ran in terms of supply and demand (though the graphic analysis was not then available) but some writers were dissatisfied with this as being superficial, explaining only the day-to-day fluctuations of prices, not their underlying, more permanent levels. There is a striking letter written in 1767 by David Hume to A. R. J. Turgot (who later became the French Minister of Finance) in which Hume says that no one denies that 'the relationship of supply and demand . . . immediately sets . . . the *current price*' but he contends that to understand the 'fundamental price' we have to look at the cost of production of the commodity (E. Rotwein, *David Hume: Writings on Economics*, 1970, p. 211). This is the direction Adam Smith took in advancing his theory of value. The history of the theory of value during the next hundred years was dominated by Smith's approach. Not until the fourth quarter of the nineteenth century did economists begin to construct explicit models of market value based on supply and demand (see Chapter 17).

In the seventeenth century, and for most of the eighteenth, the adjective 'natural' was used in many branches of science to refer to the permanent or 'essential' properties of phenomena, as distinguished from the transitory or accidental features of them that are not 'fundamental'. An idea of this sort appears to underlie Adam Smith's focus upon what he called the 'natural price'. In his view, the natural price of a producable commodity is the cost of the labour and other factors necessary to its production and, in turn, the natural prices of labour services, raw materials, machinery, land use, etc., are *their* costs of production. In this way, Smith focused the investigation of the determinants of value strictly on the conditions of production, or supply; demand factors were considered relevant only to fluctuations in the day-to-day prices of commodities, not to their 'natural prices'. The irrelevance of demand was supported by pointing out that there is no correlation between the usefulness of a commodity and its market value. Here is the famous passage in the *Wealth of Nations* where Smith expresses this view:

> The things which have the greatest value in use have frequently little or no value in exchange; and, on the contrary, those which have the greatest value in exchange have frequently little or no value in use. Nothing is more useful than water: but it will purchase scarce anything; scarce anything can be had in exchange for it. A diamond, on the contrary, has scarce any value in use; but a very great quantity of other goods may frequently be had in exchange for it. (Book I, chapter IV).

This 'paradox of value', as it was called, was frequently noted before Adam Smith (for example, by Copernicus, who wrote a bit on economic questions), but it was Smith's influence that made it an important element in directing the attention of economists solely to supply-side factors in their investigation of value. Not until a century later was the paradox resolved with the invention of the concept of 'marginal utility', which showed that the utility of *the whole amount* of a commodity might be very great while the utility of *an extra unit* of it might be very small, if the total supply of it were large. We would be willing to pay a very large sum rather than be deprived of water altogether, but not much for an extra gallon. Market transactions are normally concerned with incremental amounts, not the whole stock of anything, so it is perfectly explicable why water is very useful but low in price, and diamonds the opposite. But before the paradox of value was resolved, many streams of economic thought developed from the Smithian reservoir of value theory, most notably classical or Ricardian economics and Marxian economics. As we shall see in Chapters 9 and 13 respectively, these major landmarks in the history and philosophy of social science held fast to Adam Smith's view that value is determined solely by the conditions of production.

In one respect these later theories went even further than Adam Smith in restricting the determinants of value. Smith begins his discussion by noting that in a very primitive society, such as one whose economy is based on hunting wild game, the relative values of two types of game would be determined by the relative quantities of labour required to obtain them: 'If among a nation of hunters, for example, it usually costs twice the labour to kill a beaver as to kill a deer, one beaver should naturally exchange for or be worth two deer' (Book I, chapter VI). (A modern economist would invert this causal order and argue that producers are prepared to expend twice as much effort for a beaver as a deer because beaver is twice as valuable, not the other way round.) But, Smith notes, this is true only of an economy where labour is the only factor of production. In a more advanced economy, with established property rights to land and other natural resources, and an accumulation of the various forms of real capital (buildings, tools, etc.), the use of the services of these factors enters the picture and the relative values of goods are determined by their relative costs of production, which now include rent and interest (or profit) as well as wage costs. David Ricardo and, even more strongly, Karl Marx considered that Adam Smith had ruined a good theory of value by this amendment. They contended that the production requirements *of labour only* determine the market value of a commodity in advanced as well as primitive economies. This is the rather curious route by which the 'labour theory of value' was introduced into economic theory, with momentous consequences for the history of social science generally, its philosophy, philosophy generally, political theory, practical politics, and international relations. Some parts of this story will be told in the following pages as we continue with our (more or less) chronological history of the social sciences.

Adam Smith himself did not advance a labour theory of value (except for the 'early and rude state' of a hunting economy) but in addition to the analysis of the *determinants* of value he discussed another problem, the measurement of value, in which he gave labour a special position. This led to a great deal of confusion. Many commentators on Smith, until recent times, have described him as contending that labour is the source of all exchange value, when all that can be claimed from the *Wealth of Nations* is that he held that labour can be used as a unit in which to measure the values of other goods because it, more than anything else, possesses the requisite qualities of a satisfactory standard of measurement.

To understand this let us look again at the data given above for the market prices, in dollars, of apples, beans, and cloth. If we now write:

100 A	=	$20 in 1960
1 lb of B	=	$1 in 1970
25 yards of C	=	$50 in 1980

it is no longer possible to say:

$$5A = 1B = 0.5C$$

since the value of the dollar changed considerably between 1960 and 1980. For anything to serve effectively as a standard of measurement it must itself be constant in the property that is being measured. If we wish to compare the lengths of a desk and a table, the ruler that we use must not change its own length as we move it from the desk to the table; if we wish to compare the weights of two things we require a standard measure that is invariant in its own weight, and so on.

Smith was acutely conscious of this necessity as it applies to the problem of making value comparisons. Only one thing, in his view, remains constant in its own value over time, and between different locations – labour. So, if one records the value of anything in terms of the quantity of labour it can purchase (i.e. the ratio of its money price to the money wage rate) one is stating its value in terms of a constant unit. Smith did not have very good reasons for singling out labour in this respect. The closest he came to justifying it was to say:

> Equal quantities of labour, at all times and places, may be said to be of equal value to the labourer. In his ordinary state of health, strength and spirits; in the ordinary degree of his skill and dexterity, he must always lay down the same portion of his ease, his liberty, and his happiness. (Book I, chapter 5)

In modern economics Smith's measurement problem is handled by constructing index numbers of the 'general price level', using a large number of commodities. It is not a perfect method but it is a great deal better than singling out one thing on rather dubious psychological grounds, as Smith did. The problem of value measurement is important in the subject of economic statistics but the main significance of Smith's contention for the history of social thought is that it contributed considerable confusion to the theory of value by making it ambiguous whether a 'theory of value' deals with the *determinants* of value or its standard of *measurement*. John Stuart Mill expressed the issue clearly in his *Principles of Political Economy* (1848):

> The idea of a Measure of Value must not be confounded with the idea of the regulator, or determining principle, of value. When it is said by Ricardo and others, that the value of a thing is regulated by quantity of labour, they do not mean the quantity of labour for which the thing will exchange, but the quantity required for producing it .... But when Adam Smith and Malthus say that labour is a measure of value, they do not mean the labour by which the thing was or can be made, but the quantity of labour which it will exchange for, or purchase; in other words, the value of the thing, estimated in labour .... To confound these two ideas, would be much the same thing as to overlook the distinction between the thermometer and the fire. (Book III, chapter XV).

This would indeed be a gross error but, unfortunately, it was not carefully avoided by Ricardo, or by Mill himself, and has created a legacy of confusion that persists to the present day.

6. The 'invisible hand'

This phrase, which appears once in Adam Smith's *Moral Sentiments* and once in his *Wealth of Nations*, is a good candidate for the most widely known and least understood concept in the history of social theory. Over the past two centuries it has been quoted over and over again, usually either worshipfully or sneeringly, by innumerable writers or speakers, many of whom have known enough about Adam Smith to spell his name correctly and little more.

In the *Moral Sentiments* Smith presents a kind of moral deism. The operation of 'sympathy' and the 'impartial observer' in the psychology of individual persons forms a harmonious social whole because it was designed to be so by a wise and benevolent deity. It would not be going too far to say that if Smith had used the term 'invisible hand' freely in the *Moral Sentiments* it would have referred to the hand of God. But there is no ground for attributing any theistic conception of this sort to the *Wealth of Nations*. The general notion of natural harmonious order and its relation to social theory and social policy is important enough to warrant special treatment, so we shall defer full discussion of it to Chapter 10. Here I will only comment briefly on Smith's view of the role of markets in economic organization.

The concept of an 'invisible hand' in the *Wealth of Nations* is simply the idea that there are governing laws controlling economic processes just as there are laws governing natural phenomena. The buying and selling that goes on in a market economy is an orderly system: while each participant in the market intends only to serve his own interest, in the process of doing so he 'is led by an invisible hand to promote an end which was no part of his intention' – that is, to play his part in a co-ordinated, well functioning economic system. The idea that the chief task of social theory is to study the unintended consequences of individual actions was prominent among the eighteenth-century Scottish philosophers and its roots can be traced much earlier, but it was Adam Smith who oriented it effectively in the direction of examining the mechanism of market organization, which creates order without coercive authority and without requiring that human beings display a degree of benevolent sentiment and altruistic behaviour that is beyond their capacities. The main activity of economists since Adam Smith has been to understand the functioning (and malfunctioning) of this metaphorical 'invisible hand.' Even Karl Marx, as we shall see, considered the main task of economics to consist of the analysis of market processes and the discovery of their 'laws', though he arrived at (or started with) quite different normative valuations of their implications from those of the orthodox members of the classical school of economics.

The contrast between Adam Smith's view of social order and Thomas Hobbes's is striking. In Hobbes's *Leviathan* the chief necessity is to constrain men from doing violence to one another; in Smith's *Wealth of Nations* the main focus is upon the need to facilitate co-operation. In Hobbes's approach, a policeman is what is needed; in Smith's, what is needed is a mechanism that co-ordinates individual actions. Hobbes does not really explain why it is desirable to have social order at all, except by recognizing rather vaguely that it is necessary to 'commodious living'. The opening chapter of Smith's *Wealth of Nations* argues that commodious living is due to specialization and recognizes the need for a co-ordinating mechanism. Thus Smith's view led in a very different direction from Hobbes's: to the study of markets rather than the study of the exercise of sovereign power. To a considerable extent this distinction is still present in the different approaches of modern economists and political scientists to the problem of social order.

Smith's own investigation of the market mechanism did not lead him to conclude that it could work as an order-producing system all by itself. Individual activities cohere into a co-ordinated whole only where there is a general framework of custom or law that establishes rules of justice. (Competition among producers by each trying to find more efficient methods of production is obviously not the same as each one trying to set fire to the others' establishments.) For this a government is necessary, but the proper functions of government are not confined to the maintenance of national defence and the administration of internal justice. Smith had a great deal of confidence in the market mechanism but he did not regard it as working perfectly. If one reads the *Wealth of Nations* and notes down every occasion on which Smith calls for government action, a long agenda of state economic functions will be compiled by the time one reaches the end.

But if the reader notes every time Smith contends that the state is engaged in unnecessary or deleterious economic intervention he will also compile a long list. These passages have led some readers to interpret Smith as being opposed to intervention on principle. It is true that Smith had a low opinion of 'that insidious and crafty animal, vulgarly called a statesman or politician', but he also had a low opinion of businessmen, who, in his opinion, were always conspiring against the public interest by restricting competition and lobbying the government for special privileges. A large part of the *Wealth of Nations* is a tract against 'mercantilism', which Smith attacked not simply because it was a system of economic intervention but because of its misguided objectives and faulty scientific foundations. Smith's main objective was to improve the economic policy of the state by providing a sound foundation of economic analysis. His conclusion was that a great deal of improvement could be brought about by dismantling much of the apparatus of state intervention that had grown up in England piece by piece since Tudor times. Anyone who has looked at the economic regulations of the eighteenth century can hardly fail to conclude that Smith was right. They were very extensive, leaving hardly any aspect of economic activity untouched, but lacking any defensible, or even coherent, rationale. When one considers that these policies were administered by a government bureaucracy that was inefficient and corrupt, it is all the more clear that Adam Smith's criticisms were well placed. The main point is, however, that Smith was a pragmatist; his advice concerning economic policy was based on observation and analysis, not on the general principle of dogmatic *laissez-faire* that has so often been attributed to him.

7. The economic conception of historical stages

We noted earlier in this chapter that there was a great increase of interest in history during the eighteenth century. This was partly due to the notion expressed by Hume, that history offers a laboratory of empirical experience for the study of social laws; partly because of increased consciousness of one's society's location in a time continuum; and partly because of a factor we will examine in the next chapter, the growth of the idea of progress. In the *Wealth of Nations* there is a great deal of historical material, which would probably have established Adam Smith's reputation as a historian if it had not been overshadowed by the abstract economic analysis of the first part of the book. In this historical matter no historical *theory* is explicitly advanced but the transcripts of Smith's Glasgow lectures show that he distinctly favoured the ideas that a society necessarily evolves through certain discrete stages; that these stages are characterized by the dominant mode of economic activity (hunting, pasturage, farming, and commerce); and that the social, political, artistic, and other features of a society are derivative from the economic characteristics of the stage in which it finds itself. In advancing this view Smith apparently felt that he was moving in the direction of making the study of history scientific, by applying to it the methods of investigation developed by Newton. History was not to be simply a narrative of curious and interesting events, but a study of the fundamental forces of social evolution and the laws that govern it. It is possible that Smith's interest in economics developed from his early view that economic factors are the real determinants of history.

Many of the eighteenth-century Scottish philosophers took this general approach to history, that it should be scientific or, as they called it, 'philosophical', and also held a 'stages' view of history and regarded economic factors as fundamental. The stages idea is to be found also in French and Italian writings of the eighteenth century. So in this respect, as in many others, Adam Smith's significance does not lie in the uniqueness of originality of his ideas but in the special degree of influence he imparted to them. From the standpoint of the history and philosophy of social science, the most interesting feature of Smith's historical theories was not their origins but their reappearance again in the mid-nineteenth century in the writings of Friedrich List and, most notably, Karl Marx. I will discuss these questions again when the social theory of Marx is studied in Chapter 13 and when the philosophical problem of historical explanation is examined in Chapter 14. In Chapter 12, where nineteenth-century positivism is examined, we shall encounter the famous theory of Auguste Comte that human history is a history of man's evolution through stages that are characterized, not by the economic organization of society, but by man's intellectual development and philosophical outlook.

Chapter 8

Progress and perfection

Before we move on to the systematic developments in the social science of the nineteenth century it is worth taking time to consider some additional general ideas that were prominent features of the intellectual environment at the time of the birth of social science which exerted an important influence on its subsequent development. One such idea was the view of human society as characterized by *progress*. The importance of this was noted above in Chapter 2 B in the brief summary given there of the main characteristics and implications of the 'scientific attitude' which, the reader will recall, was described as forming the most important feature of the intellectual environment in which the modern study of social phenomena was brought to birth. Here we will examine the idea of progress, in its relation to social science, a bit further. A related idea, which also exerted a profound influence on social thought, is the conception of 'social perfection': the vision of a social order that would meet all the requirements of man's animal, social, and moral natures. This is the issue of *utopianism*, which belongs to a different tradition of thought from main-line social science but interacts with its history in a number of ways whose significance will be evident as we proceed to study the development of the social sciences during the nineteenth and twentieth centuries.

A. THE IDEA OF PROGRESS

There has been some controversy among historians concerning the idea of progress in Western thought, some contending that it can be dated back only a few centuries while others claim that the idea was evident even in medieval and ancient times. This controversy does not concern us, since the historical scope of this book is restricted to the modern era, and the historians who have debated the issue are agreed that, whether the idea was new or not, it gripped hold to an extraordinary extent during the Age of Enlightenment. Having said this, it is necessary to add immediately that it was not universally embraced by Western thinkers. No ideas ever are; but in the case of the idea of progress, differences of view led to a notable literary and philosophical controversy, most strikingly in England and France, which continued vigorously for many years. In France, following the lead of Bernard de Fontenelle and Charles Perrault, the controversy became known as the 'quarrel of the ancients and moderns' in the late seventeenth century. In the eighteenth century the quarrel continued, with especially notable contributions by Turgot and Condorcet. In England the controversy was referred to, apparently with some irony, by the title employed by Jonathan Swift, as 'the battle of the books'. David Hume contributed an important essay to the controversy, linking the issues of population growth and progress, which, as we shall see in Chapter 9, was a connection that constituted a central feature of the economic model that became known as classical political economy. The third quarter of the eighteenth century witnessed an outpouring of books in Great Britain in which the dominant theme was progress, so the era discussed in the preceding chapter as the birth-time of the modern social sciences was one in which the idea of progress (and debate over its possibility) was especially prominent in intellectual discourse – just as the work of the great inventors and entrepreneurs who produced the industrial revolution was making it a dominant issue (and a controversial one) in the real world of economic activity and social and political organization.

Once again, as so often in the preceding pages, we have to recognize the special importance of the achievements in the natural sciences. Their role in the development of the idea of progress by providing foundations for productive innovations in industry and agriculture is plain enough, but their influence upon the modern intellect was more subtle and, in the long run, more revolutionary than the steam engine or the power loom. The Renaissance era, as it rediscovered the works of art, literature, and philosophy of ancient Greece and Rome, quite naturally found it difficult to believe that those achievements could ever be matched, let alone exceeded. This would seem to settle the issue of progress, the evidence clearly demonstrating that man's capacities had deteriorated since the glorious days of the ancients. Thus even historians who contend that the idea of progress goes back further than the seventeenth century agree that it deteriorated to the point of virtual disappearance during the Renaissance.

The contention that the 'ancients' were superior to the 'moderns' might be argued even today if one were restricted to comparing the arts. But there is at least one area of human accomplishment where such a view is clearly untenable: knowledge of the laws that govern the phenomena of nature. One might argue that Rodin or Henry Moore have not matched the skill of the unknown Greeks of two and a half millennia ago who made the magnificent bronze horses that now stand in Venice's church of San Marco, or that Virgil's poetry is superior to T. S. Eliot's; but to regard Aristotle's knowledge of nature as superior to that of modern physicists and biologists would only serve as evidence of one's determination to be perverse.

From the sixteenth century on it was becoming evident that men were learning things about the natural world that no one had known before. The outstanding feature of this knowledge is that it was cumulative, new discoveries being added to the old, building a structure that is the work of many minds and is available to men of varied talents. To surpass Virgil in poetry one would indeed have to be a better poet than Virgil, but to surpass Vesalius in knowledge of anatomy one need not be especially talented, for one could easily learn all that he knew, and go further. Isaac Newton, in a letter to Robert Hooke, made the famous remark: 'If I have seen further, it is by standing on the shoulders of giants.' Newton was not noted for modesty, or for generosity to other scientists, but in this statement he captured the most essential feature of progress: if it depends on the appearance of superior persons it may not be possible, but if it depends on incremental cumulation, then moderns can easily surpass the ancients. In this way it was possible to argue for progress without denigrating in any way the quality of ancient thinkers and without arguing, as Francis Bacon had done, that progress in science requires, on principle, that previous knowledge be discarded. Because of its cumulative nature, not its individual men of genius, natural science broke the tendency of the Renaissance to revere the ancients in an idolizing way which, wherever it has dominated culture, has prevented progress. If one understands the nature of science it becomes plain that it is not necessary to choose between the ancients and moderns; one pays proper respect to the ancients, not by grovelling at their feet, but by standing upon their shoulders. Because of the developments in science, the great 'battle of the books' of the eighteenth century was never in doubt: the victory of the moderns was inevitable. The Renaissance, which could have initiated a new period of stagnation in Western civilization, became instead the beginning of its most remarkable development.

Since the modern anatomist, for example, knows all that Vesalius knew and more besides, it can hardly be denied that there has been progress in this field. But the same cannot be said of economic and social matters. The modern labourer does not have everything the medieval serf had and something more. The economic and social lives of the two are *different* to be sure, but some criteria of evaluation are necessary before one may say that there has been progress, since that involves the view that modern life is not merely positively different but normatively *better*.

In this respect, a notable feature of Western thought during the seventeenth and eighteenth centuries was the growth and spread of the idea of the worth of mundane benefits: more food and housing, better health and clothing, and suchlike. For a long period in the West, the focus of virtually all intellectual activity was upon the spiritual. St. Augustine (354–430) wrote his *City of God* in order to turn the eyes of Christians away from concern for the contemporary conditions of mundane life to the other-worldly after-life of eternity. The influence of Augustine upon Western thought was very great and lasted a long time. During the following centuries numerous writers sought to argue the merit of enjoying life in this world and the worthwhileness of increasing man's means of doing so, but it was not until the seventeenth century that this view began to be a main theme in Western thinking and took a firm grip on the intellectual world. So the era that we identify as the birth-time of social science was one in which not only had knowledge been secularized, but the principles of value judgement were also receiving a secular orientation. When historians say that the idea of progress grew in this era, what they really mean to note is that the view was becoming widespread among intellectuals, philosophers, scientists, and even some theologians, that it was possible for the conditions of mundane life to become more easy and more enjoyable; that man was acquiring the power to make this so; that this was *good*, because not only did man in fact desire to improve his material condition but the aim was morally worthy. In effect, there was in this era a revival of Epicureanism, which developed into a thoroughly secular moral philosophy, Utilitarianism, in the nineteenth century, in close connection with some branches of social science. It is difficult for us today to believe that people have not always placed high value on the pleasures and comforts of mundane life, and perhaps indeed the ordinary people, blissfully ignorant of the sophistications of philosophers and theologians, always have, but in the West such commonsense values were overlaid for many centuries by an intellectual culture in which material desires were subordinated to the conditions of spiritual salvation, that being regarded as the only goal having moral, and permanent, value.

In this discussion I have been emphasizing two aspects of the idea of progress: its connection with the growth of scientific knowledge, and its acceptance of the value of mundane life and material improvement. The connection of both these with social science is evident. The early social scientists, as I have already emphasized, hoped to construct a body of knowledge about social phenomena that was empirically sound, and they were confident that this could be done because of the example offered by the natural sciences. In addition, it is quite clear that the social scientists were equally inspired by belief in the possibility of social progress and the hope that social scientific knowledge could contribute to its promotion. Robert Nisbet notes in his *History of the Idea of Progress* (1980):

> All of the social sciences without exception – political economy, sociology, anthropology, social psychology, cultural geography, and others – were almost literally founded upon the rock of faith in human progress from Turgot and Adam Smith on through Comte, Marx, Tylor, Spencer, and a host of others. (p. 175)

This is not much of an exaggeration, if it is one at all. Consider Adam Smith, for example. In the previous chapter we noted that Smith's conception of the nature of man was that he is a dissatisfied creature, constantly wanting to improve his worldly 'condition'. It is quite evident that Smith not only noted this as a psychological fact but approved of it as a meritorious characteristic, because it leads to general progress. Adam Smith investigated 'the nature and causes of the wealth of nations' in the belief that an increase in wealth was both possible and desirable. Indeed, he carried the theme a notable step further, constructing a theory that argued not only for *more* wealth but for continuously *increasing* wealth, on the grounds, that all people, but especially the working class, benefit most from the dynamics of progress:

> It deserves to be remarked, perhaps, that it is in the progressive state, while the society is advancing to further acquisition, rather than when it has acquired its full complement of riches, that the condition of the labouring poor, of the great body of the people, seems to be the happiest and most comfortable. It is hard in the stationary, and miserable in the declining state. The progressive state is in reality the cheerful and hearty state to all the different orders of the society. The stationary is dull; the declining melancholy. (Book I, chapter VIII)

It would be difficult to find, even in the modern literature, a deeper conviction of the merits of economic growth than is expressed in this passage and, more generally, in the *Wealth of Nations* as a whole.

Another illustration, from a very different area of social science: statistics. When people began to compile quantitative data on economic and social matters in a systematic fashion in the nineteenth century, the main focus of their interest was to measure the *change* that was taking place and, in the confidence that the change was for the better, the term 'progress' was widely used as a descriptive term for these data. Thus, for example, the classic early compilation of economic and social data in England was G. R. Porter's *Progress of the Nation* (1836–43). This was shortly followed in the United States by George Tucker's *Progress of the United States* (1843) and R. S. Fisher's *Progress of the United States* (1854). Later in the century, when the issue of the distribution of income was receiving increasing attention, the Englishman Robert Giffen, who pioneered the statistical measurement of this, called the publication of his findings *The Progress of the Working Class in the Last Half Century* (1884). It was almost as instinctive as breathing for the nineteenth-century social statistician to think of his work as the quantification of progress.

Back in the early seventeenth century it was possible to believe that the world was in a state of decline. The great poet John Donne, who was also a theologian of note, contended in a sermon delivered in 1625 that decline and degeneration were evident on every hand: the weather had become less regular, he claimed, the sun was not as warm as it used to be, human beings were becoming smaller, and every year there appeared new illnesses and new species of pestiferous insects. During the nineteenth century, the era when the social sciences were developing their basic foundations, such views were treated with amusement, if they were noted at all. Classical political economy was called the 'dismal science' not because it was pessimistic, but because it was regarded by some as insufficiently optimistic. In the twentieth century the earlier faith in progress has eroded, not quite so far as to generate claims such as Donne's that the sun is discernibly cooler or that men are noticeably shorter (though equally fatuous comments are not unheard of), but enough to raise again the question whether improvement in man's economic and social life is occurring, or whether it is possible, or even whether it is desirable.

As the above quotation from Nisbet suggests, the history of the origin of the social sciences could be written as an appendix to a study of the efflorescence of the idea of progress in the later eighteenth century. The history of social science since then could also be written in the same way, but we would have to recognize that the theme of progress has been subject to a large number of major variations. Classical political economy was concerned, as Adam Smith was, with discovering the factors that promote economic growth (and those that retard it). Auguste Comte aimed at the construction of a perfect social order based upon scientific laws, which, in his view, were understandable only if one recognized that human civilization evolves through distinct stages in its intellectual culture (which Comte was confident he had discovered). Karl Marx regarded progress as governed by the materialistic laws of historical development, the discovery of which was the chief task of social science. Herbert Spencer believed that he had discovered the main law of social development, that progress is characterized by increasing functional specialization. And so on. In fact, it would be exceedingly difficult to write the history of social science as an appendix to the theme of progress because that theme split into numerous diverging streams of thought during the nineteenth century. Nevertheless, it is useful to remember that the idea of progress was the main inspiration of the earliest social scientists and it still continues, in various ways, to exert a powerful influence.

One of these streams of thought, whose antecedents go back well before the rise of the idea of progress in the seventeenth century, is the discussion not of progress itself but of its ultimate, so to speak, the perfect society. Following Sir Thomas More's famous *Utopia* (1516), this is often generically described as 'utopianism'. This line of thinking has been very influential in Western social thought, more broadly viewed than the 'social science' that is the main concern of this book. Except for a few specific cases such as the Malthusian theory of population, which will be examined in Chapter 9, the relationship between utopian thought and the attempt to study social phenomena in a scientific way is difficult to specify, but it is worth a bit of our time to look at some aspects of the history and philosophy of the doctrine of social perfection.

B. THE IDEA OF A PERFECT SOCIAL ORDER

The historian of philosophy in search of the origins of the idea of progress is easily tempted to trace it back to Greek antiquity, not only because almost every idea can be attributed to the remarkable group of thinkers who lived in Athens and other Greek cities half a millennium before the beginning of the Christian era, but because one of these thinkers, Heraclitus (*c*. 535–*c*. 475 B.C.), advanced the metaphysical notion that all worldly things are in a state of constant flux or change. While other Greek philosophers speculated that the world is fundamentally composed of tangible substances – earth, water, and air being the favourite candidates – Heraclitus opined that it is more like fire, which, we would say today, is a process rather than a substance (a distinction that Heraclitus only dimly grasped). This conception of the nature of reality made *change* its most basic characteristic. It is easy enough to see that this articulates with the idea of progress, since there can be no progress without change, though we must recognize that the idea of progress involves something more: change *for the better* in a sense that involves a value judgement.

It was not Heraclitus' metaphysical conception, however, that exerted the most powerful influence on Western thought in that period when Europeans were rediscovering the ancient Greek literature. Plato and Aristotle had far more impact, and their metaphysical conceptions were very different, oriented to thinking of the world in terms of characterizing the state of perfection in some stable sense. Plato's theory of pure 'forms' viewed perfection as an abstract idea but he contended that such forms are more real than the changing world conveyed to our understandings through sense experience, which is largely illusory in nature. As we saw in Chapter 4 A, Plato applied his metaphysical views to social and political matters in the *Republic*, which has had, and continues to have, a great influence on Western social thought, especially of the sort we will be examining in this section.

Aristotle too held a perfectionistic view of the world, but different from Plato's. Aristotle regarded all change as a transitional process inevitably directed towards a final and static end-state. The achievement of this end-state by anything is perfection because it is an inherent necessity in the thing's nature. So, for example, a falling stone achieves perfection when it comes to rest on the ground, for it is its inherent nature to be in such a state. Aristotle was struggling to develop an analytical idea that has been enormously useful in modern science: the conception of an equilibrium of forces. However, by construing it as a metaphysical truth rather than an analytical tool he confused the issue considerably and also invested the concept of equilibrium, with the view that such a state is normatively good or morally proper. These notions have clung to the concept of equilibrium in modern science, most tenaciously in the social sciences, where 'disequilibrium' is frequently used as a derogatory term without any further amplification. Among the social sciences, economics has made the most extensive use of the concept of equilibrium, and it is very common for non-economists (and some economists too) to interpret an equilibrium analysis as describing an optimum or normatively perfect state of affairs. This misinterpretation of economic models was dealt a heavy blow by

J. M. Keynes in the 1930s when he presented a model of an economy in stable equilibrium with massive unemployment: equilibrium is clearly not equivalent to desirable in such a context (see below, Chapter 17 D).

The linkage of the equilibrium idea with the idea of perfection still persists in social thought, however, perhaps because of the Aristotelian notion that everything has a 'natural end'. This was developed systematically by St. Thomas Aquinas in the thirteenth century and became an important element in Roman Catholic theology. Its influence, however, is quite apparent in all branches of utopian theory, including those of Saint-Simon, Comte, and Marx, in which the 'forces of history' are pictured as driving social development towards an end that is as ineluctable as the fate of the falling stone, and which is beyond normative criticism because, being 'natural', its merits transcend any human criteria of judgement.

This opens a vast area of social literature, dealing with the study of the perfect social order and how it may be attained. Speculative social philosophy and empirically oriented social science are not the same thing, but they intersect so frequently in both the history and the philosophy of social science that the connection cannot be disregarded even in a book that is devoted primarily to social science. In subsequent chapters we will have to note these connections as our study proceeds and, in a few cases, comment on them at length. Here my object is to give a brief sketch of the history and main characteristics of what is usually described as 'utopian' social thought.

Before we begin this we should note certain features of the relation between the idea of perfection and the idea of progress discussed in the foregoing section. According to one prevalent point of view, the notion of a perfect social state is a necessary constituent of the idea of social progress. Since the concept of progress involves change *for the better*, how can we know when a change constitutes progress without judging it according to some ideal? In this view, a perfect social order must be described by the social philosopher for the pragmatic purpose of informing our judgements, and perhaps also for guiding our action, since if we know what would be perfect we can try to propel the course of change in the direction of the ideal. (This, one should note, is very different from Aristotle's 'teleological' argument that the ideal end acts as the force which draws changes towards itself.) Those who hold such a view need not argue that a perfect social order is fully attainable in practice; it serves simply as a reference point.

One encounters this view of the relation between progress and perfection in very diverse areas of social thought. In Thomistic theology, for example, there is the idea that the laws promulgated by governments may be judged by reference to a body of 'natural law' which God has established in the realm of human relations and morals, just as he has established the laws governing physical phenomena. This view enjoys considerable appeal among social philosophers who feel that there must be some absolute criteria that one can employ in judging the actions of governments. F. A. Hayek, who is not a

Catholic social philosopher, embraces the idea of natural law in this sense in his recent trilogy *Law, Legislation, and Liberty* (1973, 1976, 1979). As another example, in a different part of social science, we should note the perfect competition model of modern microeconomic theory. This is not intended to be a description of any real economy or even a description of any realistically attainable end. Its role is to enable one to derive a set of theorems that define the conditions under which the productive resources of the economy are optimally allocated in creating the various goods and services that are desired (see below, Chapter 17 A).

One of the most important difficulties of this view of the relation between progress and perfection is that, when used to make simple judgements of particular changes, it implicitly assumes that the imperfections of the real world are independent, of one another. If they are independent then we may be certain that any change that improves a particular feature of society by altering it in the direction of the ideal contributes to *general* social improvement. But if, say, two defects tend to counteract one another, then removing only one of them may make the general situation worse. A good example is the case of a one-company town where there is no competition on the demand side of the labour market, and there is a strong trade union which prevents competition in the supply of labour as well. Both of these are 'imperfections', according to economic theory, but two imperfections of this sort may be better than one and it is not necessarily 'progressive' to remove only one of them. This difficulty, which has been explicitly demonstrated in technical economic theory, is equally relevant to general social philosophy. Even if one knows what would constitute a state of perfection, one cannot be sure that any piecemeal change constitutes progress. We could be certain that change is progress only when *all* imperfections are removed at a stroke and one moves, or rather leaps, to the state of perfection. It may be that some intuitive awareness of this is the basis of the many utopian schemes of social organization that argue the necessity of wholesale reconstruction of society rather than gradual piecemeal attempts at progress, though one should quickly add that nothing as sophisticated as this is present in the explicit arguments of the utopian literature.

Another problem in the notion that one must employ a conception of perfection in order to determine whether a change should be regarded as progress is that it must assume that one thing at least is unchanging: our conception of what constitutes a perfect social order. If this is not fixed, then we live in a much more complex world, one in which the ideal as well as the actual state of affairs is subject to change and, to make things more complex still, perhaps our conception of what is ideal changes *as a consequence* of our efforts to approach it. Some important social scientists have taken this view, most notably Alfred Marshall, whose *Principles of Economics* (1890) became the foundation book of modern microeconomic theory. Unlike the Thomistic notion of an absolute natural moral law, this adopts a relativistic stance.

Progress can be defined only with respect to tentative conceptions of perfection, which may be expected to alter. So specific changes are 'progressive' at one time, but not at another. One does not find such a view in the utopian literature. This has been written by people who, if they are not quite certain that they themselves know what is ideal or perfect, are at least confident that it is knowable in a final definitive form. We can see how the utopian literature of social thought represents a continuation of religious approaches to social phenomena rather than the mode of science, in which all knowledge, even of the laws of nature, is regarded as tentative.

One further complication must be noted. A strong and recurring theme in the literature of social thought is that change is, itself, the desired state. In such a view it is the journey that is valuable, not the destination. This brings to notice an important dichotomy in social philosophy between those whose conception of the ideal involves action, challenge, and difficulties overcome, and those for whom it means quiet, stability, and surcease from care; between those who desire to sail uncharted seas and those who crave the calm security of a snug harbour. In the paradisiacal ideal of ancient Norse mythology, one spends eternity in Valhalla fighting ferociously with sword and buckler during the day and feasting gluttonously during the night while one's noble wounds miraculously heal. In the Hindu and Buddhist ideal of Nirvana, on the other hand, supreme bliss is achieved by suppressing all worldly desire and entering a state of undisturbed calm. This difference in the conception of the ideal is mirrored in the utopian literature in a curious way. The standard portrayal of the perfect society is of one that has long since passed through its era of construction and now rests in a permanent state of order and harmony. But the authors themselves are clearly more entranced by the challenges of building the New Jerusalem than by the presumed merits of living there, and the disciples that many have gathered are typically those who value the struggle rather than the goal, more like Norse warriors than Hindu mystics.

We learn from anthropologists, who by now have studied most of the out-of-the-way societies that survive on our planet, that a common feature of most (perhaps all) of them is the belief in a society that is idyllic, providing generously for all man's material and other needs. Whether this society is regarded as located in some exotic land beyond the sea's horizon, or in a more abstract space, or in the remote past, or the far future, is not as significant as the idea itself: it brings to notice a form of social thought of exceptional importance, not only among so-called primitive peoples but prominent also in the most highly developed societies and, in the latter, among its most sophisticated thinkers. In Western civilization the earliest delineation of the characteristics and conditions of a perfect social order is, of course, the description of the Garden of Eden in the Book of Genesis. Since then, literally thousands of books have been written for the purpose of describing various visions of a perfect social order. This is in fact one of the most enduring and most popular literary genres in our intellectual history, testifying undoubtedly to the deep yearning of man to find a haven from the conflicts, fears, and deprivations of life as it has hitherto been known.

This mode of social thought has, moreover, influenced action to a surprising extent. Attempts to establish idyllic societies, based on some general or specific concept of social perfection, form an almost continuous history that gives no sign of having less energy today than, say, in the last century, when frontier America was the favourite place for a leader and a band of disciples to establish the prototype example of the perfect social order. The almost universal failure of these projects seems not to have diminished enthusiasm for new ones. Adam Smith denoted man as the permanently dissatisfied animal but he did not draw out all the implications: some dissatisfied men seek progress and improvement, but others will settle for nothing less than perfection, to be brought about by departing radically from the customary forms of social, economic, and political organization. Needless to say, this mode of social thought is not only represented by the enthusiasts who purchase a tract of land and initiate a new experiment in communal living; it is also a powerful element in more comprehensive radical political philosophies and plays a strong role in modern revolutionary movements, as it did in earlier ones such as during the Commonwealth period in seventeenth-century England and the interval between the Bourbon and Bonaparte dictatorships in France of the late eighteenth century.

The authors of the most comprehensive study yet made of the history of this mode of social thought, F. E. and F. P. Manuel (*Utopian Thought in the Western World*, 1979), note that it was prominent in ancient Greece, appearing there in a great variety of literary forms over a period of hundreds of years. Plato's *Republic* was not unique in outlining a system of social perfection. When the surviving ancient Greek texts were published during the fifteenth and sixteenth centuries, among the Hellenic legacies that were powerfully transmitted to the West were a large number of utopian social writings which Europeans of the Renaissance era read with avidity.

These Greek writings enriched and modified a tradition of perfectionist thought in which the West had already been thoroughly immersed through Christianity. If the Roman Empire had survived, it is perhaps unlikely that utopian political thinking would have had so great an influence on European history, for the Romans were earthbound and practical thinkers, more interested in the techniques of efficient governmental administration than in theoretical models of an ideal social order. The speculative temper of the Greeks and the religious millennialism of Christianity came together during the Renaissance to form a mode of social thought that has been of great importance in the West ever since. The idea of a perfect social order is not exclusively Western, but nowhere else has it had such a notable impact on social thought and social practice.

St. Augustine's fifth-century view of the order of perfection was other-worldly, referring to the regime of heavenly paradise, but there was always a strain of thought in Christianity that viewed perfection as attainable on the terra firma of planet earth. Many of the leaders of experimental ideal communities, throughout history, have been religious leaders whose band of disciples believed themselves to be especially chosen to do God's will on earth by building a social order of perfection. One of these, Thomas Muntzer, who led a peasants' rebellion in Germany in the early sixteenth century, put forward views on social organization so similar to those later advocated by Karl Marx that, despite the religious foundations of his thinking, he has been viewed by some historians as an early precursor of 'Marxism–Leninism'.

Some utopians believed that the social order of perfection had already been established on the planet by a Christian priest who had gone far away from Western Europe to perform his mission. This was the legend of Prester John, which first appeared in the twelfth century and grew with retelling over the succeeding generations. By the fifteenth century the legend was regarded by many as being as true as scripture itself. Portugal's Prince Henry, 'The Navigator', encouraged exploration down the Atlantic coast of Africa, not only to find a maritime route for trade to the Orient, but to outflank the Muslim Middle East by linking up Christian Europe with the 'Kingdom of Prester John', which was presumed to be somewhere between Africa and India. Vasco da Gama, on his voyages that opened up the sea route to the Indies around the Cape of Good Hope, carried diplomatic letters addressed to Prester John. Christopher Columbus, as part of his preparations to reach the Indies by sailing west, studied all that he could about Prester John and his idyllic Christian kingdom. By Columbus's time hardly any educated Western European believed that the earth was flat and that one could fall over its edge into the void, but many believed to a virtual certainty that one could sail to an earthly paradise. Columbus himself, in his *Letters from the New World* (1493), expressed the conviction that he had rediscovered the oldest of such paradises, the location of the Garden of Eden from which Adam and Eve had set forth to people the earth.

It was during this same period that there appeared the most famous work in this genre of all time, the one that provided its now established generic name, Sir Thomas More's *Utopia*. This has gone through more than 150 editions since its first publication, in Latin, in 1516. It is one of the very few sixteenth-century books that will be found today among the regular stock of a moderately good bookstore in American cities or university towns. Three paperback English editions of it are currently in print, selling at the lowest prices at which any book can be purchased. So, four and a half centuries after its composition, More's *Utopia* is still widely read; it continues to appeal to those who believe that man's social order could be made not merely better but perfect. The book also inspired a host of imitating authors who wrote Utopias of their own: from the sixteenth century to the eighteenth hundreds of works were composed using More's *Utopia* as model. The number of people who have been touched by Moreian ideas, directly or indirectly, has been truly immense.

Thomas More was a man of deep religious convictions, which led him to oppose Henry VIII's withdrawal of the English Church from the jurisdiction of the papacy. For this he was beheaded at Henry's order and, eventually (1935), he was declared a saint by the Roman Catholic Church. Despite More's religious feelings, his *Utopia* is not notably a portrait of a perfect social order built upon religious foundations or governed necessarily by priests. In fact it was the forerunner of the form of social perfectionist writing that rose to dominance in the eighteenth century: the vision of a *secular* utopia. We have repeatedly noted in this book that social science and social philosophy underwent a profound transformation from a religious to a secular orientation during the seventeenth and eighteenth centuries. This was also true of that branch of social thought most intimately connected with religion, the concept of a perfect social order: paradise, in effect, was brought down to earth.

In accounting for this transformation we probably have to give first place to the general intellectual change towards secularization that was taking place which, in turn, probably has to be attributed mainly to the successes of the natural sciences with their positivist–empiricist outlook. Beyond that, to be more specific, some influence of significant weight undoubtedly has to be given to the accounts that began to circulate in Europe of the nature of life in the South Pacific isles after the mid-eighteenth-century voyages of James Cook, Louis Antoine de Bougainville, and their successors. The fifteenth- and sixteenth-century explorers expected to find the Christian utopia of Prester John and were disappointed; the eighteenth-century ones, to their surprise and delight, and of those who harkened to their tales, found utopia, or so they believed, among the pagans of the South Seas. The idea of a perfect social order took on at once an air of practical possibility that appealed to the Western European empiricist outlook. Thomas More called his imaginary society 'Utopia', meaning, in Greek, 'nowhere,' which suggests that it does not exist in this our world. But now sailors reported to have seen the perfect social order with their own eyes on Tahiti and other isles where all the needs of life could be plucked effortlessly from the trees and the women were both beautiful and willing. Heretofore only the gullible could believe in a perfect social order; now that belief appeared to be substantiated by the very kind of evidence that sophisticated eighteenth-century Europeans valued most highly: direct empirical experience.

In brief, the era that gave birth to the disciplines we now group under the general heading of 'social science' was also one that witnessed a reinvigoration and modernization of ancient speculations concerning the characteristics of a perfect social order. Since its beginnings, social science has intersected with and often has entangled with utopianism, and it is very difficult for the historian or philosopher of science to keep a steady focus upon the first of these modes of thought undistorted by the other. We shall have ample evidence of this as our study of the social sciences proceeds into the nineteenth century. In preparation for this, it will be worth our while to devote a few pages to an outline of some of the main characteristics of utopian thought, so that this mode of social philosophy will be more readily recognizable.

In the article on 'Utopias and Utopianism' in the *International Encyclopedia of the Social Sciences*, the author, George Kateb, speaks of this mode of social philosophy as 'a persistent tradition of thought about the perfect society, in which perfection is defined as harmony'. This point is well worth the emphasis that Kateb gives it in his article. The most universal feature of the vast and varied utopian literature is that the perfect social order is viewed as one of peaceful communal concord: no crime or strife, war or revolution, no theft, embezzlement, violence or fraud, each member of the community functioning smoothly as part of a harmonious social whole. A number of the utopian communities that were founded during the nineteenth century were called 'Harmony', the most famous of which was in southern Indiana, on the Wabash river, where a group of German Protestant millennarians first established a religious commune to prepare for the Second Coming, and then sold out to the atheist Robert Owen, who wished there to create his own vision of a secular utopia, no less oriented to harmony than the religious disciples of Father Rapp, and so calling only for a minor change of name to 'New Harmony'. In Chapter 10 we will return to the question of perfection as harmony and undertake a more extensive discussion of its metaphysical foundations and implications for social science.

Another universal feature of the utopian literature is its handling of the question of the economic organization of the perfect social order; but in this case the universality is due simply to ubiquitous neglect of any serious attention to the subject. Utopias are typically full of specific information on the ideal society's political system, its educational system, even its architecture is often described in minute detail, but if the reader asks how the economic system is structured and how it functions, he receives no informative response. The economy is universally *presumed* to function, and indeed to function better than any known real economy, since the citizens are almost invariably described as having been relieved of the curse of economic want; but no utopian book, so far as I have been able to discover, gives any informative account of how the society organizes itself to make use of available productive resources and channel them effectively to the creation of the goods and services that are necessary to the good life. The lack of this is perhaps partially responsible for the negative connotations that cling to the term 'utopian': visionary, unrealistic, not worthy of consideration by serious minds, frivolous. One of the writers of a modern utopia, the Harvard psychologist B. F. Skinner (*Walden Two*, 1948), has his protagonist say in response to a question raised on this point: 'No one can seriously doubt that a well-managed community will get along successfully as an economic unit. A child could prove it.' Skinner apparently felt it otiose to write out this 'proof', since the book says nothing more on the matter. This contemptuous dismissal of the economic question is no better than the bizarre descriptions in the older utopian literature of lands where the mountains are made of tasty edibles and the lakes and rivers of delicious libations, treating literally the poetic description of Canaan in the Old Testament as a 'land flowing with milk and honey'. Obviously, if we lived in a world where, in the words of one of the ancient Greek utopianists,

> ... the fishes
> came perfectly willing,
> and did their own grilling,
> and served themselves up on the dishes

we would be more than half-way to the order of perfection (for man, of course). But, needless to say, or – in view of the continuing popularity of utopias without described economies, need*ful* to say – one does not solve a real-world problem by assuming that it does not exist.

In the literature of the social order of perfection there is some ambiguity towards both ends, so to speak, of the economic process: work and material wealth. Many utopias are pictured as lands of such great material wealth that all citizens live in a state of repletion, all desires fulfilled. Others depict a world in which man has learned to be content when his 'real needs' are met and not to seek fulfilment of 'mere desires', much less satisfaction to the point of surfeit. Plato distinguished between needs and desires in the *Republic* and advocated a life so reduced in its material standards that readers, even of his own day, must have regarded it as rather ascetic. Thomas More considered the desire for wealth to be the main source of evil in real societies, and his *Utopia* pictured a society in which people are content to meet basic needs and produce more only for the purpose of providing a buffer against future dangers such as drought, or attack from other states. The distinction made by Plato between needs and desires raises issues that are of continuing importance in social science and social philosophy, since it is unclear that greater material wealth makes man happier and, even if this were indubitably true as a matter of fact, it does not follow that such happiness is morally worthy. These large issues are beyond the scope of this book but we shall have to consider some aspects of them in the discussion of utilitarianism in Chapter 11.

At the other end of the economic process, utopian writers have shown mixed views about work. In some accounts it seems to be the main curse of ordinary life, and the authors construct scenarios of the idyllic society in which life is like that enjoyed by the first children of God in Eden before the fruit of the tree of knowledge was tasted. The apparent lack of regular work on Tahiti and the other Pacific isles greatly attracted the European explorers, and it is not to be wondered at (if one has any conception of the hard working life of an eighteenth-century sailor or of his compatriots back home in Liverpool or La Rochelle) that the prospect of spending one's life lying languidly on a sunny beach would seem paradisiacal in itself, even without the beautiful hedonistic maidens. But other utopian writings view labour as a positive virtue rather than a curse. In More's Utopia the citizens do no more work than is necessary to meet their modest requirements, but it is clear that More regarded such work as desirable in itself, an idea that was later embraced by Saint-Simon, the first of the modern socialist utopians, and by Karl Marx, the greatest of them. Down to the present, the view that in a good society everyone should work continues to be a feature of socialist doctrine but it is certainly not confined to it. In modern capitalistic American society, with greater material wealth than Plato or More could have imagined possible, the view is strongly held, even within the plutocracy, that life is incomplete unless one has work of some sort to do. The modern economist is made uneasy by this. In the prototypical economic model a sharp distinction is made between 'benefits' and 'costs', with work located in the latter category. If work has benefits of its own, means and ends become confused, and both positive and normative economic analysis is made much more difficult.

On one important point with respect to work there is a notable difference between the orthodox strain of social science and the perfectionist literature: the question of division of labour. As we have seen, Adam Smith considered the division of labour an indispensable feature of an efficient economic system, and as we will note in Chapter 15, Émile Durkheim regarded division of labour as equally important in creating the social solidarity that binds an aggregate of individuals into a social whole with a collective consciousness and a continuing culture. The utopian writers, and the non-utopian but non-orthodox schools of social scientists, have typically taken a different view of the division of labour, regarding it as culturally degenerative and psychologically deforming, a view that, as we noted above, Adam Smith himself expressed. The modern discussion of this has revolved around Karl Marx's concept of 'alienation', which we will examine briefly in Chapter 13 C. Marx, and his collaborator Friedrich Engels, said very little about the characteristics of communism, the ideal society that, in their view, was the natural result of the laws of historical development. They regarded such descriptions as 'utopian' in the derogatory sense of the term, but among their few remarks on this topic there are clear indications that they had a negative view of the division of labour in so far as it involves the occupational specialization of people and that they expected communism to do away with it.

This brings us to what must undoubtedly be regarded as the main focus of utopian writing, at least since Jean-Jacques Rousseau (1712–78) and Robert Owen (1771–1858): the role of society in forming the personalities and characters of those who inhabit it. As we have already seen, and will have to note again frequently in the following pages, serious students of social phenomena have always been pulled in two different directions on the subject of 'human nature', since some features of it are clearly due to the biological constitution of *Homo sapiens*, and some are equally clearly due to cultural conditioning and other features of the social environment, the line between what is 'biological' and what is 'social' being one of the most persistently disputed boundaries in the history of science.

Rousseau regarded his predecessors in social theory as having been seriously misled concerning man's basic nature. Drawing inferences from observation of existing persons, Rousseau noted, is scientifically unacceptable, since the data consist of the behaviour of persons already moulded by social institutions. The point is valid, but Rousseau's next step was purely speculative: if, he claimed, we could strip away the effects of enculturation we would see that man's basic nature is good; the bad features of human character are therefore the result of the corrupting influences of human institutions. Rousseau did not argue, as the anarchist writers (e.g. William Godwin) did, that all social organization is unavoidably evil and deleterious to character. He contended that, *hitherto,* social institutions had functioned in this fashion; but they could be otherwise, and his main message was that social institutions should be reconstructed so as to preserve man's natural goodness and to produce a process of enculturation that would suit him for life in a social order of harmonious perfection.

Robert Owen's view of man was that he is inherently neither good nor bad but whatever the social process of enculturation makes out of the wholly plastic original material. Owen was following the same line of thinking that we noted above in discussing the empiricism of Locke and Hume, and the association psychology of David Hartley, though Owen himself, a self-taught thinker who read little, was probably quite unaware of these philosophical predecessors. Owen concluded that the key to all man's problems lies in redesigning his social institutions so as to produce human beings suitable for a harmonious order. Thus he arrived at essentially the same view as Rousseau, though there is little reason to believe that, if they had met, they would have agreed on the details of the necessary social reconstruction.

Through Rousseau and Owen there occurred the modern resurrection of an idea that lies just beneath the surface, or on it, in a wide range of utopian writings: the view that man, as he now is, is unsuitable for the perfect society; it cannot be achieved without substantial changes in the human constituents. This opens the door to schemes of social reorganization that run far beyond politics and economics, since the objective is to change the human psyche. After dismissing the economic problem in *Walden Two*, B. F. Skinner states flatly that the real problems of attaining a harmonious social order are *psychological* ones, which, like many utopianists before him, he sees as being resolved only by turning our backs on human individuality and using the techniques of behavioural psychology to make man over into a creature with socially suitable behaviour patterns (see his later book, *Beyond Freedom and Dignity*, 1971). Needless to say, this view makes some people exceedingly apprehensive, especially if they feel that they are likely to be among those chosen for character modification. In recent years this line of thought has shifted from the realm of behavioural psychology to biology, where the discovery of the structure of the DNA molecule in 1953 seemed to open the possibility of genetic modification of human beings in more rapid and precise ways than had been considered by the earlier proponents of 'eugenics'. Before this scientific development took place, however, the classic criticism of it had already been written, Aldous Huxley's *Brave New World* (1932), an anti-utopia whose object was to show that a social order of harmonious perfection might not be one that a civilized person who values individuality and freedom would find attractive.

As we proceed with our history of social science we shall see that the issue of individualism versus communalism punctuates the scientific literature, as it has social philosophical thought generally, since Plato and Aristotle. Robert Owen brought to New Harmony, Indiana, in 1825 one of the most remarkable groups of individualists ever assembled in one place, but all were dedicated to building a new communal order that would demonstrate, as the prospectus for the town newspaper, the *New Harmony Gazette*, announced, 'that individuality detracts from human happiness'. Rousseau, one of the most uncompromising individualists ever to set pen to paper, celebrated the merits of a world in which the individual is submerged in society to the degree that his very personal identity, his concept of 'I', becomes derivative from or fused with the identity of the social collectivity.

Manuel and Manuel are so struck by this psychological aspect of utopian thought that they attribute its great popularity over so many centuries to the yearning of man for a return to antenatal life when, as foetus, he was secure and enclosed, and formed an organic connection with a larger entity. If Freudian psychology offers explanations of anything (which this writer doubts) it hardly serves as an explanation of utopianism, for some utopian writings are as dogmatically individualistic as others are communal. In William Godwin's perfect society even the playing of ensemble music would be unknown, since it would represent an invasion of freedom to have to accommodate oneself to the playing of others. In modern times the writing of Ayn Rand represents a utopianist vision of unalloyed individualism. It may be that some of the excesses of modern-day political tyrannies that set out to change man are traceable to the influence of Rousseau and Owen, but utopianism generally shows within itself the same conflict between individualism and communalism that characterizes the whole spectrum of modern social thought, and its history back to the ancients.

In section A of this chapter I noted the close connection that existed between the idea of progress, the rapid development of the natural sciences from the sixteenth century on, and the beginning of the social sciences in the eighteenth century. The relation of utopian thought to natural science and the social sciences is an important part of the history of modern social thought, but it is a complex relation, and a reasonably complete examination is beyond the scope of this book. The following concluding remarks are intended only to suggest some important themes.

In one respect there would seem to be a clear antithesis between the style of thought represented by utopianism and the philosophy of science that was being established by scientists like Galileo and Newton, and by philosophers like Locke and Hume. The roots of utopian theory are in ancient legends about other-worldly beings not limited by 'human nature'. The utopianists depicted model societies but they are not 'models' as philosophers of science use that term. The social order of perfection is constructed without any constraints imposed by empirical facts or laws of nature. From the epistemological standpoint this is the very opposite of a scientific model. The typical utopian scenario, ancient and modern, is an exercise in social science-fiction, but, unlike the best of science-fiction proper, it does not accept the constraint of making the story consistent with known scientific facts and accepted scientific laws. This being so, one would perhaps expect that utopian social theorists would turn their backs on science and claim other foundations of validity such as religion or personal intuition. Some of the leading utopianists, most notably Rousseau, were disdainful of science, but this was not true of secular utopian thinkers in general. By the eighteenth century science was too powerful a factor in the intellectual and practical life of the West to be disregarded. Some utopian thinkers in fact regarded themselves as applying the principles of science, even though this seems rather strange today. Charles Fourier (1772–1837), for example, whose ideas were the basis of Brook Farm and other communitarian experiments in America, idolized Newton and regarded his own design for communal 'phalanxes' as based upon laws of social attraction that were the counterpart for social phenomena of Newton's law of gravity.

The idea that the new social order of perfection would be based on scientific knowledge is traceable to Francis Bacon (1561–1626). His associated idea, that the new order would be under the governance of scientists, can be traced back to Plato, though, of course, Plato placed 'philosophers' at the top of the hierarchy of the ideal community. Francis Bacon's *New Atlantis* (1627) was widely read in seventeenth-century Europe. It pictured an ideal society in which the most important institution was a college of scientists, devoted to research and invention and, under the king, governing the society in accordance with scientific knowledge in harmony with Christian ethics. The Royal Society, founded in 1662, was inspired to some degree by Bacon's utopian views. Tommaso Campanella's *City of the Sun* (1632), another widely read utopia of the era, stressed the role that scientific knowledge must play in governing society and in changing it and its constituent individuals in the ways required to achieve the harmony of perfection.

When we come to the late eighteenth century, the most interesting figure is Condorcet. His vision of the new social order was one in which the social sciences had developed to the point where they could be effectively applied to the solution of economic problems and to the art of government. Such a set of sciences was possible, in Condorcet's view, because the mathematics of probability enables scientists to develop laws of behaviour that apply to groups of persons. It was a brilliant idea, the essential foundation of modern empirical social science. Condorcet was ahead of his time in this, but utopian to a fault in his unlimited optimism for what the social sciences would achieve once they had developed the proper mathematical foundations and the capacity to make use of large amounts of empirical data. The most important strain of utopian thought in which the perfect society is to be realized through science is early nineteenth-century French 'positivism', which we will examine at length in Chapter 12.

Chapter 9

Classical political economy

Adam Smith is the founder of economics as a branch of social science, not only because he pointed the way, but because others followed the direction indicated. No man, whatever his merits, can be a leader without followers. Unlike the Physiocrats, however, those who 'followed' Adam Smith did not do so as disciples dedicated to spreading the wisdom of the master. They were independent students of economic matters who, though recognizing the brilliance of Adam Smith in delineating the questions or problems of economic theory, were as often as not convinced that his answers were inadequate or wrong. So there developed, during the next two generations, a large body of writings on economic questions which historians now describe as classical political economy. The most important names in this literature are Thomas Robert Malthus (1776–1834), David Ricardo (1772–1823), and John Stuart Mill (1806–73). Karl Marx (1818–83) also belongs to this phase in the historical development of economic theory, but we shall study his ideas in a separate chapter (Chapter 13).

Economists did not agree with one another in the early nineteenth century any more than they do today, and it would be misleading to convey the impression that the classical economists constituted a unified school of like-minded thinkers. Malthus and Ricardo, for example, had incessant discussions on economic matters and disagreed about almost everything (except, as we shall see, Malthus's famous, or infamous, theory of population). Nevertheless, certain main lines of thought did develop, and when historians today speak of classical political economy they usually have in mind a central set of propositions bearing on the structure and dynamics of economic organization that were regarded as authoritatively established by the best thinkers and generally accepted by the wider body of those interested in the efforts to develop a science of economics. For our purposes in this chapter we will take David Ricardo as representing the received or authoritative view on economic questions. From the publication of his *Principles of Political Economy and Taxation* in 1817 through to the 1870's, Ricardo's ideas dominated economic thought. John Stuart Mill's *Principles of Political Economy* (1848), in its basic skeleton and much of its flesh a restatement of

Ricardo's theories, was *the* book in economics for many years, and new editions of it were being issued (for the use of college students) almost up to the first World War. But most historians regard classical political economy as moribund by the 1890's. A new set of developments in economic theory, starting in the 1870's, culminated in the replacement of classical political economy by neoclassical economics, which is, basically, the model structure that one still finds today in college courses in 'microeconomics'. The other branch of contemporary economics, 'macroeconomics,' is even more recent, stemming mainly from the work of John Maynard Keynes in the 1930's. The neoclassical and Keynesian economic models will be examined below, in Chapter 17.

The careful reader of the preceding paragraph will have noted that a change in terminology occurred during the nineteenth century: the subject was first called 'political economy' and later 'economics', the name it commonly wears today. The word 'economics' derives from a compound of two classical Greek words: *oikos* and *nomos*, meaning respectively 'household' and 'law'. Some writers of the Greek classical era used the word *oikonomiai* to refer to the basic principles (i.e. 'laws') of household management. This use survives today in the college subject of Home Economics, but plain Economics, as every student of it is aware, deals with the economic problems of a much larger entity – the nation and, indeed, the world as a whole. The Greek term *oikonomia politike*, referring to the management of a city-state, can be found in writings of Aristotle's time.

The term 'political economy' came into European use in the seventeenth century and became common in the eighteenth century (in France the term was *économie politique* and in Italy *economia politica*). This reflected the growth of national consciousness and the centralization of political power in nation-states that occurred in this period, and the corresponding orientation of students of economic matters to issues of political policy aimed at promoting, to quote Adam Smith's title, 'the wealth of nations.' The national focus of the subject would have been better served by calling it national economy (as the Germans did: *Nationalökonomie*) but political economy was the term that stuck. Its first use in an English book title was in Sir James Steuart's *An Inquiry into the Principles of Political Economy* (1767). 'What economy is in a family', says Steuart, 'political economy is in a state.' Adam Smith used the term political economy in the text of his *Wealth of Nations* but not in the title, perhaps because he did not wish to imitate Steuart, but by the second decade of the nineteenth century writers were not so fastidious and many who wrote general works on economics apparently could not think of entitling their books anything but *Principles of Political Economy*.

The two-word term was awkward when used as an adjective, however, and it was customary, for example, to refer to 'economic problems' or 'economic policy', not 'political-economic problems' or 'political-economic policy'. William Stanley Jevons (1835–82), one of the originators of what later became neoclassical economics, suggested that the term 'economics' would be analogous to other modern subject names such as 'mathematics', and 'ethics' and recommended it but he titled his own book *The Theory of Political Economy* (1871) none the less. At the same time Alfred Marshall, who became the chief theorist of neoclassical economics, was using the term 'economics' in his lectures and writings because he felt that the adjective 'political', which might once have referred to the whole polity or nation, had come to denote particular sectional interests within the nation, that is, 'political' in the narrow or partisan sense. When his own enormously influential treatise appeared in 1890 it was called *Principles of Economics*. But much more than the name had changed. The basic analytical model of neoclassical economics was different in some fundamental respects from that of the older classical political economy, and there was an important shift of emphasis too – away from the study of economic growth and historical development, towards a detailed analysis of how markets function and how limited productive resources can be efficiently used. So historians have retained the term 'political economy' as a handy label for the set of ideas, concepts, and theories, associated most intimately with the name of David Ricardo, which dominated economic thought during the half-century of rapid economic development that took place in Europe following the final defeat of Napoleon in 1815.

David Ricardo was the third child of a Jewish dealer in financial securities who had emigrated to England, from Holland, a dozen years before David was born. His only 'advanced' schooling consisted of spending the years between the ages of eleven and fourteen at a synagogue school in Amsterdam. Following this he returned to London and began working in his father's business. He fell in love with the daughter of a Quaker and their marriage in 1793 led to a complete break with his family. But David knew enough about the securities and financial markets by then to go into business on his own, so successfully in fact that at the age of forty-two he was able to retire to a modest country estate in Gloucestershire. Before his *Principles of Political Economy and Taxation* appeared in 1817, Ricardo was already well known because of his participation, through newspaper articles and pamphlets, in the controversies over economic policy that punctuated the Napoleonic War period. Not long after the *Principles* was published he obtained a seat in Parliament by lending the owner of the 'rotten borough' of Portarlington, in Ireland, a large sum of money in return for naming him the borough's parliamentary representative. In Parliament Ricardo participated extensively in debates, especially on economic matters. He was also a strong advocate of the extension of the franchise and other measures of parliamentary reform, despite the nature of his own seat.

Ricardo was never completely satisfied with his *Principles* and, indeed, he probably would not have published it at all but for the urging of James Mill, who was, at this time, the leading disciple of Jeremy Bentham and the chief promoter of Bentham's philosophy of utilitarianism. Ricardo did not write at all explicitly about philosophy but I think it is beyond doubt that utilitarianism exerted a very strong influence upon his economic thought, and upon classical political economy in general. Moreover, one of the features that modern neoclassical economics shares with classical political economy is that both are founded upon utilitarian philosophic principles and utilitarian empirical propositions. It was, indeed, in large part through economics that utilitarianism as a philosophy survived the romantic movement of the nineteenth century and remains to this day a powerful element in Western social philosophy. Examination of the connection between classical political economy and utilitarianism is deferred to Chapter 11, where we will study utilitarian theory more comprehensively.

A. VALUE

Ricardo begins his *Principles* by quoting Adam Smith on the distinction between 'value in use' and 'value in exchange'. He agrees with Smith that the two are unrelated and gives the same argument, that some very useful things are low in value and some things of little use are high in value. Thus Ricardo continued Smith's line of thinking on the value problem, which excluded consideration of the demand side of the market process and gave virtually exclusive attention to the conditions of production. Like Smith and other earlier writers, Ricardo accepted the proposition that the day-to-day market price of a commodity is determined by the demand for it in relation to its available supply but, like his predecessors, he did not regard this as being of much interest; the main scientific problem was to analyse the determinants of the general level around which day-to-day prices fluctuate. These 'natural prices' are not affected by demand, so the explanation requires attention only to supply, or the costs of production.

Ricardo saw more clearly than Smith had that in order to eliminate demand considerations from the theory of value something more was required than simply stating the value–usefulness paradox. That something more is the proposition that there is a definite cost of production for a commodity, which does not change as the quantity produced changes. It does not matter whether ten hats or ten million hats are produced, the cost per hat is the same. This view, we should note, is not only empirically implausible, but is not consistent with the law of diminishing returns (which says that the unit cost of production of a commodity varies with the quantity produced). Ricardo was one of the original formulators of this law and, as we shall see, it plays an important role in his theory of rent and in his view of the long-run trend of economic evolution, but, like most of the classical economists, he regarded it as an empirical generalization about the conditions of *agricultural* production; the assumption that the cost of production does not vary as the number of units changes was construed as valid for the manufacturing sector of the economy.

Ricardo tackled the problem of value determination by adopting the theory that Smith had propounded as applicable to a hypothetical 'early and rude state of society' in which there is no capital and no private property in land. As the reader will recall, Smith asserted that, in such a state of affairs, commodities will exchange in proportion to the quantities of labour required to produce them. ('If among a nation of hunters . . . it usually costs twice the labour to kill a beaver as to kill a deer, one beaver should naturally exchange for or be worth two deer,' *Wealth of Nations*, Book I, chapter VI.) Ricardo asserts that this theory of value is correct, but its validity is not restricted to the 'early and rude state'. Smith modified the theory for advanced societies, taking capital costs and land costs into account. Ricardo argued that this modification is unnecessary; in advanced societies, no less than in primitive ones, the relative value of commodities is proportional to the labour required to produce them.

It is important to note, again, that Ricardo is focusing on *relative* values. He does not deny that capital costs are part of the cost of production, but if they affect all costs to an equal degree, then they do not affect *relative* values (land costs are not included, as will be explained in section B below). In speaking of the value of a hat, Ricardo meant its price expressed in terms of another commodity, such as gold, which serves as the value numeraire or standard. Thus Ricardo's labour theory of value means that:

$$\frac{V_h}{V_s} = \frac{L_h}{L_s} \tag{1}$$

That is, the market value of a hat, expressed in terms of the standard commodity, is equal to the quantity of labour required to produce a hat relative to the quantity of labour required to produce a unit of the standard commodity. This being so for all commodities, it follows that the value of any commodity (relative to any or all others) is determined by the (relative) amount of labour required to produce it.

Ricardo knew that there were some severe difficulties with this theory, due to the neglect of capital costs. If capital could be considered as indirect labour pure and simple (we devote labour to producing a loom as an indirect way of making cloth), then capital costs would really be labour costs in another form. But capital costs are incurred *prior to* the production of the final goods (we have to devote labour to producing a loom *before* we can use it to produce cloth). Suppose it takes the same amount of labour to produce a hat as to produce a quart of strawberries, but part of the labour cost in hat production is the labour embodied in the hat factory whereas no such capital is required for strawberry production. (Strawberry gathering, which is not a manufacturing industry, is used here only for convenience to enable one to talk as if one of the industries had *no* capital cost at all.) Under such conditions, if the market value of a hat were the same as the market value of a quart of strawberries no one would produce hats. Why should anyone do so if he could get the same market value by producing strawberries and not have to wait years to recover his capital invested in a factory?

We may take capital costs into account by rewriting equation (1) so:

$$\frac{V_h}{V_s} = \frac{L_h\,W + C_h\,P}{L_s\,W + C_s\,P} \tag{2}$$

C_h and C_s are the per-unit capital costs in the hat industry and the standard-commodity industry respectively. W is the wage rate or the market price of a unit of labour, and P is the market price of a unit of capital, call it the 'profit rate'. (Since the physical units of labour are 'man hours', and for a factory are, say, 'square feet' we have to use W and P to permit aggregation.) In a perfectly competitive economy the wage rate would be the same in both industries, and the profit rate also. Ricardo assumed W and P constant in this sense. Now, under what conditions could the above equation be reduced to a labour theory of value? Ricardo seems to have realized that if the capital–labour ratio is the same in both industries, then this reduction formally follows. Equation (2) may be rewritten as:

$$\frac{V_h}{V_s} = \frac{L_h\left(W + \dfrac{C_h}{L_h}P\right)}{L_s\left(W + \dfrac{C_s}{L_s}P\right)} \tag{3}$$

It is evident that, if $C_h/L_h = C_s/L_s$, then:

$$\frac{V_h}{V_s} = \frac{L_h}{L_s} \tag{4}$$

This appears to be a labour theory of value, but the assumption that enabled us to arrive at equation (4), i.e. that $C_h/L_h = C_s/L_s$, is algebraically equivalent to saying that $L_h/L_s = C_h/C_s$. This means that, if equation (4) is valid, then so is the following:

$$\frac{V_h}{V_s} = \frac{C_h}{C_s} \tag{5}$$

Equation (4) says that the value of a hat, in terms of a standard commodity, is equal to the relative quantities of labour necessary to production in the two industries, while equation (5) says that the value of a hat in terms of the standard is equal to the relative amounts of capital necessary to production in the two industries. If (4) is a 'labour theory of value' then (5) is a 'capital theory of value' and, under the stated assumptions, one is just as valid as the other. In fact neither is a theory of value *determination*. In this phase of Ricardo's thinking all he succeeded in doing was to show some of the problems that attend the *measurement* of values.

An understanding of what is involved in equations (4) and (5) and how they relate to value measurement rather than value determination may be clarified by a simple illustration. If we are interested in ascertaining the *relative* number of cows in two fields, we could count the cows and observe that if, say, there are thirty cows in field A and ten in field B, then there are three times as many in A as in B. But if we counted the cows' horns or their hoofs we would get the same answer:

$$\frac{30}{10} = \frac{60}{20} = \frac{120}{40} = 3$$

The reason why this works, of course, is that *every* cow has one body, two horns, and four hoofs. The body–horns–hoofs ratios are the same for all cows, just as the labour–capital ratio is presumed the same for all industries in arriving at equations (4) and (5). It is true that the relative number of cows in the two fields can be *measured* by counting horns or hoofs but it would clearly be misleading to say that this is *determined* by the numbers of horns or hoofs. In the same way, given the assumption of labour–capital uniformity, the relative value of two commodities can be measured by counting the labour inputs or the capital inputs but neither can be regarded, by itself, as determining their relative value. To use another illustration: consider the relation between the number of hydrogen atoms and oxygen atoms in a water molecule. We could count the number of water molecules in a beaker by counting the number of oxygen atoms, or by counting the hydrogen atoms and dividing by two. If someone were to say that the amount of water in the beaker is determined by the amount of, say, oxygen, one might accept such a statement, but not if he went on to claim that more water would be produced if more oxygen were added. The labour theory of value has often been used to argue precisely this: that the quantity of value created in an economic process is determined by the quantity of labour employed in it, and more value is produced if more labour is used.

In addition to the theoretical problems it generates, the assumption of labour–capital uniformity is empirically incorrect. Ricardo was aware of this and, in order to sustain his theory of value, he argued that, although the ratios are not exactly the same, the labour cost is much greater than the capital cost in all industries. If this is so, then relative values are not precisely equal to relative labour inputs but *nearly* so and one can proceed to treat equation (4) as a satisfactory working approximation. Ricardo tended to lose sight of this modification in the rest of his economic theory but not to the degree that many of his successors did. The labour theory of value, as a strict economic law, not as an empirical approximation, became one of the most important propositions in nineteenth-century social science and social philosophy. The most influential line of thought stemming from this proposition will be examined when we study Karl Marx in Chapter 13, but a brief comment on the impact of the labour theory of value on political thought before Marx is appropriate here.

In the 1820's there arose in England a new and important strain of radical philosophy which differed from the long-standing utopian tradition in two ways: first, instead of depicting the excellence of an imaginary perfect social order, it focused on the miseries and injustices of the existing world; and secondly, its main argument was derived from economic theory, not directly from political philosophy and political theory. The term 'socialism' came into existence during this period, but it was not the utopian socialism of Thomas More; it was a socialism that purported to be based upon science, the science of political economy. The radical writers of this period have been called by historians 'Ricardian socialists', which is somewhat misleading, since most of them were severely critical of Ricardo and regarded his *Principles* as offering support for the *status quo* and justifying its notorious evils. Historians who have adopted this term emphasize the use made by these radical writers of the labour theory of value. Ricardo's theory, as we have seen, was hedged around with qualifications and ambiguities but it did highlight the role of labour in production and perhaps in this way acted as a stimulus to the radical thinking of the 1820's.

If one takes the view that economic science has proved that labour creates all value it is relatively straightforward to claim that labourers should receive all the value and, if they do not, to contend that they are being exploited. (We should note in passing that this sequence of argument does not disprove David Hume's contention that an ethical proposition cannot be derived direct from a factual proposition; an intermediate ethical premise is implicit in the argument: that the right to receive value is justified by, and only by, one's contribution to production.) This contention is one of the two main economic foundations of the nineteenth-century socialist movement; the other is the theory of rent, which we shall see in the next section owes even more to Ricardo than the labour theory of value does.

We noted earlier, in Chapter 5, that the Physiocrats had initiated the procedure of differentiating the members of society into economically defined classes. This was continued by Adam Smith and David Ricardo (although they defined the classes differently) and became a fundamental feature of classical political economy. The significance of this in the present connection is that it leads to the construal of exploitation in terms of class relationships: if one argues that the labour *class* creates all value, the associated ethical proposition is that this *class* is exploited if, as a collectivity, it does not receive all value. This is the foundation for the view that the socioeconomic order that Marx called 'capitalism' is characterized by class exploitation and class conflict. Because this essential feature of Marx's theory was anticipated by the 'Ricardian socialists', some historians regard their role in the history of social thought as precursors of Marxism. But even if Marx and Engels had never lived it was inevitable (or as inevitable as such things can be) that the newly developing science of political economy would be linked to general social theory and social philosophy, and it was highly likely that the labour theory of value would be employed, sooner or later, as a supportive proposition for a policy of radical social change. But whether 'inevitable' or 'highly likely' or not, this did in fact become a major role of economics in the development of nineteenth-century social philosophy.

John Stuart Mill, whose *Principles of Political Economy* (1848) became the authoritative statement of classical economics, called attention to the centrality of the theory of value in the following passage:

> In a state of society . . . in which the industrial system is entirely founded on purchase and sale, each individual, for the most part, living not on things in the production of which he himself bears a part, but on things obtained by a double exchange, a sale followed by a purchase – the question of Value is fundamental. Almost every speculation respecting the economical interests of a society thus constituted implies some theory of Value: the smallest error on that subject infects with corresponding error all our other conclusions; and anything vague or misty in our conception of it creates confusion and uncertainty in everything else.

The modern economist would cheer Mill heartily for expressing a vital point so forcefully. However, his approval would be quickly stifled, for Mill goes on to say:

> Happily, there is nothing in the laws of value which remains for the present or any future writer to clear up; the theory of the subject is complete . . . (*Principles*, III, 1, 2)

Mill was here referring to Ricardo's theory of value, which he adopted without significant amendment. His estimate of its merits expressed in this passage qualifies as one of the biggest howlers in the history of the social sciences. Far from being 'complete' and needing no revision, the explanation of market values by Ricardo was the most serious flaw in the classical economic model. That model retained acceptance, despite the weaknesses that many critics noted, because no alternative theory of value was advanced to replace Ricardo's until the development of the theory of 'marginal utility' in the last quarter of the nineteenth century (see below, Chapter 17 A). As in the natural sciences, a theory in the social sciences cannot be destroyed by mere criticism; whatever its deficiencies may be, only the construction of a better theory will remove it from the kitbag of cognitive instruments that men use in attempting to understand a complex world.

B. RENT

Numerous writers before Ricardo, and even before Adam Smith, regarded income derived from land ownership as requiring special theoretical attention, not only because it was the income of the dominant social class, but because the production factor that is the source of rent (land) apparently differed from other factors (labour and capital) in being permanently fixed in amount. But although some of these early economists made perceptive suggestions, it was Ricardo who first clearly formulated a cogent theory of rent and incorporated it into a comprehensive model of the economy. The Physiocrats of the 1760's construed rent as a production 'surplus' that is due to the employment in agriculture of factors that are free, such as rain and sunlight. Rent, according to Ricardo, is a kind of surplus; it is not due, however, to the munificence of nature in supplying free rain and sunlight, but to the limitation in the amount of fertile land. In developing his theory Ricardo utilized the idea of diminishing returns and did so in a way that foreshadowed the marginal analysis of neoclassical economics. Unlike the theory of value, modern textbooks in economics typically present rent theory in a form that differs little from Ricardo's original analysis.

A simple way to describe Ricardo's theory of rent is to consider the production of a standard commodity, such as wheat, on plots of land that differ from one another in natural fertility. (This is a simple way, but it is misleading if not modified, as I shall immediately go on to do.) Suppose that there are two equal-sized plots of different fertility; the application of a given quantity of labour and capital to the two plots will yield different amounts of wheat or, to put it differently, the cost (in terms of labour and capital applied) of a bushel of wheat will differ on the two plots. Thus, using illustrative numbers and measuring in dollars, the labour and capital costs per bushel might be:

    On plot A: $5.00
    On plot B: $7.00

In such a situation, two things are evident: plot B would not be used unless the market value of wheat were at least $7.00 per bushel; and if the market value of wheat were $7.00 per bushel, production on plot A would yield a surplus of $2.00 per bushel over cost. Suppose now that we are describing a community in which one class of people own all the land and the class that actually cultivate it are tenant farmers who rent land from the landlords. A farmer would be willing to pay any amount less than $2.00 per bushel to a landlord for plot A rather than use plot B free of charge. Thus the surplus of value over cost will accrue to the landlord as rent. If the land were owned by the farmers themselves, the $2.00 surplus would still exist, but the farmer who owned plot A would receive it himself. So rent, as an economic element, does not depend on who owns the land. The legal title to land determines who receives rent, but rent, in itself, is the consequence of differential fertility. This led to later writers characterizing Ricardo's theory as a theory of 'differential rent'.

But as I warned above, this presentation can be misleading. We can see why if we ask why plot B should be used at all. Why not produce more wheat on plot A by applying more labour and capital to it? The answer is that this is restricted by the operation of the law of diminishing returns: more wheat could be raised on plot A but only by increasing the input of labour and capital more than proportionately. Or, to put it differently, the additional bushels of wheat would cost more to produce. Again, using illustrative numbers and measuring in dollars, the labour and capital costs of production on, say, plot A considered by itself might be:

First bushel: $5.00
Second bushel: $6.00
Third bushel: $7.00

It is evident that three bushels would be raised only if the price of wheat were $7.00 per bushel, since, if it were less, say $6.50, the market value of the third bushel would not cover its cost of production. But if wheat sells for $7.00 per bushel then the aggregate value of three bushels (3 × $7.00 = $21.00) exceeds the aggregate cost of producing them ($5.00 + $6.00 + $7.00 = $18.00). This difference of $3.00, the surplus of value over cost, is Ricardian 'rent'. It is now clear that the crucial condition that generates rent is the assumption that the cost of production of the additional units of output (the 'marginal' cost in neo-classical terminology) rises as more is produced. This is the law of diminishing returns (or increasing cost).

If we put both our illustrations together it is evident that at a wheat price of $7.00 per bushel plot A would yield rent and plot B would not, and this is, indeed, due to their differential fertility. But the root cause of rent is that the 'fertility' of plot A is not constant, because its incremental, or 'marginal', productivity declines as it is cultivated more intensively.

We can now see why Ricardo insisted that rent is not a determinant of market value. The price of wheat in the above illustrations is not $7.00 because rent is paid for plot A. On the contrary, plot A yields rent because the price is $7.00. So high rents are due to high prices, they do not cause prices to be high. Adam Smith had treated rent as one of the components of market value in an 'advanced' society, no different in this respect from wages and profits. It is interesting that David Hume, reading the *Wealth of Nations* upon its publication in 1776, wrote to Smith with lavish congratulations, but demurred on his treatment of rent as a component of price. Hume may have had the essentials of Ricardo's theory in mind, but the notes he wrote on the *Wealth of Nations* during the remaining few months of his life were destroyed, so we cannot know. The law of diminishing returns was clearly stated by Turgot as early as 1768, but it was Ricardo who first built a significant theory upon it.

As we have seen in section A above, Ricardo treated manufacturing as not subject to diminishing returns and therefore not generating a rent surplus. He applied his rent theory to all of agriculture, but he saw special significance in the operation of diminishing returns in the production of wheat and other food grains ('corn', as these are generically called in England). Why this is especially significant will be evident when we consider his theory of wages and economic development below. The restriction of diminishing returns to agriculture, and emphasis upon its importance in food production, were responsible for one of the main lines of social thought of the nineteenth century and for one of the most dramatic controversies over economic policy of all time, the great debate over the 'Corn Laws' (tariffs on imported food), but they were also responsible for a serious misdirection of economic theory which was not amended until the law of diminishing returns was generalized to apply to all forms of production in the late nineteenth century. Ricardo strongly emphasized the importance of the law of diminishing returns, but its significance for economic theory was even greater than he thought.

In the *Wealth of Nations* Adam Smith reserves his harshest comments for the monopolist, the businessman who captures exclusive control of the production or sale of a commodity and eliminates competition. He had mainly in mind the monopolist whose power to control a market was due to special privileges awarded to him by the government in the form of franchises, patents, etc. Ricardo perceived that a monopoly, or something akin to it, could spring from 'natural' circumstances as well as from legal privileges. If land is naturally fixed in quantity, then its owners have a kind of monopoly. Individual landowners may be in competition with one another in their dealings with tenant farmers, but competition among the tenants assures that, whatever the rent surplus is, the owners of land will receive it. 'Rent,' says Ricardo, is 'not a creation, but merely a transfer of wealth.' One of the effects of his theory of rent was to redirect the animosity towards commercial monopolists so evident in Smith's *Wealth of Nations* against the landlord class.

It seems highly likely that a movement against the political power and social position of the landed class would have developed in nineteenth-century England even if Ricardo had never constructed his theory of rent, but Ricardo provided what many people construed as a *scientific* rationale for reforms that were widely regarded as politically desirable and morally justified. Once again we see political economy cast in the role of furnishing a scientific foundation for value judgements. Before we pursue this further, we should note four points.

Ricardo was wrong in declaring rent to be a 'transfer' of wealth. This is so only where landlords own land while others cultivate it. In a society where farmers own the land they cultivate, as in large parts of America, Ricardian rent still exists but it is not 'transferred'. The significance of this is that one must distinguish between the economic phenomenon of rent and the institutional and legal arrangements that determine who is to receive it. In itself rent cannot be regarded as just or unjust, any more than a gas that obeys Boyle's law can; the issue of justice has to do with who *ought* to benefit from it.

Secondly, Ricardo was wrong in regarding land as unique in being limited in supply. This characteristic is also true of other factors of production, even human ones. A great baseball player is limited in supply, and most of his large income is what economists call 'rent', even though others call it 'salary'. This feature of rent was not clearly realized by economists until the late nineteenth century, when Alfred Marshall pointed out that rent-like incomes are very common and, as he put it, land rent is merely 'the leading species of a large genus'.

Thirdly, rent is a phenomenon that depends upon demand as well as on the conditions of supply. Land yields rent only when there is a strong demand for its products. A great baseball player receives a high income because many people are willing to pay admission to baseball games. Land in the Nevada desert is physically limited in amount but yields no rent because there is little demand for it; a person who is exceptionally proficient at badminton cannot command a notably high income because the sport does not attract many paying viewers. So, we see, in his theory of rent Ricardo smuggled back in the demand considerations that had been excluded in his main theory of value.

Finally, rent *is* part of the cost of production of a commodity when we recognize that land has alternative uses. In the illustration above the total value of the three bushels of wheat produced on plot A is $21.00. If the plot is used for a housing site, $21.00 worth of wheat is sacrificed, so, in that sense, it is part of the cost of the housing. This point was not fully realized until the neoclassical economists developed the concept of 'alternative cost' in the late nineteenth century.

Just as Ricardo's theory of value led to an important line of radical social thought, so also did his theory of rent. The idea that the land of the nation should be owned by the government goes back well before Ricardo; for example, a book by Thomas Spence published in 1775 had argued this. But Ricardo's theory gave it a degree of intellectual support that it had not previously possessed. There were various land nationalization movements during the nineteenth century, numbering among their supporters many prominent people. John Stuart Mill was one such; another was A. R. Wallace, the independent co-discoverer (along with Charles Darwin) of the natural selection theory of organic evolution, who for many years was president of the Land Nationalization Society. The less radical idea that land rent should be a special object of taxation was argued by the Physiocrats in the 1760's. In the early nineteenth century James Mill used his influential position on the staff of the East India Company to promote a taxation system for India designed to transfer the rent of land to the public treasury. The inspiration for Mill's policy was Ricardo's theory of rent, not the vague surplus idea of François Quesnay. Ricardian rent theory was also the direct intellectual inspiration of the most influential of the land tax theories, the single-tax doctrine of Henry George. George, an American, published his *Progress and Poverty* in 1879 and during the next three decades it sold in astounding numbers in England and America. In fact it is the only book on economics ever to have been included on the standard list of publishing's 'best sellers'. Single-tax societies still exist today in the United States, though their public impact is nothing like it was in the era when many hoped (and others feared) that the movement was growing powerful enough to initiate far-reaching reforms in the economic order through the use of the fiscal power of the state.

Henry George himself was not really a radical. He felt that land rent was virtually the only important flaw in the capitalistic economy, and if it were corrected all else could be left unchanged. The most important radical movement inspired by Ricardian rent theory was the British Fabian Society, whose most prominent members were Sidney Webb and George Bernard Shaw. The latter is remembered today as the greatest English dramatist of the early twentieth century (and perhaps the greatest since Shakespeare) but he also knew a good deal of economics and was especially impressed by the theory of rent. Shaw and Webb, and others in the Fabian Society, were favourably disposed towards Marx and Engels but the Society played an important role in turning socialism away from Marxian revolutionary doctrine towards the democratic reformism adopted by the British Labour Party and similar movements in other countries. It is not too much of an exaggeration to say that the two major streams of modern socialism both found their sources in theories of David Ricardo: the revolutionary stream in his labour theory of value and the reformist stream in his theory of rent.

C. POPULATION

The question of population growth (or decline) – the analysis of its governing determinants, the prognosis of its consequences, and the debate over what (if anything) should be done about it, by individuals, or by the state and other social institutions – is one of the largest, most comprehensive, and most enduring topics in the history of social thought. Since the eighteenth century it has been the subject of a continuous debate that has extended well beyond the boundaries of even the broadest conception of social science. At one frontier, so to speak, it encounters or articulates with biology, since an important part of that science is the study of organic reproduction and the determinants of the populations of all organisms (man included) within a comprehensive ecological system. At another frontier it encounters religion, which, though it has given up much territory to social science in the past three centuries, has not abandoned its claim of special authority to render judgement on matters connected with human procreation. In a more complete history than this book aims to be, a large chapter would have to be devoted to the development of the theoretical modelling and empirical study of human populations by social scientists, and the interaction of their work with biology, theology, religion, and politics. Here we are devoting only a few pages to the subject within a chapter on classical political economy. The reason for this is that, though the modern investigation of the determinants and consequences of population growth was initiated independently of political economy, by Robert Malthus, the specific theory of population advanced by him was utilized by Ricardo as a main pillar in constructing a general theory of economic development. How Malthus's population theory fits into Ricardo's model will be sketched in the next section. The present section will outline and clarify the argument presented by Malthus in his seminal *Essay on the Principle of Population* (1798).

First, a bit of historical background. Attempts to ascertain the population of a country (probably for taxation or military purposes) are among the most ancient exercises in empirical social science. The most famous, of course, is the census of the Roman province of Judaea ordered by the emperor Caesar Augustus, which, requiring that the people should register personally in their ancestral places, occasioned the journey of Mary and Joseph to Bethlehem, where Jesus was born. Despite such early efforts, however, data on population size, even for a small area, were very unreliable before the late eighteenth century. A modern work on historical demography will give data on the population of the world at the beginning of the Christian era, for 8000 B.C., A.D. 1600, and other dates, but these are estimates made by twentieth-century demographers. Such estimates show that world population (with some major interruptions such as the period of the Black Death in the fourteenth century) has grown greatly since 'ancient times' and that the growth rate began to accelerate significantly in the late seventeenth century. But this was not known at the time. Debate over the trend of population was part of the 'ancient versus modern' controversy of the eighteenth century referred to in Chapter 8 A, with notable contributions by such outstanding figures as Montesquieu, who thought that population had declined, and David Hume, who thought it had risen. Hume's argument, presented with great skill but with little hard data in his essay 'Of the Populousness of Ancient Nations' (1752), ran counter to contemporary common opinion of the matter. Not until data began to become available in the 1760's did the view spread that population was growing. By the time Malthus wrote, the empirical controversy was over and attention had shifted to the analysis of the factors governing the size of population.

Accompanying the realization that population was growing, a change in concern occurred. When it was widely believed that population was declining, most writers, and statesmen, emphasized the dangers of depopulation and the necessity of taking measures to combat it. For example, Mirabeau, who later became the chief disciple of Quesnay, was popularly known as 'the friend of man' after the title of a book he had written, *L'Ami des hommes, ou traité de la population* (1756), in which he contended that the chief duty of a government is to promote the growth of the nation's population. But by the 1770's it was no longer clear that one acted as a 'friend of man' by promoting an increase in his numbers. Most writers began to stress the dangers of overpopulation.

Among the numerous predecessors of Malthus who argued that population tends to increase, two deserve some notice in passing. Robert

Wallace, in his *Numbers of Mankind* (1753), proceeded in a purely theoretical fashion, calculating the number of people that would result from a single pair on different assumptions as to procreation, life span, etc. Malthus's famous assertion that, if unconstrained by any 'difficulty of obtaining subsistence', population would grow 'geometrically' was clearly stated almost a half-century earlier by Wallace. In this period, the North American continent was regarded by many as a concrete instance of an environment that imposed no constraints on population growth, or nearly so. Benjamin Franklin published a pamphlet in Boston entitled *Observations Concerning the Increase of Mankind and the Peopling of Countries* (1755), arguing that the American population tended to increase geometrically, doubling every twenty-five years. His main object was to show that, before long, there would be more Englishmen in America than in England (where population growth was constrained), in order to persuade the British government to alter its colonial policies and recognize the just grievances of the American subjects of the Crown.

Malthus acknowledged in the first edition of his *Essay* that there were numerous others who had already put forward the same population growth argument and specifically named Wallace, along with David Hume and Adam Smith, in this regard. In later editions he used Franklin's figure of a twenty-five-year doubling time as the specific 'geometrical rate' for an unconstrained population. But, in the history of ideas, precursors are only precursors. It was Malthus's *Essay* that really ignited interest in the population question. So far as economic theory is concerned, the population growth thesis that Ricardo derived from reading Malthus supplied him with an element that was necessary to complete his theory of economic development.

Thomas Robert Malthus (1766–1835) was born into a comfortable middle-class family. His father, Daniel Malthus, had inherited enough wealth to permit him to follow a life of leisure, and to interest himself in the contemporary literature on philosophy and social questions. He was particularly attracted to writers with grand comprehensive views of society and radical proposals for its fundamental reconstitution. He admired the writings of William Godwin and the Marquis de Condorcet and befriended Rousseau (or tried to) when he sought political asylum in England. The two Malthuses, father and son, had many friendly arguments over the contemporary utopian or 'perfectibilist' literature that was part of a great wave of speculative social theory initiated by the French Revolution, and it was out of these discussions that Robert Malthus developed the ideas embodied in his famous book. Its full title was *An Essay on the Principle of Population as it Affects the Future Improvement of Society, with Remarks on the Speculations of Mr. Godwin, M. Condorcet and other Writers* (1798). At the time he wrote it, Malthus, an ordained minister in the Church of England, was curate of a parish in Surrey, and a fellow of Jesus College, Cambridge, where he had graduated in 1788 with honours in mathematics. The *Essay* was published anonymously but the name of its author soon became known and famous (or infamous, depending on one's reaction to the book). In 1804 he was offered the professorship in 'Modern History and Political Economy' at the East India Company's newly founded training college, where he remained for the rest of his life.

Malthus's position in the growing company of economists was second only to Ricardo's, with whom he formed a close friendship. They disagreed on almost every point in economic theory, except population, but it was Ricardo's views on value, rent, and other matters that became the accepted propositions of classical political economy. Until the work of John Maynard Keynes in the 1930's, which revived interest in Malthus as a precursor of the Keynesian theory of unemployment, the only role Malthus was accorded in the history of economics was as the originator of the classical theory of population. Malthus himself regarded the main point of the *Essay* to be his critique of the utopianist theories of Godwin and Condorcet, which occupied more than a third of its length. He was surprised to find, upon its publication that he had won fame as a social scientist, not just as a trenchant critic of speculative writers on the perfect social order.

After some brief initial remarks on 'the speculations of the perfectibility of man and society' Malthus begins his argument by laying down two 'fixed laws' of human nature: 'First, that food is necessary to the existence of man' and secondly, that 'the passion between the sexes is necessary'. Then, after a brief reference to Godwin's 'unphilosophical' (i.e. unscientific) speculations concerning the moderation of the sexual passion, he goes on to write one of the most frequently quoted passages in the history of social science:

> Assuming, then, my postulata as granted, I say, that the power of population is indefinitely greater than the power in the earth to produce subsistence for man.
>
> Population, when unchecked, increases in a geometrical ratio. Subsistence increases only in an arithmetical ratio. A slight acquaintance with numbers will shew the immensity of the first power over the second.

The application of the concept of 'geometric' growth to human population was not original with Malthus, as we have seen. To this familiar idea Malthus added the concept, also mathematical, of a law of 'arithmetical' growth for 'subsistence'. As a result, the whole argument wore a scientific aspect, being based on fixed laws of nature and expressed in mathematical terms. If Malthus's theory of population consisted, however, of nothing more than the juxtaposition of the two ratios it would be totally empty. The fact that the ratios are often referred to, even today, as the 'Malthusian theory of population' perhaps testifies to the tendency of modern science to worship mathematics in an uncritical fashion.

When Malthus talked of 'subsistence' he mainly meant man's food, which is also derived from organisms that reproduce. The capacity to reproduce is 'geometrical' in all organisms, and in those that humans use for food the reproductive potential is much greater and more rapid than man's. A wheat plant can reproduce itself fifty times over in a single year. If we were to start at year zero with, say, ten wheat plants and five pairs of humans, and each species reproduced at its full biotic potential, the humans would die from being smothered by wheat, not from lack of enough of it to eat. But, obviously, this is just mathematical play; it has little to do with the factors that explain the size of human population in the real world. Malthus's ratios are impressive but they are, at best, a statement of the *problem* that a theory must solve; they do not constitute an *explanation* of population. I say 'at best' because the problem would still exist even if human population growth were arithmetical. The area of the earth being fixed, unlimited growth of population at *any* rate will eventually produce a problem, since the area *per person* will decrease continuously as the number of persons increases. Geometric population growth simply means that this limit will be approached more rapidly than if the growth were arithmetic.

Malthus resorted to the ratios several times in his *Essay* and it is perhaps overgenerous to interpret him as merely using them as a dramatic statement of the problem. Nevertheless there is a real theory (an explanation of the determinants of population) in the *Essay*, and it is this, not the ratios, that makes it an important book in the history of social science, and the origin of a basic element in classical political economy. The main point is made by Malthus in a remark that almost immediately follows the passage quoted above: 'This implies a strong and constantly operating check on population from the difficulty of subsistence.' In a nutshell, population does not in fact grow at its biotic potential; it is controlled by the availability of food. Malthus was not arguing that this would control population in the future. He made it clear that, in his view, this factor had always acted as the governor of population. That is to say, he was not merely pointing to a problem that would arise if population continued to grow; he was offering a general explanatory theory. Well before Malthus wrote, Voltaire had pointed out that the contemporary enthusiasm for treating population as naturally growing geometrically must be wrong, since, if it were so, the world would have been overpopulated long since. Malthus's theory of population is not a prediction, but an effort to explain why overpopulation, in the gross sense of literal physical overcrowding, had not already occurred and why it never can occur. In short it is a theory of why overpopulation, in this gross sense, is impossible.

The theory is essentially very simple. There is a certain quantity of food that is necessary to sustain a man and woman and permit them to raise two children to maturity. This is what Malthus calls 'subsistence'. If the production of food (*per capita*) is greater than subsistence, more than two children will be raised and the population will grow; if production is less than subsistence, the population will decline; if production is just equal to subsistence, the population will be stable.

So far so good, but Malthus wanted to go further and argue that 'population must always be kept down to the level of the means of subsistence'. In short he contended that a stable population, neither growing nor declining, is the equilibrium point of two forces, the capacity to procreate and the ability to produce food. The theory is another example of the early use of the concept of equilibrium in the methodology of economic analysis. Malthus regarded this balancing of forces as 'an obvious truth' as he put it in the preface to the *Essay*, but it is not so obvious. Food is produced by human effort. Why cannot additional people produce additional food? As one early critic of Malthus put it, 'Does not God send two hands with every stomach?' The answer, of course, is that God does not also send additional land, so, as population grows, the ratio of land to labour (as factors of production) decreases, and though the output of food is increased it does not increase in proportion with the population. Doubling the population (and, consequently, the labour available) will increase food production but it will not double it, so *per capita* food production will decline.

Malthus's theory is incomplete without showing why more people cannot raise proportionately more food. This missing piece is the law of diminishing returns. There are a few places in the first edition of the *Essay* where Malthus seems to have this idea in mind, but they are very vague and are significant only to a reader who already knows what he should have been saying. In later editions he is more explicit, and in the discussion of population in his *Principles of Political Economy* (1820) he focuses upon the law of diminishing returns and does not even mention the geometric and arithmetic ratios. The version of population theory that Ricardo and his followers used was based explicitly on the proposition that the law of diminishing returns is an inescapable property of agricultural production.

Before we go on we should note that, even with the law of diminishing returns, the theory fails to carry conviction to the empirically minded modern reader, since population and *per capita* production of food have both increased greatly since Malthus's time. The reason is that we have experienced since then a great improvement in the technology of food production. With fewer farmers more food is raised than before. The law of diminishing returns applies only to production with a *given* technology. Of course, it still remains true that, whatever improvements take place in food production, population cannot increase indefinitely; eventually the world would become over-populated in the gross sense, since its area is fixed.

But Malthus, as I have pointed out, was not talking about what will happen in the remote future. The constant pressure of population against subsistence is, in his view, 'one of the general laws of animated nature'. God governs the world, but does so by establishing such laws, 'And since the world began, the causes of population and depopulation have probably been as constant as any of the laws of nature with which we are acquainted.' Again we see the effort of the early social scientists to discover 'laws' of the same sort that Galileo,

Kepler, and Newton had. 'The constancy of the laws of nature and of effects and causes,' says Malthus, 'is the foundation of all human knowledge,' even though one must grant that God can change the laws if he so wishes. Malthus's *Essay* is a prime example of the eighteenth-century view that the assumption that the world is law-governed is essential to the exercise of rational thought in the investigation of empirical phenomena. There can be no science and no scientific method without such an assumption. Malthus's *Essay* embraced this view and, it is worth special note, applied it to a phenomenon involving matters that people were becoming reluctant to discuss, sex and procreation. It came just in time. A generation later sexual prudery had become so great that it might have been impossible to investigate the determinants of population if Malthus had not already established it as a central problem of social science. The freedom of discussion of such matters that was part of the eighteenth-century Enlightenment was not to be experienced again until the middle of the twentieth century.

Throughout this discussion I have been speaking of Malthusian population theory as a contribution to social science. But up to this point nothing has been said that would indicate any distinction between the laws governing human population and those governing the populations of other animals. If man's procreative potential is such that population always presses against the food supply, then the factors determining population are biological, not social. In the *Essay* Malthus evinces the same ambiguity about the nature of man that we noticed in discussing the Scottish moralists in Chapter 7. On the one hand, man is an animal; on the other, he is different from all other animals. Reading Malthus, one sometimes receives the impression that he regards man, so far as population is concerned, as nothing more than a gastro-intestinal tract and a reproductive system, the one ingesting food, the other producing gametes. But unless one is determined to read him prejudicially, it is plain that, like the Scots, he regarded man as differing from the other animals in being a rational creature. If the capacity for reason has any power to control procreation, however, then human population size is not solely, or perhaps even mainly, determined by biological factors.

This aspect of the question makes an oblique appearance in the first edition of Malthus's *Essay* and a more direct one in the second (1803). In the first edition he speaks of population as controlled by 'fear of misery' as well as by 'misery' itself. If man uses his powers of reason to foresee the consequences of unlimited procreation he can avoid those consequences by limiting his procreation. Condorcet, whom Malthus criticized as a visionary utopianist, had foreseen the danger of unlimited population growth and contended that in the perfect society procreation would be controlled by contraception. Malthus pays no attention to this but recognizes, in the first edition of the *Essay*, that sexual passions can be gratified by prostitution and other 'vicious practices' that do not have the same procreational consequences as 'regular unions' of men and women. In the second edition he adds another control, 'moral restraint', by which he means sexual abstinence, not apparently being aware that, by doing so, he has undermined the significance of one of his 'laws' of human nature, the constancy of the 'passion between the sexes'. These amendments to the theory turn it from a biological theory into an economic one, since, as the modern economist would say, the number of children produced becomes a matter of rationally weighing the benefits and costs of marriage and family. But in fact the theory, from the beginning, had contained sociological elements of fundamental importance in its use of the concept of 'subsistence'.

Malthus, and Ricardo after him, frequently treated 'subsistence' as man's physiological requirement of food. But even the labouring class, at this time, spent only about half its income on food. Of course, in northern Europe clothing and shelter are as necessary to life as food, but the point is that, when one looks carefully at the texts, it appears that the early writers had in mind a minimum standard of living established by *custom*, not by physiological requirements even broadly construed, when they spoke of 'subsistence'. This becomes clear beyond any reasonable doubt in Ricardo's *Principles*, where he speaks of the worker's subsistence wage as 'the quantity of food, necessaries, and conveniences become essential to him from habit', and notes that this differs in different countries (even of similar climates) where there are 'different habits of living', and 'varies at different times in the same country'. All the leading classical economists held such a sociological conception of subsistence. Ricardo's emphasis upon food production reflects only the difficulty of incorporating such sociological factors into an analytical model, disregarding them being another of his unrealistic assumptions adopted for heuristic purposes. But this was responsible for the widespread view that the classical economists advanced an 'iron law of wages', the notion that there is no possibility of a permanent rise of the working-class standard of living above physiological requirements. In fact, however, it opened a new view of that problem, one that was much more optimistic. If the standard of living of the working class could be raised, and kept high for a long enough period, the customary conception of 'subsistence' would be raised and this, in itself, would act as an effective control on population. Instead of the population growing whenever wages exceeded subsistence, the conception of 'subsistence' could rise instead. This view was forcefully argued by John Stuart Mill, who was more concerned than any other major classical economist about the danger of overpopulation, but saw a remedy: raise the working man's aspirations for himself and his family, facilitate his desire to limit procreation by the dissemination of contraceptive knowledge and devices, and sway those who may still not be sufficiently motivated, by propaganda and social pressures against large families.

Since the later eighteenth century, discussion of the proper role of the state in regard to population has usually been motivated by fear of overpopulation. An aspect of this worth some notice here is state policy with respect to the poor. Chapter V of Malthus's *Essay* is a sustained attack on contemporary poverty policy. In it one will find all the criticisms heard today of the modern welfare system: its high administrative costs, that it encourages dependence rather than self-reliance, that it assists many who are not really needy, and promotes procreation and overpopulation. The English system of poverty relief at the time operated under a statute enacted three centuries before, at the end of the reign of Elizabeth I, which obligated each parish to support its poor from funds obtained by local taxation. Malthus was not alone in contending that the system, by encouraging indigence and population growth, was creating poverty in the process of ameliorating it. This was argued by many commentators in a great debate over the Poor Law that was already under way when Malthus's *Essay* was published, accelerated after the defeat of Napoleon in 1815, and reached a zenith with the creation of a Royal Commission of inquiry in 1832 and the subsequent passage of the Poor Law Amendment Act in 1834.

During the period from Waterloo to 1834, approximately 80 per cent of local tax revenue in England and Wales was expended on poor relief. There was little left for anything else at a time of growing need for new roads and streets, town lighting and cleaning, water and sewer services, etc. This alone would have meant that something would have to be done, sooner or later, about local finance and the burden of poor relief. The debate, as it increased in intensity, focused heavily on the Poor Law, and the opposition to the existing law became increasingly identified with the new science of political economy and its theory of population. Ricardo spoke of the 'pernicious tendency' of the Poor Law in his *Principles* and advocated the gradual abolition of the poor relief system. James Mill, also well known as a 'political economist', was severely critical of the existing system. But the most prominent figure was one whose name is familiar today only to historians of economics: Nassau W. Senior. He was the first person to occupy a professorship in political economy at a major British university – he was appointed to the newly established Drummond professorship at Oxford in 1825. He was active in politics and public affairs, and what he said was widely taken to reflect the established or orthodox theories of political economy. So when he was appointed a member of the Poor Law Commission it was natural to presume that he would represent the new science in its deliberations. Senior became the leading member of the Commission and played the major role in drafting the Bill that became the Poor Law Amendment Act.

Senior was convinced that the old Poor Law was pernicious, but he did not base this judgement on Malthusian population theory, which, unlike most other classical economists, he rejected. It is ironic that the Amendment Act was widely viewed as inspired by 'Malthusianism' and Senior frequently stigmatized as the arch-Malthusian of all political economists. We now come to the main point of this digression on the Poor Law: the debate surrounding the amendment of 1834 was the first occasion in history on which the contenders appealed to, or opposed, an argument that was purported to be based upon social *science*. Those who favoured the Amendment Act invoked the authority of political economy; those who opposed it felt it necessary to denigrate political economy and to ridicule its pretensions. Thus the debate over the Poor Law became, in significant part, a debate over the status of political economy as such. The London *Times* led the way on one side of the debate: it thundered against the Amendment Act and lost no opportunity to express its contempt for political economy. Charles Dickens, whose *Oliver Twist* became the classic critique of the Act's policy, did not disguise the low opinion he held of political economy. On the other side, Harriet Martineau, famous for illustrating the principles of political economy in a series of short novels that were widely admired as 'improving' literature (see below, Chapter 10 B), directed her talents to the support of the Royal Commission's recommendations by writing a series of four similar novels on the evils of the Poor Law, sponsored by the Society for the Diffusion of Useful Knowledge, which had taken upon itself the duty of disseminating the principles of political economy to the public at large.

We cannot devote much space in this book to the history of the role of social science in public debate and the formation of public policy. It must suffice to note here that this history began with the great debate over the Poor Law, which also contained some general features that were destined to become permanent: the attempt on the part of one faction to argue that its policy proposals are beyond question because they were 'scientific'; and the attempt on the part of another to oppose such proposals, not by criticizing the specific arguments and evidence advanced on their behalf, but by a general denigration of social science, or one of its branches. The natural sciences have, to a considerable degree, transcended this kind of factionalism. Even the modern religious opponents of the theory of evolution feel that it is necessary to criticize the substance of the theory, not the merits of biology as such. But economics, sociology, and other social sciences, have not succeeded in detaching themselves from ideological disputes and the conflicts of political factions. In all probability, they never will. This alone is perhaps sufficient to make the social sciences different from the natural sciences.

D. THE MODEL OF ECONOMIC DEVELOPMENT

In Chapter 8 we noted the importance of the idea of 'progress' in modern Western intellectual history. In discussing this development special emphasis was placed upon the significance of the view, founded upon the indisputable advances of the natural sciences, that progress in knowledge is possible; and upon the conception of human progress, also connected with natural science through its 'materialistic' focus, as an improvement in the conditions of mundane life. The rise and spread of the idea of progress, because of these features, contributed greatly to the development of the notion that history is a process governed by laws discoverable by science, and an increased interest in those aspects of the process that relate to changes in the material conditions of life of the mass of the people. The new discipline of political economy, dealing as it did with the most important element of such conditions, the economic, and aspiring to arrive at scientific laws, reflected the general intellectual ambience of the time by its emphasis upon the process of economic development. The era we are dealing with was also, of course, one of great economic change, probably the most rapid in history, to which later historians applied the label 'the industrial revolution', so the question of the historical evolution of economic life was, for the classical economists, a matter of immediate and practical concern as well as one of abstract intellectual interest.

Discussion of the philosophical problems involved in the effort to ascertain the 'laws of history' must be deferred until we have considered the ideas of Karl Marx on this subject. Here I will outline the model of economic development that was constructed by Ricardo and which was adopted by virtually all of the classical economists. This model was important in itself, since it dealt with an important question, but it also played a purely analytical role in the structure of classical political economy. So far, in the discussion the classical theories of value, rent, and population, I have made no attempt to show how they fit together in a comprehensive model of economic processes. In classical political economy, the theory of economic development plays this integrating role. One of the notable characteristics of economics, which differentiates it from the other social sciences, is its ability to construct and make use of such comprehensive models which intellectually (or, perhaps one should say, aesthetically) are more appealing than a collection of unrelated particular theories dealing with particular problems.

Ricardo's model, we should note before going on to describe it, is not the one that modern economists employ as an integrating structure. In a modern textbook of economic theory one will usually find economic development treated, if it is treated at all, essentially as an appendix, or as a field of applied economics. The integrating structure of modern economics is provided by a comprehensive model called General Equilibrium Theory in the 'positive' orientation of the subject and Welfare Economics in its 'normative' orientation. Neither of these is an attempt to delineate the determinants or laws of historical evolution.

In the discussion of David Hume in Chapter 7 we noted that his essay on the balance of international trade was especially significant in making use of the concept of *equilibrium* as an analytical device. Hume employed it in this famous essay to construct a sort of mental equivalent of the classic laboratory experiment: start with a state of equilibrium; alter one element only in the situation, keeping all others constant; trace the sequence of effects until they are finished; compare the new equilibrium with the old. (German writers later referred to this procedure as a *Gedankenexperiment*, a 'thought-experiment'.) Though the analysis was purely hypothetical, Hume's use of it to examine eighteenth-century trade policy showed that it could be a very powerful instrument for the discussion of practical problems. The central importance of equilibrium analysis in modern economics must be attributed to Ricardo, who used it as the foundation of all his arguments, whether they dealt with small questions like the effect of a tax on houses, or big ones like the long-run future of Britain's economy and the distribution of the national income between the main social classes. Ricardo's model of economic development was an application of equilibrium analysis to such 'big questions'.

Economic growth takes place, according to Ricardo, because of an increase in the nation's stock of capital; he does not consider the effects of improvements in scientific and technical knowledge. Therefore, growth is due to the devotion of a portion of the national income to investment – the creation of new production facilities. Only one of the three social classes plays a significant role in this process. Labourers consume all their income, because they are too poor to do otherwise; landowners are rich, but they are so fond of high living that they too spend all their current income. Only capitalists save a portion of their income and thereby provide the means to increase the nation's capital stock by investment. Since the income of the capitalist class is the profit obtained from industry and commerce, the amount of investment in new production facilities is determined by the size of the profit share in the national income. Adam Smith seems to have had a clear appreciation of the crucial role of profit in the dynamics of economic growth, but it was Ricardo who first incorporated it into a general model of the process.

Economic development, then, depends on profit. As long as profit is high economic growth will continue. But, Ricardo argued, it cannot continue indefinitely, because there are forces at work that will inevitably produce a decline in profit. These forces are due to the operation of the law of diminishing returns in agriculture. The scenario is as follows. Economic growth increases the demand for labour, which, in the short run, will raise wages above 'subsistence'. This, in accordance with Malthus's population theory, will lead to an increase in population which, in turn, will lead to an increase in the demand for food. But more food, because of diminishing returns, can be raised only at a higher cost of production. This rise in the price of food means that, even though the labourer may be receiving no more food than before, the cost, to the capitalist, of hiring labour rises and profit necessarily falls. The rate of profit, Ricardo repeatedly stressed, is determined by the cost of production of the labourer's food (and other necessaries) and varies inversely with the wage rate. The next step in the scenario is clear: if profit falls, less income is available for saving and investment, the rate of capital accumulation declines, and economic growth slows down. The growth process comes to an end when the rate of profit has fallen so low that capitalists can do no more than maintain the existing capital and replace it as it wears out. This is a condition of equilibrium, which became known in the later literature as the classical 'stationary state'. In this stationary state the landowners are the only permanent beneficiaries. Because they own a production resource that is fixed in quantity, they benefit from the operation of the law of diminishing returns but, in the long run, wages will be no more than subsistence, and profits will be close to zero.

The classical model of economic growth projects a rather gloomy prospect for the future, which is what some had in mind in calling political economy the 'dismal science'. Recall Adam Smith's view that the economic welfare of a nation depends upon the living standard of its most numerous class, the labourers (a view that, incidentally, Malthus also expressed in his *Essay*), and his contention that wages could be high only in the 'progressive' state, that is, while the economy was *in the process* of development. Ricardo's model supported Smith's view. John Stuart Mill, the most prominent and influential of the later classical economists, was not so gloomy, since he believed that it was possible to induce the lower orders to limit their procreation, and to persuade the governing classes to make institutional changes that would produce a more equal distribution of the nation's income. Karl Marx read a quite different message in a model that was, in respect of the long-term prospects for profit, similar to Ricardo's: that capitalism is doomed, and that its downfall is essentially due to its very success in creating growth in productive capital more rapidly than any other economic system had been able to achieve.

It is one thing to construct a hypothetical model as an instrument of analysis, another to regard the model as an isomorphic representation of the real world (see the discussion in Chapter 6 B above). When a model is viewed as an isomorphic reproduction of something as complex as an economy, it is bound to be open to the charge that it is 'unrealistic'. When it is viewed as modelling something more complex still, the evolution of an economy in real-world time, the chances that its predictions will prove to be true are next to negligible. Ricardo's model of economic development failed on all its major predictions: landowners have not been receiving a growing share of the national income; real wages have not converged to a subsistence level; food prices (relative to others) have not risen; and the rate of profit has not declined. One can always argue, of course, that the model tells us what will happen if we wait long enough. But that is no more testable than the open prediction 'It will rain in Scotland,' which would not be falsified even if the sky were to be clear there for the next fifty years, or more.

We should note, before leaving this outline of the classical model of economic development, that it shares one element in common with all the major models in economics that have been constructed since: a prediction of a falling rate of profit is derived analytically from the structure and content of the model. This historical prediction also characterizes the Marxian, neoclassical, and Keynesian economic models. The failure of the profit rate to fall therefore serves as a challenge to all these models if they are viewed as providing foundations for long-run historical predictions. This is an important challenge in the case of the Ricardian theory because of the role of the development model as the framework for integrating the specific theories of value, rent, wages, and profits. It is important for Marxian theory because its central purpose was to make historical predictions. It is not important for neoclassical or Keynesian theory, which both focus upon short-run phenomena and have little, if anything, to say about the course of history.

In the discussion of Malthus's theory of population, we made note of the fact that it played a role in the debate over the Poor Law that preceded and followed the Amendment Act of 1834. This was the first occasion on which a specific proposition of an established social science was a conspicuous element in popular discussion of public policy. But it was not the last, of course, and its uniqueness was short-lived, since there developed, in the 1840's, an even more intense controversy on economic policy, this time having to do with international trade, which, coming to a head in the repeal of the corn laws in 1846, ushered in the first period of substantially free international trade in modern history. The contribution of classical political economy to this debate cannot be fully appreciated until we have examined Ricardo's theory of international trade in the next section, but one aspect of it is closely connected with the Ricardian theory of economic development. If the basic cause of a slow-down in the rate of economic growth is the increased cost of producing food, which results from the limited supply of land, then it can be counteracted by importing food from other parts of the world not so intensively cultivated as England. International trade, by which England would exchange manufactured goods for food, would act as if the agricultural land of other countries were added to that of England. A growing population in England would not then have the immediate effects on wages and profits described in Ricardo's theory of development. Economic growth could continue longer; perhaps for a very long time. Some historians of classical economics have argued that the whole purpose of Ricardo's *Principles* was to lay a theoretical foundation for an attack upon contemporary tariff policy; that, in short, it should be considered as a tract on behalf of free international trade rather than as an objective attempt to lay down the scientific 'principles of political economy'. This is a distortion of Ricardo, but a reading of his followers' comments on the corn laws indicates that they were not overly scrupulous in their use of those principles as propaganda on behalf of the campaign for free trade.

E. INTERNATIONAL TRADE

Even those historians of economics who are highly critical of classical political economy and emphasize the various ways in which it misdirected economic theory into blind alleys concede that in one area – the theory of international trade – it made important and lasting contributions. The discussion of international trade in current textbooks on economic theory reproduces theoretical arguments developed between the middle of the eighteenth century and the middle of the nineteenth, mainly by Hume, Ricardo, and J. S. Mill, and the more complex parts of the modern theory are extensions and elaborations of the original classical analysis. The most interesting and important aspect of this is the principle of 'comparative advantage' – interesting because it appears to contradict common sense; important because it demonstrates that the opportunities for mutually advantageous international trade are very extensive. This principle can be found, once we know what we are looking for, in the arguments of numerous eighteenth-century writers, but it was David Ricardo who first formulated it in a clear and explicit fashion.

If Ricardo had written no more than the twenty-odd pages comprising chapter VII 'On Foreign Trade' of his *Principles of Political Economy and Taxation*, he would deserve a prominent place in the history of economic theory and, because of the importance of economic factors in the relations between sovereign states, a significant role in the general subject of international relations and the practical matter of foreign policy. The fact is, however, that the principle of comparative advantage hardly appears at all in modern discussions of international economic relations and foreign policy, in contrast to its central importance in economic theory. The main reason for this, I think, is the counter-intuitive nature of the principle. Even students who learn it on college courses and pass examinations on it will soon thereafter discuss international trade issues as if they had never heard of it. For this reason it is worthwhile if we approach an explication of the principle somewhat obliquely, by first considering the more general subject of the sources of gains from trade of any kind.

Aristotle classified trade as a purely 'acquisitive' activity, in contrast to the 'productive' activities of farming and other occupations that produce goods not otherwise available. In accordance with this way of thinking we should also classify such activities as transport and storage as non-productive, since they do not increase the physical quantity of goods. In the limit this argument degenerates into the proposition that there are no 'productive' activities at all, since, in accordance with the conservation laws of physics, the total of mass and energy in the universe can be neither increased nor diminished. This *reductio ad absurdum* indicates that when we speak of economic production we must focus upon activities that alter the *form* of matter and energy, or its *location* in space or time, or its *distribution* among people, so that it is more useful in serving human wants and needs.

By the eighteenth century the discussion of economic questions had advanced considerably in sophistication but Aristotle's dichotomy was still embraced so far as international trade was concerned. Such trade was generally viewed as adding nothing to the quantity of goods available. If some nations gain from trade, other nations must lose. Accordingly, the object of national policy in this area was to assure that one's own nation would be a gainer, not a loser. The policy described as 'mercantilism' held that this object would be attained if a nation achieved a 'favourable balance of trade', more exports than imports. In itself this would seem to violate common sense, since it contends that a nation gains by giving more goods than it receives. Mercantilism is not a tightly modelled body of theory, because different writers advanced different justifications for the policy of promoting a favourable trade balance. One of the most prominent of these was the argument that, when a nation's exports exceeded its imports, there would be an inflow of precious metals, which were construed as constituting the nations's 'wealth'. The significance of David Hume's essay 'Of the Balance of Trade' (1752), which was discussed above (Chapter 7 B), is that although he regarded this conception of wealth as foolish, he undertook to show that, even if increasing the stock of gold and silver were a desirable objective of national policy, it would be unattainable by the methods advocated by the supporters of the favourable balance of trade doctrine.

Hume's argument was important as foreshadowing the practice in modern economics of considering the analysis of the probable effects of a policy as more important than debate over the merits of what it *intends* to achieve. Adam Smith, whose *Wealth of Nations* is a sustained attack on the whole range of eighteenth-century British economic policy, laid special emphasis upon foreign trade policy. He advocated free trade on the ground that it would increase wealth. But, unlike Hume, he did not argue that the objective of mercantilist foreign trade policy was unattainable. He contended that it was *undesirable*, since, in his view, the wealth of a nation does not consist of its gold and silver but of the quantity of useful goods available for consumption by the people. (He knew Hume's balance of trade argument but it makes no appearance in the *Wealth of Nations*.) In fact, Smith did not put forward a specific theory of international trade; he regarded free trade across national borders as simply another way of 'extending the market'. Productivity can be greatly increased by 'division of labour' but this is not possible unless there is a large market in which the increased output can be sold. By enlarging the market, says Smith, international trade permits greater specialization and thereby increases productivity. Smith would not have argued that trade, as such, increases the quantity of goods, but he pointed out that trade is a necessary part of a system of specialization that produces more.

In Adam Smith's presentation, international trade does not differ in any important way from trade within a nation's borders. Ricardo's contribution was based on noting that there *is* a difference between domestic and international economic activity: labour and capital move freely within a nation but not, for various reasons, between nations. He argued that under such conditions international trade in commodities can benefit all the participants. He accepted Smith's contention about the connection between trade and division of labour, but he did not focus upon this as the source of increased output. Even with no improvement of technology and productivity, trade could increase output, simply by altering the geographical location of industry. He arrived at the surprising conclusion that trade is beneficial to a nation even when it imports goods that it can produce more efficiently itself. This is the argument that runs so counter to intuition that, even today, more than a century and a half later, it has not won recognition beyond the limited circle of professional economists. We can best approach Ricardo's principle of 'comparative advantage' by first looking at the more clear-cut case of 'absolute advantage'. (The following illustrations are identical to ones contained in modern elementary textbooks.)

Let us consider two countries, say England and France, and note their respective production abilities in two commodities called 'clothing' and 'food'. In the following table we record what an English and a French worker can produce, under the technological conditions existing in the two countries:

	Units of clothing	Units of food
England:	3	2
France:	4	1

France is here depicted as superior to England in clothing production, while England is superior to France in food production. Under these conditions it is not difficult to imagine that the total output of clothing and food would be greater if France specialized in clothing and England in food and they traded with each other instead of each producing both food and clothing for itself. If France shifts a unit of labour from food to clothing, one unit of food is lost but four units of clothing are gained. Meanwhile, in England, by switching a unit of labour from clothing to food, three units of clothing are lost but two units of food are gained. Summarizing:

	Change in output of	
	Clothing	Food
England :	−3	+2
France:	+4	−1
Total	+1	+1

Thus, taking England and France together, there is an increase in the production of both food and clothing without any change in technology, simply by specializing. This can only be done, of course, if England and France trade with one another; so trade, in this sense, is a 'productive' activity.

The above case, where England has an absolute advantage over France in food production while France has an absolute advantage over England in clothing production, is hardly surprising. It is no more profound than recognizing that grapes *can* be grown in England (in hothouses) but that it would probably be wiser to let the French do it. But Ricardo went on to show that gains are possible even if one country is superior to another in the production of *everything*. Consider the following production possibilities, again recording what one unit of labour can produce in each country:

	Units of clothing	Units of food
England:	6	3
France:	4	1

In this case England is more productive than France in both clothing and food. Ideally the workers of France (and French capital too) should migrate to England, but if there are barriers against this, some gains are achievable by having the food and clothing travel instead, i.e. by trade. These gains can be obtained if England specializes in food, where her *comparative advantage* over France is greater (3:1 compared with 6:4) and France specializes in clothing, where her *comparative disadvantage* is less (4:6 compared with 1:3). If, for the sake of illustration, England switches one unit of labour from clothing to food and France switches two units of labour from food to clothing, we get:

	Change in output of	
	Clothing	Food
England:	–6	+3
France:	+8	–2
Total	+1	+1

Again we find that specialization increases total output, and that England and France can both gain by sharing the increase. Trade in this case, like the other, is a necessary element in a system of economic arrangements that is more productive.

This result appears mysterious at first sight but the reason for it is really quite simple. In the above illustration England has two ways of obtaining clothing, by producing it herself or by trading food for it with France. England can produce clothing cheaper than France can, but she can obtain it more cheaply still by producing food and exporting it in exchange for clothing. Similarly, in France, food is more costly to produce than in England, but it can be obtained more cheaply by producing clothing and trading it for food. England would be better-off if clothing exchanged for food at any rate greater than 2c for 1f. France would be better-off at any rate less than 4c for 1f. At a rate such as 3c for 1f both countries gain.

The above illustrations of absolute and comparative advantage show that production can be increased when trade permits increased specialization. Is it permissible to say that trade is a *cause* of productivity? If we recall the analysis of causation in Chapter 3 A 3 we see that this is so. Trade is *I*nsufficient to increase productivity by itself; it is a *N*ecessary element in a set of factors that increase productivity. But increased productivity could result from another set (including, for example, improvements in science and technology as an element), so the set including trade is *U*nnecessary; it is only *S*ufficient to cause an increase in productivity. In accordance with the INUS model of causation, therefore, trade can be called a *cause* of increased productivity.

We can see why classical political economy played a prominent role in the great debate over the British tariff in the 1840's. The proponents of free trade could apply one of the strongest policy arguments yet developed by economists: the argument that free trade would benefit or, at least, could benefit everyone. Moreover, the theory seemed to indicate that England would gain even if she adopted a free-trade policy unilaterally, without waiting for other nations to see the light. This she did, repealing the corn laws in 1846 and following up in the next few years by the virtual elimination of all import tariffs. France followed suit in 1860, and other countries too, ushering in the first period in modern history of general free trade. It was a short-lived system. Various countries began to raise tariff barriers in the 1880's; protectionism accelerated in the early years of the twentieth century; and the depression of the 1930's produced a collapse of international trade and a revival of high-tariff policies that seemed at the time to end for ever the hopes that had begun with Adam Smith. After the first World War, however, as part of the reconstitution of international relations generally, a new period of free trade (relatively speaking) began.

Throughout this period since the 1840's economists have been more consistent, and more in agreement, on international trade than on any other issue of public policy. This is probably due mainly to the power of Ricardo's theory of comparative advantage, which, though it has had to be amended in important ways (most importantly in relation to an economy experiencing unemployment), is sufficiently compelling for even the most enthusiastic proponents of state intervention to be made to feel somewhat abashed when arguing for tariffs and other forms of interference with international trade.

The great debate over the corn laws of the 1840's left a legacy behind that has dogged orthodox economists down to the present. Most of the classical economists argued for free international trade but very few of them, and none of the most prominent, proposed a general policy of non-intervention in the economy on the part of government. One can find proponents of such a view during the classical era, but they are, without significant exception, not economists, unless one uses that term to include journalists and lobbyists, and social philosophers who dabbled a bit in economics. During the debate over the corn laws the distinction between free trade and a general policy of *laissez-faire* was muddied, and the economists who favoured one were construed erroneously as being advocates of the other. We will not consider the issue of *laissez-faire* further here; its importance in the history and philosophy of social science warrants devoting a separate chapter to it, which we go on to after completing our survey of classical economics.

Note: Specialization and productivity

In the preceding section we examined Ricardo's theory of international trade, which aimed at showing the benefits that can accrue to both trading partners, even if one of them is more efficient than the other in producing both the traded commodities. This theorem is not confined to the special case of two countries and two commodities. It applies also to 'multilateral' trade among many countries in many commodities. It is important also to note that the theorem is not confined to the special case of *international* trade. To demonstrate this, all one needs to do is reconstruct the numerical illustrations of absolute and comparative advantage given above to refer to two American states instead of England and France, or two Indiana counties or, for that matter, two individuals. Strike out 'England' and 'France' and write 'Smith' and 'Jones'; similar conclusions follow. Total output is increased if they specialize instead of producing independently, and this is true even if Smith, say, is better than Jones in both lines of production. This conclusion can also be extended to many persons and many commodities.

Though he did not realize it, Ricardo had demonstrated that production can be increased by all forms of specialization – of regions, industries, persons, etc., as well as nations – so long as it is in accord with existing absolute and comparative efficiencies. Adam Smith traced the productivity gains of division of labour to improvements in human skill, its saving of time, and its stimulus to technical improvement. Ricardo's theorem says that, even without any of these, an improvement in productivity can result, simply by allocating the various tasks in the appropriate way. In Adam Smith's pin factory, for example, if it were organized according to Ricardian principles, each person would be set to work at the particular part of the process in which he had a comparative advantage over the other workers. Even if one person, say, could perform all processes more efficiently than his colleagues, he should specialize too – in the one in which his efficiency is, comparatively, the greatest.

Moreover, the same theorem applies to other factors of production, not just human labour. Reconstruct the above numerical illustration by substituting 'land plot No. 1' and 'land plot No. 2' for England and France, or 'machine No. 1' and 'machine No. 2' for these countries; the same conclusion follows, that production can be increased if land plots and machines are specialized in accordance with the principles of absolute and comparative advantage.

I am labouring this point because the argument that Ricardo constructed for the limited purpose of showing that tariffs and other interferences with international trade impair productivity is much more important than he realized. Indeed, it is the central proposition in what is today called 'microeconomics'. In Chapter 17 A and B we shall see that the fundamental objectives of modern microeconomic theory are to determine the rules that define the *optimum* specialization of an economy's productive resources, the role of markets in achieving this optimum, and the reasons why markets may fail to achieve it, which may call for the intervention of the state.

Despite the generality of the theories of absolute and comparative advantage, most modern textbooks discuss it, as Ricardo did, when dealing with international trade. The only reason for this is the historical fact that the theory was first developed in connection with international trade. This is a prime example of the influence of the past on present modes of thought. Even in science, the way we think today is partly due to the history of science, and even to features of that history that were only transitory, or accidental.

F. METHODOLOGY

Though Ricardo had made his fortune by dealing in financial markets, he seldom spoke of their institutional organization and practices, or those of any other line of business, in his writings on political economy. Instead he attempted to analyse how markets work by showing logically how they *must* work if certain basic 'principles' and conditions hold. Ricardo was a man of practical affairs, with very little formal education, but he was more of a pure theorist than most academic scholars, and his demonstration of the power of theoretical modelling in the *Principles* was the factor primarily responsible for its establishment as the basic methodology of economics. In this respect, economics remains today much as it was in the early nineteenth century. The difference between classical political economy and neoclassical economics lies in the content of their models, not their scientific methodology.

We noted earlier, in Chapter 7, that David Hume had put forward a prototypical economic model in his essay 'Of the Balance of Trade'. We also saw there how Adam Smith marked out the area of investigation of economics and identified some of its most fundamental problems. The first hundred pages of the *Wealth of Nations* are devoted mainly to theoretical construction and exposition, but the work as a whole is packed with historical, institutional, and descriptive material. One may call it a book of economic *theory* only if one adds that it was only partially so and that the theory it contained, while very suggestive, did not form a complete system.

In this sense, then, Adam Smith must be viewed as a precursor; the credit for constructing the first comprehensive model that focused strongly upon the organization of economic processes by the market mechanism must go to Ricardo. Part of the reason for this undoubtedly lies in the fact that ground-clearing is messier work than architecture. Smith was very conscious, in writing the *Wealth of Nations*, that it was necessary to hack away directly at the jungle of tangled economic policies of the 'mercantilist' era. Ricardo devoted himself to more abstract matters, which he did initially by means of critical study of the theoretical sections of the *Wealth of Nations*. But the difference between Smith and Ricardo was perhaps more fundamental, since Smith, along with the other Scottish moralists, was somewhat suspicious of purely deductive analyses of social questions, and insisted, in line with the philosophy of empiricism, on the need to connect economic theory closely with historical and contemporary factual material. It has even been suggested by one distinguished historian, Elie Halévy, that the real source of inspiration for Ricardo, so far as methodology is concerned, lay across the English Channel rather than across the river Tweed – in France rather than in Scotland (*The Growth of Philosophic Radicalism*, 1928, pp. 272–3, 282). Certainly the French, admiring Descartes much more than Hume or Locke, were more attracted to abstract reasoning and system-building than the English. But it is impossible to establish the source of Ricardo's scientific inspiration, whether it derives from Scotland, or Paris, or from the Sephardic synagogue in Amsterdam, or, indeed, from something that was unique and original in his own mental constitution, a chance confluence of genes providing a filter of experience that turned a practical stockbroker into one of the most influential abstract social theorists of Western intellectual history.

What we find in the *Principles* is certainly abstract. Ricardo constructs a model, which is simple in the sense that it consists of only a small number of elements and relationships, and then he uses the model rigorously to deduce conclusions concerning such things as the effect of tariffs on wages, profits, and general economic development; the effects of different kinds of taxes on the distribution of the national income among the great social classes – landlords, capitalists, and labourers; and so on. If Ricardo's conclusions had been intuitively obvious his abstract modelling would probably have generated little interest, but they were not. Many of them were counter-intuitive, flew in the face of common sense, and certainly did not agree with widely held views concerning the effects of contemporary economic policies. The demonstration that unexpected, and sometimes unwanted, consequences often flow from actions established economic theory as a permanent and important element in Western social thought. To Ricardo must be given the credit for driving home the vital point that, since the effect of an action is not controlled by one's intentions, it is necessary to analyse the causal connections of economic phenomena in a sophisticated way. To act effectively means to act on the basis of sound science, which, for Ricardo, meant sound *theory*.

This methodology became the dominant scientific stance of classical political economy, defended by all the leading figures of the school. Nassau W. Senior, disagreed with Ricardo on numerous points of substance, but he thoroughly embraced the view that good economics consists primarily of logical deductions from a few intuitively axiomatic initial premises, such as the proposition that every person acts so as to 'better his condition'. John Stuart Mill, writing 'On the Definition of Political Economy' in 1836, described it as an essentially abstract science, using the techniques of deductive logic to arrive at principles of general applicability. Later, in his *System of Logic*

(1843), he expressed a strong preference for induction rather than deduction as a general philosophy of science, but he advocated deduction as the proper method for the social sciences. John Elliot Cairnes, second in prominence only to Mill as an economist of the mid-century period, gave the subject book-length treatment in his *The Character and Logical Method of Political Economy* (1856) in which he tenaciously defended the notion that the Ricardian methodology was the proper way to investigate economic phenomena. All true sciences, he contended, aim at the construction of abstract models, and the ability to do so is simply a sign of their intellectual maturity. This view was, however, not universal. In England it was challenged by Richard Jones, who was encouraged in this by the great polymath William Whewell. In Europe it was the subject of an acrimonious and protracted controversy, known as the *Methodenstreit*, between the leading German and Austrian economists in the last quarter of the nineteenth century.

Richard Jones, who succeeded Malthus on the faculty of Haileybury College, attacked classical economics root-and-branch in various writings: condemning its introspectively derived utilitarian assumptions, its policy recommendations and, above all, its methodology. What the study of economics requires, he argued, is the inductive examination of economic phenomena, not the construction of theoretical models. He was a precursor of the later 'historical' and 'institutional' schools of economics, but he attracted few immediate disciples, and his name now appears only as a minor reference in histories of the discipline. William Whewell, a close personal friend of Jones, was far more prominent in the intellectual life of the time. He was one of the foremost scholars of Cambridge University, respected for contributions to many fields: linguistics, mathematics, history, science, the natural sciences and their history, and the philosophy of science. He also wrote three papers in which he tried to render the Ricardian model in mathematical form, apparently in order to attack it as being insufficiently rigorous. Though he supported Jones's views on the methodology of economics, his own public statements on the matter were so ambiguous that they failed to displace English political economy from the path that Ricardo had blazed.

In Germany, however, the story was very different. Teaching and research in economics in the German universities were closely connected with history and, in the later decades of the nineteenth century, a school of economists rose to dominance there that rejected altogether the theoretical methodology dominant in England. Gustave Schmoller, the leader of this school, insisted that the proper way to do economics was by means of detailed specific historical research of a severely inductivist sort, without the aid of any theoretical notions. The general 'laws' of economics would, he felt, reveal themselves in due course, after a sufficient volume of factual studies had been accumulated. Schmoller was a powerful figure in German academic politics and, during his heyday, it was virtually impossible for any economist who favoured a theoretical methodology to secure an appointment in a German university. In Vienna, however, free from Schmoller's authority, a school of economists arose that, while disagreeing with the content of English classical political economy, strongly approved of Ricardo's methodology. Carl Menger, the leading member of this school, delivered a frontal attack on the Schmollerians in a book published in 1883 (translated into English as *Problems of Economics and Sociology*). The result was an acrimonious and long-lasting dispute across the Austro-German frontier, which sharpened the issue of the methodology of economics, and renewed discussion of it in England, which was, at the time, the acknowledged centre of economic scholarship.

Henry Sidgwick, one of the leading academic philosophers, who had written a book on economics himself, addressed the British Association in 1885 on 'The Scope and Method of Political Economy', a talk in which he criticized the German historical school and its followers elsewhere for misunderstanding the methodology and content of classical economics. Six years later, another Cambridge philosopher, John Neville Keynes, published his *Scope and Method of Political Economy*, which became, and remained for many years, the definitive statement of the subject. The study of economic phenomena, he argued, can be separated from other aspects of social life; unrealistic postulates are permissible in constructing heuristic theories; the aim of economics, like other sciences, is to develop theoretical models that embody nomological propositions of general validity; ethical propositions can be, and must be, separated from scientific ones. Keynes, in effect, accepted all the main contentions of the Austrians, and rejected those of the Germans, but his book merely restated the methodological views that had been dominant in English economics during the preceding seventy years. Keynes's book was not displaced in the reading lists for college students until 1932, by Lionel Robbins's *Essay on the Nature and Significance of Economic Science*, which, if anything, took an even harder stance in defence of the deductive methodology.

In the United States the methodological battle was less one-sided than in England. In the latter part of the nineteenth century and the early twentieth, many Americans went to Germany to do postgraduate work in the social sciences and one might have expected them to return to the United States imbued with the ideas of the German historical school. Some indeed were, and from them originated the American school of 'institutional economics' which has played a minor, but not negligible, role in the history of American economic thought. For a considerable period (up to the 1950s or thereabouts) the institutionalists dominated certain applied sub-fields, such as labour relations and agricultural economics, but the leading American economists at the major universities were caught up in the new wave of economic theory that came from England and Austria with the advent of neoclassical economics and, whatever they might have brought back from Germany in their intellectual baggage, the methodological message of the historical school did not remain for long a guiding principle in their research.

As we shall see in Chapter 17, a great deal of classical political economy was swept away by the 'revolution' in economic theory that took place in the last quarter of the nineteenth century, but one of the things that remained was the conviction that the scientific study of economic phenomena requires the use of analytical models. In no other branch of the social sciences is this view so deeply entrenched. Before we take leave of this subject, let us note four matters that deserve brief attention at this point: (1) the distinction made by J. S. Mill between 'laws of production' and 'laws of distribution'; (2) the resort to introspective knowledge; (3) the role of *ceteris paribus*; and (4) the use of mathematics.

1. John Stuart Mill's *Principles of Political Economy* (1848) became the virtual textbook from which most students learned economics during the latter half of the nineteenth century. Its theoretical structure was Ricardian, with only minor modifications. But, in the preface, Mill asserts and emphasizes that his book differs from others in trying to present theoretical principles in close conjunction with practical problems, and in recognizing that this requires consideration of a broader range of social and ethical matters than most economists are accustomed to examine. So we find in Mill's book far more material of a historical and descriptive or institutional nature than in Ricardo's. From the standpoint of the philosophy of social science the most important proposition that Mill drew from his larger view of political economy was a categorical distinction between the 'laws of production' and the 'laws of distribution'. Here is the famous passage in which he states this:

The laws and conditions of the Production of wealth partake of the character of physical truths. There is nothing optional or arbitrary in them. Whatever mankind produce, must be produced in the modes, and under the conditions, imposed by the constitution of external things, and by the inherent properties of their own bodily and mental structure. Whether they like it or not, their productions will be limited by the amount of their previous accumulation, and, that being given, it will be proportional to their energy, their skill, the perfection of their machinery, and their judicious use of the advantages of combined labour. Whether they like it or not, a double quantity of labour will not raise, on the same land, a double quantity of food, unless some improvement takes place in the processes of cultivation .... The opinions, or the wishes, which may exist on these different matters, do not control the things themselves .... We cannot alter the ultimate properties either of matter or mind but can only employ those properties more or less successfully to bring about the events in which we are interested.

It is not so with the Distribution of wealth. That is a matter of human institution solely. The things once there, mankind individually or collectively, can do with them as they like. They can place them at the disposal of whomsoever they please, and on whatever terms .... The distribution of wealth, therefore, depends on the laws and customs of society. The rules by which it is determined are what the opinions and feelings of the ruling portion of the community make them, and are very different in different ages and countries; and might be still more different, if mankind so chose. (Book II, chapter I)

Mill is here asserting that the laws governing the production of wealth are fundamentally different from those governing its distribution. The first are laws of nature, like the law of gravitational attraction or the ideal gas laws; the second are like laws passed by legislatures or established by custom, such as those that bear on the inheritance of property after the death of its owner, or the division of property and income in a divorce. Obviously the term 'law' does not mean the same thing in these two usages, and Mill would have rendered good service if he had simply pointed this out. But his emphatic insistence that production is governed *solely* by laws of nature, and distribution *solely* by institutional arrangement, is extremely misleading. In Chapter 8 we noted that utopian theorists seldom say anything about the economic organization of the perfect society. A reason for this is their tendency to think of production as simply a matter of engineering, agronomy, and other applications of natural science, and distribution as a separate matter of ethics, leaving no room for economics in either branch. Mill's categorical distinction was frequently quoted by utopian and other writers who wished to contend that the only real source of poverty was maldistribution of wealth and income, which could easily be altered by the exercise of political power.

Mill himself leaned towards socialism, but he was not a utopianist by either temperament or conviction. In fact, neither in the *Principles of Political Economy* nor in any of his other writings do we find him actually adhering to the categorical distinction stated in the above quotation. In practice, he treated both production and distribution as governed by a combination of natural and man-made laws; and he recognized that these economic processes are interdependent, the quantity and composition of production being affected by the distribution of income and wealth, and vice versa. This view, rather than the demarcation, was embraced by the mainstream of economic theory.

2. In the examination of the political theory of Thomas Hobbes in Chapter 4 we observed that he put forward the view that, since men are very similar to one another, one can obtain valid empirical knowledge of human nature in general by examining one's own self. In effect, this contends that personal introspection is a reliable way of obtaining certain kinds of empirical knowledge – about the basic nature of man's wants, aspirations, and fears. This view was one of the few elements of Hobbes's thought adopted by the Scottish moralists and, via Smith and Ricardo, it became a central element in economic theory. It remains so to the present. Look into any book in modern economic theory and one will find that man is assumed to behave rationally, and in

accordance with certain straightforward desires or preferences. In stating these assumptions economists do not resort to psychology as practised by professional or academic psychologists but, as Hobbes did, to simple introspection. Numerous writers, especially over the past half-century or so, have criticized economics for lacking a proper basis in psychology, but no one has so far offered a union of the two disciplines that has met with more than lukewarm and transitory interest.

Now, if introspection is a valid means of obtaining empirical knowledge, it provides such knowledge about the *individual*. This can be generalized by making the assumption that human entities are similar to one another. But it would be clearly erroneous to claim that introspection can provide direct knowledge about compound social things such as nations, corporations, the working class, capitalism, and so on. One of the reasons why classical economics adopted the principle of 'methodological individualism' – reducing social phenomena to the actions of individual persons – is that its use of introspection tied it to the level of the individual. Modern mainstream economics continues to embrace methodological individualism, in large part because the theory with which it works relies upon introspection for some of its primary factual propositions. This is not the whole story, by any means, since methodological individualism is clearly connected with political and ethical individualism. However, even one who is prepared to accept the theory of 'emergent properties', viewing social wholes such as 'nations' or 'classes' as in some sense more than aggregations of their component individuals, might well be wary of abandoning methodological individualism for some form of 'holism', since introspection, while it may be a dull tool of knowledge, is better than some others. When holists assert, as they are wont to do, that they possess direct, immediate knowledge of the nature of such things as 'the state', 'capitalism', 'imperialism', and so on, they are not resorting to introspection but to *intuition*, a very different thing.

3. The Latin term *ceteris paribus*, meaning literally 'other things equal (or constant)', is often used in science to call attention to the fact that most 'laws' are conditional statements. For example, a physicist may say that 'the volume of a gas will increase when its temperature rises *if pressure remains constant*'. Or he may say, more generally, 'the volume of a gas will increase when its temperature rises, *ceteris paribus*', meaning if *none* of the non-temperature factors that can affect volume alters. This is a potentially dangerous way of talking, because, if we are not careful, we would simply be saying that a rise in temperature increases gas volume except in those cases in which it does not! But science could not proceed without making statements of *restricted* laws, which is what a *ceteris paribus* statement is, and it is very convenient and scientifically useful if instead of always saying vague things like 'The volume will most likely increase' we can say, 'If certain conditions are fulfilled, the volume *will* increase.' An experiment is, of course, a way of fulfilling the *ceteris paribus* conditions with a high degree of empirical reliability. Modern

statistical methods are devised to enable one to approximate similar *ceteris paribus* conditions in non-experimental work.

Any theory, whether in natural or social science, must employ *ceteris paribus*. Otherwise every theory, no matter how small, would have to take everything in the universe into account. So there cannot be any serious criticism of classical political economy simply on the ground that it constructed *ceteris paribus* theories. However, Ricardo and other classical economists were not as clear about this matter as they should have been. Ricardo sometimes spoke of the conclusions he had arrived at as 'tendencies' and sometimes as if they were certain. Properly stated, the conclusions were *analytically certain* under the conditions of *ceteris paribus*, but they could be construed only as *empirically probable*, because in the real world 'other things' are not constant.

The chief source of difficulty with the *ceteris paribus* clause is that it can be employed in four quite different ways, as follows. First, it can be used in order to state, formally and precisely, the conditions under which a theory applies, such as specifying the conditions of the Newtonian model when using it to construct a theory of the movements of a pendulum. Secondly, it can be used as a shorthand way of saying something like 'Other factors are not constant, but their influence is very small, so we can proceed pragmatically *as if* they were constant.' Thirdly, it can mean that other factors *are* constant, or have been *made* constant, as in a laboratory experiment. And finally, the *ceteris paribus* clause can be used as shorthand for 'Other factors are not constant but our procedure is to build a simple model first by *temporarily assuming* that they are and then go on to relax this assumption by taking the other factors systematically into account in constructing progressively more complex models.'

Obviously, there is considerable room for confusion as to what a theoretical model is if its use of *ceteris paribus* is not clear. Ricardo and the other classical economists were indeed not clear and, when attacked, they often resorted to shifting their position on this methodological issue. Hardly any of Ricardo's long-term predictions have been verified by the course of economic history since he wrote. This means that, even if the internal logic of his model is sound, it is not very useful if it locks up empirically important factors in the *ceteris paribus* clause. Saying that the theory *would* apply if the real world were different does not rescue a theory. Social scientists have more difficulty in accepting this than natural scientists, because the 'positive' and the 'normative' are more entangled together in social science. As pointed out in Chapter 3 D, a positive proposition is tested by the real world but a normative proposition serves as a test *of* the real world. When a positive proposition disagrees with reality the theory should be altered, but when the reality disagrees with a normative proposition this serves as ground for contending that efforts should be made to alter the world. The necessity for conceptual differentiation of positive and normative propositions is easy to appreciate, but it is difficult to achieve in the social sciences.

4. Leafing through a modern textbook in elementary economics, one is struck by the copious use of diagrams, which are used not merely to plot empirical information for visual inspection, or to illustrate a theory geometrically, but to carry out theoretical analysis and provide logical proofs of propositions. In advanced textbooks diagrams are rare but mathematics is omnipresent. Economics has become the most mathematical of the social sciences, more mathematical indeed than most of the natural sciences. This is not surprising in view of the extent to which theoretical modelling has been a central feature of economics since Ricardo's construction of abstract arguments about the functioning of economic processes. Recalling the admiration of the eighteenth-century social theorists for the achievements of natural science and their desire to emulate Galileo and Newton, one would expect that mathematics would have been pressed into service early in the history of economic theory. The Scottish moralists of the eighteenth century were passionately enthusiastic about the use of mathematics in all fields of investigation that aimed to be scientific. But, in fact, they made little effort to apply mathematical techniques to economics or the other social sciences. In Adam Smith's *Wealth of Nations* or Malthus's *Principles of Population* (1798) or his later *Principles of Political Economy* (1820) there is neither geometry nor algebra, despite the fact that Smith probably and Malthus certainly possessed a good knowledge of mathematics. Ricardo had no training in mathematics. In his *Principles* he made extensive use of numerical tables, but these served mainly to illustrate theoretical propositions that Ricardo argued in verbal terms.

There were some efforts to employ geometrical and mathematical techniques for analytical purposes in the early nineteenth century, most notably by a Frenchman, Augustin Cournot, in his *Recherches sur les principes mathématiques de la théorie des richesses* (1838), but these excited no general interest. Mathematics and geometry did not really begin to be employed until the development of neoclassical economics got under way in the 1870's. Alfred Marshall firmly established the use of geometry by his *Principles of Economics* (1890). Leon Walras's *Eléments d'économie politique pure* (1874) is now regarded by historians as a landmark, in economic theory itself and in the use of mathematics, but few economists followed this lead; mathematics did not come into general use by economists until the middle of the twentieth century.

We cannot devote space in this book to an extensive examination of the history of mathematics in economics (and other social sciences), though it is an aspect of the philosophy of social science of some importance. My object in these few paragraphs is historical – to point out that though the methodology of analytical abstraction that Ricardo established was 'mathematical' in nature, he did not use mathematics explicitly, nor did his successors in classical political economy. Marx mainly used numerical illustrations, as Ricardo had. There is a bit of algebra in *Das Kapital* but it is so simple that it cannot be described as mathematical analysis. At the urging of his great friend and collaborator Friedrich Engels, Marx studied differential calculus but neither he nor Engels was able to make effective use of it in his social science writings.

Obviously, the methodology of modelling can be applied by a science only if the worldly domain it investigates is orderly. If it were utterly chaotic, no laws, or even loose generalizations, could be made. The ultimate form of the view that the world is orderly is the notion that it is a *perfectly harmonious* order, i.e. that it cannot be improved, in the normative sense, by human intervention. This view has its roots in seventeenth-century metaphysics and, in the nineteenth, became prominent in regard to the social domain, through the doctrine of *laissez-faire*. The examination of this is the subject of the next chapter.

Chapter 10

The idea of harmonious order

In our consideration of the philosophy of social science up to this point attention has been mainly focused upon the branch of philosophy called epistemology – the theory of knowledge. In tracing the origins of social science special emphasis was put upon the importance of the physical sciences which, during the period from Copernicus to Newton, established canons of scientific method that the early social scientists aspired to emulate. Only occasionally, as in discussing utopian social thought in Chapter 8, has it been necessary to make reference to another branch of philosophy – metaphysics. In this chapter I pursue this further in order to examine more fully the foundations of the view that the organization of humans into social collectivities is an aspect of a more general harmonious order of nature, and to assess the influence of this view upon the development of modern social science. I undertake this discussion following the examination of classical political economy in the preceding chapter, since one of the prevalent contentions in nineteenth-century social thought was that the science of political economy had demonstrated, or claimed to have demonstrated, that the principle of natural harmonious order was operative in man's economic relations with his fellows.

A. THE METAPHYSICS OF HARMONY

The notion that the world is a harmonious order, despite the manifest appearances of conflict, muddle, and formless happenstance, has a long history, going back to the great Greek thinkers of the classical era, but we will confine our attention here to the development of the doctrine in the seventeenth century. The accelerated interest of philosophers in non-theological metaphysics in that period was in great part due to the scientific advances then taking place, especially in physics and astronomy. Science was challenging deeply held notions about the nature of the world, stimulating a great burst of speculative thought which was the beginning of modern philosophy. The immediate issue that gave rise to the metaphysical literature of the seventeenth century was a problem in empiricism first clearly formulated by René

Descartes (1596–1650). Descartes's work initiated an unending debate in philosophy that centred on the relation of physical phenomena to mental phenomena – the problem of 'dualism'. Descartes made a hard categorical distinction between 'body' and 'mind', which stimulated intense efforts by metaphysicians to re-establish a monistic unity, which still continues in the present day. Even philosophers who regard metaphysics as meaningless nonsense, and are scornful of these early attempts to resolve the Cartesian dualism, have nevertheless had to contend with some very difficult problems that are posed by it.

The specific issue raised by Descartes concerns this relation between mental and physical phenomena. If they are *categorically* different, how can they be conjoined, as common sense believes them to be? If one observes, say, the fall of a leaf from a tree, there are two distinct occurrences: the fall of the leaf as a physical phenomenon, and the perception of a falling leaf in the mind. Common sense tells us that the two events are linked, but are they? And if they are, how? We cannot here survey, even briefly, the various answers to these questions that have been offered during the past three centuries, for that would amount to a virtual précis of a large part of modern philosophy. Nor is it possible to state the conclusion philosophers have come to on this issue, since no proposed solution of Descartes's dualism has been able to withstand fatal criticism. A distinguished modern philosopher, writing in 1982, states that 'the question of what is implied by saying that one and the same event has both mental and physical characteristics still waits for a sufficient answer' (A. J. Ayer, *Philosophy in the Twentieth Century*, 1982, p. 190). It must suffice for our purposes here simply to note that if it is possible to demonstrate that the world is a complete harmonious order then all parts or aspects of it are in harmony with all other parts or aspects; the harmony between a perception in the mind and an event in the world is merely an instance of the harmonious nature of the general order of things. This is the line of response to Descartes's problem that gave rise to much of metaphysical philosophy during the era of the scientific revolution. I will here confine discussion to the ideas of Gottfried Wilhelm Leibniz (1646–1716).

Seventeenth-century thinkers, impressed as they were with mechanical inventions, especially clocks, often inclined to treat the mind–body problem as being similar to that posed by the synchronization of two clocks, one representing external phenomena and the other mental consciousness. We could, for example, take two pendulum clocks and link their pendulums together by a rigid rod so that they perforce must move together. This has many difficulties as an analogy of the linkage of mind and body which we cannot go into here. Another approach is to consider two clocks that are perfectly made so that each keeps perfect time. If the two clocks are both set going upon the same instant, they will keep in synchronization throughout eternity, even though they are quite independent of one another. At first sight this seems unpromising as an explanatory analogy for the mind–body relationship but it is, essentially, the one that predominated in seventeenth-century metaphysics.

Before continuing further it may be worth our while to consider a different metaphor, which provides us with three analogical possibilities of harmonious synchronization. This, I believe, is more trenchant in orienting the issue to the question of *social* harmony which is of course our main concern, even though, at the moment, we may seem to be digging in unpromising ground. Consider the ways in which the actions of the musicians in an orchestra can be synchronized to play 'in harmony'. (1) The first corresponds to the second of our clock analogies. If the musicians were trained to follow a score perfectly, and the score contained all necessary instructions, and the score itself had been designed to harmonize the roles of the various instruments, then all that would be necessary is for a starting signal to be given and the music would be perfectly played by synchronized musicians. This corresponds to the analogy of the perfect, but independent, clocks. (2) A harmonious orchestral performance could also be attained if all the musicians obeyed the instructions of a conductor. In principle, only the conductor need know the score, which he could, of course, modify or even create *de novo* as the performance proceeded. The actions of the various musicians would be synchronized with one another, even though each musician operated independently of the others. Of course, to make this metaphor plausible we have to assume that the conductor somehow issues completely detailed instructions and that the musicians obey virtually as automata. This analogy is not without significance in applying the orchestra metaphor to social phenomena. (3) The third analogy is to conceive of the musicians as linked to one another through the information each receives by listening to the sounds made by the others. In such a case there is no need for a conductor. In principle there is no need for a score, either, since the music could develop as the playing went along, as a collective phenomenon, such as occurs, say, in some jazz concerts. The history of social theory, oriented as it is to the problem of how order is attained in human activities, could be written in terms of these three orchestral analogies, some thinkers having stressed the pre-established harmony of (1), others the centrally directed harmony of (2), others the interactive harmony of (3); while still other thinkers, less inclined to metaphysics, have focused, in a pragmatic way, on how these three elements can be used as instrumental methods that may be mixed and combined in order to promote co-operative social organization.

1. The Leibnizian doctrine of harmony

Leibniz is the outstanding figure among those whose line of thought has been governed by the metaphysical conception of the world as a 'pre-established harmony' – this phrase is, in fact, his own description and, according to Bertrand Russell, it was this that he regarded as his greatest contribution to philosophy (*A Critical Exposition of the Philosophy of Leibniz*, 1937, p. 136). Leibniz did not simply assert that the world is a harmonious order, he attempted to demonstrate this as a conclusion following rigorously from two primary axioms: (1) the existence of God, a perfect being, who created the world; and (2) the principle of 'sufficient reason' – that nothing exists or occurs without a reason and, moreover, nothing fails to exist or fails to occur without a reason. The specific features of the world are in no way accidental, for God himself does not (cannot?) act capriciously. The world cannot be different from what it is, since, given the above axioms, the possibility of alternative forms of existence for the things that actually exist is logically contradictory.

God, according to Leibniz, created the world according to this principle of sufficient reason, but he does not act as a continuing governor of it. Thus, to advert to the second of our orchestral analogies, God is not construed as the immediate conductor of on-going worldly events. The fundamental constituents of the world are irreducible elements that Leibniz called 'monads'. These are described as entities that are totally independent of one another. They cannot interact, so the world is not constructed according to the third of our orchestral analogies either. The world is a harmonious order because God designed it to be composed of monads that are 'compossible', as Leibniz put it; i.e. capable of existing together without contradiction. Each monad, however, plays its role in the collective enterprise spontaneously, without direction and without affecting, or being affected by, other monads.

Leibniz's metaphysical conception corresponds to our first orchestral analogy, or the analogy of the two perfect clocks. The harmonious nature of worldly events is inherent in the initial constitution of things, so it is a 'pre-established' harmony. The world, then, is not after all a causal order, since the usual conception of 'cause' would require that monads can affect one another. Thus, according to Leibniz, the commonsense conception of causality is merely an illusion, due to a failure to appreciate that everything is as it is, and occurs as it does because of God's pre-arrangement. Leibniz's metaphysics constructs a completely determined system. But the world is not deterministic because everything is governed by laws of nature in a causal order; it is deterministic because everything that occurs has already been written in the score, so to speak, and the players in the orchestra function as automata. This implication of his metaphysics worried Leibniz a great deal. He was unwilling to accept determinism altogether and struggled mightily to escape it sufficiently to provide room for free will and individual responsibility. It cannot be said that his efforts in this regard did anything but add additional obscurities to his metaphysical theory.

The main features of seventeenth-century metaphysics that are of special interest to the historian of social science are the idea of the world as a continuous plenitude of existence; and the doctrine that it is, of all the possible worlds that could be, the 'best'. The first of these is the subject of a famous book by Arthur O. Lovejoy, *The Great Chain of Being* (1936). I shall draw heavily on this in outlining the idea of continuous plenitude and, indeed, throughout the remainder of this section.

The notion that the world is a continuous plenitude of existence is, briefly put, the view that the whole universe is filled with beings and that each of these differs from those adjacent to it only to an infinitesimal degree, so that the whole forms a continuous 'great chain of being'. The physicist's dictum that 'nature abhors a vacuum' means little more today than a colourful way of expressing the fact that gases and liquids flow down a pressure gradient, but the modern saying reflects the seventeenth-century theological view that God, literally speaking, can tolerate no void, and so *filled* the world with objects. The dictum *natura non facit saltum* (nature does not make leaps) is, similarly, employed today mainly as a colourful way of expressing the continuity of temporal change, such as the process of organic evolution, but in seventeenth-century metaphysics it expressed the view that a static world is a continuum of infinitesimally differentiated things. There may appear to be voids in the cosmos, such as the apparently vast empty spaces between the stars, and there may appear to be discrete differences between the entities of God's creation, such as, for example, between a rock and a tree, but these are only appearances, due to our inability to see the whole chain of being. If we cannot perceive the continuous plenitude of existence, how do we know it to be? By logically deducing it as an implication of the proposition that God is perfect. In the late seventeenth century, and more so in the eighteenth, many theologians attempted to ascertain the properties of God by inductive inference from the perceived properties of nature, but metaphysicians such as Leibniz were arguing in the opposite direction, deducing the 'true' properties of nature from the 'undeniable' properties of God.

Though this line of thinking looms large in Christian theology, its fundamental roots are in Plato and Aristotle. Plato argued (though he presents it as a 'myth') that God created the world because a failure to do so would have been inconsistent with his perfection. To deny existence to other beings is an act of envy, and enviousness is no property of God. (We can begin to see here the grave difficulties of this theory: if envy, and other imperfections, characterize the creations of God, how can God have created properties of which he himself was totally devoid?) God, then, according to Plato, necessarily had to create other beings and, indeed, he had to create *all possible* beings, making the world full, a plenitude. The conception of continuous gradation is implicit in this but it was made explicit by Aristotle, who, as a biologist, was struck by the fact that the various organic species can be arranged in a sequence, with no sharp distinctions between adjacent forms. Even the broad distinction between animals and plants is not sustainable, since there are some forms – the zoophytes – that belong to both classes. Long before the discovery of viruses, Aristotle extended his view of the continuity of nature to claim that no categorical distinction can even be made between living and non-living forms of existence. The invention of the microscope in the seventeenth century, disclosing as it did myriads of living and non-living forms hitherto invisible to human perception, gave empirical support to that era's metaphysical conception of the world as a continuous plenitude. The invention of the differential calculus by Leibniz, and independently by Newton, provided powerful support also by showing how the infinite gradations of continuous nature may be subjected to quantitative analysis, a process previously possible only for phenomena ordered in discrete classes.

Since the seventeenth century the concepts of plenitude and continuity, especially the latter, have enjoyed great appeal, outlasting the popularity of seventeenth-century metaphysics. In natural science, apart from the general use of the differential calculus, the main impact of the idea of continuity has been on biology. Darwin, like Leibniz, was very fond of declaring that nature does not make leaps. Occasionally, as in modern ecological romanticism, one finds a recrudescence of the whole compound of seventeenth-century metaphysics: continuity, plenitude, and natural harmony. In one area of science, however, the principle of continuity has suffered a major blow – in quantum mechanics, where physicists view nature at the sub-atomic level as characterized by discrete packages and capable of making rather astonishing leaps. The influence of the concept of continuity on social science has been very large. The seventeenth-century concept, joined to Darwinism in the nineteenth century, was an especially powerful influence on social science. We leave this for later examination but it is worth noting here that on the title page of the most important book in the development of modern economic theory, Alfred Marshall's *Principles of Economics* (1890), one finds the Leibnizian motto: *natura non facit saltum*.

The concept of continuous plenitude involves something more: the idea that the world is composed not merely of an infinite number of beings but of an infinite number of *kinds* of beings. Plenitude alone could be achieved by simply filling the universe with identical objects, like filling a jar with beads. But this would not have the property of continuity, since that involves differentiation. Plato contended that God's creative power necessarily resulted in a pluralist universe composed of all possible kinds. Leibniz argued along the same lines. The modern saying 'It takes all sorts to make a world' has a sardonic resonance but it could stand as a literal description of the seventeenth century's conception of the constitution of the plenitude. In the social sciences, the closest we can come to identifying a similar notion is Herbert Spencer's doctrine that evolutionary development is characterized by increasing differentiation, which, being a cosmic 'law' in his opinion, characterizes social evolution as well as all other forms of progressive change (see below, Chapter 15 A 4).

There seems, however, to be a contradiction in Leibniz's views on this point in that existence is conceived to be both pluralistic and monistic. Leibniz's attempt to resolve this involves one of the most obscure features of his metaphysics: the idea that the world is composed of a plurality of 'monads' each of which independently 'mirrors' the one whole. The efforts of philosophers to translate Leibniz's metaphor of the mirror into more direct language have not been successful hitherto and I will not attempt it here. Seventeenth-century metaphysicians were often satisfied to represent the pluralist–monist character of existence simply by a motto, which was already ancient in their time: 'The One in the Many, and the Many in the One'. This rather obscure saying was frequently expressed by Leibniz, and Alfred Marshall used it as the epigraph of his second major book on economics (*Industry and Trade*, 1923). Marshall had little interest in metaphysics and almost certainly had never read any Leibnizian philosophy. Moreover, as a social scientist he was clearly not a harmonist, but the appearance of Leibniz's two favourite metaphysical dicta in such prominent places in his writings is curious. Perhaps it means that modern utilitarian social thought has been affected more than it is wont to recognize by the metaphysics of the era that witnessed the rise of science. Perhaps it says something also about the nature of the intellectual evolution in a continuous culture like that of the West: the immortality of fundamental ideas. Empires rise and fall; races and nations flourish and then disappear; preachers of new doctrines are crucified or burnt at the stake; heretical books are destroyed; but basic ideas never die. The culture absorbs them, like an organism digesting the nutriment essential to its existence, and the elements reappear, time and again, in new forms.

More germane to the immediate subject of this chapter is the Leibnizian view that the world is endowed with inherent moral properties as well as physical ones. This addressed itself to the ancient problem of the status of evil. In the early Christian era a flourishing line of thought, derived from pre-Christian sources, was Manichaeism, the doctrine that the world is a kind of battleground between the forces of good and the forces of evil, the ultimate outcome of which may be in doubt. St. Augustine embraced this doctrine in his youth but rejected it upon his conversion to Christianity. As a way of accounting for the existence of evil it has a strong appeal, and it has never been fully extirpated from Christian theology, but it is clearly inconsistent with the view that God is both all-powerful and good.

Leibniz's solution of this problem was to derive the existence of evil as a necessary feature of a world that is a plenitude of existence. Evil not only does exist, it necessarily *must* exist in order to complete the plenitude. Recall Leibniz's 'principle of sufficient reason': nothing exists or fails to exist without a reason; the reason for the existence of evil is that there would otherwise be voids in the plenitude. But recall also the doctrine of 'pre-established harmony'. How is this made consistent with the existence of evil? Leibniz's answer is that of all the worlds that God could create with 'compossible' constituents, he perforce created the best possible world, which is, despite the existence of evil, a manifestation of his goodness. In a passage quoted by Lovejoy, Leibniz declares:

> It is true that one can imagine possible worlds without sin and without suffering, just as one can invent romances about Utopias . . . but these worlds would be much inferior to ours. I cannot show this in detail; you must infer it, as I do, *ab effectu*, since this world, as it is, is the world God chose . . . . (*The Great Chain of Being*, p. 225)

There is a certain circularity in this argument. God chose the best possible world because he is good, and we know that it is the best because God chose it. If the word 'good' has independent meaning, it cannot be made equivalent to 'best possible'. At most, Leibniz only demonstrated that evil is necessary. But even this introduces a serious difficulty: if evil is a necessary constituent of the world, man cannot be held morally responsible for his evil acts, as Leibniz considered him to be.

The doctrine that this is the best possible world had numerous precursors before Leibniz, but since the seventeenth century it has been indelibly associated with his name. As a monumental example of the misuse of intellect, what Israel Zangwill called 'the higher foolishness', it is without equal. In the eighteenth century Voltaire wrote a classic burlesque based on it, *Candide*, in which Leibniz appears as Dr. Pangloss, who, despite an endless succession of terrible events, comforts the hero with assurances that this is the best of all possible worlds. The black comedy potential of the doctrine is apparently inexhaustible: in recent years Italian readers have been entertained by Leonardo Sciascia's anti-communist novel *Candido* and American theatregoers by Leonard Bernstein's musical *Candide* ('What a day! What a day, for an auto-da-fé!'). Justifying the ways of God to man can be hazardous work.

2. Harmony and evolution

In Chapter 8 our attention was drawn to the antithesis between the idea of progress and the idea of perfection. As our examination of utopian social thought there showed, the scenarios of perfect social orders are not simply more imaginative and less constrained versions of the idea of improvement, but belong to a categorically different domain of thought. The ideas we have been examining so far in this chapter, though more cosmic in scope, belong to the utopian category. The fundamental conflict between progress and perfection became evident in the eighteenth century, when Western thought was reoriented to an historical conception of man and society, and the idea of progress became dominant in social theory and social philosophy. The shift in the utopian literature from locating the perfect society in another place (like the kingdom of Prester John) to locating it at another time was paralleled by a shift in the metaphysics of harmony to a temporal mode. In the same era, and not unconnectedly, both utopian social thought and metaphysics became more secular, appealing less to the perfection of God and more to the perfection of the laws of nature. Without an appreciation of the temporalization and secularization of metaphysics it is difficult to see any connection between the grand cosmic theories we have been discussing in this section and the more mundane matters we will examine in section B.

The logical incompatibility between seventeenth-century metaphysics and the idea of progress is evident upon a little reflection. Recall that the perfection of existence is due to a *pre-established* harmony. To advert again to the comparable orchestral analogy, it is a property of the musical score. One must necessarily infer from this that any innovations on the part of the musicians would introduce disharmony. The logic of seventeenth-century metaphysics forbids progress as well as regress: if the world is worse now than it was, it is clearly not perfect now; but if it is better now than it was, it cannot have been perfect then. The concept of perfection belongs to the realm of hard statics; it is incompatible with any kind of change.

It is difficult to believe that this crystalline view of the world was held by even the most devoted believers in the great chain of being. Leibniz himself expressed such an unequivocal belief in the possibility of progress and, indeed, of progress without end that Robert Nisbet, in his recent *History of the Idea of Progress* (1980), gives him a prominent role in the development of this feature of modern Western thought (pp. 157 ff.). But, whether or not anyone ever seriously embraced a static view of the world, it is clear that by the later seventeenth century, and certainly by the eighteenth, the concept of the chain of being was being overwhelmed by the idea of progress. The Western intellect was entering its evolutionist era.

This transformation of thought wrote an end to the metaphysics we have been discussing, but not to its component elements. Most of them found a secure place in the new evolutionary model of existence. The concept of the plenitude was less prominent, but the concept of continuity was even more so than in the static model of the chain of being. The idea of harmony was also reoriented to evolutionism, and the moral judgements embedded in it were recast in terms of progress. In his *Essay on Man*, Alexander Pope declared that all the evils we observe are really but part of the 'universal good' that is embodied in God's plan for the evolution of the world. Malthus tempered the gloomy conclusions of his *Essay on Population* by suggesting that the pressure of population growth against the supply of food is part of God's plan to secure the progressive development of man's moral character by providing him with challenge. The same view is contained in Immanuel Kant's 'The Idea of a Universal History from a Cosmopolitan Point of View': the wise Creator endowed man with selfishness, envy, and other 'unsociable' qualities that generate social conflicts, for, otherwise, man would live a simple life of peace and contentment that would not promote the development of his 'rational capacities'. In the twentieth century the same essential idea forms the foundation of A. J. Toynbee's ten-volume *A Study of History* (1934–54), in which man's cultural evolution is seen as the product of 'challenge and response'.

Tracing the ramifications of the metaphysics of harmony as it encountered the idea of progress and changing conceptions of man's own nature is beyond our scope. We cannot even trace its full impact upon social thought, or on social science more narrowly construed. Our study of social harmonism will be restricted to the development of the idea that one part of the social order, the economic system, is governed by laws which, in all essential respects, are analogous to the Leibnizian pre-established harmony.

B. THE IDEOLOGY OF *LAISSEZ-FAIRE*

The idea that the world as a whole is a harmonious order does not necessarily mean that every part of it is such an order considered by itself. Consequently, it is not necessary for a metaphysical harmonist to contend that any particular aspect or sector of the world is harmonious. Nevertheless, there is a strong temptation for the harmonist to view any part of the world that he considers especially important as harmonious in itself. In this section we examine the notion that the economic organization of a society can be a natural harmonious order.

As industry and commerce grew in importance during the latter part of the eighteenth century and in the nineteenth, increasing attention was devoted to the properties of the market system of economic organization. Specialization and trade go back as far as archaeologists have been able to trace the record of human social life, but they began to increase with extraordinary rapidity in the eighteenth century. These developments, plus the great prestige of the natural sciences, which we have already emphasized, led to efforts to construct similarly scientific theories of the market system. In view of the great influence of seventeenth-century metaphysics on all branches of European thought it would be surprising indeed if the concept of inherent harmony were totally absent from discussions of the structure and mechanics of economic organization. In the outline of classical political economy in the previous chapter we paid no attention to this and in the next chapter it will be argued that economic theory was dominated by a very different philosophical outlook, utilitarianism, but this does not mean that the harmonist view made no significant appearance. In fact many historians have contended that nineteenth-century economics was fundamentally harmonist, inspired by the view that the market economy, if left to work by its own automatic processes, would create the best of all possible worlds. Adam Smith's 'invisible hand' was, in this view, a reflection of the Leibnizian doctrine of pre-established harmony, through which the activities of the independent entities are ordered without requiring the visible and tangible hand of any directing authority. This is the doctrine of *laissez-faire* or, at least, the extreme version of it. The notion that a hard ideology of *laissez-faire* was deeply embedded in classical political economy and that it also dominated the actual economic policy stance of the nineteenth-century state is an image of the era that modern historical research has very greatly modified but it still persists strongly in popular opinion.

In investigating this matter some preliminary remarks are necessary about terminology. Some nineteenth-century writers used the term 'laissez-faire' to refer to the conception of the world, or at least that part of it embraced by the market system, as a natural harmonious order in something like the Leibnizian sense. But others used the term simply to mean that the market system is capable of performing co-ordination functions, without contending that it can do so perfectly, or that it can function without the extensive operation of auxiliary co-ordinating instruments such as those provided by the coercive and constraining power of the state or by established custom. Others used the term to mean that in considering the exercise of governmental power the burden of proof should be on those who propose to constrain private actions rather than on those who contend that they should be let alone. In investigating here the role of *laissez-faire* as an ideology we are not interested in such moderate and tentative defences of the market system, even though the phrase *laissez-faire* was sometimes used as a label for such views. We are looking for evidence of a stronger and more doctrinaire contention: that the market system is capable of providing a perfect mechanism of economic organization with no more assistance from the state than the prevention of criminal acts against life and property and, in the civil sphere, the enforcement of private contracts.

The qualification made at the end of the preceding sentence is necessary in order to render correctly the views of most of those whom we shall characterize as espousing an ideology of *laissez-faire*. Few of these writers contended that a harmonious social order could function without government altogether, but before we begin our study of the ideology we should take brief note of the fact that such an *ultra-laissez-faire* doctrine occupies a position of some importance in the literature of nineteenth-century political philosophy. This is the theory of 'anarchism'. It is the polar opposite of Thomas Hobbes's political philosophy, which we examined in Chapter 4. Not only is it not necessary that the state should exercise unlimited power, but it is not necessary to have a state at all. In the mid-nineteenth century, anarchism became associated with socialist theory through the writings and political activities of Pierre Proudhon and Mikhail Bakunin, but this was before 'socialism' became identified, as it is today, with the advocacy of state power and comprehensive governmental control of the economy.

The first person to give a clear formulation of anarchist theory was William Godwin, in his *Inquiry Concerning Political Justice* (1793), and in numerous other writings. His son-in-law Percy Bysshe Shelley, one of the great romantics of the era, expressed Godwin's views in his poetry, most notably in his long lyric drama, *Prometheus Unbound* (1820). Godwin's central idea was that any interference with individual freedom is both unnecessary and unjust. If people were left to exercise their individuality without constraint, a perfect harmonious order would result. In Godwin's view the argument that a government is necessary to assure that people act justly towards one another is ludicrous, since government itself is the chief cause of injustice.

> With what delight [says Godwin] must every well-informed friend of mankind look forward to . . . the dissolution of political government, of that brute engine, which has been the only perennial cause of the vices of mankind, and which . . . has mischiefs of various sorts incorporated with its substance, and no otherwise to be removed than by its utter annihilation! (*Political Justice*, chapter 24)

Godwin declares in this passage that government is the 'only perennial cause of the vices of mankind', but there are also others not 'perennial'. In fact he disapproved of any kind of collective activity that requires the individual to accommodate to other persons, including such things as theatrical productions and orchestral music, speaking of them as involving an 'absurd and vicious co-operation'. Godwin's perfect social order can hardly be described as 'social' at all. His extreme individualism projects one back to Leibniz's conception of the world as a pre-established harmony of totally independent 'monads', and forward to the individualist element in nineteenth-century romanticism and, in our own day, to such writers as Ayn Rand.

Anarchism is important in the general history of modern social thought, but not in the history of social *science*. Like other utopians, Godwin made no effort to construct theories or models of social phenomena that went much beyond simple intuitive assertion. All he had to say about the economy was to offer the assurance that it would work much better in a regime of unconstrained individualism, but he does not say anything about *how* it would work. In the remainder of this chapter we will look at the doctrine of *laissez-faire* which, though it remains in its extreme form a branch of anarchism, focuses specifically upon the economic aspect of social organization and the role of the market system as an automatic mechanism that co-ordinates the activities of independent individuals. The questions that will concern our attention are the extent to which that doctrine reflected a metaphysical view of natural harmony, and its connection with the development of systematic economic theory.

1. Before the classical economists

As we noted in Chapter 5, the first systematic model of the economy was constructed by the Physiocrats in the third quarter of the eighteenth century. François Quesnay and his disciples are often represented in the history of economic thought as deriving from their economic system a rigid doctrine of *laissez-faire* but, as we shall see, such an interpretation cannot be sustained, and one suspects that the mere fact that the doctrine has no native English name but is designated by a French term is, in part at least, responsible for its ascription to the Physiocrats. Similarly, the fact that there is no word for the doctrine in German, which earlier used the term *Smithianismus*, later replaced by *Manchestertum*, may account for the fact that in Germany it is regarded as an English doctrine.

The associated French phrases *laissez-faire*, *laissez-nous faire*, and *laissez-faire, laissez-passer* were not, in origin, due to the Physiocrats, but seem to have come into use as early as a century before. The second of these ('leave us alone') was apparently uttered by a merchant, one LeGendre, about 1680, as a pointed reply to the solicitous inquiry of Colbert (chief economic adviser of Louis XIV) as to what the state might do to assist industry. The Marquis d'Argenson and Vincent de Gournay (first half of the eighteenth century) used one or other of these terms fairly freely in their writings. The Sieur de Boisguillebert (1646–1714), whose theories are of more interest to the historian of economics, used the phrase *laissez-faire* in a manner that suggests that he may fairly be considered a natural harmony ideologue.

It was their disposition to express themselves for literary effect in the metaphysical terms of an *Ordre naturel et essentiel des sociétés politiques* (the title of a book by Mercier de la Rivière) that undoubtedly was largely responsible for the Physiocrats being looked upon as doctrinaire harmonists by later commentators. But this is, at best, a superficial interpretation of their views. Ronald Meek, the most thorough student of the Physiocratic literature, points out that their identification of agriculture as the only source of 'net product' in the economy was in fact used by them as the basis of a plea for intervention by the state, positively, by stimulating demand for agricultural products and encouraging investment in farming and, negatively, by removing the host of constraints and interferences with which that industry was encumbered at the time (R. L. Meek, *The Economics of Physiocracy*, 1962, pp. 23 f.). Colbert's economic policy, which was still in the ascendant, employed the influence of government on behalf of manufacturing and commerce. The Physiocrats were trying to orient it in another direction. In using the phrase *laissez-faire*, as they did, they seemed to mean only that if the king wished to be wise as well as energetic in promoting the economic growth of his nation he would do well to use his power in accordance with the laws of nature. This was not an ideology of non-intervention, but the very different view that if one wishes to manipulate the economy successfully, the laws that govern its behaviour must be known and taken into account.

Physiocratic interventionism was not confined to agriculture, either. The Physiocrats favoured state poor relief and education, and other activist policies. Some of their contemporaries even accused them of excessive paternalism. On freedom of trade and commerce, the issue that became the prime object of *laissez-faire* dogma in the nineteenth century, they argued only for freedom of internal commerce for agricultural products, and freedom of exports. But they regarded the import trade as a worthy object of special regulation, since, according to their theory, imports contribute nothing to the 'net product' and, moreover, they impair the achievement of national self-sufficiency, which was held to be a desirable objective of state policy.

In England, nothing that corresponds intellectually to the Physiocratic grand system of the economy made its appearance prior to the nineteenth century. With few exceptions, the writings of the so-called 'mercantilist' period held the view that harmony in economic processes does not spring from the natural play of individual interest, but must be created by the wise governor. The necessity of state action in this fashion is to be found, for example, in the economic writings of George Berkeley and Bernard Mandeville in the early eighteenth century, and later in those of Sir James Steuart, who, if Adam Smith had not written the *Wealth of Nations*, might well have initiated the science of economics with his *Inquiry into the Principles of Political Economy* (1767). Mandeville's proposition that 'private vices' lead to 'public benefits' in his famous *Fable of the Bees* (1714) has sometimes been interpreted as an expression of harmonist doctrine, but more careful reading shows that, like most of his contemporaries, Mandeville was seeking to discover the opportunities for beneficial state action in the economic sphere rather than to promote a doctrine of *laissez-faire*.

As the capitalistic market-oriented economy developed during the eighteenth century and businessmen grew in power and influence, they urged upon government both state intervention and *laissez-faire*. There is no mystery in this. Men of business, then as now, desired the positive aid of the state in some things but also wished it to refrain from other activities that they regarded as objectionable. If we fix attention exclusively on the first, the eighteenth century appears to be an age of almost ubiquitous state interference with private economic activity; if we focus on the other, it appears an age when *laissez-faire* was in the air. The general image of this period that has come down to us in the historiography rests mainly upon the first of these two alternatives, and the term 'mercantilism', when used to denote more than the emphasis of the period on international trade and gold, usually implies a general economic policy of state intervention, even 'economic planning' in something like the modern sense.

In the wider angle of view that time affords, however, it is clear that the trend towards the relaxation of old restrictions on economic activity was the more significant development. Many of the restrictive statutes of mercantilist Britain were, in fact, never repealed but simply allowed to fall into disuse. Acts of explicit repeal were often due to the fact that old statutes had been rummaged out of the archives by those opposed to the economic changes that were taking place in order to enlist the power of the courts on their behalf. The manner by which the freeing of private enterprise thus took place in the eighteenth century is itself significant. It demonstrates that the most powerful influence at work was the press of economic events, not a general theory or philosophy of economic policy.

2. The classical economists

As a phase in the history of economic thought and policy, *laissez-faire* is usually regarded as a nineteenth-century phenomenon, and an English one. The established resonances of the term harmonize so well with the other standard stereotypes of the Victorian age – narrow-mindedness, harshness, sanctimonious moralism, philistinism, etc. – that it evokes immediate images of the hard-eyed English manufacturer or merchant, ruling his business, as he ruled his household, with stern confidence in his knowledge of what was best for all. This is a general picture that modern historiography has greatly revised, and, with it, a revision in our understanding of Victorian social thought and policy has also begun to take place. The Victorian Age now appears to modern students of the period as a rather confused mixture of conflicting themes. If we had to give the era a name to match the Age of Reason and Age of Enlightenment for earlier periods we should perhaps call it the Age of Ambiguity. In nineteenth-century England there emerged the world's first truly pluralist society – differentiated within itself in economic power, political authority, religion, and ideas. It does not resolve crisply under the historian's microscope, because it did not in fact resolve within itself.

A prominent feature of the earlier historiography of Victorian England is that influential opinion was represented as dominated by the ideology of *laissez-faire*, which, in turn, was traced to the theories of classical political economy. A professor of history at Princeton, writing in 1913, characterized Victorian England thus:

> a paralysis of mind and soul crept abroad; for the spider's web, fragile yet clinging, enclosed and covered man, a web of *laissez-faire*, spun ceaselessly by the metallic and remorseless brains of Ricardo, Poulett Thompson, Nassau Senior, and the whole troop of classical economists. (Water P. Hall, 'Certain early Reactions against Laissez-faire', American Historical Association *Annual Report*, Vol. 1, p. 130)

The language is more extreme than that of most other commentators, but this view of the Victorian era enjoyed wide currency until modern historical scholarship began to undermine it. The popular view of the era, however, is still dominated by the stereotype of a doctrinaire *laissez-faire* that was promoted by the leading economists of the period.

In Chapter 7 we saw that Adam Smith, whose name is most often associated with *laissez-faire*, did not espouse it as a doctrine, and the concept of the 'invisible hand' in the *Wealth of Nations* does not reflect Leibnizian metaphysics or any other variant of the view that the world is an inherently harmonious order. On the contrary, Smith did not regard it as possible for an economy to work without the exercise of governmental powers by the state, not only to provide a legal framework for private activities but to furnish numerous services that are beyond the capacity of the market system. That

Smith regarded many of the economic activities of the eighteenth-century state as doing more harm than good and advised their cessation is a testimony to his good sense, not to the grip of a *laissez-faire* doctrine. The same is true of the major figures who subsequently developed the analytical models of classical political economy. Some of them used the term *laissez-faire* but more as a part of their generally pragmatic and expedient view of the role of government than as a motto expressing a philosophic conviction. The classical economists entertained a general presumption against governmental interference and even tended to speak of non-intervention as a 'principle', but they did not make use of it as a maxim which rendered direct judgement on particular questions of governmental intervention. In fact they favoured, on simple pragmatic grounds, a great deal of specific intervention. This feature of classical economics is supported by any reading one chooses to do for oneself of the original texts, and in increased proportion to the amount of that reading.

A detailed examination of the classical economists on this point is not possible here, but some discussion of them is necessary in order to come at the question of the place occupied by the *laissez-faire* doctrine in our intellectual history. Little need be said, in this connection, about David Ricardo. His writings were too constrained by the requirements of rigorous analysis, and he was too little given to philosophic generalization, to provide grounds for characterizing him as a harmonist. Ricardo is often named in the literature identifying classical economics with *laissez-faire*, but specific statements of his are not quoted or referred to, and it seems apparent that his name is included among the company of *laissez-faire* ideologues primarily because of his distinction as the acknowledged theoretical leader of the classical school. Aside from Adam Smith, J. R. McCulloch and Nassau W. Senior are the classical authors that require most attention in this connection, for it is with them that the doctrine of *laissez-faire* has been most distinctly connected as an influence upon contemporary policy.

John Ramsay McCulloch (1779–1864) was the chief expounder of the theories of classical political economy before this role was taken by John Stuart Mill. In the first half of the nineteenth century he represented the classical school to a greater extent than any other figure. He wrote voluminously and with lucidity; he participated vigorously in public discussion of economic questions; and his works were extensively reprinted and translated into foreign languages. He wrote the important article on 'political economy' for the *Encyclopaedia Britannica* in 1824, and this, turned into a monograph on *The Principles of Political Economy* (1825), became virtually the first extensively used textbook in economics. Before J. S. Mill's *Principles of Political Economy* was published in 1848, McCulloch's works were generally used as the chief sources for the orthodox corpus of classical economics. Because of his public prominence as an expositor of political economy McCulloch became an object of hatred and ridicule by those who were opposed to it for one reason or another. Thomas Carlyle, who viewed classical economics as a symptom of a decaying civilization, regarded McCulloch as the very incarnation of its devilish work. In Thomas Love Peacock's satirical novel *Crotchet Castle*, McCulloch appears in the character 'MacQuedy' (the reference is to the use of *Q.E.D.* in mathematical proofs) as a representation of the rather special kind of intellectual foolishness and narrow-mindedness that Peacock considered to be characteristic of the political economists.

In the 1840's, when the great debate over the corn laws took place, a *laissez-faire* ideology existed to be sure, but it is significant that McCulloch was not then identified with it. The London *Economist*, for example, which ran a doctrinaire crusade for general *laissez-faire* as a part of its campaign against the tariff, regarded him as worthy enough when he produced editions of Smith's and Ricardo's works, but his own productions were viewed as evincing a deplorable lack of firmness on the great question of the role of the state in economic affairs. By the 1880's, however, it was almost customary among economists to blame McCulloch for the doctrinaire image of classical economics, and this has persisted down to the present. If one consults McCulloch's own writings, however, it becomes clear that the view that he was a *laissez-faire* ideologue is not sustainable.

This is not to say that occasional passages implying such a doctrinaire view are not to be found in McCulloch's works. His *Encyclopaedia Britannica* article on 'political economy', and his *Principles*, could be quoted selectively in this way. His *Discourse on the Rise, Progress, Peculiar Objects, and Importance of Political Economy* (1824) also might reasonably lead the reader to infer that he held a harmonist viewpoint and advocated a *laissez-faire* policy. But against such passages one must place explicit rejection by him of *laissez-faire* as a general principle: in the *Principles* he notes that 'An idea seems . . . to have been recently gaining ground, that the duty of government in regard to the domestic policy of a country is almost entirely of a negative kind, and that it has merely to maintain the security of property and the freedom of industry.' The matter, he felt, was 'by no means so simple and easily defined as those who support this opinion would have us believe'. 'The principle of *laissez-faire*,' he observes in another publication, written in 1848, 'may be safely trusted to in some things but in many more it is wholly inapplicable; and to appeal to it on all occasions savours more of the policy of the parrot than of a statesman or a philosopher.' One of McCulloch's favourite points was that the physical sciences differ essentially from the 'moral and political sciences' in that the principles of the former are *always* true and that those of the latter are only true most of the time. In the *Encyclopaedia Britannica* article and in the *Discourse* he pointedly applied this specifically to the question whether people should be left free 'to follow the bent of their own inclinations, and to engage in such branches of industry as they think proper' and came to the conclusion: usually, but not invariably.

The list of recommended specific interferences that can be compiled from McCulloch's works is long enough to satisfy any utilitarian. Public education, the relief of poverty, control of working conditions in factories, and public health legislation, all items of sharp controversy in McCulloch's day, received his strong endorsement. He supported working men's combinations on the simple pragmatic ground that they would increase the strength of labour in the wage bargain, and an article by him in the *Edinburgh Review* in 1823 was influential in persuading Parliament to repeal the laws prohibiting trade unions. He deplored monopoly practices by business and advocated governmental supervision of business in industries where monopoly was unavoidable, such as water supply and railways, and in banking, where competition could not be expected to lead unambiguously to the public good. He recommended the establishment of training standards and the compulsory licensing of physicians, and the governmental certification of articles that could not safely be tested by the buyer himself, such as firearms and ships' anchors. He advocated the governmental provision of postal services. Unfettered individual enterprise was, in his view, the primary instrument of progress, but *laissez-faire* could not be a universal rule.

> Freedom [of economic activity] is valuable only as a means to an end; and whenever it can be shown that the end – the *salus populi* or public advantage – will best be secured by the imposition of restrictions, they ought, unquestionably, to be imposed.

The principle, then, to which McCulloch had final reference is not a metaphysic of harmony and its derivative of doctrinaire *laissez-faire*, but a utilitarian conception of the general welfare.

The object of the most intense obloquy by those who identified classical economics with *laissez-faire*, and held both notions in contempt, was neither Adam Smith, the founder, nor J. R. McCulloch, the leading expositor, of classical economics. That distinction was reserved for Nassau William Senior, the most prominent economic statesman of the period. Senior was the chief economic adviser of the Whigs. He was a member, and an exceptionally influential one, of a number of the important Royal Commissions of the mid-century era. No economist of the period had a larger immediate influence on governmental policy than he.

In his first term as Drummond Professor of Political Economy at Oxford (1825–30) Senior advocated in his lectures a narrow caretaker-state role of government, but this was a neophyte opinion and did not long remain his attitude on the issue. He quickly adopted an essentially pragmatic stance, viewing the responsibilities of government as determined primarily by the wishes of the community in question, limited only by the practical problem of the government's ability to achieve the end desired. Senior was, however, the inspiration and author of the famous (or notorious) report of the Poor Law Commissioners of 1834 and the storm of controversy that focused on this report and the subsequent Poor Law Amendment Act, did much to fasten on to him (and all economists) an image of hard-hearted Malthusianism, with which doctrinaire *laissez-faire* was closely identified by critics. In addition, he was the originator of the 'abstinence' theory of interest; was widely thought to have advanced the proposition that businessmen's profits were due to the 'last hour of labour' of their work force; and wrote some rather silly passages that romanticized the conditions of work in factories. For these he was subject to much ridicule as an apologist for the rising capitalist class, an attitude regarded by many as intimately associated with a doctrinaire espousal of *laissez-faire*. This image has clung to Senior's name down to the present day.

If we examine Senior's career, however, it is clear that he was, above all else, a pragmatist. It is one of the ironies of history that while he was one of the few economists of the early Victorian period who rejected the Malthusian theory of population, his greatest work, the Poor Law Amendment Act of 1834, has been generally characterized by historians as inspired by Malthusianism. The Amendment Act did not in fact spring from Malthusian population theory, but from the simple fact that the old Poor Law system had become an administrative, economic, and financial monstrosity, and its revision required the work of men endowed with practical and innovative capacity, not ideology. Popular opinion of the 1830's created a whole string of derogatory characterizations of 'political economy' and it is perhaps not surprising that Senior, the author of the hated Poor Law Amendment Act, was labelled with them all, including the characterization of being a doctrinaire advocate of *laissez-faire*. Senior may have been sensitive to this popular image of him when, in the lectures he gave upon returning to Oxford in 1847, he made unmistakably clear his attitude to the role of the state. Noting that some had argued that since governmental intervention often fails to achieve its intended results or even produces the opposite,

> They have declared that the business of government is simply to afford protection, to repel or to punish internal or external violence or fraud, and that to do more is usurpation. This proposition I cannot admit. The only rational foundation of government . . . is . . . the general benefit of the community. It is the duty of a Government to do whatever is conducive to the welfare of the governed. The only limit to this duty is its power. And . . . the only limit to its power is its moral or physical inability. (Quoted in Marian Bowley, *Nassau Senior and Classical Economics*, 1949, p. 265)

Nevertheless, the notion persists that Adam Smith, Ricardo, McCulloch, Senior, and the other leading economists of the classical period were united in espousing a general doctrine of *laissez-faire*. Henry Sidgwick's lecture to the British Association in 1885 on 'The Scope and Method of Economic Science' pointed out that it was erroneous. This was the first of numerous attempts to set the historical record straight on this matter, all of which have so far failed to dislodge the popular myth that the work of the early economists was inspired by the metaphysical doctrine of natural harmony. For some reason, many historians of nineteenth-century thought still appear to have a compelling need to believe it.

3. Economic policy, popular political economy, and public debate

Let us move now from the plane of economic theory to the level of action and popular opinion. During the heyday of classical political economy, was there a *laissez-faire* ideology at work guiding the policy decisions of Parliament and government and the public debates thereon? A strong current of economic liberalization was in fact in motion even before the publication of Adam Smith's *Wealth of Nations*. This trend was not reversed even by the national crisis of the Napoleonic wars. Britain did not revert to a policy of economic regulation under the stress of what was, for the time, 'total' war, but allowed economic activity to operate under the degree of freedom it had by then acquired. This might be viewed as evidence of the strength of *laissez-faire* ideology, but no one who writes of the existence of such a doctrine of economic policy dates it as established as early as this and, moreover, it is implausible that any abstract doctrine could have stood in the way of state mobilization of the economy in the cause of national survival under conditions of such intense fear of the French as then prevailed. It is more plausible to interpret the policy stance of the British government in this period as indicating that, by this time, few men of influence viewed the older types of intervention as efficient. With the onset of peace, the current of liberalization resumed and quickened. The second and third decades of the century witnessed a great and almost continuous freeing of economic activity from state regulation. Britain was now clearly embarked upon a new approach in her economic policy. But this trend does not, in itself, prove the existence of a guiding economic ideology such as *laissez-faire* is supposed to have been. It is evidence, to be sure, but only *prima facie*, not conclusive.

Again, there is no lack of accusers, both contemporary and retrospective, giving witness to the dominance of ideology over reason and humanity in the economic policies of the Victorian Age. But, upon examination, the issue becomes replete with ambiguity. To illustrate this, I draw attention here to two well known contemporary writers, Charles Kingsley and Samuel Smiles, whose political philosophies and reactions to the florescent industrial and commercial capitalism of their time could not have been more different.

Kingsley was one of the founders of 'Christian Socialism', the first radical movement to penetrate significantly into one of the established estates of the realm, the Church of England. He was a radical activist both inside the Church itself and outside, in working men's movements and associations. He wrote voluminously on social questions in essays, letters, poetry, and fiction. Literary scholars remember him more today as the person who goaded John

Henry Newman, upon the latter's conversion to Catholicism, into writing his great *Apologia pro Vita Sua* (1864) than for his own creations, but he was an exceedingly popular author in his own day and some of his fiction is still read for enjoyment by the young. His most important social novel, *Alton Locke* (1850), is now almost forgotten, but it was a best seller (in both England and America) when first published. As a story it is a real Victorian tear-jerker. Alton Locke is a poor lad, apprenticed to a sweatshop tailor, but he thirsts for learning and beauty and begins to read books. He is befriended by an old Scots bookseller of radical views who guides his education. He writes poetry, which brings him to the notice of some members of the upper classes and clergy, who encourage him and promote the publication of his poems, though not without some political editing which he later deeply regrets. Of course, he falls in love with a beautiful girl of this class, and equally 'of course' it is impossible that his love should be requited. He becomes a Chartist, is involved in a riot, arrested and sent to prison. Later he takes part in the great Chartist agitation of 1848 but emerges disillusioned. Physically ill and sick at heart, he takes ship to America, but dies *en route*. In the process of taking Alton Locke through this stereotyped romance, Kingsley gives horrifying descriptions of the working conditions of the poor, advocates working men's associations, and preaches to his fellow Anglican clergy that their proper mission is to spearhead and guide the movement for social and political reform.

As one might guess from the narrative skeleton of *Alton Locke*, Kingsley's democratic sympathies were, to say the least, uncertain. He was equally ambiguous towards political economy. He liked to regard himself as a man of scientific attitude and advanced thought; to think well of and be thought well of by the new intelligentsia; but there was much in political economy and the idea of laws of nature in the social sphere that he deplored. In the course of discussing the miseries of the labouring poor in *Alton Locke*, Kingsley puts these words into the mouth of Crossthwaite, a needleworker:

> But you can recollect as well as I can, when a deputation of us went up to a member of Parliament – one that was reputed to be a philosopher and a political economist, and a liberal – and set before him the ever increasing penury and misery of our trade, and of those connected with it; you recollect his answer – that, however glad he would be to help us, it was impossible – he could not alter the laws of nature - that wages were regulated by the amount of competition among the men themselves, and that it was no business of government, or anyone else, to interfere in contracts between the employer and the employed, that those things regulated themselves by the laws of political economy, which it was madness and suicide to oppose.

Now that seems to be plain enough, and it is a double-barrelled shot; it identifies political economy as the intellectual basis of *laissez-faire* ideology and it certifies the effective penetration of that ideology into Westminster.

But if we use such a passage as an indicator of Kingsley's own view of the responsibilities of the state, we are on treacherous ground. A few years later, when the price of bread rose sharply during the Crimean War and there was threat of rioting, we find him taking a different stance. At a meeting of one of the working men's associations in which he was active, a member asked why the government did not adopt what he called 'Joseph's plan', that is, buy up grain to prevent speculation and provide fair distribution. To this Kingsley replied:

> Yes, and why ain't you and I flying about with wings and dewdrops hanging to our tails? Joseph's plan won't do for us. What minister could we trust with money enough to buy corn for the people, [and] power to buy where he chose?

Then he went on to give the questioner an orthodox lecture on political economy (M. Kaufmann, *Charles Kingsley*, 1892, p. 181). The fact is, even those who castigated the state for insensitivity and inaction, and deplored the theory they thought it was based upon, quailed at the prospect of intervention when they considered the character of the government and bureaucracy that was to do the intervening.

Samuel Smiles has achieved historical immortality as the very symbol of Victorian individualism. He celebrated the orthodox virtues in books devoted to *Self-help* (1859), *Character* (1871), *Thrift* (1875), and *Duty* (1887). The first of these sold an astounding 20,000 copies in its first year and was translated into all the major languages of the world. A whole series of other books sang the praises of the great men of business and industry who, by practising these virtues, had created the industrial economy that had made Britain first among the nations of the world. He even practised the virtues himself, sometimes to the despair of his family. If there is any author of the Victorian Age in whose writings we should expect to find the government advised to restrict itself to a severely limited role it is Samuel Smiles, and so we do; but note this passage from *Thrift*:

> When typhus or cholera breaks out, they tell us that nobody is to blame.
> That terrible Nobody! How much he has to answer for! More mischief is done by Nobody than by all the world besides. Nobody adulterates our food. Nobody poisons us with bad drink. Nobody supplies us with foul water. Nobody spreads fever in blind alleys and unswept lanes. Nobody leaves towns undrained. Nobody fills jails, penitentiaries and convict stations. Nobody makes poachers, thieves and drunkards.
> Nobody has a theory, too – a dreadful theory. It is embodied in two words: Laissez-faire – let alone. When people are poisoned by plaster of paris mixed with flour, 'Let alone' is the remedy. When *Cocculus Indicus* is used instead of hops, and men die prematurely, it is easy to say, 'Nobody did it.' Let those who can, find out when they are cheated: *Caveat emptor*.

When people live in foul dwellings, let them alone. Let wretchedness do its work; do not interfere with death.

This is the most powerful indictment of *laissez-faire* to be found in the literature of the Victorian Age. It beats anything in Carlyle or Dickens. 'Let wretchedness do its work; do not interfere with death.' Who would not blench upon hearing that characterization of his social philosophy? Its date is 1875 and its point of focus is the presumed theory of classical political economy, with its presumed dominance over social and economic policy. Following this passage we find Samuel Smiles urging that there ought to be a law, indeed a whole series of laws, about drainage, water, paving, ventilation, etc. – all this from the leading apostle of Victorian self-reliance!

There is no doubt that the self-help doctrine was a fundamental constituent of nineteenth-century liberalism. It is ubiquitous in the social literature of the period, regardless of the political colouration of the author. There is no doubt, either, that the appeal of such ideas was a ready-made lever for *laissez-faire* propaganda; but when we find the leading popular apostle of individualism exclaiming so bitterly that its tenets are excessively applied, we have to pause and consider whether the Victorian faith in self-help was quite as simple and straightforward as we have been led to believe. Read by themselves, the passages quoted above from Smiles and Kingsley seem to certify that an obtuse and insensitive doctrine had entrenched itself in the bosom of the state, that government had chained itself to *laissez-faire* doctrine. But, read with an eye to the surrounding ambiguities, passages of this sort mean something else. They testify to the inactivity of government in a purely *relative* sense – relative to the growing needs of the time. The world was changing very rapidly, and the arts and acts of government were lagging behind developments in industry and commerce. In such a situation even Samuel Smiles was urging the state to be more active.

And, indeed, the Victorian state *was* active. Its seeming sluggishness was only relative to the problems that economic change was presenting with such rapidity, and it is this gap that contemporary and retrospective observers have mistaken for ideology or torpor. But, relative to what preceded it, the Victorian state was full of energy and innovation and was continuously straining against the practical boundaries set by its political and administrative capacities. The historian W. L. Burn remarks that some of the legislation of the period 'contained startling exceptions to the laissez-faire doctrine' over a wide field of concern (*The Age of Equipoise: a Study of the mid-Victorian Generation*, 1964, p. 153). But it is 'startling' only because of the stereotype that has come down to us. If we think of Britain as the first society in the history of the world to experience the impact of industrialization, urbanization, and the replacement of communal social organization by the factory system and the widespread proletarianization of labour, our interpretation changes and we see her struggling to cope with large and novel problems.

As one surveys the legislative and administrative activity of the Victorian period it seems impossible to state any general principle that would define what the state then found it legitimate to do and what to leave alone. Some inconsistencies approach the grotesque. For example, the government did practically nothing to regulate the operations of railway companies, despite the large number of accidents and the clear evidence of elementary negligence; yet, at the same time, it enacted many measures to control the operation of passenger ships. One might think that *laissez-faire* and *caveat emptor* were regarded as the right rules for continuing British residents, but those who voyaged or emigrated abroad would have to risk the moral dangers of a regulated trade. Surveying the legislation of the mid-century decades, Burn comes to the conclusion that 'As "evils" came to light they were dealt with but it is very difficult to see any principle of selection behind the dealing' (pp. 160 f.). If we go further and try to discover how the 'evils' came to light, we will often discover a Samuel Plimsoll or an Edwin Chadwick, men dedicated, even obsessed, not by a general ideological principle, but by the need for particular improvements. There were indeed those who deplored such a loose and *ad hoc* attitude on the part of government, wishing to see the general principles of state policy clearly defined and rigorously applied; and there were those among them who argued that practical problems would be best solved by the free play of the market, and the unconstrained exercise of self-interest. But those who regarded this as the whole *vade mecum* of the legislator were few, and they did not succeed in binding the practice of government to a hard doctrine of *laissez-faire*.

We have to remember that the institutions of government in Victorian England did not possess much capacity for the efficient administration of an interventionist economic policy. Many who opposed the market system found themselves in a dilemma, because they were also reluctant to call for the adoption of new responsibilities by a state apparatus which they regarded, with considerable justification, as corrupt and incompetent. Charles Dickens, for example, though he wrote in derogatory terms about the political economists, and abhorred the market economy that they favoured, was also a fierce critic of the government of his day and, on the few occasions on which he expressed an explicit political philosophy, he made it plain that he entertained little hope that the state could be a constructive force in social improvement (see Humphry House, *The Dickens World*, 1942, chapter 7). No advocate of *laissez-faire*, before or since, has produced as scathing a portrait of governmental bureaucracy as Dickens's description of the 'Circumlocution Office' in *Little Dorrit* (1857).

Anyone who has been squeezed reluctantly through a college course in modern economics, with its recondite graphs and diagrams, will find it hard to believe that it was ever a popular subject. But in the second quarter of the nineteenth century it was popular in England, even to the point of being a fad in some quarters. Young middle-class ladies of 'accomplishment' were admired if they could prattle political economy as well as play the piano or sing in tune. Instruction in political economy for the working classes was a rather more serious business. The middle and upper class-sponsors of working-class education held it as essential that the true principles of political economy should be taught to the lower orders. And it was never too early to begin – in the Birkbeck and other schools the working-class child was instructed on the 'laws of political economy' as soon as he could read, or even before. When Charles Dickens created his unforgettable schoolmaster, Mr Gradgrind, that immortal portrait of fatuity was not entirely a work of imagination; it was modelled upon real teachers, real schools, and real books.

The schooling of the Victorian working class recognized little distinction between education and indoctrination. For that matter, neither did the schooling of the comfortable and the wealthy. But whereas in the latter case the objective was the social enculturation of the young, in working-class schools the indoctrination had another purpose as well – the production of political quietude. The advocates and practitioners of popular education in political economy did not preach working-class resignation. They were in fact full of advice as to how workers might improve themselves. Moreover, they did not even advocate that class distinctions should be rigidly maintained. On the contrary, many held the view that permanent improvement was most assured for those labourers who adopted middle-class standards of behaviour, personal habits, and aspirations. This didactic literature had political objectives, however, in that it attempted to induce the working classes to forswear violence and collective action of a class nature. It was not working-class hopes of a better life that made the establishment uneasy; it was fear that these yearnings might be channelled into revolutionary action. The message of the economics teachers and preachers to the working class was: 'Do not be led into the ways of wickedness by political and labour agitators. These are false friends. Your true friends are the laws of nature, including the laws of political economy. Properly understood and properly heeded, they point to improvement and happiness for all. Have faith in an economic system of enterprise and competition, and in personal habits of thrift, hard work, and self-reliance, which invariably lead to individual success in such a system.' It is, seemingly, but a step from this to the doctrine that the beneficent properties of nature will be made manifest if it is left entirely unfettered, and many popular writers made this 'small' extension. In the eyes of Carlyle, political economy, middle-class apologetics, mammonism, capitalism, and *laissez-faire* were all of a piece and should be flung into the abyss in a clean sweep. But one did not have to be as angry and bitter as Carlyle to arrive at equations and judgements of this sort. It is not difficult to see how a calm and rational reader of mid-nineteenth-century popular renditions of political economy could have reached the same conclusions.

So far as the working classes themselves were concerned, there is little evidence that these efforts were very effective. Their leaders were, for the most part, able to see the political economy instruction of the schools for what it mainly was: an attack upon their own growing political strength by the anciently entrenched landed class and the new middle class, different in form but not in essentials from the repressive measures by which working-class radicalism had been combated in the disturbed years after Waterloo. Britain was becoming more civilized, and the grosser forms of coercion were giving way to more subtle and urbane ones: propaganda, in the educational system and the mass media.

It is not possible here to review the various efforts at propagandization by means of political economy, but in order to give the foregoing general statements some concreteness I would like to pay some attention to one of the most notable of these: Harriet Martineau's series of novelettes published under the general title of 'Illustrations of Political Economy' in 1832–4. At first Martineau had difficulty in finding a publisher for her plan to write stories which would illustrate the true principles of political economy as she perceived them to be, but her conviction that the lower orders desperately needed instruction of this sort proved to be in correlation with the market, even though it is doubtful whether the working class provided many of her actual purchasers. The stories were from the first an immense success. Her publisher made a fortune, and Harriet Martineau herself was launched upon a career as novelist, journalist, essayist, travel writer, popular philosopher, and pundit so outstanding that she finds a prominent place today in the history of feminism as one of those remarkable nineteenth-century women who first breached the established male enclaves of status and power.

The stories, it must be said at once, were not immortal literature. They were a cut above the worst of the cheap novels, to be sure, but there is little in them in the way of character creation, narrative development, description, or any of the other aspects of literary art that would serve to explain their great popularity without reference to their didactic purpose. The largest part of the explanation must be found in the Victorian passion for improving, instructional, and inspirational reading, upon which was superimposed a great interest in the new science of political economy. In the tales themselves there was no direct instruction in political economy, and if the author had not appended a 'Summary of Principles Illustrated in this Volume' at the end of each, the didactic point of many of them would have remained an enigmatic puzzle to the reader. It is difficult to say how important these summary appendages were to the success of the novels, or to use them to chart their influence upon contemporary thought. I myself cannot recall a single instance of seeing them quoted in contemporaneous literature. It is possible that the general title of the series and the summaries acted primarily as certificates of indulgence; in an era when novel reading was regarded by the middle and upper classes as a wasteful and possibly dangerous use of time, as television is today, one could read Harriet Martineau without feeling wicked. It was an age when anything that would permit one to take pleasure and leisure openly and without a sense of guilt enjoyed a strong demand.

If there are mysteries in Harriet Martineau's popularity as a novelist, there is no mystery in the message she wished to convey. All twenty-five of the 'Summaries of Principles' are worth reading *in toto*, but our purpose must be served by a briefer series of quotations from them:

> The interests of the two classes of producers, Labourers and Capitalists, are ... the same: the prosperity of both depending on the accumulation of CAPITAL. (No. II)

> By universal and free [international] exchange . . . an absolutely perfect system of economy of resources is established. As the general interest of each nation requires that there should be perfect liberty in the exchange of commodities, any restriction on such liberty, for the sake of benefiting any particular class or classes, is a sacrifice of a larger interest to a smaller – that is, a sin in government. (No. XVII)

> Free competition cannot fail to benefit all parties: consumers, by securing the greatest practicable improvement and cheapness of the article; producers by the consequent perpetual extension of demand; and Society at large, by determining capital to its proper channels. (No. XVIII)

> The duty of government being to render secure the property of its subjects, and their industry being their most undeniable property, all interference of government with the direction of the rewards of industry is a violation of its duty towards its subjects. (No. XXI)

> As public expenditure, though necessary, is unproductive, it must be limited. . . . That expenditure alone which is necessary to defence, order, and social improvement, is justifiable. (No. XXIII)

> A just taxation must leave all the members of society in precisely the same relation in which it found them. (No. XXIV)

Here we have the whole doctrine of *laissez-faire*, bag and baggage: the perfection of the competitive system; the harmony of interests that reigns within a society so organized; the illegitimacy and perverse consequences of governmental interference. It is not a Panglossian picture in that it does not urge the reader to resign himself to a vile and miserable world because it is the best possible; but it presents a harmonist thesis, promising eternal progress if only natural economic laws are permitted to function.

In Harriet Martineau's tales we find the true fusion of ideas and confusion of understanding that is the essence of the doctrine of *laissez-faire*. She could not distinguish between the 'laws of political economy' as a simple abstract model whose focus is the heuristic one of assisting one to analyse the complex processes of the real economy; 'laws' which are the findings of such an analysis; and 'laws' which are ethical precepts. The same air of certainty, indeed necessity, is given alike to statements that are logical deductions, empirical predictions, and moral exhortations. 'Principle' was one of Martineau's favourite words, but she could not distinguish the difference between saying that a person is a 'man of principle' and the transitivity law as a 'principle' of mathematics. Nor could she accept the fact that scientific knowledge is partial and tentative; its certainty and completeness, too, were matters of 'principle'.

But let us regain perspective. Is it possible to believe that the great myth of Victorian *laissez-faire* was the independent creation of myopic popularizers of classical political economy such as Harriet Martineau? I think not. A much larger part of the explanation must be traced to the use made of such versions of political economy in public debate on concrete political issues. Another series of Harriet Martineau's didactic stories entitled *Poor Laws and Paupers*, which she wrote at the request of Lord Brougham and the Society for the Diffusion of Useful Knowledge to drum up support for the recommendations of the Poor Law Commission, was probably more important. They did not sell well, but they identified the laws of political economy with one side of a political issue on which interest and feelings ran high. Discussion of Poor Law policy was so intense and general that one did not actually have to read the stories to be aware of the claim that 'political economy' had spoken. As historians now know, the leading economists of the day were not simple-minded Malthusians and laissez-fairists on the poverty question. Moreover, the Commission's recommendations and the resulting legislation were, if anything, the opposite of *laissez-faire* ideology in the type of poor relief and the degree of central government administration proposed. A true devotee of *laissez-faire*, a believer in the social order of individualism and the complete beneficence of the market system would, in logic, be compelled to advocate a Poor Law system by which the poor, if assisted at all, would be given grants of money to spend in accordance with their own preferences. The intent of the Amendment Act to shift the system from 'outdoor relief' (i.e. cash payments) to the construction of houses where the lives of the poor would be regulated by the parish guardians was the antithesis of *laissez-faire*; it was a paternalistic philosophy of poverty policy. Nevertheless, in the popular mind the debate over the Poor Law in the 1830's became a contest between hard-hearted and tight-fisted individualism on the one side and compassionate generosity and concern for communal values on the other. The oracular Miss Martineau left no doubt that political economy was wholly on the former side.

Classical economics thus got a bad name in the 1830's, in large part because of its putative stand on the poverty and trade union issues, but the label of *laissez-faire* was not firmly riveted upon it until the 1840's, as a result largely of the great debate over the tariff on imported food, the corn laws. This was a controversy that punctuated, and for a time dominated, the whole range of English political life: newspapers, journals, pamphlets, tracts and books, the speaker's platform, the political club, the pub, the shop and factory, Parliament, the political hustings, the farmer's cottage, the working man's kitchen, the middle-class parlour, the upper-class drawing room. It was a debate like a civil war, and it left a mark upon politics comparable only to the political controversy accompanying the actual civil war of the seventeenth century. The seventeenth century established the importance of political *theory* in Britain's political life; the nineteenth the power of its modern vulgarizations: propaganda and 'public opinion'.

The corn laws were not merely a tariff; they were a symbol, an emblem of the old constitutional order. The attack upon them was nothing less than an attack upon the established order of privilege. The fact that the controversy focused on an economic question is in certain respects fortuitous, but at all events, it exerted a great impact on the history of economic thought and the interpretation of that history. The character of the controversy, and the fact that it resulted in a 'great victory' that dominated English politics in subsequent decades, invested with special significance and qualities all that had been involved in it. The corn law controversy was a prodigious political foundry, full of noise and heat, in which were cast some of the most distinctive moulds of Victorian stereotype. The facts of the case provide little ground for interpreting the controversy as a debate over the general issue of *laissez-faire* rather than the specific and much more limited one of free international trade, and less for the view that the leading economists were unambiguously ranged on one side of the issue. Like all groups, the economists had mixed opinions. Some of them, like Malthus, strongly opposed free trade in corn. Even the 'Manchester school' free-traders who spearheaded the fight for repeal of the tariff and financed the massive attack did not have a homogeneous set of ideas on economic policy. But the view became firmly established that free trade was an application of the more general doctrine of *laissez-faire* and that the political economists supported it, not on the basis of Ricardo's theory of international trade, but as an aspect of the essential harmony of the market system.

In considering the relationship between the anti-corn law campaign and the ideology of *laissez-faire*, it is essential to recognize that, for the great bulk of free-trade advocates, it was free international trade itself that was the basic faith. The leading orators and publicists of the Anti-Corn Law League were willing to employ almost any instrument that would aid their cause, and sometimes they spoke fervently of the harmony of an economic universe left free to move according to the laws of nature. But an examination of their thinking discloses no underlying Leibnizian metaphysic. The occasional bit of *laissez-faire* harmonism in their expressions served merely as oratorical rococo which the Leaguers found congenial and useful. They had a faith, to be sure, but its bedrock was the unqualified merit and constructive power of an international policy of free trade.

There are, however, some notable cases of free-trade advocacy that were clearly derivative from a general doctrine of *laissez-faire*, the most striking being the weekly commercial magazine *The Economist*. It was created, in 1843, to promote the anti-corn law cause, but its founder and editor, James Wilson, had earlier become a convinced *laissez-faire* doctrinaire. In the pages of the *Economist* during the first dozen years of its life one will find a *laissez-faire* ideology that was fully developed and consistently applied to all issues of contemporary policy. This magazine contains the most elaborated and consistent *laissez-faire* ideology to be found in the English literature of the Victorian Age (see Scott Gordon, 'The London *Economist* and the High Tide of Laissez Faire', *Journal of Political Economy*, 1955).

Despite such instances as Harriet Martineau and the *Economist*, it is incorrect to equate free trade with the doctrine of *laissez-faire*. The equation of *laissez-faire* with classical political economy is equally incorrect. James Wilson of the *Economist* regarded the classical economists as insufficiently firm on the principle of *laissez-faire* and, generally, he viewed Ricardian economics with hostility. Harriet Martineau referred to political economy for support of her harmonism but her knowledge of its theories was slight. The conclusion we must arrive at is that a Leibnizian metaphysical outlook can be found, but not easily, in nineteenth-century economic thinking. The reason for this is that the outlook of the Victorian Age, in matters that concerned economics and economic policy, was dominated by a very different philosophy – utilitarianism – which we shall examine in the next chapter. Before we leave this subject, however, it is worth shifting our attention briefly across the Atlantic, to America, where the doctrine of *laissez-faire* found more fertile soil.

4. *Laissez-faire* and political economy in the United States

The picture that emerges from a study of *laissez-faire* in nineteenth-century Britain is that, when viewed as an ideology, it is difficult to locate, and is more commonly to be found in the eye of the beholder than in the object of his attention. An examination of the intellectual history of the United States, however, drives one to a different conclusion. There is an authentic *laissez-faire* tradition in American economic thought; its advocates are neither few, nor unimportant, nor are they exclusively popular writers or interested parties; and the doctrine is not confined to brief or restricted periods of American history.

Within the space that can be devoted to this topic, only a brief survey of the history of American political economy is possible, but before we can begin even this it is essential to note a characteristic that differentiates much of American economic thought in the nineteenth century from the orthodox British tradition: the difference between a nationalistic and a cosmopolitan orientation of political economy. In the framework of classical economic theory both orientations can find a compatible housing. Adam Smith effectively established a cosmopolitan orientation by his attack on the mercantilist trade restrictions, and by the extension of his principle of division of labour to international economic activity. One of the most notable of Ricardo's achievements was the analytical demonstration that, under almost all conceivable (static) conditions, international trade is mutually beneficial to the parties. The widely held mercantilist view that in such trade one nation's gain is necessarily another nation's loss was thus overthrown, at least among the *cognoscenti* of economic theory, and cosmopolitanism (which assuredly had other strong bases of support as well) became an almost universal characteristic of British economic thought. Even Richard Cobden, the greatest of all the free-trade propagandists of the Anti-Corn Law League, was fundamentally a philosophical cosmopolite, dreaming of a world of universal and continuous peace secured by knitting together the various sovereign nation-states by the bonds of mutually beneficial commerce.

But another, and contrary, orientation lay at the centre of political economy in that it took the nation-state as the basic unit of collective action. Thus *political* economy was, and is, inherently *national* housekeeping, and policy was, and is, *national* policy. This could be overlooked to a considerable degree in nineteenth-century Britain, enjoying as she did the hegemony of world economic and political power, but in an undeveloped country like nineteenth-century America the case was different. American economic thought was often explicitly nationalist, and oriented towards the promotion of national development. Without analytically demonstrating the point in any succinct way, numerous American economists intuitively perceived that the Ricardian theory of international trade did not necessarily apply in a national context of economic development. No British advocate of *laissez-faire* could have been a protectionist, but the tariff does not serve even as a preliminary index of *laissez-faire* ideology in the United States. There were *laissez-faire* ideologues in American economic thought who were free-traders and there were equally committed ones who were protectionists. For the latter group, *laissez-faire* was a prescription for *domestic* policy, and the harmony of interest was viewed only as an intranational law of nature. The basis of protectionist economic thought in America was laid very early by one Tench Coxe, who wrote the famous document known as Alexander Hamilton's *Report on Manufactures* of 1791. The theory there embodied was never made analytically explicit but it had a profound and long-lasting effect on American economic policy.

The first American economist to receive any widespread international attention was Henry C. Carey. His father, Mathew Carey, was an ardent advocate of forced industrialization by means of the tariff, writing most of the Addresses of the influential Philadelphia Society for the Promotion of National Industry after the War of 1812, when the issue of industrial protection was hotly debated, and continuing his advocacy thereafter in a long series of books and pamphlets. Henry Carey followed his father in the publishing business, in independent authorship, and in advocacy of a nationalist economy policy. But, beyond such practical matters, he was a man with a grand metaphysical vision, which informed all his writings, from his first *Essay on the Rate of Wages* (1835) through numerous other books, including two three-volume treatises on *Principles of Political Economy* (1837–40) and *Principles of Social Science* (1858–9), to his final effort to describe the complete order of the universe in his *Unity of Law* (1872). Carey saw human society as coalesced with the physical and natural world, all of which displayed the design of a beneficent Creator. He admired Alexander Pope's *Essay on Man*, the poetic expression of Leibnizian metaphysics. The title page of Carey's *Principles of Political Economy* contains as an epigraph the line from Pope that embodies the crucial assumption underlying the application of this metaphysical theory to the social order: 'All discord, harmony not understood.' Carey's mission was to persuade man to understand the harmonious design of nature.

Within such a natural harmonious order there would seem to be no need for government; Carey's metaphysical view was coherent with philosophical anarchism. But he made two major amendments: first, he did not consider the law of harmony to rule in international relations between countries at different stages of economic development, so the action of the sovereign national power is necessary to promote progress in an underdeveloped country; and secondly, he regarded man as an imperfect creature, not to be relied upon to follow the golden rule without constraint, so there will be an indefinite need for governmental power to preserve the security of person and property. Beyond this, and within the national context, there is no need for governmental action, the sole duty of legislators being 'to refrain from every measure tending to impair the right of individuals to determine for themselves the mode of employing their time and their property'. If the common stereotype of the English classical economists as *laissez-faire* harmonists were correct one would expect Carey to have been a disciple, but since it is not, one should not be surprised to find him a strong, even bitter, opponent of them. He regarded classical economics as not merely inapplicable to American conditions (a view held by many other American economists) but as inherently erroneous. He spent much effort in attempting to refute the central classical theories of population and rent, because he considered them as falsely picturing the social world to be invested with the disharmonious element of conflict of economic interest.

The quality of Carey's philosophical reasoning cannot delay us here, but it is worth noting that he was not a very good economist. His attack upon Ricardo's theory of rent displayed serious misunderstanding of the law of diminishing returns upon which it was based, and his 'refutation' of Malthus on population was nothing more than an assertion that the Creator, in his benevolence, could not have ordered the world so and had, indeed, ordered it differently by establishing the laws of conservation of mass and energy! In his later books he often evinced strong hostility towards 'commerce', that is, buying and selling, as opposed to producing and consuming, and he did not seem to conceive of the harmony of economic activity as resulting from the play of competitive forces in a system of markets. As one reads Carey one comes gradually to the conclusion that his economic harmonism was not founded upon any economic model at all. His metaphysical belief was not merely antecedent to his economic theory; the former rendered the latter unnecessary as a serious intellectual challenge. But no matter; an economic ideology does not necessarily have to be based upon a coherent economic theory.

Carey viewed himself not only as advancing the law of harmonious order but as having been the first to discover it. He virtually accused Fréderic Bastiat, the leading French publicist of *laissez-faire*, of having plagiarized him in the latter's *Harmonies économiques* (1850). Karl Marx, who was a keen student of the history of economic ideas, accepted this claim and pictured Carey to be the originator of European harmonism, as represented not only by Bastiat in France, but also by Eugen Dühring in Germany and the free-trade *laissez-faire* ideologues of England. To one brought up in the orthodox historiography this seems to present a strange picture of the diffusion of ideas. But the more one examines the intellectual history of the nineteenth century the more one appreciates the impact of America upon European and English thought, even in the early nineteenth century.

Henry Carey was extremely influential in early American economic thought. In a recent study of him, Paul K. Conkin says that, in the pre-Civil War period, 'he became something of a cult figure to many businessmen, politicians, and journalists' (*Prophets of Prosperity*, 1980, p. 309). But, so far as the scientific aspects of economics are concerned, he was no American Adam Smith or David Ricardo. He did not initiate the construction of a body of economic theory that rivalled classical political economy as an analytical model. So, in this sense, despite the large number of admiring disciples he attracted, he founded no alternative school of economics. But he did effectively begin an authentic American tradition in what might be called the 'political philosophy of political economy' by his effective promotion of the view of society as a natural harmonious order. Let us look briefly at some of the writers who continued to promote that philosophy in the development of American economics.

One of the most prominent of these was Francis Wayland. He was President of Brown University and Professor of Moral Philosophy when he published his *Elements of Political Economy* in 1837. The book became the leading textbook of economics in the United States and remained popular for several decades. Despite Wayland's insistence that economic questions should be kept separate from moral issues, a strong odour of moralism, to the point of sanctimoniousness, pervades the volume. The rights of property and the duties of individual responsibility (except for those who are poor owing to the 'visitation of God') were presented by him as basic conditions of order and progress. Wayland considered the tariff at some length in the *Elements*, and concluded that it was both unwise and unjust. Beyond the provision of 'wise, wholesome and equitable laws [which] protect the individual in the exercise of his right of person and property' Wayland considered that the role of the state might be extended to education, the promotion of science, and the encouragement of industrial experimentation. The last especially would seem to have great elastic potential, but it is clear that Wayland had a very small role in mind. He concluded his consideration of the question of state intervention by saying that the government 'can do much by confining themselves to their own appropriate duties, and leaving everything else alone'.

Our next writer, Francis Bowen, was primarily a philosopher, whose chief interest was in harmonizing philosophy with Christianity. He was, for a time, editor of the influential *North American Review*. He was appointed to the Harvard faculty in 1853, and three years later published his *Principles of Political Economy, Applied to the Condition, the Resources, and the Institutions of the American People*. Here, and in his later *American Political Economy* (1870), Bowen argued for a distinctively American science of economics. He was a nationalist to the point of isolationism, and there is a general air of disdain for other nations in his writing. He opposed classical political economy not only as being inapplicable to American conditions but as indefensible in itself. But both his books begin with a firm statement of the general principle of *laissez-faire*. The system of private enterprise and competition is divinely ordered and the proper role of the state is to remove impediments in its functioning and to prevent one person from infringing the right of another to be 'let alone' in his own sphere. Under such a regime no class has any cause of complaint, for it is impossible that any should be improperly favoured. Inequality will still exist, because it is a law of nature. This picture, however, is confined to the domestic role of the state. In international matters the state has much larger responsibilities. It should impose tariffs and embargoes whenever required to protect America from the economic or political power of other nations. This, says Bowen, is 'not an infringement but an application of the *laissez-faire* principle [since] it is designed to procure for [the American people] a larger liberty than they would otherwise enjoy'. The key to Bowen's thought is nationalism. Cobden's idea that free trade would knit the world together economically and usher in an era of peace and prosperity was anathema to him. God had ordained not only that there should be a *laissez-faire* economy but that the world should be divided into nations, and only within each nation did the laws of natural harmony prevail.

One can go on, finding such distinct representatives of *laissez-faire* ideology among American economists – up to the close of the nineteenth century. Amasa Walker, who was widely regarded, both abroad and at home, as the leading American economist of the mid-century period, definitely qualifies.

His widely read *Science of Wealth* (1866) was filled with the characteristic clichés and moralistic certitude that are authentic indexes of *laissez-faire* ideology, and his investigation of economic questions did nothing to contradict his general conclusion that 'Economically, it will ever remain true, that the government is best which governs least.' Arthur Latham Perry of Williams College, whose *Elements of Political Economy* (1865) was for more than two decades the most widely used textbook in economics, was similarly doctrinaire, though not quite so florid in his rhetoric as Walker or Bowen. He was a dedicated fighter in the cause of free trade and pursued an unremitting attack on the tariff. But, more generally, he was a firm believer in the general concept of natural economic harmony, which he apparently derived from Bastiat rather than from Carey, and was critical of classical economics because the theory of rent raised doubts about this harmony.

> There are [he declared] no deep-seated antagonisms within the sphere of exchange; not even between landlords and the foodless poor. If there be such antagonism . . . it comes from the maladministration of men in government, not from the fundamental laws of Economy.

And then, of course, there is William Graham Sumner of Yale, who was first inspired to study political economy when he read (and avidly re-read) Harriet Martineau's *Illustrations of Political Economy* as a young teenager. So much has been written about Sumner's *laissez-faire* doctrinairism that there is little need to say more here. The picture of him as a 'Social Darwinist' is somewhat misleading in that it construes his social philosophy deriving its fundamental inspiration from the biological theory of evolution. There is no doubt that Sumner found support in Darwin, but his basic vision of the order of nature was formed by what he conceived to be the message of political economy, not biology, and it was to the philosophy of political economy that he devoted his life's work.

Beyond the academic political economists there are good representatives too. Simon Newcomb, who was one of the best known of American physical scientists of the later nineteenth century, wrote a theoretically significant *Principles of Political Economy* (1886) and many articles on economic and political questions in the *North American Review* and other journals. There were some ambiguities in his thought, and he tried to draw an interesting distinction between the 'let alone' principle and the 'keep out' principle of political economy, but there can be no doubt that he held a *laissez-faire* view in the sense required by our terms of reference in this chapter. The influential magazine *Dial*, having in mind no doubt that he was an astronomer by profession, presented his *Principles of Political Economy* as embodying a 'vivid conception of economic life as a symmetrical organism or system in which there is constant harmonious circulation', The issue of 'socialism' was at this time reviving in public debate. Newcomb disposed of it summarily in the penultimate chapter of his *Principles* with the assertion that:

The fact is that, under the present arrangements, men are working for each other in the most effective way that it would be possible for them to work under the supervision of the wisest government. We have already a system of socialism marvelous in its perfection. The most admirable feature of it is that those propensities of men which we consider most selfish lead them to work for the good of their fellow-men.

In the field of public service, there was David A. Wells, who was chairman of the important Revenue Commission of 1865, became a leading expert on public finance, and also played a large part in the development of governmental statistical services. He held important offices and enjoyed a close association with the senior levels of bureaucratic power, even up to the presidency. He was well known abroad, too, and was chosen foreign associate of the French Academy of Political Science in 1874 to fill the vacancy left by the death of John Stuart Mill. In a series of articles, books, and reports Wells persistently promoted the principle of *laissez-faire* as the best rule of government. The David A. Wells essay prize at Harvard, which became the most prestigious award to which a young American economist could aspire, was established under a grant from him which, as a condition, ruled out any essays of a radical character.

With Wells, Sumner, and Newcomb, the *laissez-faire* tradition in American intellectual history extends to the end of the nineteenth century and into the twentieth. In some of the historiography it is this era (which Mark Twain both lamented and baptized as the 'Gilded Age') that is depicted as the zenith of *laissez-faire*. The picture is ambiguous, however; many historians present *laissez-faire* in this period not as a philosophy of political economy founded upon an economic theory or a metaphysical theory, or both, but as a simple slogan used by the growing plutocracy of business to support its own self-interest and to keep governmental power either at bay or in alliance. The thesis has been advanced, most fully by Benjamin Twiss (*Lawyers and the Constitution: How Laissez-faire Came to the Supreme Court*, 1942), that *laissez-faire* became in this period an established legal ideology, embraced and promulgated by the highest court of the land. There can be no doubt that the Supreme Court was generous to business in its interpretation of the constitution, but some question remains whether one can interpret this as a victory of *laissez-faire* ideology. A non-lawyer is ill advised to enter very far into these labyrinthine passages, but it seems to me that the cases upon which this interpretation rests have as much, or more, to do with defining the legal status of the corporation as with the issue of non-intervention by the governmental power. The two questions are not unrelated, of course, but they are by no means the same thing. A legal decision to give corporations the same status and rights as natural persons says nothing in itself about the limits deemed to be imposed upon government in interfering with those rights. The matter requires further study.

Despite people of the stature of Sumner, Newcomb, and Wells, the continuing use of Perry's textbook in the colleges and universities, and the possible extension of *laissez-faire* ideology into the bureaucracy and the judiciary, the hegemony of *laissez-faire* as a philosophy of professional economics in America really came to an end in the 1880's. A new period opened then, with a great influx into the colleges and universities of young and energetic economists, many of whom were committed to the view that there were unnecessary evils and injustices on vivid display in the world, and that a good society should use the sovereign power of the state in their amelioration. The American Economic Association, now the professional society of American economists, was founded in 1885 by young men seeking to overthrow the established *laissez-faire* orthodoxy of academic economics. Richard T. Ely, the initiator of the Association, expressed himself as wishing to draw together 'economists who repudiate *laissez-faire* as a scientific doctrine' which he further declared to be 'unsafe in politics and unsound in morals'. This view sufficiently prevailed at the founding meeting for item I of the 'Statement of Principles' there adopted to aver that 'We regard the State as an agency whose positive assistance is one of the indispensable conditions of human progress.' When Charles Dunbar, who succeeded Bowen in the Chair of political economy at Harvard, became the first editor of the first professional economic journal in the English language, the *Quarterly Journal of Economics*, he devoted his lead article in the inaugural issue of 1866 to 'The Reaction in Political Economy', saying that the new school of economists were in agreement on the point that there was need for 'a vast increase in the functions and activity of the State'.

The American Economic Association and the other social science societies appraised the status of *laissez-faire* at their 1917 meetings. They thereupon officially declared the doctrine deceased. But ideas that have had a strong impact upon a culture over a lengthy period never really disappear. Although the dominance of *laissez-faire* in American professional economics ended a century ago, there have been repeated revivals in the economic literature down to the present. If we consider social science more broadly, and include notice of popular social philosophy and politics, the ideology of *laissez-faire* and, indeed, anarchism as a political philosophy remains a continuing feature of American social thought.

Chapter 11

Utilitarianism

On numerous occasions in the preceding chapters the early development of modern social science was described as taking place in an era that was powerfully influenced by the philosophy of utilitarianism. In the present chapter we shall examine this aspect of the history and philosophy of social science, which requires that we pay more attention than we have heretofore to that branch of philosophy called 'ethics'. Our main interest in this book centres upon epistemology, but just as we found it necessary in the previous chapter to give some consideration to metaphysics, so we must now do likewise for ethics. Utilitarianism was the first and most important attempt to develop a thoroughly secular theory of ethics, oriented to man's palpable welfare in this world rather than to any presumed requirements of his transcendent spirit or his relation to God. This alone is sufficient to make utilitarianism an important part of the intellectual history of the West with special significance for any efforts to develop scientific theories of social phenomena.

The reader who is familiar with nineteenth-century history may object at once that it is a gross distortion of that era to represent it as dominated by the utilitarian philosophy. It was also the era of romanticism, a very different set of ideas, which undeniably had an enormous impact on the Western intellect, especially in literature, music, and the arts generally, but also in political and social thought, and in formal philosophy. Romanticism will be discussed briefly below in an appendix to this chapter, but we shall be mainly concerned here with the development and influence of utilitarianism.

As an ethical theory, utilitarianism is the doctrine that man's worldly happiness is the only good, and the only test of his social institutions. To a very considerable degree Thomas Hobbes was a utilitarian in arguing that unlimited sovereign power is justified as a necessary condition to assure security of life and property and permit man to enjoy 'commodious living'. John Locke also was a utilitarian in considering human happiness to be the highest good. But Hobbes and Locke should not be singled out in this regard, since the basic idea, that social institutions must be judged by reference to the criterion of man's worldly welfare, is a theme that recurs repeatedly in the older literature, going back at least as far as ancient Greece and Rome. The philosophy called Epicureanism, named after Epicurus of Samos (341–270 B.C.), is virtually a synonym for utilitarianism. Titus Lucretius Carus (c. 99 B.C.–c. 55), the Roman whose remarkable poem *De Rerum Natura* we took special note of in Chapter 2, held a utilitarian view of ethics as firmly as he held a materialist epistemology. It is obvious from our discussion of the Scottish Enlightenment in Chapter 7 that a focus upon worldly happiness was a central element in the ethical philosophy of the Scottish moralists. Francis Hutcheson, the first member of the group, was the one who coined the motto that later came to represent the utilitarian credo: 'the greatest good of the greatest number'. But precursors are only precursors, after all. It is Jeremy Bentham (1748–1832) who must be acknowledged the founder of utilitarianism, because he did not merely state the principle; he commenced to build upon it an edifice of positive and normative social analysis, which his followers elaborated and extended throughout the nineteenth and twentieth centuries, without diminution of influence down to the present day.

Young Jeremy Bentham was a precocious child who read adult literature at the age of three and had a good knowledge of Greek and Latin by the age of six. His father expected great things of him and aimed his son for a career in law. At twelve years old he was ready for university, so he was sent to Oxford, where William Blackstone, the most renowned authority on law in Britain, was teaching. After graduation he went on to one of the London Inns of Court, the next step in becoming a practising barrister. But young Bentham had a mind of his own that survived the assiduous efforts of parent and teachers to turn him into a great lawyer. His study of law convinced him that what the law needed was not another practitioner who could argue cases with a great display of learning and scholastic reasoning, but someone who would undertake to reform the English legal system, root and branch, changing not only the substantive content of the law but its basic philosophical foundations. So Bentham's father educated a son to become a distinguished lawyer, perhaps even a Lord Chancellor and elevate the Bentham family line to the aristocracy, only to have raised instead a thoroughgoing radical, who never practised, never held office, and, since he remained a bachelor, did nothing even to continue the Bentham name, let alone raise it to the peerage.

The term 'radical' has a somewhat different meaning in our day than it did in Bentham's. It is derived from the Latin word *radix*, meaning 'root', as in a tree, say. Bentham's followers called themselves 'philosophic radicals', by which they meant to describe themselves as those who get to the root of things, by philosophic method. As we saw in Chapter 7, 'philosophic method' meant, to the eighteenth-century thinkers, proceeding by the methods established in the physical sciences. Early in youth Bentham decided to abandon the logic-chopping scholasticism practiced by orthodox jurists and apply to law the methods of Bacon and Newton. At the age of twenty he had an inspiration as to how this could be done, which guided all his future work: the principle of utility could serve in social science the role that gravity plays in Newton's model of the physical universe.

So far as the legal system of England was specifically concerned, Bentham mounted a frontal attack upon Blackstone, whose Oxford lectures, published as *Commentaries on the Laws of England* (1765–9), formed the first comprehensive synthesis of English law and jurisprudence. Blackstone held that the essential law of England is embodied in the decisions of judges and juries more than in the statutes passed by Parliament. He was not merely arguing that the English system of case law regards judgements on old cases as precedents that are germane to new ones; he viewed the accumulation of case judgements as embodying a steadily refined moral wisdom which is superior to any explicit ethical philosophy or any rational assessment. The moral merit of the law lies in its tradition. Good law is that which is continuous with customary practice. Reason, thought Blackstone, is a fragile instrument whose serviceability in dealing with the complex problems of social life is severely limited, but man can draw upon something that is much more reliable: the transcendent wisdom of tradition. To Bentham this was sheer mysticism. Customary practice might be morally defensible, but not because it was customary. The law is a human artefact that man makes, and changes, to serve his purposes. Whether the law is good or not has nothing to do with its history, but only with its consequences or effects, which must be rationally and empirically assessed, and evaluated according to the criterion of 'the greatest happiness of the greatest number' of the members of society.

In Bentham's view the utilitarian criterion applies not only to law but to all social institutions and practices. His followers, inspired by this, asked searching and often embarrassing questions about politics, economics, religion, and all aspects of the social order. To the modern ear the term 'radical' has the connotation 'subversive'. The philosophic radicals did not form revolutionary cadres dedicated to overthrowing the established order by force, but they were subversives in their own way, placing the institutions of society under philosophical attack by challenging their defenders to demonstrate that they contributed to the general welfare. The inability to deflect that challenge made the nineteenth century the Age of Reform.

The basic legal system was less immediately affected by utilitarianism than other aspects of the social order were. In England, and countries whose legal system is derivative from England (including the United States), Blackstone's theory of law continued to dominate throughout the nineteenth century. During the twentieth, however, even the lawyers became infected with philosophic radicalism, a development that has accelerated recently with the insertion into legal theory and practice of the findings and methodology of modern economics and sociology. But in one area of legal practice utilitarianism led to significant reforms much earlier. Bentham's contention that public policies must be judged in terms of the greatest happiness of the greatest number, when coupled with the view that criminals are members of society like everyone else, led to the proposition that punishment inflicted upon the criminal can be justified only by a greater benefit to others. This did a great deal to undermine the view that punishment is the proper retribution for immoral acts or that it is justified because the offender has broken God's law, not merely one enacted by the state. The vicious barbarity of criminal justice in Bentham's time was greatly ameliorated during the nineteenth century because it failed to meet the utilitarian challenge. One has only to look at the practice of criminal justice in countries where it is still dominated by religious or political fundamentalism to recognize the contribution of the philosophic radicals to the growth of a humane civilization.

A. BENTHAM AND THE MILLS

In the opening section of his *Introduction to the Principles of Morals and Legislation* (1780), Bentham announced the central principles of utilitarianism:

Nature has placed mankind under the governance of two sovereign masters, *pain* and *pleasure*. It is for them alone to point out what we ought to do, as well as to determine what we shall do. On the one hand the standard of right and wrong, on the other the chain of causes and effects, are fastened to their throne. They govern us in all we do, in all we say, in all we think: every effort we can make to throw off our subjection, will serve but to demonstrate and confirm it. In words a man may pretend to abjure their empire: but in reality he will remain subject to it all the while.

If we read this carefully we see that Bentham advanced two fundamental propositions, not one: first, the psychological proposition that man is by nature a being whose behaviour is governed by desire for 'pleasure' and aversion to 'pain' (i.e. 'happiness'); and secondly, the ethical proposition that this is the only objective that is morally worthy. If Bentham had contended that the second is justified by the first he would have committed the error that Hume pointed out in his argument that 'ought' statements and 'is' statements are categorically different and that one cannot be derived from the other. In his anxiety to become the Newton of moral philosophy Bentham frequently spoke as though he had found a solid foundation for ethical judgement in facts of nature, but it is not necessary to argue in this fashion to be a utilitarian. One can take the view that the two propositions, one positive and the other normative, are both valid, but each has its own independent validity, neither being dependent on the other. Since Bentham, proponents and critics of utilitarianism have frequently connected its positive and normative propositions intimately together, but most of the main utilitarian writing does not, and I shall, in what follows, treat the psychological and ethical propositions of utilitarianism as logically independent.

As a positive proposition in human psychology Bentham's greatest happiness principle is open to some doubt. All of us have observed actions, by ourselves and others, that clearly seem to contradict it. There is something in the claim that men can and do act out of motives that are 'higher' or 'nobler' or, at least, different from those of individual material self-interest. Of course, one may argue that such actions are only 'apparently' non-utilitarian; that 'at bottom' they are motivated by the desire to further one's own happiness. The man who gives up his place in a lifeboat to another, or the person who murders his family and commits suicide, can be described as one who believed that doing so would make him happy. But if we argue in this way the happiness principle is turned into a tautology: happiness is the motive of human acts, but we know what makes a man happy by observing his acts. This gets us nowhere. In order to make utilitarianism viable as a psychological principle the much looser proposition must be held that people sometimes do act against their personal interests but that 'generally' or 'for the most part' they do not, and, in analysing social phenomena, it is reasonably safe to assume that they will act according to these interests. Bentham himself was inclined to hold the utilitarian principle as an exceptionless proposition in psychology, but many of his followers, most notably J. S. Mill, were content to adopt the looser version as a pragmatic or instrumental assumption that is useful in the analysis of social phenomena.

Moreover, if it were true that people always act out of self-interest, it would be meaningless to assert that they ought to do so. An act is subject to moral evaluation only if the doer could have acted differently. In a deterministic world there can be no ethics, utilitarian or otherwise. In framing social policy designed to promote the greatest happiness, it may be useful to assume that people will generally pursue their own interests, and in analysing social policy it may be wise to assume that those who frame it will also be motivated by self-interest, but in making moral valuations of social policy it is necessary to believe that the world could be different (better or worse) than it is. The utilitarians who promoted the political and social reforms of the nineteenth century pressed their psychological and ethical principles very far but one of their notable characteristics is that they did not press them to the point where they became nonsensical. Utilitarianism, because of its rather loose, commonsense character, was the first ethical philosophy that obtained wide popular support without being the object of extensive religious or political indoctrination. Because of their tolerance of incompleteness in their ethical philosophy, the utilitarians were able to promote social progress in a pragmatic spirit, not becoming enchanted and spellbound by the utopian dream of social perfection.

In the discussion of Adam Smith in Chapter 7 we noted that an important feature of the *Wealth of Nations* is that the 'nation' is conceived by Smith as embracing all its people. The idea that the 'lower orders' are full members of society whose welfare counts in considering the wealth of the nation was not widely held in Smith's day but it became an increasingly important feature of nineteenth-century social thinking. At least part of this development must be attributed to the firmness with which the utilitarians asserted that the greatest happiness principle means the happiness of *all*. As we have already seen, Bentham would not even exclude criminals from the calculus of pleasure and pain; the pain of punishment to them must be justified by a greater benefit to others. He would not totally exclude animals, either: 'The question is not, Can they *reason*? nor Can they *talk*? but Can they *suffer*?' (*Morals and Legislation*, chapter XVII). This line of thought shifts attention from the maximization of happiness to the minimization of misery, which is sometimes described as 'negative utilitarianism'.

How do we compare the criminal's punishment with the benefit it confers on others in doing our utilitarian accounting? For that matter how do we compare anyone's utility with that of anyone else? Bentham took the view that such comparisons are inherently impossible. 'One man's happiness,' he asserted, 'will never be another man's happiness: . . . you might as well pretend to add twenty apples to twenty pears' (quoted by M. P. Mack, *Jeremy Bentham: an Odyssey of Ideas*, 1963, p. 244). This is the main difficulty of the greatest happiness principle as a normative rule for social policy. Very few social policies do not have a mixture of benefits and harm to different individuals. How then do we ascertain the net balance without making interpersonal comparisons? The pragmatic utilitarian reformers did not worry greatly about this. They were prepared, as we have already noted, to apply the utilitarian principle in a rather rough-and-ready fashion. The main implication they drew from this problem is that not only should social policy be aimed at the general welfare but the political process, which generates and administers social policy, would be more effectively utilitarian the wider the participation in that process by the people at large. This view was a powerful force in the political reform movement of the nineteenth century which led to the creation of the modern democratic state.

Not all utilitarians were content with such a loose philosophy. In the social sciences, economics embraced utilitarianism more firmly than any other branch but it has devoted much effort to the problem of dealing with the aggregation of pleasures and pains. In the later nineteenth century F. Y. Edgeworth, an important figure in the development of neoclassical economics, looked forward to the day when a science of 'hedonometry' would have been created which would permit quantitative measurement of pleasures and pains and therefore calculation of the net value of a social policy (*Mathematical Psychics*, 1881). But most of the economists followed Bentham in regarding this as inherently impossible. The modern branch of economic theory known as 'welfare economics' holds to the principle that interpersonal comparisons are technically impossible yet accepts the fact that the pragmatic necessities of social policy require such comparisons (see below, Chapter 17 B).

Edgeworth's vision of a science of hedonometry is unrealistic but it is worth noting that even if it were possible it would not solve the main problem of utilitarian ethics. Suppose that psychologists and engineers had succeeded in constructing a device that would measure pleasure and pain in standard cardinal units as a calorimeter, say, measures energy. If we could calculate the aggregate happiness by adding up the several happinesses of the members of society, would it follow that social policy should be aimed at maximizing this aggregate? Not at all. The aggregate happiness is not, in itself, the happiness of any one person, so why should we maximize it? There are two possible answers to such a question. The aggregate might be regarded as constituting the happiness of some external observer such as God; or one might conceive of the social collectivity as, in itself, a sentient being and the aggregate utility as 'its' happiness. One can see how by means of such reasoning a theist or a believer in the organic conception of society might be persuaded to adopt a practical utilitarianism, but a true utilitarian individualist would have to reject these contentions.

Ethical controversy would not end if we were able to construct and install an Edgeworthian hedonometric system. The plane of discourse would only be shifted. We would no longer dispute whether a policy would in fact raise or lower the aggregate happiness, for that could be ascertained direct from the empirical data. Instead, we would debate the merits of the *distribution* of the aggregate happiness. We would have to ask whether it was right or just for Albert, say, to have five times the happiness of Bertha even if the aggregate happiness would thereby be maximized. Also, we would have to consider the ethical merits of those things that give people pleasure. If the data were to show that the public execution or flogging of criminals would increase the aggregate happiness, should we do it and have the proceedings televised? There are at least some who would be dubious about the ethical merits of such a policy. One cannot be ethically neutral concerning *what* it is that makes people happy, and especially so since that is not a universal given of 'human nature', but is a component of culture and a consequence of enculturation. As a society changes, the internal mechanism of the hedonometer would undergo alteration, giving more weight to some pleasures and pains, and less to others, and one cannot regard such changes in values with ethical indifference. In effect, there is no way by which the utilitarian can avoid the fact that, when he says it is good that people should be happy, he does not thereby render meaningless the proposition that it is also desirable that people should be made happy by 'good' things and not by 'bad' ones.

Let us now give some further attention to the influence of utilitarianism on the political thought of the nineteenth century. The main figures in this are James Mill and his son John Stuart Mill. The Age of Reform is notable not only for adopting the utilitarian criterion of social policy but also, and perhaps more importantly, for the steady growth of the view that the utilitarian objective is best furthered by a democratic and liberal political system. As a social philosophy, utilitarianism is not inherently democratic or liberal. One can argue that a dictatorship is the most efficient way of producing the

democratic liberalism have argued that the acceptance of this social philosophy during the nineteenth century was merely a reflection of the developing market economy of the period. That contention is valid, except for the 'merely'. To some minds, competition is the antithesis of co-operation and must be stamped out of social processes and removed from man's psyche if a humane civilization is ever to be achieved. This is, in my view, erroneous scientifically and dubious ethically. Adam Smith argued that economic competition and co-operation are not inherently antithetical; given appropriate conditions they are complementary. James Mill's *Essay on Government* and John Mill's *On Liberty* were efforts to show that the same is true of political and intellectual competition. Whatever the defects of their arguments, that feature of them is valid, and of great importance to social philosophy.

John Mill was not a totally convinced utilitarian. He was attracted, at least emotionally, to certain features of romanticism. One aspect of this should be noted. In his essay *Utilitarianism* (1861) he tackled the problem of how one may compare different types of pleasure, since, in his view, some are 'higher' or more worthy than others. He began by arguing that if we observe that a person capable of appreciating two pleasures chooses one and eschews the other it is apparent that the former is superior to the latter. As the argument proceeds, however, it undergoes a significant transformation, with Mill contending that some persons are superior to others in evaluating the cultural and moral qualities of different types of pleasures. Pushed to its conclusion, this would propose that a cultural or moral aristocracy should be established, the superior members of society determining what is best for others. Some nineteenth-century, writers, particularly the romantics, did not shrink from this conclusion, but Mill himself did, despite his own argument. Like many others who value progress but are suspicious of perfection, Mill was prepared to leave his position on the matter ambiguous.

As noted above, one of the features of the utilitarian philosophy, as it was used by the pragmatic reformers, was its commonsense antipathy to rationalistic extremism. The history of philosophy shows that intellectual space has, so to speak, a curvature in it which makes ideas, when logically extended very far, turn back upon themselves and become the antitheses of their originals. Christianity, the doctrine of universal love, led to the Inquisition and the wholesale murder of the Albigenses and other heretics. Marxism, which originally viewed the state as an instrument of oppression, became the foundation of the modern totalitarian state. Romanticism, which celebrated the value of individualism, became a doctrine claiming that 'society' is an organism and individual persons are merely its members. Utilitarianism could have become a repressive ideology too, but because of its disciples' tolerance of ambiguity it developed into a philosophy of democratic liberalism and a consistent opponent of the absolutist doctrines that were generated in abundance during the nineteenth century.

B. HENRY SIDGWICK

As the main animating force of social policy in democratic societies utilitarianism still functions today with the momentum provided by the initial formulation of Jeremy Bentham and the contributions of James and John Stuart Mill. But any sketch of the place of utilitarianism in the history and philosophy of social science must also pay some attention to the work of Henry Sidgwick (1838–1900). Unlike Bentham and the Mills, Sidgwick spent his life in the university. As a student at Cambridge he achieved first division honours in both mathematics and classics and became a fellow of Trinity College. He was appointed to the Chair of moral philosophy in 1883. He played an important role in making Cambridge the leading centre of academic philosophy that it became in the last quarter of the nineteenth century, and continued to be for half a century after his death. He was also important in the rise of Cambridge to outstanding prominence in the social sciences. He lectured on economics until Alfred Marshall was appointed Professor in 1885, and his book *The Principles of Political Economy* (1883) is, though only recently fully recognized by historians, an important landmark in the development of the theoretical foundations of state intervention in the market economy. The orientation of Marshall's work to what is today called 'welfare economics' was due in part to Sidgwick's contribution to economic theory and his connection of it to the philosophy of utilitarianism. He also wrote a book on political science, *The Elements of Politics* (1891), which contains an important argument concerning the problem of interpersonal comparisons. F. Y. Edgeworth, who, as noted above, looked forward to the solution of this problem through the construction of a science of 'hedonometry', was a great admirer of Sidgwick and embraced the version of ethical utilitarianism that Sidgwick advanced in his most important philosophical work, *The Methods of Ethics* (1874).

In the following discussion of Sidgwick's utilitarianism I shall, in the interest of brevity, sketch it in much more definite terms than he himself did. Like the other utilitarians he had an aversion to philosophic finality, dreading the dogmatism it generates. When arguing a point Sidgwick not only gives all the arguments for his own position but all those against it as well, often including objections which no one else had thought of. More than one of his Cambridge colleagues remarked that whenever Sidgwick proposed something in college or university councils it was invariably judicious, liberal, and wise, but if no voice of criticism was raised, he would go on to elucidate the flaws and weaknesses of his proposal himself!

In his *Methods of Ethics*, Sidgwick made a strong distinction between 'intuitionism' and 'utilitarianism' as different 'methods' of moral reasoning. He did not intend to reject the role of intuition altogether, recognizing that no ethical theory can be constructed without using some primary intuitive principle. His object was to restrict intuition to this unavoidable role. The intuitionism he opposed was the view that man possesses an inherent moral sense that enables him to construct *a priori* a complete code of specific moral rules that, in themselves, give direct judgements concerning actions or classes of actions without reference to the *consequences* of the actions, and without establishing general principles to which particular cases may be referred. His own first principle was Bentham's: the purpose of human existence is human happiness, and whether something is good or bad depends upon its effect on that happiness. He followed Bentham, too, in regarding happiness as a concept that is meaningful only for the individual; social collectivities are not sentient beings, and social happiness is only the aggregate of the happiness of individual persons. The ethical problem then becomes a matter of dealing with the existence of conflict between the interests of different individuals. Bentham thrust this problem aside by emphasizing the principle of psychological hedonism (that all men are by nature driven to seek only their own benefit) and, as we have seen, the problem of politics for James Mill was, consequently, one of devising a constitutional organization that would channel the actions of egocentric governors to the social good. Sidgwick rejected this 'method' of 'egoistic hedonism' as he called it, in favour of 'universalistic hedonism'.

Man, according to Sidgwick, has a capacity for objectivity. He is not a mere behavioural respondent to his own pleasures and pains. He can take the happiness of others into account and, as a consequence, he is capable of making moral judgements. As we saw in Chapter 7, this was the view Adam Smith had put forward in his *Theory of Moral Sentiments*. The fundamental issue then becomes the matter of weighting: how much weight ought one to give to another man's happiness compared to one's own? Sidgwick's answer was that they must be given equal weight: to act ethically means that one must not discriminate between oneself and others. In one's personal behaviour and, *a fortiori*, in the determination of social policy, all human beings must be treated as equally capable of happiness. Recall the interpretation of Hume's ethical theory given above in Chapter 7: Hume argued that man has the capacity to take the welfare of others into account but that an individual is justified in discounting the welfare of others to the extent that they are distant from him in space, time, biological relationship, culture, or other factors. Sidgwick's contention was that no such discounting is ethically permissible. This is what he meant by describing his utilitarianism as 'universalistic'.

Despite his aversion to philosophic finality Sidgwick attempted to construct a complete system of ethics on the basis of his principle of non-discrimination. His system breaks down, as all philosophic systems do, when we try to extend it very far. The merits of Sidgwick's universalism are plain enough when we apply it to gross cases of bigoted discrimination against others who differ from ourselves only in race, religion, or sex, but Sidgwick's application of universalism was not restricted to such cases. Let us look at some of the difficulties this creates.

In considering our own welfare as compared to that of future generations, do we give persons yet unborn the same weight as those now living? In effect do we apply a positive rate of interest as a discounting factor in determining social policy concerning such things as capital investment and the conservation of natural resources? In Sidgwick's view we must not discriminate between ourselves and others, so such discounting is ethically impermissible. We cannot here analyse the consequences of such a rule but a moderate acquaintance with economic theory is sufficient to convince one that it is a prescription for inefficiency and waste in the use of resources. In effect it treats time as economically irrelevant, which may be true in heaven, but not on an earth inhabited by people who have finite life spans and, reasonably, value the known present above the unknown future.

In recent years we have had demonstrations of the difficulty that is involved here in the practical efforts at economic planning undertaken by socialist countries such as the Soviet Union. In Marxian theory there is a strong objection to interest rate discounting on the ground that it represents the exploitation endemic to a capitalistic economy. This is a different argument from Sidgwick's but its practical import is the same. The issue has been the subject of much debate and analysis by both Marxist and neoclassical economists and it now seems clear that a policy of zero discounting is unacceptable on simple grounds of economic efficiency. The economic planner or policy-maker cannot be indifferent as between production processes (of identical physical output) which require different lengths of time. Time is scarce, and without a positive rate of interest the organization of economic processes (whether capitalist or socialist) would be very wasteful. The real policy dilemma that resides here is that we know that there must be some discounting of the future; but there is no way of establishing what rate is the correct one to employ. Neither the capital market of a capitalistic economy nor the administrative processes of a socialist planned economy can generate a magnitude that one could call a 'true' rate of time-preference for social policy; but we do know that it cannot be zero.

The application of Sidgwick's universalism to social distance is equally difficult to fulfil. One would have to regard the pleasures and pains of all members of contemporary humankind as equal in weight to one's own and one's family and friends. A man could not sit down to eat his dinner in ethical peace unless he had ascertained that there was no one else in the world who would enjoy it more. The fact is, not only do we discount the happiness of others in some proportion as they are distant from us, but we must do so in order to make practical action possible.

Bentham's ethical principle that happiness is the only good, when construed to mean that the sole criterion of social practices and policies is the maximization of *aggregate* happiness, does not permit one to make any independent value judgement concerning the distribution of that aggregate. If, in a society of two persons, one is ecstatically happy while the other is minimally so, it cannot be asserted that it would be a better arrangement if there were greater equality in the distribution of happiness, unless such a redistribution would raise the aggregate. It is not correct to say, as some interpreters of utilitarianism have, that utilitarianism is indifferent to or disregards the distribution of happiness (or income, or power). What is implicit in Bentham's formulation of the utilitarian principle is that distribution, as such, does not have any ethical merit. That specific distribution is best, whatever it may be, which maximizes the achievable aggregate. Sidgwick was convinced that human happiness is good, and the more of it the better, but he was unwilling to accept the distributional implication of Bentham's principle. If, in our hypothetical society of two persons, each were to disregard the condition of the other, they would be practising 'egoistic hedonism', which Sidgwick regarded as morally unacceptable. Sidgwick's universalism does not require the abandonment of the greatest happiness as an ethical principle; it means that in considering what will maximize it one must not discount the happiness of others solely because they are others. If Alfred will be made more happy by a piece of pie than Bertha he should have it; Bertha herself is ethically obligated to give it to him without recourse to considerations other than the capacity of the pie to generate happiness. If Bertha's ability to turn pie into happiness is greater than Alfred's, even though she has already eaten two pieces and Alfred none, she is obligated to consume the next piece herself. Neither self-sacrifice nor selfishness is permissible in Sidgwick's moral world.

The difficulties of Sidgwick's prescription are severe. In order to determine whether Albert or Bertha should have the pie, it is not sufficient that Bertha should disregard characteristics that are palpably irrelevant such as Alfred's sex or the colour of his skin, she must be able to compare his 'utility function' with her own. This is difficult to do within a small social organization such as a family whose members are well known to one another; the difficulties increase enormously as one widens the domain to embrace other members of society, including, as Sidgwick did, those of future generations. Sidgwick's contribution would have been negligible if he had been content to advance his principle of universalism as a superior ethical intuition, regarding the practical problems of implementing it as none of his concern. His most important contribution resulted from his efforts to deal with the deficiencies of his own doctrine of universalistic hedonism, the crucial issue being that of determining the proper distribution of economic goods and political power.

An ethical person may be morally obligated not to discount the *happiness* of others but, Sidgwick recognized, this tells one nothing about the proper distribution of *wealth and income*, since that is dependent upon an empirical matter, the utility functions of different persons (i.e. their capacity to turn objective wealth and income into subjective happiness). If one rejects Edgeworth's view that it is possible to construct a scientific 'hedonometry' which will provide this empirical information, one must, instead, make some *assumption* about utility functions. If no specific assumption is more tenable than any other, then utilitarian social philosophy cannot provide guides for social policy on the basis of the greatest happiness principle. Concerning the distribution of economic goods, for example, it is demonstrable that different assumptions concerning utility functions lead to quite different distributional conclusions. If Albert's utility function and Bertha's are identical, and both are characterized by diminishing marginal utility, then it follows that the aggregate happiness will be maximized by an equal distribution of the available pie. If the utility functions are identical, but characterized by constant marginal utility, it does not matter how the pie is distributed; all distributions generate the same aggregate. If Albert and Bertha equally enjoy the first bit of pie but Alfred's marginal utility is constant while Bertha's diminishes, then maximizing aggregate utility requires that Albert get virtually all the pie and Bertha virtually none. Other assumptions about utility functions lead to the conclusion that the proper distribution of pie depends critically on how big the pie is; for example, it is easy to construct a case, without making psychologically bizarre assumptions, in which the pie should be shared unequally if it is either very small or very large, but a pie of intermediate size should be shared equally.

The utilitarian ship of state would seem to be afloat upon an uncharted sea; no one knows how to set a course for the land of maximum happiness, since it can lie in any direction. But *some* course must be set, none the less. Is it possible to do so by arguing that one of the possible assumptions about utility functions is more tenable than any other? Sidgwick did not attack this problem in the explicit analytical terms I have employed here but he was able to make a powerful argument on behalf of equality of distribution, rather than merely asserting it as an intuition or deriving it from the questionable assumption of zero discounting.

If we cannot make empirical utility comparisons in order to determine the proper course for social policy, then any course we do adopt is very likely to be in error. But there is no reason to think that all policies are subject to the same *degree* of probable error. If it is determinable that one assumption about utility functions is exposed to less error than any other, it would be plausible to contend that this is the one that should be adopted. This is the prudential 'minimax' rule of modern decision theory: adopt the policy that minimizes the maximum error exposure.

To explain this, let us suppose that one is a participant in a game of chance which consists of making blind draws from a box in which black balls and white balls have been placed. If information is given concerning the proportion of black to white balls in the box, the chance of losing is minimized by making one's bet in accordance with that information. If the proportion in the box is known to be two-to-one in favour of black, then one should expect that, in a series of draws, black will be drawn twice as often as white, and bet accordingly. But suppose that one is given no information at all concerning the proportions; what *assumption* minimizes the maximum risk of loss? The rational gambler should proceed on the assumption that the chance of a black being drawn is the same as a white. This is the same strategy that it would be rational to adopt if one knew that white and black balls are present in equal numbers. Utopians are, by contrast, not rational gamblers. They always bet their 'favourite' colour regardless of the odds against it. They prefer any small chance of being right over any large chance of being wrong. Or they proceed with confidence that they know what colour will be drawn regardless of the empirical facts, or lack of them. Utopians, in effect, are either imprudent in the face of known facts, or they regard facts as irrelevant.

The important point about this is that rational analysis prescribes that when one knows nothing about a distribution, the minimum exposure to error is achieved by acting on the assumption of equal probability. John Locke, in his *Letter on Toleration* (1689), used a similar argument, noting that there is a danger that *everyone* will be in doctrinal error if all obey a single religious authority, whereas, if everyone obeys his own conscience, the danger will be smaller. So, he concluded, tolerance of all religious doctrines is prescribed. Since we do not know which one is correct, we must proceed on the assumption that all are equally likely to be correct. Two centuries later, Sidgwick argued this way concerning utility functions. If we know nothing about the utility functions of Alfred and Bertha, the proper distribution between them is the same as if we know them to be identical. The pie must be equally shared. In Sidgwick's view, this leads one to unambiguous conclusions in the domain of politics. All members of society must be presumed to be equally capable of exercising political power. There is, therefore, no warrant for restricting the franchise or other opportunities for participation in political processes. Sidgwick did not contend that all persons *are* equally wise, equally competent, or public-spirited to an equal degree. It is not necessary to make such a questionable factual assertion in defence of democratic liberalism; it is sufficient to recognize that empirical assessment of comparative political worth is impossible. Everyone must be *assumed* equal in the political domain because their merits are hidden from view, and will always remain so. The ship of state minimizes the chances of sailing to absurdity when all aboard have an equal opportunity to participate in the collective decision-making process, though this does not guarantee that it will not do so.

The observant reader will have noted that the preceding discussion of whether utility functions may be compared was carried out in terms of the economic problem of the distribution of income, but, in indicating the implications of the minimax principle, attention was shifted to the political problem of the distribution of power. Sidgwick was well aware that parallel arguments can be made on these two issues. If the minimax principle requires one to regard all members of society as equally worthy political entities, why does the same reasoning not compel one to conclude that the best distribution of income is a perfectly equal one? Sidgwick was emotionally drawn to egalitarianism in all respects, but he rejected equality of income on the ground that such a rule of distribution would seriously impair the productive efficiency and growth of the economy. Economic goods must be produced in order to be distributed, and if their production requires human activities that will not be undertaken unless rewarded, it follows that the best distribution may not be an equal one. Indeed, it is very unlikely to be equal, since, if everyone knew that he would receive a *pro rata* share of the national income regardless of his own productive effort, little such effort would be likely to be forthcoming. The production system is interwoven with the distribution system in a complex way, since distributions act as production incentives.

This is a theme that recurs over and over again in the modern literature of economics and the other social sciences. Many (perhaps most) social scientists have strong leanings towards economic equality as a normative criterion of social policy, either on simple intuitive grounds, or because they believe that all people are in fact identical in their utility functions, or because of Sidgwick's minimax argument. But the equality of universal poverty has little appeal, so we find that while modern pragmatic utilitarians are inclined to argue that economic inequality should be reduced, they rarely advocate its complete elimination. Once again we find that there is a great difference between those who seek progress and those who will settle for nothing less than perfection.

C. UTILITARIANISM AND ECONOMICS

Utilitarianism makes little appearance today in the writings of professional philosophers. Part of the reason for this is that it was not a complete philosophical system, since it had very little to say about any branch of philosophy besides ethics. But even ethical philosophers are not inclined to view utilitarianism with much favour. John Rawls, whose *A Theory of Justice* (1971) comes as close to espousing the greatest happiness principle as any late twentieth-century utilitarian might wish, is nevertheless at pains to describe his ethical theory as non-utilitarian. Philosophers seem to view the role of utilitarianism in the history of their discipline as something of an embarrassment and, at any rate, now deceased. But utilitarianism, in much the form given it by Bentham and the Mills, lives on in two areas of modern thought: in the unsophisticated social philosophy of ordinary people, journalists, and those engaged in practical politics; and in the theoretical models of neoclassical economics.

The utilitarian roots of economic theory go back well before Bentham. Both psychological hedonism, the positive proposition that men act in accordance with their material interests, and ethical utilitarianism, the normative proposition that human happiness is the highest good, are evident in much of the mercantilist literature, and even the Physiocrats can be loosely described as utilitarians. The presence of positive and normative utilitarianism in the economic writings of David Hume and Adam Smith is not merely a secondary characteristic of their thinking but provided the epistemological and ethical foundations of it. Bentham's explicit statement of utilitarian principles supported a line of development in scientific economics that would probably have continued without him but it provided much intellectual comfort for the classical economists of the early nineteenth century, living as they did in an age when it was still considered necessary for any science to have the imprimatur of philosophy.

Virtually all the classical economists were utilitarians. Their essential conception of human nature was Bentham's. All the classical theories, concerning value, wages, rent, profit, population, and economic development, depend upon viewing human action as motivated by desire for 'pleasure' and aversion to 'pain'. Man plays his role in the classical economic models as a being whose essentially hedonistic nature is not appreciably altered by such things as religious beliefs, philosophical principles, or the characteristics of his particular culture. In classical political economy the secular and individualistic conception of man was embraced more fully than in any other branch of social science. Likewise, in their discussions of state policy, concerning the Poor Law, the tariff, factory regulation, or other matters, the classical economists adopted the utilitarian view, evaluating any policy in terms of its consequences for the general happiness rather than according to any criteria of inherent merit. When the classical economists disagreed over policy, their contradictory proposals reflected differences in specific positive analysis, not in their normative objectives.

The classical economists, however, did not provide explicit models of how men act as individual producers or consumers. Nor did they provide a coherent model that defines the theoretical conditions under which the general happiness would be maximized. Utilitarianism was therefore only half visible beneath the surface of their theories. The explicit and detailed use of utilitarian positive and normative assumptions that one finds today in all standard textbooks of economics is due to developments that began in the 1870's when utilitarianism was combined with the differential calculus. This development of economic theory is sometimes referred to as the 'marginal utility revolution'. In the sense that this introduced into economic theory the incisive concept of the 'margin' it was indeed a revolution, a revolution of analytical technique; but in that it focused upon 'utility' it was no revolution at all, being rather a continuation of the utilitarian tradition in economics. All the great figures in the development of neoclassical economics, such as W. S. Jevons, Léon Walras, F. Y. Edgeworth, P. H. Wicksteed, Alfred Marshall, and Vilfredo Pareto, were utilitarians or, if they had doubts about utilitarianism, as J. S. Mill had, they thrust them into the closet when it came to doing economics.

The history of economics was not completely utilitarian, however. Karl

Marx was fiercely opposed to utilitarianism in all its aspects, and the line of economic theory extending from him is distinctly non-utilitarian. Economic historians, until recently, did their work in a non-utilitarian mode which emphasized the cultural continuity of social life rather than the role of the happiness-oriented individual. The strong opposition of the members of the historical school, such as Gustav Schmoller in Germany and William Cunningham in England, to abstract modelling in economics was motivated in part by aversion to the utilitarian foundations of the procedure. The opposition to economic theory by American institutionalists such as Thorstein Veblen and John R. Commons had a similar foundation. But these lines of scholarship were peripheral to the mainstream of development in economics.

APPENDIX: ROMANTICISM

Historians of ideas generally agree that one of the most important forces shaping modern Western thought was the romantic movement of the early nineteenth century. In current literature this is most often treated as a development in the world of the fine arts that witnessed a general transition from the rational and objective to the emotional and subjective, as represented by the difference in styles, for example, in the poetry of Dryden and Pope as compared to that of Coleridge and Wordsworth, in the music of Bach and Haydn compared to Beethoven and Brahms, and in the painting of Gainsborough and Reynolds compared to Turner and Delacroix. But the romantic movement was equally important in philosophy and social thought. There is no article on romanticism in the *International Encyclopedia of the Social Sciences*, but that stands as a reproach to its editors, not as evidence that the romantic outlook was not, or no longer is, a significant feature of social thought.

Though historians generally agree on the importance of romanticism, they are far from clear when undertaking to describe it. The romantic style in poetry, painting, and music is unmistakable, but when one tries to state what constitutes romantic social philosophy and the romantic approach to the study of society the subject proves to be elusive. One historian calls romanticism 'a complex clutter of ideas' (Crane Brinton, 'Romanticism', *Encyclopedia of Philosophy*, 1972) while another suggests that the best way to describe it is 'contradictoriness' (H. G. Schenk, *The Mind of the European Romantics*, 1966, p. xxii). I shall not attempt to bring order into this 'complex clutter' but will focus upon those features of romanticism that are, even though contradictory, germane to understanding its role in the history and philosophy of social science.

Along with many other observers of the early nineteenth-century social scene the romantics were repelled by the economic changes that we now call the industrial revolution. After much controversy on the matter modern historical research has shown that the standard of living of the English working class was not deteriorating during this time (except perhaps for a brief period during the Napoleonic wars and the depression that followed) but it would have been difficult for the ordinary contemporary observer to believe that. The poor, previously hidden away in the countryside, were now all too visible in the new factory towns. The dirt and smoke of the factories and the architecture of the new towns were an offence to anyone with aesthetic taste, and the conditions of employment, especially since women and children were included in the factory work force, repelled anyone with even moderately refined sensibilities. Thomas Carlyle, enraged at what he had seen in the factory towns, published the most scathing indictment of industrialism, *Past and Present*, in 1843, but well before this many others had expressed serious misgivings at the direction of change in the British economy and society.

One line of reaction to this was taken by the reform movements, which attempted to use the authority of the state to modify working conditions, town life, and other aspects of industrialism. But the romantics took a different view. Britain's troubles, they felt, were not due to the steam engine and the power loom; these were merely the surface manifestations of a profound spiritual and philosophical malaise that was the inevitable consequence of two centuries of growing reliance upon science and reason as sources of knowledge, and the resulting suppression of religious faith, intuition and imagination, feeling and emotion. Coleridge, for example, at first an admirer of Hartley's association psychology (see above, Chapter 7 B, Note 2) later rejected it totally because it represented the human mind in a materialistic way, not accounting for its most important features, its creative freedom and its capacity for intuitive insight. These powers, in the romanticist view, are stunted and suppressed by the detached, rational, and empirical approach of the scientist. Truth comes from within man, not from the formulation of coherent theories and empirical evidence.

In formal philosophy the classical expression of this aspect of romanticism was given by the German philosopher Arthur Schopenhauer (1788–1860), who celebrated the human 'will' as being more real than material phenomena. Moreover, this will is unknowable and unpredictable, moving the world in inexplicable ways. The English romantics did not go quite so far but their philosophy was essentially anti-rationalist, anti-materialist, and anti-empiricist, emphasizing, as Schopenhauer did, the supreme importance of the ineffable powers of man's 'spirit'. A common theme running through the romantic literature is that it is a philosophic illusion to believe that there is objective truth. The real philosopher does not seek truth, he *creates* it by the power of his imagination. The romantics did not merely claim that empirical observation contains subjective elements and is 'theory-laden', a view that many modern philosophers have admitted; they went much further than that, making a high philosophic virtue out of what many others would regard as an unfortunate infirmity of empirical science.

The romantics made no attempt to attack the physical sciences in any specific fashion. At bottom they were more interested in social and political questions than in science. They viewed utilitarianism and the new science of political economy as prime examples of the decline of civilization. Thomas Carlyle was the most outspoken critic. Utilitarianism was, in his judgement, a 'pig philosophy' and political economy a blasphemy in its attempt to interpret man as subject to scientific law. There is no evidence that Carlyle had read any of the classical economists; he did not need to. Samuel Taylor Coleridge was more open-minded and he was certainly acquainted with the economic literature. He regarded Sir James Steuart as a more important economist than Adam Smith, probably because of Steuart's argument that close governance of economic processes is necessary, which fitted Coleridge's view that society should be firmly guided and directed by its superior members. Unlike Carlyle, Coleridge thought that political economy could be a worthy discipline if it were rescued from utilitarianism. His own efforts to write on the subject, however, were negligible, or worse. John Stuart Mill, who admired Coleridge's poetry and was attracted to some of his social ideas, said of him that 'in political economy . . . he writes like an arrant driveller, and it would have been better for his reputation had he never meddled with the subject'. Despite some recent attempts to rehabilitate Coleridge as an economist, Mill's judgement still stands.

Of the English romantics the one who made most of the necessity to construct a 'true' political economy to replace the detestable doctrines being promoted by Ricardo and the other utilitarians was the great art critic and essayist John Ruskin. He attacked orthodox economics in articles in the *Cornhill Magazine* in 1860 which raised the ire of the utilitarians. He wrote a small book, based on public lectures, called *The Political Economy of Art* (1857) and made numerous comments on economic matters in his other writings. Ruskin regarded himself as an important economist and was bitterly indignant that this view was not widely shared. In fact he did not write on the subjects that the classical economists were debating and he once remarked that the only economist he had in fact read was Adam Smith. His writing on 'political economy' was directed more at sociological questions, and some commentators regard him as a precursor of modern 'social economics', whose supporters contend that the disciplines of economics and sociology should be joined more closely than they now are. Despite its defects and limitations, economic theory has had to work with the conception of man laid down by Bentham in his doctrine of psychological hedonism. The romantics were unwilling to accept such a conception even as a heuristic device. They regarded it as both false and immoral, symptomatic of the general degradation of culture and society by scientists and rationalists.

The romantics devoted much of their energy to deploring the state of contemporary society, and its trends as they perceived them. This accounts for a great deal of their popularity: woe and calamity have always had a ready market. But their role as dissenters goes only a short distance in explaining the longer-run impact of romanticism. That influence is largely due to their vivid expression of both the individualistic and holistic conceptions of man and society.

In *The Great Chain of Being* Lovejoy argues that romanticist individualism was an outgrowth of the idea that in completing the plenitude of existence God had filled it with an infinity of *different* beings, each one of which is unique. Whether or not this intellectual connection is sustainable, it is certainly true that romanticism was a celebration of the uniqueness of the individual personality. This was carried to the point where the romantics saw great value in personal behaviour that recognized no constraints or rules. Bizarre, quixotic, or capricious behaviour was regarded, not as deplorable, but as welcome evidence of individual freedom. Romanticism and utilitarianism were both individualistic, but in ways that were so different that no common term can correctly be applied to them.

On the other hand, one of the most important features of romanticism in nineteenth-century social thought is the view that the human individual is part of a larger entity – society, the race, the nation – which is itself a kind of living organism, and one that is more philosophically significant than its constituent members. On this aspect of romanticism the most important philosophers were J. G. von Herder (1744–1803) and G. W. F. Hegel (1770–1830). Some historians describe Hegel as the most influential philosopher of the nineteenth century. This is mainly due to his influence on Karl Marx and Friedrich Engels and his impact on formal academic philosophy, but it is also due in part to his role in the romantic movement of giving expression to what has become known as the 'organic theory of society'. Bentham never tired of asserting that society is an aggregation of individuals and has no interests apart from that of its members. Coleridge, and other romantics, regarded this as totally wrongheaded. Society is an entity in itself, with interests of its own that transcend those of the individual both factually and morally. Thus we can see that on the one hand romanticism was much more individualistic than utilitarianism and, on the other, much less. This may seem contradictory, but it is part of romanticism's great appeal. Everyone wants to be free to do as he pleases and to have his individuality respected, while at the same time being a member of a social group and feeling united with others in communal oneness. Most serious social philosophers have felt a need to face up to this contradiction, taking one side or the other, or sketching the constitution of some middle course. The romantics were content to leave it as it was (after all, life is contradictory, is it not?) and so their writings gave inspiration to individualists and communalists alike.

Some historians have drawn a straight line from Schopenhauer and Hegel, through the romantic movement, to Adolf Hitler and the racist nationalism of German fascism. There is something in this contention, as the Nazi literature celebrating the transcendent value of the German *Volk* shows, but it must not be carried to the point of arguing that human behaviour is a 'necessary' consequence of philosophy. That would simply be another form of determinism; the Nuremberg court that condemned the Nazi leaders should have issued a posthumous damnation of Hegel and Schopenhauer instead. Christianity did not 'necessarily' result in the Inquisition, or Marxism in Stalinism, or utilitarianism in commercial television. The test of a philosophy is what people do with it more than what it 'inherently' is. But, given the strong currents of racism and nationalism that ran in Western thought during the nineteenth century, it was fortunate that the utilitarian emphasis upon mundane Epicurean values was present to act as a counterweight to the romantic vision of the transcendental virtues that lie beyond the understanding of ordinary men and require, for their realization, that the artist should be king.

Note: Some passages in this chapter have been taken from my *Welfare, Justice, and Freedom* (New York: Columbia University Press, 1980).

Chapter 12

French positivism and the beginnings of sociology

It would be helpful if we could begin this chapter with a clear definition of the term 'positivism' but, unfortunately, that is not possible, since it has been, and continues to be, employed in varied ways. In the context of French social thought the terms 'positive science' and 'philosophy of positive science' were apparently first introduced by Madame de Stael, a popular novelist and a leading figure of French romanticism, in her influential book *De la littérature considérée dans ses rapports avec les institutions sociales* (Literature Considered in its Relation to Social Institutions, 1800). Inspired more by Condorcet's utopianism than by Montesquieu's analytical approach to social questions, de Stael was the centre of a group of French intellectuals who contended that the perfectibility of man and society is possible, since all social problems are soluble by the use of scientific methods and the application of scientific knowledge in a state governed by scientists. As we shall see, a similar view played a central role in the development of positivism by Saint-Simon and Comte. But this is as far as one should go in trying to define early nineteenth-century French positivism in a general way. It is best to allow its meaning to emerge from a specific examination of the ideas of its main figures.

The term 'sociology' is almost as problematic as 'positivism' when one sets out to discover its 'beginnings'. Some historians of sociology start with the ancient Greeks, or earlier (see, for example, H. E. Barnes, *An Introduction to the History of Sociology*, 1948) while others are reluctant to go back even as far as the early nineteenth century, as we are doing in this chapter (see, for instance, the articles on 'Sociology' in the *International Encyclopedia of the Social Sciences*, 1968). The subject matter of sociology is much more difficult to specify than that of the other social sciences. When a writer discusses the tariff, or the supply of gold, or market prices, we know that he is at least talking about economic matters and it is relatively easy to determine whether he is making use of a theoretical model or being otherwise systematic. But when a writer discusses the family, or crime, or culture he *may* be doing sociology, but not necessarily, since the frame of his discourse may be theology, or political philosophy, aesthetics, ethics, psychology, or . . . . And even if he is indeed talking about sociological phenomena it is not always easy to ascertain whether he is proceeding in a systematic way, since such phenomena do not lend themselves to the degree of conceptual and empirical quantification that economics can achieve by the use of the common numeraire of money measurement. Moreover, sociology embraces substantively all social pheno-mena, and such boundaries as it imposes upon itself are purely conventional. Human intellectual activity is itself a social phenomenon, so sociology includes within its subject matter the study of the social organization of science, including social science, not excluding itself. This point is of more than passing interest, since, as we shall see, one of the most important features of the thought of the early French sociologists was their focus upon the organization and development of science and other intellectual activities, as social phenomena. Auguste Comte's main thesis was that there are laws of intellectual evolution which govern the development of the human mind. He used the term 'positivism' to describe the epistemic culmination of this development and invented the word 'sociology' to denote the science that he himself would create as the final synthesis of all knowledge.

In Chapter 1 we noted that man is an extraordinarily 'altricial' animal, the young of the species requiring many years of growth and preparatory training before they can assume the functions of mature persons. During this time a process of 'enculturation' takes place which fits the individual for life in a par-ticular society or culture. We also noted that, as a social animal, man is unique in being 'multisocial', that is, the individual may belong simultaneously to numerous social groups such as occupational associations, religious associ-ations, recreational associations, etc., whose membership may overlap. If we consider the discipline of sociology to be the branch of social science that is especially concerned with these aspects of human sociality the beginnings of soci-ology should probably be located in eighteenth-century France and Scotland.

In France, the Marquis de Condorcet should be mentioned, since his emphasis upon the development of man's knowledge and intellect as a phenomenon of social evolution focuses upon the aspect of sociality that became the centrepiece of Comte's sociology. His *Esquisse d'un tableau historique des progrès de l'esprit humain* (Sketch for a Historical Picture of the Progress of the Human Mind, 1795) was one of the great pieces of literature reflecting the outburst of enthusiasm for social reconstruction of the early period of the French Revolution and, through Saint-Simon and Comte, one of the most influential. But more important as a sociologist was Montesquieu, whose *De l'esprit des lois* (1748) had more influence on social thought and theory in Scotland and America than in France. Montesquieu's emphasis upon the enculturating role of social institutions, the great diversity of such institutions, their causal role in historical events, and their interaction within a culture that can be viewed as a whole system, supports the contention of some historians that he should be considered the first sociologist.

The Scottish moralists of the second half of the eighteenth century have already been discussed (Chapter 7 A) and it is clear that they must be regarded as at least precursors of modern sociology. Recent historians have singled out Adam Ferguson and his *Essays on the History of Civil Society* (1767) for special notice in this regard, but strong claims can be made on behalf of all the main figures of the Scottish Enlightenment, including David Hume and Adam Smith. The chapter headings of Louis Schneider's book of selections from the writings of the Scots (*The Scottish Moralists*, 1967) reads almost like a syllabus for an introductory course in sociological theory. Nevertheless, I will say no more here about Montesquieu and the Scots. As a social phenomenon a science 'begins' when a line of continuous development can be traced back to such an origin. This is the sense in which Montesquieu, Hobbes, and Locke can be regarded as the originators of political science and Adam Smith as the founder of economics. By the same criterion, the claim may be made that Saint-Simon and Comte should be regarded as the founders of sociology.

Once again, however, we should note that many modern sociologists would deny any intellectual indebtedness to Saint-Simon and Comte, and the historian has no warrant to foist upon the practitioners of a science a lineage that they reject. The sociology of Saint-Simon and Comte was very different from that which one finds today in a modern university curriculum, especially in the United States. Its closest modern counterpart is the academic and research sociology of the Soviet Union and other Marxist countries. Saint-Simon and Comte were engaged in what might be called Grand Sociology, the attempt to construct a comprehensive theory embracing in a unified synthesis all aspects of human sociality and its historical evolution down to the present and, beyond, into the future. Their most notable aspirant to this was Karl Marx but we should also include James Frazer, Herbert Spencer, and historians such as Oswald Spengler and A. J. Toynbee as non-Marxist practitioners of Grand Sociology. Émile Durkheim and Max Weber did not have quite so large a view of sociology but the discipline did not really commence to lose its grandeur of scope until the twentieth century. Today, Marxists again excepted, sociologists emphasize empirical research and, to the extent that they use theoretical constructs which are more than *ad hoc* empirical research instruments, they employ what Robert K. Merton has aptly called 'theories of the middle range'.

The social theory we will examine in this chapter belongs to a period in the history of Western Europe that witnessed a climactic transition between two worlds: from an old world of small agriculture, handicraft industry and limited trade, social localism and intimate community, and the confinement of political power to a small hereditary oligarchy; to a new world of large-scale machine industry, ubiquitous commerce, urbanization and the proletarianization of labour, a social psychology of nationalism, and the emergence of new classes to positions of political influence and power. Without excessive exaggeration it may be claimed that the social sciences are the products of social change, being intellectual responses to great and rapid alterations in traditional modes of social organization and the disorder, often punctuated by violence, that accompanied them. Without much more distortion, modern political science may be regarded as a product of the English Civil War of the seventeenth century and the American Revolution of the eighteenth, economics as a product of the industrial revolution, and sociology as a product of the French Revolution.

The destruction of the *ancien régime* in 1789 brought forth in France a great flood of literature, espousing all sorts of social theories, and grand plans for reconstruction of the social order, which continued in spate throughout the successive phases of the revolution, the Napoleonic dictatorship, and after Waterloo. The English Civil War generated a similar flood, but in the discussion of the beginnings of modern political theory in Chapter 4 our attention was restricted to the writers who were of dominant importance in the subsequent development of the subject, Thomas Hobbes and John Locke. Similarly, in this chapter we will focus only upon the two commanding figures, Henri Saint-Simon and Auguste Comte, neglecting others who, in a more complete history, would require notice. I shall not undertake here to sketch the general historical background of French positivism and sociology detached from specific examination of Saint-Simon and Comte but, before concluding this introduction, it will prove useful later if we take some brief notice of the French system of higher education.

Saint-Simon and Comte both adopted an idea of Condorcet's, which he in turn had derived from Francis Bacon: the conception of a utopian social order governed by men of science. In the England of Bacon's time this was seen to call for the creation of a great new institution with unquestionable status, prestige, and authority, which was brought to pass, some thirty years after Bacon's death, by the establishment of the Royal Society. In nineteenth-century France the necessary structure was already in existence, in Comte's view, in the form of the Institut de France, its several academies, and the system of special schools, chief among which was the École Polytechnique.

State policy in eighteenth-century France sponsored the creation of specialized senior institutions for training and research outside the established universities, which, because of their roots in medieval scholasticism and Renaissance humanism, were considered unsuitable for the proper promotion of science and technology. The great school of public works engineering, the École des Ponts et Chaussées (School of Bridges and Roads), was established as early as 1715. By the time of the revolution there were more, and better, higher institutions of science and technology in France than in any other country in Europe. They were prestigious institutions, admission to which was in itself a certificate of intellectual superiority, and because of their state sponsorship entry was sought not only by those who wished to practise a profession, but also by the sons of families who desired to elevate their social prestige and to secure a better place in the hierarchy of political power. The aristocracy, seeing their traditional status thus threatened, tried, with some success, to restrict admission to the children of aristocratic families, but this, like the rest of the apparatus of the *ancien régime*, was swept away by the revolution. Not the schools themselves, though; their importance was appreciated, and they were promoted, by the successive revolutionary regimes, by Napoleon, and by the rulers of France after Waterloo. The modern historian of the École Polytechnique, Terry Shinn (*L'École Polytechnique, 1794–1914*, 1980), notes that during the half-century after 1830 the graduates of the special schools, now coming mainly from the middle class, not only dominated the professional sectors of French society but exercised great political influence. This was the period when Auguste Comte was constructing his positive philosophy.

A. HENRI SAINT-SIMON (1760–1825)

Henri Saint-Simon was born into an aristocratic family of modest wealth and social status. He was a rebellious youth and although he was the oldest son he was left no inheritance when his father died in 1783. At the age of sixteen he obtained a post as an officer in the French army and, after rising to the rank of captain, he volunteered to serve in the expeditionary force sent to assist the American revolutionaries. He was in America for only two months but it was during the decisive phase of the revolutionary war and he participated as an artillery officer in the battle at Yorktown in 1781. In later years he was inclined to exaggerate his role as one of the founders of American liberty but more important than his effect on America was its effect upon him. He was greatly impressed by a society without an aristocracy, which could even achieve great military successes with an army that was led by officers drawn from the people. The emphasis in his subsequent writings on the importance of individual talent and ability, not restricted by hereditary caste, was due to his brief American experience as well as his personal rebellion against his family.

When the French Revolution broke out in 1789 Saint-Simon was one of the first to renounce his aristocratic title and to identify himself with the revolutionaries. This did not save him from the Terror, however. He was arrested in 1793 and only narrowly escaped the guillotine. His eleven months of imprisonment, under constant fear of execution, made a lasting impression on him, reflected in the emphasis in his later writings on the evils of anarchy and the supreme importance of social order. Like Thomas Hobbes, whose political theory was moulded by the turbulence and uncertainty of the English Civil War, Saint-Simon's social thought was permanently dominated by his own, more personal, experience of the consequences of civil disorder. Imprisonment also had an enduring psychological effect upon him, or served to exacerbate neuroses to which he was already subject. He suffered from hallucinations, in one of which Charlemagne appeared before him and predicted that he would become a great philosopher whose ideas would regenerate the civilization of Europe. In later years he repeatedly experienced similar hallucinations and sometimes regarded himself as the literal reincarnation of Socrates or Descartes, a messiah destined to change the world through the power of ideas, as Charlemagne had done by force of arms. He suffered a nervous breakdown in 1812 and spent some months in a mental institution. In 1823 he attempted suicide. The modern student of his writings and of the activities of his disciples who is familiar with Saint-Simon's personal history is easily tempted to categorize the Saint-Simonian doctrines as madness but, if so, it must be recognized as a madness that has had profound effects upon modern social thought.

During the early years of the revolution Saint-Simon became heavily engaged in speculative enterprises mainly having to do with the sale of land and property that had been confiscated from the Church and the aristocracy. These activities were the immediate cause of his imprisonment. After the fall of Robespierre he renewed his speculations and became very wealthy. But he spent lavishly, entertaining persons of high status, including especially the professors of the École Polytechnique. His luck in business ran out as well, and by 1805 he was penniless. By this time, however, he had begun to write on social questions, and the realization of the prediction made to him in prison by Charlemagne became the dominant purpose of his life. He obtained money wherever he could and without scruple, but only to buy the necessities that were essential for his great work.

Saint-Simon did not, however, conceive his mission to be that of a scholarly philosopher who would construct, all alone, a new system of social thought. Charlemagne had not conquered Europe single-handed; he was the commanding genius who had inspired others and had organized them for the task. So, likewise, Saint-Simon viewed his role as providing the leadership for an intellectual crusade that would be carried out, under his direction, by the best scholars and scientists of the day. Throughout his life as a writer he aimed to become the impresario and conductor of a great co-operative enterprise that would achieve a complete systematization of all knowledge on new philosophical foundations. Unlike the other social scientists we have studied so far, Saint-Simon's ideas cannot be located in a single great treatise or a few major works. He spent his energy writing pamphlets, prospectuses, and periodical articles, never completing any methodical or comprehensive statement of his ideas. Nevertheless, in these disorderly pages one finds a system of ideas or, at least, the embryonic elements that developed into the positive philosophy of Auguste Comte.

Saint-Simon was, apparently, a brilliant conversationalist and it was his talk rather than his writings that began finally to attract the disciples he longed for. Augustin Thierry, who later won fame as a popular historian, became his assistant in 1814 and three years later Comte succeeded Thierry. During Saint-Simon's last years a band of young intellectuals gathered around him, forming after his death a movement dedicated to the creation of a new religion and to spreading its doctrines throughout Europe, led by Prosper Enfantin, an engineer who had received his training at the École Polytechnique. Within a few years some hundreds of young graduates of the École joined the movement and, for a period, it seemed that Saint-Simon's dream of a new religion based upon science would sweep through Europe. The Saint-Simonians sent evangelical emissaries to England and elsewhere, published numerous periodicals and newspapers, and gave public lectures that attracted large audiences. But internal dissension and the adoption of bizarre rituals that invited ridicule and generated repugnance weakened the movement. Enfantin, who now called himself the 'Father of Mankind', was arrested and imprisoned, along with other leaders, and the movement came effectively to an end in 1832. Saint-Simonism revived in the 1840's, and obtained the support of Napoleon III in the 1850's, but it again declined as the original disciples died out. Its main impact on modern social thought was through Auguste Comte and Karl Marx.

The disorderly and flimsy character of Saint-Simon's writings, compared with Comte's systematic and weighty treatises, invites one to discount the role of Saint-Simon in the development of positivism. But reappraisal of Saint-Simon by modern historians has established his importance beyond reasonable doubt. The rudiments of positivism are present in his early writings, even before Thierry became his assistant. Comte first met Saint-Simon when he (Comte) was nineteen and remained a devoted disciple for four years. Despite his later insistence that he owed nothing to Saint-Simon, it is unlikely that Comte's experience as Saint-Simon's young assistant, fresh from the École Polytechnique, revelling in his release from its strict discipline and heavy curriculum of studies, was unimportant in his intellectual development. Nevertheless, it must be acknowledged that Saint-Simon's writings before his association with Comte, and after, contain only the undeveloped and unsystematized *elements* of positivism, and I shall not attempt to treat them as more than that.

One of the confusing features of positivism as a philosophy of science is that it seems to be both rationalistic and empiricist. The modern philosopher, whether or not he calls himself a 'positivist', inclines to resolve this conflict by recognizing the complementary roles of theory and empirical evidence in the advance of knowledge. Saint-Simon's resolution was of a different kind. He had the idea that *a priori* theory and the *a posteriori* study of facts operated not as collaborative methods but as temporally alternating modes of scientific investigation. This is the Saint-Simonian *'law of alternativity'*. European science, in Saint-Simon's view, had been for more than a century in a fruitful phase of empiricism, under the influence of Newton and Locke, but its constructive potential was now exhausted and it was necessary to shift to the other mode and move forward to a new rationalistic synthesis. He saw himself as the leader of such a development.

Saint-Simon's writings contain nothing of interest on any substantive topic in physical science or mathematics and, in fact, he knew very little about them. His scientific knowledge consisted only of what he picked up from the table-talk of the scientists he had entertained when he was a man of wealth, before he embarked on his mission to regenerate the civilization of Europe. But he was confident that his genius transcended the workaday activity of scientists and that his vision would point a way that they would follow.

In his earliest writings Saint-Simon's admiration of science was an idolatry which he not only celebrated as a personal conviction but recommended for general adoption. In his very first publication, *Lettres d'un habitant de Genève à ses contemporains* (Letters from a Resident of Geneva to his Contemporaries, 1803), he proclaimed the foundation of a 'Religion of Newton' and recommended the creation of a 'Council of Newton' composed of twenty-one distinguished scientists, scholars, and artists who, taking their inspiration from physical science, would be the authoritarian priesthood of a new social order. Like Madame de Stael and her circle, Saint-Simon entertained the hope, briefly, that Napoleon would be the instrument of such a new order, but disappointment in this did not substantially alter his utopian vision. The same essential idea of a world governed by an elite in accordance with principles of science is contained in his last work, published shortly before his death, *Nouveau christianisme* (New Christianity, 1825). Between his first and last writings there occurred, however, a significant change in Saint-Simon's thought, from physics as the paradigm for social science to biology and physiology, and from intellectuals as the elite class to men of industry and commerce; but he did not alter his initial conviction that experts should, and will, become the governors of society and that peace, order, justice, and the welfare of the masses required that they should have unrestricted authority. The role of such an elite, in contrast to the aristocratic elite that had constituted traditional political authority, was described by him in a striking passage that has become known as 'Saint-Simon's parable':

Let us suppose that France suddenly loses fifty of her first-class doctors, fifty first-class chemists, fifty first-class physiologists, fifty first-class bankers, two hundred of her best merchants, six hundred of her foremost agriculturists, five hundred of her most capable ironmasters, etc. . . . . Seeing that these men are its most indispensable producers, makers of its most important products, the minute that it loses these the nation will degenerate into a mere soulless body and fall into a state of despicable weakness in the eyes of rival nations, and will remain in this subordinate position so long as the loss remains and their places are vacant. Let us take another supposition. Imagine that France retains all her men of genius, whether in the arts and sciences or in the crafts and industries, but has the misfortune to lose on the same day the king's brother, the Duke of Angoulême, and all the other members of the royal family; all the great officers of the Crown; all ministers of state, whether at the head of a department or not; all the Privy Councillors; all the masters of requests; all the marshals, cardinals, archbishops, bishops, grand vicars and canons; all prefects and sub-prefects; all government employees; all the judges; and on top of that a hundred thousand proprietors – the cream of her nobility. Such an overwhelming catastrophe would certainly grieve the French, for they are a kindly disposed nation. But the loss of a hundred and thirty thousand of the best-reputed individuals in the State would give rise to sorrow of a purely sentimental kind. It would not cause the community the least inconvenience. (Quoted from *L'Organisateur*, 1819, by Charles Gide and Charles Rist, *A History of Economic Doctrines*, 1915)

Despite his sojourn in America, Saint-Simon did not consider that a republic could also be a democracy. The leaders of men can be recruited from the people but they must rule over them with unlimited power.

Saint-Simon's political theory was intimately connected with his philosophy of science. It is a profound mistake, in his view, to regard scientific knowledge as growing by the simple accumulation of the results of methodical research. The many working men of science must be commonly inspired by the insight of the philosophical genius who, in an intuitive fashion, grasps the inner meaning of the phenomena of nature. Without him there can be no scientific progress. Likewise, the governing elite of society must be united by a common devotion to realizing the social vision of the unique genius who understands the essence of social phenomena and is able to perceive the laws, hidden to lesser men, which govern human history. This genius need not be a scientist or scholar; his intuitive insight provides truths of a more profound sort than methodical research can discover. This is no mere speculation, for such men of genius have walked on earth before, and now one has come again to save Europe in her hour of crisis – who else but the author of these thoughts himself? In Saint-Simon's megalomania we see a union of the philosophy of science and political ideology, or, more correctly, the subordination of the former to the latter, which repeatedly reappears in the history of nineteenth- and twentieth-century social science and social philosophy.

In the modern literature of the philosophy of science there is a continuing controversy concerning the role of that discipline, whether it should restrict itself to describing the methodology of scientific practice, or attempt to ascertain the rules of correct practice and employ them as critical criteria and prescriptive norms. In early nineteenth-century French positivism, the descriptive and prescriptive orientations of the philosophy of science were fused together in the view that man's intellectual development proceeds necessarily through three stages, the 'theological', the 'metaphysical', and the 'positive'. This is the so-called *'law of the three stages'*, a central pillar of Comte's philosophy of history. Positivism, on this view, is not only a descriptive term for the most recent stage, but also a prescription of methodological rules that should henceforth govern all scientific practice. The essentials of the law of the three stages are contained in Saint-Simon's writings of 1813, four years before he met Comte.

One of these 1813 publications is entitled *Mémoire sur la science de l'homme* (Memoir on the Science of Man). The scientific study of human social phenomena, in Saint-Simon's view, must adopt the methodology of the natural sciences. Saint-Simon had entertained this view from the time of his earliest writings on social matters, and perhaps earlier, since this may have been one of the reasons why, when he was a man of wealth, he had taken up residence near the École Polytechnique and sought the company of its distinguished scientists and mathematicians. Saint-Simon's philosophy of science, however, went beyond the claim that the study of social phenomena could be effectively modelled after the natural sciences. He was convinced that all phenomena, whether physical, chemical, biological, or social, reflect the operation of a single principle. After much consultation of his intuition he concluded that this monistic principle was Newton's law of gravitational attraction. As usual, however, he did not explain this but wrote a pamphlet, *Travail sur la gravitation universelle* (Work on Universal Gravitation, 1813), urging scientists to follow his insight, and claiming that the civilization of Europe could be rescued if they were to do so. Terms describing the science of society as 'social physics' or 'social physiology' in the early positivist literature prior to Comte's introduction of the neologism 'sociology' reflect Saint-Simon's epistemic monism.

From his earliest thinking on social questions it is evident that Saint-Simon felt that a new social science can, and must, be created that would, like modern natural science, be 'positive'. But after a few years of association with the engineers and mathematicians of the École Polytechnique (who then showed no inclination to become his disciples) he shifted his residence to the vicinity of the École de Médecine and cultivated the company of physicians, physiologists, and biologists. Society, he came to believe, is a living organism, not a machine or a planetary system, and a scientific social science must be modelled upon the life sciences.

The view of society as a kind of super-organism, in which individual men and classes of men play roles akin to cells and organs, can be traced back to Greek antiquity, but it began to play a prominent role in social thought only during the nineteenth century. The first profoundly influential philosopher to advance this view was the leader of the early German romantic movement, Johann Gottfried von Herder, most notably in his four-volume *Outlines of the Philosophy of the History of Man* (1784–91). Saint-Simon probably did not read Herder, or Hegel, who presented a similar view of society, but he adopted the concept of society as organism and was an important conduit through which the idea penetrated into social philosophy and social science. Auguste Comte and, subsequently, Émile Durkheim and Herbert Spencer were deeply influenced by it. Durkheim in particular was profoundly impressed by

Saint-Simon's idea that a society, being an organism, possesses a consciousness of its own, which transcends and, indeed, determines that of its member individuals (see below, Chapter 15 B). The concept of collective consciousness or, in its most extreme form, the notion of a 'group mind' was enlarged subsequently by Carl Jung, second only to Sigmund Freud as father of psychoanalysis, who contended that each society also has a collective subconsciousness, lying beneath the shared beliefs and mental perspectives that are its sensile culture, which preserves in subliminal memory its past history as a collectivity. The impact of this set of ideas on modern literature and art, and their perceptions of social phenomena, has been enormous.

Throughout the modern history of social science the concepts of organism and mechanism have warred against one another, and still do. The conflict between holism and reductionism as methodologies of social research is in considerable part a reflection of these two alternative metaphysical concepts of society. This also characterizes one of the notable distinctions between sociology and economics as social sciences, sociology leaning towards organicism and holism, mainstream economics towards mechanism and reductionism. I say 'mainstream' economics because one of the outstanding features of Marxian economics, the historical school, institutionalism, and social economics has been an emphasis upon the organic and evolutionary features of society. But even mainstream economics has not been impervious to the appeal of holism and organicism; in the writings of Alfred Marshall, the most important figure in the early development of neoclassical economics, one finds that he viewed his own contributions to economic mechanics as preliminary to the development of an organic theory of society. Social scientists have always had difficulty with the concept of 'society', in large part because they have been reluctant to regard society as a categorically distinct existential entity. Some social scientists tend to view societies as merely aggregations of individuals while others regard them as organisms, or at least 'like' organisms. The war between these concepts reflects the monism that characterizes academic philosophy, each side claiming to be the true metaphysical One. But organisms are not the same as mechanisms and societies are not the same as either. Metaphysical pluralism is not neat, but one of its merits is that it permits one to view societies as societies, and to study their organization without excessive dependence upon analogical crutches.

The organic conception of society was firmly welded to the theory of evolution in the period following the publication of Charles Darwin's *Origin of Species* (1859), but a similar conjunction of organicism and evolutionism is present in Saint-Simon's writings of half a century before, and even earlier in Herder's philosophy of history. There is, however, a fundamental difference between Herder and Saint-Simon on this point. In Herder's view, every age and every society has its own unique character, just as every organic species is distinct from others. History, therefore, is a record of the pluralistic development of culturally different societies. Saint-Simon, on the other hand, viewed the variety of cultures as merely superficial. All social development takes place according to an underlying plan; human history is no less governed by monistic law than the planets are in their motions. Saint-Simon was not the first writer to hold such a view of history but he was the first to contend that conflict between economic classes constitutes the central dynamic force of social evolution. Independently of Hegel he had the idea of dialectical history, and prior to Marx he identified the economic class aspects of society as its foundation. Thus he may be regarded as the originator of dialectical materialism.

Saint-Simon had no doubt that man's social future is as law-governed as his past. The laws of history are the laws of destiny, which will inevitably conduct society to a determined end, the perfect social order that his intuitive vision had revealed. Saint-Simon was not, however, an absolute determinist. That is equivalent to fatalism and would make nonsense of any programme of social action such as he constantly urged. The *general* laws of history are unbreakable and their ultimate end is inevitable, but it is within man's power to affect details and, most important, the ease and speed with which these laws work. Moreover, not only can the individual affect the historical dynamic in this way, but he is morally obliged to act in harmony with historical law. It is a moral crime for one to try to stop or alter the force of history and a moral virtue to assist and hasten it. Thus, in effect, one is morally as well as intellectually obliged to acknowledge Saint-Simon as lord and guru and to join the Saint-Simonian movement. There is a great deal in the thought of Saint-Simon that resembles views later expressed by Karl Marx and developed by his disciples. Marx and Lenin criticized Saint-Simon for engaging in a utopian delineation of the detailed structure of the future social order but, none the less, an obelisk stands today in Moscow's Red Square which includes the name of Saint-Simon among those honoured as significant precursors of Marxism-Leninism.

In modern Marxist theory a distinction is drawn between 'socialism' and 'communism' and between 'utopian socialism' and 'scientific socialism'. The term 'communism' is reserved for the ultimate end of the process of social evolution, while 'socialism' refers to the transition period following the revolution and preceding the establishment of 'communism'. The distinction between 'utopian' and 'scientific' socialism in Marxian theory reflects the basic difference Marx and Engels saw between themselves and the long line of writers we surveyed above in Chapter 8 B who drew sketches, and sometimes complete blueprints, of a perfect social order. This was most clearly stated in Engels's *Socialism: Utopian and Scientific* (1880), which was aimed immediately at the writings of Eugen Karl Dühring, a German critic of Marx, but was also a general attack upon all utopianists. The construction of plans for a new social order, in Marx's and Engels's view, is idle speculation, devoid of scientific foundation. A socialism that is truly scientific does not concern itself with this but concentrates upon the analysis of the dynamic processes that will bring about the destruction of capitalism and the inauguration of a new historical era. Thus 'scientific socialism', in Marxian terminology, does not mean that the new era is characterized by the scientific organization of society, as Saint-Simon and Comte advocated, but refers to the 'laws of history', discovered by Marxist science, which demonstrate that the coming of socialism is inevitable.

Engels was more sympathetic to Saint-Simon than Marx, perhaps because he perceived in Saint-Simon's disorderly writings, in addition to description of a new social order, the contention that he was also *predicting* a historical development that must come to pass. Saint-Simon does not really qualify as a precursor of Marxian 'scientific socialism', since he offered little in support of this prediction beyond revealing it as an intuitive vision. From his first writings to his last, however, he made much effort to describe, in considerable detail, how the new society would be organized. In this respect, therefore, Saint-Simon was a 'utopian'. Whether he should be called a 'socialist' is a question on which interpreters disagree. The first appearance in French of the term *socialistes* has been traced by historians to the Saint-Simonian newspaper *Globe*, in 1832, where it was introduced as a description of the believers in the New Christianity. But, like most political labels, 'socialism' and its cognate terms have gone through many variations during the past century and a half, and it is a waste of time to argue over whether Saint-Simonism is accurately characterized by a word that now embraces a polymorphous miscellany of ideas.

We noted above that Saint-Simon's imprisonment during the Terror impressed upon him the supreme value of social order. Such order, in his view, requires unlimited control by the sovereign power of the state. He rejected the concept of spontaneous order that was a central thesis of classical political economy and was hostile to the pluralistic liberalism taking root in England. The new society that he advocated, and predicted, was to be authoritarian and totalitarian, with all the activities of its members subject to the control and direction of a governing elite. Saint-Simon provided the foundations for this in his own writings, in which he constantly argued that the solution of all man's problems is to be found in the organization of his society by deliberate general planning and detailed administrative direction.

Like all utopians, Saint-Simon and his followers had little to say about the economy of the new society. Their negative view of the market system was sufficient to convince them that a planned economy would be superior, but one finds no discussion in their writings of the technical problems of economic planning and how they would be handled. Some historians of Saint-Simonism have interpreted it as an economic theory but this is incorrect. It is primarily a political and sociological theory, whose occasional notice of economic issues is unilluminating. Like many utopians, also, Saint-Simon is somewhat ambiguous in his view of government. On the one hand, government is the instrument that controls and directs society; on the other hand the full maturity of the new society will be characterized by such profound alterations in man that it will operate smoothly without need of coercion. In Saint-Simonism we find the germ of Marx's idea that under full communism the state will 'wither away' and Lenin's view that central economic planning is a matter of simple clerical 'administration'.

Leaving such visions of the ultimate aside, Saint-Simon's delineation of the organization of the new society is a blueprint for an authoritarian totalitarianism. It differs from the *ancien régime*, however, in two important respects: the governing elite will be recruited from all sectors of society, according to talent rather than birth, and the duty of the elite is to govern for the benefit of all. In Saint-Simon's writings one finds frequent quotation of Bentham's formula 'the greatest happiness of the greatest number', and the first expression of the rule that Marx later made famous, 'from each according to his ability; to each according to his needs'. We do not, however, find any recognition of James Mill's problem, how to structure a constitutional order so that the governors, however they are recruited, will act in the interests of the whole. In Saint-Simon's view, unlike Mill's, the governors of the new society could be relied upon to suppress their personal interests and perform their duties as trustees of society conscientiously.

The new society was to be a society of inequality. The elite would rule and the mass of the people would obey. This, in Saint-Simon's view, would be in harmony with nature, since men are by nature unequal in their talents and abilities. In his early writings Saint-Simon regarded scientists, scholars, and artists as constituting the natural elite; later he placed more emphasis upon the tycoons of industry, commerce, and finance, viewing them as engineers who are capable of dealing with the practical problems of the new social order. It should be clear, Saint-Simon felt, that such an organization of society is in the interests of the masses, and he first addressed his message to the proletariat as well as to the graduates of the special schools. But he later came to the conclusion that the proletariat were too ignorant to appreciate his philosophy. Recognizing the effectiveness of religion as an instrument of social control, he advocated the creation of a new religion to serve this function in the new social order. The elite would be devotees of positive philosophy, sophisticated masters of pure and applied science; but the proletariat would be indoctrinated into a faith appropriate to their limited capacities and designed to fit them for their role as complaisant workers. This faith, in terms of the title of his last pamphlet, was to be a 'New Christianity'. Saint-Simon considered himself a Christian, but it is doubtful that he meant this in any theological sense or that he believed in the existence of any supreme being, let alone the divinity of Jesus. What he really believed in was *history*, and he had no doubt that he had been selected to fulfil its great plan. In the service of that transcendent end, no means are forbidden.

Modern interpreters of Saint-Simon have represented him as fitting into the intellectual and political history of the nineteenth and twentieth centuries in various ways: as a precursor of Marx; as an advocate of central economic planning and opponent of the market system of economic organization; as precursor of fascism and other modern forms of totalitarian social philosophy; as an early political philosopher of technocracy, the doctrine that the world should be governed by engineers; as the originator of 'scientism', the view that the methodology of the natural sciences is the appropriate methodology for the study of social phenomena; and as an early metaphysical philosopher of 'historicism', the conception of man's past and future as governed by general 'laws of history'. From our survey of Saint-Simon's ideas it is evident that there are solid grounds for all these contentions. Since he did not produce any systematically integrated philosophical treatise, it is difficult to capture the various elements of his thought by a single term. But some further understanding of Saint-Simon's place in the history and philosophy of social science may be attained by recognizing the close affinity of his main ideas to those outlined in the appendix to Chapter 11, and classifying them under the heading of romanticism. In that discussion we noted the antipathy of the romantics towards the growing market economy of their time and to classical political economy and utilitarianism; their emphasis upon the great value to society of its few members who are endowed with creative talent and the gift of intuitive insight; their claim that ordinary rules of conduct do not apply to such 'heroes', to use Carlyle's term; their view that the mass of mankind should, in their own true interests, worship such men of genius and submit to their governance; their conception of society as an organism that is healthy and happy when each part of it plays its proper role in the communal whole. Many of Saint-Simon's ideas can be stated in similar terms. His political theory, especially the idea of the need for a reconstituted state religion suitable for an organic society, bears much resemblance to Samuel Taylor Coleridge's *Constitution of Church and State* (1830) the most important political treatise of the English romantic movement.

Some of Saint-Simon's views seem to be opposed to romanticism, most notably his views on industrialism and science, but upon closer examination they too have romantic properties. Many of the romantics viewed the growing industrialism of their time with abhorrence and praised the civilization of earlier periods, especially the Middle Ages, when life was, in their view, simpler and more communal, society more organic and hierarchical, and the individual less alienated. They initiated the practice, which is still prominent in social thought, of distorting the past in order to condemn the present. Saint-Simon celebrated the merits of industrialism, but the new society he envisaged was one in which the great virtues of the medieval era would be restored through a new communalism. He opposed the Enlightenment belief that there had been progress, arguing that true progress awaits the emergence of a perfect social order in which the modern industrial economy would be incorporated in a political and social system that will be a centralized version of medieval feudalism. The romantics were hostile to science and especially to the idea of a scientific study of man and society, while Saint-Simon admired natural science and urged the application of its 'positive' epistemology to social phenomena. But Saint-Simon was severely critical of classical political economy, as the romantics were, and, when we look closely, we find that natural scientists and social scientists do not occupy the topmost position in his hierarchy of talent. That position is reserved for the 'genius' who discovers truth by intuition rather than through methodical research and analytical modelling.

The romantic movement and the development of social science during the nineteenth century are usually viewed as antithetical and antagonistic streams of social thought. Generally speaking they were, but Saint-Simonism was a conduit through which romanticism penetrated into social science. It would perhaps be naive to believe that, but for Saint-Simon, modern social science would not be infected with romanticism, but it is he who played the historical role of first distributing that pathogen widely in Europe.

B. AUGUSTE COMTE (1798–1857)

Auguste Comte was born into a middle-class family at Montpellier in the south of France a year before the French Revolution was ended by the *coup d'état* of Napoleon. His parents, who had remained steadfast supporters of the Bourbon monarchy throughout the revolution, were also ardent Catholics and baptized the child Isidore August Marie Francois Xavier, including among his preparations for this world the name of the founder of the Jesuit Order. Their son would, however, renounce Catholicism when still a boy and spend his life laying the foundations for a new religion which, though it did not succeed in becoming the official faith of civilized nations as its author hoped, has had a large, and still potent, influence upon Western social thought.

After schooling in Montpellier Comte gained admission to the École Polytechnique in Paris in 1814. He was a brilliant student and would probably have gone on to become a faculty member of the École or one of the other prestigious special schools if he had not offended the strict discipline of the institution by leading a student rebellion. He was expelled just before he would have taken his final examinations. His relations with the École were not completely broken, however; he was permitted to act as a mathematics coach for École students. Prior to becoming Saint-Simon's assistant, and again after the rupture of their relations, Comte earned his living in this fashion, and later as an examiner for the École, which gave him the free time he needed for his writing. After his work became known he was able to count on fees and royalties, and occasional donations by admirers, to sustain his modest style of living.

Comte married in 1825 but the marriage was not a happy one. A year later he suffered a mental breakdown which culminated in attempted suicide. He recovered, but not completely, and the rest of his life was marked by periods of mental instability and a melancholia that even his faith in the coming of a new social order could not banish. At the age of forty-seven he fell deeply in love with a woman whose death, a year later, left him inconsolable.

It was while he was a student at the École Polytechnique that Comte conceived the idea that philosophy could be constructed on purely scientific foundations and that scientific methods could be applied to social problems, yielding results as certain as those of physics, chemistry, and mathematics, thereby eliminating the differences of opinion that are such potent sources of political instability and social conflict. Comte felt that his few years at the École Polytechnique had equipped him with all he needed to know about science and he studied little thereafter. Moreover, he feared that a creative genius such as himself risked contaminating his originality by too much reading of the works of others and he practised what he called 'cerebral hygiene', reading nothing except a bit of poetry while engaged in the composition of his own works. This, as modern scientists and scholars would be quick to recognize, has its own dangers. No matter how good one's initial education, and no matter how brilliant one is, obsolescence comes rapidly if one disregards the work of others. Some of Comte's pronouncements upon contemporary science demonstrated this amply: he opposed, for example, cellular theory in biology; the shift by astronomers from the solar measurement of the earth's rotation to the use of the fixed stars as points of reference; the development of probability theory; and, in general, he denigrated the use of experimental procedures to obtain empirical data and to test theories. These views, and his own reliance upon intuition and *a priori* methodology, made his 'positive philosophy' unattractive to working scientists, but it was precisely Comte's view that he knew enough science to construct a scientific philosophy and a science of society that attracted as disciples men of literary and artistic bent who had little taste for laboratory work or analytical modelling. To be assured that one may safely disregard the substantive content of science and yet speak of one's views as having the authority of science was (and is) a great comfort. Three centuries before, Giordano Bruno had taunted the theologians who felt that they had no need of science in evaluating the Copernican theory. 'Ignorance is the most delightful science in the world,' he remarked, 'because it is acquired without labour or pains and keeps the mind from melancholy.' The high benefit–cost ratio of such 'science' was rediscovered in the nineteenth century, assisted greatly by Comtean positivism.

Comte wrote an enormous amount. Unlike Saint-Simon, he was methodical and embodied his ideas in large, systematic treatises. The first of these was the *Cours de philosophie positive* (Course of Positive Philosophy), which was originally begun as a series of lectures in 1826 and was finally published in six volumes between 1830 and 1842. In this work he surveyed all scientific knowledge, attempted to establish the general philosophy of positivism, and commenced its application to social matters. His second major work was *Le Système de politique positive* (System of Positive Polity), which appeared in four volumes between 1851 and 1854. This outlined his conception of a society organized on positivist principles. At his death in 1857 he was at work on another large treatise on technology.

There has been some difference of opinion among historians as to the uniqueness and originality of Comte's main ideas, especially his degree of indebtedness to Saint-Simon. Comte was Saint-Simon's assistant for seven years before he began his own work, and, in my view, all the central propositions of what today is called 'Comtism' were anticipated by Saint-Simon. The reader will find that the following outline of Comte's ideas parallels those discussed in section A with only minor differences. Comte and Saint-Simon broke their association in 1824, but there is no evidence of any substantial disagreement between them on points of philosophic doctrine, social analysis, or conception of the new social order. Their rupture primarily reflects only Shakespeare's observation that 'when two men ride one horse, one must ride behind'. Neither Saint-Simon nor Comte, both megalomanic personalities, was prepared to take second place in the Pantheon of greatness.

Like Saint-Simon, Comte lived in the dark shadow of the French Revolution. He had no personal experience of waiting day after day to be called to the guillotine, as Saint-Simon had during the Terror, but he was no less fearful of social disorder. The motivating force of his social thought was the supreme importance of avoiding the kind of political and social anarchy that gripped France after 1789 and had been only imperfectly and temporarily suppressed by Napoleon. When he began writing the *Cours* he was convinced that he had discovered a philosophy that would banish disorder from human civilization forever and make it permanently harmonious, just, and prosperous. It was not, or so he thought, a political or an ethical philosophy, but a scientific philosophy, as solidly grounded in reality as Newton's laws of physics. By calling it the 'positive philosophy,' Comte meant to emphasize its absolute certainty, which distinguished it from all other philosophies previously conceived.

Comte nowhere gave a succinct definition of positivism, perhaps assuming that any reader who knows what science is will know what positivism is. In all his voluminous writings there is no significant extended discussion of the problems that have occupied the attention of philosophers under the heading of 'epistemology', so we cannot compare his specific views directly with those of Hume or Kant, or with modern 'logical positivism', or any other school of the philosophy of science. In general terms, however, he makes his position clear. Under the heading 'The Character of the Positive Philosophy' in the *Cours* he says:

> the first characteristic of the Positive Philosophy is that it regards all phenomena as subject to invariable natural *Laws*. Our business is . . . to

pursue an accurate discovery of these Laws, with a view to reducing them to the smallest possible number.

The governance of these laws embraces human and social phenomena as well as physical and biological phenomena, for they are all part of a seamless order of nature. In Comte's view, the task of the positive philosopher in so far as human and social matters are concerned, is to discover the laws that have governed and will continue to govern the historical evolution of civilization. Comte did not conceive of this as requiring an investigation of economic history or political history; the fundamental laws concern man's *intellectual* history, the evolution of his way of thinking about himself and the world around him. Thus restricted, Comte was convinced that he had fulfilled the basic requirements of the positive philosophy by discovering what he called the *law of the three stages* and its corollary, the *hierarchy of the sciences*.

As we noted in Chapter 7, the idea that human history proceeds according to some pattern and that this pattern is essentially a succession of distinct 'stages' is present in the writings of the Scottish moralists of the eighteenth century. Comte applied this, by his day familiar, idea to intellectual development. In this he had precursors in Turgot, Condorcet, and Saint-Simon, as well as the Scots, but the idea is now indelibly associated with Comte's name because of his extensive exposition of it in the first volume of the *Cours* and his utilization of it as the keystone of the positive philosophy. It deserves to be emphasized, however, that Comte did not regard the law of the three stages as a heuristic device constructed by the scholar to assist him in the study of history, but as constituting the essential nature of historical evolution. He had not devised the law of the three stages any more than Newton had devised the law of gravity. The law had been at work since the beginning of man's life on earth. Comte was not its inventor but its discoverer. Attention to this point is important, since, throughout the history of science, and perhaps most significantly of social science, there has persisted a fundamental difference of view concerning the nature of scientific laws, some regarding them as representing inherent properties of nature and others as man-made artefacts, hypotheses employed in the attempt to ascertain the properties of nature. Comte clearly belongs to the former category as a philosopher of science. As he succinctly put it:

From the study of the development of human intelligence, in all directions, and through all times, the discovery arises of a great fundamental law, to which it is necessarily subject, and which has a solid foundation of proof, both in the facts of our organization and in our historical experience. The law is this: that each of our leading conceptions – each branch of our knowledge – passes successively through three different theoretical conditions: the Theological, or fictitious; the Metaphysical, or abstract; and the Scientific, or positive . . . .

In the theological state, the human mind, seeking the essential nature of beings, the first and final causes (the origin and purpose) of all effects – in short, Absolute knowledge – supposes all phenomena to be produced by the immediate action of supernatural beings.

In the metaphysical state, which is only a modification of the first, the mind supposes, instead of supernatural beings, abstract forces, veritable entities (that is, personified abstractions) inherent in all beings, and capable of producing all phenomena. What is called the explanation of phenomena is, in this stage, a mere reference of each to its proper entity.

In the final, the positive state, the mind has given over the vain search after Absolute notions, the origin and destination of the universe, and the causes of phenomena, and applies itself to the study of their laws – that is, their invariable relations of succession and resemblance. Reasoning and observation, duly combined, are the means of this knowledge.

In other words, Comte felt that in the earliest stage man's view of nature was theistic or animistic; all natural phenomena are regarded as resulting from the operation of forces essentially similar to human powers of will and action, whether these powers are exercised by a single supernatural being, or by particular spirits that inhabit stones, trees, and other natural objects. This 'theological stage' lasted, in Europe, up to the fourteenth century. The 'metaphysical stage' was characterized by a belief in Aristotelian 'essences'. The phenomena of nature are not attributed to man-like forces but to abstract properties that are part of the inherent nature of physical objects. This stage, according to Comte, dominated European thought from the fourteenth century until the French Revolution. The true significance of the revolution was not that it was a landmark in Europe's political history but that it dated the beginning of a momentous transformation in man's intellect, the beginning of the 'positive stage', the mature age of science, which would in due course explain all phenomena in terms of the operation of laws of nature and usher in a new social order.

Another passage from Comte's *Cours* is worth quoting:

The progress of the individual mind is not only an illustration, but an indirect evidence of that of the general mind. The point of departure of the individual and of the race being the same, the phases of the mind of a man cor respond to the epochs of the mind of the race. Now, each of us is aware, if he looks back upon his own history, that he was a theologian in his childhood, a metaphysician in his youth, and a natural philosopher in his manhood. All men who are up to their age can verify this for themselves . . . .

Comte was here generalizing his own intellectual development as he saw it – his personal passage from the theological stage to the metaphysical when he renounced his parental religion at the age of thirteen, and his maturation into the positive stage during or shortly after his studies at the École Polytechnique. As verification of the law of the three stages Comte cited his personal experience during his attacks of melancholia: he found himself regressing into the metaphysical stage and then into the theological, the process being reversed as he recovered. Comte obviously regarded intro-spection as a reliable empirical procedure but he relied upon it to supply data of much more cosmic scope than we noted above in our studies of Hobbes and Adam Smith. We also see here indications of Comte's organicist view of human society and anticipation of the theories developed later by Durkheim and Jung, which attributed to society the property of a collective 'mind' with conscious and subconscious components.

Comte was an able mathematician and in his early years he was attracted to Laplace's view that one could construct a mathematical model of the physical universe which, when supplied with the necessary existential data, could predict exactly all future phenomena and completely reconstruct the past. In the beginning of the *Cours* he toyed with Saint-Simon's idea of reducing all phenomena to the 'law of universal gravitation.' He never lost his faith in Laplace's cosmic view of the power of science, but he came to the conclusion that mathematics and physics, though necessary, are insufficient to deal with human history. Mathematics is the most general of the sciences, a necessary basis for astronomy, which, in turn, is a necessary basis for physics, and so on, with chemistry and biology occupying successively higher positions, dealing with increasingly complex phenomena. This is his theory of the Hierarchy of the Sciences. The history of the development of the various sciences exemplifies the law of the three stages, all of them having passed through the theological and metaphysical stages in their early development, and now being mature, i.e. 'positive' disciplines. This having been accom-plished, says Comte, it is possible to complete the positive stage in man's intellect by constructing the crowning science of the hierarchy, the science of man as a social creature, which would disclose the laws by which human history is governed. This new science, which Comte himself set out to create, was first described as 'social physics' but later, in the fourth volume of the *Cours*, he compounded Latin and Greek roots into a new term, sociology.

One should note the absence of economics in Comte's hierarchy of the sciences. He did not view the economic aspects of society as important in human history and he had a very low opinion of classical political economy. It was Marx who gave weight to the idea that the key to understanding the laws of history lies in the analysis of economic relations in society in its different stages of economic evolution. Marx, to use his own term, 'materialized' the sociology of Comte.

As a sociologist Comte must be viewed mainly as a practitioner of what I have called Grand Sociology, which many modern Western sociologists, especially in the United States, would regard as too speculative a mode to be called sociology at all. But there are some elements in his thought that provide more substantial grounds for treating him as, at least, a protosociologist. Unlike the classical economists, he did not approach the study of social phenomena by examining the behaviour of man as an individual but insisted on viewing him, as Montesquieu had emphasized, as inherently social in nature. For Comte, sociology is the study of the social whole, which is not reducible to its individual members. The individual, indeed, having been shaped by his culture, is not an independent entity, and to treat him as such is to engage in the kind of abstraction characteristic of the 'metaphysical' stage of intellectual development. Society as a whole is more primary, and indeed more concrete, than individual persons. Though he carried his holism to extremes, Comte did draw attention to the fact that human society is not a mere aggregation and that, in attempting to understand how it functions as an organized structure, one must examine the cultural elements that create social solidarity and serve to integrate the behaviour of individuals into a communal enterprise. This aspect of human consciousness, which is undeniable as a simple matter of fact, was overburdened by Comte's rather mystical organicism, but those who interpret him as the progenitor of even American sociology can find support in his view that one needs to know how individuals view their world, how they think, and what they believe, in trying to understand and predict how they will behave.

In Comte's third, or 'positive', stage of human evolution, sociology is established as the 'Queen of the Sciences', but the role of the sociologist is not restricted to a purely intellectual sovereignty. As we noted in beginning our examination of his thought, Comte was motivated by the conviction that social disorder is the greatest of all evils and he embarked upon writing the *Cours* in the conviction that he had found a complete and permanent cure for this recurrent disease of the social body. From the beginning of his work, he intended that the new science he would build should be a practical one, having the same relation to politics as physiology to medicine. In a famous aphorism he announced that 'to know is to predict, and to predict is to act'. We proceed now to examine the main features of the new social order that Comte proposed as the remedy for the malaise of civilization.

Just as the various sciences naturally constitute a hierarchical order, so, in Comte's view, do the various elements of a society. Thus a peaceful and progressive social order must be based upon social differentiation. This was construed as not only desirable but inevitable, since the study of history reveals that as societies evolve there come about both increasing specialization of individual functions and increasing integration of the whole. Comte abhorred the pluralistic liberalism that was steadily becoming more characteristic of English society. This, in his view, meant only that society would be racked by repeated upheaval. Individualism of this sort he called 'the disease of the Western world'.

For a brief period after Waterloo Comte was attracted to the doctrine of economic liberalism and the conception of an economy built upon competitive enterprise and organized through markets. He was a close friend of Jean-Baptiste Say (1767–1832), sometimes called 'the French Adam

Smith', but he soon realized that economic liberalism was incompatible with his social philosophy and came to regard competitive economic activity as symptomatic of society's disorder rather than an ordering mechanism, as classical political economy contended. Comte followed the utopian tradition in saying very little about how the economy of the new society would function. In the light of his general political theory one must assume that he viewed it as being centrally directed, as everything else was to be. Unlike Marx, he saw no special significance in the ownership of industrial property, since, in the new society, the owners of such property would, like other members of the higher orders of the hierarchy, eschew individual self-interest and manage their property in the spirit of social stewardship.

The role of government, as we have seen, was somewhat ambiguous in Saint-Simon's vision of the new society, but not in Comte's. The state does not 'wither away' but is strengthened in its powers and enlarged in the scope of its duties, becoming in fact authoritarian and totalitarian in the fullest senses of those terms. In the interest of the social organism all private rights are to be suppressed, for order requires that the individual be subordinated to the life of the social organism. This harmony, in Comte's view, can be achieved only by force. Non-state institutions, customs, and conventions are potent instruments through which force can be exercised, but they are secondary powers, functioning effectively only under the supervision, control, and directing leadership of the sovereign state. Comte recognized only one political philosopher of significance in the twenty-two centuries that had elapsed between Aristotle and himself – Thomas Hobbes. It is not surprising that John Stuart Mill, who was greatly impressed by Comte's theory of intellectual development, drew back in horror when he saw the political direction in which the positive philosophy was going.

The top tier of Comte's social hierarchy was to be occupied by positive philosophers, the bottom by the mass of the proletariat. Comte did not think that there would be dissatisfaction in such a rigidly stratified society, for the proletariat would appreciate the benefits they received from a social order that eliminated war and domestic conflict. They would accept their low status uncomplainingly and play their roles quietly and efficiently in a society which had the capacity to achieve a hitherto unknown degree of social solidarity. Indeed, Comte looked upon the proletariat as the element in existing society that would force its transmutation into the new order. Their lack of education, as well as their misery, would make them receptive to the message of the positive philosophy. At times Comte toyed with the idea that the new order would be established from above, through the conversion of Napoleon III or Czar Nicholas I of Russia, but the encouragement he received from these quarters was inadequate. Nevertheless, the Laws of History cannot be repealed and they do not depend upon the actions of individuals. The transmutation of society would, if necessary, take place from below, at the insistence of the proletariat or, rather, through the alliance of intellectuals with the proletariat in a common cause – a union of 'brains and numbers', to use the felicitous title of a recent book on Comtism (Christopher Kent, *Brains and Numbers: Elitism, Comtism and Democracy in mid-Victorian England,* 1978). Through such a union the intellectual class, or at least those of them who embrace positivism, would at last find a mission worthy of their abilities and would cease to be alienated from society, graciously accepting the duty of becoming its future governors after that mission is completed.

The new governors in Comte's vision of the positivist social order would not be 'philosophers' in Plato's sense, but more like those envisaged by Francis Bacon and Condorcet. They would be drawn from the topmost tier of scientists, doctors of the new science of sociology, which involves mastery of all the other disciplines in the hierarchy of the sciences. Comte did not envisage government by men of ethical superiority or refined artistic sensibility, as many of the romantics proposed. It was to be government by experts, a technocracy. Comte himself, of course, stood ready to assume the topmost role. He did not say what should be done during those periods of insanity in which he would regress from positivist enlightenment into the mists of metaphysics and theology. Perhaps if he had addressed himself to this problem, he would have made an important contribution to the political theory of totalitarian dictatorship.

As noted above, Comte had great hopes for the role of the proletariat in establishing the positivist society, and he spoke of the complaisance with which they would play their role in it once it had been established. In due time the scientists and technologists of the new society would create a new species of man requiring little nourishment, reproducing without sexual intercourse, and otherwise more suited than *Homo sapiens* to citizenship in positivist society (like the new species of Aldous Huxley's *Brave New World*), but in the meantime the positive philosophers would have to deal with man as he is, and it was only realistic to recognize that the proletariat might not in fact accept their subordinate status without complaint. The stability of the new society would require careful and skilful management of the proletarian mind. To achieve this Comte proposed the creation of a new Church, which would properly indoctrinate the lower levels of society in what he called 'the Religion of Humanity'.

Comte himself was an atheist, and had been so since the age of thirteen, when he rejected Catholicism, but he appreciated the power of religion as a means of social control. In the outline of his proposed Religion of Humanity he reproduced many features of Catholicism – a trinitarian focus of worship, priestly mediation, vestments, sacraments, hymns, catechisms – designed to produce awe and veneration, and an uncritical acceptance of doctrine. The priests were to be positivist sociologists, free of any illusions concerning the transcendental claims of the religious doctrine, but appreciative of the power of propaganda, and skilled in the use of it. In all this he was repeating and elaborating upon the argument of Plato, who, living also in a time of social disorder, proposed the reconstitution of Athens as an autocracy under the leadership of a philosopher-king and, recognizing that those in the lower ranks would have to be persuaded to accept their inferior status, advised the construction and promulgation of a religious myth to justify the position and power of the elite. 'A high value must be placed upon truth' (says Plato's protagonist in the *Republic*); 'falsehood is useful to men only as a medicine and, clearly, the use of medicine must be confined to our doctors.' The ordinary citizen must be truthful at all times but, for the 'guardians' of society, a great 'noble lie' is permitted because it is necessary to ensure obedience and social order. The sacrifice of truth to power by intellectuals who are certain that they know what is best is no new development; it has been a prominent element in Western political philosophy since its beginnings in ancient Greece.

C. THE INFLUENCE OF POSITIVISM

The reader cannot have failed to notice that the writer has a low opinion of Saint-Simon and Auguste Comte. This is generally shared by the mainstream of academic social scientists in the West, though some students of the history of sociology might say that I have been over-zealous in noting the bizarre and foolish features of their thought and have not given sufficient credit to their constructive contributions in emphasizing the unity of social systems and the role of social institutions as intermediaries between the individual and society as a whole. Historians of social science, whether hostile or sympathetic to French positivism, agree that its impact upon modern social thought has been very large, and some discussion of this is indispensable in any effort to sketch the main outlines of the history and philosophy of social science. In order to examine the impact of early French positivism I will differentiate between its influence on social and political philosophy, and its influence on the substantive content of academic or professional social science. No line of hard demarcation can be drawn between such matters but we will proceed to discuss the influence of French positivism by focusing upon each in turn.

If South America had been more important in nineteenth-century social thought than it was the historian would have to direct his attention there, since positivism became especially popular among intellectuals who opposed the role of the Catholic Church in Latin American society. But social ideas are much less cosmopolitan than scientific discoveries. The general importance of propositions in social philosophy, and even in social science, depends greatly on the language in which they are expressed and the country of their provenance. In the mid-nineteenth century no social philosophy could have wide influence unless its language was French, German, or English, and its protagonists lived in France, Germany, Great Britain, or, increasingly, the United States.

The main initial impact of positivism was not in France, its place of origin, but in England. An extraordinary number of the leading figures of English intellectual life were attracted to Saint-Simon and later to Comte. Thomas Carlyle translated some of Saint-Simon's writings so that they could work their benefits more easily upon the English, who, then as now, did not trouble to learn other European languages. Harriet Martineau, whom we met in Chapter 10 as the publicist of *laissez-faire,* abridged and translated Comte's *Cours.* George Eliot, the great Victorian novelist and essayist, considered herself a positivist. Her common-law husband G. H. Lewes, editor, critic, and distinguished biographer of Goethe, wrote a book on Comte's philosophy of science and a number of others expounding it and applying it to philosophical and social questions. John Morley, biographer of Voltaire, Rousseau, Cromwell and others, and editor of the influential *Fortnightly Review*, played an active role in the English positivist movement. George Grote, the author of a twelve-volume *History of Greece* (1846–56) which became a classic of historical scholarship, was a Benthamite but was also greatly impressed by Comte's writings. So also was John Stuart Mill, who referred to Comte in the most favourable terms in his book on the philosophy of science, *A System of Logic* (1843), promoted the reading of the *Cours* among the members of his intellectual circle, corresponded extensively with Comte, and arranged financial assistance by English admirers when he lost his position as examiner for the École Polytechnique. The presence of Grote and Mill in this list appears to support a connection between positivism and utilitarianism, but not on closer examination, since, like numerous others who admired Comte, they distinguished between his philosophy of science and his social philosophy and made it plain that their endorsement was confined to the former.

None of the persons cited above held a position in a British university, but the main centre of English positivism was in fact there, and specifically at Oxford. A group of positivists gathered at Oxford under the leadership of Richard Congreve. In addition to Comte and Congreve they were inspired also by Thomas Arnold, who had founded the great English 'public' school, Rugby, as a forcing-house to train an elite to govern England, and who, in his brief tenure as Regius Professor of Modern History at Oxford, had taught that nations are like organisms and history is the science that investigates the laws of their development.

Comte himself, disappointed at the little notice that was taken of him in his native land, was delighted with his success in England, began to dream that the positivist new order would commence there, and offered advice and counsel to his English disciples. Mid-Victorian England provided the most hospitable climate in Europe for the direct reception of positivist ideas. Comte's followers included persons of high distinction in English intellectual circles and some who were prepared to dedicate their full energies to the promotion of positivism – Congreve, and his student, Frederic Harrison, most notably. But despite such auspicious beginnings, positivism did not take firm root in English political life. Its influence did not spread much beyond a small group of middle-class intellectuals. Congreve founded the London Positivist Society in 1867 as the evangelical arm and central administration of the movement. That year became one of the great milestones of English political history, but for a different reason, the passage by Parliament of the second Reform Bill, which greatly broadened the electoral franchise and placed England firmly on the course of fully participant democracy. Comte's hope that a new political era would be brought into being by the union of the proletariat and positivist philosophers was not realized. The English positivists met in London to celebrate a great Festival of Humanity in 1881 but this proved to be a vain attempt to establish the movement as a significant political force. It virtually disappeared from view shortly thereafter, though, at Oxford University, Comte's influence continued to persist even into the twentieth century (see Alon Kadish, *The Oxford Economists in the Late Nineteenth Century*, 1982). Looked upon in retrospect, the English positivist movement of the Victorian period strikes one as a rather strange aberration in England's intellectual history.

In support of the contention that French positivism had a great impact upon modern social and political philosophy we must look elsewhere, to Karl Marx and Friedrich Engels and the development after them of what is now called 'Marxism–Leninism'. The similarities between the thought of Saint-Simon and Comte and that of Marx and Engels have been noted occasionally in this chapter and will become more evident in our study of Marxian theory in Chapter 13. As a revolutionary movement Marxism succeeded in constructing an effective union of proletariat and intellectuals. In Lenin's *What is to be Done?* (1902) we find a restatement of the positivist view of the dynamics of history and a recognition, similar to Comte's, of the special role in it that must be played by a small cadre of intellectuals who are both firmly dedicated to the doctrine and expertly skilled in the art of manipulating the masses. The tracing of philosophic influences is subject to much uncertainty, since ideas that are highly similar or even identical may have been arrived at independently. Marxism might have arisen and developed as it did even if Saint-Simon had been called to the guillotine and Comte had been successful in attempting to drown himself in the Seine. But I leave this matter without further comment, since it raises large and difficult questions that we cannot enter into here: the assessment of historical causation and the role of ideas in the evolution of human society.

The influence of French positivism on the development of the social sciences is only somewhat less problematic. Concerning sociology, there is considerable disagreement as to when it can be said to have originated, and many modern sociologists regard Comte as only the one who named, not the one who founded, the discipline; with even less credit awarded to Saint-Simon. There is considerable difference, however, in how sociology is practised today in different countries and there is corresponding difference of view on the role of French positivism in its history.

In France itself, Émile Durkheim (1858–1917) is considered the key figure in the development of sociology, and this view is shared by some English and American sociologists. Durkheim was the first French academic sociologist, teaching initially at the University of Bordeaux and later at the Sorbonne in Paris. He founded and edited *L'Année Sociologique*, a journal whose importance in the development of European sociology was very large. But it is not clear how much Durkheim's sociological thought owes to Saint-Simon and Comte. Some writers view Durkheim as virtually a conduit by which their ideas were embodied in later sociology, while others treat their influence upon him as a youthful enthusiasm which he later rejected. The editor of the English translation of Durkheim's *Socialism and Saint-Simon* (1958), Alvin W. Gouldner, regards him as engaging in a 'deep-going polemic' against Comte in his major works, while Anthony Giddens regards Comte's influence upon Durkheim as fundamental ('Positivism and its Critics', in Tom Bottomore and Robert Nisbet, eds, *A History of Sociological Analysis*, 1978). We have already noted that the organicism of Saint-Simon and Comte was adopted by Durkheim, and the importance of it in his thought will be evident when we come to study Durkheim's sociology in Chapter 15. But Durkheim made no use of Comte's theory of history, the law of the three stages, or the hierarchy of the sciences.

In English and American sociology the influence of French positivism has been less than in France. Sociology as an independent academic discipline hardly developed at all in England until the mid-twentieth century, owing in part no doubt to the low repute with which the English positivists came to be regarded. In England, therefore, the influence of positivism on sociology was negative, slowing its development. Today the names of Saint-Simon and Comte are noted favourably by some English sociologists, but only those who consider themselves Marxists. In the United States, where quantitative sociological research had its beginnings, the influence of French positivism has been small. Lester F. Ward (1841–1913), a botanist and geologist turned sociologist, was an avowed admirer of Comte. He shared Comte's view of the need for a science of society that would be the queen of all the sciences to serve as a guide for the wholesale regeneration of the social order, ending the anarchy and individualism of capitalism. Ward was elected president of the newly founded American Sociological Society in 1906, but his work shortly thereafter fell into almost total neglect by sociologists. A stronger candidate as founder of modern American sociology is Albion W. Small (1854–1926), who was appointed to the first Chair in sociology at an American university, the newly established University of Chicago, in 1892, where he built a department of outstanding quality and long influence on American sociology. He founded in 1895, and edited for thirty years, the *American Journal of Sociology*, the leading academic journal in the discipline. Like Ward, he was critical of capitalism, and the influence of Marx upon him is evident, but he was hostile to French positivism and criticized Ward for promulgating the 'myth' that American sociology is indebted to Comte. In Small's view, sociology began with Adam Smith's social psychology in his *Theory of Moral Sentiments*. Small's methodology was, however, like Ward's, non-quantitative, and his influence upon modern sociological research was negligible, despite his prominent role in establishing sociology as an independent academic discipline. The country where French positivism has had, and continues to have, the largest impact on academic sociology is the Soviet Union, where the task of the sociologist is regarded as furnishing a comprehensive view of (mainly capitalist) society as a whole and the further delineation of the laws of history. This style of sociology, the Grand Sociology as I have called it, owes its immediate inspiration in the Soviet Union to Marx, so any assessment of its debt to French positivism depends on one's view of Marx's debt to Saint-Simon and Comte.

Saint-Simon and Comte were writing before the development of the various social sciences, but there was one that was already recognized as an established discipline: economics, or 'political economy', as it was then called. The question of the influence of French positivism on economics therefore deserves some brief notice.

Saint-Simon knew very little about classical political economy. One commentator on him remarks that he left this branch of social science to Comte. But Comte was not interested in the subject, either. In all his voluminous writings there is no extended discussion of any of the topics considered in Chapter 9 above and it is likely that he knew little, if anything, about the classical theories of value, rent, population, international trade, or, despite his central interest in the laws of historical evolution, the Ricardian theory of economic development. Without knowing its specific content, Comte was hostile to classical political economy, becoming more extreme in this as his aversion to market capitalism grew more intense. In line with his view of the unity of all science he objected to the classical economists' efforts to construct an independent science of economics and especially their use of the concept of 'economic man', which divorced economic activities from their social and cultural context. The new premier science of sociology would include economics within a general theory of society without bothering itself about unimportant matters such as the formation of market values, international trade, and suchlike. There is some similarity between Comte's view of economics and that of J. C. L. Simonde de Sismondi (1773–1842), whose *Nouveaux principes d'économie politique* (New Principles of Political Economy, 1819) was a sweeping attack on Ricardian economics, but there is not much evidence that Comte was directly influenced by Sismondi. Following Comte's lead, the English positivists adopted as an important part of their programme the combating of what they considered to be the deleterious influence of classical political economy on English social thought. Their efforts in this regard may have had some influence upon the development of the study of economic history in England (and America), which, until quite recently, was dominated by scholars who were hostile to the analytical modelling of orthodox economics and eschewed the use of economic theory in their work.

Aside from its influence upon economic historians and on those who described themselves as institutionalists or social economists, the impact of positivism on economics was negligible. The mainstream of the discipline continued to employ the methodology established by Ricardo. John Stuart Mill, as we have seen, was sympathetic to Comte and made very favourable reference to him in his book on the philosophy of science, *A System of Logic* (1843), but it is difficult to find any influence of Comtean philosophy in his *Principles of Political Economy* (1848), which dominated the study of economics in England and America until the end of the century. J. E. Cairnes, second only to Mill in later classical economics, launched a frontal attack upon Comte in the *Fortnightly Review* in 1870. This was answered by Frederic Harrison on behalf of the positivist movement, but the mainstream of economists sided with Cairnes.

One of the striking features of modern social science is the difference between economics and sociology in their approach to the investigation of social phenomena. Some sociologists, including Albion Small in the last century and Dennis Wrong and Jonathan Turner recently, have described sociology as originating in protest against the methods and content of traditional economics. Raymond Aron attributes the continuing hostility between sociologists and economists in French universities to the acceptance by the former of Comte's view that economic theory is excessively abstract and makes an unacceptable separation of economic matters from other social phenomena. It is doubtful that this is due to Comtean positivism as a philosophy of social science, but it is undeniable that modern economists and sociologists do not have a high opinion of each other's discipline, and this is not confined to France. Students majoring in sociology in American universities are not required, or even encouraged, to take courses in economics, nor are students in economics advised to study sociology. Modern sociology and economics are both strongly empirical and stress the use of sophisticated quantitative methods, but economists regard sociology as too descriptive, verging on raw empiricism, while sociologists find economics too boldly theoretical, verging on metaphysics. This may owe something to sociology's positivist origins and the connection of economics with utilitarianism but, in my view, it is mainly due to the fact that economics continues to be quite severely reductionist and embraces methodological individualism as a fundamental principle of science, while sociology is more holist and emphasizes the emergent properties of social associations. Given a set of data showing, say, that the allocation of family income to different uses (the proportion spent on housing, food, entertainment, etc.) differs for families of different incomes, the sociologist is likely to interpret it as evidence that different social groups or classes have different styles of life, while the economist would say that it shows that different commodities and services have different 'income elasticities of demand'. The sociologist considers that he has found an explanation of differences in behaviour in social differentiation and stratification, while the economist clings tenaciously to the view that all people are basically the same. When F. Scott Fitzgerald remarked to Ernest Hemingway, 'The rich are different from us,' he was thinking like a sociologist, and when Hemingway replied, 'Yes, they have more money,' he was expressing the economist's point of view.

Attempts to unite sociology and economics have been made by institutionalist economists and social economists and by modern sociologists who employ the 'exchange' paradigm of social behaviour. With only a little stretching, we could interpret John Stuart Mill's emphasis upon institutional arrangements in his *Principles of Political Economy* and his hope that a scientific study of the formation of human character ('ethology' he called it) would one day be developed, and Alfred Marshall's emphasis upon the sociological character of the demand side of the market and his expectation that economic theory could be developed into a comprehensive science of 'economic biology', as steps towards, and encouragement for, the union of economics and sociology. But, again, we must turn to Marxism for the most important attempt to forge such a union. Marx's analytical economics continued in the tradition established by Ricardo, as we shall see in the next chapter, but Marx viewed economics in a much broader context. Ricardo's theory of economic development does not have the cosmic character of Marx's theory of history or the import of his 'laws of motion of capitalism'. Marx's broad perspective can be regarded as an attempt to construct a comprehensive theory of society through a union of the sociology of Saint-Simon and Comte and the economics of Ricardo (freed of its utilitarianism and individualism). The attempt to find an emulsifying agent for this intellectual oil and water remains a central concern of modern Marxist social science.

D. FRENCH POSITIVISM AND THE PHILOSOPHY OF SCIENCE

Despite their reverence for science and their emphatic insistence that the study of social phenomena must be scientific, neither Saint-Simon nor Comte discussed any aspect of epistemology in more than a superficial way, and it is not possible to synthesize a coherent philosophy of science from their writings. Modern interpreters of French positivism are sometimes boldly assertive in describing and evaluating its philosophy of science, but this is sustained by focusing on some aspects of Saint-Simon's and Comte's work and disregarding others, or by insistence on fitting it into the author's own procrustean bed of historical interpretation. Some interpretations take at face value Saint-Simon's and Comte's demand that the methodology of investigation must treat reality as objectively existent, independent of our preconceptions, and construe French positivism as a continuation of eighteenth-century empiricism. But it must be plain from our survey of Saint-Simon and Comte in this chapter that the tradition of empiricism in the philosophy of science and French positivism are poles apart; whatever similarity they possess is confined to Saint-Simon's and Comte's rhetorical exhortations and is not evident in their own methodological practice. The fact that they did not follow their own epistemological precepts does not, in itself, disqualify Saint-Simon and Comte as philosophers of science but it means that we cannot resort to their writings to amplify and clarify their epistemological views.

The lack of any direct discussion of the epistemology of science in the writings of Saint-Simon and Comte hampers any effort to identify their philosophy of science as a prescriptive norm but it is of some historical significance none the less. Along with many other writers of their time, and since, Saint-Simon and Comte did not consider it necessary to delineate the principles of scientific investigation, since they regarded words like 'science' and 'scientific' as being, in themselves, complete and unproblematic designations of those principles, not requiring further amplification. The historical significance of French positivism in this connection is that it contributed greatly to the tendency to use the words 'science' and 'scientific' as encomiastic labels for one's own doctrine, irrespective of its content. Today we see terms such as Scientific Socialism, Christian Science, Scientific Creationism, Scientology, the Science of Astrology, Spiritual Science, and more; any and all points on the modern intellectual compass can be described as 'science'.

Throughout the preceding chapters of this book we have seen the powerful influence upon Western thought of the development of the physical sciences. Not only did this make possible the separation of social investigation from theology and ethics, and its release from the control of established religious and political authority, but it provided methodological inspiration as well. A listing of early social scientists who aimed to follow the epistemological footsteps of classical astronomy and physics is almost identical to a complete roster of the important names, and only moderately smaller is the number who explicitly described themselves as the Galileos or Newtons of social science. In this respect, Saint-Simon and Comte were merely following a well established tradition, but their invocation of 'science' shows graphically that it is not at all clear what is meant by contending that social investigation should be patterned after the physical sciences. It may be useful here to anticipate some epistemological issues that cannot be fully appraised until our survey of the history of social science is more complete. In saying that the study of social phenomena must follow the lead of the physical sciences a number of different propositions may be intended, as follows.

1. The most simple-minded view is that the social sciences should imitate the methodology of the natural sciences in an uncritical fashion. When a social scientist claims scientific credentials for his work by pointing out that

in physics, or biology, or some other branch of natural science similar procedures are employed, he is using natural science as the final norm of methodological reference. This is not a defensible position, since it means that the credentials of social science are derivative from the practice of natural science without reference to *its* credentials. This resorts to the *prestige* of natural science, not its epistemological foundations. Moreover, natural scientists work in a wide variety of ways. The research methods of astronomy, organic chemistry, ecological biology, and plate tectonic geology share little in common beyond recognition that there is an objective world, and even this seems to fade from view in some of the theories of modern physics. A social scientist with only moderate ingenuity would have no difficulty in finding research work somewhere in the natural sciences that is methodologically similar to his own.

2. A related view is that the natural sciences are quantitative, and social investigation is scientific to the degree that it too is quantitative. But one would not contend that falsified data have scientific merit, so this criterion of science has to be referred to other criteria of good scientific practice, and cheating is not the only procedure it forbids. Quantitative data, even honestly obtained, may be meaningless or irrelevant. A vague qualitative proposition may be more empirically germane than a precise numerical one.

3. In recent years, led by economics, social scientists have been enthusiastic about the potentialities of mathematical modelling and sometimes one hears the contention that the identifying mark of a scientific proposition is that it can be expressed in mathematical language. This would in fact rule out a great deal of the work of natural scientists, making the remaining corpus of science rather small. Moreover, that corpus would not necessarily be empirical, or even meaningful, since one can talk nonsense in any language, including mathematics.

4. Among professional philosophers of science, a more common view than any of the above is that there are valid general principles of epistemology which are applicable to all fields of empirical investigation, and the significance of the natural sciences is not that they themselves provide the criteria of science but that they exemplify them most clearly. This would be a powerful argument if there were even moderate agreement as to what these general principles are, but philosophers of science today hold many different views on this (see Chapter 18 A). The idea that there are general principles of epistemology that are discoverable, though not yet discovered, tends to degenerate into (1) above, since many philosophers proceed in ways that seem to imply that those principles may be discovered by analysing the research methods of natural science, especially physics. The view that there are general epistemological principles applicable to both the natural world and the world of human behaviour and social phenomena has been hotly contested, most prominently by F. A. Hayek, who has derogatorily labelled this 'scientism' and traced it to Saint-Simon and Comte (*The Counter-revolution of Science: Studies in the Abuse of Reason*, 1955).

5. Another view of social science is that it can achieve true scientific status only by basing itself substantively upon the findings of biology. Human behaviour, and therefore social phenomena, are governed by man's biological constitution, runs this argument, and the social sciences must build their models on foundations provided by biology. Comte seems to have held this idea, which is implied in his 'hierarchy of the sciences', where biology occupies the position immediately below sociology. In the current literature this view has resurfaced in 'sociobiology', whose leading protagonist, Edward O. Wilson (*Sociobiology: the New Synthesis*, 1975), has proposed, contrary to Comte, that the study of human sociality should be made a sub-discipline of biology, with its experts solidly trained in neurology and genetics.

6. Finally, in delineating the various propositions that are embraced by the contention that social science should follow the lead of natural science, we must note the comprehensive view that social phenomena are governed by general laws and the task of the social scientist is to discover them. If we take this a step further to the thesis that these laws are like those governing natural phenomena in being spatially universal, temporally constant, and impervious to any modification by human activity, we arrive at the central proposition in Saint-Simon's and Comte's view of human sociality, its history, and its future.

Reviewing these six propositions, it is evident that the invocation of 'science' by the French positivists was based mainly on (6), and secondarily on (4) and (5). I do not think that there is much ground for attributing (1), (2), and (3) to them in any significant way.

Understanding the relation of early French positivism to the philosophy of science has been muddied considerably by attempts to trace a connection between the views of Saint-Simon and Comte and the modern school of philosophy initiated by the Vienna Circle which, during the 1930's, was called 'logical positivism'. One can discern a certain affinity to early French positivism in the manifesto of the Vienna Circle, published in 1929. This was drafted by Otto Neurath, a sociologist. Neurath was a Marxist and played a role of some importance in the development of the idea that, under communism, the market system would be replaced by central planning and administration of economic processes. This, as we have seen, was a notable feature of Comte's vision of the new social order, so, in this respect, Neurath may be regarded as linking this conception of economic organization to modern Marxism. But this has to do with social philosophy, not epistemology. Most of the members of the Circle were logicians, mathematicians, philosophers, and physical scientists whose common interest was in the philosophy of natural science. On that subject the only similarity between them and Comte was their strong condemnation of transcendental metaphysics and their plea for its replacement by 'the scientific conception of the world'. French positivism and logical positivism are two distinct philosophies which happen to have the same name. The positive philosophy initiated by the Vienna Circle, and its relation to the social sciences, will occupy our attention in the final chapter of this book.

Chapter 13

The Marxian theory of society

Before we begin to examine the content of Marxian theory some terminological clarification is necessary. The eponymous term 'Marxian' itself raises the question of the role of Marx's friend and collaborator, Friedrich Engels, in the initiation and development of the ideas that are designated by it. Five years after Marx's death, Engels noted that, while he had had 'a certain independent share', Marx was the leading member of the team and 'could very well have done without me' (*Ludwig Feuerbach and the End of Classical German Philosophy*, 1888). This modest assessment of his relationship with Marx has been rendered questionable by recent historical research. It is now evident that Engels had developed, in writing, some of the basic propositions of Marxian theory even before his collaboration with Marx began in the fall of 1844. For example, Engels's 'Outlines of a Critique of Political Economy', which was written in 1843, contains many of the ideas that are prominent in Marx's first writings on social science, now known as the 'Paris Manuscripts' (or by the title under which they were first published, in the 1930's, as *The Economic and Philosophical Manuscripts of 1844*). Before he met Marx, Engels had arrived at the view that class conflict, due to society's economic structure, is the prime factor in social change. It was Engels's insistence on this point that persuaded Marx to shift the main focus of his scholarly work from philosophy to economics. Throughout their forty-year friendship Engels played an important part in the development of Marxian theory. The famous *Communist Manifesto* (1848), for example, was composed in its final form by Marx but it was based upon a manuscript written by Engels called 'The Principles of Communism' (1847). If Engels had accepted Marx's offer to include him as joint author of *Capital*, there would perhaps be less neglect today of his role in the development of Marxian theory among those who regard the economic analysis presented in that book as the core of Marxian thought. Virtually all Marx's major work after 1844 was discussed with Engels and, even if there were no explicit documentation on the matter, it would not be possible to relegate Engels to a minor place in the development of Marxian theory.

Engels's role in the *promotion* of Marxian theory was also important. His numerous reviews of Volume 1 of *Capital* (with their authorship disguised) introduced it to a wide audience, especially in Germany. Engels's own first major work, *The Condition of the Working Class in England* (1845), prepared the way for a favourable reception of the Marxian analysis of the evils of capitalism and the view that communism is the only solution to the social problems created by industrialization. One of his later works, *Anti-Dühring* (1878), which he read aloud to Marx from the manuscript before publication, contained an exposition of Marxian theory that exercised a strong influence upon socialists and intellectuals, motivating them to a study of Marx's writings. Three chapters of this book were published as a pamphlet, *Socialism, Utopian and Scientific* (1880), which was translated into many languages and has probably been read by more people than any of the other writings of Marx or Engels except the *Communist Manifesto*.

After Marx's death Engels's role became even more important. As Marx's literary executor he prepared the second and third volumes of *Capital* for publication; he undertook to defend Marx from all critics; he became the acknowledged authority on Marxian theory, to whom all disciples of Marx appealed on doubtful or disputed points of interpretation. The period between Marx's death and Engels's (1883–95) was exceptionally important in the development of European socialist thought and Engels played the leading role in the branch of it that drew inspiration from the Marxian theory of society.

I do not mean to suggest that Engels was *more* important than Marx in the origination or development of 'Marxian theory'. It is only necessary to point out that their separate contributions cannot be satisfactorily disentangled, and I will not attempt to do so in this chapter. For literary convenience I will often refer to 'Marx' when the ideas in question were those of Engels as well. The term 'Marxian theory' will similarly refer to Engels as well as Marx. (For a recent study of the role of Engels in the development of the basic ideas of Marxian theory, see Terrell Carver, *Marx and Engels: the Intellectual Relationship*, 1983.)

While it is not important, for the history of social science and social thought, to distinguish between Marx and Engels, it is essential that their ideas should not be fused with those of later writers who consider themselves to be their followers. Over the past century, interpretations and extensions of Marxian theory have been published in profusion, and many of them bear only a tangential relation to the ideas of Marx and Engels. I cannot here undertake to do more than make occasional reference to this literature. For terminological clarity I shall use the words 'Marxism' and 'Marxist' to refer to the literature published since Engels's death, and 'Marx' and 'Marxian' to refer to the views expressed by Marx and Engels themselves.

Some Marxists hold that one must be a committed Marxist in order to understand Marxian theory. This furnishes a convenient defence against criticism, but lacks epistemological merit, being not unlike the proposition that spirits appear only to those who believe in them. The reverse of this view is in fact more defensible: if one reads the Marxian literature with an unshakable determination to agree, it is certain that one will not understand it. Many bizarre distortions of Marxian ideas have resulted from such an approach. But it is equally true that if one reads the Marxian literature for the sole purpose of condemning it one will not understand it, either. In order to comprehend Marxian theory, or any other body of ideas for that matter, one must read *critically*. An appreciation of the weaknesses and flaws of any theory is essential to understanding it. But one cannot criticize what one considers to be nonsensical or diabolical; one can only call it names. In this chapter I shall try to present Marxian theory as a coherent set of ideas. It will be evident to the reader that I view much of Marxian theory as fatally flawed, but my object is critical explanation, not condemnation. Marxian theory and Marxism have exerted an enormous influence upon the history and the philosophy of social science, and on social thought generally. I do not disguise from the reader that I regard its influence as pernicious, but one must study Marxian theory not, as Marx would say, to 'settle accounts with it', but in order to comprehend an important part of the intellectual and political history of the modern world.

A. KARL MARX AND FRIEDRICH ENGELS

1. Karl Marx (1818–83)

Karl Marx was born in the small German city of Trier in the Mosel valley, not far from the borders of France and Belgium. His father, Heinrich, and his mother, Henrietta, were of Jewish ancestry, with many rabbis in both their family lineages. Heinrich Marx was a lawyer employed in the city administration of Trier. When the city came under Prussian rule after the defeat of Napoleon in 1815 his livelihood was threatened on account of the Prussian law which prohibited Jews from occupying public posts or practising the professions. He thereupon converted to Christianity. Marx's mother was reluctant to renounce Judaism and to break her family ties as her husband had, and did not become a Christian until both her parents were dead. Karl, the third of nine children, was baptized at the age of six and confirmed at sixteen but he did not have a religious upbringing, either Judaic or Christian, and there seems to have been only a brief period in his youth when he was attracted to religion as a personal philosophy or ontological outlook. An essay 'On the Jewish Question' written when he was twenty-five, and numerous scurrilous remarks about Jews in his later works and letters, have led some commentators to speculate that Marx's hatred of bourgeois society reflected the religious ambiguity of his childhood in the household of Heinrich and Henrietta Marx, but posthumous psychoanalysis of this sort is never more than marginally useful in the study of history. Whatever his attitude to Judaism and Christianity may have been, it did not differ, in his mature years, from his view of all religions. He regarded belief in God as illusory and all organized religions as repressive.

After schooling in Trier, where the curriculum emphasized classical languages, Marx entered the law school of the University of Bonn. He spent a great deal of his time drinking, duelling, and participating in student affairs and his father decided, despite the fact that he did well in his courses, that he should move to the University of Berlin. Marx found there a group of students who were intensely interested in the philosophy of G. W. F. Hegel (1770–1831) and the new literature of the German romantics, which soon became an absorbing intellectual interest of his own. He was especially influenced by Bruno Bauer, who developed an atheistic version of Hegelian philosophy in his lectures and writings. Marx decided to work towards a doctoral degree, with the aim of pursuing an academic career. Bauer moved to the University of Bonn in 1839 and hoped to arrange for Marx to join him in the philosophy department there. Marx obtained his doctorate in 1841 with a thesis on classical Greek philosophy, but shortly thereafter Bauer lost his post at Bonn and this ended any real chance Marx had of securing an academic appointment.

During the next seven years Marx was a journalist, writing for and editing magazines in Bonn, Cologne, Paris, and Brussels. Early in this period he became a committed socialist. The atheistic and socialistic stance of his writings, as well as his fierce criticisms of governmental policy, attracted the hostile attention of the authorities and he was summarily deported from France and Belgium. He started a new paper in Cologne in 1848 but was expelled again. Now married, with three children and a fourth on the way, he moved to England, where he lived for the rest of his life. Marx's friendship with Engels dates from his period as a journalist. They met briefly in 1842 and their close association began with correspondence concerning Engels's 'Outlines of a Critique of Political Economy', which was published in 1844 in the *Deutsch–Französische Jahrbücher* edited by Marx. They spent a good deal of time together during the next few years discussing philosophy and economics and participating in radical political activities. As already noted, they jointly wrote the *Communist Manifesto* in 1848. With the failure of the European revolutions of that year, which they had hoped were the beginning of a new social era, Marx and Engels both moved to England; Engels to Manchester, where a branch of his family's business was located, Marx to London, where the library resources of the British Museum provided him with the materials he needed for the research that occupied most of his time during the rest of his life.

A major source of Marx's income during the thirty-four years of his life in England was Friedrich Engels. Engels was convinced that Marx's scholarly work was of great importance to the socialist movement and the future of mankind. From the beginning of their association Engels supplied Marx with funds and sought in other ways to enable him to pursue his researches. After he had established himself as manager of the family firm's Manchester branch, Engels's income was quite high and, over the years, he gave Marx substantial sums. Marx had other sources of income as well – contributions by other admirers, inheritances, and earnings from his writings. From 1851 until 1862 he was a correspondent for the *New York Daily Tribune* and received a substantial income from his contributions (about a quarter of which were actually written by Engels). Between 1857 and 1860 he contributed sixty-seven articles to the *New American Encyclopedia* (fifty-one of which were actually written by Engels) at quite generous rates. Marx and his family lived in London at a level that can be described as 'comfortable middle-class'. They were constantly in financial difficulties, periodically approaching crisis proportions, but this was due to the fact that neither Marx nor his wife Jenny had much ability to manage their resources, not to any serious lack of them.

Engels's insistence on the importance of economics, and the great free-trade debate of the early 1840s which demonstrated the political signif-icance of economic theory, motivated Marx to study the literature of political economy. As early as 1846 he signed a contract with a publisher for a book on the subject, but he made little progress until he settled in London three years later. All Marx's work on economics was subject to numerous delays while he diverted his attention to other subjects. Not until 1859 did his first book on economics, *A Critique of Political Economy*, appear in print. In the meantime, in addition to his articles for the *New York Daily Tribune* and other papers (about 700 in all), he wrote extensively on philosophy, history, and politics. Marx did not regard these distractions from his economic research as unwelcome, since economics was not the subject that engaged his intellectual interest most strongly and, indeed, he found it rather tedious. As early as April 1851 he wrote to Engels that he hoped soon to 'be through with the whole economic shit'. This was, however, only the first time that he would give vent to similar views. The scope of his work on economics, however, kept expanding as his studies proceeded and, in fact, he never completed it. The *Critique of Political Economy* was only part of the first volume of what, by 1859, Marx planned to be a six-volume work. (The lengthy manuscripts that Marx had written by this time but did not include in the *Critique* were first published in 1939–41, and are now usually referred to as the *Grundrisse*, or 'foundations'.) In the summer of 1865 Marx wrote to Engels, who was constantly pressing him on the matter, that he was reluctant to publish any part of what was now to be called *Capital* until the whole was finished but, he said, it was almost done. Engels urged him to prepare the first volume for publication, since the other volumes would quickly follow, and Volume I of *Capital* was published in Germany in 1867. Following this, however, Marx did little further work on economics. He fended off Engels's urgings that the rest of the book be sent to the printer, and hid the fact that it was far from complete. Engels discovered this only after Marx's death in 1883 when he undertook to edit the manuscripts for publication. Volume II of *Capital* was published in 1885, but Volume III, on which depend some of the crucial points in Marxian economic theory (which have been intensely debated down to the present) was in very poor order and Engels was not able to construct a publishable text until 1894. Engels intended to publish Marx's lengthy studies of the history of economic theory as Volume IV of *Capital*, but he did not complete editing them before his death. The manuscripts were prepared for publication by Karl Kautsky in three volumes under the title of *Theories of Surplus Value* (1905–10).

Marx's writing style was mixed. His philosophical work was written in the obscure and convoluted style of Hegelian metaphysics. His economics employed the abstract analytical modelling of Ricardo. By contrast with both of these, Marx's popular writing was direct, lucid, graceful, and dramatic, and passages of this sort are to be found interspersed in the texts of his 'heavy' works such as *Capital*. This stylistic mixture was probably of some considerable significance in the development of Marxism as a modern intellectual genre. Union of the fervour and drama of romanticism with the power of scientific method and the insight of transcendental vision makes a potent compound. In forging such a union Marx had no equal in the history of social thought, before him or since.

2. Friedrich Engels (1820–95)

Friedrich Engels was born in the German town of Barmen (now Wuppertal), near the Dutch border. His family were wealthy industrialists engaged in textile manufacturing. Friedrich's parents were staunch Protestants, belonging to a strict Puritan congregation, and were intensely loyal to the Hohenzollern monarchy. Young Friedrich was brought up to accept without question the virtues of fealty to the God of Calvin and to the King of Prussia. But question them he did, and quite early. Before he was well into his twenties he had rejected not only Calvinism but all religions; and not only the Hohenzollern monarchy, but all monarchy and, indeed, all governments that exercised power by the privileged few over the mass of the people.

Engels attended the town school in Barmen and then the senior school in the nearby town of Elberfeld, but he left school before graduating. His parents apparently felt that working in the family business would modify his rebellious disposition. It did not, and relations between him and his family were always quite strained. There was no overt breach, however, and his father was content, despite the increasingly embarrassing views and political activities of his son, that he should be associated with the family business. Engels never enrolled at a university but, while he was doing his military service in Berlin in 1841, he attended some lectures at the university and associated with the students, who were avidly discussing philosophical questions. He became a Hegelian and a socialist. When his father proposed to send him to work in the firm of Ermen & Engels in Manchester, he welcomed the opportunity to get away from Barmen and to visit England, where, he was convinced, the social conditions produced by industrialism were speedily proceeding to a revolutionary climax. His first major writing, *The Condition of the Working Class in England* (1845), was based upon his first-hand observation of working-class conditions and showed his exceptional ability to write clear and powerful prose. During this period in Manchester he began to study the literature of classical economics and became convinced that a properly scientific economic analysis was a necessary element in the promotion of the socialist movement. His 'Outlines of a Critique of Political Economy', which led to his friendship with Marx, was written during this first period in Manchester.

Engels did not enjoy business administration, though he was good at it. In 1844 he returned to Germany and spent the next five years in revolutionary politics, during which his friendship with Marx was cemented. With the failure of the revolutions of 1848 Engels decided to return to work at Ermen & Engels in Manchester. He expected that the great revolution he and Marx had predicted in the *Communist Manifesto* was not far distant, but in the meantime it was necessary that Marx, whose scholarly ability he greatly admired, should construct the new scientific economics that would reveal the evils of capitalism and the inner contradictions that would lead to its downfall. The biographer of Engels, W. O. Henderson, says that:

> Engels worked in Manchester in an office which he detested not to oblige his father but to secure a regular income in order to help Marx financially. In his view it was imperative for the communist cause that Marx should devote himself entirely to the study of economics. (*Life of Friedrich Engels*, 1976, p. 201)

The great upheaval did not come, and Engels spent the rest of his life in England. He wrote a great deal himself, and was active in socialist politics, but he never altered his view that supporting Marx in his scholarly work was to be his most important contribution to the future of mankind. He was highly successful as a businessman and was able to send Marx regular stipends and to respond to the repeated financial crises of the Marx household. He did not marry, perhaps because he felt that he should not incur family responsibilities that might take priority over Marx's needs. He lived with a former employee, Mary Burns, for many years, but they had no children. In 1869 he was wealthy enough to retire, so he at last left the Manchester factory and moved to London, where he took a house close to Marx's and spent the rest of his life promoting Marxian theory and, after Marx's death, editing the unpublished volumes of *Capital*.

Engels's formal education ended without completing high school but he was extremely intelligent and had an interest in scholarly and scientific matters that went far beyond that of the typical political activist or, indeed, the typical university graduate. He had an unusual talent for languages. At the age of nineteen he offered to teach his sister Danish, Spanish, or Portuguese, and said that he could understand twenty-five languages, including Turkish and Japanese. He spent a great deal of time, especially in his fifties, studying natural science and mathematics. His mathematics remained mediocre but he succeeded in learning a great deal about the natural sciences and was familiar with contemporary developments in numerous areas of them. His knowledge of science was much greater than Marx's, and he frequently furnished Marx with information and advice on scientific matters. Military science and military history were of special interest to Engels, going well beyond the view he sometimes expressed that these studies would prove useful in the forthcoming revolution. He wrote extensively on military topics, his many articles appearing in papers, journals, and encyclopaedias in England, Germany, and the United States. He was 'one of the few civilians in the middle of the nineteenth century who became an acknowledged master of the theory of warfare and an authority on the technique of armed insurrection' (Henderson, p. 415). In 1845, chafing at his life in Manchester, Engels tried to obtain a post on the London *Daily News* as a writer on military topics but the editor decided that his work was too professional for the readers of the paper. After his retirement from Ermen & Engels in 1869 he spent a great deal of time on military journalism. His intimate friends called him 'the general'. Marx's and Engels's political and economic writings continually use military metaphors in the description and analysis of social phenomena, as does the modern Marxist literature. This is probably due mainly to the importance of the notion of class struggle in Marxian theory, but it may also owe something to Engels's interest in military science and military history.

As noted in the introduction to this chapter, Engels cannot be regarded as a figure of minor, or even secondary, significance in the development of Marxian theory. Engels without Marx may have achieved only a small place in the history of social thought, but Marx without Engels might well have achieved no more. The importance of Engels was not merely a matter of financial support for Marx, but of substantive significance in determining the direction and content of Marxian theory. When he was in Germany supervising the publication of Volume I of *Capital*, Marx wrote to Engels saying that 'it has lain heavily upon my conscience that your wonderful powers should have gone to rust in the world of business mainly on my account' (Henderson, p. 400). But it may be doubted that Engels's powers went to rust in Manchester; their undiminished strength and keenness were evident in his own writings such as *Anti-Dühring*, and in the pages of Marx's *Capital* itself.

3. The problem of interpretation

Some commentators on the writings of Marx and Engels find them so filled with ambiguity that no coherent interpretation is possible – or any interpretation is possible. Others contend that there is a tightly organized basic model in their writings which, when explicated and understood, will show that all the various parts of their thinking, even those that seem to contradict one another, are linked together in coherent unity. The discussion of Marxian theory in this chapter will lean towards the latter view, but not to the extent of attempting to resolve all ambiguities, which can only be done by shaving and bending Marx and Engels to fit a mould of one's own making. In his preface to Volume III of *Capital*, Engels urged that one should study the works of an author 'above all without reading anything into them that they do not contain'. This is a difficult precept to follow, but it is good advice none the less. Before we begin to examine the content of Marxian theory, however, it is worth taking a few moments to consider why the problem of interpretation is encountered to an especially great degree in the writings of Marx and Engels.

First we must note the extraordinary volume and range of the Marxian works. The collected German edition of Marx's writings alone, which is not entirely complete, runs to thirty-nine volumes. A Marx–Engels bibliography published in 1956 (Maxmilien Rubel, *Bibliographie des oeuvres de Karl Marx, avec en appendice un répertoire des oeuvres de Friedrich Engels*) lists 901 items. These cover subjects that would today be classified as philosophy, history, political science, economics, sociology, psychology, anthropology, natural science, military science, and literature. Various items now considered of great importance were not accessible until many of the unpublished works were printed in the 1930s. It is not surprising that different interpretations of Marxian theory can be reached by emphasizing different writings. In particular, the publication of Marx's *Paris Manuscripts*, written in 1844, has led to a reinterpretation of Marxian theory that is important in assessing its place in the history and philosophy of social science. At the time these manuscripts were written Marx had not read much of the literature of classical political economy. He was, clearly, not very familiar with the work of David Ricardo, whom he later recognized as the leading classical theorist. The greater part of the manuscripts deals with philosophical matters and social psychology, especially the issue of 'alienation'. Some modern interpreters of Marxian theory place their main emphasis upon the *Paris Manuscripts*, heavily discounting the importance of economic theory, and arguing that there is a great deal of difference between the 'young Marx' who was a 'humanist' and the 'older Marx' who constructed nomological economic models like those of Ricardo. The reader will see that I do not follow that line of interpretation in this chapter. There is no doubt that many of the basic components of Marxian theory, such as its view of historical development and its conception of the essential nature of capitalism, are present in the early writings of Marx and Engels, but Marxian economics is a central pillar which bears the weight of all the rest of Marxian theory. Marxian economics may be incomplete without Marxian sociology and the Marxian theory of history, but the latter two without the first would be, as the saying goes, like a production of *Hamlet* edited to eliminate the role of the Prince.

Even if one regards economics as central to Marxian theory, interpretive differences do not disappear. Some scholars regard the unpublished manuscripts known as the *Grundrisse* as equal in importance to *Capital*, or even more. Clearly, Marx did not so regard them, since he did not publish them. But, as we have noted, he did not complete all of *Capital* either, and there are important differences between its volumes. Volume I, for example, has much in it that reflects Marx's interest in German idealist philosophy, while Volumes II and III are severely disciplined to the construction of economic models. How much of this was due to Engels's editing of Marx's manuscripts is an issue not yet examined fully by scholars.

There are also semantic problems. The English translator of Marx's *Paris Manuscripts,* for example, notes that the German word *Wesen* can have various different meanings and that Marx 'frequently plays on' two or more of these, even in a single sentence. The English term 'alienation' is the customary rendering of two German words of different meaning, *Entfremdung* and *Entaüsserung*, which Marx sometimes used even in the same sentence. In addition, the crucial economic terms 'value', 'price', 'profit', 'subsistence', 'labour', and so forth are subject to various interpretations. A great deal of the modern literature on Marx consists of semantic controversy which sometimes degenerates into the proposition that the essence of capitalism is revealed in the meanings of certain words.

Finally, difficulties are presented by the fact that many of Marx's and Engels's writings on theoretical matters are not presentations of their own theories but critiques of the theories of others. For example, the Marxian view of the nature of communism is not described in any systematic fashion in their writings but can only be (vaguely) surmised from scattered comments on views expressed by other socialists such as Proudhon, Dühring, or Lassalle. It is easier to ascertain Marx's and Engels's views of others than to determine their own, but the former is itself not easy, since their critical writings frequently degenerate into invective and, though much of it is brilliant as literature, the reader finds himself wishing for more use of simple declarative sentences. Almost all the work of Marx and Engels was polemical, and much of it was composed in connection with the fierce disputes that punctuated the revolutionary politics of the time, making it difficult to separate tactics from strategy, and both of these from social science and philosophy, in the original Marxian literature.

At any rate, multiform interpretations of Marxian theory abound in the flood of writing that has been produced since the death of Engels. Before Engels's death, and even before Marx's, schools of Marxists were developing theories that Marx and Engels themselves were anxious to disown. Many of the phrases that are now commonly presented as capturing the essence of Marxian theory were never used by Marx and Engels, and many of the arguments of modern Marxists are conspicuously non-Marxian on any reasonable reading of the original texts. Writing to Marx's daughter Laura in 1890, Engels complained:

For the past 2–3 years a crowd of students, literary men and other young declassed bourgeois has rushed into the Party, arriving just in time to occupy most of the editorial positions on the new journals ... and, as usual, they regard the bourgeois universities as a socialist staff college which gives them the right to enter the ranks of the Party with an officer's if not a general's brevet. All these gentlemen go in for Marxism, but of the kind you were familiar with in France ten years ago, and of which Marx said: 'All I know is that I am no Marxist!' And of these gentlemen he would probably have said what Heine said of his imitators: 'I sowed dragons, and reaped fleas.' (W. O. Henderson, *The Life of Friedrich Engels*, 1976, p. 645)

It is impossible to hope that one can present an exposition of Marxian theory that would be generally regarded as 'authentic', but I will try in this chapter to discuss its main elements without, as Engels advised, relying more on my own inventiveness than the original texts.

B. HISTORY

In introducing the subject of French positivism in Chapter 12, we noted that Saint-Simon and Comte lived in a Europe that was experiencing a rapid transformation in its economic, social, and political life. By Marx's time (he was born fifty-eight years after Saint-Simon), this transformation was much more advanced, especially in England. The handicraft system of production and small-scale industry had given way to the large factory, employing hundreds of workers within the walls of a single enterprise. Agriculture had also been greatly affected by developments that created economies of scale, and thousands of displaced farmers and farm labourers flocked to the new factory towns to become part of the largest class in society, the industrial proletariat. Two years before the *Communist Manifesto* was published, England repealed the corn laws and embarked on a policy of free trade. In 1851 the Great Exhibition was held in London, evidencing and celebrating the arrival of the industrial age and the shifting of political power from the landed to the middle class. The Second Reform Bill, which began the extension of the franchise to the 'lower orders', was passed the same year that Volume I of *Capital* appeared.

Intellectual developments were equally revolutionary. The admiration for science was widened and deepened by the new technological marvels of the age as well as by continued discoveries in pure science. Charles Darwin's *Origin of Species*, which undermined the last bastion of religious authority in the understanding of nature, was published in 1859, the same year as Marx's *Critique of Political Economy*. The secular social sciences, especially economics, were being accepted as belonging among the respected intellectual disciplines. Academic philosophy took a different road, especially in Germany, and, linking itself more to trends in the arts than in the sciences, reasserted the primacy of metaphysics over epistemology.

Some historians of Marxian theory view it as the set of ideas that links two great events in the political history of Europe, the French Revolution of 1789 and the Russian Revolution of 1917. As part of modern intellectual history it is also a link between or, perhaps more correctly, a synthesis of English classical economics, French positivist sociology, German metaphysical philosophy, and the utopianist political literature that flooded from the presses of Europe after the destruction of the *ancien régime* in France. Marx undertook the construction of a Grand Sociology, a comprehensive and unified model of human sociality in all its aspects. Reflecting the heightened historical consciousness of his time, he constructed his social science within a general theory of historical development. Most of the Marxian social science writings deal with the most recent stage of this evolutionary progression, the stage to which Marx gave the name 'capitalism', but to understand these writings we must first examine the Marxian theory of history and its conception of the essential characteristics that distinguish capitalism as an historical stage.

1. The theory of history

History, for Marx, was not merely a temporal sequence of events that the conscientious historian can describe, but events which may be *explained*, in the way that the phenomena studied by natural science may be explained – that is, by the discovery of the laws that govern them. The study of history can be a scientific enterprise, and the historian can take his place among scientists if he directs his attention to the underlying forces that control the evolution of human societies. Every specific society behaves in accordance with its own 'laws of motion', but these reflect the operation of more general laws that govern all human history. These specific and general laws, if correctly grasped, enable the historian, like the natural scientist in his own field, to predict the future course of social development. Marx saw no conflict between Saint-Simon's view that all history proceeds according to a single plan and Herder's emphasis upon the distinctiveness of different societies. Capitalism evolves according to 'the laws of motion of capitalism', just as feudalism followed its own laws, but there are universal elements in all historical development, which must be discovered before the social scientist can understand any specific society or type of social organization.

The idea that the historical evolution of human society conforms to a general law had been expressed by Auguste Comte in his celebrated 'law of the three stages' and, in the mid-nineteenth century, it was widely held by those who felt that the investigation of social phenomena could be made truly scientific. John Stuart Mill, for example, in explaining his 'inverse deductive method' (*System of Logic* VI, X), observed that the factors that act as the immediate causes of social phenomena operate within the conditions of a given 'state of society'. The analysis is incomplete unless this state is also explained in terms of the operation of governing laws.

The proximate cause [says Mill] of every state of society is the state of society immediately preceding it. The fundamental problem, therefore, of the social sciences, is to find the laws according to which any state of society produces the state which succeeds it and takes its place.

Marx and Engels agreed that this is the 'fundamental problem' and addressed themselves to the task of discovering the laws of history, which, in their view, required the adoption of a particular philosophical outlook, a 'materialist conception of history'.

Like most young German intellectuals of the mid-nineteenth century, Marx and Engels were greatly intrigued by the philosophy of G. W. F. Hegel. Hegel's basic philosophical view was that history is the progressive development of what he called *Geist*, or 'spirit', to give it the closest rendering that is possible in English. Marx and Engels accepted the Hegelian view that there is a coherent and systematic scheme in historical evolution, but they rejected his view that it is essentially spiritual in nature. They also rejected Comte's view that social evolution is fundamentally the progressive development of man's mental outlook, from the 'theological stage', through the 'metaphysical stage', to its final maturation in the 'positive stage', and Mill's notion, derived from Comte, that the dominant factor in social evolution is man's knowledge and beliefs. In the materialist conception of history, neither God's will nor man's ideas are fundamental. Society evolves through stages, but the factors that are the basic constituents of each stage, and those which result in a transformation from one stage to another, are the 'material' elements of social life which, in Marx's and Engels's view, are the *economic* characteristics of production and its concomitant social organization. The idea that the distribution of property ownership is the basic determinant of political organization was clearly expressed by James Harrington in the seventeenth century. The 'stages' conception of historical development was anticipated by Adam Smith, Saint-Simon, and numerous other late eighteenth-century and early nineteenth-century thinkers. But it was in Marxian theory that these ideas reached their full development as a philosophical outlook and became the foundation of a grand edifice of social science.

Despite the importance of the materialistic conception of history in Marxian theory, no systematic exposition of it is to be found in the writings of Marx or Engels. Among the fragmentary expressions of it, the most succinct are in Marx's preface to his *Critique of Political Economy* and in Engels's *Anti-Dühring*:

In the social production which men carry on they enter into definite relations that are indispensable and independent of their will; these relations of production correspond to a definite stage of development of their material powers of production. The sum total of these relations of production constitutes the economic structure of society – the real foundation, on which rise legal and political superstructures and to which correspond definite forms of social consciousness. The mode of production in material life determines the general character of the social, political and spiritual processes of life. It is not the consciousness of men that determines their existence but, on the contrary, their social existence determines their consciousness. At a certain stage of their development, the material forces of production in society come in conflict with the existing relations of production, or – what is but a legal expression for the same thing – with the property relations within which they had been at work before. From forms of development of the forces of production these relations turn into their fetters. Then comes the period of social revolution. With the change of the economic foundation the entire immense superstructure is more or less rapidly transformed. (Karl Marx, *A Contribution to the Critique of Political Economy*, preface)

The materialist conception of history starts from the principle that production, and with production the exchange of its products, is the basis of every social order; that in every society which has appeared in history the distribution of the products, and with it the division of society into classes or estates, is determined by what is produced and how it is produced, and how the product is exchanged. According to this conception, the ultimate cause of all social changes and political revolutions are to be sought, not in the minds of men, in their increasing insight into eternal truth and justice, but in changes in the mode of production and exchange; they are to be sought not in the *philosophy* but in the *economics* of the epoch concerned. (Friedrich Engels, *Herr Eugen Dühring's Revolution in Science*, III, II)

In his criticism of Dühring, Engels asserted that it is a mistake to interpret history, as most historians had done, as a struggle for political power and the exercise of physical force. These are merely means to a more fundamental end, the desire to acquire economic advantage, and to preserve it.

Since economic factors are fundamental in historical evolution, it follows that the central social science is economics. The modern orthodox economist is unlikely to demur, but an important difference between the economic theory of the modern college curriculum and Marxian theory should be noted at this point. Orthodox economics analyses both consumption and production, and the economy is viewed through the perspective of a system of markets in which 'demand' factors and 'supply' factors interact. In a certain sense more emphasis is placed on demand, since, in microeconomics, the use of labour and other production factors is construed as responding to consumer demand, and, in Keynesian macroeconomics, aggregate demand plays the central role in determining the total volume of production. Marx's economic analysis, by contrast, continued, and increased, the emphasis of Ricardian theory on the supply side of the market, and extended it beyond economics, to a general analysis of society and history. Whether we are considering Marxian economics, sociology, or philosophy, or the Marxian view of capitalism, or its preview of the future stage of communism, the main focus of attention is on man's work activities, the operation of the system of production, and the relations between different classes in that system.

Marx and Engels distinguished four stages in the historical development of human societies, each characterized by different technologies of production and different class relationships, the latter reflecting the mode of use of the factors of production and the form of ownership of them. The first stage, Primitive Communism, was like Adam Smith's 'early and rude state' in which hunters and gatherers made use of communal natural resources with tools so simple that they were not essentially different from a person's clothing or household goods. In short, there was no significant exclusionary private property in the 'means of production' and, therefore, no class structure. Marx described this stage as 'communism' because it was, in his view, a *classless society*, a definitional criterion he consistently adhered to. With the second stage, Slavery, there began the long odyssey of man's social development, characterized on the positive side by an increase in the ability to produce, and on the negative side by the emergence of class differentiation, private property in the means of production (including labour in this stage), and the exploitation of one class by another. In the third stage, Feudalism, social and economic organization was more complex, reflecting the development of more advanced production technologies, but class and property relationships remained essentially the same. So too in the fourth or current stage, Capitalism: the propertyless labourer is no longer a slave or a serf, he sells his labour power in a free market, but he is exploited none the less, and this exploitation cannot end until yet another stage dawns, Advanced Communism, in which there is no private property in the means of production and, therefore, no class differentiation. In the *Communist Manifesto* Marx and Engels wrote:

> The history of all past society has consisted in the development of class antagonisms, antagonisms that assumed different forms at different epochs. But whatever form they may have taken, one fact is common to all past ages, viz., the exploitation of one part of society by the other. (Section II)

Capitalism is a system of class exploitation no less than slavery or feudalism. One of the main objectives of Marx's economic analysis is to show that this has not been altered by the development of free markets, and to combat the view of orthodox economists that exploitation is due to monopolistic privileges and the restriction of competition. Under capitalism exploitation is less obvious than under slavery or feudalism but it still exists, and in certain respects is more intense.

The Marxian historical stages, one should note, are not classificatory categories that the historian has constructed for heuristic purposes. Other early (and later) stage theorists may have taken such an epistemological view, but Marxian theory construes the stages metaphysically, that is, they are regarded as essential properties of history itself. The study of history can be scientific only if it focuses upon the stages of social evolution, because history *is* the evolution of society through stages. The laws of history are not invented by the historian, they are *discovered* by him. As we shall see, Marx and Engels modified this view somewhat in their later work, putting forward a teleological view of history which emphasized the inevitability of communism more than the necessity of the various stages leading to it.

Marxian theory does not view each historical stage as static. Changes are taking place in the society's technology of production. The transformation from one stage to another occurs when these changes have accumulated to the point where the prevailing system of property ownership has become obsolete. Exogenous and 'superstructural' factors such as geographic discoveries, epidemic diseases, and dynastic conflicts have been mistakenly construed by historians as the operative factors in historical evolution. In Marxian theory the important factors are endogenous and concern the 'base' of the social structure: the forces working *within* the social system that alter its mode of production. Climactic events such as wars, and revolutions, may act, to use Marx's graphic expression, as the 'midwife' of social transformation, but the new society has already developed within the 'womb' of the old. The birth of a child is a discrete event, but it is only the end-product of a gradual development, and it does not occur until the process is complete.

Certain ambiguities of Marxian theory on this point have given rise to a large literature on its view of the nature of social transformation and the role of revolution, and, especially since the Russian Revolution, on the question whether the process can be accelerated to the point where most or even all of an historical stage is skipped. Marx and Engels, in their roles as active revolutionaries, found themselves in an ambivalent position, which has troubled many Marxists since. If one argues that history proceeds according to laws that are independent of man's autonomous actions, what is the point of revolutionary activity? The doctrine that man is truly free when acting in accordance with transcendent 'necessity' is difficult to accept. It may be inspiring to believe that 'history' is on one's side, but discouraging to be told that one's individual efforts and sacrifices count for nothing in the larger scheme of things. If Marxist revolutionaries can influence events, why cannot others? And, if they can, does this not mean that the laws of history can be bent, or even broken? This threatens their status as metaphysical propositions. Marxism is, of course, not the only doctrine that suffers from the dilemma of determinism. All religions, in one way or another, force their adherents to dodge between the horns of fatalism and freedom. V. I. Lenin escaped this dilemma by simply calling the determinist features of Marxian theory 'economism' and declaring it heretical (*What is to be Done? Burning Questions of our Movement*, 1902), but it continues to be a serious problem in the philosophical appraisal of the Marxian theory of history.

The central problem in the materialist conception of history is that it raises the issue of the role of non-'material' elements, such as ideas, and political and social institutions, in the historical process. The Marxian theory of history, like a great deal else in Marxian theory generally, was originally developed as a critique of other views – in this case as a critique of Hegel's idealistic conception of history as the progressive realization of *Geist*. In confronting Hegel, Marx and Engels asserted the opposite and, as they so often did, expressed themselves in rather extreme and dogmatic fashion. The passage quoted above from Marx's preface to his *Critique of Political Economy* was intended to summarize his reactions to Hegel's idealism. The quotation from Engels's *Anti-Dühring* must, similarly, be read in the light of Engels's intention to combat Dühring's emphasis upon the historical importance of political factors.

Some interpreters of the Marxian theory of history construe it as a strictly deterministic theory which contends that economic or, indeed, technological factors are all-important, ideas and political phenomena being strictly derivative from them. Others interpret the theory as only arguing that economics and technology are *more* important than ideas and politics or that the former sets limits on the scope of the influence of the latter. Still others have convinced themselves that in Marxian theory history is not law-governed at all but may be created by man's autonomous actions virtually without constraint. It is not possible to settle this question simply by reference to the writings of Marx and Engels, since all these interpretations can find support there. Engels, who had originally coined the term 'the materialist conception of history' in 1859, acknowledged later that he and Marx had not been sufficiently clear in delineating its meaning and were therefore partly to blame for the excessive emphasis on economic factors by some of the younger Marxists. In a letter written in 1890 to Joseph Bloch he said:

> According to the materialist conception of history, the *ultimately* determining element in history is the production and reproduction of real life. More than this neither Marx nor I have ever asserted. Hence if somebody twists this into saying that the economic element is the *only* determining one, he transforms that proposition into a meaningless, abstract, senseless phrase . . . .
>
> We make our history ourselves, but . . . under very definite assumptions and conditions. Among these the economic ones are ultimately decisive. But the political ones, etc., and indeed even the traditions which haunt human minds also play a part, although not the decisive one. (R. C. Tucker, *The Marx–Engels Reader*, 1972, pp. 640–1)

This letter, which is frequently quoted in the modern literature on Marxian theory, does not clarify the issue much. It seems to say both yes and no to the question whether the course of history can be significantly affected by autonomous human choice and action. To say that certain factors are 'ultimately' determinative can be interpreted as meaning that they are the only factors of importance, or that they are not, depending on whether one is focusing on the long run or the short.

The character of the Marxian theory of history – whether it is deterministic and, if so, what the determining factors are – has been a persistent subject of debate within Marxist circles as well as by non-Marxist scholars. With the Russian Revolution the Soviet leaders took upon themselves the role of acting as a Papal Curia in matters of Marxist doctrine. Lenin abandoned his criticism of 'economism', rejected Karl Kautsky's insistence on the importance of non-economic factors in history, and embraced the economic determinist views of Nikolai Bukharin, who was installed as the authoritative spokesman on matters of doctrinal interpretation. Bukharin was executed during the Stalin purges of the 1930s, but Stalin himself held fast to the view that history is governed by unbreakable laws which operate independently of the will of man (see his *Problems of Socialism in the U.S.S.R.*). Leon Trotsky, who eluded Stalin's reach for a time, came to the conclusion that the laws could be modified so much as even to make the course of history reverse itself, with retrogression to barbarism being as possible as Marx's prediction of unilinear progress to communism.

Part of the difficulty with the Marxian theory of history is that it is presented as a scientific theory which explains historical events in terms of their *antecedent* causes, and yet contains a substantial component of Aristotelian teleology, which explains events in terms of the *future* state which is the culmination of the line of development. What Aristotle called a 'final cause' is subsequent to the events it controls. In Aristotle's view, the embryological development of an organism, for example, represents the operation of the material factors as immediate causes but the whole process is governed by its end or purpose, the ultimate emergence of a viable organism. In their anxiety to construe history as meaningful Marx and Engels resorted to the Aristotelian view, which Hegel had firmly embraced in his own theory of history, that the *meaning* of historical events, and therefore the scientific explanation of them, must be modelled in terms of the end-state to which they lead. Marx and Engels rejected Hegel's notion that this end-state was the full realization of *Geist*, replacing it with their conception of communism. 'Communism,' says Marx in the *Paris Manuscripts*, 'is the riddle of history solved, and it knows itself to be this solution.' Under the pressure of events, and the findings of historians, Marx modified his theory of historical stages and the role of economic factors but he continued to be confident that, whatever the immediate causes and the particular patterns of historical events might be, the ultimate end of the process is the realization of man's full potential in a classless society. Most of his scientific work was devoted to the analysis of capitalism. This will be the focus of our examination of Marxian sociology and economics in sections C and D. As a preliminary to it we will note his view of the characteristics which identify capitalism as a distinct type of social organization.

2. Capitalism as an historical stage

'Modern capitalist production,' says Engels in his *Anti-Dühring*, 'is hardly three hundred years old and has only become predominant since the introduction of large-scale industry, that is, only in the last hundred years.' Considering as they did that the downfall of capitalism was imminent, Marx and Engels regarded it as a stage in historical development that would prove to be much shorter than the previous stages. The reason for this is that the endogenous forces of change in the capitalist system work with extraordinary power and, as a consequence, the historical mission of capitalism is completed with great rapidity. This mission (to use a term no more grandiloquent than Marx and Engels were accustomed to employ) is to accomplish such a great increase in productive powers that the stage of communism inherits an economy capable of providing material plenty for all and can devote itself to developing and fulfilling man's higher aspirations. The first pages of the *Communist Manifesto* are devoted to describing the changes that have occurred since the beginning of the capitalist era and include a striking statement concerning the great increase in productive power that has been brought about:

> The bourgeoisie, during its rule of scarce one hundred years, has created more massive and more colossal productive forces than have all preceding generations together. Subjection of nature's forces to man, machinery, application of chemistry to industry and agriculture, steam-navigation, railways, electric telegraphs, clearing of whole continents for cultivation, canalisation of rivers, whole populations conjured out of the ground – what earlier century had even a presentiment that such productive forces slumbered in the lap of social labour?

Marx and Engels speak here of the 'bourgeoisie', a term that was later supplanted by the stage designation, 'capitalism'. This, and Marx's decision to call his main work *Capital*, have led to some confusion which we should clear up at this point. In orthodox economics the term 'capital' refers to the artefactual means of production such as factories, roads, machines, etc., as distinguished from 'labour' and 'natural resources' as factors of production. In Marxian terminology, capitalism is not uniquely characterized by the use of such 'capital' in the production process. Previous stages used capital, and the stage of communism will be one in which there is such an abundance of capital that there is little need for any further accumulation of such artefacts. The view of some modern Marxists that communism will be a less technological and less industrial society, with people content to receive the smaller material benefits of a simpler economy, is not what Marx and Engels had in mind.

There is also some confusion over the identification of 'capitalism' with an economy that employs the market mechanism as its primary system of organization. This is due in part to Engels's view of market processes as inherently chaotic and his assertion that under communism the co-ordination of economic activities would be accomplished by a system of centralized planning and administration. Despite this, Marxian theory is unclear on the economic organization of communism, but whether it is viewed as a planned economy or not, capitalism is not uniquely identified by the market system of economic organization. Such a system is necessary because capitalism is an economy in which the means of production are privately owned. But it would also be necessary if all producing units were independent co-operatives, or were owned by their workers, or even if they were all owned by the state (if they were left free to make their own production decisions). In Marxian theory the feature of capitalism that constitutes its essential characteristic is that productive property is privately owned by a distinct class, the 'bourgeoisie' or 'capitalists', while another class, the 'workers', possess no appreciable means of production that they can call their own. Capitalists, as owners of the means of production, are the buyers of 'labour power', the workers live by selling it. Capitalism therefore, like slavery and feudalism before it, is a class society. It differs from them in that the labourer cannot be owned as property and he is no longer bound by the rules of serfdom. He is free to sell his labour power to whomever he wishes, but the only buyers are those who own the complementary factors of production.

In Chapters 5 and 9 we saw that the Physiocratic model employed a class structure (agriculturalists, artisans, landowners) that was defined in terms of economic roles rather than in traditional political and religious ones, and that the Ricardian model worked with similarly defined class categories (labourers, capitalists, landlords). Marxian theory continued this economic definition of class, but reduced the number of classes to two: capitalists and labourers, those who own means of production and those who do not. Marx and Engels were acute in perceiving that one of the great permanent changes taking place in their time was the decline in the social, political, and economic importance of land ownership. A strong theme in Marx's *Paris Manuscripts* is that the distinction between land and other forms of private property, and between the landlord and capitalist classes, is fast disappearing. Landlords and capitalists now form a single class, the owners of the means of production. Whether these means consist of land or man-made instruments is no longer important. (Thirty years later, in his 'Critique of the Gotha Programme', Marx criticized the Lassalleans for failing to recognize landowners as a distinct class, but his own economic analysis in *Capital* dissolves them into the capitalist class.) The working class, which under feudalism had certain rights to the use of land and other productive factors, has been completely separated from them. The legal owners are no longer bound by any traditional rules, and the workers have no rights other than the right to sell their labour power as a commercial transaction. One would not say that the slave-worker had 'rights', but under slavery, like feudalism, there was a union of labour with other productive factors embedded in the institutional structure of society. Under capitalism all such connection has been sundered. The freedom of the worker to sell his labour power is simply a corollary of the fact that he has been alienated from the means of production.

Under capitalism, then, two categorically distinct classes confront one another, locked in an unresolvable conflict which becomes ever more severe as economic development proceeds. The main object of Marx's economic analysis is to demonstrate that a capitalistic economy is a system that perpetuates the exploitation of labour – more subtly than under slavery and feudalism but, if anything, with increased intensity. In Engels's 'Outlines' and Marx's *Paris Manuscripts* the exploitive nature of capitalism is strongly asserted, but no explanation is offered as to how this comes about in a competitive economy with free labour. As we shall see, the explanation is contained in Marx's later development of the theory of 'surplus value', which Engels regarded as his friend's principal discovery in economics.

The reason why exploitation is less obvious under capitalism than under slavery or feudalism, according to Marxian theory, is that the market mechanism masks the significance of the ownership of the means of production. Commodities are produced for sale rather than for direct use and the prices at which they are exchanged in the market appear as relations between the commodities, disguising the fact that they reflect the more fundamental relations between the social classes. The task of economic analysis is to penetrate beneath the surface phenomena of market prices to reveal the conflict between workers and capitalists, which is the fundamental characteristic of the system. The sociological character of capitalism is not less important than its economics: it is a type of society in which all relations between human beings have been reduced to commercial relations, estranging men from one another, and from society in general. Labour power itself has become a commodity, sold for a price in the market, and other things 'such as conscience, honour, etc.', though not commodities in themselves, 'are capable of being offered for sale by their holders, and of thus acquiring, through their price, the form of commodities' (Marx, *Capital*, Book I, p. 102). In the *Communist Manifesto* capitalism is described as a system in which all the relations of human beings have been reduced to the 'cash nexus' of the market place, a phrase that Thomas Carlyle had coined to express his abhorrence of the modern age. Engels praised Carlyle's *Past and Present* (1843) in his *Condition of the Working Class in England* (1845) and wrote a favourable review of it for a German periodical. Long before Marx had developed his economic theory of value and exploitation, he and Engels were convinced that the sociological and psychological characteristics of the capitalist system of 'commodity production' render it inimical to the proper development of man as a social being. One can see the reasons for the debate, which continues down to the present, over whether the fundamental core of the Marxian theory of capitalism is its sociology or its economics.

According to the Marxian theory of history, all past stages have proved to be impermanent because of endogenous developments that created 'contradictions' between the 'forces of production' and the 'relations of production'. Capitalism will come to an end for the same reason. The concepts enclosed above by quotation marks were not made entirely clear by Marx and Engels. But, speaking generally, it seems that by 'forces of production' are meant the technical components of the production system: its supply of factors of production, including man-made instruments, its technological capacity, and the productivity of its labour force. The 'relations of production' refer to the organizational structure of the economy: its system of property ownership, the ways in which productive labour is used, the methods by which production decisions are made, and the mechanism that distributes the output of the production process among the members of society. Greater difficulties are encountered in trying to comprehend what Marx and Engels meant by 'contradictions'. Some interpreters view this as the Marxian version of Hegel's conception of history as 'dialectical', which does not make it any easier to understand. More concretely, it is the thesis that every system of economic organization will, over time, become progressively incapable of accommodating to the technical developments in production that are taking place and thus act as a 'fetter' which restricts their further development. In capitalism specifically, the factory system is a method of 'socialized production', while the ownership of the means of production is still private. This contradiction develops naturally, owing to forces working within the dynamics of capitalism – which thus creates its own fetters. In the past, such contradictions have been resolved through the emergence of a new stage in the historical process, and a similar development will take place as capitalism matures.

Note : Marxian historical theory and Darwinian evolutionism

Charles Darwin's *The Origin of Species* was published in 1859. It fell like a bombshell upon the pious Victorian world and has since exerted an influence upon the modern intellect second only to the doctrine of mechanism enunciated by the philosophers and scientists of the seventeenth century. Historians of the nineteenth century have discerned a variety of connections between the Darwinian theory of evolution, the capitalistic economic system, classical economics, Western political theory and social philosophy, and the Marxian theory of history. Some of these connections will be explored more fully below in Chapter 16, but it is useful at this point to note the impact that the *Origin* had upon Marx and Engels.

Marx and Engels read the *Origin* soon after its publication and were very enthusiastic about it. Writing to Ferdinand Lassalle in January 1860, Marx said that 'Darwin's book is very important and serves me as a basis in natural science for the class struggle in history'. Marx and Engels regarded the Darwinian theory as verification of their general conception of history and especially their view of the competitive market economy of the capitalist stage. Engels remarked in his 'Dialectics of Nature' (written in 1875–6) that Darwin had unconsciously written a 'bitter satire' which showed that the struggle for existence in the animal world had not been essentially modified in human society, and would not be until the market system was replaced by one in which 'production and distribution are carried on in a planned way'.

Marx and Engels, however, were not totally favourable towards Darwin's theory. In a letter written in 1875 to Peter Lavrov, a Russian sociologist and a leader of the populist Narodnik movement, Engels expressed objections to the theory of natural selection as excessively Hobbesian, failing to give proper weight to co-operative features that were evident even in the non-human organic world. Marx and Engels were particularly hostile to Darwin's use of the Malthusian theory of population, which they detested so much that they were averse to admitting its relevance anywhere.

Despite these *caveats,* Marx and Engels continued to regard Darwin's *Origin* with great favour. Engels, who was more interested in, and knew more, natural science than Marx, was especially firm in his conviction, and on at least one occasion persuaded Marx against supporting an alternative theory of evolution (by one Pierre Tremaux). At the graveside of Marx in 1883 Engels declared that 'Just as Darwin discovered the law of development of organic nature, so Marx discovered the law of development of human history', and in his preface to the English edition of the *Communist Manifesto* in 1888 he predicted that the Marxian theory of class struggle 'is destined to do for history what Darwin's theory has done for biology'.

These are the bare facts – the view of Darwinism explicitly expressed by Marx and Engels. Assessment of the affect of the *Origin* on Marxian theory is more difficult. One modern historian, E. M. Ureña ('Marx and Darwin', *History of Political Economy*, winter 1977), comes to the conclusion that there is little similarity between Marxian and Darwinian theory and suggests that the parallelism stated by Marx and Engels was mere puffery, aimed at vicariously strengthening Marxian theory's claim to scientific credentials and to draw attention to it. Lewis S. Feuer ('Marx and Engels as Sociobiologists', *Survey*, autumn 1977), however, argues that Darwin's *Origin* induced Marx and Engels to abandon the Hegelian concept of dialectic, in favour of an evolutionary view of history which stressed the gradual and cumulative nature of social change.

Since neither Marx nor Engels made more than brief occasional remarks directly on the question, and the influence of evolutionary biology is not specifically evident in their sociological and economic analysis, it is impossible to arrive at any firm conclusion on the issue. By one of those ironies of which intellectual history is full, it seems that the direction of influence may have been mainly the other way round. Some modern biologists, most notably Stephen Jay Gould (who regards himself as a Marxist), have attempted to revise the accepted scenario of organic evolution through the concept of 'punctuated equilibrium' (see his 'Evolution as Fact and as Theory', *Hen's Teeth and Horse's Toes*, 1983). The thesis is that species tend to be stable over a long time and are then transformed quite rapidly (in terms of geological time, that is) to a new equilibrium that embodies the incremental changes that have been accumulating in the old one. The similarity between this and Marx's theory of social contradictions and historical transformation is evident.

C. SOCIOLOGY AND SOCIAL PSYCHOLOGY

One of the most important features of Marxian theory is its emphasis on the social nature of man – that he lives in a social environment, which is itself composed of differentiated social groups, and that, as a mature individual, he is the product of strong processes of enculturation. Though this was stressed often by previous writers, most notably by Saint-Simon and Comte, it did not constitute a fundamental element in any body of social analysis prior to the development of Marxian theory. Classical political economy, as we saw in Chapter 9, constructed a model of social organization based upon the conception of man as a utility-maximizing individual. Marx followed classical economics closely in his economic analysis, but even if we regard Marxian economics as the central pillar of Marxian theory, our understanding of that theory will be seriously incomplete unless its economic analysis is viewed within the more general framework of its sociology. Marxian theory is reductionist in the sense that it relies heavily upon psychological propositions, but these are propositions in *social* psychology, not, as in utilitarianism, propositions about man's fundamental nature as an autonomous individual. Marx repeatedly asserted that human consciousness is a product of sociological factors (which, in turn, reflect economic factors). His view of social organization as creating the individual, rather than individuals creating social organization by their autonomous actions, is one of his main points of departure from the classical model of a market economy as a system of social co-ordination. The exchanges that take place in markets are viewed by Marx as only superficially constituting value relations between 'commodities'; more fundamentally they represent the social relations that exist between persons as members of social classes. The Marxian 'labour theory of value' which we shall examine in section D is designed not only to show how market prices are determined, but also to reveal the nature of social class relationships, which, under capitalism, have become much more covert than they were in previous historical stages.

1. Human nature and consciousness

In the *Paris Manuscripts* Marx makes numerous comments on human nature which have given rise to a great deal of interpretive discussion, since they are not easy to understand and it is not clear when Marx is criticizing Hegel for identifying human nature with self-consciousness and when he is presenting his own views. Some modern Marxists, most notably Louis Althusser, argue that Marxian theory is scientific because it does not rely upon questionable propositions about human nature, but others take a diametrically opposite view. In a recent book John McMurtry (*The Structure of Marx's World View*, 1978) attacks Althusser's contention, arguing that the very core of Marxian theory consists of the proposition that man differs from the other animal species in the possession of a special innate capacity which enables him to foresee the result of his actions and, therefore, to work purposefully and creatively instead of merely instinctively. What McMurtry calls 'projective consciousness' in Marxian theory reminds one of Adam Smith's discussion of the uniqueness of man as the animal that can make and keep explicit agreements with his fellows, in the second chapter of the *Wealth of Nations*.

Since most of Marx's writings deal with capitalism, it is difficult to tell what human characteristics, if any, he regarded as basic, and what were regarded as the product of the enculturational processes of bourgeois society. But a clue at least to the former is offered by the fact that Marx often condemned capitalism because it had warped and distorted human nature, and applauded the coming of communism because it would in his view restore man to a more natural state. If we pursue this line of thought it seems evident that Marx did indeed regard man as having a basic human nature and, though he said too little about it to enable one to explain it in detail, it was clearly bound up with the Marxian concept of *freedom*.

In the *Communist Manifesto* Marx and Engels speak scathingly of the kind of 'freedom' that is fostered in bourgeois society - freedom from constraint in one's economic activities – and contrast it with the forthcoming classless society 'in which the free development of each is the condition of the free development of all'. This introduces a subject that has played an important role in the literature of political philosophy down to the present. Some writers hold the 'negative' concept of freedom, defining it strictly in terms of the absence of constraints upon one's actions imposed by other persons (who may or may not be acting as agents of society as, say, policemen do). Others construe freedom in a 'positive' way, focusing on the power one has to achieve one's goals. (The classic discussion of this is Isaiah Berlin, *Four Essays on Liberty*, 1969.) When Marx talked of the existence of 'free labour markets' in a capitalistic economy he was using what he himself characterized as the bourgeois concept (i.e. the negative concept) of freedom; but it is obvious that Marx did not think that the worker has much freedom to realize his aspirations in such an economic system.

The basic nature of man, for Marx, is the desire to be free, the realization of which in his conception did not recommend the anarchism of William Godwin or that of his great rival for control of the First International, Mikhail Bakunin, but a planned society like that advocated by Charles Fourier, Robert

Owen, and other utopianists, where men would be free in the sense of having the ability to realize their potential for personal development. Marx did not think of freedom in terms of the material circumstances of life, though material plenty was a necessary condition of it. The self-realization of the individual, in his view, consists fundamentally in the fulfilment of his creative and artistic potential, which is not only a desire but a need that is inherent in man's nature. This need can be met only in a classless society. Through its conception of freedom Marxian theory connects closely to the romantic movement of the nineteenth century and its successors down to the present.

The desire and need for freedom are a basic constituent of human nature but, in Marx's view, one cannot construct a model of society upon such a proposition, for, as he put it in his *Contribution to the Critique of Political Economy*, 'Man is in the most literal sense of the word a *zoon politikon*, not only a social animal but an animal which can develop into an individual only in society'. In particular the social scientist must pay attention to the system of production of the society he wishes to examine, for it is the most basic constituent of social organization. Thus, in order to understand capitalism as an historical stage in social evolution, one must consider the effect of the capitalistic mode of production and its system of property ownership upon the psychological constitution of the individuals who are the members of such a society. The 'bourgeois' political economists, in Marx's view, had committed three fundamental errors: they had built their economic analysis on the conception of man as a self-seeking individual, disregarding the fact that the human individual is necessarily a *zoon politikon*; they had seriously mis-construed the meaning of freedom as denoting no more than the absence of constraints upon one's economic activities; and they had created the ideology that a competitive economy is the most perfect and historically ultimate form of economic organization, instead of recognizing its gross defects and its transitory nature.

2. Alienation

Marx's most important attempt to examine issues that would today be classified under the discipline of social psychology was his discussion of what the English literature now calls 'alienation'. This occupies a prominent place in the *Paris Manuscripts* of 1844 and in some of his other unpublished work. Since the publication of these manuscript materials in the 1930s there has been a great deal of discussion of the concept of alienation and its role in the Marxian theory of society and social evolution. On the latter point there is much divergence of opinion among modern scholars. George Lichtheim, one of the most widely read interpreters of Marx, contends that Marx's interest in the idea of alienation did not outlast his youthful speculations on social philosophy and that he had virtually abandoned the notion by the time he came to write *Capital* (*Marxism: an Historical and Critical Study*, 1964, p. 197).

On the opposite end of the spectrum there is Piero V. Mini, who contends that all Marx's economic analysis was constructed to provide a scientific proof of the social-psychological proposition that capitalism is characterized by alienation (*Philosophy and Economics: the Origins and Development of Economic Theory*, 1974, p. 189). Both these views, and all in between, are defensible and I will not argue the issue here. Obviously, though, the place that one assigns to the concept of alienation in the interpretation of Marxian theory depends upon what it means, so we must devote our attention primarily to that question.

As we noted in section A 3 above, interpretation of Marx and Engels is frequently bedevilled by semantic problems. These appear in a particularly difficult form with regard to the term 'alienation'. Even the English word is ambiguous, since it can be used to refer to a psychological phenomenon or a legal matter. A generation or so ago it was not uncommon to refer to mental diseases by the generic term 'alienation' (and to the psychological therapist as an 'alienist'); now it has a more distinctively social meaning in its psychological mode, indicating the feeling of being isolated from the other members of one's society or social group. The legal meaning of the term refers to the transfer of rights of ownership, as for example in describing a property as having been alienated. (The term 'inalienable rights' in the American Declaration of Independence draws upon the legal meaning in claiming that individuals have rights that cannot legitimately be taken from them and, moreover, cannot be voluntarily given away or sold by their possessors.) The psychological and legal concepts are quite different, yet, as we shall see, both are related to the use of the term in Marxian theory. Marx used two and sometimes three different German words to express the varied notions that are denoted by the English word 'alienation'. I shall here summarize the meanings that have been most prominent in the interpretive literature, in ascending order of importance (as it seems to me) with regard to the significance of the concept in the general corpus of Marxian theory.

Estrangement. This is the most purely psychological meaning of the concept of alienation. It refers to the feeling that a person may have of not belonging fully to a social group or not being accepted by its other members. Obviously this is a common psychological phenomenon. It may, however, be due to a variety of reasons. The artist or composer who creates works in a novel style, the scientist whose theories are idiosyncratic, or the religious zealot whose views are unconventional, may well feel isolated from his society. Even the hermit or recluse who, as a matter of preference, lives as solitary a life as possible is alienated in this sense. This interpretation of alienation, which could be supported by numerous quotations from, for example, the *Communist Manifesto*, relies upon a rather romanticized view of communal life in pre-capitalist societies, and fails to take account of the fact that, as we noted in Chapter 1, man is a 'multisocial' animal, belonging not just to one (geographically defined) social group but, simultaneously, to many. In view of the fact that Marx stressed the growing class-consciousness and solidarity of the proletariat under capitalism (and of the capitalists too), it is doubtful that this interpretation of alienation focuses upon an important aspect of Marxian theory. The union of modern Marxism with nationalism has perhaps played some role in promoting the interpretation of alienation as psychological estrangement, since it emphasizes the geographically defined nation-state as man's basic 'community', but Marx and Engels clearly did not have this in mind.

Powerlessness. This interpretation connects alienation to the positive conception of freedom outlined above. If a person is greatly constrained in his ability to give effect to his desires, he may be said to be 'alienated'. In this sense of the term the individual capitalist is no less alienated than the individual worker in a competitive market economy, since both are powerless to affect events by their own autonomous actions. But capitalists, as a class, have power, while the workers, as a class, do not. It may be that Marx had this in mind when describing workers as alienated, i.e. excluded not only individually but as a class from the institutions of society through which the power to affect events is exercised.

Ethical normlessness. The criticism of capitalism by Marx and Engels on the ground that it reduces all human actions to commercial activities and all relations between persons to the 'cash nexus' may be construed as a form of alienation in that the behaviour of individuals is not guided by any ethical norms that transcend the desire for personal gain. Capitalism extirpates all considerations of sentiment, altruism, loyalty, or concern for the general welfare, establishing Adam Smith's 'economic man' as the archetypical man, the man whose sole ethical imperative is to shun all ethical imperatives. Again, there are passages in the *Communist Manifesto* and other writings that represent capitalism in this light but, in view of the fact that Marx and Engels consistently avoided any systematic discussion of ethics in their writings, regarding it as unscientific, it is doubtful that this aspect of alienation can be viewed as playing a major role in the corpus of Marxian theory.

In my view (which seems to be the one taken by most students of the Marxian writings), none of the above three interpretations of the concept of alienation is of more than marginal interest. Let us proceed, then, to outline the two that are more intimately connected with the basic structure of Marxian social science. In both of these, the legal and institutional denotations of the term are the foundations of its psychological content. The editor of the Moscow edition of Marx's *Paris Manuscripts* says that:

> By 'estrangement', or 'alienation', Marx meant the forced labour of the labourer for the capitalist, the appropriation by the capitalist of the product of a worker's labour and the separation of the labourer from the means of production, which, being in the capitalist's possession, confront the labourer as an alien, enslaving power.

There are two ideas here that should be distinguished: the separation of the worker from the means of production, and his separation from the product of his labour. I will call the former the idea of 'divorcement' and the latter 'dissociation'.

Divorcement. In the light of our examination of the Marxian view of the essential nature of capitalism in section B 2 above, this notion is quite straightforward. In pre-capitalist societies the worker, while not an owner of the means of production, had certain rights to their use through customary and institutional arrangements such as, for example, the feudal rules which bound him to his manor and its land. With the coming of capitalism all such ties are dissolved. The land, the mills, and other instruments of production which he has been accustomed to work with year after year, as his ancestors had, are transformed into private property, upon which he has no claim sanctioned by custom or law, just as he has no claim upon the new means of production being constructed in the factory towns. Thus divorced from any association with the means of production, both natural and artefactual, he must earn his living by selling his labour power to their owners as a purely commercial transaction.

A great deal of Marxian theory, especially the key doctrines of value and exploitation, hinges upon the conception of capitalism as an economic system composed of two distinct classes: those who own the means of production, and the alienated class, those who have been divorced from any share in that ownership. This must be a main focus of attention below, in considering Marxian economics.

Dissociation. As a consequence of the worker's divorcement from the means of production under capitalism there comes about a corresponding dissociation between him and the products of his work. Because the capitalist owns the means of production and hires labour power under the same terms as he, say, buys raw materials, the worker's association with the product of his labour ceases when he departs from his place of work with his wage payment in hand. Regardless of how much that wage may be, the worker has fallen into a degraded state under capitalism, Marx contends, since he no longer identifies with the product and must regard his work as no more than the means by which he earns his income. 'The worker,' says Marx in the *Paris Manuscripts*, 'is related to the *product of his labour* as to an *alien* object.'

In order to understand this denotation of the Marxian concept of alienation it is necessary to appreciate the Marxian view of 'work', and the difference between it and the treatment of work in classical and modern orthodox economics. In orthodox theory work is treated as 'disutility', one of the 'pains' in the Benthamite pleasure–pain calculus, having no positive value in itself. In Marxian theory, work is a human *need*, an expression of man's desire to create, having value in itself because the most basic element of human nature is the desire for positive freedom, the freedom not merely to be unconstrained by others, but the freedom to realize one's creative potential.

Under capitalism, with its purely negative conception of freedom, work has indeed become nothing more than a disutility, since man is dissociated from the product of his labour. The divorcement from the means of production produces dissociation from the products and creates a society in which the ultimate form of alienation is experienced – man's alienation from *himself*. What in earlier eras was inherent in the concept of a God whose will determines all that occurs, leaving no room for the creativity of man, has now been reproduced in secular society through an economy based upon private property in the means of production. Once again it is evident that Marx was greatly influenced in his youth by the romantics, who, in poetry and other arts, celebrated the nobility of man as a creator and viewed the good society as one in which all men would be like themselves: artists who rejoiced in their work, and could view its product as the objectified realization of their inner selves.

There has been some discussion in the modern literature of the extent to which the concept of alienation is connected, in Marxian theory, with the practice of occupational specialization, since there are numerous passages in the writings of Marx and Engels which suggest that alienation is due to the division of labour. As we can see from the above catalogue of ideas, the basic source of alienation is found in the private ownership system of capitalism. Division of labour is a necessary element in such a system and serves to exacerbate alienation by dissociating man from the product of his labour, and therefore from himself as a creative individual.

3. Class and class conflict

It is evident from our discussion of Marxian theory so far that the concept of class plays a central role in it. No other notion appears so ubiquitously throughout the whole range of the Marxian writings. We have already seen its importance in the Marxian theory of history and in Marxian social psychology; we shall see below that it is equally central to Marxian economics and political theory, and the Marxian view of the nature of the forthcoming communist society. It can be said without much distortion that Marxian social science is fundamentally the analysis of class differentiation in human societies. On this ground some interpreters of Marx consider him primarily as a sociologist, but this simply attempts to squeeze him into one of the now traditional divisions of academic social science. The Marxian conception of social class is based upon the notions of 'economic relations', and 'forces of production', so it is essentially economic in nature. Any attempt to separate Marxian sociology and Marxian economics can only produce a serious distortion of both. Marx did not become an economist until he was in his thirties, when, at the urging of Engels, he began to study the literature of classical political economy, but it is not useful to divide his intellectual career in two, describing him as a sociologist in youth and an economist in maturity. Because of the centrality of class in his thinking he was always a sociologist, and because of the nature of his concept of social class he was always an economist, even before he knew anything about the literature of the subject and had begun to develop his own economic theories.

The view of societies as hierarchically ordered is, of course, a very old one. The social writings of ancient and medieval times seldom discuss the matter, because it was commonly taken for granted as a natural characteristic of social organization. The complacent view of a natural social hierarchy was left unaffected by the frequent political upheavals of the pre-Renaissance era, since these, except for rare events such as the Roman slave rebellion led by Spartacus in 73 B.C., were contests between rival moguls of power and did not involve any serious attempts to alter the vertical structure of the social order. From the early sixteenth century on, however, events began to accumulate that served to bring the established view of hierarchy into question. The Protestant Reformation, the first of these, had a momentous impact upon the concept of hierarchy, which was only with difficulty kept from spreading beyond the sphere of religion into politics; the rise of science introduced a more subtle, and in the long run more powerful, subversion of the idea of hierarchical order and authority; the English revolutions of the seventeenth century questioned established hierarchy directly in the political sphere, as did the American and especially the French revolutions of the eighteenth century. By the end of the eighteenth century the idea of class was widely employed as a focus of social thought, and many historians and political writers discoursed in terms of what Marx later called the 'class struggle'. The modern terminology was not established until the nineteenth century (see Asa Briggs, 'The Language of "class" in Early Ninteenth-Century England', in Briggs and John Saville, eds, *Essays in Labour History*, 1960). In earlier writers such as Adam Smith, words such as 'orders' or 'ranks' were used to express the idea. The word 'class' was used before the nineteenth century in the sense of a category in a classification as for example by biological taxonomy and, in human terms, to refer to a group formed for educational purposes. These two uses survive in modern speech but they do not, of course, have the sociological connotations that are attached to the term in Marxian theory. In England the term 'working class' came into use about 1815 and 'middle class' a decade or so later. In Germany the equivalent language was in widespread use by the middle of the nineteenth century. In France there was a school of historians in the early nineteenth century, led by Saint-Simon's disciple, Augustin Thierry, who wrote history in terms of class conflict, but common use of class terminology did not develop before the twentieth century and was probably due to the influence of Marx.

In England during the early and mid-nineteenth century the most prevalent use of the concept of class was in popular literature and politics rather than in social science more narrowly defined. We cannot examine this in detail here but as background for understanding the Marxian focus on class and class conflict it is worth our while to note the appearance of these notions in the most widely read form of literature of the period, the novel. Many of the writers of the time whose names are prominent in modern courses in English literature wrote 'social novels', dealing with what became known in the early nineteenth century as the 'condition of England question', which was, essentially, the question of the relation of the social classes to one another.

The novels of Jane Austen (1775–1817) form a bridge between the literature of the eighteenth century, which concentrated upon the amusing foibles, manners, and dilettantism of the propertied classes, and that of the nineteenth, which treated the relations between the classes as a much more serious subject. *Pride and Prejudice, Sense and Sensibility*, and *Mansfield Park* seem to concern themselves with the recurring minuet of courtship and marriage but their underlying theme is the relationship between love and *property*. The working class may have lacked class consciousness at this time, but the middle-class and upper-class characters of Austen's novels certainly did not. Indeed, they were obsessed by it; terrified by anything that might threaten their social status, which depended upon property. Marx and Engels, in their explicit criticism of 'bourgeois' values, were no more scathing than Austen in her more subtle critique of the materialism of the 'gentlemanly' way of life. Charles Dickens (1812–70) went much further, depicting the misery and degradation of the underclasses of society in a long series of fictional constructions, which left no room for doubt that the deplorable condition of England in the Age of Industry was due to the selfishness of the upper orders. Anthony Trollope (1815–82), the most reportorial of the Victorian novelists, in his 'Barsetshire' series of novels painted a detached yet merciless picture of the pettiness, vanity, selfishness, and ignorance of the upper orders that, if it had not been presented as fiction, would surely have been recognized as subversive literature. In his later, and most pessimistic, novel, *The Way We Live Now*, he depicted England as having fallen into the hands of a special class of capitalists, the financiers and speculators, a theme of growing importance in radical social thought, including that of Marx and Engels. George Eliot (1819–80), the most philosophically sophisticated of these writers, studied political economy and contemporary economic conditions in preparation for writing *Felix Holt*, which attributed the degradation of the working class, and class differentiation itself, to the division of labour which was the product of capitalistic industrialism. Numerous other writers could be cited who employed similar themes, such as Mrs Gaskell, Charles Kingsley, W. M. Thackeray, and Benjamin Disraeli, who became leader of the Conservative Party and Prime Minister.

One should not assume, on the basis of the themes and rhetoric of their works, that these writers were proto-Marxists. In fact they all favoured the retention of the established hierarchical order and saw the solution of the 'condition of England' problem as lying primarily in an acceptance by the governing class of more responsibility for the stewardship of society and a revival of the feudal concept of the duty of the powerful to accept paternal obligations toward the lower orders. Marx and Engels scoffed at that; their solution demanded no less than the elimination of all class distinctions. The roots of the Marxian theory of class extend into the general ambience of social thought that is well represented in the nineteenth-century social novel, but its main sustenance was drawn from the scientific literature of political economy. As we have already seen, the Physiocrats, Adam Smith, and Ricardo, all constructed their analytical models with class categories, defined not merely in terms of relative wealth or income, but as entities that play distinct roles in economic processes. The Physiocratic distinction between the 'productive' and 'sterile' classes, and Ricardo's theory of rent, are clear anticipations of Marx's distinction between the class that creates value and the class that does not, thus laying the foundation for the Marxian theories of exploitation and class conflict. Marx and Engels may have been impressed by Saint-Simon's distinction between the class of 'producers' and the class of 'parasites', but it was the economics of Ricardo that showed the way to develop a model of capitalism that revealed its so-called freedom of competition to be a disguised system of class exploitation. Ricardo, in Marx's opinion, was the first economist who could lay valid claim to scientific credentials, because his analysis focused directly upon the issue of class relations and class conflict, unlike the 'vulgar economists' who strove to suppress it. For Marx, class conflict was not a conclusion reached by analysis but a plain matter of fact which it was the business of science to explain.

This discussion of the concept of class in the pre-Marxian literature is not meant to denigrate the significance of Marx by questioning the originality of a notion that plays such an important role in Marxian theory. In fact Marx himself never claimed that he had originated the concept of class or the class-conflict view of society. In a letter written in 1852 he explicitly denied that he had, and said that:

> What I did that was new was to prove: (1) that the existence of classes is bound up only with specific historical phases in the development of production; (2) that the class struggle leads necessarily to the dictatorship of the proletariat; (3) that this dictatorship only constitutes the transition to the abolition of all classes and to a classless society. (W. O. Henderson, *The Life of Friedrich Engels*, p. 602)

This statement does not give one much assistance in attempting to understand the Marxian concept of class and the role of class structure in a capitalistic economy. Unfortunately, it is as explicit a statement on the subject as one can find in the writings of Marx and Engels. Perhaps because they lived in a society where everyone took its hierarchical structure for granted and many talked of class conflict and its evils, they did not think it necessary to discuss these conceptions in a systematic way. As Marx said in the passage quoted above, the really new thing was to 'prove' that hierarchical structure is not essential to social order, that it could be done away with, and that it would. The result is that numerous questions remain unanswerable in connection with this aspect of Marxian sociology. We do not know, for example, how Marx and Engels viewed the phenomenon of multisociality, the simultaneous membership of the individual in numerous overlapping social groups; we do not know how they regarded the growing phenomenon of upward social mobility, or an opposite phenomenon, the identification by members of the bourgeois class such as themselves with the aspirations and historical mission of the working class; we do not know whether they thought that the economic condition of the worker is sufficient to create in him a sense of class consciousness and solidarity with his fellows that goes beyond that represented by the formation of trade unions to *political* class consciousness, or whether something more – an ideology, or a philosophy – is necessary; we do not know how they would have responded to the claim that man has a discriminating nature which leads him to join in solidarity with others like himself against those who differ, not only in economic status, but in religion, race, language, geographic location, sex, ideology, and in countless other ways.

The role of the concept of class in the social science that has developed over the past century is mixed. Some historians and political scientists, and not only Marxist ones, have found it useful as a heuristic device in systematizing the complex phenomena with which they deal. Sociologists, again not only Marxist ones, tend to treat class as a primary social fact, so to speak, not just a heuristic artefact of their own construction. In orthodox economics, however, it has almost completely disappeared. The social classes that Ricardo identified with 'land', 'labour', and 'capital' no longer serve as analytical categories. The neoclassical model of economic processes treats 'factors of production' as abstract entities which bear no fixed relationship to persons who are identified as belonging to a specified social class. Marxist economists still focus upon class but, at least in the West, it now has the character of an ideological fretwork appended to a structure of analysis that is essentially the same as that employed by orthodox economists.

D. ECONOMICS

The French sociologist Raymond Aron, noting that Marx 'was an economist who wanted to be a sociologist at the same time' says that *Capital* must be read as 'a book of economics which is at the same time a sociology of capitalism and also a philosophical history of man' (*Main Currents in Sociological Thought*, I, p. 124). It is important to keep this in mind as we examine the structure and content of Marxian economics in this section. But it is equally important that the reader who is not much interested in economic theory or comfortable with its abstract method should resist the temptation to skip over this discussion lightly. Even though Marx himself regarded economic theory as rather tedious, he agreed with Engels that a properly scientific appraisal of the social characteristics of capitalism and sound predictions concerning its future development must rest upon a penetrating economic analysis. Marx and Engels had harsh words for the 'vulgar economists' who neglected the sociological aspects of capitalism, but they would have had much stronger criticisms of those modern Marxists or interpreters of their views who treat the economic aspects of Marxian theory as peripheral to its main argument.

Among those who acknowledge the importance of economics to an understanding of Marxian social and historical theory there has been some dispute as to what should be regarded as its most important statement. The *Grundrisse* manuscripts, which were only published sixty-five years after Marx's death, are regarded by some as a more authentic source of Marx's economics than *Capital*, and there has been a continuous dispute also concerning the relative importance of the different volumes of *Capital*, only one of which was published in a form that Marx himself determined. I cannot enter into this issue here in any constructive way, so let me simply state that in this section I will treat Marxian economics as it appears in *Capital* and will not make any important assertions that rest upon the contention that some part or parts of the two volumes that Engels edited should be viewed as more important than the one that Marx himself delivered to the printer.

Even so, interpretation of Marxian economics is difficult. There is hardly any important propositions in it that cannot be given very different interpretations, all supported by direct quotation. But the scholarly work of the past hundred years has helped considerably to clarify, if not resolve, the most important of these difficulties, and I shall not attempt here to offer an interpretation of Marxian economics that departs significantly from the main view of it that is to be found in the current literature. However, among the numerous mythologies that have grown up about Marxian theory there are some that relate to the content of Marxian economics as found in *Capital*, so the reader must bear with me as I take a few moments to clear the ground by noting what *Capital* is *not*.

1. There is so much discussion in the modern Marxist literature of the tendency of developed capitalistic economies to experience the growth of very large firms that are able to exercise discretionary power in the markets in which they operate that some writers who are imperfectly familiar with the economic analysis of *Capital* presume or infer that it examines an economy of imperfect competition, or even one characterized by outright monopolies in the various markets. Marx did indeed speak frequently of the tendency of capital to concentrate into fewer and fewer hands, but he did not construct an economic model of capitalism as a system of imperfectly competitive markets. He recognized the scientific weakness of any argument about social phenomena that attributed them to the activities of powerful individuals, since he aimed at emulating the natural scientists in explaining phenomena in terms of the operation of general 'laws'. He did not have access to the modern theory of imperfect competition, which was constructed only in the 1930's, and he did not develop such a theory himself. In his basic model of the capitalistic

economy Marx followed the classical economists in assuming, as a heuristic device, that a state of perfect competition exists in all markets, including the markets for labour and other factors of production as well as those for consumer goods. Marx did not modify this model in any significant respect to take imperfections of competition into account. This has been viewed by some modern Marxists as the principal weakness of Marxian economic theory. The most notable attempt, so far, to repair this presumed weakness in Marxian economic analysis is Paul A. Baran and Paul M. Sweezy, *Monopoly Capital: an Essay on the American Economic and Social Order* (1966). This has not won a great deal of acceptance as a satisfactory revision of Marxian economics and it is not possible, at present, to delineate a modified Marxian model that incorporates imperfect competition while retaining the Marxian propositions concerning value and surplus value, on which hinge the theories of exploitation, class conflict, and the demise of capitalism. The reader should keep in mind, as we proceed to examine the structure of Marxian economics, that the perfect competition assumption, which we shall have frequent recourse to, is Marx's assumption, not mine.

2. Marx and Engels made many comments on the role of the state in capitalist society, and their theory of the state as an instrument of class exploitation is an important feature of Marxian theory generally. But the analytical model of *Capital* is that of an economy without the state playing any significant role as a regulator of private economic activities or as the agency for the provision of what are now called 'public goods' and 'transfer payments'. The state appears in the Marxian model in the same restricted way it does in classical political economy: as the sovereign power that determines the laws of property and enforces private contracts. In short, Marx did not view economic events as reflecting the operation of state power any more than he viewed them as reflecting the power of private monopolies. The forces that operate in the Marxian model are those of Adam Smith's 'invisible hand'.

3. The rhetoric of modern Marxism is so punctuated by reference to 'imperialism' that one might reasonably infer that this was a primary concern of Marx himself. This feature of Marxism, however, was developed mainly by Rosa Luxemburg and V. I. Lenin in the early twentieth century, and represents a union of Marxian theory and nationalism that Marx and Engels would almost certainly have rejected. Luxemburg (and the non-Marxian economist John A. Hobson) made the argument that imperialism is due to a failure of a capitalistic economy to generate sufficient demand for commodities to maintain full employment; markets are developed abroad in order to meet this problem. This argument was clearly expressed by Hegel in his *Philosophy of Right*, and Marx must have encountered it in his study of Hegel, but he did not use it in his own work or even refer to it. In *Capital* the economic model is that of a closed economy. Though the existence of separate sovereign states is recognized, no important proposition in Marxian economics hinges upon this.

4. Finally, we should note that *Capital* is about capitalism, not socialism. If one combs the three volumes for discussion of how the future socialistic and communistic economies will work, one emerges with virtually nothing. In fact, very little is to be found on this subject in all the writings of Marx and Engels, published and unpublished. Some critics of Marxian theory regard this as its principal defect, but Marx and Engels viewed discussion of such matters as a purely speculative exercise, characteristic of 'utopian socialism'. In their judgement, 'scientific socialism' demonstrates that capitalism is, inevitably, a transitory phase in historical evolution that is destined to be succeeded by socialism. To modify Galileo's famous remark about heaven, the task of science is not to show how socialism goes, but how one goes to socialism. The analysis of the organizational mechanics of what Engels called a 'planned economy' dates only as far back as the early twentieth century.

These remarks should not, however, be taken to mean that one must discount Marx's class conception of society in evaluating his economic analysis. Capitalists compete fiercely with one another, yet they nevertheless constitute a class; just as labourers do, despite the fact that each one sells his labour power individually. In fact the whole point of Marxian economic theory is to show how these apparently individualistic actions result in consequences that constitute the exploitation by capitalists *as a class* of workers *as a class*. For Marx, the two social classes are real entities, not mere classifications constructed by economists for heuristic purposes. Each class is more than a mere aggregation of persons, and the economy is not properly understood if it is viewed (along the lines of modern orthodox economics) as reducible to the actions of individuals. There are some very difficult problems involved here, since, as we shall see, Marx's theory of value is severely reductionist in nature while his theory of exploitation is essentially holistic. This is the source of some of the philosophical difficulties in interpreting Marxian theory, and it is also the root of the issue that has been much debated by economists under the title of 'the transformation problem'.

The discussion of Marxian economics in the following pages will make use of the concept of 'equilibrium', which may strike the reader as a clear distortion of a theory which aims at showing the dynamic nature of capitalism and the forces working within it that create unresolvable 'contradictions'. But Marx in fact employed the same kind of equilibrium analysis as Ricardo did, and he attempted, like Ricardo, to utilize an equilibrium model for the purpose of describing the process of economic development under capitalism. We have to keep in mind that Marx, much more so than Ricardo, regarded the analysis of economic development as the central problem of economic theory. In a certain sense, all the propositions of Marxian economics are aimed at ascertaining the 'laws of motion' of capitalism. Some critics of Marxian theory would see its principal weakness as an inability to do this, but an acquaintance with the modern literature on the theory of economic development is sufficient to temper this criticism considerably, since, after some forty years of intensive work, orthodox economists have been unable to discover any laws that are more reliable than Marx's. Science, says Sir Peter Medawar, is 'the art of the soluble'. Unfortunately, one sometimes does not know when a problem is insoluble until much time and effort has been expended, which creates a disposition to resist criticism in the interest of preserving the putative value of the accumulated intellectual capital.

1. Value

In an economy organized by means of the market mechanism, the composition of production and its distribution among the members of the society are controlled by the prices of commodities and of their factors of production. The central problem therefore in the economic theory of a market economy is the explanation of how this structure of prices emerges from the independent actions of the large number of persons who appear in the various markets as buyers or sellers of commodities or factors. Recognition of the importance of this is one of the main reasons why Adam Smith is considered to be the founder of economics as a systematic discipline. We saw in Chapter 7 how Smith endeavoured to explain the formation of market prices, and in Chapter 9 we examined Ricardo's modification and extension of Smith's argument, which became the accepted 'theory of value' of classical political economy. In order to refresh the reader's memory, I will briefly summarize the essential features of Smith's and Ricardo's value theories before going on to outline Marx's.

The idea that market prices are determined by the forces of supply and demand was widespread in the literature before Adam Smith, but the early writers on economic questions did not possess the analytical apparatus that is necessary to construct a proper model with it. Penetrating scientific thinkers such as Hume and Smith leaned to the view that the forces of supply and demand are responsible only for the transitory day-to-day prices of the market place, offering no insight into the more permanent factors that govern the general levels around which these prices fluctuate. Smith concluded that a satisfactory explanation of this more important question must rest on an analysis of the conditions of production, thus beginning the classical economists' rejection of the importance of demand, which continued to be characteristic of the orthodox theory when Marx was constructing his own. The classical emphasis on production in their theory of value harmonized with Marx's emphasis upon it which we have already seen in the above discussion of the Marxian theory of history and Marxian sociology.

Adam Smith argued that labour input is the sole determinant of value in a very primitive economy that has no capital equipment and recognizes no private property rights in land and other natural resources but, in more 'advanced' societies, labour must share the value-determining role with other factors. Ricardo contended that labour is the sole determinant of the values of all competitively produced commodities in advanced as well as primitive economies. His theory of rent enabled him to eliminate natural factors but, as we saw, his explanation of value ran into great difficulty over the handling of the role of capital. The assumption that he adopted to deal with this, that the ratio of capital inputs to direct labour inputs is the same in all industries, is not only empirically incorrect but converts the 'theory of value' from an explanation of the *determinants* of value to a proposition about the *measurement* of value.

Early in the first volume of *Capital* Marx proceeds to develop his analysis of value along the same lines as Smith and Ricardo. Exchange value is an equational expression (X units of one commodity equal Y units of another), and an equation can have meaning only if the entities on either side of the equation sign are commensurable in some respect. Like Smith and Ricardo, Marx rejected the notion that the common property is the usefulness of commodities, thereby rejecting demand factors as operative in the determination of exchange values. Immediate demand and supply may influence the day-to-day fluctuations of prices, but their general levels are determined by the conditions of production of commodities under normal (long-run equilibrium) conditions. These determinative conditions of production consist solely of the relative quantities of labour that are required to produce the different commodities. The use of capital equipment and natural resources have nothing to do with the determination of value. Failure to recognize this opens the door to 'vulgar political economy' in Marx's terminology, by hiding the fact that the two classes that compose society play categorically different roles in the economic processes of capitalism. Moreover, Marx follows Ricardo in insisting that the level of wage rates plays no role in value determination, for value does not reflect the money cost of production but its cost in terms of the quantity of society's available supply of labour that is required to produce the various commodities. This is what Marx called the 'law of value'. 'A commodity has *value*,' he says in a summary of his theory that he prepared for a meeting of the General Council of the First International in 1865:

> because it is a *crystallization of social labour*. The *greatness* of its value, or its *relative* value, depends upon the greater or less amount of that social substance contained in it; that is to say, on the relative mass of labour necessary for its production. (*Value, Price, and Profit*)

In the preceding paragraph I have been careful to refer to value as concerning 'commodities'. This is Marx's terminology, the significance of which is that Marx regarded capitalism as an economic system in which production does not take place for direct use but for sale. In a schema that he frequently employed, Marx represented capitalism by the notation M–C–M' in order to indicate that the capitalist begins with Money, purchases labour power, raw materials, and other things in order to produce Commodities, which he then sells for Money to complete the process. The modern distinction between 'commodities' and 'services' has led to the erroneous view that the Marxian law of value applies only to tangible goods and does not cover such things as transport services, medical services, etc. As we shall see, Marx did exclude some services from the law of value, but it was not his intention to exclude all of them. The term 'commodities' was used to focus attention on the part of the economy that is 'capitalistic' in the sense that production is undertaken for the purpose of profitable sale in markets rather than for direct use by the producer.

By comparison with the analysis that one finds today in the orthodox textbooks of microeconomic theory, the crucial features of the Marxian theory of value are the exclusion of demand-side considerations and the elimination, or reduction, of all non-labour supply-side factors. Land and other natural factors are eliminated as value-generating factors by Marx without any analytical explanation, on the ground that they are 'supplied by nature'. If a factor of production

> is not the product of human labour [says Marx] it transfers no value to the product. It helps to create use-value without contributing to the formation of exchange-value. In this class are included all means of production supplied by Nature without human assistance, such as land, wind, water, metals *in situ*, and timber in virgin forests. (*Capital*, I, chapter 8)

Production factors such as factory buildings, machinery, and partially processed materials *are* products of human labour, which Marx called 'constant capital'. They transfer to the finished commodity the value that is embodied in them by the 'crystallized labour' they represent, but they make no additional contribution to its value. This vital aspect of the Marxian theory of value is severely reductionist: all 'constant capital' is reducible to the labour it embodies, and no value is attributable to the conjunction of labour with other factors, or to specialization, or to the organization of the production process. Marx did not adopt Ricardo's device of eliminating the influence of capital on value by assuming a uniform ratio of labour to capital in all industries but, as we shall see, his method created a similar difficulty, the celebrated 'transformation problem' in the Marxian theory of value.

One of the criticisms that had been levied against Ricardo's theory of value was that he had spoken of 'labour' as if it were a homogeneous thing, failing to recognize that labourers differ greatly in their productivity, owing to such things as their natural abilities, their prior training, and the intensity of their work effort. In numerous passages in *Capital* Marx takes note of this problem and says that the labour that enters the value equation of the market place is not the concrete working time of particular labourers but labour as measured in 'abstract' units. An hour's labour of a skilled workman, for example, must be counted as a larger amount of this abstract labour than an hour's labour of an unskilled workman. He does not, however, indicate how the reduction of concrete labour to abstract labour takes place. In some passages he suggests that the coefficients of reduction are determined by the different market values of the commodities produced by different kinds of labour, but this is a circular argument; one cannot say that value is determined by labour input and at the same time ascertain how much labour input occurred by reference to the magnitude of value produced. In other passages he suggests that the coefficients are determined by differential wage rates (which is how modern orthodox economics tackles this problem) but this too is a circular argument within the framework of Marxian theory, since wage rates are also market prices and are asserted to be determined by the law of value like everything else that is bought and sold in capitalistic markets. In one passage early in the first volume of *Capital* Marx simply says that the reduction of concrete labour to abstract labour is 'established by a social process that goes on behind the backs of the producers' and goes on to tell the reader that henceforth he will be speaking of unskilled labour or its equivalent in order to 'save ourselves the trouble of making the reduction'. This can hardly be regarded as a solution of the problem. Engels, in his *Anti-Dühring*, acknowledged that this way of dealing with the heterogeneity of labour refers to a 'process which, at this point in the development of the theory of value, can only be stated but not as yet explained' (p. 236). This matter has not received much attention in the modern Marxist literature. Some Marxists have expressed the view that it represents a serious difficulty in the Marxian theory of value, but most of their attention has been devoted recently to a similar problem in orthodox economic theory: the heterogeneity of the 'capital' that is included in its model as a non-reducible factor of production.

A much more important feature of the Marxian theory of value is that it does not include all human effort as 'labour'. In order to count as value-creating labour, says Marx, an activity must satisfy two criteria: it must be devoted to the production of goods that will be useful to others (i.e. there must be a demand for them), and 'the time occupied in the labour of production must not exceed the time really necessary under the given social conditions of the case' (*Capital*, I, chapter 7). Marx gives illustrations to clarify the latter point. For example:

> If under normal, i.e. average, social conditions of production, A pounds of cotton ought to be made into B pounds of yarn by one hour's labour, then a day's labour does not count as 12 hours' labour unless 12A pounds of cotton have been made into 12B pounds of yarn; for in the creation of value, the time that is socially necessary alone counts. (*loc. cit.*)

If a technological development, such as the invention of the power loom, decreases the time necessary to produce cloth, then a hand-loom weaver who spends ten hours producing the same amount of cloth that a power-loom weaver could produce in one would be contributing only one hour of 'socially necessary' labour. The market will not pay more for a bolt of cloth produced on a hand loom than an identical one produced on a power loom. In counting the labour time that produces value one must count the time that is necessary under the most efficient conditions of production that are available to the society at the current stage of its economic development. The influence of natural factors must also be considered, since, for example, in a good growing season a certain amount of socially necessary labour may be embodied in eight bushels of corn, while in a poor season it is embodied in only four. There seems to be a circularity in Marx's argument here, since it resorts to the market price to ascertain the magnitude of the factor that is supposed to determine market price. This appears more strikingly in Marx's argument that if the price of a commodity falls because it is produced in excess of the demand for it, some of the labour used in its production must not be counted as socially necessary.

Marx's notion of socially necessary labour plays a more vital role in Marxian theory than the notion of abstract labour, which is evident when one considers the various sorts of human activities that are categorically excluded from the process of value creation. These consist of a large number of activities that Marx regards as having to do with the marketing of commodities rather than their production. Labour expended in sorting, packaging, storing, wholesaling, and retailing is not socially necessary. These activities are undertaken in a capitalistic economy in order to enable the capitalist to 'realize' the value that is embodied in commodities (i.e. to complete the M–C–M' process) but they make no contribution to that value. Moreover, it is evident that a host of other activities are considered in the same light: those of lawyers, priests, stockbrokers, civil servants, soldiers, and so on, including of course the activities of capitalists themselves. Capitalists (as distinct from the managers of producing enterprises) are engaged in a great deal of activity, but this does not count as value-creating labour. Their incomes are derived by appropriating some of the value produced by the socially necessary labourers. Capitalists share this 'surplus value' with a large number of other persons because they perform essential roles in the 'exploitation' process by which some of the value is diverted from those who have created it. In the future communist society capitalists will have disappeared and, along with them, all these exploitation-mediating functionaries.

Marx was severely critical of J. S. Mill for contending that the 'laws of production' are categorically different from the 'laws of distribution', insisting that production and distribution are part of one unified capitalistic process. But he himself dichotomized the economy through his concept of 'socially necessary labour'. Marx's notion reverts back to the distinction made by Aristotle between 'productive' activities and 'acquisitive' activities. It can hardly be denied that this distinction is valid; theft, for example, is clearly an acquisitive activity that contributes nothing of positive value to the production process. Other activities that are legal in themselves may have the same characteristics, such as gambling (except for the pleasure it may give to its participants). But one cannot determine what is a productive activity and what an acquisitive one without an economic analysis of their effects. Marx's main objective was to show that the capitalist plays no productive role in the economy, and his theory of surplus value, as we shall see in the next section, was designed to explain why this is so. In doing this, however, he restricted the concept of 'socially necessary labour' to exclude the activities of many who are not capitalists. Marx did not provide any reasons for his long list of exclusions, apparently relying upon the Aristotelian notion that some activities are *inherently* unproductive. By such a procedure one is free to characterize arbitrarily as unproductive any activity one has a mind to, which permits some modern Marxists to claim that only Marxist social scientists are productive workers, the others playing a part in the subtle process by which value is stolen from those who create it.

These difficulties in the Marxian theory of value relate to problems that one would encounter when translating it into quantitative terms in an empirical analysis of a specific capitalist economy. In order, for example, to determine whether the extent of 'exploitation' is great or small, or whether it is increasing or decreasing, one would have to be able to differentiate non-arbitrarily between 'necessary' and 'unnecessary' labour and find a way of measuring the former in 'abstract' units. Marx and Engels were not interested in such problems. Their object was to provide a theoretical model of the capitalistic economy in general. The difficulties that we have noted above are not negligible, but they are not fatal to Marxian *theory*. Leaving them aside then, the 'law of value' may be expressed by the equation

$$W = L$$

where W represents the aggregate value of the commodities produced in the economy during a specific period, and L represents the aggregate quantity of abstract socially necessary labour that has been devoted to their production.

If Marx's law of value is construed to be a theory that explains how value is *determined*, the modern orthodox economist would criticize it as requiring the very strong assumption of strict proportionality between the labour input and the value produced (which, incidentally, Marx did not always adhere to). If this is not maintained, then the amount of labour required to produce a unit of a commodity varies with the quantity of the commodity produced and the market price is not determinate without bringing in the demand side of the market process as a co-determining factor. There are also some serious difficulties encountered in passing from a theory of *relative* values to an aggregative proposition such as Marx's law of value. But these are problems that arise if Marx's theory of value is construed as an explanation of value *determination* in a capitalistic economy. It is not at all certain that the Marxian theory of value should be interpreted in this way. Marx and Engels gave ambiguous directions on this point and there has been much discussion, by Marxists and non-Marxists, of this vital issue. In the early years of the Soviet

Union, the doctrinal authorities there decided that Marx's theory should be construed as a theory of value determination, but this did not end debate on it.

Some interpreters of Marxian theory regard the law of value as dealing with the technical problem of value *measurement* rather than value determination. If magnitudes are to be compared, or aggregated, one must employ some numeraire that does not itself vary in the quality being measured. We examined this problem above in Chapter 7 in discussing Adam Smith, who, we noted, argued that labour time is the most reliable unit in which to measure value because an hour's labour involves the same disutility regardless of when or where it is performed. Marx did not accept Smith's contention but he did speak frequently in terms that suggest a similar use of labour as a value numeraire. The only extended discussion of this point in the Marxian literature is in Engels's *Anti-Dühring* (III, IV), but it does little to clarify the issue and Engels, like Marx, frequently speaks of value measurement and value determination as if they are synonymous. It is true, of course, that if one measures the output of a process in terms of one of the inputs then the magnitude of the output will be equal to the magnitude of the input, but this equality cannot be construed to mean that the value of the output is causally determined by the input used as the numeraire. This is evident from the equation $W = L$ that I have used in expressing Marx's law of value. If W is measured in labour units, then the equation says nothing about the determinants of W. Even if some other commodity, such as gold, were used as the unit of measurement, it necessarily follows that $W = L$ for the economy as a whole if is assumed that the amount of labour embodied in an ounce of gold is a specific magnitude.

Another common interpretation of the law of value construes it to be a definitional proposition. Marx is regarded as saying neither that labour determines value nor that it can serve as a measurement of it, but that value *is* labour. If this interpretation simply means to call attention to Marx's language, it does little to assist us in understanding the content of Marxian theory. One is free to use words any way one pleases, but the world is not governed by the words we use, and a definition has no explanatory power in itself. There is more to it than that, however, since there are some strong grounds for the view that the law of value was construed by Marx as a statement about the *essential* nature of the capitalist economy. That is to say, it is a metaphysical proposition, dealing not with causally connected phenomena but with the inherent nature of capitalism, a matter too fundamental to be doubted and not subject to empirical test. Marx spoke of labour as the sole determinant of value, but he also noted that such a statement is a 'tautology', since value *is* labour (*Critique of Political Economy*, I, I). I do not think that Marx meant to imply that the law of value is a proposition in formal logic or that he was merely referring to his own linguistic usage. In view of the other substantial elements of Aristotelian essentialism that are present in Marxian theory, it is not surprising that Marx invested his law of value with similarly metaphysical qualities. But I would disagree with those who contend that the law was meant to be strictly a definitional or an ontological proposition, not a causal law in the sense in which the term 'law' is used in natural science.

Yet another interpretation of the Marxian law of value construes it to be fundamentally a normative proposition, stating something that *ought to be* rather than something that *is*. There is no doubt that Marx's theory of value plays a vital role in his theory of exploitation, and the latter is, of course, a normative or ethical proposition. Marx may have felt that the law of value serves as an empirical proposition from which it is possible to derive directly an ethical proposition. If this were his essential view of it, Marxian theory would have to be regarded as offending against Hume's principle that empirical facts and value judgements are categorically disjunct. Moreover, even within its own framework, the Marxian theory could not demonstrate that labour is exploited, since its own market price is determined by the law of value like that of any other commodity. Some interpreters have argued that Marx demonstrated that justice prevails when all commodities sell at their labour values, and condemn capitalism on the ground that some things do not do so in an economy based on private ownership of the means of production. This interpretation has been supported by the doctrinal decision of the Soviet authorities that the law of value must govern economic processes in a socialist regime. Engels confused the issue considerably by contending in a 'Supplement' to Volume III of *Capital* that the law of value applies only to pre-capitalistic economies, and arguing in his *Anti-Dühring* that under socialism it would reassert itself 'naturally' without the managers of the planned economy having any need for a numeraire to serve as an instrument of value calculation or exchange, while contending in the same book that Marx did not apply the law of value to anything except the pricing of commodities in a capitalistic economy.

The interpretations of the Marxian theory of value outlined in the preceding three paragraphs are, in my view, totally unacceptable, notwithstanding the support that can be given to them by direct quotation from the writings of Marx and Engels. If the law of value is not intended to be an explanation of how market prices are determined in a capitalistic economy, then *Capital* is not an analysis of capitalism at all, since it advances no *other* theory of this vital constituent of a market economy. The theory of value determination is not a secondary feature of a model of capitalism that can be discarded without fatal consequences. Marx understood this clearly. The lengthy discussions of the mechanism of value determination in *Capital* form the core of his analysis of capitalism and, whatever the defects of his theory of value might be, it cannot be abandoned without bringing about a collapse of the whole structure.

It is not impossible to construct a theory of exploitation that relies upon an economic analysis different from the law of value. But the point is, Marx *did* use his law of value for this purpose. His condemnation of capitalism does not rest upon a simple assertion that it is an exploitive system, or the contention that exploitation is so obvious that it requires no analysis. On the contrary, Marx's view was that the market system of voluntary exchange disguises the phenomenon of exploitation, which, in the earlier regimes of slavery and feudalism, was clear for all to see. Capitalism is a regime that cannot be understood at all without economic theory, and its exploitive nature cannot be revealed without an analysis of value determination. If we are interested, not in what Marxian economics *could* have been or what it *should* have been, but what it *was*, the labour theory of value determination must be viewed as playing a crucial role in it. We go on now to examine how Marx proceeded to build his theory of exploitation upon his law of value.

2. Surplus value and exploitation

The word 'exploitation' is used in common speech in two quite different senses. One of these is descriptive, or explanatory in a non-normative sense, such as when one says, for example, that the growth of New York was due to exploiting the advantages of its location as a salt-water harbour, or when one refers to a chess player as exploiting the opportunities offered by his king's pawn position. When used in other ways, however, the term involves a moral judgement, as for example when one says that West Virginia coal miners are exploited by their employers. This double meaning of the word is unfortunate, since it invites unclarity and offers opportunity to smuggle moral valuations into a discourse that purports to be scientific. The word itself, originally French, dates back only to the mid-eighteenth century, when it began to be used in its descriptive sense. The moral denotation was a creation of the Saint-Simonians, whose catch phrase 'the exploitation of man by man' quickly passed into common speech. (See Arthur E. Bestor Jr, 'The Evolution of the Socialist Vocabulary', *Journal of the History of Ideas*, June 1948.)

In Engels's 'Outlines of a Critique of Political Economy', which led to his friendship with Marx, he said that the only difference between capitalism and previous systems of economic organization was that 'unscientific swindling' had been replaced by 'licensed fraud'. This feature of capitalism, for which Marx and Engels adopted the term 'exploitation', is hidden from view by the market process and can be revealed only by economic analysis. This was the main reason why Engels urged Marx to divert his scholarly abilities from philosophy to economics. Marx's explanation is contained in his theory of 'surplus value', later described by Engels as 'the most epoch-making achievement of Marx's work'. It had created *scientific* socialism by showing that, without overt cheating or the use of force, capitalists deprive workers of that which properly belongs to them (*Anti-Dühring*, II, VII).

The theory of surplus value is expounded in *Capital* with the systematic use of the general equation:

$$W = C + V + S$$

where W represents the aggregate value of the economy's production during a period of time, C and V stand respectively for what Marx called 'constant capital' and 'variable capital', and S for 'surplus value'. The theory of surplus value hinges upon the content of C and V and the reasons why Marx calls the former 'constant' and the latter 'variable'. Since they are both called 'capital', however, we must begin by explaining Marx's use of this word, which differs considerably from the sense in which it is employed in orthodox economics.

The classical economists used the term 'capital' to refer to one of the three main categories of the factors of production: things such as factory buildings, tools and machines, transport facilities, partially processed stocks of goods, etc., which are neither 'labour' nor 'land'. Modern economists employ the term in a similar way. In this usage there is no particular connection between 'capital' and 'capitalism'. A slave economy or a feudal one could make use of 'capital', as could a communist one. Marx retained some features of the classical use of the term but his fundamental definition of it involves a reference to its *ownership*. Marx speaks of land and labour services, or money that may be used to purchase them, as forms of 'capital', and the general notion he seems to have in mind is that, whatever its specific form may be, 'capital' is the property of the capitalists that is employed in the process of production. The M–C–M' schema of capitalism refers to the fact that the capitalist begins with Money-capital, purchases labour power, raw materials, machines, and other concrete forms of 'capital', turns them into Commodity-capital, and sells them for Money again. Throughout the process the capitalist is the owner of all the means of commodity production. In this sense there is no distinction between labour and the other production factors. In Marx's view, however, there *is* a vital difference between labour and the other factors of production, which the classical economists had failed to see. This difference is embodied in Marx's distinction between 'constant capital' and 'variable capital' which, he noted, he had been the first to grasp.

In concrete terms the items that enter the above equation under C consist of the expenditures made by the capitalist for raw or partially finished materials and for such things as buildings and machinery. Each individual capitalist purchases these in the market (from other capitalists) at prices which are their 'values' expressed in money units. In what sense are such items 'constant'? Marx explains that this part of capital 'does not, in the process of production, undergo any quantitative alteration of value'. By contrast, 'that part of capital represented by labour-power does, in the process of production, undergo an alteration of value' (*Capital*, I, VII). In short the materials, machines, and other C-items that the capitalist purchases transmit to the commodity produced in his enterprise the same value he has paid for them. They cannot therefore yield a profit to the capitalist. This is the crucial implication of Marx's characterization of them as *constant* capital.

'Variable capital', V in the above equation, consists specifically of the expenditures made by the capitalist for the purchase of (socially necessary) labour services. These too are paid for at their 'value' but, unlike the C-items, they have the ability to create *more* value than is represented by their wages. This, says Marx, is a 'gift of Nature' which is a quality only of the 'living labour' that is directly employed in a production process. This additional value is what Marx calls 'surplus value' and is represented by S in the above equation. The labour that is embodied in constant capital yielded surplus value when it was used in the process of producing the machines, buildings, etc., but it is now 'dead labour' which, being 'crystallized' or 'locked up' in a commodity, transmits its value to the other commodities it may be used to produce, but does not add to it. Marx's notion of labour as *variable* capital is an effort to solve a problem that is encountered in any exclusively supply-side theory of value: if the magnitude of an output is determined by the magnitude of its input, how can there be any *net* output? Marx's answer to what would seem to be a violation of a conservation law is that this occurs because of the unique properties of living labour, which, so to speak, is a productive engine with greater than 100 per cent efficiency, producing more output value than its own input value.

The surplus value produced by the labourer becomes, in a capitalistic economy, the property of the capitalist. When he hires labour for a wage, the capitalist possesses the full 'labour-power' that the worker is able to perform during the stipulated time period. The commodity produced is the property of the capitalist and, when sold at the value determined by the labour embodied in it, will yield a surplus. The labourer creates this surplus but the capitalist, because of the private ownership of the means of production, appropriates it as his own. Marx often refers to this surplus as 'profit' but it is clear that it also includes what orthodox economists call 'rent' and 'interest', and a large part of their 'wages and salaries' category as well, since Marx includes in V only the payments made for 'socially necessary' labour. Ricardo, in Marx's view, had touched the theory of surplus value in his own analysis of profit, but he was unable to grasp it firmly because he had failed to appreciate the fundamental difference between constant and variable capital.

Schematically, Marx's theory of value and exploitation can be presented as follows. The value of the output of any industry, or of the economy as a whole, during a specified period of time, is equal to the (socially necessary) labour embodied in the commodities produced. This 'law of value', which was previously written as $W = L$, can be rewritten to distinguish between the labour used immediately in production and the labour embodied in the raw materials, tools, and other constant capital items:

$$W = L^l + L^d$$

where the superscripts l and d refer respectively to what Marx sometimes described as 'living' and 'dead' labour. If we now look at the distribution of the value, we have:

$$L^l = V + S$$

and

$$L^d = C$$

That is to say, the value created by living labour is divided between the wages paid to workers, V, and the surplus value, S, obtained by capitalists. The payment for dead labour is what capitalists have to expend for the constant capital, C, used in production. Thus we obtain Marx's equation:

$$W = V + C + S$$

We can now see how this equation compares to the 'law of value' as expressed by the equation $W = L$.

The law of value (which Marx did not write, as I have, in equational form) states that the value of a specific commodity, and of all commodities taken together, is determined by the input of socially neccssary labour. The equation sign in $W = L$ must be read as inferring a causal statement. The equation $W = C + V + S$ describes how the value of a commodity, or of all commodities taken together, is accounted for in wage payments, payments to other factors of production, and surplus value. It is an accounting statement, not a causal one. By comparison with modern national income accounting $C + V + S$ corresponds to the 'gross national product' of a year (if C refers to the constant capital depreciated during that period), and $V + S$ to 'net national income'.

The ground for construing surplus value as 'exploitation' in the moral sense of the term is the ethical proposition that one ought to have what one produces. Marx and Engels did not make this explicit in their writings, and though it was not viewed by them as the rule of distribution under communism, it was the basis of their moral condemnation of capitalism. In order to sustain this, Marx devotes a great deal of space in *Capital* to explaining why constant capital produces no net value and why the activities of capitalists in accumulating capital and administering it do not create value. Some of his sharpest invective was aimed at the followers of Ricardo who, in Marx's view, acted as apologists of capitalism by attempting to show that profit and other surplus value incomes were the required recompense for socially necessary functions.

Some important elements of Marxian theory depend upon the view that the *degree* of exploitation under capitalism, which Marx expresses as the ratio of surplus value to wages, S/V, is large, and tends to increase. This is, however, part of Marx's analysis of the dynamics of capitalism and has no necessary connection with his theory of exploitation. Marx's implicit ethical criterion of just distribution condemns *all* surplus value regardless of its magnitude, and regardless of whether the personal incomes of capitalists are large or small. Contrary to a widespread modern view, the condemnation of capitalism advanced by Marxian theory does not rest upon the proposition that under it there is great inequality in the distribution of income. Even if there were complete equality of income, those who play no necessary role in the value-creating process would still be exploiting those who do.

Any valuational judgement such as the Marxian theory of exploitation requires two elements, a normative criterion, and an empirically valid positive proposition. The normative criterion identifies what *ought* to be; the positive proposition, what *is*; and the judgement consists of comparing the two. In Marxian theory the positive proposition consists of the law of value and the value distribution equation, and the (implicit) normative criterion is that the whole economic value of a production process ought to belong to those who create that value. Since Marx's death there has been little discussion of his normative criterion. Many writers treat it as so obviously true as to be beyond discussion, a view that is not supported by any acquaintance with the literature on ethical philosophy. The discussion of Marxian economics has focused primarily on the empirical validity of the law of value and the internal consistency of the model that Marx erected upon it. Most modern economists, including many who consider themselves Marxists, have rejected the law of value. The Marxist economic literature continues to condemn capitalism as unjust, but one finds today little disposition to base this judgement on the Marxian theory of value. The predominant theory of exploitation in modern neoclassical economics connects it with monopolistic conditions and other imperfections in the market mechanism of a private enterprise economy.

A survey of the decline and fall of the labour theory of value is beyond the scope of this book. In Chapter 17 A we shall examine the value theory that replaced it. As part of our present concern, however, we must devote some attention to the attempt by Marx to cope with the difficulties of his theory of value that were advanced by critics and were clearly evident to himself. This mainly concerns what has become known as the 'transformation problem'. It has generated a large body of literature, but I shall be brief, and will stick close to Marx's own attempt to deal with it.

3. The transformation problem

In numerous places in *Capital* Marx recognizes that production requires time, and that commodities may differ greatly in the length of their production processes. However, he did not modify his theory to take account of this as Ricardo did. He was, apparently, aware of the serious damage this would do to his exploitation thesis. In those passages where the matter is noted, Marx simply asserts that non-labour time does not create value (see, for example, *Capital*, II, V), despite the fact that no capitalist would undertake to produce a long-process commodity when a short-process one would generate the same profit. Nevertheless, the same problem that Ricardo encountered emerged in his own theory in terms of the ratio of constant to variable capital or, as he called it, the 'organic composition of capital'.

In *Capital* Marx makes extensive use of three ratios for analytical purposes:

$$\frac{S}{C+V} = RP \text{ [the 'rate of profit']}$$

$$\frac{S}{V} = RS \text{ [the 'rate of surplus value']}$$

$$\frac{C}{V} = OC \text{ [the 'organic composition of capital']}$$

Marx assumes that the magnitude of RP must be uniform throughout the economy. This is an equilibrium condition that pertains owing to competition: if the rate of profit in one industry were different from another, capitalists would shift their investments, and would continue to do so until RP was equal in all industries. Similarly, competition in the labour market assures that RS will be uniform throughout the economy. Given the law of value, RS is determined by the hourly wage rate, and some other factors such as the 'intensity' of labour. If these were different in different industries labour would move among industries until an equilibrium equality of RS was attained. These two propositions, which are simply implications of the general assumption of perfect competition, lead, however, to a third, since it can be shown by simple algebra that if RP and RS are uniform then OC must be also. This third proposition is empirically unacceptable, since it is quite clear even from casual observation that the ratio of constant capital to variable capital differs greatly among industries.

Marx noted this difficulty while he was working on *Capital* and constructed a solution for it. But he did not include discussion of the problem or his solution in Volume I. Not long after its publication in 1867, a number of readers perceived the problem and some fastened upon it as a serious analytical flaw in the Marxian model. Marx did no further work on this after 1867 and it was left to Engels to respond to the criticisms when he came to edit the second and third volumes of *Capital* after Marx's death. In his preface to Volume II, Engels took note of the criticisms that had been based upon the apparent inconsistency of assuming uniformity in the rates of profit and surplus value while acknowledging the non-uniformity of the organic composition of capital. He announced that Marx had constructed a satisfactory solution of the problem and that he intended to include it in Volume III. The publication of this did not take place until 1894, nine years later, and, in the meantime, there was a good deal of discussion, by Marxists and critics, of the possible ways in which the matter could be resolved. So when Volume III finally appeared, an exceptional amount of interest centred upon the solution that Marx had worked out. In Volume I Marx usually treated 'price' as 'value' expressed in money units, drawing no distinction of analytical importance between them. In Volume III his solution of the ratios difficulty rested upon a distinction between value and price, contending that under capitalism the commodity values determined according to the law of value are 'transformed' into commodity prices, the latter being the 'phenomenal form' that actually appears in market transactions. Since 1894 this issue has been known as the 'transformation problem'.

Marx constructs his value–price transformation with the use of a numerical illustration which, with a bit of simplification, is as follows. (The reader will find Marx's discussion in *Capital*, III, II.)

Industry	C	V	S	Value	Price	Price–Value
I	80	20	20	120	130	+10
II	70	30	30	130	130	· 0
III	60	40	40	140	130	– 10
Sum [Σ]	210	90	90	390	390	0

$$\text{Value} = C + V + S \qquad \text{Price} = C + V + RP(C + V)$$

$$RP = \frac{\Sigma S}{\Sigma C + \Sigma V} = \frac{90}{300} = 30\%$$

In this illustration we have three industries which differ only in the organic composition of their capitals. Marx assumes that the rate of surplus value, S/V, uniform throughout the economy, is equal to 1, so S = V in all industries. (There is no analytical significance in this; any positive number will serve.) The first step in the transformation is to calculate the overall profit rate of the economy, which in the above illustration is 30 per cent. Since, in competitive equilibrium, all industries must have the same rate of profit, RP must be applied uniformly to the production expenditures of all industries (C + V) in order to arrive at the prices at which their several commodities will be sold. This is how the column labelled 'Price' in the above table is calculated.

It is evident that the only commodity that sells in the market at its labour value is that which is produced with an organic composition of capital equal to the *average* composition of the economy as a whole – industry II in the above illustration. An industry whose OC is above the average sells its commodity at a price above its value, while an industry whose OC is below the average sells its commodity at a price below its value. What this means is that the individual capitalist does not receive the surplus value generated in *his* firm through the exploitation of *its* labour force. The total surplus value of the economy goes into a common pool, so to speak, and each capitalist receives a share of it such as to make the profit rate of all capitalists equal, irrespective of the composition of their capitals. This equalization is accomplished by the requisite deviation of prices from values. If this were not so, says Marx, 'it would be as plain as day that the surplus-value, and thus value in general, must have an entirely different source than labour, and that political economy would then be deprived of every rational basis' (*Capital*, III, VIII).

The arithmetic of Marx's discussion is plain, but the economic process it represents is not. Sometimes he speaks of the 'tendency' of all industries to move towards an organic composition of capital equal to the average composition of the economy as a whole, which would mean that the deviation of prices from values is a transitory disequilibrium condition; under full long-run equilibrium all prices would equal values. Sometimes he speaks of the tendency for capitalists to shift from industries with a high OC to industries with a low OC (which, incidentally, is inconsistent with Marx's view of capitalism as characterized by the rapid growth of constant capital) and says that the resulting change in the relationship of supply to demand of the various commodities will bring about the equalization of profit rates. Sometimes he says that the prices of raw materials or wage rates can be unequal among industries, thus bringing about a deviation of prices from values. Sometimes he speaks of the deviation as constituting an 'infraction' of economic laws, or notes that the individual capitalist may garner a larger share of the pool of surplus value by means of 'the sharpness of his business wits'. Comments of this sort invite one to make various interpretations: for example, that Marx abandoned his labour theory of value; or that it was never meant to be a theory of the market process; or that he did not really analyse capitalism in terms of a model of perfect competition, except as a first approximation.

Every interpretation (and these are only a few of those that have been advanced) generates difficulties of its own. If Marx abandoned the labour theory of value, what then is the status of his theory of exploitation? If the theory is not an analysis of market processes, then *Capital* lacks an explanation of the central organizing mechanism of a capitalist economy. If capitalism is not modelled on the assumption of perfect competition, then where do we find Marx's true model, since it is not in *Capital*? The discussion of the transformation problem has continued unabated since Volume III of *Capital* was published and has overshadowed all other aspects of Marxian theory in the literature of technical economics, Marxist and non-Marxist economists, with few exceptions, viewing the solution of the transformation problem as an issue upon which Marxian theory as a whole stands or falls. The debate has become increasingly complex, not to say scholastic, and there seems to be no end of it in sight.

Without claiming to offer a definitive interpretation of Marx's reasoning, I think we may obtain some useful insight into it by examining again the numerical illustration given above. Marx proceeds by assuming a certain rate of surplus value as a datum (RS = 1 in the above illustration). This enables him to calculate the aggregate surplus value of the economy (90). The several prices are then calculated by redistributing the aggregate surplus value so as to make RP equal in all industries. Why not proceed in the opposite direction? We could start with a certain RP as a datum (30 per cent), calculate the aggregate profit of the economy from it (90), and then redistribute it among the industries so as to equalize RS in all of them. In this way we would be 'transforming' prices into values rather than values into prices.

I have no doubt that Marx would have objected strongly to this alternative transformation as a gross misunderstanding of his theory of value. Value, in Marx's view, is *prior to* price. Price is merely the 'phenomenal form' of something more fundamental, though hidden – value. In scientific analysis one attempts to penetrate through the phenomenal appearances to the underlying forces and laws that govern them. The difference between Marx and the customary procedure of scientific analysis is that the latter undertakes to *infer* the underlying forces and laws from the observable phenomena, and regards such inferences as tentative and empirically testable. Marx viewed his law of value as unquestionably true; it is a metaphysical truth about the inherent nature of capitalism. We see here the elements of Platonic idealism and Aristotelian essentialism that Marx retained from his youthful studies in philosophy.

Many of the criticisms of Marx's theory of value focus upon its deficiencies as an explanation of the prices of commodities *relative* to one another. No theory of a market economy can be satisfactory without an adequate theory of relative prices, since it is these that constitute the main co-ordinating mechanism of such an economy. But Marx was fundamentally interested in the economy as a whole, and the relations of the capitalist class as a whole to the working class as a whole. The distribution of surplus value among industries and the sharing of it among the capitalists is a minor matter, compared to its aggregate magnitude. In the above numerical illustration we see that Marx arbitrarily assumed a rate of surplus value equal to 1, giving the working class and the capitalist class the same aggregate share of the net national income. Obviously, the extent to which capitalism is exploitive in Marxian terms depends upon this magnitude. The degree of exploitation varies directly with the size of RS and there would, of course, be no exploitation at all if RS were zero. The magnitude of RS depends upon a number of factors, the most important of which is the wage rate that the capitalist pays for the purchase of labour-power. We go on now to examine Marx's theory of the determination of the wage rate.

4. Wages

Any comprehensive model of a market-organized economy must account for the distribution of the national income as well as its production. This becomes very complex if the model attempts to incorporate the interactive effects of production and distribution on one another. Virtually all the prominent economists since Adam Smith have recognized this interaction, but prior to the modern development of 'general equilibrium' theory it was not possible to deal with it in a systematic way. Some interpreters of classical economics (and Marxian economics), most notably Samuel Hollander, view them as attempting to present a general equilibrium model of the economy that was deficient, not in basic conception, but in the limitations of the analytical tools they had to hand. A good case can be made for this but it seems to me that, even if the older economists had the concept of general equilibrium in mind, they were so far from constructing an explicit model of it that simpler renditions are more accurate delineations of their actual achievements. One must resist the temptation to overinterpret earlier thinkers in the light of more modern knowledge. In Chapter 9 Ricardo's theory of distribution was presented in terms of accounting for the sharing of an already determined national income, and the same approach underlies the treatment of Marxian theory in this chapter. Ricardo worked with three factors of production, land, labour, and capital, corresponding to three classes of persons, landlords, labourers, and capitalists. Marx and Engels reduced the class structure to two categories, workers and the owners of the means of production, whose incomes consist respectively of wages and surplus value. The latter, we should remind ourselves, includes not only what is usually called (and Marx often called) 'profit', but also rent, interest, taxes, and the wages and salaries of those whose activities are not 'socially necessary' to the process of production.

Marx's theory of distribution is like Ricardo's in that one of the distributive shares is determined as a residual. Ricardo had three distributive categories, so he needed to construct primary theories of distribution for two of them, which are his theories of wages and rent. Marx had two categories and needed only one such primary theory, which is his theory of wages. Marx's 'surplus value', like Ricardo's 'profit', consists of the part of the national income that is left over. So our discussion of Marx's theory of wages in this section is, in fact, a general outline of his theory of income distribution. (Marx made no attempt to explain how aggregate surplus value is distributed between capitalists proper and the other recipients of it, and usually treated it simply as profit *tout court* in his analytical work.) Marx noted that the magnitude of surplus value is affected by such things as the length of the working day, the number of wage-earners in the family, and the intensity of work and other factors that influence its productivity, but his main focus was on the daily wage rate and I shall restrict the discussion here to his analysis of its determinants.

In the examination of Marx's theories of value and surplus value above we noted his insistence that the law of value applies to labour power just as it does to other commodities. Surplus value is due to the fact that when a capitalist hires a labourer for a day he obtains the right to have him work, say, X hours; but he pays him a wage that represents a smaller number of hours, say Y, since that is the amount of labour embodied in the commodities that the labourer can purchase with his wage. Surplus value, measured in labour hours, is simply $X - Y$. To say that the wage rate is determined by the labour embodied in the commodities purchasable by the wage is, however, not a theory of the wage rate unless one couples it with an explanation of the determinants of this basket of commodities – the 'real wage', in modern terminology.

Marx asserts that the real wage rate is determined by the quantity of commodities necessary to produce a labourer and to replace him; that is, by the 'subsistence' requirements of himself and his family. In the *Paris Manuscripts* and the *Communist Manifesto* the worker is pictured as living at the edge of subsistence in the strictly physiological sense, but in *Capital* Marx follows Ricardo and the other classical economists in using the term 'subsistence' to refer to a standard of living that is the established norm in the society: 'the necessities of life habitually required by the average labourer' (*Capital*, I, XVII). This standard of living is a datum in any particular time and place in Marx's view, but it may vary over time and be different in different societies. Marx did not provide any explanatory analysis of such variations in the subsistence norm and his theory of wages is therefore indeterminate for the same reason that Ricardo's is.

The notion of subsistence was incorporated into the Ricardian model as the basis of a proposition concerning the long-run supply of labour. Ricardo adopted Robert Malthus's theory of population, which stated that population would increase continuously if the wage rate were above subsistence, and decrease continuously if it were below it. The supply of labour was construed to be a simple function of population size, so, in effect, Ricardo argued that the wage rate could not deviate for long from the subsistence level, since changes in the supply of labour would always tend to bring it back to that level. As we saw in Chapter 9, the post-Ricardian classical economists, especially John Stuart Mill, argued that permanent improvement in the standard of living of the labouring class was conditional upon control of their procreational capacity. This could be achieved only by a rise in the worker's conception of 'subsistence'. If the standard of living were raised, and kept high long enough to become established as a social norm, workers would control their procreation and thus prevent the erosion of wages that would otherwise take place through a growing labour supply. In this way the variability of the notion of subsistence, though it introduced an element of formal indeterminacy in the classical economic model, was made the basis of their theory of sustainable economic progress. Adam Smith had noted earlier that a nation cannot be considered rich if the great majority of its members, the labourers, are poor. A century later, the most important of the neoclassical economists, Alfred Marshall, argued the merits of an 'economy of high wages' which, by controlling population through elevation of the subsistence norm, and by increasing the productivity of labour, would assure that the nation would become rich in Adam Smith's sense of the term (see below, Chapter 17 C).

This line of argument, which was becoming prominent in 'bourgeois' economics in Marx's time, was, of course, not in accord with his theory of capitalism or his prognosis of its historical development. Within the framework of his own economic model he could have used the Malthusian theory of population to explain why the working class could not expect any permanent amelioration of their miserable condition without the kind of fundamental changes in society that he envisaged as a consequence of the replacement of capitalism by communism. But Marx and Engels were totally opposed to the Malthusian theory. In his 'Outlines of a Critique of Political Economy' (1844), Engels called it 'the crudest, most barbarous theory that ever existed', expressing a view that Marx later adopted.

The notion of subsistence, despite its appearance in Marx's contention that the wage rate is determined by the law of value, does not play an important role in his economic model. For an understanding of his view of the determinants of the wage rate we have to look elsewhere. Some interpreters of Marx have focused upon remarks in *Capital* that suggest what modern terminology calls a 'bargaining power' theory of wages, the view that the wage rate is determined by the relative ability of workers and capitalists to force wages up or down by affecting the short-run supply of or demand for labour power. Since the capitalist can hold out longer than the worker can, he has the greater bargaining power and wages are therefore forced down to a minimum. This conception of the labour market, which Adam Smith expressed clearly in his treatment of wages, is consistent with Marx's view that the organization of workers into labour unions can effect an increase in wage rates above the level that would be in accord with the law of value. In *Value, Price, and Profit*, which was written when his work on *Capital* was nearly finished, Marx argued, against the contention of the classical economists, that labour unions can alter the distribution of the national income between workers and capitalists. But this argument is not consistent with the perfect competition assumption of Marx's economic model, which leaves no room for bargaining power in the determination of market prices. Most modern interpreters of Marx look elsewhere for an understanding of his theory of wages, focusing upon his view that capitalism is characterized by unemployment, which, by providing a 'reserve army of labour', exerts downward pressure upon the rate of wages.

Unemployment plays the same role in the Marxian model that Malthusian population theory does in the classical model. It explains why wages are held down to the subsistence level by the behaviour of the supply of labour. In order to complete the Marxian explanation of wage rates, a theory of unemployment is required. Marx disagreed with Ricardo's contention that unemployment, as more than a transitory disequilibrium condition, is impossible in a market economy, and totally rejected 'Say's law' upon which this was based, calling it a 'childish dogma'. Some interpreters of Marx see him as a forerunner of John Maynard Keynes, who, in the 1930s, constructed the first theory of unemployment that orthodox economists found analytically acceptable, but this is an example of overinterpretation, requiring a reading into *Capital* of modern ideas that are not demonstrably there.

Marx does not present a systematic discussion of unemployment in *Capital* or elsewhere in his writings but from scattered remarks one can construct two embryonic theories: that the technological dynamism of capitalism steadily displaces labour from older occupations and forces workers to throw themselves on the labour market; and that the cyclical character of economic activity under capitalism (which Marx viewed as becoming steadily more severe) recurrently forces many workers into the reserve army of the unemployed. The first of these notions goes back to the eighteenth century, when industrialism was beginning to displace workers from the handicraft industries and there was much discussion as to whether they could be absorbed in the new occupations, a discussion that continues today. Ricardo considered the question in his *Principles of Political Economy* (1817) in an ambiguous way which raised qualifications to his general acceptance of Say's law (for which Marx complimented him). The cyclical behaviour of the market economy became a matter of considerable discussion during the mid-nineteenth century, which focused mainly upon the not infrequent financial 'crises' that were often followed by depression conditions. Engels used the term 'reserve army' to refer to the unemployed in his *Condition of the Working Class in England* (1845) and connected unemployment with the periodic crises of the economy in his 'Outlines'. The empirical analysis of cycles began with Clément Juglar's *Les Crises commerciales et leur retour périodique en France, en Angleterre et aux Etats-Unis* (1862). Although Marx did not construct a systematic theory of economic cycles, many historians of economics credit him with a pioneering role in their investigation. This has less to do with the role of cycles in Marx's theory of wages than with his proposition that increasingly severe fluctuations in economic activity are one of the 'laws of motion' of capitalism, which we shall examine in the next section.

One of the main difficulties of Marx's theory of wages is that it does not seem to be consistent with his view of capitalism as a social order that is characterized by exceptionally rapid accumulation of productive facilities such as factories, machinery, and the other things he included under the category 'constant capital'. If constant capital yields no surplus value, why does the capitalist invest in it? A sum of money used to purchase machines and buildings returns no more to the capitalist than what he has paid for them, while a similar sum paid out in wages yields a profit through the unique capacity of 'living labour' to generate surplus value. Even if one were to accept Marx's value–price transformation and grant that the individual capitalist does not retain the surplus value generated in his own enterprise, it is difficult to see why capitalists should be motivated to invest in constant capital, either individually or as a class. This raises two associated problems: What accounts for the tendency for constant capital to be accumulated at an unprecedently rapid rate during the capitalist stage of historical evolution? And why do capitalists not demand the profit-generating part of capital, that is, labour, with such avidity that the wage rate rises, and keeps on rising until there is no surplus value at all? Marx did not address these problems directly, and it is not possible to say with assurance what his response would have been. Some interpreters of Marxian theory argue that the individual capitalist is construed as being able to obtain a transitory increase in profit by introducing cost-decreasing constant capital in his own enterprise, and this motivates all to do so. This is consistent with neoclassical economic theory, and perhaps even with Volume I of *Capital*, but it cannot be argued within the framework of Volume III, for there, as we have seen, Marx contends that the individual capitalist does not retain the surplus value generated by his own labour force. One may perhaps resolve this difficulty by recognizing that Marx views the capitalist as having motives that are somewhat different from those assumed by the classical economists or by orthodox modern ones. In those models the capitalist maximizes profit in order to enjoy a high standard of living. Marx's capitalist is different. It is not the enjoyment of use or consumption that he seeks, but the pleasure of pure *possession*. If the motive of the capitalist were personal consumption, capitalism would be destroyed 'root and branch', says Marx, since capital would not be accumulated. The driving force of the system, however, is that the desire to accumulate wealth dominates the behaviour of the capitalist class. For this class there is only one maxim: 'Accumulate, accumulate! That is Moses and the Prophets!' (*Capital*, I, XXIV). Such a conception of capitalist psychology may be invoked to explain why capitalists invest in constant capital while it is variable capital that generates surplus value.

I do not know whether this notion played such a crucial role in Marx's thinking, since he did not argue explicitly in this fashion. It may be worth noting, though, that the conception of the economic agent (not just the capitalist) as desiring to acquire wealth is implicit in the classical economists' disregard of consumption as an economic phenomenon. John Stuart Mill stated firmly that political economy is concerned only with production and distribution, not with consumption, and that it restricts its conception of man to that of 'a being who desires to possess wealth ... it shows man accumulating wealth, and employing that wealth in the production of other wealth ... ('On the Definition of Political Economy'). In construing the capitalist in this way, Marx was not deviating from the conception of economic agents that the orthodox economists adopted for heuristic purposes in limiting their attention to the supply side of the market mechanism. Moreover, it would be hard to deny that the desire to accumulate wealth acted in fact as a strong motivation of action in Victorian England. Even after the analysis of consumption had been developed, and integrated into the corpus of economic theory, the desire to save, in order to accumulate wealth, has continued to be emphasized, most notably perhaps in Max Weber's famous thesis on the connection between Calvinism and the development of capitalism (see Chapter 15 C 3) and in John Maynard Keynes's analysis of the problem of unemployment (Chapter 17 D).

5. The laws of motion of capitalism

In the discussion of the Marxian theory of history in section B above we noted that the laws of historical evolution lie on two levels. The *general* laws consist of the propositions that historical events are governed by 'material' factors; that historical development proceeds through distinct stages; that all stages are characterized by class conflict; and that the transition from one stage to another takes place because of endogenous developments that create incompatibilities or 'contradictions' between the system of production and the mode of economic organization. The *specific* laws are propositions that detail how the last two of these general laws function in a particular historical stage. In this section we examine the Marxian analysis of the specific laws of capitalism. Following the practice of most commentators, these will be treated as four related propositions: (1) the tendency for the rate of profit to decline; (2) the increasing misery of the working class; (3) the tendency for the ownership of capital to become concentrated; and (4) the increasing severity of economic fluctuations. These propositions have been subject to a great deal of discussion and criticism over the past century, since upon them hinges the validity of Marx's prediction that capitalism cannot be sustained indefinitely and is doomed to break down from its own internal contradictions. Marx and Engels were convinced that this breakdown was imminent in England and Western Europe in their own day. The failure of this to occur, and the rise of communist states in other countries, has generated a large literature, but we cannot undertake to survey it here, or to examine the extensive literature criticizing and interpreting the Marxian 'laws of motion of capitalism' in theoretical terms. As elsewhere in this chapter, the main object is to provide a critical explanation of Marxian theory.

We might note before we begin to examine these laws of motion that they are contained in embryo in the earliest writings of Marx and Engels on economic questions. The proposition that the rate of profit tends to decline can be found in Marx's *Paris Manuscripts*; the increasing misery of the working class in the *Communist Manifesto* and other early writings; and the tendency to concentration and to increasingly severe economic fluctuations in Engels's 'Outlines of a Critique of Political Economy'. Without unreasonable distortion, *Capital* can be viewed as aimed at amplifying, and providing a scientific basis for, these very early ideas of Marx and Engels.

1. *The falling rate of profit*. The law of the falling rate of profit is the primary 'law of motion' in the Marxian theory of capitalism, since it is the one that is derived most directly from Marx's economic model, and the other laws, at least in certain interpretations of them, are based upon it. The reasoning that forms the basis of the falling rate of profit is quite straightforward. Recall the ratios that Marx used in his economic analysis: the rate of profit ($RP = S/C + V$), the rate of surplus value ($RS = S/V$), and the organic composition

of capital (OC = C/V). If we take the RP equation and divide the numerator and denominator of its right side by V we obtain:

$$RP = \frac{RS}{OC + 1}$$

It follows immediately from this that RP is determined by RS and OC, varying directly with the former and inversely with the latter. With RS a given magnitude, the law of the falling rate of profit is a consequence of the growth of constant capital, which Marx held to be an outstanding feature of capitalism. The contradictory nature of capitalism is thus plain: the unlimited desire of the bourgeois class to accumulate private property leads to an erosion of the source of that accumulation.

We saw in Chapter 9 that Ricardo had also argued that the rate of profit tends to decline, but his theory was quite different from Marx's. Ricardo's model was based upon the law of diminishing returns in agriculture, which, by increasing the cost of food production as population increases, raises the wage rate that is necessary to provide subsistence for the labourer, and thus lowers profit. The law of diminishing returns is also the basis of the proposition one finds in modern neoclassical theory and in Keynesian theory that the rate of profit tends to fall as capital is accumulated. But Marx did not use the law of diminishing returns in his economic model. It is difficult to extend his reasoning about the declining rate of profit beyond the above equation to the *economics* of the matter without the law of diminishing returns, but Marx was almost certainly aware that the use of that law would fatally undermine his basic theories of value and surplus value.

In comparing Marx's theory of profit to classical and modern economics, a more serious error would be to de-emphasize the different implications drawn from them by their proponents. Ricardo concluded that the economy would proceed over the long term to a 'stationary state' which would be stable. John Stuart Mill, the most widely read of the classical economists, argued that the stationary state could be a good society, if appropriate institutional arrangements were made to decrease the inequality of income. Alfred Marshall contended that the future looked even brighter than the previous century of progress because the growth of capital and other factors would raise the real wages of the working class, without consequences to the capitalist system beyond making it more civilized. John Maynard Keynes, the founder of modern macro-economics, argued that the capital stock of a country like England could be increased in one generation to the level that any sensible person could desire, with a corresponding worthy decline in property income ('the euthanasia of the rentier'), if full employment could be maintained. The implications that Marx drew from his law of the declining rate of profit were very different: capitalism is doomed to be destroyed as completely as feudalism was, or more so. Marx would have no truck with the social meliorists of his own day such as Mill, and he would not have had any with those who have dominated the literature of Western economics and social thought since then.

Marx refers to the law of the falling rate of profit as a 'tendency', recognizing that there are numerous factors that can offset it. One of these, increased labour productivity, is a serious admission. If it is granted that machinery and the other components of constant capital increase labour productivity, then in terms of the above equation that defines the determinants of the rate of profit, OC and RS increase together and it is not possible to say anything about RP without knowing which increase is the greater, an issue that Marx did not address. Theoretical difficulties aside, there is no empirical evidence that the rate of profit has experienced a secular decline in mature capitalistic economies. This is so even for profit as defined in orthodox economics, so Marx's profit, which includes rent, interest, taxes, and a substantial part of wage and salary income, has proved to be even more impervious to what he considered to be the inexorable processes of a capitalist economy. Many modern Marxists have abandoned the notion that there is a 'law of the falling rate of profit'.

2. *Increasing misery.* Marx's 'immiseration' law, the proposition that the lot of the worker tends to worsen under capitalism, may be derived directly from his law of the falling rate of profit, though the two seem to contradict one another at first sight. Marx's argument is that the capitalist, pressed by the tendency of the profit rate to decline, presses the worker in turn, forcing down wages, increasing the length of the working day, speeding up his machinery and adopting other means of increasing the 'intensity' of labour.

In the mid-nineteenth century very little systematic information was available on trends in real wages and working conditions, even in England, where the best data were to be had. Marx and Engels were not alone in their opinion that the worker was suffering a progressive deterioration in his condition under industrialism. The anecdotal evidence furnished by witnesses before Royal Commissions inquiring into such matters, which Marx quoted at length, painted a ghastly picture that horrified the educated members of the upper classes. Not until the 1880s did reliable data become available, which showed that real wages had been rising, probably since the end of the Napoleonic wars. At any rate, it can no longer be argued today as a general proposition that the material condition of the working class tends to fall in capitalist societies, since, during the past century at least, real wages have risen, the length of the working day has been reduced and there are more holidays, and the intensity of labour has declined in most occupations.

Observing these developments in the later nineteenth century, Eduard Bernstein called for a basic revision in Marxian theory (*Evolutionary Socialism*, 1898), but Karl Kautsky, who had taken Engels's place as its authoritative interpreter, contended that Marx had never argued a thesis of *absolute* immiseration and that Marxian theory still stood firm, since the *relative* standard of living of the working class was declining. Both interpretations of immiseration can be supported by numerous quotations from *Capital* and other texts. Kautsky's interpretation, however, is insufficient to save the immiseration law from empirical attack, since the burden of statistical evidence seems to show that the relative income of the working class has not been falling and, most probably, has been rising over the past century.

3. *The concentration of capital*. Marx did not present a sustained discussion of the forces that lead to the concentration of capital but in scattered remarks he anticipated the essential elements of the modern theory of imperfect competition. The classical economists generally followed Adam Smith in attributing restrictions of competition to governmental policies that gave special privileges to the favoured few by limiting the ability of firms to enter exceptionally profitable industries. Marx was hostile to any explanations of economic phenomena that resorted to such optional actions rather than to the functioning of objective laws. He predicted that capital would become concentrated because the technical nature of industry makes it advantageous to produce in large enterprises. In modern terminology, he saw 'natural' concentrations as emerging owing to 'economies of scale'. Large enterprises produce more efficiently than small ones, because of the greater opportunities they afford for division of labour. The smaller enterprises cannot survive in the competitive market and disappear, with their owners joining the ranks of the proletariat. Marx did not suggest that concentration enables the surviving firms to manipulate the economy at will. They are in fierce competition with one another, and economic phenomena are still governed by economic laws: the view one finds today in a standard textbook treatment of 'oligopoly'. The increasingly large amounts of capital required run beyond the personal resources of the individual capitalist, so capital must be drawn together from many sources, which is facilitated by the development of the financial system of capitalism. Marx saw clearly the technological and organizational factors that have been prominent in the development of industrial economies during the century following his death.

Unlike the modern orthodox theorist, however, Marx did not consider that this tendency to concentration would lead to a stable state. What was happening, in his view, was the development of inefficiencies in the use of productive resources despite the economies of scale and, more significantly, workers were becoming increasingly 'socialized' in the large establishments while the capitalists were still engaged in a competitive struggle with one another. This prepares the way for the breakdown of capitalism, by strengthening the solidarity of the proletariat and preventing the capitalist class from forming a united resistance when the day of revolution dawns. One of Marx's most frequently quoted apocalyptic passages makes a direct connection between the growth of concentration and the breakdown of capitalism:

> The monopoly of capital becomes a fetter upon the mode of production, which has sprung up and flourished along with it, and under it. Centralisation of the means of production and socialisation of labour at

last reach a point where they become incompatible with their capitalist integument. This integument is burst asunder. The knell of capitalist private property sounds. The expropriators are expropriated. (*Capital*, I, XXXII)

4. *Economic fluctuations*. Marx was not the first economist to draw attention to the phenomenon of economic fluctuations but he was the first to discuss it as requiring a general theoretical explanation in terms of factors endogenous to the market economy, rather than attributing particular cycles to specific exogenous events such as wars or bad harvests. Such occurrences, in Marx's view, acted as no more than the immediate causes of developments that were really due to the contradictory nature of capitalism. Engels, who viewed the market economy as chaotic, attributed the cyclical behaviour of capitalism, like many other of its features, to its 'planlessness', but this is too general to constitute an explanatory theory. Marx's discussion of the problem recognizes that a good theoretical explanation must be sufficiently general to embrace a large number of non-identical instances of a phenomenon and yet not so general that it embraces everything else as well.

Marx did not devote a major section of *Capital* to the discussion of economic fluctuations but he frequently commented upon the subject in the discussion of other matters. From these brief passages what emerges cannot be described as a systematic theory of the cyclical phenomenon, but a number of suggested explanations which anticipate almost all the major lines of cycle theory that have been developed during the past century. For example, Marx noted the intimate connection between fluctuations in production and the behaviour of the monetary system; he anticipated the Keynesian emphasis upon the lack of synchronization between saving and investment; he suggested the possibility of undesired inventory changes due to a lack of adjustment between production and sales; he realized that Ricardo's admission that there can be an imbalance between the commodity structure of production and that of demand was more serious than Ricardo was willing to admit; he anticipated Joseph Schumpeter's contention that cyclical behaviour is intimately connected with the process of economic growth.

Most of the commentators on this aspect of Marx's economics have emphasized two more general suggestions that focus on the downward side of the cycle rather than the cycle as a whole: the effect of a discrete reduction in the rate of profit; and the difficulty of 'realizing' surplus value. Concerning the first of these, Marx seems to have had the idea that, in the short run, an exceptionally rapid accumulation of capital can result in demand pressure on the labour market, which raises the wage rate. The resulting discrete fall in the profit rate creates a crisis which ends the boom and sends the economy into a depression. The realization problem results from the inequality of income distribution. The income of the working class cannot provide sufficient aggregate demand for the commodities that are produced, and the capitalist class, intent as it is upon accumulating rather than consuming, does not fill the deficiency. The result is that capitalists find that they cannot 'realize' the surplus value they have extracted from the workers; that is, they cannot complete the M–C–M' process of turning commodity-capital back into money-capital. The capitalist system is contradictory, which becomes manifest here in the phenomena of falling prices, falling profits, and depression. This argument was emphasized by one of the leading Marxist economists of the early twentieth century, Rosa Luxemburg (*The Accumulation of Capital*, 1913), and more recently by Paul Baran and Paul Sweezy (*Monopoly Capital*, 1966), who argue that a law of rising surplus value should replace Marx's law of the falling rate of profit as the fundamental proposition in the dynamic model of capitalism. The notion of realization easily connects with the idea that a capitalist economy is driven to imperialism in order to obtain markets for its surplus production and, through this, it has become one of the prominent features of modern Marxism.

None of these arguments is sufficient to sustain the contention that capitalism is characterized by *increasingly severe* economic fluctuations. During the 1930s this was commonly regarded as a proposition that needed no analytic demonstration and, until the publication of J. M. Keynes's *General Theory of Employment, Interest, and Money* (1936), Marxian theory was regarded even by many non-Marxists as offering clues at least to the most serious malaise of capitalism. The decline of Marxian economics since the second World War is due largely to the development of Keynesian macroeconomics and to the fact that the fluctuations in economic activity that have occurred have been mild. No one can deny that any economic system that fails to use its productive resources fully while there are many needs and wants unsatisfied is 'contradictory', but it seems less likely today than in Marx's time that such difficulties presage the breakdown of economies that use the market mechanism as their primary mode of organization.

6. The economics of communism

We noted above that in *Capital* Marx undertook to present an economic analysis of capitalism. In all the more than two thousand pages that constitute its three volumes there are no more than a few scattered remarks referring to the economic order that Marx envisaged as the successor stage in the historical process. Some further material on this can be gathered from other writings of Marx and Engels, but the total is meagre in the extreme. One of the *Paris Manuscripts* deals with the future society, but it focuses almost entirely upon its social-psychological characteristics and provides little information concerning its economy. In the *Communist Manifesto* Marx and Engels put forward a ten-point programme concerning what will occur immediately after the revolution when the proletariat comes to power, and twenty-seven years later Marx wrote some twenty pages of notes in criticism of a programme advanced by the Lassallean socialists ('Critique of the Gotha Programme') which afford some information on this question. These, and some scattered remarks in other texts, are all one has to go on in attempting to ascertain the Marxian conception of communism. At a meeting in Brussels in 1846 Marx demanded that Wilhelm Weitling, who advocated immediate open warfare against the propertied class, should furnish a detailed account of what the proletariat might do when they had won such a struggle. When Weitling failed to meet this demand, Marx shouted that 'ignorance has never yet helped anyone' and stormed from the room (Isaiah Berlin, *Karl Marx: His Life and Environment*, 1959, p. 110). But he himself never provided such a programme.

From the materials available, one can say that Marx and Engels envisaged communist society as having a technologically advanced system of production which would provide a high material standard of living, with a working day shortened to allow much free time for other activities. They did not have in mind the restoration of a simpler, predominantly agrarian, economy. They rejected totally the idea that man's freedom from economic necessity is to be found in diminishing his wants rather than increasing his productive powers, as was argued by Proudhon and Bakunin. They rejected also the view held by orthodox economists since Adam Smith that division of labour was essential to high productivity. It may have contributed to productivity in an earlier period but was no longer necessary in an era of high technology and great capital accumulation. Under capitalism the division of labour had become the basis of class division, the enslavement of the worker to the owners of capital, and the degradation of creative work into meaningless toil. Under communism there would no longer be division of labour in the sense of personal specialization, and work would become man's way of satisfying the creative urge which is the most fundamental constituent of human nature. The capitalist system of commodity exchange, using money as its medium, would disappear, since there would no longer be 'commodities' identifiable as the products of specific labour. All such labour would be undifferentiated parts of 'social labour' and all specific goods would be part of a common pool of social production. In the initial stages of the transformation after the revolution, workers would deliver their production to this common pool and receive in return certificates denominating the amount of labour it represented; these certificates would then permit each worker to withdraw an equivalent amount of goods from the common pool for his personal use. Under full communism this system of distribution would no longer be necessary, being replaced by the general rule: 'From each according to his ability, to each according to his needs'.

These comments on the nature of communism strike responsive chords among modern scholars who look at Marxian theory from the standpoint of sociology and political science, but economists, including Marxist ones, are left uneasy about them. They give no indication as to how the communist economy will be organized as a co-ordinated system. How will the allocation of labour and other productive resources be determined so as to produce the mixture of consumer goods that people want? What will assure that the total production equals what the members of society seek to withdraw from the common pool to meet their 'needs'? How will provision be made for what modern economics calls 'public goods', such as roads, street cleaning, sewage disposal, etc.? How will provision be made for the replacement of worn-out capital? Will the capital stock of the society be increased and, if so, how will it be determined how much of society's productive potential should be devoted to this purpose rather than immediate consumption? Such issues are not mere technicalities; no sketch of a social system is minimally adequate without satisfactory answers to them.

Marx and Engels furnished very little information that would enable one to construct a model of the communist economy which addresses these matters. In his criticism of the Lassallean 'Gotha Program', Marx pointed out that it was naive to suppose that the workers could receive the total proceeds of their labour, since provision must be made for capital replacement and expansion, insurance against accidents and natural calamities, administrative costs, public goods, and the support of those unable to work; but he gave no indication, there or elsewhere, as to how these provisions would be determined. Engels mentioned similar issues, and there is some reason to believe that he had given more thought to the economic organization of communism than Marx, since he repeatedly noted that a fundamental feature of it would be the organization of the economy by means of a system of centralized economic administration or 'planning'. Though Marx himself said virtually nothing on this score, the conception of a planned economy has become the main identifying feature of communism and is regarded by many as the central doctrine of Marxian theory. Engels's comments on this point, however, are too vague and too inconsistent to enable one to construct from them a coherent model of communist economic organization. One might naturally assume that when private property is abolished the state becomes its formal owner, and that economic planning becomes a state function, but it was Engels also who advanced the proposition that after the revolution the state progressively 'withers away' and under communism no such entity remains. Communism is not a market economy and yet Engels argues at one point (in his preface to the first German edition of Marx's *Poverty of Philosophy*, 1884) that a price system is absolutely necessary to economic organization and that only competitive market processes can furnish a correct structure of prices. His remark, forty years earlier in his 'Outlines', that capitalist competition must not be confused with *'true* competition, such as will be established when the time comes', does not clarify matters.

So far as economic planning itself is concerned, Engels said nothing as to its procedures. Occasional remarks indicate that he regarded it as such a simple matter that it could be carried out by clerks and accountants with ease.

This notion, which has antecedents in the utopian literature, was strongly expressed by V. I. Lenin in his *State and Revolution*, written just weeks before he became the leader of the new Soviet state. Needless to say, events proved unkind to the theory and, after many difficulties, and changes in economic policy, the U.S.S.R. became the most state-dominated of modern economies and the one most committed to comprehensive centralized planning and administration of economic processes. The idea of a planned economy has become a central tenet of almost all schools of modern Marxism and, as the recent upheavals in Eastern Europe indicate, the notions of central economic planning and the political dominance of committed Marxists stand or fall together.

Some critics of Marxian theory reserve their strongest condemnation for its failure to provide any significant information on the structure and functioning of the communist economy. This is indeed a serious omission if one regards the debate between market organization and central planning as bearing upon a matter of human valuation and choice. How can one say that economic planning is superior to the market mechanism without even a conjectural model of the former? This is, however, not a trenchant critique of Marx within the framework of his own philosophy. In Marx's view, 'material conditions' govern events, and the course of historical development is not determined by any valuational or optional factors. Capitalism *will* break down and communism *will* succeed it. The economic organization of communism will be determined by the new relationship that pertains between the 'forces of production' and the 'relations of production'. According to Marx, this is all that a scientist can say about it without abandoning science for speculative utopianism.

E. PHILOSOPHY

Marx's first scholarly interest was in philosophy. This developed when he was a student at the University of Berlin under the influence of the engrossing academic interest there at that time in idealistic philosophy and the revival of metaphysics by the followers of G. W. F. Hegel. If it had not been for the hostility of the authorities to the early expressions of his political radicalism and the dismissal of his patron, Bruno Bauer, Marx would probably have obtained an academic position instead of embarking on a career of radical journalism which led, through his friendship with Engels, to his devoting the most creative period of his life to economics. Nevertheless, he remained a philosopher, and his economic theory is intimately connected with his philosophical outlook. In discussing Marx's economics, and the other aspects of his social science, in this chapter we have had to refer repeatedly to his philosophical position in order to clarify our understanding of matters that the modern social scientist regards as having little to do with philosophy. In this section I will try to draw the philosophical references of the preceding sections together and provide a more coherent elucidation of Marxian philosophy.

In Marx's writings there is a great deal of discussion of philosophical questions, but there is no systematic extended presentation of his views on epistemology, metaphysics, or ethics. In fact, the most complete statement of Marxian philosophy in a single document was written by Engels, his *Anti-Dühring*, which itself is mainly a critique of another philosophy rather than a systematic presentation of the Marxian one. Nevertheless, Marxian social science rests upon Marxian philosophy and we must try to piece the latter together in order to understand the former. In this section I shall proceed by discussing Marxian philosophy under the conventional headings of Epistemology, Metaphysics, and Ethics. This would probably not be accepted by Marx and Engels, since they regarded their philosophical outlook as an integrated whole, and I shall not be able to stick rigorously to it, but it will serve for purposes of exposition.

1. Epistemology

Throughout this history of the social sciences I have repeatedly stressed the significance of the development of the natural sciences on Western social thought. The physicists of the seventeenth century, by detaching their areas of human inquiry from theology, paved the way for social thinkers to do likewise. In demonstrating the effectiveness of a method of investigation that united empirical observation with formal analysis, they provided not only an inspiration but a methodological guide. Some writers on social matters claimed affinity to Galileo and Newton purely for promotional reasons, but most of the great figures in the development of the social sciences sincerely attempted, not always with success, to construct social theories that would satisfy the epistemological principles exemplified by natural science. Marx and Engels, the latter especially, were very impressed with the natural sciences and, as socialists, they sought to replace the traditional dependence of socialist thought upon speculation and utopianism with a scientific theory of society. A great deal of philosophy, in their view, was no more than theology with a different terminology, and a great deal of social theory was no more than propaganda on behalf of the ruling class. The task of 'scientific socialism' that they set themselves, was to construct a theory of society based upon the 'material' constituents of social life. Hegel had pointed the way to a scientific analysis of society through his concept of 'dialectic', but had turned things upside down by regarding man's history in terms of the operation of spiritual factors instead of material ones.

The only social theories prior to their own that Marx and Engels regarded as approaching scientific status were the economic models of the Physiocrats and Ricardo. But these too, they believed, had been converted into apologetic instruments by the 'vulgar economists' and it was necessary to construct a scientific analysis of society virtually from the ground up. Marx and Engels felt that ideological rationalization always plays a role in human thought, even in science, but this can be overcome by a strong determination to be objective and a proper appreciation of the principles of scientific method. Marx was confident that he had accomplished this transcendence in his own work. Today the sharpest point of controversy between Marxists and non-Marxists relates to this issue, Marxists contending that Marxian theory, despite its weaknesses on specific points, is *the* objectively scientific theory of society, while non-Marxists see it as epistemologically flawed, some even regarding it as belonging more to speculative metaphysics than to positive science (see, for example, M. Blaug, *A Methodological Appraisal of Marxian Economics*, 1980).

As a philosophical outlook, modern Marxism is frequently described as 'dialectical materialism'. Marx and Engels never used this term themselves. It was coined by the Russian Marxist G. V. Plekhanov in the 1890s. Lenin adopted it as a way of distinguishing Marxian theory from other types of materialism and, after the Russian Revolution, it became the established term for the philosophical description of communism. Whether Marx and Engels would have approved of this we do not know, but they did regard their philosophical outlook as 'dialectical' and 'materialistic', so it would not seem improper to join these notions together. The concept of 'materialism' has already been discussed, especially in section B of this chapter, dealing with the Marxian theory of historical development. Here I will try to give an account of what is denoted by the term 'dialectic'.

The word itself is derived direct from a classical Greek one which referred to the mode of philosophical discourse initiated by Zeno in which the writer presents his argument in the form of a conversation between two or more parties. In the *Republic*, which is in this form, Plato uses the term 'dialectic' more specifically to refer to the method by which the true philosopher may transcend the mere empirical appearances of particular phenomena and acquire knowledge of the universal 'pure form' of reality. Beyond saying that this method relies upon 'reason and understanding' rather than upon information furnished by the senses, Plato gives no indication of what he means by 'dialectic'. Presumably he viewed the *Republic* as defining it by example. As used by Marx and Engels, the concept derives more directly from epistemological and metaphysical propositions advanced by Hegel.

Throughout the eighteenth century, the philosophy of empiricism, which was becoming ever more dominant in natural science, failed to win the degree of approval among European philosophers that it did in the English-speaking world. Descartes's view, that the nature of the real world can be deduced logically from a few self-evident primary propositions, was accepted by many of the leading European philosophers. In his *Critique of Pure Reason* (1781), Immanuel Kant attempted to provide a compelling criticism of Cartesian 'rationalism', while at the same time rescuing empiricism from the sceptical implications of Hume's insistence that mental processes cannot go beyond the data received through the senses. Kant's argument, in which he used the term 'dialectic', made a strong impact, but the thrust of his philosophy of science was blunted by Hegel, whose writings, though extremely obscure, turned German philosophy away from empiricism towards idealism and metaphysics. As we have already noted, it was Hegelian philosophy that was the object of great interest among professors and students in Germany when Marx and Engels were in their youth.

Hegel's concept of dialectic is usually presented in the form of a triadic sequence: thesis, antithesis, synthesis. Hegel never used this schema explicitly but it seems to be a satisfactory way of capturing his concept of dialectic. Marx and Engels did not use the triadic expression, either, but their terms 'negation' and 'negation of the negation' seem to embody the same essential idea as Hegel's dialectic. The 'seem to' hedges in the above two sentences indicate that it is not at all clear, even after many years of scholarly effort, what Hegel, or Marx and Engels, meant by dialectic. The only extended discussion of it in the Marxian literature is in Engels's *Anti-Dühring*, which does not provide much clarification, and includes some examples of what Engels regarded as dialectical processes that are so patently absurd that they have been gleefully quoted ever since by anti-Marxists. (One recent writer contends that dialectic was 'invented' by Engels, and represents a distortion of Marx's epistemological views: Terrell Carver, *Marx and Engels*, 1983, chapter 4.) Marx and Engels made no explicit use of the dialectic as a methodology in their social science writings, so it is not possible to elucidate its meaning by reference to their practice.

The most general idea that is associated with the concept of dialectic in the Hegelian and Marxian texts is an emphasis upon the non-static character of reality, which harks back to the view expressed by Heraclitus, a fifth-century B.C. Greek philosopher, that reality is in a continuous state of motion and change. The world, said Hegel, is always in a process of *becoming* something different from what it is at any moment. Every seemingly static state of affairs necessarily generates an opposing tendency; the new state which results from the conflict, however, is no more stable than the former, for opposing forces appear again, and so the process that J. G. Fichte characterized as 'thesis–antithesis–synthesis' continues. The history of the world is not repetitious, however, for each successive synthesis represents a higher stage of development than its predecessor. The Marxian view that every social system experiences an endogenously generated conflict between the forces of production and the relations of production which eventuates in the emergence of a new social system is in accord with Hegel's concept of dialectical process. As Marx and Engels noted, their only disagreement with Hegel on this point was that he had identified the basic dialectical forces as spiritual rather than material. Hegel's philosophy was dialectical but not materialistic; the philosophy that followed Bacon and Locke, however, was materialistic but not dialectical. A true philosophy, which aims at comprehending a world of constant motion and change, must be both. One can see here the ground for the enthusiasm of Marx and Engels for Darwin's theory of evolution, since it dealt with the phenomenon of change by reference to material factors, and in a way that, with a little stretching, could be considered dialectical.

A limited interpretation of dialectic construes it as referring primarily to the process by which man acquires knowledge about the natural world rather than to the natural world itself. According to this view the dialectic is a proposition in intellectual sociology or descriptive epistemology. Knowledge increases as a result of a process that is conflictual: a thesis or theory is advanced, it is opposed by an antithesis, an alternative theory, and in due course a resolution is attained which includes elements of both in a new synthesis. As a description of the history of science this is virtually beyond dispute. Theories are effectively challenged only by other theories; the process of scientific development involves much dispute between the protagonists of an old theory and a new one; and intellectual development, like the evolution of organic species, is an historical process in which the present corpus reflects the route by which it developed from the past. As a *prescriptive* epistemology of science this interpretation of dialectic is indistinguishable from the liberal contention that scientific inquiry should be free from censorship and that any claims to authority by persons or established institutions should be rejected. Marx and Engels sometimes spoke in such terms. Engels pointed out that it would be 'sheer nonsense' to suppose that knowledge could reach a limit beyond which no further progress was possible, and all knowledge of reality must remain tentative (*Anti-Dühring*, I, III).

Much more questionable is the proposition that all science *must* be dialectical because the real world *is* dialectical in its essential nature. As we have seen, Marx and Engels took this view of social phenomena, arguing that all social development occurs because of the 'contradictions' that accumulate in social systems. Marx's description of communism as 'the negation of the negation' in the *Paris Manuscripts* and in *Capital* would be incomprehensible without recognition of its reference to dialectic. The idea that social evolution takes place through conflict, or what Marxian theory calls 'contradiction', or, if one insists, 'negation' and 'negation of negation', is not incomprehensible or, indeed, implausible as a social theory, but what is one to make of Engels's notion that *all* phenomena are dialectical? What is the negation and the negation of the negation in the orbits of the planets, or the process of cell division, or Mendeleev's table of the elements? Undoubtedly one could, with sufficient ingenuity, shave and batter natural phenomena to fit a dialectical schema, but one could do the same for any schema. Engels says, in the preface to the 1885 edition of *Anti-Dühring*, that he had undertaken to examine mathematics and natural science

in order to convince myself in detail – of which in general I was not in doubt – that amid the welter of innumerable changes taking place in nature, the same dialectical laws of motion are in operation as those which in history govern the apparent fortuitousness of events . . . .

This refers to a text which claims that the concepts of negation and negation of negation are exemplified by such things as the germination of a barley seed and the fact that the square of a negative quantity is a positive quantity.

More important than these absurdities is the contention that dialectic is really a new and superior type of logic. Although Engels made one or two remarks suggesting this, it is doubtful that he and Marx construed dialectic in this way. The modern Marxists who do so rest their interpretation on the notion that the Marxian concept of 'contradiction' is applicable to the basic axiom of formal logic known as the 'law of non-contradiction', which asserts that it is impermissible to hold directly contradictory propositions. For example, the statements 'The moon is made of cheese' and 'The moon is not made of cheese' cannot both be true. Marx and Engels did not use the term 'contradiction' in this logical sense; it was simply a strong way of referring to the empirical fact that in a changing world there are conflicting elements, such as the disharmony between the forces of production and the relations of production in advanced capitalism. If we were to construe this to mean that a study of empirical phenomena reveals that *formally* contradictory statements are logically permissible, the implications would be momentous. We could then assert with equanimity both that the moon *is* made of cheese and that it is *not*. What some Marxists seem to say when they claim that dialectic is a higher logic than orthodox logic is that the latter depends upon the acceptance of the law of non-contradiction, while the former does not. Armed with such a conception of dialectic, a Marxist could dismiss all the criticisms of Marxian theory we have noted in this chapter on the grounds that they employ orthodox logic. This may be effective as a debating stratagem but it destroys all ability to engage in constructive discourse, since, as K. R. Popper has shown (*Conjectures and Refutations*, chapter 15), rejection of the law of non-contradiction makes any and all propositions logically admissible. By using such a notion of dialectic one could dismiss Marxian theory too (or at least those parts of it that are logically coherent), and there would be no way of making an epistemological distinction between scientific propositions, untestable speculations, fantasies, or, indeed, totally meaningless strings of words and phrases. Hegel, the great protagonist of dialectic, advanced few scientific hypotheses, but wrote a great deal about the world as he fantasized it, and much that was incomprehensible.

As an epistemological doctrine, the notion of dialectic has made little headway among natural scientists, who, to the extent that they are influenced by philosophers at all, have deviated little from the methodology established by the scientists of the seventeenth century. The only exception worth comment is in the field of biology. More than any other branch of science, biology is concerned with phenomena of developmental change, and biologists with philosophical interests have never been fully satisfied with the mechanistic view of the world and the reductionist method of analysis. Repeatedly, efforts are made to orient biology towards a 'vitalist' view of phenomena and to promote a 'holistic' methodology. Among biologists who regard themselves as Marxists this frequently takes the form of asserting the superiority of the dialectical view of nature. One finds, for example, in Garland Allen's *Life Sciences in the Twentieth Century* (1978) the contention that modern biology has been flawed by failure to replace 'mechanistic materialism' with the 'dialectical materialism' that Marx had employed in his social science. The well known modern geneticist, R. C. Lewontin, has made similar pleas for the construction of a 'dialectical biology' (see, for example, *New York Review*, 20 January 1983). The rise of Trofim Lysenko as the authoritative leader of Soviet biology in the 1930s was due in no small part to the official adoption there of dialectics as the true philosophy of science. The disastrous effect of Lysenko on Soviet biological science and practical agriculture did a great deal to cool enthusiasm for the dialectical view, but it did not destroy it, since the understandable dissatisfaction of biologists with the mechanistic ontology and reductionist methodology remains.

In recent years, the espousal of 'holistic epistemology' has become prominent in Marxist literature. The connection between it and any of the above conceptions of dialectic, however, is unclear; the common ground that they are presumed to share may consist only of the obscurity that surrounds each. Moreover, it is not evident that Marx and Engels themselves consistently advocated, or practised, a holistic epistemology. In his preface to the first edition of *Capital*, Volume I, Marx claimed that his analysis of capitalism followed the epistemological mode of physics, without adding any of the qualifications one would expect if he were hostile to reductionism. There are passages in the writings of Marx and Engels suggesting a commitment to methodological individualism that are as definite as any that advocate holism. It is doubtful whether Marx and Engels gave much thought to this issue; at any rate they did not discuss it explicitly as a philosophical problem. Marxian social science in practice was a compound; the theories of class conflict and exploitation, for example, have distinct holistic qualities, while the theory of value is reductionist in the extreme.

Since the Scottish Enlightenment social scientists have tried to navigate the uncertain water between Scylla and Charybdis, recognizing on the one hand that social phenomena result from the decisions and actions of individuals, and on the other that mature persons are the products of social enculturation and that society is an entity in itself, not merely an aggregation of persons. Marx and Engels did not resolve the issue of reductionism versus holism, but criticizing them for failing to do so is demanding of them something that no one since, Marxist or non-Marxist, has succeeded in doing; indeed, it is doubtful whether it *can* be done. Methodological individualism, as a heuristic procedure, has demonstrated great power in modern economics, but the immaculate versions of it that one finds, for example, in 'Austrian economics' or the economics of the 'Chicago school' are inspired more by political ideology than by any general philosophy of science. (See Chapter 18 B 2 for further discussion of the individualism–holism issue in the philosophy of science.)

A great deal of the epistemological debate that has taken place in the social sciences concerns whether they can, like the natural sciences, construct explanatory models of universal applicability. Natural scientists have never doubted that this is the object of their work. When a model fails to agree with empirical experience, this is taken to mean that the model is defective or incomplete, not as evidence that different laws of nature operate at different times and places. Even the most convinced biological holist would not argue, say, that different laws of genetics are at work in Brazil and Australia, or that they are different now from what they were a century ago. Most natural scientists would regard such a time- and place-specific conception as destructive of science altogether. In the social sciences, however, model specificity is a respectable doctrine. Most sociologists, anthropologists, and political scientists are suspicious of models that claim unlimited generality, and some historians reject models altogether, claiming that historical events are too diverse to be brought under the rubric of any general laws. In fact, only economics has constructed models that are claimed to have the kind of universality that is characteristic of the natural sciences.

The position of Marx and Engels on this point seems, at first sight, to be ambiguous. In the *Paris Manuscripts* Marx says that all science must be based upon sense-perception, and predicts that, in time, a unified science will be constructed that embraces human and non-human phenomena in one comprehensive model. There can be little dispute as to the universality of the Hegelian–Marxian notion that dynamic phenomena are dialectical. On the other hand, Marx emphasized that every historical epoch is governed by laws that are specific to it, and his economic analysis of capitalism was aimed at discovering the 'laws of motion' that are peculiar to a competitive economy operating in a regime of private ownership of the means of production. He criticized the classical economists for claiming that their 'laws of political economy' are universally valid, not only because he regarded them as faulty, but because he considered any such claim to be epistemologically unacceptable. Engels, in *Anti-Dühring*, fiercely attacks the idea that it is possible to arrive at ultimate general truths in science, especially in the social sciences, where the basic nature of the phenomena is their inconstancy.

> Anyone [he says] who sets out in this field to hunt down . . . truths which are pure and absolutely immutable will bring home but little, apart from platitudes and commonplaces of the sorriest kind – for example, that generally speaking man cannot live except by labour; that up to the present mankind for the most part has been divided into rulers and ruled; that Napoleon died on 5 May 1821, and so on'. (I, IX)

Even logic and dialectics, he goes on to say, cannot be regarded as providing universal truths concerning the laws of human thought.

Marx and Engels were not unique in being much more critical of other theories than they were of their own. It is easy to accuse them of inconsistency in criticizing other social thinkers who viewed scientific laws as universally valid while frequently claiming this quality for their own model of society. Such an accusation is blunted, however, when we consider that, even in the most stringently modelled science, physics, laws are not really construed to be universal when it comes to explaining, or predicting, empirical phenomena. The law of gravitational attraction, for example, describes a universally operative force, but its applicability to specific empirical events depends upon the satisfaction of certain auxiliary conditions, such as the existence of a vacuum. The fact that leaves may fly upward in a wind, or that an aeroplane rarely approaches the earth with an acceleration of thirty-two feet per second, does not disprove the universality of the law; it demonstrates that the word 'universal' does not always mean what the dictionary says. The relation between 'laws' and 'conditions' is too complex a matter for us to examine here (even if philosophers had an agreed opinion on it), but it is sufficient for our purposes to note that the assertion that social laws are relative to time and place does not necessarily undermine the proposition that social phenomena are law-governed and may be modelled. It simply calls attention to the fact that all scientific models are human artefacts, heuristically constructed for analytical and practical purposes. There is little point in trying to impale Marxian theory on the horns of the universalist–relativist dilemma, and less merit in claiming that failure to grasp one of the horns leaves it in an epistemological void, since all scientific models are located there. In *Capital* we find a model constructed according to the same epistemological canons that Smith and Ricardo had adopted and that have been accepted by all the main schools of economics since: an abstract model, severely restricted in its elements, and relying upon a general *ceteris paribus* clause to define the conditions under which it operates.

The value of a scientific model depends upon (1) the degree to which it enables one to tackle the problems for which it was initially designed, compared to other models that are applicable to the same problems; (2) one's ability to relax its assumptions and still retain a coherent model; (3) the extent to which events that fail to conform to the model's predictions can be explained by a manageable examination of its 'conditions'; (4) its ability to generate propositions about the real world that are not attainable through simple observation and common sense; and (5) its fruitfulness in leading to the construction of a new and better, perhaps more general, model. The Marxian model has retained its power over the past century with respect to the first of these criteria, and finds favour among modern social scientists whose main interest derives from the perception of the capitalist market economy as a system of exploitive class relationships and the conviction (or hope) that it generates endogenous 'contradictions' which will lead to its ultimate destruction. On the other criteria, Marxian theory has proved, so far at least, to be unsturdy; but that is a scientific weakness, not an epistemological one. Many modern Marxists use the models of orthodox economics freely and without apology, grafting on to them, sometimes no more than rhetorically, references to such things as exploitation, class conflict, and the contradictions of capitalism.

2. Metaphysics

Most metaphysical systems are based upon religious or spiritual notions, but they need not be. In fact the significance of the development of the natural sciences since the seventeenth century is that they were creating a new world outlook, moulding the Western mind to the metaphysical view that reality consists of 'material' factors, matter and energy, with man's consciousness developing as an emergent property of their organization, from below, so to speak, not from above. Many still find this outlook too limited to satisfy the desire for meaning, but others would agree with Darwin, who said on the last page of his *Origin of Species* that 'there is grandeur in this view of life'. Scientists have adopted it, not merely as a heuristic procedure, but as their ontological conception of the world.

Marx and Engels embraced materialism early in youth, before they had met one another. Each had read the writings of Ludwig Feuerbach, which convinced them that Hegel's metaphysics was fatally flawed by its idealism. But they resolutely accepted another feature of it: the view that reality is fundamentally a process of developmental change. In their view, Hegelian idealism and mechanistic empiricism are both wrong, but a correct world-view can be constructed by uniting the historical orientation of the former with the materialism of the latter. For Marx and Engels a philosophy of historical materialism can satisfy man's desire to find meaning in existence. The world is meaningful, and its meaning is understandable, not because it is God-governed, but because it is law-governed. Man's past can be explained, his present state analysed, and his future predicted, by the application of materialistic science to a world in process of development. This view has a powerful appeal, especially for the modern intellectual who requires that life have a meaning and purpose that transcends utilitarian concerns but cannot find it in religious faith.

Like virtually everything else in philosophy, the materialist conception of existence can be traced back to the ancient Greeks. However, the most important of these philosophers, Plato and Aristotle, were not materialists, and the influence of Greek philosophy on Western thought in the medieval period supported the idealist thrust of Christian theology. One cannot find anywhere a more distinct expression of the materialist outlook than in the Latin poem *On the Nature of Things*, written by Lucretius in the first century before Christ, but it had no impact upon Roman philosophical thought, or Christian, and began to be read as a metaphysical argument only when new editions of it were printed in the sixteenth century. The mechanistic materialism of Ptolemaic astronomy apparently had no impact on philosophical thought during the fifteen centuries it reigned unchallenged as a model of the universe. Pierre Gassendi (1592–1655) is frequently mentioned by historians of philosophy as one of the earliest thinkers to oppose frontally the Aristotelianism of the Church (of which he was a priest) and present a materialist view of nature. Thomas Hobbes (1588–1679), whom we studied in Chapter 4 as one of the first modern social scientists, is also frequently named as an initiator of the materialist philosophy. From these dates it is evident that the ascendancy of materialism is a seventeenth-century phenomenon, making its way into philosophical thought in the same era that saw the birth of modern science, and meeting no strong opposition until idealism was revived by romantic philosophy in the nineteenth century.

Materialism has never been accepted by those who embrace a religious faith, but it has not been completely accepted by atheists, either. It is one thing to deny the existence of spiritual powers, but quite another to claim that man's consciousness is no more than a chemical and physical phenomenon of a material brain. Even the doctrine of emergent properties is insufficient to account for consciousness, since it would have to be extended to claim that mental phenomena somehow, in fact inexplicably, transcend the material phenomena of the brain. This is the 'mind-body problem', which has been discussed incessantly by philosophers since it was formulated clearly by Descartes in the seventeenth century.

As materialists, Marx and Engels had no difficulty in rejecting the notion that reality contains spiritual elements, but they had the same difficulties concerning the role of human consciousness that other materialists have had. There are numerous passages in the writings of Marx and Engels that seem to espouse an unqualified, fully deterministic, materialism. Ideas, theories, and other phenomena of mind are treated as direct derivatives from material factors, which, for them, include the organizational structure of society and its economy. 'It is not the consciousness of men that determines their existence, but, on the contrary, their social existence [that] determines their consciousness' (preface to *Critique of Political Economy*). It is doubtful, however, whether Marx and Engels regarded their own consciousness and their own theories as no more than 'epiphenomenal' features of the capitalist society in which they lived. If one takes the view that an idea that one dislikes simply reflects the material conditions of its proponent, how does one escape the return thrust of the same dagger? If the materialist admits that his own ideas are also epiphenomenal, then indeed life is meaningless. It would even be meaningless to say that it is meaningless, for one could not 'say' anything, only make noises. An unqualified materialism fails to meet what philosophers call the 'test of self-reference'. On the other hand, if one claims exemption from materialistic determinism for one's own ideas, there is no warrant for denying a similar exemption to the ideas of others.

Some ingenious explanations have been offered as solutions to this problem, such as the proposition that the proletariat class (and its honorary members recruited from the intellectual bourgeoisie) are free of the ideological fetters that bind the propertied class, or the proposition that the world ceases to be determined by material factors after the socialist revolution, but it is claims of this kind that have given metaphysics a bad reputation among serious philosophers. Like other philosophies, materialism makes sense only if it is not pushed too far. Marx and Engels did not confront the problem directly, and they did tend at times to express extreme materialist views, but, to their credit, they did not follow their materialist philosophy to its self-destructive end.

The mind–body dichotomy intersects with another one that has been especially important in the social sciences and in social philosophy generally: the dichotomy between 'facts' and 'values'. We noted this earlier in discussing the distinction between 'positive' and 'normative' propositions in Chapter 3 D. Despite the fact that some have espoused this dichotomy as part of an effort to eschew metaphysics altogether, it is itself a metaphysical notion, since it rests upon a view of the nature of existence. Statements concerning facts and statements concerning values are construed to be categorically different, so reality is metaphysically dualist in this respect, even if it is not in any other respect. There is no escape from this in saying that a value statement is simply a factual statement recording that someone has a certain value. The statement 'John Smith considers truthfulness to be good and lying bad' is indeed a positive statement about John Smith but it has very little, if any, meaning unless the words 'good' and 'bad' are intelligible in themselves, any more than a statement like 'John Smith is pale' would be meaningful to a blind person. Numerous efforts have been made to escape this dualism without falling into moral blindness, such as by means of the Thomistic concept of 'natural law', or Bentham's union of psychological and ethical utilitarianism, or, most recently, by E. O. Wilson's claim that a moral code can be constructed from knowledge of the neurophysiology of the lower brain. None of these convincingly dislodges Hume's contention that *is* and *ought* are categorically different.

As part of his metaphysical monism, Hegel denied the dualism of facts and values. Marx and Engels followed Hegel in this, being monists themselves, but they did not accept his solution in terms of the notion of *Geist*. Their own resolution of the fact–value dichotomy is not clear, since they did not discuss it directly. Their writing is punctuated with moral judgements, but they did not explain the metaphysical, or the epistemological, status of their values. They seem to have had the view, in accord with the philosophy of materialism, that values, like other mental phenomena, are reflections of material conditions. This does not, however, offer a resolution of the fact–value dichotomy that is any more satisfactory than its response to the mind–body problem. Further discussion of Marxian ethics is deferred to the next section.

So far, in examining Marxian metaphysics, we have focused upon materialism. It cannot be denied that Marx and Engels regarded themselves as philosophical materialists, but this does not mean that they consistently adhered to materialist principles in their social science. Non-materialist elements appear there in important places, and some interpreters contend that, in practice, they were not materialists at all. The reader of the *Paris Manuscripts*, or the first part of *Capital*, Volume I, would have no ground for construing Marxian theory as materialistic and, if he read further, he could compile a large file of examples in support of a non-materialist interpretation of Marxian theory.

To begin with a very general point, the economic factors that Marx and Engels considered to be the foundations of social phenomena are not 'materialistic' in the philosophical sense of that term. To the strict materialist, the only basic constituents of existence are matter and energy. A materialist analysis of organic, or social, phenomena must necessarily be rigorously behaviourist, tracing such phenomena to the physical and chemical constituents of physiology. Marxian theory is clearly not behaviourist, at least to this degree. In calling economic factors the 'material' bases of social phenomena, Marx and Engels were using the word in one of its customary senses, but it is not what philosophers mean by it. When we say in common speech that 'John Smith is a materialistic person,' we do not mean that his behaviour is explicable in terms of the laws of physics and chemistry. In the Marxian analysis of capitalism, the 'relations of production' do not refer to the kind of relations that a strict materialist has in mind, since the entities involved do not merely *have* relations with one another, but the fundamental nature of each *involves* such relations. The individual, and the social classes, are not independently definable, because what they *are* consists of the relations between them and other such entities. To the materialist, the world consists of 'things'; but to Marx and Engels its basic constituents are the 'relations' through which the things themselves are defined. This 'holistic' view is a prominent feature of Hegelian philosophy which they did not discard. As a metaphysical outlook it has certain merits, especially in respect of organic and social phenomena, but it is not, strictly speaking, a materialist conception of existence.

Much more questionable, in my view, is the tendency of Marxian theory to resort, at crucial points, to the Aristotelian notions of 'essentialism' and 'teleology'. The first of these takes the view that individual entities are members of generic classes because of some essential quality that all members share. The proper way to study real-world phenomena is by penetrating below the surface appearances of the individual cases to the underlying essences, for the phenomena are manifestations of those essences. Thus, to Aristotle, a rock behaves as it does because of the essential nature of rocks, and a tree behaves differently because trees have a different essential nature. Marx frequently resorts to this kind of argument, for example in his treatment of classes, in his identification of historical stages, and in his labour theory of value. The difficulties of this conception are so great that modern philosophers are generally hostile to it. No scientific work is possible without using generic categories, but the argument that the categories represent fundamental 'essences' is not helpful, since there is no way of distinguishing between an empirical appearance and an essence, and, moreover, it opens the door for anyone to assert whatever he fancies about the world without having to respond to any empirical challenge.

The Aristotelian notion of teleology is the argument that events are governed by the ends or purposes that are achieved by them. A pine seed grows into a pine tree because its essential nature contains that objective. The mature pine tree is, in Aristotle's language, the 'final cause' of the various processes through which the seed germinates and the seedling develops. The same idea, on a cosmic scale, is contained in Hegel's conception of reality as the process through which *Geist* realizes itself. In Marxian theory this notion is present in numerous places, most prominently in the theory of history which treats social development as a process controlled by the end or purpose served by it, the emergence of the communist society. The doctrine of final cause reverses the temporal order of cause and effect that materialistic science employs; the final cause is subsequent to the effects that one empirically observes. For this reason it is regarded with suspicion by most philosophers and with derision by natural scientists. Some social scientists occasionally flirt with it on the ground that human action is purposive and can be explained only in terms of ends. This is a simple mistake, however. Human actions are undertaken *now* in accordance with desires that the actors *now* have and the ends they *hope* to achieve. Social phenomena are determined, in part, by what men do; not by the desires or intentions that motivate their actions, but by the actions themselves. There is no teleological element in this.

Essentialism, teleology, and strict materialism are alike in one respect: they are deterministic. Everything said above about Marxian metaphysics would seem to lead to interpreting it as a deterministic view of reality. But we have already seen (especially in section B 1 on the Marxian theory of history) that Marx and Engels were unwilling to accept a deterministic interpretation of their views. Engels's remark that he and Marx claimed only that economic factors 'ultimately' determine the course of history does not clarify their metaphysics so much as reveal an element of ambiguity in it. Whether Marxian theory is deterministic or not has been much debated, non-Marxists usually arguing that it is deterministic, and Marxists claiming that is not; the former often transparently motivated by the desire to skewer Marx with an easy thrust, the latter desiring to escape what they recognize as fatal to their political posture. It would be unprofitable to review this debate here, especially since it now seems clear that the ambiguity of Marxian theory on this point cannot be resolved. I shall only make a few brief remarks in order to clarify the issue and to indicate some of the more important non-deterministic features of Marxian metaphysics.

Determinism is not equivalent to the assertion that empirical phenomena have causes. Nor does it hinge upon whether some phenomena are probabilistic, or whether indeterminacy reflects the incompleteness of our knowledge about the world. The heart of the issue is whether human mental states can function as causes and, if they can, whether they have any autonomy, that is, whether they are not themselves totally determined by non-mentational factors. Though a strict behaviourist would disagree, the first requirement is, in my view, beyond dispute. Purposes, tastes, and beliefs motivate and guide men's actions, and therefore function as causes of the events that are produced by the actions. The second requirement is not beyond dispute, but it is beyond test, since there is no way that one can demonstrate the autonomy of mental entities, or the contrary.

The interpretation of Marxian theory on this point then becomes a matter of ascertaining its view concerning the autonomy of mental entities. Marx and Engels frequently argued that ideas, and social factors closely connected with them, such as politics, are 'epiphenomenal', reflecting the operation of more basic material factors. This would seem to deny that mental entities can be autonomous, and leads to a deterministic interpretation of Marxian theory. But, on the other hand, Marx and Engels claimed that certain persons, such as themselves, are able to escape these fetters, and that there are certain times, such as when society is in a state of revolutionary upheaval, when large numbers of people transcend their material conditions and generate independent ideas. More generally, they sometimes expressed the view that history is a process through which man acts in a creative way, reaching its culmination in the communist society where the final barriers to his creative self-realization are removed. Taking the view, as they did, that the basic feature of human nature is the desire for individual creativity, it would have been difficult for them to adopt a deterministic metaphysics. The closest one may come to a coherent statement of the Marxian view on this point is to interpret it as saying that, in a society based upon private property, men are so held in thrall by their material conditions that their mentational autonomy is small, but it is not zero, and, given the right social conditions, it can become large.

A connected issue is the role of human knowledge in enlarging man's mentational autonomy. The strict determinist is forced to contend that the more we learn about the world and ourselves, the more we realize that we are not free, and cannot be free. For Marx and Engels, freedom is enlarged by knowledge, since it increases the scope of purposive action. An ignorant person may have some mental freedom, but he does not know how to turn it to practical use. Marx and Engels were inspired by the idea that scientific knowledge is a necessary complement to freedom. They set out to construct a science of society, not merely to predict where history is going, but as an inspiration and guide for those who are willing to play an active role in it. The Hungarian Marxist Gyorgy Lukàcs argued in the 1920's that ideas play a role in history, but he was suppressed by Stalin. As Lenin had demonstrated by his own writings and actions, the revolutionary activist has an interest in claiming the power of ideas, but the dictator's interest lies in presenting himself as the product of more transcendental forces.

3. Ethics

Marx and Engels did not develop a systematic ethical theory, and they made very few comments that indicate the general ethical philosophy they entertained. Some other aspects of Marxian theory that were not systematically discussed by Marx and Engels can nevertheless be constructed from their criticisms of other theories, but the original Marxian texts contain very little critical examination of the ethics of Aquinas, or Leibniz, or Kant, or utilitarianism, or any other moral system. The best one can do is to try to infer some of the main features of Marxian ethical theory from other materials – without much confidence, one should add, that Marx and Engels would have accepted such inferences. Under the circumstances, it may well be doubtful whether anything of value can be added to this survey of Marxian theory by discussing the subject of abstract ethics at all. But we must undertake it none the less, since the writings of Marx and Engels on social questions are replete with strong and explicit moral judgements, and some of the propositions that are critical to Marxian social science, such as the theories of surplus value and exploitation, are heavily loaded with implicit ethical principles. After noting, in *Anti-Dühring*, that even science, dialectics, and logic as well, are incapable of furnishing absolute truths, Engels goes on to say that much less progress has been made in discovering the principles of good and evil (I, IX). Later in the same work he declares that 'From a scientific standpoint . . . appeal to morality and justice does not help us an inch . . . ; to economic science, moral indignation, however justifiable, cannot serve as an argument, but only as a symptom'. The 'indignation of the poet', he goes on, cannot *prove* anything (II, I). Marx and Engels regarded themselves as scientists and, like most of the scientists of their day, and ours, they had a low opinion of moral discourse. In addition, they aspired to construct a 'scientific socialism', which meant rejecting the utopian tradition, which relied heavily on comparing the ethical qualities of existing society with the one proposed. Moral fervour punctuated almost everything Marx and Engels wrote but, presumably, they regarded this as poetic embroidery, not intimately connected with their fundamental analysis.

This is about all that one can say, based on explicit remarks. But if some liberty of inference is permitted, there seems to be more to Marxian ethics than scientific abstemiousness. As we saw in the preceding section, one of the aspects of Hegel's philosophy that Marx and Engels accepted was its rejection of the distinction between facts and values. If they are not categorically different, there is no ground for declaring ethics and science to be unconnected. Ethical values can play a role in the determination of scientific truth, or scientific truths can serve as the foundation of ethics. The writings of Marx and Engels permit one to infer that they entertained both these connections. The first has received little support in Western philosophy, especially since the Church disgraced itself by the trial of Galileo, but the latter has been a phoenix, many times destroyed, but always appearing again in a new incarnation, the latest being the philosophical claims of 'sociobiology' as espoused by E. O. Wilson and his followers. This is the doctrine of 'ethical naturalism', which contends that a moral system can be constructed from empirical components, without resort to spiritual elements or to the contention that man has capacity to form ideas that are not wholly determined by material factors.

The variant of ethical naturalism that can be inferred from Marxian theory derives from the teleological element in its conception of historical development. If the end of the developmental process is predetermined as its 'final cause', it is ethically good to promote the rapid and easy achievement of that end. Actions that work against it are not only empirically fruitless; they are ethically iniquitous. Social phenomena that are essential elements of the historical process are neither good nor bad, they simply *are*. Working with such an ethical system, Marx and Engels could praise, or condemn, or be neutral towards, any specific event or practice, depending on how they were inclined to evaluate its relation to the stream of history. Capitalists could be denounced for stealing surplus value from the workers, or lauded because they accumulate capital, or sympathized with as actors in an historical process over which they have no more control than the workers. Just as the priest can justify any event as being 'God's will' or condemn any as 'the work of the Devil', so one can arbitrarily declare anything to be in accordance with 'the laws of history', or contrary to them, as one pleases. Such ethical systems have the power of flexibility. Moral judgements can be changed without challenge of inconsistency. Marx and Engels themselves adopted a moral stance that has become one of the notable features of modern Marxist politics.

The resilience of ethical naturalism derives from the fact that it promises release from the burdens and uncertainties of moral judgement. If ethical principles could be made scientific there would be no more reason to agonize over such things as poverty policy or the criminal law than over the law of gases or the process of cell division; and the application of moral rules would be no more problematic than engineering. A scientific morality would be as certain and as objective as other scientific laws. It would be a non-discriminatory code, governing as impartially as the law of gravity. The appeal of this illusion is understandable, but it is still an illusion. Nature responds to empirical questions, when they are cleverly framed, but she is mute when asked moral questions. The result is that ethical naturalism rotates a half-circle. Instead of listening to nature we are asked instead to pay heed to her 'authoritative spokesmen'. Ordinary men are deprived of their role in moral discourse and made subservient to those who are arrogant enough to present themselves as moral experts, and have the power to compel obedience. History is no more articulate on moral matters than nature is, or God. When morality is presumed to be derived from such sources, the result is rule by a priesthood and, instead of objectivity and equity, we have arbitrariness, discrimination, and caprice.

Chapter 14

The methodology of history

In the opening chapter of this book I emphasized the fact that man is not only a social animal but also an altricial one. At birth the human individual is not an independently viable organism. His body must grow and his brain must be 'programmed' before he can function. The programme consists not only of those instructions that are necessary to the effective performance of functions that are biologically essential, but also those that shape his behaviour in accordance with the customs, values, and ontological conceptions of the society to which he belongs. This process of enculturation plays an essential role in creating the social solidarity and stability that enable the human individual to engage in co-operative activity with other members of his species. Needless to say, it also plays a role in creating the sense of distinctiveness of social groups which often leads to destructive conflict between them.

There are few human societies in which the *history* of the group does not play an important role in the enculturation of the young. Stories are told, songs and dances and rituals are performed, telling of the past glories and sufferings of the group, the feats of its great men, and the actions of its gods. Through this history the identification of the individual with the group is deepened and his appreciation of its ways is made to transcend their utilitarian functions. In literate societies the process of enculturation becomes more elaborate and more intellectual. In Western society, before the seventeenth century, religion played the leading role in the process of enculturation, and theology was its intellectual helpmate. With the secularization of thought that was brought about by the rise of science, history became the main instrument of enculturation, and the historian replaced the theologian as the authentic source of the sophisticated knowledge that defines and identifies a social group, and differentiates it from others.

Not all historians are happy to play such a role. Some regard themselves as unpretentious empiricists, studying the past only in order to discover what 'really happened,' but even they find their writings pressed into the service of social enculturation. The development of history as an intellectual discipline in the eighteenth century, and its continued growth since, are due in part to its socializing role. Today that role is accepted almost automatically. This is the main reason why history, alone among the social sciences, is an obligatory school and college subject. To say of any group that it 'has no history' does not mean that it came into existence yesterday, but that it is not *aware* of its past, and the remark is a deep reproach, implying that such a group's level of civilization, even its humanity, is inferior.

We shall be mainly concerned here with the epistemological problems that are encountered in the attempt to investigate the human past. Is it possible to pursue such an enterprise in an objective way, searching for truth in a 'scientific' spirit? Can the historian adopt the investigatory modes of the natural sciences? Is the main object of the historian the discovery of general 'laws' that govern the particular phenomena? If the historian does not adopt the modes and objectives of science, how does he *explain* past events or render them coherent or intelligible? What is the relation between history and the other social sciences? Does knowledge of the past enable one to predict the future? What is the relation between the actions of individual persons and their shared experience as members of the groups (nations, classes, etc.) that the historian talks about? These are the questions we shall focus upon. During the last decade of the nineteenth century and the first two of the twentieth, European historians engaged in a fierce dispute concerning the epistemological status of their craft, but English and American historians paid little attention to the problem. Recently, however, initiated by an essay by a philosopher, Carl G. Hempel ('The Function of General Laws in History', *Journal of Philosophy*, 1942), there has been a continuing debate in the English-language literature. We shall begin by examining the thesis advanced by Hempel and the main criticisms of it that have been put forward.

A. HISTORICAL EXPLANATION AND THE NATURAL SCIENCE MODEL

1. Hempel's thesis and its critics

The philosophy of science has two objectives: to *prescribe* the procedures that *must* be employed if one aims to make true statements about empirical phenomena that penetrate beneath their surface appearances; and to *describe* the procedures that *are* in fact employed by practising scientists and scholars. Epistemological criticism consists of comparing the information furnished by the latter activity with the principles derived from the former. In examining the epistemology of the various fields of knowledge, the mixture of prescription and description differs greatly. When considering physics, philosophers tend to be almost entirely descriptive; in examining other disciplines, prescription (and criticism) increases, roughly in inverse proportion to their use of experimental methods and mathematics. Among the many influences upon Western thought of the development of the natural sciences, one of the more important is the disposition to regard the practices of physicists as providing the epistemological principles that all other disciplines should embrace.

Hempel's 1942 essay on history is a notable example of this. Contending that there is a universal method of analysis that is applicable to all empirical phenomena, he argues that historians can provide valid explanations of past events only by casting their narrative accounts in a form that is fundamentally the same as that employed by the natural sciences. Unless this is done, Hempel asserts, the historian is reduced to contending that the events he examines are due to 'chance', and to explaining them by means of 'divination'. One of Hempel's objectives was to question the epistemic credentials of two particular modes of historical explanation that will be discussed below in sections B and C, but the main thrust of his argument was broader, amounting to a criticism of the prevailing methodology of historical scholarship in general.

The debate that was initiated by Hempel's paper cannot be reviewed here in detail; we shall concentrate on the main points made by defenders and critics. Two aspects of it should be immediately distinguished: some commentators focus upon whether, in prescribing for historians, Hempel has given a correct description of the epistemology of the natural sciences themselves; others are concerned with his contention that history, since it deals with empirical phenomena, must employ the same methodology as the other empirical disciplines. Some critics of Hempel claim that he has misconstrued the methodology of natural science and has therefore advocated erroneous epistemic principles, while others argue that this is beside the point, since his doctrine of epistemological monism is itself unacceptable and, whatever may be appropriate for natural science, the disciplines that deal with human social phenomena require the application of different methods of investigation – the doctrine of epistemological pluralism. As one can see, Hempel's argument goes far beyond the assessment of the practice of historians, raising issues that are central to the methodology of social science and, indeed, to epistemology in general.

Hempel's account of the epistemology of science is aimed at emphasizing the importance of 'general laws.' Sometimes he focuses upon the *discovery* of such laws, and sometimes on the *use* of laws already established in providing explanations of specific events. As the title of his paper indicates, however, Hempel is mainly concerned with the latter. His contention is that any explanation of an historical event involves the use of general laws that provide the warrant for the inference that connections exist between empirical phenomena. This 'covering law model', as it has come to be called, was initially presented by Hempel as consisting of three components: (1) an event that one wishes to explain; (2) another event (or set of events) that suffices to produce event (1); and (3) a valid *general* law (or set of laws) that describes a necessary connection between events of type (2) and events of type (1). In this construction, the occurrence of the specific event (1) is explained deductively; that is, it is logically entailed by statements of the form (2) and (3). Later, Hempel modified his position somewhat, recognizing that some 'universal hypotheses' or 'laws' are probabilistic statements and cannot be expected to hold in every specific case ('Explanation in Science and in History', in R. G. Colodny, ed., *Frontiers in Science and Philosophy*, 1962), but he did not budge from his central contention that to offer an explanation of any empirical phenomenon involves using general laws to link the event to be explained with the events that are construed to be its determinants. In effect, an historical explanation, according to Hempel, shows *why* an event occurred by demonstrating it to be a specific instance of a general law that applies to all events of a similar sort.

One can easily see why narrative historians may be hostile to the covering law model. In explaining Germany's invasion of Russia in June 1941, for example, the historian concentrates on describing the events that led to it, and he usually has few qualms in saying that they caused it, but he would find it exceedingly difficult to specify the empirically validated general laws that give warrant to the linkage. Most practising historians regard Hempel's epistemology, not as a prescription for the improvement of historical research, but as a virtual demand that they abandon their craft, since they do not, and very probably cannot, meet his canons of scientific respectability. In defence, some claim that the historian transcends the narrow rules of empirical epistemology, reaching a higher level of understanding not open to scientists. Others say that the historian is a literary artist, who writes about the past as a novelist or dramatist might, not primarily intent upon explaining events, but using them to tell a story.

Hempel recognizes the difficulties that would be encountered in trying to meet the requirements of his model. In practice, he notes, the historian only provides an 'explanation sketch', which is 'a more or less vague indication of the laws and conditions considered as relevant' to the event to be explained. But, insistently prescriptive, he contends that the historian should aim to provide a full explanation, by specifying explicitly the general laws that would 'fill out' the explanation sketch. Presented in this way, the covering law model can be viewed as an epistemological *ideal*. That it is not fully realizable in practice is not an admission of its irrelevance, and the historian is not rebuked by failure to realize it. Like all ideals, it serves as a guide for practice.

Historians may derive little comfort from this, considering that it is not much easier to use the covering law model as a guide than to fulfil its requirements to the letter. In rejecting the model as a guide, critics have pointed out that phenomena can be brought under a covering law only if they are similar. Natural scientists deal with phenomena that can be grouped into homogeneous classes; historians, it is claimed, do not. The law of gravitational attraction or the Mendelian laws of inheritance can be applied to many specific phenomena because all bodies have mass, and many organisms reproduce by means of sexual union. But what is it that 'revolutions' or 'wars' have in common that could be covered, even ideally, by a general law? Can the American, French and Russian revolutions all be explained in terms of a general 'law of revolutions'? Natural scientists are interested in the differences between phenomena as well as the similarities, but they have many similarities to work with and, indeed, it is precisely because of this that differences are noteworthy objects of investigation. The phenomena the historian deals with have so few similarities that it almost seems as though terms like 'revolution' or 'war' have different meanings in different cases, not representing much that can be regarded as inherently characteristic of, or common to, the events they denote. Because of this lack of homogeneity in the material that the historian studies, it seems evident that it would amount only to a slavish mimicry of natural science if historians accepted the covering law model, even as an ideal.

Historical phenomena may be more heterogeneous than natural phenomena (a biologist might question this), but the argument in the above paragraph is not fatal to Hempel's thesis. The covering law model does not require the historian to search for, and apply, general laws that embrace wars and revolutions. Laws that refer to human behaviour will serve just as well or, some would claim, a great deal better. To utilize an illustration that appears frequently in the recent literature on this question, one does not have to explain why an automobile radiator filled with water cracked on a cold night by invoking a 'law of cracking radiators'. Instead, one has recourse to laws that deal with the expansion of certain forms of matter in passing from a liquid to a solid state, and the laws of stress resistance in metals. In a similar way, the historian may refer to laws of human behaviour in explaining a specific revolution. Just as the engineer or mechanic draws upon physics and chemistry in explaining why a radiator has cracked, the historian can draw upon economics and sociology.

This does not mean that history is necessarily a parasitic or secondary discipline, though some historians talk as though it reflects unfavourably upon the honour of their trade to have anything to do with 'social science'. The point of the above argument about cracking radiators is that explanation of empirical phenomena requires *reduction*. Large events like wars and revolutions must be decomposed to a level where some secure generalizations of an economic, sociological, or psychological nature may be applied. Some critics of Hempel contend that the decomposition required by adoption of the covering law model involves one in an infinite regress, every explanatory factor having to be explained by other factors, and these in turn by other factors, without end. But this problem is not unique to history. One *could* insist, when the mechanic explains why the radiator cracked, that he explain why water turns to ice, why molecular motion is slowed by a drop in temperature, and so on, pursuing the hapless fellow relentlessly until he admits that he does not know. Fortunately, it is not necessary to know everything in order to know something. The historian, like the scientist, must reduce his phenomena, and he must also know when to stop reducing.

The infinite regress argument and the heterogeneity argument have persuaded some prominent historians (e.g. Charles Beard and Michael Oakeshott) that their discipline is not concerned with explanation at all, at least in the sense of the word 'explanation' that demands an answer to 'Why?' questions. This view contends that the historian is concerned solely with 'What?' questions (though Oakeshott seems to argue that when one has properly described what happened this serves in itself as an explanation of why it happened). It is ironic, however, that the narrative historian is in a weaker position in criticizing the covering law model on this ground than the natural scientist. When Vesalius engaged in anatomical dissection and Malpighi employed the newly invented microscope to examine finer structures, they were not explaining but describing. A great deal of the work of modern scientists is similarly descriptive in form. Many modern biologists and geologists would be nonplussed by Hempel's demand that they write their papers in the mode of the covering law model. The historian may claim that he is simply describing events, but the narrative form unavoidably invites the reader to infer that he is explaining why the events occurred. An historian who undertook to be abstemiously descriptive would produce only tables and lists. This would be uninformative, as well as dull. The historian cannot escape from the demand for explanation, but he can reject the claim that explanation requires conformity to the covering law model.

The infinite regress argument opens another issue that we should briefly note. If every factor that one introduces in explaining an event must itself be explained, does not this mean that one's conception of the world is deterministic? Some scholars (e.g. Isaiah Berlin) reject the covering law model primarily on the ground that it is incompatible with human freedom and responsibility. As we have seen, however, the model does not necessarily involve an infinite regress and, although a supporter of it could adopt a deterministic philosophy, he is not compelled to do so (see an excellent paper by Ernest Nagel, 'Determinism and History', *Philosophy and Phenomenological Research*, 1960). The reader must forgive my reluctance to pursue any further a debate that has gone on for centuries without prospect of resolution.

2. Non-causal modes of explanation

The Aristotelian notion of teleology regards an event as governed by its 'final cause', which, being the end or purpose of the event, lies subsequent to it in time. Teleology still survives in modern thought, and historians who view events in terms of a grand, comprehensive Law of History are among its most prominent champions but, since Hume, the concept of causation has generally been construed in terms that reverse this temporal order, regarding the cause of an event as necessarily antecedent to it. Since the narrative historian writes of a sequence of events, it may seem that he is engaged in causal explanation, but this need not be so. All *causal* explanations require statements of temporal sequence, but not all *explanations* require them, and not all statements of temporal sequence are explanations, much less causal explanations. Hempel's covering law model construes the historian's narrative account as offering a Humean causal explanation of events. Some critics of the model contend that historians do not offer explanations at all; others claim that they do offer explanations but not causal ones; while others say that though they operate with a causal model, it is one that, emphasizes elements whose importance is not appreciated by Hempel. In this section we will examine the second of these views, but it is useful to begin with the third, since the notion of non-causal explanation can be clarified if we regard it, not as categorically distinct from the Hempel model, as some scholars (e.g. William Dray) insist, but as a distinction of emphasis.

In the literature of the debate over the covering law model, numerous commentators have pointed out that a causal explanation of a particular empirical event consists of two elements: a statement of the 'cause' of the event; and a specification of the 'conditions' under which that cause operated. William H. Dray, in his excellent selection of papers from this debate, notes the distinction between causes and conditions as one of the prominent features of the discussion (*Philosophical Analysis and History*, 1966, 1). While Hempel and other philosophers of science do recognize this distinction, critics regard them as failing to appreciate its great importance in dealing with historical phenomena.

In order to clarify this matter we may refer to the INUS model of causation outlined above in Chapter 3 A 3. This was originally constructed as a theory of historical explanation (K. Marc-Wogau, 'On Historical Explanation', *Theoria*, 1962). According to the INUS model, (1) all events are due to a *set* of circumstances; (2) events of a similar type may be due to different sets of circumstances; and (3) when we say that a specific event was caused by a specific factor we mean that, while this factor was not sufficient, in itself, to cause the event, the set of circumstances, of which it is a necessary element, was sufficient to cause it. In such an account, we describe the factor that completes a sufficient set as the 'cause' of the event, and the other elements in the set as the 'conditions'. Hempel's model and the INUS model do not differ in any fundamental way, since Hempel's argument can be construed simply as insisting that any statement of a sufficient set should include the relevant covering laws, as well as the facts of the case, among the conditions. The debate between Hempel and (some of) his critics thus reduces to this: Hempel emphasizes the role of covering laws, while the critics emphasize the distinction between causes and conditions.

This does not mean that the debate over the covering law model can be easily resolved and its doctrine of epistemological monism reaffirmed. In a narrative history we find that most of the text is devoted to describing the conditions that pertained at the time and place in order to explain why certain specific causes (usually the acts of particular persons) had certain specific consequences. In the text of a natural science document much less space is devoted to this, and sometimes it is virtually absent. For example, an account of the resolution of the dispute between the Venetian Republic and the Pope in 1606–7 would treat the decision of the Venetian senate very briefly, but would give a lengthy account of contemporary economic and other conditions, noting that many of the Venetian nobles had become more interested in mainland enterprises than in maritime ones, the changing sources of Venetian state revenues, the distribution of political power, etc. By contrast, a scientific paper explaining the cause of sickle-cell anaemia would focus on the irregularity of one amino acid on one chromosome, simply taking for granted that the reader would fill in for himself the relevant facts about human genetics, organic chemistry, etc.

The reason for this difference in explanatory style is plain. The natural scientist explains in terms of 'conditions' as well as 'causes' but, since the conditions are so similar in many cases, he has no need to specify them. The historian deals with phenomena that occur under such dissimilar conditions that, by contrast, he must devote most of his attention to them. In terms of the INUS model, the natural scientist works with phenomena that can be explained by a limited number of sets of factors, while the historian's world contains many sets, perhaps even a different one for every event. A forest fire caused by lightning may be explained by a set of factors that shares a great many items with one caused by a camp fire (dryness, presence of brushwood, etc.) but two revolutions may be so dissimilar in their conditions that many historians prefer to avoid language that implies causality. Confronted with the heterogeneity of historical events, a mode of explanation is employed that focuses on the coherence of the factors that were present concurrently at a particular time and place, rather than on a temporal sequence of cause and effect, and when the particular actions of persons are noted, they are treated not as independent factors (like lightning, say) but as actions that one might expect rational persons to undertake, given their aims, in the particular circumstances. We can now see that the argument that historical events are heterogeneous, even the contention that each one is unique, does not mean that no explanation of them can be given. It requires that explanation must be non-causal in form and must focus primarily on the circumstances that were present when individuals made decisions to act (or, of course, to refrain from acting). The narrative form that the historian employs is not a causal analysis, but an intelligible account of the conjunction of such circumstances at a given time and place. The central concepts that are involved in this view of historical explanation are 'intelligibility', 'coherence', and 'situational rationality'. In invoking such concepts the critics of the covering law model are not concerned with its deficiencies as a prescriptive epistemology, or as a descriptive epistemology of natural science. They are attempting to show that it does not correctly describe the methodology of history. Since the supporters of the covering law model are prepared to admit that the traditional methodology of narrative history does in fact succeed in furnishing empirical knowledge, the real problem is to show how this is accomplished.

The emphasis on the function of general laws in Hempel's model calls attention to the fact that an empirical phenomenon is rendered intelligible if we perceive it to be a particular instance of a general class. A particular instance of a stone falling is understood when one knows that all bodies obey the law of gravitational attraction. But this is not the only way of rendering empirical phenomena intelligible and, indeed, it is not suitable at all for some of them. If an observer notes that the prows of Venetian gondolas have six functionless projections and asks for an explanation, his guide may say that the projections represent the six districts of the city and go on to sketch the history of the custom. The observer is not furnished with any covering laws which explain, in scientific terms, *why* the gondola builders behave as they do; he is offered a description of *what* the projections represent and *how* the tradition came to be established. A clever epistemological monist could no doubt recast such an explanation in the deductive mode of Hempel's model, but such a scholastic performance would subtract more than it would add to one's comprehension of the phenomenon. In order to achieve intelligibility, the narrative historian tells a story, utilizing a mode of intelligibility that has been effectively practised at least since the Old Testament was written. A good story has a beginning, a middle, and an end. In adopting the narrative mode the historian distorts the human experience, which is all middle, but one should not reject this as a heuristic procedure unless another mode is shown, by actual practice, to be superior.

In the Newtonian model of the solar system an account of the planetary motions is furnished that shows how they 'fit together'. That is to say, the law of gravitational attraction enables one to construct a model of the solar system that is *coherent*. General equilibrium theory in economics, similarly, provides a model of a market economy that describes how the parts of the economy, functioning according to certain general laws, fit together in a coherent way. The historian may claim that he also presents a coherent model, even though it may not be one that relies upon any laws of the sort that Hempel has in mind. In giving an account, say, of the Protestant Reformation, the historian is at pains to show how various trends 'came together' in early sixteenth-century Europe, and how the various events of the time 'interacted' with one another. An historian may be led to doubt the authenticity of a document ascribed to Martin Luther, say, because it seems to be anachronistic, while he may suggest that another document was probably written by Luther because it is consistent with other facts. One historian may criticize another's account of the Reformation on the ground that the elements cited by the latter do not fit together, or that he has neglected certain elements that are necessary to complete a coherent picture.

One might argue that coherence is coherence, whether it is employed as an explanatory criterion in astrophysics, economics, or history, but it would be very difficult to state the general laws that underlie an historical narrative. Since the historian does succeed in producing a coherent account of events, and employs the criterion of coherence in evaluating the empirical validity of an account, it would seem that application of the covering law model is not the only way of achieving coherence. J. H. Hexter has argued, giving a striking example, that, in some cases, the use of the narrative mode is the only way of producing a coherent explanation of an event ('Historiography: I. The Rhetoric of History', *International Encyclopedia of the Social Sciences*, 1968; see also Terry Pinkard, 'Historical Explanation and the Grammar of Theories', *Philosophy of Social Science*, 1978). This emphasizes once again that the methodology of an enterprise must be suited to the task it undertakes to perform. The momentous paper by J. D. Watson and F. H. C. Crick describing the structure of the DNA molecule is only a page long (*Nature*, 25 April 1953), providing a coherent model without any account of the procedures employed in constructing it. The subsequent book by Watson (*The Double Helix*, 1968), describing how he and Crick arrived at the structure, is written as an historical narrative. One learns a great deal from both, but not the same things. If the Watson–Crick paper had been written in narrative form, and Watson's book in the terse mode of a scientific report, we would learn little from either.

As we have noted, the historian typically devotes much more space to describing the conditions pertaining at a particular time and place than the specific actions of persons. Nevertheless, such actions play an indispensable role in an historical narrative. An account of the Fourth Crusade, in noting that the crusaders attacked the Christian cities of Zara and Constantinople before proceeding to the Holy Land, would have to say that the leaders of the crusade 'decided' to do so, but such an apparent perversion of the crusade's aim would not be intelligible without an explanation of the circumstances under which the decision was made. In short, the historian does not treat the actions of persons as capricious or inexplicable, but as rational, given their aims and the circumstances. Historical events are explained by invoking the notion of 'situational rationality'. The historian contends not that the economic, political, etc., circumstances of the time determined events, but that they constitute the conditions that made it rational for individuals to undertake the actions that played a role in bringing them to pass.

Numerous supporters of Hempel's thesis have advanced the contention that explanation (by means of covering laws) has the same logical form as prediction. A prediction shows that an event is a necessary consequence of certain causes and conditions because it is logically deducible from them; an explanation shows what causes and conditions would logically entail the event in question. Explanation, therefore, is simply 'prediction in reverse'. In practice, however, it is frequently possible to explain phenomena that could not have been predicted. For example, a biologist can explain how the zebra evolved from earlier organic forms, but he would not claim that it could have been predicted to occur. The strong supporters of the covering law model regard this as due to lack of information: *if* all the facts and relevant laws had been known before the zebra had evolved, its emergence *could* have been predicted. (For a good example of this argument see May Brodbeck, 'Explanation, Prediction, and "Imperfect" Knowledge', *Minnesota Studies in the Philosophy of Science*, 1963.) According to this view, one could have predicted that the forces of the Fourth Crusade would attack Constantinople; that this would have so weakened the Byzantine empire that the Turks would extend their territorial control into Europe; that, however, they would be stopped at Vienna; and so on. In short, the old problem of determinism is raised again.

In the effort to escape from the notion that we live in a world that could have been predicted by a Laplacean intelligence at the time of the big bang, commentators have resorted to many considerations, from the indeterminacy principle of quantum mechanics to the notion that God occasionally intervenes in worldly affairs. Karl Popper argues in his *Poverty of Historicism* (1957) that the notion is *logically* untenable: if the future were predictable, men would act on the basis of those predictions, thus altering events from what they would otherwise be and proving the prediction false. This is not a compelling demonstration, since it inserts freedom of action into the premises of an argument that sets out to prove its existence. What lies at the bottom of the notion of situational rationality is the idea that one may explain human actions by construing them as resulting from the decisions that rational persons would make, without claiming that they were *compelled* to make them. This is the kernel of all claims that the historian employs non-causal modes of explanation. Defenders of Hempel contend that such modes are causal after all, but many of them are as unwilling to accept determinism as the critics. The notion that humans have power to alter their future requires one to believe that events have causes, and these causes in turn have causes, and so on, but, somewhere in the chain, there are elements that may act as causes but are themselves uncaused. Though I hold this view myself I do not undertake to defend it here. Determinism and freedom are notions that can be clarified by discussion, but any effort to prove or disprove them draws one into terrain that is swamp, all the way down.

B. METAPHYSICAL HISTORY

In this chapter we have so far paid no explicit attention to what is often described in the literature as 'the philosophy of history'. This phrase refers to the notion that past events are manifestations of a universal design, the apprehension of which is the chief task of the historian. This is the 'covering law model' writ large, so to speak: instead of calling upon the historian to state the general empirical laws that govern particular events, as Hempel does, it contends that all events are governed by One Great Law. Since the present and future, as well as the past, are manifestations of this design, the historian who can grasp it transcends the picayune attempts of economists, sociologists, and other social scientists to analyse contemporary conditions and assess their trends. The phrase 'philosophy of history' is too broad for this genre, while the terms 'historicism' (Karl Popper and F. A. Hayek) and 'historiosophy' (Isaiah Berlin) are too narrow. I refer to it here as 'metaphysical history' because it approaches historical events in the metaphysical mode, that is, in terms of their 'essential nature' rather than their concrete 'appearances'.

In our examination of the idea of 'harmonious order' in Chapter 10 we noted that A. O. Lovejoy, in his study of the metaphysical conception of the world as a *Great Chain of Being* (1936), pointed out that this idea, which originally viewed reality in static terms, began to be 'temporalized' in the eighteenth century: the great chain of being was transformed into a great chain of *becoming*. Instead of conceiving the world as a plenitude in which all possibilities of existence *do* exist, metaphysicians began to regard it as an evolving system in which all consistent possibilities are destined to come into existence through the slow unfolding of time. History, according to this view, is the process by which the inner design of the world is progressively realized. Discovering 'the One in the Many' is therefore the task of the historian rather than the analytical philosopher, since the One is concretely manifest as a dynamic force in the sequential events that the historian studies. This notion was in fundamental disagreement with the view, growing steadily since the seventeenth century, that the empirical natural sciences represent the mode of investigation appropriate for all phenomena. Idealist metaphysics, in retreat during the Age of Enlightenment, was infused with new vigour, which derived not from its old association with theology but from a new association with history. By the time that natural science had itself begun to colonize the territory of history with Darwin's theory of organic evolution, metaphysical history was a powerful intellectual force, with intimate links to other important developments in nineteenth-century thought, most notably romanticism, socialism, and nationalism.

The idea that the One that is in the Many is revealed in history can be found in many eighteenth-century and early nineteenth-century writers. Carl Menger, in his fierce polemic against the German historical school of economists (see above, Chapter 9 F), observed that the various proponents of a 'philosophy of history' agree that there is an inner essential singularity at work within history's phenomenal diversity, but identify it quite differently:

> The proof of the constant advance of the human race in its historical development (Perrault, Turgot, Leroux); the proof that the development of the human race takes place in definite epochs (Condorcet); the proof that history is the progressive realization of the idea of freedom (Michelet),

an education of the human race (Lessing), a progress toward the realization of the idea of humanity (Herder); the proof that the history of individual nations shows a rising line, a peak, and a falling line of development (Bodin, Vico); the proof that the ultimate goal of all history is the formation of a state in which freedom and necessity attain harmonious union (Schelling); indeed, even the proof that French civilization is the type of human civilization in general (Guizot) - these have all been designated already as philosophy of history. (*Problems of Economics and Sociology*, 1883/1963, p. 121 n.)

This is a nice passage, but Menger does not mention explicitly the writer who was most important in introducing metaphysical history into Western thought, G. W. F. Hegel. In Chapter 13 we noted the influence of Hegel on Marx and Engels, but his impact on the European intellect was much broader than this. Most modern readers of Hegel find him attempting to explain the incomprehensible by means of the inscrutable, and it would serve no useful purpose to try to describe here Hegel's conception of history as the process by which *Geist* progressively realizes itself. At any rate, Hegel's main impact derived from his promotion of the general *idea* of metaphysical history rather than his particular metaphysical conception and the details of his argument. Most of those who were inspired by Hegel, like Marx and Engels, felt free to construct their own metaphysical histories or social theories, devoid of Hegel's specifics, or select whatever Hegelian elements they wished, or turn them upside down.

Since René Descartes's *Discourse on Method* (1637), Western philosophy has been much concerned with the 'mind-body problem': the existence of two distinct, and seemingly disjunct, types of phenomena, human thought and consciousness on the one hand, and the material world on the other. (In Chapter 10 A we examined Leibniz's attempt to solve this problem, since his conception of harmonious order is relevant to some major issues in social theory and social philosophy.) The problem continues to be debated, because there are only two synoptic solutions of it, both of which are unacceptable. One of these contends that mind is really matter; consciousness is a phenomenon of the material brain, not categorically different from other physiological functions or, indeed, from any phenomena of the non-organic world. The other solution contends that matter is really mind; even phenomena that appear to be non-organic, such as the gravitational attraction between masses, is the work of a force akin to human consciousness. The monistic doctrine of *mechanism*, which regards men as like stones, is no more convincing than monistic *animism*, in which stones are like men, but the natural sciences were able to progress as they did by adopting metaphysical mechanism as a heuristic ontology. The rejection of this by the idealist philosophers of the late eighteenth and early nineteenth centuries was, in considerable part, a rebellion against science and a struggle against the application of its methodology to the study of man and society.

For the romantics a prime defect of the mechanistic philosophy was its denial of human freedom. Emphasizing as they did the importance of the individual, and his power to influence events, they rejected the view that the world is law-governed in the way that the natural scientists asserted, and the social scientists were beginning to claim. But, at the same time, they regarded the events that result from individual actions as controlled by a cosmic design and, following J. G. von Herder, they insisted that the individual person is a member of a larger whole, a society, which is an organic entity in itself. Hegel appealed to the romantics because his conception of history seemed to provide a resolution of these apparently conflicting views. Hegel's concept of 'the cunning of reason' was an elaboration of Giambattista Vico's argument that Providence realizes its intent through the history that men make by their actions. Men are free to act, but the desires that motivate them (as social beings) are part of a cosmic plan: 'freedom' and 'necessity' are one. The logic of this is questionable, but it struck a responsive chord with the romantics, who regarded the individualism of utilitarian theory, classical economics, and capitalism as a false individualism, insufficiently cognizant of the holistic nature of society and the transcendent mission of human history.

We can now see the connection between metaphysical history and political philosophy through its impact on the romantic movement of the nineteenth century. Romanticism, despite its individualism, was allied with the growing sentiment of nationalism, and with socialism construed as a form of society that would replace the mechanistic procedures of capitalism with the organic unity of social purpose. Metaphysical history appealed to the romantics by assuring them that, despite their defeats of the previous two centuries on the fields of thought and practice, ultimate victory would be theirs, for human history has a transcendent purpose or goal. Like all who embrace such a conception of history, they interpreted this goal as the realization of a society that would embody their own ethical and political values. Empirical history, however, fails to pay attention to philosophers, since humans perversely refuse to obey the laws they claim to have discovered. But it would be erroneous to convey the impression that the conception of history as governed by general laws appealed only to thinkers who regarded metaphysical philosophy as capable of finding deeper truths than empirical science. John Stuart Mill, for example, who shared none of these views and wrote his great treatise on epistemology (*A System of Logic*, 1843) to support the empiricist stance of science, nevertheless held that 'the course of [human] history is subject to general laws, which philosophy may possibly detect'. He lauded Auguste Comte for pioneering work in this and expressed regret that English thinkers had not followed the lead of continental ones in searching for these laws. Mill himself did nothing to advance this mode of historical investigation and, despite his exhortation, metaphysical history did not successfully migrate to England. For a long time after, a notable difference between English and continental (including Marx and Engels) social scientists continued to be that many of the latter aimed to detect, by 'philosophy', the transcendent governing laws of historical evolution, while the former addressed their efforts to the achievement of more modest objectives.

C. HISTORICAL EXPLANATION AS ART

In Hempel's 1942 essay he contrasts his methodological thesis with 'the familiar view that genuine explanation in history is obtained by a method which characteristically distinguishes the social from the natural sciences, namely, *the method of empathetic understanding*'. According to this view, the historian must go beyond the specific empirical evidence revealed through examination of documents and statistics; he must study the general culture of the time and place, its literature, art, language, etc., in order to arrive at an understanding of what life was like, how people thought, their hopes and fears, their conception of themselves, their society, and the world. Only by such means can the historian who belongs to one culture give an accurate and penetrating account of events that took place in another. Few historians would deny that this is a necessary part of the historian's craft, but some advance the larger contention that it is the essential nature of history, making it, as Hempel notes, a profoundly different enterprise from physics or biology, more like one of the arts than any of the natural sciences. This view is frequently encountered in the debate over historical method, often under the rubric of a German term, *verstehen*, which means 'to understand', as opposed to *wissen*, 'to know'. The most prominent names in the twentieth-century expression of this view are Max Weber (1864–1920), Benedetto Croce (1866–1952), and R. G. Collingwood (1889–1943), but it will assist our comprehension of it if we go back to its origins in the eighteenth century in the writings of Giambattista Vico (1668–1744) and J. G. von Herder (1744–1803). (Isaiah Berlin, himself a strong supporter and exemplary practitioner of the approach to history we are examining here, has written excellent essays on these two figures: *Vico and Herder: Two Studies in the History of Ideas*, 1976.)

There are aspects of Vico's view of history that identify him as a 'metaphysical' historian, since he believed that historical events reflect the working of a cosmic design of development that was God's intention when he made the world. These were noted in the previous section; here we are concerned with Vico's epistemology, his view of how man, who is not God, can conduct an empirical investigation of history. Only God knows history in its totality, because he made the world, but the specific events of history can be understood by the human intellect, says Vico, because they are made by human actions. The historian shares the quality of humanity with those men, great and small, whose actions create the phenomena of history. This enables him to enter *inside* the historical process, thus achieving a subjective understanding of it that is more profound than the objective knowledge attainable by the natural scientist, who is compelled to remain *outside* the phenomena he studies. The historian can understand what it was like to be Henry of Navarre and change his religious allegiance from Protestantism to Catholicism. No one can know what it is like to be water molecules changing from a liquid to a solid. As Berlin puts Vico's view, 'in history we are the actors, in the natural sciences mere spectators'. By this reasoning Vico made the bold claim that one can discover laws of social development that are more certain even than the laws of physics. In calling his book *New Science* (1725) he meant to contend that the science of history furnishes the most precise and most irrefutable form of human knowledge. Historians, and other social scientists, have no need to consider themselves inferior to natural scientists, or to try to mimic their methodology, for a categorically different, and superior, methodology is available to them. Vico's views received little notice during his own lifetime, but in the nineteenth century they found a sympathetic response in the romantic movement, which rebelled against the prestige of natural science and rejected its claim to represent the universal methodology of knowledge. In Chapter 15 C below we shall encounter a similar idea to Vico's, but not a romantic one, in the methodological thought of the sociologist Max Weber.

If Vico had argued, as Hobbes and the Scottish moralists had, that the process of personal introspection enables one to arrive at universally true propositions concerning 'human nature' which may be employed as premises in analytical models of social phenomena, he would not have been saying anything that a social scientist would find incompatible with the methodology of objective science. But Vico held that men live in societies that differ greatly in their cultural characteristics. The historian can investigate a society that has now passed from the scene, not by applying universal principles of human nature, but by achieving an intimate understanding of what it was like to have been a member of such a society or one of its leaders.

Herder did not make the same grandiose epistemological claims as Vico, but he played an important part in promoting the notion of history as the art of cultural understanding by amplifying the conception of cultural diversity and stressing its importance for historical research. In Herder we find the compound of cultural pluralism, social holism, and expressionistic individualism that was to become characteristic of romanticism. The desire for individual self-expression is fundamental to man's nature but, says Herder, the individual can develop his capacities and realize his potential only by belonging to a community, united with other members of it by sharing a common culture. Culturally homogeneous societies are, for Herder, the natural units of human existence. This does not mean, though, that all societies are culturally the same, or that they should be. On the contrary, cultural diversity is a natural characteristic of human social existence, just as it is natural that each individual identifies with his own culture. In order to study a culture that differs from one's own, it is necessary to do as Vico advised: enter into the communal life of its people, study their art and language and ways of thinking, do more than *know* what they do, *understand* them as social beings. The historian, even when he studies the past of his own society, must make such efforts, since culture changes over time.

In the writings of Benedetto Croce and R. G. Collingwood we find strong reaffirmation of these views. The importance of economic, geographic, and other material factors in history is not denied, but they are made subordinate to the mental factors that motivated men to act as they did. The historian must know the facts, but he must, more importantly, understand the mentalities of those whose actions created the events of history, and he can accomplish this by transporting himself, so to speak, into their minds. The historian, according to this point of view, is like an actor who, trained in the 'method' school of Constantin Stanislavsky, plays a role by 'becoming' the character. To project Shakespeare's Lear to an audience, the actor must get 'inside' the character to such a degree that when he appears upon the stage he *is*, for a few hours, a naive and foolish king who does not appreciate the true qualities of his daughters. When the historian sits down to write of Henry IV's religious conversion, he thinks himself into the mind of a newly crowned late sixteenth-century king of France, faced with the problem of consolidating his power. In order to project to the reader, the narrative historian must employ the techniques of literary art, writing the true story of real events as the novelist tells a story about imaginary ones. Croce and Collingwood wished to preserve and promote the craft of history as an artistic discipline. They rejected the contention that the epistemology of science is appropriate for the study of man's past and, in particular, fought against the growing attempt to apply the theories and methods of the social sciences to historical phenomena. Few modern historians are prepared to accept the extreme contentions of Vico and Herder, or Croce and Collingwood, but in the typical history department of a modern university one finds historians who see themselves as literary craftsmen, different from their colleagues who construct statistical measures and apply economic and sociological theories to the investigation of the past. (For a good defence of the view that history cannot be and should not be a science, by a modern master craftsman of literary history, see Isaiah Berlin, 'History and Theory: The Concept of Scientific History', *History and Theory*, 1960.)

In my view, this conception of history has merit and, moreover, has justified itself by performance rather than by mere methodological preaching. One cannot read the best works of literary history without admitting that they tell us some things about the past that are good to know. There is no need to say that they tell us *everything* we want to know in order to defend their claims to territory. The employment by such historians of the techniques of literary art may excite the suspicion of the plain-speaking scientist, but such techniques can be efficient devices of communication and there is no reason why they should not be used. The main complaint that can be levied against the craft of literary history is that it lends itself to political propaganda, and to a powerful form of it in societies where people look to their past as a definition of their culture. When the historian persuades himself that he is the ordained steward of a people's culture, and that his mission is to sing of the glories of his race or nation (as he conceives them to be), he is likely to understand the past no better than a scientist who is determined to make the data conform to his theory. That some literary historians write propaganda is no ground for a general condemnation, however; some scientific historians grind their own axes exceedingly broad.

D. HISTORICAL EVENTS AND SOCIAL LAWS

In the preceding sections I have talked about 'historical phenomena' and 'historical events' without offering any definition of them. This is not as unproblematic as it may first appear. The events that took place at Pearl Harbor on the morning of 7 December 1941 can be called 'historical' in a loose sense, but their specific historical import may be variously described, for example, as 'the bombing of Pearl Harbor by Japanese aircraft', 'the attempt by the Japanese to obtain naval predominance in the western Pacific', 'the entry of the United States into the second World War', 'the beginning of a new phase in the struggle between democracy and dictatorship', and so on. As historical phenomena, events do not carry natural descriptions, and different historians will describe them differently, each adopting a different focus for his narrative, depending upon whether he sets out to write a military history, a political history, an economic history, a religious history, etc. Every statement that one can make about events is an 'historical' statement, since all events have a time locus, but, paradoxical though it may appear, there are no strictly *historical* statements, since every sentence that one may write about events refers to an empirical phenomenon which substantively belongs under some other heading: politics, economics, geography, etc. Even the metaphysical historian cannot write about history in itself, though he may often use language that implies that he is doing so.

Further difficulties are encountered when the historian attempts to discuss events under a generic heading such as 'war', 'revolution', or 'business cycles'. Not only do the different instances differ, but in some cases the existence of the generic category may be subject to doubt. The term 'business cycle', for example, implies that certain economic events have a regular periodicity, but the facts fail to demonstrate this, and the historian who focuses too rigidly upon such a generic category may spend much time explaining a non-existent phenomenon. The stock market crash of 1929 is a fairly definite historical event, the Great Depression of the 1930s less so, and the 'business cycle' so much less so that it may be like the unicorn, existing in the mind rather than in the world.

Difficulties accumulate in profusion when the historian sets out to cultivate a domain that is defined in normative terms. An account of 'capitalist exploitation', for example, requires some theory of 'exploitation' as well as a satisfactory generic description of 'capitalism'. Some historians regard such investigations as the chief task of history, but the reader is frequently left to supply these elements for himself, the writer considering them too obvious to warrant explication or, at any rate, disdaining to offer any.

Narrative history of the traditional sort avoids these problems to a considerable degree. The problem of generic categories does not enter if the historian restricts himself to giving an account of events that occurred at a specific time and place. A history of the War of 1812 can be written without any necessary reference to 'war' as a generic social phenomenon. The problem of aspect is considerably eased if the historian adopts the view that *one* aspect of events is his primary concern. The long tradition of narrative history, now in decline, is that the proper subject matter of history is *politics*, the actions of governments and their leaders. A traditional narrative history of the War of 1812 would necessarily have a good deal to say about economics, geography, etc., but its main emphasis would be on political events in the United States, Britain, and the Canadian colonies. Modern historiography has been departing from this tradition in two ways: by laying much greater emphasis on the economic and sociological aspects of past events, and by utilizing the theories and empirical techniques of economics and sociology in the study of them. Defenders of traditional narrative history do not object greatly to the former, but they have strong reservations concerning the latter, as we have seen in our examination of the debate over Hempel's thesis on historical methodology.

In order to clarify this matter it is necessary to distinguish the contention that there are laws of history as such from the much more modest claim that there are laws of social phenomena that may be applied to the study of historical events (see Maurice Mandelbaum, 'A Critique of Philosophies of History', *Journal of Philosophy*, 1948). The first of these regards the historian as engaged in the *discovery* of laws, while the second argues that he should *use* laws already established by social scientists. This point can perhaps be made clear by an analogical illustration. Let us consider a 'wake-up machine' of the sort that the cartoonists Rube Goldberg and Heath Robinson used to draw: the descending weight of a grandfather clock trips the catch on a container, causing a heavy iron ball to fall on the bulb of an old-fashioned automobile horn. The resulting sound startles a cat, whose tail is tied to a rope, the other end of which is attached to a bucket of water which tips over, spilling its contents on the sleeper. The emptying of the water causes the bucket, which had been balanced by a rope over a pulley attached to a weight, to rise, and the weight to fall. In its rise the bucket strikes a switch which turns on the coffee pot while the descending weight moves the setting on a thermostat controlling the furnace. These events can be explained, but not in terms of a comprehensive 'law of Rube Goldberg machines'. What serves the purpose are a number of more specific laws concerning falling bodies, the effect of the rapid passage of air through a small aperture, the behaviour of startled cats, etc. Historians are correct in rejecting the notion that we should search for laws of war, or revolution, or the rise and decline of civilizations, but they are wrong if they insist that no laws at all operate in such events.

Traditional narrative historians have been as critical of metaphysical history as any other scholars, and few would wish to defend even milder versions of the notion that there are general laws of history already known or awaiting discovery. But their opposition to the claim that the work of the historian can be improved by the application of modern social science is less defensible. William Dray, one of the most tenacious critics of Hempel's thesis, declares that 'there are few historical events that we can hope to explain in terms of theories borrowed from the special [social] sciences' (*Laws and Explanations in History*, 1957, p. 66). This seems to me to be mistaken.

Rejection of the application of social science theories and techniques to the study of historical phenomena may be due in part to the traditional emphasis of narrative history on politics. Dray would be on more solid ground if he had said that the discipline of political science contains few general theories of politics. In fact, political scientists borrow most of their theories from economics and sociology. This does not mean that historians cannot be borrowers too, though it does suggest that political historians might do better to borrow their economics and sociology direct rather than third-hand. More important is the view that historians, whether they focus upon politics or other aspects of past events, cannot borrow from *any* science, because science deals with the similarities of phenomena while historians deal with unique events. This comes down to the contention that probabilistic concepts and statistical empirical methods, which is what social and other scientists employ in dealing with non-homogeneous phenomena, are inapplicable to many of the things that historians study and, in particular, to those that form the main subject matter of narrative history. As Ernest Nagel puts it, a distinction is drawn between two categorically different types of disciplines, 'the nomothetic, which seek to establish [he should have added "or apply"] abstract general laws for indefinitely repeatable processes; and the ideographic [*sic*], which aim to understand the unique and nonrecurrent', history being one of the latter ('Some Issues in the Logic of Historical Analysis', *Scientific Monthly*, 1952). The terms 'nomothetic' and 'idiographic' in this connection were first coined by the Kantian philosopher of history Wilhelm Windelband.

At first sight there seems to be much merit in the claim that economists and sociologists may be able to convert idiographic phenomena into nomothetic ones by the use of statistical reasoning but historians cannot. The economist can accept the fact that, when the price of a commodity changes, individual consumers may respond in very different ways, without abandoning the law of demand, because it refers to the aggregate behaviour of many consumers.

There may have been many wars, but they do not share enough in common to be grouped under a generic heading, and therefore, it is claimed, neither war in general nor any single instance of war can be explained by using laws that apply probabilistically to large numbers of similar events. This contention rests on two misapprehensions. First, one need not claim that social science can explain events like wars; in order to do so a Law of War would indeed have to be advanced, and few social scientists are bold enough to do that. Instead, social science laws are deemed to apply to economic and social conditions, and the same laws apply to conditions that are not at all restricted to wars. The historian is urged to apply economic theory not directly in explaining the War of 1812 but in analysing factors such as U.S. foreign trade, which he indeed discusses in his account of that war. Wars may be too heterogeneous to be made the subject of a nomothetic discipline, but international trade is not.

Secondly, in rejecting probabilistic reasoning, the proponent of idiographic history is referring only to a particular type of probability theory, that which construes a probability as a statement of the relative frequency of one type of event within a larger class of similar events, such as the frequency with which a seven, say, will occur in a large number of throws of a pair of dice. This view of probability is prominent in statistical practice but it has recently given way to conceptions that are not restricted to events of such homogeneity. If one were to adopt the notion of probability which construes it in terms of the relation between the event one predicts, or explains, and the evidence one has for making a predictive or explanatory assertion, probabilistic reasoning would not be ruled inapplicable to the kind of events that even the most idiographic historian undertakes to examine.

Finally, we may note that the historian who is adamant in rejecting the use of economics and sociology will find himself forced into some contentions about the methodology of these disciplines as well as his own. If economic theory and its empirical techniques are applicable to the study of current events, why do they become inapplicable when those events recede into the past and become 'history'? Some writers on the epistemology of social science argue that the methodology of natural science is unsuitable for the study of human social phenomena, whether current or past. The rejection of social science by traditional narrative historians is, in perhaps large part, based on the view that social scientists, in following natural science, have adopted a methodology of social investigation that is fatally flawed. This is a much larger issue than we are concerned with in this chapter. We have already touched upon it and will do so again below.

Chapter 15

The development of sociological theory

Discussion of the history of sociology poses some special difficulties, since it is not easy to define the subject matter of sociology in a way that differentiates it distinctively from the other social sciences, and there is little agreement among sociologists as to which older writings ought to be regarded as the most significant landmarks in the development of the modern discipline. Chapter 12, which dealt with the ideas of Henri Saint-Simon and Auguste Comte, was called 'French Positivism and the Beginnings of Sociology' but, though Saint-Simon and Comte were important in the development of nineteenth-century social thought, their writings were too speculative and metaphysical to be regarded as antecedents of what is denoted by either 'positivism' or 'sociology' in modern discourse. Through Marx and Engels, the notion of a comprehensive social science embracing all social phenomena in a unified theoretical model that would provide a scientific account of human history, explain contemporary society, and predict the future, derived a powerful impetus that has carried it through to the present day as an intellectual and political ideal. However, the mainstream tradition of modern sociological research, especially in the United States, neither practises nor professes to find much inspiration in such Grand Sociology. Most sociologists would not refer to Saint-Simon or Comte as precursors, much less founders, of their discipline; so the title of Chapter 12 is not one that could be defended very strongly.

In tracing the beginnings of modern sociology as an empirical science that uses theoretical constructs, not as metaphysical verities, but as heuristic concepts and models, our attention must be directed at the literature of the later nineteenth and early twentieth centuries. In this era a large number of writers contributed to providing a shape and focus for modern sociology, but three of them tower above the others, and this chapter will be devoted primarily to them: Herbert Spencer, an Englishman, Émile Durkheim, a Frenchman, and Max Weber, a German. As we shall see, these writers did not reject altogether the style of Grand Sociology that Saint-Simon and Comte represented so strikingly but, in their work, distinct progress is evident in the direction of examining human social phenomena in the methodological mode that modern social science has embraced. In their substantive studies of social behaviour and in their extended discussions of methodology Spencer, Durkheim, and Weber effectively defined the subject matter of modern sociology and developed many of the concepts that sociologists have since found useful in theoretical and empirical research. Their work therefore marks the transition between the older conception of sociology, in which the proportion of empirical science to metaphysics is small, to the modern one, which aims at the inverse ratio. During the period that saw the emergence of sociology as a distinct academic discipline it advanced more rapidly in America than in Europe, but it was these European thinkers who were most important in the initial development of its scientific foundations.

A. HERBERT SPENCER (1820–1903)

Herbert Spencer was born in the English Midland town of Derby. His mother may have been subject to the RH Factor disease, since she gave birth to nine children but only the first, Herbert, survived. He was educated privately by his father, who was a teacher by profession, and later by an uncle who was a clergyman. Neither of these imposed a strict course of studies; his own interests were allowed to determine the curriculum. He emerged from this educational regimen with a very different fund of knowledge from that of the typical product of the English schools of the period: a good command of mathematics and physics, but almost no knowledge of classical languages and literature. He was, in terms of the standards of the time, inadequately prepared for university work, but he seems not to have been much interested in attending university anyway. At the age of seventeen he obtained employment with a railway company and, quite rapidly, was doing the work of a professional civil engineer.

Except for an early article on the Poor Law, Spencer's first publications were on engineering and related subjects (see Jay Rumney, *Herbert Spencer's Sociology*, 1966, for a bibliography of Spencer's writings). A pamphlet on *The Proper Sphere of Government* (1843), consisting of letters originally published in the *Nonconformist* newspaper, initiated Spencer's career as a writer on social subjects. From this point on, his dominating interest was in what, following Comte, he called 'sociology'. His early work in natural science, as a student and practising engineer, had convinced him that the combination of theoretical modelling and empirical evidence that formed the characteristic methodology of natural science was the appropriate procedure for the study of all phenomena. Given his youthful studies of physics and mathematics, and his work as an engineer, one might have expected Spencer to look to Newtonian mechanics for a modelling paradigm, but he sought inspiration elsewhere, in biology rather than physics. The intellectual and philosophical impact of developments in biological science during the Victorian era was profound and widespread, affecting Western thought to a degree matched only by the revolution in physics of the seventeenth century. Spencer's work in sociology, to a greater extent than that of any other major social scientist, forged a connection between the study of social phenomena and the field of biology. He was not the first, nor the last, to utilize biological concepts and biological findings in social science, but he was exceptionally important in the manner in which he did so, and in the influence of his sociological theories in an era that witnessed the great challenges to traditional thinking that attended the delineation of the theory of species evolution by Charles Darwin.

In 1846 Spencer went to London and obtained employment as an assistant editor of the *Economist*. This weekly newspaper, which is still published today, was founded in 1843 as a vehicle for the promotion of the free-trade policies of the Anti-Corn Law League. As we noted in Chapter 10, the *Economist* deserves mention in connection with the history of the doctrine of 'harmonious social order', since, in promoting the cause of free trade, it appealed to the more general principle of *laissez-faire* in economic policy, which it derived from the even more general principle of metaphysical natural harmony. The views that the *Economist* put forward in its columns were similar to those that Spencer had expressed in his pamphlet on *The Proper Sphere of Government*. Spencer did not write articles for the *Economist*; his work there was concerned mainly with editing the commercial news and statistical information published in it. He was engaged at this time in composing a book that would elaborate and clarify the ideas of his *Proper Sphere*, and took the editorial post at the *Economist* as a way of earning a living in an occupation that would allow time for his own writing. In 1850 he published this book, *Social Statics*, which brought him immediate recognition and opened the doors of the leading journals to contributions by him. A legacy received upon the death of his uncle in 1853, plus the growing prospect of earning income from his writings, enabled him to resign from the *Economist*. From that point on he devoted himself entirely to research and writing. He never married, lived frugally, and devoted a good deal of his income to defraying the costs of comprehensive compilations of empirical data that he felt were necessary for work in sociology.

The first and last of Spencer's major works, *Social Statics* (1850) and *The Man versus the State* (1884) suggest that his main abiding interest was in political theory. So it was, but Spencer did not pursue this interest in the traditional style of political philosophy, in which the main object was to derive propositions about the legitimacy of state power by deduction from postulated 'primary principles' of theology, moral philosophy, or meta-physics. Spencer's cast of mind was more like Montesquieu's or the Scottish moralists' than that of Hobbes or Locke, Aquinas or Hegel. In Spencer's way of thinking, political organization is part of a larger structure, social organization in general, and scientific study of society is necessary to the derivation of sound propositions about politics. Though Spencer's main interest may have always been strongly focused on the issue of the relation of the individual to the state – the central problem of political philosophy – he early embraced the view that it must be examined from a comprehensive standpoint, one that examines the individual as a member of a society, and treats the state as one among its many institutional structures.

By 1858 at the latest Spencer had also developed the notion that social phenomena must be viewed in terms of evolutionary change. He wrote, in that year, a 'Prospectus of a System of Philosophy' in which he outlined the 'Synthetic Philosophy', the work to which he intended to devote his life. The 'Prospectus' projected an initial volume dealing with 'First Principles', that is, the philosophy of science, which would be followed by comprehensive multi-volume surveys of biology, psychology (on which Spencer had already published a book), and sociology, and conclude with two volumes on 'The Principles of Morality'. The 'Prospectus' was not published until 1860. In the meantime Darwin's *Origin of Species* had appeared, creating the impression that Spencer was seeking to capitalize on the intense interest in evolution that was generated by Darwin's work. In fact, Spencer had developed his evolutionary viewpoint independently and, indeed, he even anticipated the publication of the *Origin* in suggesting that evolutionary development results from what Darwin called 'natural selection'. Darwin and Spencer were the two great evolutionary thinkers of the Victorian era. Everyone then knew their names; today, everyone still knows who Darwin was, but Spencer has been forgotten by all but specialists in intellectual history.

Even more remarkable than Spencer's 'Prospectus' was that he actually followed it. *First Principles* appeared in 1862; *Principles of Biology*, in two volumes, in 1864 and 1867; *Principles of Sociology*, in volumes and 'parts' of volumes between 1876 and 1896, overlapping with the *Principles of Ethics*, which was published, similarly, between 1879 and 1893. Nor was this all. In addition, he published several other books and many articles. The collected edition of his works runs to twenty-one volumes. From the standpoint of the history of modern sociology, special note should be made of the anthropological data compiled by his research assistants which Spencer began to publish in 1873 under the title of *Descriptive Sociology*, and a book that he wrote in response to a request for a statement of the problems involved in making a scientific study of society, *The Study of Sociology* (1873). The first of these stands as a landmark in the study of comparative anthropology because of its systematic organization of ethnographic data, which inspired G. P. Murdock in creating the Yale University 'Human Relations Area Files', now found in every large library. The second deserves reading today, not only for what it tells us about Spencer's views, but for trenchant discussion of the factors that continue to stand in the way of objective examination of social phenomena.

To survey all Spencer's writings here would take us far beyond the scope of this book. Our attention will be focused on those aspects of his thought that were of special importance in the history of sociology or in the debate over the philosophy of social science.

1. The scientific study of society

Spencer's first book, *Social Statics*, contains a mixture of incompatible philosophical views, reflecting the lack of coherence typical of the autodidact who has not yet digested the materials obtained from voracious private reading. One finds in it expression of the relation between sense data and mental phenomena that resembles Hume's radical empiricism; a metaphysical harmonism that reminds one of Leibniz; Aristotle's teleological causality; a view of progress that is as secular as Bentham's in its focus on human happiness, but also deist in attributing this to divine design; a determinism as complete as Laplace's, but an insistence on the freedom of the individual comparable to that of the romantics; a political philosophy of extreme individualism, denigrating socialism and even the milder measures of collective action embraced by contemporary liberals, yet asserting confidently that progress will eventually transform men into altruistic beings who will value the happiness of others as much as their own. Over the next decade Spencer shed some of these youthful notions and reconsidered the rest. By the time he wrote the Prospectus for his life's work he had developed a coherent philosophy, centring on the conception of man and society as natural phenomena which can be understood by applying the methods of investigation that had been adopted in the natural sciences. As we have seen, this was not a new idea. Spencer did not claim to have originated it; he felt, with good reason, that, except in political economy, such methods had not yet been applied to human social behaviour. He adopted Comte's term 'sociology' for a more comprehensive study of social organization that would deserve to be called scientific.

The word 'sociology' was not common in England in the 1860's, except among the disciples of Comte. In adopting it, Spencer did not intend to declare himself a Comtean, and he made no attempt to associate himself with the positivist movement of Congreve and Harrison which was then growing rapidly in intellectual circles (see Chapter 12 C). In fact, Spencer was anxious to differentiate his views from those of Comte, which he regarded as scientifically erroneous and politically pernicious. In 1864, responding to a French review of his *First Principles*, describing him as a follower of Comte, he wrote an essay entitled 'Reasons for Dissenting from the Philosophy of M. Comte' in which he rejected Comte's central doctrines of the three stages of intellectual evolution and the hierarchy of the sciences, and noted that his own political philosophy was the very antithesis of Comte's. He pointed out that because Comte had distinguished 'positive philosophy' from theology it did not mean that everyone who rejected theological explanations of worldly events was a follower of Comte, since this would make many people 'followers' who had lived long before; and, moreover, Comte had not correctly understood the nature of scientific method. Spencer amplified his disagreement with Comte on general matters by noting specific points on which they differed. As to similarities, Spencer admitted that he and Comte drew analogies between the individual organisms studied by biologists and the 'social organisms' that were the subject matter of sociology, but pointed out that many others had preceded both of them in this respect, and averred that his own inspiration in this connection was derived, not from Comte or any other social theorist, but from the empirical work in embryology of natural scientists such as William Harvey and Karl Ernst von Baer. Spencer's proposition that social evolution is characterized by increasing differentiation of component parts and the specialization of their functions was anticipated by Comte (see above, Chapter 12 B), but his persistent practice of illustrating this by analogy with the tissue differentiation that takes place in embryological development leaves little room to doubt his assertion that von Baer was the source of this central proposition in his sociology. Spencer's paper should have put the matter of his relation to Comte to rest, but it did not, and even today one finds commentators on Spencer saying that he was indebted to Comte, on no more ground, apparently, than that he adopted the term 'sociology' and regarded social phenomena as governed by laws.

What did Spencer mean in contending that sociology could be a science? In his view, science is characterized by the construction of theoretical models supported by empirical evidence. Social phenomena can be modelled because they are governed, as natural phenomena are, by causal laws. In taking this stance Spencer abandoned altogether the deism of his youth and also set himself in opposition against those who interpreted history in terms of the autonomous actions of 'great men'. Much of what he had to say about scientific sociology, on this plane, is similar to the argument we noted in Chapter 14 as having been made recently by Carl Hempel concerning the validity of historical explanation. According to this view, explaining a phenomenon involves reference to the 'general laws' which 'cover' it. Such explanation is possible, at least in principle, for all phenomena that are law-governed, which, in Spencer's view, did not exclude human social behaviour and the history of social development.

Adopting this view did not lead Spencer to regard the creation of a scientific sociology as an unproblematic application of the established methods of the natural sciences. He recognized that special difficulties are encountered in the scientific analysis of social phenomena. In 1875, immediately before commencing to write his *Principles of Sociology*, he was invited by an American admirer, Edward L. Youmans, who was editing the 'International Scientific Series', to write a book on sociology for it. This book, *The Study of Sociology*, was Spencer's most sustained discussion of the methodological problems of scientific sociology. It became one of his most influential works, especially in the United States, much more widely read than his *Principles of Sociology*. In the first courses in sociology taught in American universities it was frequently used as a textbook. Few of Spencer's writings are read today, except by students of intellectual history. His substantive sociological theory is archaic. But *The Study of Sociology* retains its original interest, since the special problems of social science that Spencer discusses there have not diminished during the past century.

These special problems, in Spencer's view, do not arise from the great complexity of social phenomena or the difficulty of quantitative measurement. Natural phenomena are also exceedingly complex, and natural scientists are incapable, in many areas, of furnishing explanations, or predictions, that reliably go beyond qualitative statements. The most important difference between the natural and the social sciences lies in the relation between the scientist and his material. The sociologist investigates the properties and problems of a collectivity to which he himself belongs and in whose ambience he has been nurtured from infancy to maturity. Even the exceptional man cannot detach himself completely from his own culture; his inferences and, indeed, the empirical data on which they are based are unavoidably contaminated by preconceptions and value judgements that distort his understanding of both his own and other societies. In addition, there are distortions that result from 'biases' that *can* be avoided by a careful scientist who wishes to be objective, but ensnare those who are doctrinaire and uncritical of their own beliefs, including those who regard the adoption of unorthodox or unpopular beliefs as certification of their scientific or philosophic superiority. Spencer goes on, in successive chapters, to point out the biases resulting from religion, and from dogmatic denigration of religion; from nationalistic loyalty and patriotism, and from the anti-patriotism of those who see no good at all in their own nation; from formal education, and from ignorance; from political partisanship, class identification, and so on. Spencer was over-optimistic in believing that such biases, once identified, can be guarded against, but his *Study of Sociology* is as good as anything that has been written since on the 'emotional' and 'intellectual' difficulties of social science, as Spencer called them.

On the more positive side, Spencer advocated that anyone who hopes to do scientific work in sociology should prepare himself by study of the natural sciences. The good sociologist must be able to think both abstractly and concretely, and he must be able to synthesize as well as analyse. These various 'habits of thought' can best be obtained from the study of natural science. No single science possesses all the requisite qualities, so one must study all of them; but one of the natural sciences is more important to the sociologist than the others: biology. The 'Science of Life' utilizes theoretical conceptions that apply equally well to social phenomena and it 'yields to the Science of Society certain great generalizations without which there can be no Science of Society at all'. Much of Spencer's sociological theory revolves around these 'great generalizations' furnished by biology. His view of the relation between the two sciences should not be confused, however, with the notion that social phenomena are determined by biological factors. Spencer did not intend to argue that social organization and social change are governed by laws that operate at the biological level of human life. On the contrary, he regarded social phenomena as governed by *social* laws. The biological material that is omnipresent in his sociological works is not introduced in order to explain the determinants of the social practices under consideration. It has a quite different import, reflecting two of Spencer's most strongly held views: that there is a parallelism between biological and social organization; and that organic life and social life reveal, each in its own sphere of existence, the process of evolution that is going on, everywhere, in the cosmos. These two notions must not be confounded. As we shall see, Spencer used the first as a heuristic analogy; the second, however, was, for him, a metaphysical truth.

2. The purpose of social organization, and its modes

In the first chapter of this book we noted that the concept of 'society' involves more than the empirical observation that certain species 'live together in groups'. The contiguity of pine trees does not mean that the pine is a social species. Even animals such as domesticated sheep or cattle, which tend to stay close together rather than dispersing themselves, are 'gregarious' rather than truly 'social'. The notion that man is 'by nature' a social animal points to the apparent gregariousness of the human species, but it fails to supply significant insight into the foundations of social organization, much less explain warfare and other phenomena of conflict between human groups. In order to provide a useful footing for the analysis one must recognize society as a type of association that enables the individual members to co-operate with one another in order to achieve objectives as a collectivity that cannot be achieved by independent individual action. *Homo sapiens* is not the only species that is social in this functional sense. Bees and ants are, in some ways, more social than man. But the forms of co-ordination that have developed in human societies are unique. The study of these is the main object, not only of sociology, but of all the social sciences.

One of the most notable features of Herbert Spencer's sociology is his adoption of this utilitarian conception of society. (See, for example, *Principles of Sociology*, V, II). Humans co-operate with one another, not because of God's plan, or because they love one another, or because sociality is part of their intrinsic nature, but because their mundane individual interests can be furthered thereby. According to Spencer, this has been the essential characteristic of social organization from its earliest primitive origins, and throughout its evolution into the complex social systems of civilized societies. Spencer observed that social organization has been oriented to different objectives in different societies, and its structure, accordingly, has taken different forms, but it has always, and everywhere, been primarily instrumental, enabling the members of a society to do things that they cannot do when acting independently of one another.

Spencer distinguished two fundamentally different types of societies, the 'militant' and the 'industrial'. The first type consists of those societies that utilize the increased effectiveness of co-ordinated action in the exercise of force, in aggressive warfare, and in defence against the aggression of other societies. Co-operation, in such societies, is achieved by compulsion, effectuated by means of a hierarchical structure of power and authority, the status of each member being clearly defined in a linear chain of superiority and subordination. Such societies are 'militant' in both their purposes and their organizational form. They are, in effect, like armies: 'The militant type is one in which the army is the nation mobilized while the nation is the quiescent army, and which, therefore, acquires a structure common to army and nation' (*Principles of Sociology*, II, X).

The 'industrial' type of society aims to achieve a different objective – the increased productivity that springs from the division of labour. Its primary mode of organization is not political, and does not require coercion. Co-operation is voluntary, achieved by means of the exchange of goods and services in open markets. The 'industrial' system is a society where the relations between the individual members consist of *ad hoc* 'contracts', which are freely entered into, rather than fixed 'status', a distinction that Sir Henry Maine, a contemporary of Spencer, had been emphasizing in his own writings on comparative social institutions and the history of legal systems. Like Maine, who viewed social evolution as a progressive movement from 'status' to 'contract', Spencer believed that one can perceive in man's history an evolutionary development from the 'militant' form of social organization to the 'industrial'.

One can easily see here the dependence of Spencer's sociological theory on the perception of market transactions as a system of economic co-ordination that had been developed by the classical economists in explicating Adam Smith's notion of the 'invisible hand'. Spencer himself, however, did not write much that can be described as economic theory. One does not find any discussion in his books of the matters that occupied our attention in Chapter 9 above on 'Classical Political Economy'. He seems to have been familiar with the general view of the market system advanced by the classical school (see, for example, *Principles of Sociology*, V, II), but there is no evidence that he had studied the specific theories of value, distribution, and economic development that they had constructed, or that he was aware of the many criticisms of classical economics that had been advanced, or of the work of Marx and Engels, or that he devoted any attention to the revolution in economic theory in the 1870's and 1880's that was transforming the economic analysis of the market mechanism (see Chapter 17 below). Unlike Comte and Durkheim, Spencer had a high opinion of economics as a branch of social science, but his opinion was not based on a more profound knowledge of the subject than they had.

Spencer intended his militant–industrial dichotomy to serve as a scheme for the empirical classification of societies, but it is important to note that he did not regard real societies as organized exclusively through one or the other of these modes. The detailed data compiled by his research assistants made it plain that private property exists, and voluntary exchange of goods and services takes place, even in militant societies, and though he viewed his own society as industrial, he did not disregard the importance of political power in its organizational structure. In beginning his discussion of the militant–industrial dichotomy Spencer points out that these two modes coexist in real societies, the significant difference being that societies differ 'immensely' in the relative importance of these modes. A few pages later he speaks of the 'extreme forms' of these as 'diametrically opposed' and adds that 'the contrasts between their traits are among the most important with which Sociology has to deal' (*Principles of Sociology*, II, X). The point that deserves to be noted is that the militant–industrial dichotomy was, in Spencer's main use of it, an instrument of theoretical analysis rather than a scheme of empirical classification. The two modes of social organization were paradigmatic forms, what Max Weber called 'ideal types' (see below, section C 1).

Since Spencer's time, sociologists have devoted a great deal of effort to devising schemes for the classification of societies. Spencer's militant–industrial typology did not find a permanent place in the sociological literature, but it was adopted by economics as a basic framework of analysis. Like Spencer, modern economists consider real economies as mixtures, in differing proportions, of two fundamentally different modes of organization, which are usually called the 'central planning system' and the 'market system'. The analysis of how these function as ideal types is embodied in standard university courses, the former under titles such as 'The Economics of Socialism' or 'The Theory of Economic Planning', the latter in courses on 'Microeconomics' or 'General Equilibrium Theory'. The comparison of these forms in practice is called 'Comparative Economic Systems'. Economists do not acknowledge Spencer as an antecedent, but in classifying societies as 'militant' or 'industrial' he made a distinction that economic analysis has found indispensable. We noted in Chapter 13 that Marx and Engels said very little about the form of economic organization that they expected to obtain in the post-capitalist world, and it is not clear that Marx, at least, thought that it would be some sort of planned economy; but Marxist nations have emphasized central economic planning, and most Marxist social theorists have embraced this mode of economic organization as a fundamental feature of an authentically Marxist society. A great deal of the modern debate over the comparative political, social, economic, and ethical merits of capitalism and socialism revolves around the distinction that Spencer sought to capture with his militant–industrial dichotomy. Spencer was not the first to draw this distinction, but his emphasis upon it deserves recognition as focusing the attention of social science upon an issue that is now generally recognized to be of cardinal theoretical and practical significance.

3. Society as a super-organic entity

Two conflicting philosophical interpretations of Herbert Spencer jostle one another in the literature. On the one hand he is represented as a *nominalist*, holding the view that terms such as 'society' and 'nation' are merely names that we use to refer collectively to individuals who share some common characteristics. On the other hand he is treated as adopting the *realist* position, which views such terms as denoting entities that have an autonomous existence of their own. The nominalist interpretation is supported by Spencer's utilitarian view of the purposes of social organization, his analysis of the difference between the 'militant' and 'industrial' modes of organization, and his hostility towards state regulation of the economic activities of private persons. Often described as an extreme example of 'individualism' in political philosophy, Spencer also provided sufficient grounds for one to call him a 'methodological individualist' or 'reductionist' in his philosophy of science. The realist interpretation derives mainly from Spencer's description of society as an 'organism', and his extensive use of biological analogies in his investigation of social phenomena.

Spencer's writings in fact are ambiguous on this issue. For example, in the same year (1860) in which he published the 'Prospectus' of the work to which he intended to devote his life, he wrote an article for the *Westminster Review* entitled 'The Social Organism', but in it he expressly repudiated the notion that societies *are* organisms, or are even *like* organisms in more than certain specific respects. In 1876 he expressed great objection to having the idea ascribed to him that there is 'any special analogy between the social organism and the human organism', referring specifically to the organic analogies of Plato and Hobbes (*Reasons for Dissenting from the Philosophy of M. Comte and other Essays*, 1968, pp. 69–73, 81); but he himself uses many biological–social analogies in *Principles of Sociology*, and one of its chapters bears the seemingly plain title 'A Society is an Organism' (II, II). Spencer strongly objected to the political propositions that Plato and Hobbes supported by construing society as an organism, but it is not immediately apparent that his disagreement with them rested on deeper philosophical foundations.

Nevertheless, I think it is possible to sort out Spencer's views on this matter. He *did* regard society as an entity. But it is not an organism; it is a 'super-organic' entity. Spencer uses the adjective 'super-organic' in the opening pages of the *Principles of Sociology* in defining the subject matter of sociology. The term is not intended, however, to carry the connotation that human society is a superior kind of organism or, indeed, that it is any kind of organism at all. It is an entity *composed* of organisms – human individuals – which is organized at a level that lies above, or is 'super' to, such organisms. The functional dynamics of the individual organism must be explained in terms of biological and physiological laws; but to understand a society one must discover the higher-level laws of social organization. Biology and physiology have a great deal to contribute to sociology, not because societies are organisms or because social phenomena are determined by biological factors, but simply because there are suggestive similarities between organic and social phenomena.

Part II of Spencer's *Principles of Sociology*, entitled 'The Inductions of Sociology', begins with the question 'What is a Society?'

> This question [says Spencer] has to be asked and answered at the outset. Until we have decided whether or not to regard society as an entity; and until we have decided whether, if regarded as an entity, a society is to be classed as absolutely unlike all other entities or as like some others; our conception of the subject-matter before us remains vague.

He goes on to reject nominalism explicitly and states that society must be regarded as a 'thing' in itself.

> But ... what kind of thing must we call it? It seems totally unlike every object with which our senses acquaint us. .... Between a society and anything else, the only conceivable resemblance must be one due to *parallelism of principle in the arrangements of components*' [Spencer's italics].

Societies resemble organisms in respect of this 'parallelism'. If one keeps this statement in mind, and is not distracted by his frequent asseveration that societies *are* organisms, the philosophical status of Spencer's constant references to biological structures and physiological functions becomes clear: they do not reflect a metaphysical notion about the ontological nature of society; they are employed heuristically in the empirical investigation of social organization.

This is how Spencer's organicism differs from Plato's. Though rejecting nominalism and adopting realism to the extent of recognizing the existence of society as a 'thing', Spencer did not follow Plato in claiming for society a more real existence than its component individuals. In examining the relation between a society and its individual members Spencer stressed their reciprocal interaction (see *Principles of Sociology*, I, II). But, if anything, he emphasized the role of the individual in this interaction: holding fast to the notion that there is a basic human nature, he says that:

> Society is created by its units, and ... the nature of its organization is determined by the nature of its units. The two act and react; but the original factor is the character of the individuals, and the derived factor is the character of society.

Jay Rumney, who quotes this passage (*Herbert Spencer's Sociology*, 1966, p. 20), remarks that this notion creates some serious difficulties for Spencer's theory of social origins and development but, in defence, one might contend that they are not as great as those that would result from a rigorous adoption of the opposite position. Spencer seems to have had in mind the notion of 'emergent properties' sketched in Chapter 3 B above. Just as new properties appear when chemical elements are combined into molecules, and when molecules combine to form organic and inorganic substances, new properties appear when individual persons combine to form societies. It is in this sense that society is a super-organic entity, and sociology is the study of its special properties and organizational modes.

Spencer did not do much original biological research, but his knowledge of the subject was extensive, and up-to-date. His *Principles of Biology* (1864, 1867) was highly regarded, and outstanding biologists such as Charles Darwin and T. H. Huxley respected his opinion. In the history of biology Spencer deserves a permanent place as the first person to go beyond the making of simple assertions about the factors that influence inheritance by postulating a hypothetical mechanism to explain how hereditary transmission might work so as to produce the results that one actually observes in successive generations. Darwin did not suggest a theoretical mechanism of transmission until 1868, four years after Spencer. Spencer's theory was wrong (as was Darwin's) but it raised an issue that contemporary biologists recognized as of vital importance. The investigation of it led, in time, to the modern science of genetics. (For a brief summary of Spencer's, and other, early theories of genetic transmission see Ernst Mayr, *The Growth of Biological Thought*, 1982, pp. 668 f.) The analogies between biological and social phenomena that fill many pages of the *Principles of Sociology* strike the modern reader as rather forced, and some of them induce spontaneous hoots of laughter, but in Spencer's own time they were regarded as reflecting a keen empirical sensitivity and the exercise of an exceptional capacity for scientific analysis.

Spencer's notion that there are parallels between biological and social phenomena apparently originated very early in his thinking on social questions, but his interest in exploring the analogy was greatly increased in 1851 when he encountered the biological work of Henri Milne-Edwards and K. E. von Baer. Milne-Edwards drew an analogy between the division of labour as Adam Smith had explained it, and the physiological specialization of the organs of an organism. Von Baer pointed out that the embryological development of the individual organism consists of the differentiation of initially homogeneous tissue into the heterogenous structures that form the various organs of the body. Later, Spencer often referred to 'the transformation of the homogeneous into the heterogeneous' as 'Von Baer's Law'. He broadened the scope of this 'law' into a principle of development applicable to societies as well as to individual organisms. (Indeed, as we shall see in the next section, it became for him a cosmic law of evolution.) The central idea that seized Spencer's imagination was that a complex organism is composed of differentiated somatic structures which perform specialized physiological functions; the organism as a whole is an integrated *organization*, a co-ordinated arrangement of these entities into a higher entity. So it is, too, with human societies: individuals are functionally specialized in their economic and social roles, and their society is itself an entity.

At the time that Spencer encountered the work of von Baer he had been working for five years at the *Economist*, whose weekly issues not only made frequent use of the organism–society analogy but repeatedly stressed the significance of Adam Smith's analysis of the productivity of the division of labour in the opening chapters of the *Wealth of Nations* (see above, Chapter 7 C 4). These were favourite ideas of the paper's owner and editor, James Wilson. In his *Study of Sociology* Spencer attributes the conception of 'the physiological division of labour' to Milne-Edwards rather than von Baer, but adds that it 'obviously originates from the generalizations previously reached in Political Economy' (chapter XIV). In later life Spencer was inclined to discount any influence that his association with the *Economist* had had on him (see his *Autobiography*, 1904) but, if the *Economist* did not impress the significance of functional specialization upon him, it must have at least prepared the way for his response when he encountered it in the field of biology.

Spencer's first extended discussion of the parallels between biological and social phenomena was in his 1860 essay entitled 'The Social Organism'. He outlines there the specific features common to individual organisms and societies which differentiate them from non-living things. He goes on immediately, however, to point out the differences between individual organisms and societies. He notes four such differences: that societies have no specific physical forms as organisms do; that the tissues of an organism form a 'continuous mass' while the individuals of a society do not; that the parts of an organism cannot alter their locations and functions, but individual persons can; and that there is a localized seat of consciousness in an organism while, in a society, all the parts are endowed with consciousness. Spencer is anxious to argue that these differences are not sufficient to impair the usefulness of the organism–society analogy, but he emphasizes the significance of the last point. The text here is worth quoting, since it highlights an issue that was not only important in Spencer's thinking but remained prominent, and continues to be, in the methodological and political debate between individualists and holists. The 'contrast between bodies politic and individual bodies' says Spencer,

> is one which we should keep constantly in view. For it reminds us that in individual bodies, the welfare of all other parts is rightly subservient to the welfare of the nervous system whose pleasurable or painful activities make up the good or evil in life; in bodies politic the same thing does not hold, or holds to but a very slight extent. It is well that the lives of all parts of an animal should be merged in the life of the whole; because the whole has a corporate consciousness capable of happiness or misery. But it is not so with a society; since its living units do not and cannot lose individual consciousness; and since the community as a whole has no corporate consciousness. And this is an everlasting reason why the welfare of citizens

cannot rightly be sacrificed to some supposed benefit of the State; but why, on the other hand, the State is to be maintained solely for the benefit of citizens. The corporate life must here be subservient to the lives of the parts; instead of the lives of the parts being subservient to the corporate life. (J. D. Y. Peel, ed., *Herbert Spencer on Social Evolution*, 1972, p. 60)

Spencer's utilitarianism is here plain – in the Benthamite language employed and, more importantly, in the view expressed of the status of collective institutions such as the state. Spencer regarded society as an entity because of the interdependence of its component individuals; it is a 'living' entity, but it does not have feelings, desires, and purposes of its own. In one respect Spencer extended, or at least clarified, utilitarian theory. The statement that the welfare of citizens 'cannot *rightly* be sacrificed to some supposed benefit of the State' (emphasis added) is a moral proposition, not a factual one. If it were supposed to be the latter, it would be amply refuted by empirical evidence, since history is full of such sacrifices. The proposition that sacrificing the individual for the collectivity, though possible, is morally impermissible, is a cardinal principle of utilitarian ethics. Spencer was attempting to base this moral rule, however, on a factual proposition: that collectivities of humans lack sensory organs and nervous systems and, therefore, do not possess consciousness. However much one might be persuaded that this factual proposition is correct, Spencer's (or any other) moral proposition cannot be derived from it without eliding David Hume's categorical distinction between facts and values. Whether it is irredeemably fallacious to derive moral propositions from factual premises is still under debate, but even if Hume's contention were rejected, any argument proceeding from factual premises to a moral conclusion would lose its force if the factual premises themselves were shown to be empirically untrue. Spencer's premise that collectivities such as nations or classes or cultures are lacking in consciousness (or anything akin to it) has not been universally accepted as an indisputable scientific proposition. In the next section of this chapter, for example, we shall note that Émile Durkheim's concept of *conscience collective* came very close to postulating the existence of such a phenomenon.

For scientific purposes, Spencer focused attention on the similarities between organisms and societies. His *Principles of Sociology* explores these to a degree that can only be described as excessive. In reading these pages, however, one should not lose sight of the fact that he treats the similarities as *analogies*, a term that he repeatedly uses. At the end of Part II of *Principles of Sociology* there is a brief chapter entitled 'Qualification and Summary' in which one finds the following explicit statement of the epistemological status of the organism–society parallelisms that fill the preceding pages:

Here let it once more be distinctly asserted that there exist no analogies between the body politic and a living body save those necessitated by that mutual dependence of parts which they display in common. Though, in foregoing chapters, sundry comparisons of social structures and functions to structures and functions in the human body have been made, they have been made only because structures and functions in the human body furnish familiar illustrations of structures and functions in general . . . .

But now let us drop this alleged parallelism between individual organizations and social organizations. I have used the analogies elaborated but as a scaffolding to help in building up a coherent body of sociological inductions. Let us take away the scaffolding: the inductions will stand by themselves.

If we accept Spencer's own description of his methodology, we have to regard his organic analogy as a heuristic device, employed in the service of empirical investigation. Spencer pursues the analogy so extensively that one is tempted to characterize him as holding a metaphysical organicism, but this is incorrect. His sociological work is more vulnerable to the criticism that, in using the analogy, he frequently committed the fallacy of *ignoratio elenchi*, setting out to demonstrate a specific proposition about societies and showing instead that it is demonstrable about organisms. Analogy is a hazardous form of argument and Spencer was insufficiently sensitive to its dangers. There *is* an element of metaphysical organicism in Spencer's sociological thought but it involves, not his views on social organization as such, but his notion of social *evolution*.

4. Cosmic evolution

The Latin verb *volvere* literally means 'to roll' but it was used in a broad sense to refer to motion, and processes for which the concept of motion served as a metaphor. The companion verbs *evolvere* and *revolvere* were more explicit, denoting, respectively, a 'forward' motion, and a reversal or 'rolling back' as, for example, in unrolling and rerolling a scroll. The noun form of the latter, *revolutio*, came into use in astronomy in the fourteenth century; by Copernicus's time it referred, not to backward motion, but to the entire orbit of a planet. It is one of those curiosities of language that the political meaning of the term 'revolution', which dates from the early seventeenth century, denotes a sudden jump rather than a continuous 'roll' and – by those who favour it, of course – a jump forward. Etymologists trace the word 'evolution' back to *evolvere*, but it apparently did not come into use until the mid-eighteenth century, when Charles Bonnet, a Swiss naturalist, used it in respect of the embryological development of an organism. In modern biology the word denotes something quite different, the notion that the great variety of organic species that now inhabit the earth are modified descendants of earlier species which, in turn, were similarly descended, forming a continuous chain of life going back to the single-celled organisms that first appeared on the planet. In political discourse 'evolution' frequently denotes change that is slow and continuous, in contrast with 'revolution'. In the context of biology, the word 'evolution' immediately evokes the name 'Darwin', but Darwin was not the first to advance the view that current biological species, including man, had come into existence through modification of earlier ones. The French biologist Jean Baptiste de Lamarck (1744–1829) had even suggested a plausible mechanism by which the process might work. Darwin's distinction is due to his having suggested an even more plausible one.

The theory of evolution has influenced the modern mind to a degree that defies comparison with anything except the scientific revolution, as it is now called, of the seventeenth century. It was an extension of that revolution to the phenomenon of life, a giant step in the replacement of theology by science. Its impact spread far beyond the particular issue of the origin of organic species and the science of biology; like Newtonian mechanics, it modified profoundly the way that ordinary folk, as well as scientists and intellectuals, regard themselves and their world. In this transformation no one played a more important role than Herbert Spencer. His influence was at its height during the period after the publication of Darwin's *Origin of Species* (1859), when the great debate over evolution took place. His writings not only contributed to the victory of the Darwinians, but extended the idea of evolution from biological to social phenomena and, beyond these, to the consideration of the whole cosmos of existence.

According to his own account (*Autobiography*, I, pp. 200 f.), Spencer's conviction that species had evolved resulted from reading Charles Lyell's *Principles of Geology* (1830–3) at the age of twenty. In this book he encountered an outline of Lamarck's theory of species evolution. Lyell had set out to demolish Lamarck, but the effect on Spencer was the reverse; from that point on he was an evolutionist, and a Lamarckian. Darwin's *Origin of Species* did not appear until nineteen years later; in the meantime the idea of evolution was developing in Spencer's mind, and, with *Social Statics* (1850), it began to appear in his writings. Two articles published in 1852 are worth noting. In 'The Development Hypothesis' the deism of *Social Statics* was discarded, evolution taking the place of the traditional Christian doctrine of special creation as the explanation of the variety of life forms. Darwin read this paper in 1858, expressed his admiration in a letter to Spencer, and noted that he was at work on the same subject (R. L. Carneiro, ed., *The Evolution of Society*, 1967, p. xvi). The other paper, 'A Theory of Population Deduced from the General Law of Animal Fertility', is noteworthy because, though Spencer does not refer to T. R. Malthus by name, he employs arguments and forms of expression that appear to be drawn direct from Malthus's *Essay on the Principle of Population* (1798). Darwin and A. R. Wallace, independent co-discoverers of the theory of species evolution by the process of natural selection, both expressed their indebtedness to Malthus as having furnished the essential clue to this line of thought. Spencer might well have made a similar acknowledgement.

The distinction between the Lamarckian theory of evolution and that which Darwin advanced in the *Origin* is as important in the social sciences as it is in biology. Lamarck contended that the germ plasm of an individual organism is altered by that individual's life experiences. Its 'acquired characteristics' are, therefore, transmitted to its progeny. The long neck of the giraffe, for example, may be explained as resulting from many generations of animals stretching their necks in order to crop the foliage of trees. Darwin observed that the progeny of an animal are not identical, which suggested to him that they had inherited different characteristics despite their common parentage. The pressure of overpopulation means that some individuals must suffer an early death, but they are not condemned at random; those surviving are the individuals possessing variations that give them an advantage over others in food-gathering, defence, etc. The long neck of the giraffe is the cumulative result of the higher survival rate, over many generations, of those individuals that had inherited slightly longer necks than their fellows. Darwin called this mechanism 'natural selection' and later described it, borrowing a phrase from Spencer, as 'the survival of the fittest'. Neither Darwin nor Lamarck had access to information about hereditary transmission that would support their theories, but later discoveries in genetics and embryology revealed that Darwin was on the right track and Lamarck was not.

Darwin did not reject altogether the notion of the inheritance of acquired characteristics. The *Origin* contains unmistakably Lamarckian arguments, from its first edition until the last, published by Darwin in 1872. The distinction between the two mechanisms was, however, sharpened by other biologists, and Spencer found himself in the role of being one of the leading defenders of Lamarck. In the early 1890's he engaged in a protracted controversy with the distinguished German biologist August Weismann, who had discovered that the cells constituting the germ plasm of an organism are walled off from the rest of the soma early in embryological development. Weismann was unable to convince him that Lamarck was wrong. Why was Spencer so insistent in combating the conviction of professional biologists on this point? To answer this question we have to keep in mind that Spencer's main interest was in sociology, not biology. To the observer of social phenomena it should be plain beyond dispute that social 'characteristics' originating *de novo* at one time may be retained by the culture for a long time thereafter, outlasting the life-spans of the individuals who first initiated it. A new religion is founded, for example, or a new production technology is developed; these are passed on, becoming established elements of the social structure. Spencer was trying to understand the mechanism of *cultural* evolution as an adaptive process, and especially that pertaining to an 'industrial' society in which the 'survival of the fittest' results from civilized competition, not primitive warfare. It is incorrect to describe the process of cultural evolution as 'Lamarckian', since Lamarck's theory of hereditary transmission between discrete generations of organisms differs significantly from the continuous history of a society but, if one had to choose between applying Darwin's or Lamarck's theory to cultural evolution, the latter would be more appropriate. But why did Spencer defend Lamarckianism as a *biological* theory? He could have admitted that the Darwinian mechanism applies to species evolution and the Lamarckian to social evolution. This way was impossible for Spencer because he had come to believe early in his career, and became more convinced as his work progressed, that evolution is a singular transcendental principle that pervades all existence. Weismann's attack on Lamarckian theory was therefore perceived by him as endangering the fundamental metaphysical presumption of his own work. Spencer's metaphysical evolutionism, like his biological–social parallelism, may be discarded without loss, but the notion that social evolution is Lamarckian, which he was the first to enunciate clearly and discuss extensively, is sufficient to give him an important place in the history of social science. The description of social evolution as 'Lamarckian', though in my view misleading, has become a common locution in modern social thought.

Spencer believed that there was ample empirical evidence for his proposition that evolution in all realms of existence, inorganic, organic, and super-organic, displays a persistent increase in heterogeneity. But he wished to go further, to show that this universally observed phenomenon is a matter of necessity, resulting from the metaphysical nature of the cosmos. There are some passages in Spencer's writings that remind one of Leibniz, who argued that the cosmos is a plenitude containing every conceivable kind of thing. Leibniz deduced this from the proposition that the nature of God is such that he would not wish to deny existence to anything that could exist (see above, Chapter 10 A). If Spencer had retained his youthful religious faith he might have followed a similar line of argument but, having discarded theology for science, he sought to demonstrate that increasing heterogeneity could be deduced from scientific principles. The most basic of all such principles, Hume notwithstanding, is universal causality – the proposition that all phenomena have causes. Spencer argued that the 'law of increasing differentiation' was, at bottom, due to an even more basic law, which he called 'the law of the multiplication of effects' or 'fructifying causation'. Briefly put, this notion is that every cause has more than one effect and, since every effect in turn becomes a cause, the effects proliferate: like the branching of a tree, but unlike a real tree in that a greatly varied foliage is produced. Spencer did not deny the importance of Adam Smith's observation that division of labour increases productivity, or Durkheim's contention that it generates social solidarity by making individuals dependent on one another, but functional specialization in human society, like all differentiation, was seen by him to reflect a more fundamental force that is at work in all existence. C. Lloyd Morgan, who played an important role in the early development of experimental psychology, remarked in his Herbert Spencer Lecture at Oxford in 1913 that reading Spencer's essay on 'Progress: its Law and Cause' in youth had 'served to quicken that craving, which is, I suppose, characteristic of those who have some natural bent towards philosophy – the imperative craving to seek and, if it may be, to find the one in the many' ('Spencer's Philosophy of Science', *Herbert Spencer Lectures, 1905–1914*, p. 4). 'The One in the Many', as we noted above, was one of Leibniz's favourite mottoes.

This aspect of Spencer's thinking, while it may have inspired readers of a philosophical, or perhaps one should say metaphysical, turn of mind, left no mark on the social sciences and need not concern us further. But we might note before we leave it that its empirics and its logic were both faulty. In modern textbooks in biology one will frequently find a schematic 'evolutionary tree' depicting the branching of forms that Spencer had in mind, but the author will point out that 'convergence' as well as 'divergence' takes place in the process of speciation, and explain both in terms of the principle of natural selection. Spencer's law of increasing differentiation is not validated by either the theory of evolution or the historical record of species change. The notion of 'fructifying causation' is also unacceptable. In the limit, it leads to the contention that every phenomenon is unique, having causal antecedents that differ from all other phenomena, a proposition that is altogether incompatible with the scientific conception of causal explanation as the specification of general laws that cover classes of phenomena.

The importance of Spencer's evolutionism in the history of modern thought was not due to its metaphysical foundations. He forged a connection between the theory of evolution and the idea of *progress* which had developed, from the eighteenth century, into one of the central notions of secular Western social philosophy (see above, Chapter 8). In Spencer's hands this connection appeared to open the way to the resolution of a problem that had deeply troubled the Western intellect since the onset of the scientific revolution: the disjunction of science and ethics. Some regarded Darwin as having made the divorce between them complete and irrevocable, but even before the *Origin* was published Spencer had expressed the contrary view, that science had in fact become the very foundation of ethics, since the law of evolution is also the law of progress towards the good. Spencer was not the first to argue for what G. E. Moore called 'naturalistic ethics' (*Principia Ethica*, 1903, chapter II), and by the time he came to write the final book in his Synthetic Philosophy he had changed his view on this matter, but he was the first to attempt to derive ethical inferences from a conception of nature that was based upon the concrete findings of a specific science. Moore, following in Hume's footsteps, declared naturalistic ethics fallacious and singled out Spencer for special attention, since he was, then, the best known advocate of it. Moore's criticism may have played some role in the decline of Spencer's repute, but he did not succeed in delivering a fatal blow to the 'naturalistic fallacy'. The desire to base ethical judgements on something more solid than personal opinion, less relative than social *mores*, higher than materialistic ends, and more accessible than God, was too strong to be set aside by logical argument. Efforts to show that ethical propositions can be derived from factual ones have continued to the present day, and when writers attempt to do this, not merely in principle, but specifically, they most commonly resort, as Spencer did, to evolution. In Chapter 17 we shall encounter this line of thought again and consider its most recent formulations. In the following section Spencer's enunciation of a naturalistic ethics, and the response to it, will be briefly outlined.

5. Evolution, ethics, and social philosophy

Shortly before he wrote the Prospectus for his Synthetic Philosophy, Spencer published 'Progress: its Law and Cause' in the *Westminster Review* (1857). Virtually the whole complex of main ideas that guided his future work can be found in this brief essay: the necessitarian conception of universal evolution; the attribution of this to the nature of causality; the view that the evolutionary process generates steadily increasing heterogeneity, manifest in human society in functional differentiation of institutions and individuals; and the identification of evolution with progress. The last point is the core of Spencer's social philosophy; evolution, as he put it, is a 'beneficent necessity'.

As we have already observed, Spencer viewed social evolution, and progress, in terms of a steady decline of the 'militant' mode of social organization, and its replacement by the 'industrial' mode; the former characterized by coercion, the latter by voluntary action. Spencer did not write a Utopia describing the perfect social order, but he did make some remarks bearing on this that we should note. In *Social Statics* he says:

> When the change at present going on is complete – when each possesses an active instinct of freedom, together with an active sympathy – then will all the existing limitations to individuality, be they governmental restraints, or be they the aggressions of men on one another, cease. Then, none will be hindered from duly unfolding their natures . . . . Then, for the first time in the history of the world, will there exist beings whose individualities can be expanded to the full in all directions.

Another, similar, passage from *Social Statics* is quoted by Spencer as the concluding sentences of *Principles of Sociology*. In his 'Reasons for Dissenting from the Philosophy of M. Comte' he notes that Comte's 'ideal of society is one in which *government* is developed to the greatest extent' and states his own view as follows:

> That form of society towards which we are progressing, I hold to be one in which *government* will be reduced to the smallest amount possible, and *freedom* increased to the greatest amount possible – one in which human nature will have become so moulded by social discipline into fitness for the social state, that it will need little external restraint . . . . one in which

individual life will be pushed to the greatest extent consistent with social life; and in which social life will have no other end than to maintain the completest sphere for individual life. [Spencer's emphasis]

These passages read like Karl Marx's view of the ideal state of communism after the state has 'withered away'! They reflect in fact a combining of themes that were prominent in later nineteenth-century thought: not just evolution and progress, but the notion that social progress means an enlargement of individual freedom. In his recent *History of the Idea of Progress* (1980, p. 229), Robert Nisbet describes Spencer as 'the supreme embodiment in the late nineteenth century of both liberal individualism and the idea of progress'. There is, however, another theme in Spencer's thinking, which is evident in the foregoing quotations: the notion that the ideal social state requires a change in human nature. This is a standard proposition in the utopian literature, before Spencer's time and since. Spencer thought that it would come automatically, as a product of evolution, but history records numerous instances in which the development of a properly formed 'social man' has been embraced as a prime objective of governmental policy, leading to events that can hardly be described as sanctioned by a philosophy of 'liberal individualism'. Spencer believed that one could help the process of evolution along (see, for example, the final pages of *The Study of Sociology*), but he did not have in mind actions to transform the human constituents of society of the sort that were adopted in the twentieth century by Adolph Hitler's Germany or Pol Pot's Cambodia.

Spencer's identification of evolution and progress, though it united two of the dominant ideas of the age, did not go unchallenged, and it was T. H. Huxley, as close a personal friend as Spencer allowed himself to have, who made the most pointed attack. Huxley was the leading promoter of Darwin's theory of evolution in England after the publication of the *Origin of Species* in 1859 and he defended it for four decades against all criticisms, by biologists, theologians, or others, with the vigour and enthusiasm of one who was utterly convinced that evolution had been established as a scientific fact. As late as 1886 he argued that the mechanism that had produced the various organic species could be defended as morally worthy. But in 1888 he began to express a different view in an essay entitled 'The Struggle for Existence in Human Society'. Invited to deliver the prestigious Romanes Lecture in 1893, Huxley devoted it to the subject of 'Evolution and Ethics'. Without referring to Spencer by name, he attacked the notion that there is a necessary connection between evolution and progress. Indeed, not being content to argue that natural processes such as evolution are ethically neutral, he gave the screw an additional turn by declaring that it is frequently necessary to *oppose* the mechanism of natural selection in order to achieve objectives that are morally worthy.

Huxley's lecture became a classic item in the continuing debate over the relation of science and ethics, but its only effect on Spencer was to lower his opinion of his erstwhile friend. If Huxley had been willing to recognize the operation of a Lamarckian mechanism in social evolution, and if Spencer had been less insistent on the metaphysical unity of all evolutionary processes, the differences between them might have been resolved. But, in Spencer's view, Huxley had committed the egregious error of placing man and nature 'in antithesis', thereby abandoning science for 'old theological notions' (J. D. Y. Peel, ed., *Herbert Spencer on Social Evolution*, 1972, p. 174). Spencer did not continue to regard the theory of evolution as providing a foundation for moral philosophy. In Part V of the second volume of his *Principles of Ethics*, published in 1893, he admitted that 'The doctrine of evolution has not furnished guidance to the extent I had hoped. Most of the [ethical] conclusions, drawn empirically [from it], are such as right feelings, enlightened by cultivated intelligence, have already sufficed to establish.' He could accept the proposition that science does not provide a set of ethical principles, but he continued to reject Huxley's notion that the processes of nature might be in opposition to ethical precepts derived from 'right feelings'.

If this were all that need be said about Spencer's social philosophy, we could represent him as an example of the general harmonist doctrine described above in Chapter 10 and, on the specific question of the role of the state in economic matters, as great a devotee of *laissez-faire* as Harriet Martineau, or James Wilson, his old employer at the *Economist*. Spencer has been so described by numerous commentators but, in fact, his antipathy to the state as an institution did not extend to the adoption of a philosophical anarchism, nor did he employ the principle of *laissez-faire* as a fundamental criterion of judgement to which particular cases might be referred. In the pages of the *Economist* during Spencer's employment there, governmental economic policies were consistently condemned on the ground that they violated the principle of *laissez-faire* (see Scott Gordon, 'The London *Economist* and the High Tide of Laissez Faire', *Journal of Political Economy*, 1955). Spencer did not resort to this kind of argument in his own attacks on the governmental policies of the day. His position was more like that of Adam Smith (see above, Chapter 7 C 6), who argued that state intervention in economic activity is not the sole foundation of order, since private economic activity is itself law-governed, and criticized many of the state policies of his own day as tending to produce deleterious rather than beneficial effects. That a bad policy may be worse than no policy in specific cases does not mean that *laissez-faire* should be adopted as a *general* rule. Like Adam Smith, Spencer emphasized the errors committed by government (social scientists still do), and he was deeply suspicious of the state as an institution because of its historical origin in the 'militant' form of social organization, but he specifically repudiated the term 'laissez-faire' as descriptive of his philosophy (*The Study of Sociology*, chapter XIV). His main point was that state action, where it is necessary, works beneficially when it is in harmony with economic and sociological laws. The purpose of social science is to discover those laws, so that the state may be properly guided in what it undertakes to do, and dissuaded from doing those things whose long-run costs exceed their short-run benefits. By modern standards, Spencer envisaged a very small role for the state, but his general stance was no different in principle from that adopted today by pragmatic economists and sociologists.

This view of Spencer's social philosophy is at variance with the picture of him presented in the historical literature of the past half-century or so. There he appears as one of the most extreme doctrinaires of his (or any other) age, a rather ridiculous figure, whose main significance in the history of Western thought is that he created an ideology found serviceable for political propaganda by the tycoons of modern industry, justifying their rapacious accumulation of wealth through the creation of monopolies and cartels. In the United States especially, there is supposed to have been a period of 'Social Darwinism' in the latter part of the nineteenth century, and Spencer is described as its philosopher. Spencer visited the United States in 1882, and the leading American men of business lionized him. But this episode, much referred to by historians who argue the Social Darwinism thesis, hardly serves as conclusive evidence that the great tycoons viewed him as providing a philosophical defence of their drive for power. Spencer's principal host during the visit was Andrew Carnegie, probably the only one of the tycoons who had actually troubled to read his books. But a comparison of Spencer's ideas with Carnegie's own writings on social philosophy reveals more notable differences than similarities and, moreover, Carnegie did not advance the thesis, as the Social Darwinists are supposed to have done, that successful men of business owe their eminence to the laws of nature. The tycoons who were trying to create monopolies could not have derived much comfort from Spencer's celebration of the 'industrial' system as one of open competition, for it was competition that they were busily endeavouring to suppress.

Spencer's books were widely read in the United States and were extensively used in college courses, but the vogue of *laissez-faire* in American economic theory antedated Spencer and derived from native sources (see above, Chapter 10 B 4). By the time of Spencer's visit in 1882 it was already in eclipse among professional economists. The American Economic Association was founded in 1885 at the initiation of Richard T. Ely of Johns Hopkins University in order to unite 'economists who repudiate *laissez-faire* as a scientific doctrine' which, he declared, is 'unsafe in politics and unsound in morals'. It rapidly became the leading professional organization. The thesis that Spencer played a role in a late nineteenth-century era of 'Social Darwinism' might still be argued if the history of American economic *policy* showed evidence of the operation of such a doctrine, but it does not. The stance of federal and state governments had been far more interventionist than the principle of *laissez-faire* would allow, continuously from the time of the Revolution, and there was no appreciable reversal of this in the later nineteenth century. So far as the great tycoons were concerned, what they may (erroneously) have taken to be Spencer's authorization of their monopolies and trusts was unavailing. The Sherman Antitrust Act was passed by Congress in 1890, extending to interstate commerce policies that had previously been adopted within their limited jurisdictions by several states. This Act, indeed, made the United States more active than any other industrial country in using the arm of government to combat concentrations of economic power. The business giants may have liked to think of themselves as having demonstrated their superior 'fitness' by winning a Darwinian struggle for existence, but the legislators obviously took a different view.

If one wishes to trace Spencer's influence on economic policy, a better case can be made for Japan! His books were widely read there and the leaders of Japanese society and government sought advice from him as their nation emerged from its long isolation into economic, political, and intellectual contact with the Western world. In 1892, responding to such a request from a Japanese Cabinet Minister, Spencer urged his government to introduce policies to preserve the continuity of indigenous social institutions and to keep foreigners 'as much as possible at arm's length' by such measures as prohibiting them from owning or leasing land or making business investments, or engaging in coastal commerce (J. D. Y. Peel, ed., *Herbert Spencer on Social Evolution*, 1972, chapter 24). The Japanese did indeed maintain the continuity of their social institutions to a remarkable degree as the nation modernized, developing the new industrial *zaibatsu* within the framework of, and in accord with, the social structure and mores of the old feudal system; and they did adopt a policy of severely restricting the role of foreigners in their economy. How much credit (or debit) Spencer deserves for this is probably undeterminable; my own guess is that it is small. For the historian of ideas, the most interesting feature of Spencer's advice to the Japanese is that it pointed in the direction of preserving the 'militant' rather than the 'industrial' form of social organization, amounting to a virtual abandonment of his own theory of evolutionary progress. But no matter. Spencer's importance for the history we are tracing in this book derives not from his influence on politicians or businessmen, but upon the intellectuals who were engaged in advancing the scientific study of social phenomena.

6. Spencer's place in the history of social science

Spencer's importance as a contributor to the corpus of modern social science is evident from the above discussion. In summary we might note the following points. (1) He provided a clear conceptualization of society that was based on the concrete material advantages of the division of labour rather than relying on the rather vague notion of man's 'social nature', or excessive resort to his capacity for altruistic action. He thereby extended Adam Smith's discussion in the opening chapters of the *Wealth of Nations* beyond the area of private economic activity to the achievement of collective objectives by means of social organization. The modern analysis of 'collective choice' does not derive any of its specifics from Spencer, but he may be regarded as advancing a general conception of society that serves as its foundation. (2) He viewed society as an entity in itself, not making the mistake of attempting to deny the phenomenon of culture. But he construed this in terms that preserved the role of the individual as the locus of judgement and decision-making instead of resorting to the holistic mysticism of the Comteans, romantics, and Hegelians. The 'action frame of reference' emphasized by Talcott Parsons and his followers in modern American sociology, and attributed by them to Max Weber, has a lineage in which Spencer was, at one time, prominent. (3) Spencer's emphasis on Adam Smith's notion that social order may be generated through the interplay of voluntary individual activities as well as by means of coercive power preserved and developed a distinction that now occupies a central place in comparative studies of economic organization and in contemporary debates in political philosophy. His idea that social evolution is inevitably characterized by movement from the use of coercion to reliance upon the spontaneous mechanisms of organization has not found a place in social science but, less generally construed, it is a prominent theme in the historiography of the modern West. (4) Spencer approached the study of social institutions from a utilitarian point of view. That is to say, he studied their structures in terms of the functions they perform in social organization. Modern sociologists do not resort to analogies from anatomy and physiology, but 'structuralism' and 'functionalism' in contemporary sociological theory are, in essence, a continuation of Spencer's view of social institutions. (5) On the empirical side, Spencer pioneered in the comprehensive and systematic compilation of empirical data. Modern scholars may not approve of the way that he used his data, but he played an important role in moving sociology from a purely theoretical discipline to an empirical one. As a separate discipline, anthropology is indebted to him for the comparative perspective afforded by his taxonomic arrangement of ethnographic information. (6) Finally, we should note again that Spencer's *Study of Sociology* is an important work in the methodology of social science, especially because of the extended examination there of the various 'biases' that social scientists are subject to in studying an entity of which they are a part, with the unavoidable engagement of interest and emotion that this creates. (If we were to extend our survey to the study of sociality in species other than *Homo sapiens* we would also have to note that the pioneering work in this field of biology by Alfred Espinas, *Des sociétés animales* (On Animal Societies, 1878), was inspired by Spencer's writings.)

Nevertheless, Spencer's name hardly appears at all, even as a footnote, in the literature of modern social science. Even writings that are concerned with the historical antecedents of the social science disciplines generally pass him by. For example, Robert A. Nisbet's *The Sociological Tradition* (1966), which has been widely used in college courses, contains no indication that sociology may owe anything of significance to Spencer's work. Raymond Aron's *Main Currents of Sociological Thought* (1967) contains chapter-length studies of Montesquieu, Comte, Tocqueville, Durkheim, Pareto, and Weber, but Spencer is only mentioned in passing in the chapter on Durkheim. Spencer was, in his own day, 'a towering figure in the world of learning' (R. L. Carneiro, 'Spencer, Herbert', *International Encyclopedia of the Social Sciences*, 1968). His books were used in university courses in biology, psychology, sociology, anthropology, and philosophy. His repute extended beyond English-speaking countries to Europe, Russia, and the Orient. But his decline was as swift as his eminence was great; within a decade after his death, he was almost unknown. Writing in his private notebook at the age of sixteen (1888), Bertrand Russell coupled Spencer's name with Shakespeare's as exemplifying the highest qualities that the human species had attained (*My Philosophical Development*, 1959, p. 30), but he did not mention him at all in his *History of Western Philosophy* (1945). Charles H. Cooley, one of the most prominent sociologists during the discipline's foundation period in the United States, in a paper read on the centenary of Spencer's birth, began by saying that 'nearly all of us who took up sociology between 1870, say, and 1890 did so at the instigation of Spencer', but quickly added that 'it is certain that nearly all of us fell away from him sooner or later and more or less completely'. Cooley then went on to present a severely negative appraisal of Spencer, concluding that 'his way of seeing and thinking was not sociological' ('Reflections upon the Sociology of Herbert Spencer', *American Journal of Sociology*, 1920). This view was virtually universal until a decade or so ago, when scholars began to re-examine Spencer's own writings and rediscover the reasons for his great prominence in the late Victorian era.

Spencer's decline might be attributed to a variety of factors. To the degree that his repute as a social thinker was due to his credentials in natural science, these were eroded by his insistence on defending the Lamarckian mechanism of species evolution. On the other hand, those who did not understand the difference between the Lamarckian and Darwinian theories regarded his evolutionism as celebrating the virtues of low cunning and naked force, in domestic relations as well as war. Towards the end of Spencer's life an important change was taking place in the dominant social philosophy of the West. The institution of the state, having been tamed by the development of constitutionalism, and reoriented by the growth of democracy, was beginning to be regarded with less suspicion and appealed to more broadly as a vehicle for the amelioration of social evils. The nineteenth-century liberal who had emphasized freedom from government was becoming the twentieth-century liberal who called for its enlargement, a transformation that made Spencer's view of the state not merely 'conservative' but obsolete. Most important, however, was the change that took place in the view that social scientists took of their task. The idea that economists or sociologists should undertake to discover the fundamental laws that govern the human experience, so that we might know where our civilization came from and where it is going, was being abandoned for more modest aims. Social scientists were beginning to view themselves less as philosophers and more as craftsmen. The grandeur of Spencer's vision became an embarrassment rather than a source of inspiration to professional social scientists. The contributions that Spencer had made to the craft of sociology were retained, but they were no longer identified with his name.

B. EMILE DURKHEIM (1858–1917)

Durkheim was born in the town of Épinal in eastern France on the Moselle river, not far from the German border. His parents were Jewish; his father was descended from a long line of rabbis and was himself a rabbi. His mother came from a merchant family and supplemented the meagre income of her husband by operating an embroidery workshop. Like other children of orthodox Jewish families, Émile studied Jewish religious philosophy and Hebrew in the synagogue school as well as attending the usual secular school. It was assumed that he would follow his father into the rabbinate but, apparently at a quite early age, he rejected this. About the age of thirteen, under the influence of a schoolteacher, he had a mystical experience that interested him in Catholicism, but shortly thereafter he abandoned Judaism without adopting any other religion, and remained a secularist for the rest of his life. His rejection of Judaism, however, was not a rebellion against his Jewish origins. As a mature man he looked back upon his childhood in the close-knit Jewish community of Epinal without any tinge of regret or recrimination. Indeed, the prominence of social solidarity in his sociological theory may reflect a continuing appreciation of the collective values that had been impressed upon him in that community.

After finishing his schooling in Épinal, Durkheim went to Paris to prepare for the entrance examinations to the École Normale Supérieure, one of the most prestigious of the *Grandes Écoles*. After two unsuccessful attempts he was admitted in 1879. He was more interested in philosophy and science than the classical languages and literature that dominated the curriculum of the Ecole, and he graduated near the bottom of his class, but he encountered there other students who, like himself, represented a new wave of intellectuals who were to exert a profound influence upon French thought and culture. Durkheim's role in this was the creation of a new discipline, sociology. He regarded it as a peculiarly French science, which had its original roots in the thought of earlier Frenchmen such as Montesquieu, Rousseau, Saint-Simon, and Comte, and for its practical objective the regeneration of French society, the need for which had been made manifest by the disunity that had brought defeat in the Franco-Prussian War and the disastrous civil upheaval of the Paris Commune.

Upon graduation from the École, Durkheim taught philosophy for a few years in high schools. When, about 1884, he decided to study the subject that Comte had called 'sociology' he found that the most interesting work along these lines was being done in Germany. He visited several German universities, talked to the scholars who were studying social and psychological subjects, and returned to France determined upon the direction of his life's work. In 1887 he was appointed to the faculty of the University of Bordeaux, and there created the first university course in France devoted to sociology. He was, by all accounts, an enormously influential teacher and, when he began to publish the results of his sociological studies, he was recognized throughout France as one of the nation's leading innovative thinkers. In 1902 he was appointed to the faculty of the Sorbonne in Paris, where he remained until his death. It deserves to be noted that, both in Bordeaux and in Paris, Durkheim was responsible for teaching and administering courses in education for students who were being trained as schoolteachers as well as lecturing on social science. A good deal of his influence on French society was due to his strategic position in training those who were responsible for the education of youth. Not only in France, but wherever sociology has become an established discipline, one of its main avenues of influence has been through its impact upon the philosophy of education and the conception of the social role of the teacher. Durkheim's view that the school, rather than the church or the home, was the main institution through which the child should receive his moral education as well as his training in intellectual skills is one that is now widely held by secular professional educators. Durkheim did not originate it, but he played an important role, at least in France, in promoting it concretely and in linking it with the new academic discipline of sociology.

Durkheim's main works are *The Division of Labour in Society* (1893), *The Rules of Sociological Method* (1895), *Suicide* (1897), and *The Elementary Forms of the Religious Life* (1912). He founded the journal *L'Année Sociologique* in 1898 and, thereafter, most of his work appeared in it. *L'Année* was established by Durkheim in order to promote research in sociology by drawing together the diverse studies of social phenomena being done by various scholars. It was not the first sociology journal in France; Frédéric le Play had established one as early as 1881 and, by 1896, four such periodicals were being published. Durkheim felt the need for another, to provide a vehicle for his own views and those of others who shared them. By this time there was a distinct Durkheimian school of French sociologists who, institutionally united through *L'Année* (which was edited by Durkheim down to the most minute detail) became, though not without opposition, the dominant force in French social science and social philosophy, exerting an influence that persists until the present day. Writing in 1915, Durkheim said that the purpose of *L'Année* was not only to promote sociological research but 'to bring the sociological idea down into [the other social] disciplines in such a manner as to make true social sciences of them' (Kurt H. Wolff, ed., *Émile*

Durkheim, 1858–1917, 1979, p. 381). Durkheim's conception of sociology was that it was not merely a branch of social science but the foundation of all social science. Until the disciplines of history, politics, law, anthropology, and economics were placed upon sound sociological foundations, they could not be scientific. As we saw in the preceding section, Herbert Spencer felt that a sociologist must prepare himself by studying the natural sciences and psychology. For Durkheim, sociology is the basic science, even more basic than the natural sciences, since science itself is a sociological phenomenon and the philosophy of knowledge is an aspect of culture.

By contrast with Durkheim's view of sociology, economists were constructing a discipline that was construed as severely limited in scope, and independent of the other social sciences. Except for the simplest postulate in utilitarian psychology, economic theory relied not at all upon theoretical propositions or empirical evidence drawn from other fields. This approach to the analysis of economic phenomena, initiated by the classical economists, was continued, and intensified, in the 'neoclassical' economics that was emerging during the period when Durkheim was doing his work. Durkheim's writings give no indication of this development in economics. Though one of the main figures in it was a Frenchman, Léon Walras, Durkheim does not seem to have been aware of his work, or of that of any of the other leading economists of the period. The few remarks he makes about economics indicate that he had a low opinion of it. What is important for us to note is that he considered the work of the classical economists to be fatally flawed by its individualistic orientation. The attempt to derive 'laws' for any area of social phenomena by deduction from postulates about individual 'human nature' was, for him, so wrongheaded as to deserve summary dismissal. Man is a *social* animal, and his 'nature' is created for him by society. Others before had stressed this point, but Durkheim made it the central pillar of a complex and coherent structure of social theory.

This was also the reason for Durkheim's rejection of Spencer, whose writings were widely read and admired in France. One of those influenced by Spencer, as we noted above, was Alfred Espinas, whose pioneering work on the social behaviour of animals was inspired by the concepts Spencer was advancing. It was Espinas who, as Dean of the Faculty of Letters at Bordeaux, brought Durkheim to the university, creating a new position in social science and education for him. In Durkheim's first book, *The Division of Labour*, Spencer is referred to more frequently, by far, than any other writer. In this early period of his scholarly life, the conception of society as an organism, the significance of functional differentiation, and the notion of social evolution through increasing heterogeneity, made a deep impression on him. But he could not abide Spencer's commitment to individualism, either as a methodological principle or as a moral and political precept. Later, in speaking of the development of sociology as a scientific discipline, Durkheim passed Spencer by and named Saint-Simon and Comte as the outstanding early thinkers. He acknowledged that they had not carried the concrete study of social phenomena very far, and he did not see much merit in Comte's doctrine of the three stages of intellectual evolution, or in his hierarchical classification of the sciences, but he credited Saint-Simon and Comte with having emphasized the need for a scientific study of society that focused on the problem of social order; with perceiving, in terms of order, the functional nature of social institutions; and, above all, with understanding that the fundamental constituent of a culture is the moral and intellectual ideas that are held in common by its members. What Comte had called 'consensus' was an antecedent of Durkheim's *conscience collective*, the keystone in the structure of his sociological theory. Historians of sociology differ greatly in appraising Comte's substantive influence upon Durkheim, but Durkheim himself frequently described it as profound.

Despite his claim that he had provided the foundations for the scientific study of society, Comte did not succeed in establishing sociology as a recognized field of scholarship in France. In fact, by Durkheim's time, Comte's main followers were to be found in England. In his own country Comte was in general disrepute, and the word 'sociology' only denoted one of the transitory fads of the tempestuous intellectual history of the post-revolution period. Durkheim set out to demonstrate, to his fellow intellectuals and to the general public, that Comte had been correct in at least two respects: society could be studied scientifically; and such a study, properly conducted, could provide knowledge of great practical value. In considering Durkheim's role as one of the major figures in the creation of modern sociology, both these points must be kept in mind. As Raymond Aron remarks, Durkheim 'wanted to be a pure scientist; but this did not prevent him from maintaining that sociology would not be worth an hour's trouble unless it enabled us to improve society' (*Main Currents in Sociological Thought*, 1967, II, p. 66).

Durkheim did not write a Prospectus for his life's work as Spencer did, but, in his first lectures at Bordeaux, he made it plain that he was a man with a mission – 'to found a doctrine, to have disciples, to establish a true science of society and thus to play a role in the social reconstitution of France . . . . ' (Harry Alpert, 'France's First University Course in Sociology', *American Sociological Review*, 1937). The Franco-Prussian war was then seventeen years in the past, but the self-doubt that it had created was still prominent in French thinking and the political stability of the Third Republic was tenuous. This was, in broad terms, the practical problem that Durkheim felt could be solved by sociology. Like Spencer, in the deepest level of his being he was a political philosopher. Social science could provide guidance for political organization, not only by revealing the laws of human behaviour, but by providing a scientific understanding of the foundations of ethics. Durkheim stood aloof from the partisan politics of the day (except for the great debate over the Dreyfus case), but he considered himself a socialist, and socialism was, for him, not only, or mainly, a different form of economic organization from market capitalism; it involved a change in the motivation and moral outlook of the members of society. To quote directly from his first lectures:

> Our society must regain the consciousness of its organic unity; the individual must feel the presence and influence of that social mass which envelops and penetrates him, and this feeling must continually govern his behavior . . . [sociology] will enable the individual to understand what society is, how it completes him and what a small thing he is when reduced to his own powers. It will teach him that he is not an empire enclosed within another empire, but the organ of an organism, and it will show him what is valuable in conscientiously performing one's role as an organ. (Quoted in Steven Lukes, *Émile Durkheim*, 1973, p. 102)

As we can see from this passage, Durkheim's organicism was more like Plato's and Hobbes's than Spencer's. Despite his own organic view of society, Spencer belongs to the classical nineteenth-century liberal position in political theory, emphasizing the autonomy and rights of the individual rather than his social dependence and duties. Durkheim places society first, the individual after. They differed, too, in their views of the state. For Spencer, the state must be constrained in the interests of individual freedom; for Durkheim it must be reconstituted, and its scope enlarged, in order to promote the solidarity that is necessary to social order. Durkheim did not think, as Marx did, in cosmopolitan terms. He was an ardent nationalist, and when he spoke of 'society' he thought of France. Sociology, in his view, was a French science, because only the French possessed the qualities that are necessary to create it and to use it. But, in terms of political theory, views similar to Durkheim's took deep root on all the continents of the world. It is difficult to determine causality in these matters, but it seems likely that Durkheim's sociology played a role of some importance in forging the union between socialism and nationalism that has been so prominent in twentieth-century political thought and practice.

1. The objective reality of 'social facts'

From his earliest writings in sociology, Durkheim emphatically put forward the view that society is an entity in itself, not merely an aggregate of individual persons. This became a hallmark of the Durkheimian school and one of the main points of attack on it by critics. In the preface to the second edition of *The Rules of Sociological Method* (1901), Durkheim defended his view that, as he put it, 'social phenomena are external to individuals'. Responding to critics, he pointed out that this assertion is simply a recognition of the reality of emergent properties, a proposition that has been freely accepted in the scientific analysis of physical phenomena. The hardness of bronze does not reside in the copper and tin of which it is composed, and the fluidity of water does not reside in its hydrogen and oxygen. If physical scientists regard the properties of hardness and fluidity in such cases as real phenomena, why cannot the social scientist do likewise? Indeed, he argued, sociology can be a science only if it concerns itself with the objective reality of social phenomena.

In considering the notion of emergent properties above (Chapter 3 B and C), we noted that there is an important respect in which the parallel between individuals combined in a society and chemical elements combined in a compound does not hold. Hydrogen and oxygen do not change their properties, as elements, when they combine, but human individuals do. In fact it is misleading, from the sociological standpoint, to speak of individuals 'combining' into a society, if this is meant to imply that they bring their already formed personalities to it, from outside, so to speak. All mature individuals are products of enculturation; their personalities are formed within the societies in which they have been nurtured. Durkheim did not explicitly note that social phenomena differ from the physical reality in this respect but, in fact, his sociology was based on the proposition that the characteristics of individual persons are created by their social milieu. Though claiming that his social analysis was sanctioned by the realist outlook of the natural sciences, he vehemently rejected the reductionist methodology that had become traditional in them. Economics, in Durkheim's view, was flawed by its reliance upon propositions concerning basic human nature that were construed to be common to all men and independent of their social ambience. Sociology would be more scientific because it focused upon society itself as the generator of 'social facts'. In the great methodological debate between 'individualism' and 'holism', which continues unabated to the present day, Durkheim looms above all other major figures as a proponent of holistic sociology.

Durkheim is remembered today mainly for his theoretical work, and it is this that will occupy our attention. But he was also an empiricist. His studies of suicide and religion in particular are filled with statistical data. In fact he played an important part in the creation of modern empirical sociology, using quantitative data to classify and describe sociological phenomena and to test specific theoretical propositions. The inspiration for this empirical work was his conviction that social phenomena are objective 'facts' that can be observed and measured just as physical phenomena can. The second chapter of the *Rules*, entitled 'Rules for the Observation of Social Facts', begins with the following imperative: 'The first and most fundamental rule is: *Consider social facts as things*' (Durkheim's emphasis). Durkheim never tired of reiterating this command. He did not intend to claim that social phenomena have a material existence, such as bronze and water do, but they are no less real. In short, like Herbert Spencer, Durkheim rejected nominalism; he insisted upon regarding society as an independent real entity. Unable to say 'what kind of thing' society is, Spencer resorted to the organism analogy as a heuristic device. Durkheim was also strongly attracted by the organism analogy, and indeed some of his contentions, and language, suggests that he, rather than Spencer, should be regarded as the leading social organicist of this foundation period in the history of sociology, but, at any rate, he shared Spencer's view that a society is a type of entity that differs from any other. The main influence of the organic analogy upon his sociological theory was, as in the case of Spencer, that it heightened his conviction that social institutions must be viewed in functional terms. If one can see clearly what a society is, and understand what is necessary to its maintenance and growth, one will be able to make a scientific analysis of its institutions in terms of the social functions they perform. It will then be possible to determine what is 'normal' and what is 'pathological' in social life, and prescribe remedies for the latter.

Durkheim's central methodological principle was derived from his ontological conception of society as an autonomous entity. Causal explanation in sociology, he insisted, must always locate itself at the social level of existence. Social facts are caused by other social facts, and the general laws that scientific sociology seeks to discover must be propositions that link social phenomena to one another without recourse to other factors. He rejected any resort to metaphysical propositions which attempt to explain social phenomena by reference to forces that transcend the experiential reality, and he also rejected reductionism, the attempt to explain social phenomena in terms of the psychological or biological characteristics of human individuals. On the same principle, he excluded from sociological analysis factors such as climate and geography, since these did not lie within the domain of the social. Durkheim was especially insistent on making the point that sociological explanation must not rely upon psychology. In the *Rules* he states as a methodological principle that *'the determining cause of a social fact must be sought among the social facts preceding it and not among the states of individual consciousness'* (p. 110, Durkheim's emphasis). Social phenomena are 'psychological', but not in the sense that they derive from the psychological properties of individuals; society is a living entity in itself and, as a collectivity, has a consciousness of its own. Sociology is the study of this collective consciousness.

> Individual minds, forming groups by mingling and fusing, give birth to a being, psychological if you will, but constituting a psychic individuality of a new sort. It is, then, in the nature of this collective individuality, not in that of the associated units, that we must seek the immediate and determining causes of the facts appearing therein. The group thinks, feels, and acts quite differently from the way in which its members would were they isolated. If, then, we begin with the individual, we shall be able to understand nothing of what takes place in the group . . . . Consequently, every time that a social phenomenon is directly explained by a psychological phenomenon, we may be sure that the explanation is false. (*Rules*, pp. 103–4).

Durkheim regarded economics, based as it was on the assumption that men are primarily motivated by individual self-interest, as flawed by a psychological premise that is empirically untrue, but his main critique was that the economists, like others who have attempted to explain social phenomena by reduction to the level of the individual, had committed a fundamental methodological error.

It is evident from his methodological 'rules' that Durkheim's conception of society differs greatly from the view of it as a utilitarian artefact that men construct in order to enable them to achieve objectives which require co-operative action. For Durkheim, society is prior to the individual. Obsessed by the phenomenon of enculturation, he carried this notion to extremes; as Morris Ginsberg remarks, the concept of society had 'an intoxicating effect on his mind' (in Robert A. Nisbet, ed., *Émile Durkheim*, 1965, p. 151). Although he warned against the use of metaphysical concepts in scientific sociology, Durkheim's conception of 'society' has more than a tinge of metaphysics in it. In the history of social science Durkheim continued and extended a line of thought that was given prominent expression a century earlier by J. G. von Herder (see above, Chapter 14), in which the fundamental unit of social analysis is the culture rather than the individual.

In the opening pages of the *Rules* Durkheim states what he considers to be the true relationship between individual behaviour and 'social facts'. A behaviour is not 'social' simply because all persons engage in it. Everyone eats and sleeps, for example, but if we were to regard such phenomena as social phenomena because they are universal, then 'sociology would have no subject matter of its own, and its domain would be confused with that of biology and psychology'. Sociology deals with universal behaviour such as speaking a common language or using a common currency, and with common ways of thinking such as religious beliefs or the acceptance of moral obligations. These are matters that are defined *for* the individual, by social facts such as customs or laws, which are *external* to him. Social facts 'acquire a body, a tangible form, and constitute a reality in their own right, quite distinct from the individual facts which produce it'. The social fact 'is to be found in each part because it exists in the whole, rather than in the whole because it exists in the parts'.

Why is this the proper way to construe the direction of the relationship between society and the individual? Because, according to Durkheim, the main significance of social facts is that they exercise 'coercive' powers over the individual members of society. These powers function in the educational process and in the other procedures through which the young are enculturated into their society, and they act upon mature individuals, constraining and directing their ways of acting, thinking, and feeling. Durkheim speaks of these social forces in terms that are analogous to the way in which one might refer to physical forces. As members of a society, individuals are no less governed in their behaviour by customs, laws, and other social facts than they are by the facts of physics and biology. Indeed, it is the existence of such powers that enables the sociologist to identify a social fact:

> A social fact is to be recognized by the power of external coercion which it exercises or is capable of exercising over individuals, and the presence of this power may be recognized in its turn either by the existence of some specific sanction or by the resistance offered against every individual effort that tends to violate it. (*Rules*, p. 10)

As a scientific discipline, the domain of sociology is the study of the coercion of the individual by the collectivity. But one thing more must be added: sociology focuses upon the *functions* performed by this system of coercion. In focusing upon them it is essential to keep in mind that social facts serve social, rather than individual, ends:

> The function of a social fact cannot but be social, i.e. it consists of the production of socially useful effects. To be sure, it may and does happen that it also serves the individual. But this happy result is not its immediate cause .... *The function of a social fact ought always to be sought in relation to some social end*. (*Rules*, pp. 110–11, Durkheim's emphasis)

Reading such passages, one is tempted to conclude that Durkheim simply reversed the central canon of utilitarian social philosophy. Instead of regarding society as an artefactual construction designed to serve the needs of individuals, he seems to say that, on the contrary, the individual is fabricated, so to speak, by society, to serve *its* needs. Durkheim did not intend to go quite so far. His desire to combat the individualism that he perceived to be dominant in the social thought of his time led him to linguistic excess on many occasions. His main aim, however, was not to prove that the individual is merely an instrument in the hands of a higher being, but to emphasize the dualism of human nature, a nature in which the individualistic and the social elements are combined. The fundamental characteristic of a stable and healthy society is *solidarity*; when that exists, the needs of both the individual and society are met through mutual service to one another. A central task of sociology, therefore is the analysis of the conditions of solidarity.

2. Social solidarity

What are the forces that hold society together? This question has been a central concern of all the social sciences, and the answers that have been proposed to it differentiate the various social sciences from one another. Thomas Hobbes is one of the founders of modern political science because he stated in emphatic fashion the thesis that social order depends upon the existence of an institution that possesses an incontestable degree of coercive power. Society is made possible by a 'sovereign', without whose control it would fly apart under the force of individual self-interest. The theory of constitutional democracy has considerably modified Hobbes's thesis, but political science is still primarily concerned with the analysis of how the state operates to control the centripetal energies of immediate egocentric interest. Adam Smith is the founder of economics because he initiated the analysis of how social order is created by a different means, the mechanism of market exchange.

In Durkheim's first lecture course in sociology at Bordeaux, he defined sociology as the study of the bonds that hold people together and unite them into a society, and the rest of his life was devoted to the study of these bonds. He was dissatisfied with the economists' argument that a spontaneous order arises out of the private commercial transactions that individuals enter into with one another and he felt that traditional political science had not penetrated below the surface in its analysis of the role of the state. Every society has a government and an economy, which serve utilitarian purposes, but the fundamental cementing forces are such things as established customs and conventions, shared values and beliefs, common historical experiences, and the self-identification of individuals as members of a community. Durkheim's first major work, *The Division of Labour*, is a study of the forces that hold a society together. He distinguishes here between two types of societies, characterized respectively by 'mechanical solidarity' and 'organic solidarity'. The former are relatively primitive communities in which there is not much economic specialization or status differentiation. The members of such a community 'resemble' one another and the social bond between them is due to this resemblance. The argument parallels, but in less psychological fashion, that advanced in the mid-eighteenth century by Adam Smith in his *Theory of Moral Sentiments*. Smith had maintained that man's natural egocentrism is constrained by his 'sympathy' and 'fellow feeling', which springs from the individual's recognition that other persons have the same desires and feelings as himself (see above, Chapter 7 C). Organic solidarity, on the other hand, characterizes more economically advanced societies in which there is extensive division of labour and much more differentiation among individuals. Contrary to Auguste Comte, who viewed the development of division of labour negatively, as tending to loosen the bonds that bind individuals together, Durkheim argued that it strengthens the social bond by making the members of society more dependent upon one another. This solidarity is called 'organic' by Durkheim because it resembles the way in which the parts of a biological organism are joined together, the viability of each depending upon the functional services of all in maintaining the life of the whole.

Durkheim accepted Herbert Spencer's extension of 'von Baer's law' to the social domain; social evolution is characterized by increasing heterogeneity. The main problem of sociology is to discover how social solidarity is maintained in a heterogeneous society. Karl Marx had argued that, under capitalism, social solidarity is undermined; the society becomes polarized into classes which have opposed interests, leading, ineluctably, to social breakdown. Spencer contended that social solidarity becomes less necessary as society evolves from the 'militant' to the 'industrial' type, since the market mechanism produces order without requiring individuals to orient their behaviour to the welfare of the whole. Durkheim accepted neither of these theses. In *The Division of Labour* he argues that functional differentiation does not make the achievement of social solidarity either less necessary or more difficult. In fact it is the very thing that promotes a different type, the 'organic' type, of solidarity. As we shall see, Durkheim shifted his ground on this point, perhaps in the course of writing *The Division of Labour* itself (see Robert A. Nisbet, *Émile Durkheim*, 1965), and settled on an explanation of the social bond in functionally differentiated societies that relies upon the continuance in them of the basic factors that are the foundations of mechanical solidarity. But before examining this feature of his mature thought, we must pay some further attention to the argument concerning organic solidarity that he initially advanced.

It will assist our understanding of Durkheim on this point if we compare his thesis to the other great discussions of the division of labour in the literature of social science: Plato's *Republic*, Aristotle's *Politics*, and Adam Smith's *Wealth of Nations*. Durkheim did not emphasize social solidarity more heavily than Plato and Aristotle had twenty-three centuries earlier. Plato speaks of the 'city' as like an organism, which flourishes only when its members are bound together in unity. The valuable citizen, says Aristotle, is not the person who has the ability to do many things, but he who can do one thing excellently and confines himself to it. This division of labour has two salutary effects: it increases efficiency, and it makes the citizens dependent upon one another for the satisfaction of their needs. Adam Smith focused on the first of these consequences noted by Aristotle; Durkheim on the second. Plato's famous argument concerning political organization follows immediately after his discussion of the division of labour. Like other activities, the task of government must be a specialized function, performed exclusively by those who, owing to their natural talents and training, have the appropriate qualities. The general citizenry submit to the absolute authority of the 'guardians' because they have been induced to believe that, in a good society, each has his proper place. Durkheim's assertion that the individual realizes himself most fully when he is like an organ in an organism resembles Plato's view of the well ordered city. Durkheim's political theory will engage our attention below; at this point we should note that his analysis of the processes that make the individual content to be an 'organ' is different from Plato's. In the *Republic*, the submission of the citizenry to the guardians is achieved by chicanery, the deliberate promulgation of a 'noble lie'. In Durkheim's thinking the individual's acceptance of his role reflects the coercive power of 'social facts'. Some might say that this is a distinction without a difference, but Plato's thesis only directs attention to the art of political propaganda, while Durkheim's opens the analysis of much larger matters, the phenomenon of enculturation and the operation of conventional norms in controlling individual behaviour.

Adam Smith's discussion in the first three chapters of the *Wealth of Nations* is historically significant not because it points to the increase in productivity that can be achieved by the division of labour. On this matter he makes little advance beyond what had been said by many earlier writers, back to Plato and Xenophon. The significance of Smith's discussion is that it serves as preamble to the analysis of economic organization. The technical advantages of the division of labour cannot be utilized unless there is a system of institutions that permits the output of each producing unit to be exchanged for that of others. Put in Durkheimian terms, Smith regarded social order as necessary to the practice of specialization. But, in Durkheim's view, Smith had misunderstood the connection. Social order depends upon solidarity, and this, in turn, is due to the division of labour. Functional specialization does not depend upon social solidarity as a precondition; it is the main factor that creates solidarity of the 'organic' type. For Adam Smith, specialization generates a problem, how to dispose of the production; for Durkheim it is the solution of a problem, how solidarity may be achieved in a heterogeneous society.

In this outline of Durkheim's notion of organic solidarity I have tried to avoid expressions suggesting that it is traceable to the rationality of human individuals in assessing their interests. If we were to say that in a functionally specialized society each individual *knows* that his welfare is dependent on the services rendered by others and that he *consciously* suppresses his immediate interests in order to promote his long-run welfare as a member of a community, we would not, according to Durkheim, be speaking 'socio-logically', since a social phenomenon cannot properly be explained by resort to factors which lie at the level of individual consciousness. While working out his analysis of the division of labour, Durkheim arrived at his methodological principle that social phenomena must be explained solely by other social phenomena. If we are forbidden to explain social solidarity in terms of the individual's rational perception of the interests he shares with others, how then do we explain it? Durkheim's answer is that the individual is *coerced* into behaving communally, not by the state, but by the norms of his cultural milieu. The established customs and conventions of his society, its commonly accepted values and beliefs, are 'social facts', which he responds to unconsciously and non-rationally. These factors operate as social bonds in all societies from the most primitive to the most advanced.

Durkheim speaks of the factors that produce social solidarity as constituting, in each society, a distinctive *conscience collective*. This term cannot be easily translated and most modern commentators on Durkheim who write in English retain Durkheim's original French expression in discussing this aspect of his thought. In English, the words 'consciousness' and 'conscience' have quite distinct meanings, the first referring to the general phenomenon of mental awareness, the second, more restrictedly, to the awareness of the distinction between right and wrong. Both of these are rendered in French by the same word, *conscience*. The adjective *collective* in Durkheim's phrase implies that he believed that society, as an entity in itself, possesses one, or both, of these capacities. As we saw above, Herbert Spencer argued that the lack of a localized seat of consciousness in societies is the most important factor that distinguishes them from organisms. A society does not have a brain and, therefore, it does not have a mind. Did Durkheim believe that there is such a thing as a group mind, distinct from the individual minds of persons? It is not possible to answer this question with confidence. English commentators on Durkheim retain the French term *conscience collective*, not only because *conscience* has two quite different meanings, but because it is not altogether clear how far Durkheim meant to go in using *collective* as its modifier.

The notion of group mind was explicitly stated by Auguste Comte in connection with his famous 'law of the three stages'. The intellectual development of the individual from the 'theological' way of thinking in childhood, through the 'metaphysical' way in youth, to the 'positive' way in maturity, recapitulates the intellectual evolution of man as a species: 'the phases of the mind of a man correspond to the epochs of the mind of the race'. Wilhelm Wundt, whom Durkheim knew personally, postulated the existence of a 'group soul' (*Volkseele*) in his pioneering work in experimental psychology, and Gustave LeBon, in his famous book on crowd psychology, used a term (*l'âme de la foule*) that suggests the same notion. Mind-like properties are also present in Hegel's concept of *Geist*, which was familiar to every nineteenth-century European intellectual. The notion of an intelligence located outside the human brain is, of course, also a feature of Judaeo-Christian theology. Was Durkheim's *conscience collective* a secularized version of this? In saying that, in modern life, moral imperatives derive from the functional needs of society rather that the will of God, was Durkheim conceiving society as not only an entity, but an entity possessing mind? On the whole, I think we must acquit him of this egregious error. At any rate, his sociological theory does not depend upon it. His mode of argumentation in using the notion of *conscience collective* is analogical. The way in which the behaviour of the individual is constrained by his social milieu is *like* the way in which it is constrained by beliefs that are located internally in his own mind and which may be uniquely his own. The *conscience collective* is more like Aristotle's *ethos* than *Geist*, *Volkseele*, and other reified concepts. Aristotle used this term, which in classical Greek usually refers to the character of an individual person, to denote the commonly held values and beliefs that constitute the character of a community. Durkheim's *conscience collective* could be rendered as 'ethos' in English translations of his texts, since that word, in Aristotle's usage, has found its way into our language, but it would be no better than using the word 'culture', as sociologists customarily do when they wish to refer to such phenomena. Neither rendering of *conscience collective* would carry much information, however, because the phenomenon of culture still remains, in spite of the sociological research of the past century, as difficult to understand as it was in Durkheim's day.

Durkheim sometimes speaks as though the normative mentality of the individual is created entirely by his social milieu, its content consisting entirely of internalized objective social 'facts'. If this were his fundamental view, the notion of group mind would be essential to his sociological theory, whether he recognized it or not. If individual mind is derivative, it must derive from something, and that something, in the context of Durkheimian sociology, can only be the existence of a group mind. This parallels the celebrated issue of the relation between mind and brain or, more generally, the mind–body problem, which has occupied the attention of philosophers since Descartes. Durkheim did not address this issue but, in considering the relation between the individual and society, he adopted a dualistic stance, as Descartes had in dealing with the relation between physical and mental phenomena. Durkheim's clearest expression of this feature of his thought is contained in an essay entitled 'The Dualism of Human Nature and its Social Conditions'. This was written late in life (1914), but it reflected views that he had always entertained. The following paragraph from this essay deserves quotation:

> It is not without reason . . . that man feels himself to be double: he actually is double. There are in him two classes of states of consciousness that differ from each other in origin and nature, and in the ends towards which they aim. One class merely expresses our organisms and the objects to which they are most directly related. Strictly individual, the states of consciousness of this class connect us only with ourselves, and we can no more detach them from us than we can detach ourselves from our bodies. The states of consciousness of the other class, on the contrary, come to us from society; they transfer society into us and connect us with something that surpasses us. Being collective, they are impersonal; they turn us towards ends that we hold in common with other men; it is through them and them alone that we can communicate with others. It is, therefore, quite true that we are made up of two parts, and are like two beings, which, though they are closely associated, are composed of very different elements and orient us in opposite directions. (Kurt H. Wolff, ed., *Émile Durkheim*, 1979, p. 337)

In this same essay Durkheim speaks of the 'struggle between the two beings within us' and 'the painful character of the dualism of human nature'. Such remarks, and similar expressions in other writings, suggest a parallel between Durkheim's work in sociology and the psychological theories of Sigmund Freud. The Freudian concept of 'superego' resembles Durkheim's *conscience collective*, and the conflict between the 'ego' and 'id' in Freud's analysis of the human psyche resembles the tension between the individual and society that Durkheim speaks of. R. A. Nisbet remarks that 'Durkheim shares with Freud a large part of the responsibility for turning social thought from the classic rationalist categories of volition, will, and individual consciousness to those aspects of behavior which are in a strict sense nonvolitional and nonrational' ('Conservatism and Sociology', *American Journal of Sociology*, 1952). The significance of this point is enlarged if we recast it in terms of Durkheim's conception of the dualism of human nature and connect it with the dualism of Descartes. The philosophy of materialism, in its global form, views all phenomena in terms of physical entities and forces, denying any real existence to what we humans are disposed to describe by such terms as 'volition', 'reason', etc. Descartes sought to preserve a domain for these by postulating an ontological dualism, a metaphysical proposition that lies beyond refutation, or verification, by natural science. With the development of scientific sociology, the territory thus declaratively identified as the sovereign republic of mind was attacked from a different direction, 'society' rather than matter claiming hegemonic authority. Durkheim, who led this attack, did not wish to destroy the sphere of individual autonomy altogether, only to reduce it considerably. His insistence upon the existential nature of society was not meant to lay metaphysical foundations for a claim that the *conscience collective* occupies the whole domain that Descartes had reserved for mind. Nisbet is correct in saying that Durkheimian sociology played an important part in orienting Western social thought away from rationalism and individualism, but its deepest philosophical import was that it converted the Cartesian dualism into a trinitarian ontology, with matter, organic life, and society sharing the domain of existence as categorically different realities. We shall consider this trinity further in Chapter 18 B 1.

3. The sociological point of view

Durkheim aimed to establish sociology, not merely as a discipline that investigates a delimited area of social phenomena or specific problems such as the basis of social solidarity, but as the foundation science for all social research. In his view, economics, political science, history, and the other conventionally defined areas of social research cannot achieve scientific status until they adopt the methodological principle that social phenomena must be explained by other social phenomena. The study of the material realm of existence had become scientific by undertaking to explain events in terms of general laws that link material effects to material causes, eschewing theological and other concepts that are non-materialistic in nature. So, likewise, since the social realm has its own ontological autonomy, a truly scientific study of social phenomena aims at the discovery of laws that are exclusively social. Durkheim regarded the social sciences of his time as flawed by their inclination to explain social phenomena in terms of factors that operate at the level of individual consciousness and volition. History and political science typically attempt to explain social events in terms of the thoughts and decisions of kings and generals; economics enlarges the domain of explanation to include less magisterial beings but, in accordance with utilitarian psychology, their behaviour is construed as reflecting the operation of individualistic rationality and motivation. Durkheim's 'sociological point of view' was an attack upon the tradition of reductionism in the social sciences.

One of the reasons why Durkheim is regarded as the father of modern sociology is that, not only did he assert the sociological point of view as a matter of epistemological principle, but he exemplified it by specific studies. The most important of these are his books on suicide and religion. Some brief attention to these is useful in furthering one's understanding of Durkheim's insistence that one must rigorously adhere to the domain of the social, neither descending below it nor ascending above it, in seeking the causes of phenomena that bear the mark of sociality.

In *The Rules of Sociological Method* Durkheim points out that in attempting to identify a 'pathological' social condition one must employ as a standard of reference not some abstract conception of the ideal state, but empirical evidence of what is 'normal' in societies of the type under consideration. Crime, for example, is not necessarily pathological, since, in normal circumstances, there will be a certain incidence of crime. When the crime rate exceeds what is normal for a society of that type, it is due to social factors and, therefore, must be explained in sociological terms. The same is true of suicide. Each suicide, like each crime, is an individual act, but a suicide rate higher than the normal is evidence that some individuals are driven to acts of self-destruction by social causes. Durkheim's analysis of suicide as social pathology centres on his view of the importance of social solidarity. In *The Division of Labour* he refers to the weakening of solidarity by the degeneration of social bonds as a condition of 'anomie.' In *Suicide* he develops this further. Some suicides are 'egoistic' (e.g. the suicide of a person suffering from a painful illness); some are 'altruistic' (e.g. the act of a soldier who throws himself on a grenade to protect his fellows); some are performed by persons who suffer from a sense of dissociation from their society, a condition of 'anomie' so acute that life is unbearable (e.g. the suicide of a person who has been ostracized; this and the preceding illustrations are my own, not Durkheim's). Under normal conditions there will be a certain rate of suicide, including some suicides that are due to anomie. But a suicide rate that is significantly higher than normal can only be due to an erosion of solidarity which generates more widespread, and more intense, anomie; its causes, therefore, are *social*.

This capsule summary of Durkheim's theory of suicide is perhaps sufficient to illustrate how he applied his general methodological principle in the study of a specific phenomenon. The significance of *Suicide* in the history of modern sociology, however, is not only, or even mainly, due to this. The notion of anomie became a central concept in sociological theory, applied to a much larger range of phenomena than suicide. Also, Durkheim's attempt to demonstrate the validity of his theory of suicide by analysis of quantitative data was pioneering work in empirical sociology. *Suicide* exemplifies the usefulness of what R. K. Merton has called 'theories of the middle range' – theories that are neither so abstract that no contact between them and empirical evidence can be established, nor so concrete that they are devoid of generality. Even sociologists who reject Durkheim's methodological precept and/or his explanation of variations in suicide rates, acknowledge that *Suicide* is one of the outstanding landmarks in the development of scientific sociology.

Durkheim's analysis of religion is even more important from the standpoint of modern intellectual history. On numerous occasions in this book we have noted that the social sciences, like the natural sciences, were engaged not in uncontested cultivation of vacant territory, but in the insurgent invasion of domains hitherto occupied by theology. With Durkheim's analysis, the very citadel of religion was brought under siege. Science, already opulent with conquests, recognized no frontiers. In the development of modern secularism Durkheim's *Elementary Forms of the Religious Life* was as important as Darwin's *Origin of Species*. Perhaps, indeed, it was more important, since Darwin only undermined the biblical account of man's material origin, while Durkheim focused upon the source of his moral values, denying that they derive from God, and relegating religion to the subordinate role of reflecting the secular *conscience collective*. Theology could have accommodated to Darwin by adopting the view that evolution is God's work, as many theists who accepted the theory of evolution argued, but a theist could not embrace Durkheim's theory of religion without abandoning all claim to religious authority on moral questions.

Durkheim's basic thesis is that, in all societies, the source of moral values is society itself. In the *Division of Labour* he had argued that certain acts are considered criminal because they offend the shared consensus of what is right and proper. The function of punishment is not to deter, but to give expression to this consensus. In *The Elementary Forms* he elaborated upon this thesis with reference to the role of religion. Religion does not furnish moral precepts; it simply reflects those that society embraces. Religion is a powerful force in deterring individuals from certain acts but these acts are condemned by the *conscience collective*, not by God. Those things that religion holds 'sacred' derive their special status from the service they render in preserving social solidarity. Sacerdotal functions have a wholly secular purpose. What is held to be the will of God is in fact the needs of society. In Dostoyevski's great novel *The Brothers Karamazov* (1880), Ivan asks whether man's moral values are not, necessarily, dependent on the existence of God: 'If God did not exist, would not all acts be permissible?' Durkheim would have answered that the existence or non-existence of God is irrelevant. All acts would be permissible if the *conscience collective* did not exist. The totems of primitive religions and the sophisticated conceptions of the sacred in modern ones are alike in that they are no more than *représentations* (a favourite Durkheimian word) of the *conscience collective*. Social solidarity is promoted by a common religion but any religion will serve. In different societies men may worship different gods; but in all societies what they really revere is their own society.

Intellectual revolutions, like political ones, purge many erstwhile partisans in the process of consolidating the new authority. Any natural scientist who might have exulted over Durkheim's dethronement of theology would have been sobered by the realization that it was sociology, not physics or biology, that Durkheim intended to place in command. He applied the sociological point of view also to the natural sciences and found their epistemic credentials to be no less derivative from social facts than were the moral credentials of religion. In *The Rules of Sociological Method* Durkheim seems to argue that scientific concepts derive from sense perception. If he had adhered to this view, his philosophy of science would have been as individualistic as Hume's. However, he rejected the Humean theory of 'ideas' and also Kant's notion that basic concepts such as space, time, and causality have *a priori* status as innate to the human mind. Such concepts, according to Durkheim, are social in nature; they are in the individual mind only because the individual lives within a society. So, for example, he explains that the concept of time derives from the sequential observance of communal festivals; space is a geographic concept that owes its origin to the locational separation of different communities; causality is a generalization from the coercive power of parents, political authorities, and the *conscience collective*. These concepts, which scientists regard as naming objective properties of the material world are, in fact, *représentations* of the social world. Space, time, and causality are impersonal, not because they are material, but because they are collective.

Durkheim's explanation of the source of these fundamental concepts has been disregarded by philosophers. The *Encyclopedia of Philosophy* (1967), for example, does not so much as mention his attempt to offer an alternative to the theories of Hume and Kant, even in the article it contains on him. Commentaries on Durkheim by modern sociologists typically treat this aspect of his thought as not meriting serious consideration. Nevertheless, if we detach our attention from Durkheim's attempt to explain the origin of such basic concepts as space, time, and causality, it is evident that the application of his sociological point of view to science has found its way into modern thinking. Many philosophers of science acknowledge that, even in the experimental sciences, empirical observation of the material world is mediated by the theories that scientists construct; these intellectual artefacts play a role in generating the very data that are supposed to test their validity. Perceived 'facts' are 'theory-laden' and, some argue, the theories inevitably contain elements that reflect the social milieu. Such elements are the main interest of scholars who write 'externalist' histories of science. In the field of sociology itself an important sub-discipline, the 'sociology of science', has grown up, which studies the personal relationships among scientists, the roles of the various institutions in which they work, the influence of political and ideological convictions, competition for prestige, national and other loyalties, and other social factors that influence the direction of scientific research, and its findings. In these developments, Durkheim's theory of the social origin of the concepts of space, time, and causality exercised no influence, but his general thesis that all human activities are social has led to a more sceptical appraisal of the enterprise of science. Scientists are still admired, but reverence for them as priests of the Holy Grail has been tempered by recognition that even the greatest of them are much like ordinary men.

4. Sociology and politics

Writing a decade after Durkheim's death, a French sociologist noted that the Durkheimian school was motivated by the view held by its founder that sociology should be 'a pure science, without a mingling of philosophy or politics' (P. Fauconnet, 'The Durkheimian School in France', *Sociological Review*, 1927). It is evident from our survey of Durkheim's work, however, that he did not regard this precept as imposing much constraint on the domain or content of sociology. He felt that the academic scholar should distance himself from partisan politics; he himself joined no political faction and, except for the Dreyfus affair, avoided direct participation in contemporary political controversies. But politics in a larger sense of the term was in fact the inspiration of his life's work. Social questions caught his attention as a young man, not primarily because of the intellectual challenge they presented to one who wished to be a pure scientist, but because the investigation of them promised to provide solutions to the profound problems of modern civilization and, more specifically, to furnish scientific guidance for policies that would reverse the decay of French culture. He wished to be both a scientist and a moral mentor. In the latter role he adopted a consequentialist stance, arguing that the moral quality of acts and institutions is to be determined by reference to the ends they serve. The role of scientific sociology is to clarify this relationship, thereby combating ignorance, wishful thinking, and deceit. He rejected the utilitarian consequentialism that had devolved from Bentham and the Mills because of its focus on the ends of the individual; in his view, society has ends of its own. Durkheim could be described as a 'holistic utilitarian', but he did not consider it necessary to devise a term to describe his philosophy, since, from his youth, he regarded his essential views on morality, and science, to be adequately represented by the word 'socialism'.

The last quarter of the nineteenth century was a transition period in European socialist thought. The modern conception of socialism as denoting the replacement of the market mechanism by an administrative system of economic planning centralized at the level of the nation-state, despite the clear expression of it by Saint-Simon several decades earlier, was then only in embryo and would not definitively appear in political philosophy until concrete examples of such a mode of economic organization had been provided by the military-oriented economies of the major European states in the first World War. Many who described themselves as socialists, such as the English Fabians, were concerned mainly with the inequality of the distribution of income, and took their inspiration from David Ricardo's theory of rent, either directly, or indirectly via Henry George's popularization of its thesis in *Progress and Poverty* (1879). Socialists who regarded themselves as followers of Marx and Engels focused their intellectual attention on the Marxian theories of value and exploitation, and their political energies on the promotion of the class struggle that was fated to destroy capitalism, without any substantial delineation of the socialist mode of social order that would succeed it. The older ideas of the utopian writers were reflected in socialist theories advocating a world composed of small autonomous communities in which the sense of social solidarity that had been eroded by capitalism and industrialism would be regenerated. Some writers, on the other hand, took socialism to denote a heretofore unknown liberation of the individual not only from the constraints imposed by institutions such as churches and governments, but from those mandated by less formal pressures to conform to communal standards of behaviour. Oscar Wilde, for example, one of the greatest eccentrics of the age, construed socialism as a world of sublime individualism, one in which everyone could indulge his personal idiosyncracies without fear of law or convention ('The Soul of Man under Socialism', *Fortnightly Review*, 1891).

In his scientific sociology, as we have seen, Durkheim strongly opposed individualism as methodologically flawed and substantively erroneous. In his political philosophy he similarly rejected the ethical claims of classical liberalism. The central pillar of his thinking, as scientist and as moralist, was the need for social solidarity. This is not only necessary to maintain the integrity of the social order, but it is the essential condition of man's existence as a moral being. To live morally is to conform to the dictates of an authority that is external to oneself. Some say that God is this authority, but scientific sociology, according to Durkheim, reveals that the real source of morality is society; God only serves as a conceptual representation of society. The notion of a divine authority has served social needs, but it will not be necessary in a socialist society that is informed by scientific sociology, since the secular foundations of morality will then require no mythic representations.

Durkheim was far more interested in the sociological and moral merits of socialism, as he conceived it, than in its superiority as a mode of economic organization. He viewed a socialist economy as one that would contain a high degree of functional specialization and, apparently, he assumed that these activities would be co-ordinated by means of central administration rather than by the automatic forces of competition and exchange. But he did not undertake to describe how such a central administration would work and he paid no attention to the discussion of this that was beginning to appear during the last two decades of his life. Likewise, he was uninterested in the economic criticisms of capitalism, devolving from Ricardo and Marx, that many socialists of his time took as their main sources of inspiration. In short, Durkheim occupies no place in the development of the economics of social-ism. Indeed, if he deserves mention in this connection, it is as one who perpetuated the naive view that the organization of a socialist economy is so simple that it requires no scientific analysis. Lenin's view that, following the revolution, the operation of the economy could be left to a few accountants and clerks was not derived from Durkheim, but nothing that Durkheim had to say on the matter would have warned him that the construction of a new system of economic organization might prove more difficult than the destruction of the old one.

Durkheim's place in the history of political science is much more significant. The methodological view that political structures and processes should be studied in sociological terms, which has greatly influenced modern research in political science, is due more to Durkheim than to any other person. In addition, he was a major advocate of a particular form of political organization called 'syndicalism' or, less commonly today than in Durkheim's time, 'corporatism'. This deserves our attention, not only because it was the central institutional element in Durkheim's practical programme for social regeneration, but because an examination of it reveals, more generally, the main defects of his scientific sociology.

The democratizing political trends of the nineteenth century gave rise to much theoretical discussion of constitutional organization. If one accepts the assumption that the nation should be, or must be, the sovereign political entity, the problem arises as to how such a large unit, containing millions of persons, can be provided with an institutional structure that effectuates the democratic notion that political power should be widely shared. The democracy of ancient Athens, in which all citizens met in general assembly to determine public policy, was clearly inappropriate for the nation-states of modern Europe. Some form of *representative* democracy was necessary. The dominant trend of political evolution was to modify the feudal system, in which the aristocracy consisted of regional authorities, by simply extending regional representation to a broader spectrum of the population. In modern democracies, the coercive power of the state is exercised by assemblies whose members represent the people who reside within constituencies that are geographically defined.

This trend was rapidly becoming the established mode of political organization in Durkheim's day. He opposed it, advocating instead that another feudal institution should be adopted as model: the guild, which was a union of persons in the same occupation or trade. National 'corporations' should be created, defined economically rather than geographically, consisting of all persons engaged in the same industry, employers and workers alike. These corporations would have power to regulate their industries, under the supervision of the state. The general idea that the political organization of society should reflect its economic organization in this way antedates Durkheim and was advocated in his day by a large number of prominent political thinkers in all the countries of Europe (H. E. Barnes, 'Durkheim's Contribution to the Reconstruction of Political Theory', *Political Science Quarterly*, 1920). In Italy, a decade after Durkheim's death, corporatism was adopted and implemented by Benito Mussolini, becoming an established feature of fascist political theory and practice which, in the 1930s, migrated to Germany and Spain. It is doubtful that Durkheim's writings played any direct role in the development of fascist political thought, but if Mussolini had read them he would have found Durkheim congenial to his way of thinking, not only on the specific question of political organization, but also in expressing his own view of the fundamental nature of society. For example, the opening paragraph of Mussolini's 'Charter of Labour' says:

> The Italian nation is an organism having ends, life, and means of action superior to those of the separate individuals or groups of individuals which compose it. It is a moral, political, and economic unity that is integrally realized in the fascist state. (George H. Sabine, *A History of Political Theory*, 1937, p. 765)

Change 'Italian' to 'French' and 'fascist' to 'socialist' in this statement, and it could have been written by Durkheim.

Like everything in Durkheim's thought, his political syndicalism was derived from his view of the incontestable importance of social solidarity, and his analysis of its conditions. In a perfect world, there would be a solidarity of all humanity, but man is not capable, or is not yet capable, of forming social bonds with all other members of his species. He can identify only with a smaller group. Even the nation may be too large, as the continuous inter-necine conflict and repeated political upheavals in France since the Revolution would seem to certify. The 'corporation', a collectivity of all engaged in the same industry, would meet the conditions necessary to the achievement of solidarity. Durkheim's proposal for political reorganization would therefore appear to be consistent with his basic sociological theory, but this is questionable on two counts: it relies upon the operation of factors that lie at the level of individual psychology rather than 'social facts'; and it runs counter to his argument concerning the foundations of 'organic solidarity'.

If Durkheim had conceived of corporations as associations of professional persons such as physicians or lawyers, it might be arguable that, by virtue of their common training and their commitment to a code of professional ethics, the members of such associations function within the constraints of a *conscience collective*. Commentators on Durkheim frequently refer to his corporations as 'professional associations' or 'occupational groups', but if we look to the regulative functions that the corporations are expected to perform in the economy, it is evident that they correspond to *industries*. Is it plausible to suppose that in, say, the steel industry there is a *conscience collective* that subjects unskilled labourers and skilled ones, foremen, engineers, accountants, managers, *et al.* to common moral imperatives? If we are trying to explain the solidarity that such different people display on certain matters such as, for example, the tariff on steel, or its price, the assumption that individuals act out of self-interest will do at least as well as the notion that a *conscience collective* is at work. In fact Durkheim resorted to this individualistic premise in explaining how the corporation might be expected to serve as the focus of solidarity. In doing so he abandoned the 'sociological point of view' for the reductionist mode of analysis.

As we have seen, Durkheim argued in *The Division of Labour* that 'mechanical solidarity' is based on the similarity of persons, 'organic solidarity' on their functional differentiation. Apparently, however, he assumed that organic solidarity is limited to specialization within an industry; strong social bonds cannot be formed between those engaged in different industries. For this reason, a strong state is necessary, to weld the separate solidarities of the corporations into a national solidarity. This undermines the whole notion of organic solidarity. Instead of arguing that increased specialization promotes a different kind – indeed, a superior kind – of solidarity through mutual dependence, Durkheim seems to have allied himself with the many critics of specialization who regarded it as a source of conflict and social dissolution. Economic development does not automatically generate new forces that promote social solidarity; it increases the centripetal dynamic that drives the components of society apart. Organic solidarity therefore, at the level of the nation, must be created by the state, through the exercise of its sovereign power to make law and compel obedience to it. Some commentators on Durkheim's political programme interpret it as a proposal for a pluralistic society, utilizing the mechanism of checks and balances to control the exercise of power (see, for example, R. A. Nisbet, *Émile Durkheim*, 1965, pp. 59 f.; Steven Lukes, *Émile Durkheim*, 1973, p. 282), but an at least equally strong argument can be made that Durkheim should be regarded as having anticipated the fascist policy of using the institution of the corporation as a vehicle for the more effective exercise of totalitarian state power.

The political inheritance that derives from the syndicalist theory of constitutional organization is not our main concern. Nor is the discrepancy between Durkheim's syndicalism and his sociology of more than minor interest in itself. The point of these last few paragraphs is to enable us to bring into sharper focus the fundamental flaw in Durkheim's theoretical model of societies such as France and other Western nations. That flaw is social *monism*, the passionate insistence that society is One. In the first chapter of this book we noted that modern Western nations are characterized by 'multi-sociality', that is, they are socially pluralistic; or, perhaps one might even say, 'meta-pluralistic', since their diversity goes beyond any simple scheme of mensuration. To speak, for example, of 'American society' may be a locutional convenience, but even one who regards 'society' as an ontological entity cannot seriously intend to say that there is, within the geographic confines of the United States, *one* society, with ubiquitous cultural characteristics. There are many different cultures in the United States, definable on regional, racial, religious, linguistic, occupational, and numerous other dimensions. We cannot even say that there are N cultures in the United States corresponding to N dimensions, since some enclose others and some overlap.

Durkheim's sociological theory, in itself, is not committed to the notion that a nation is one cultural entity. It could have accommodated itself, for example, to the empirical fact that there are many regional cultures in France. But his notion of solidarity requires that, while there may be many cultures within a nation, every individual belongs to one, and only to one. Social bonding requires undivided loyalty. The segregation of people into discrete social units is therefore a precondition of solidarity. Durkheim's syndicalism was not a recognition of pluralism but a proposal to replace geographical location by occupation as defining the unit to which the individual belongs. Recognition of the fact that a Frenchman may be, simultaneously, a Breton, a Catholic, a communist, a physician, a chess-player, a conservationist, etc., and belong to associations representing all these features of his personality, beliefs, and interests, would have undermined his sociological theory by calling into question the usefulness of the notion of solidarity in explaining social order. In an article on 'Sociology and its Scientific Field', published in 1900 in an Italian journal, Durkheim says that 'social life is nothing but the moral milieu that surrounds the individual – or, to be more accurate, it is the sum of the moral milieus that surround the individual' (Kurt H. Wolff, ed., *Émile Durkheim*, 1979), but he did not modify his sociological theory to accommodate this 'more accurate' pluralistic conception of sociality. In the same article he restates the virtual identification of 'society' with the nation-state that pervades his sociological writings and dominates his political philosophy. While he made many contributions to sociology, Durkheim's social monism prevented him from perceiving that modern societies are held together as functioning entities in ways that do not rely, or at least do not rely so heavily as he supposed, on the coercive power of the *conscience collective*. Social scientists are only now beginning to understand what the co-ordinating forces are and how they function. Solidarity is still regarded as an important social and psychological phenomenon, but it is not construed in monistic terms, and it does not occupy the key position in social science that it did in Durkheim's thought. At the levels of political action and social policy the doctrine of social monism was fiercely embraced, with disastrous consequences, by the philosophers of Nazism but, as we shall see in Chapter 16, the early development of this line of thought by the German Monist League under the leadership of Ernst Haeckel drew its inspiration from biology rather than sociology, from Darwin rather than Durkheim.

Note 1: Karl Popper's 'world three'

The conception of society as an irreducible ontological entity is not one that is easily accepted by philosophers. Having struggled for three centuries with the problems created by Descartes's duality of mind and body, it is understandable that the notion that there is yet another primary domain of existence might be resisted. K. R. Popper, however, has adopted ontological pluralism, which he sees as offering a solution to the most fundamental problems of epistemology, ethics, and political philosophy. His epistemology has had a notable impact on methodological discourse in modern economics; many economists have embraced his view of the relation between empirical data and theoretical propositions almost as gospel (see Mark Blaug, *The Methodology of Economics*, 1980). This will demand our attention later, in Chapter 18. At this point, while Durkheim's sociology is fresh in our minds, a brief digression on Popper's metaphysical doctrine may be useful. Popper's 'world three' does not correspond exactly to what Durkheim meant by 'society', but they are both attempts to deal with the phenomenon of *culture* by postulating the existence of an entity that is neither material nor mental.

In an essay 'On the Theory of the Objective Mind', Popper rejects all monistic efforts to resolve the problems created by Descartes's dualism. He adopts, instead, a pluralist view of existence which he expresses as follows:

> In this pluralist philosophy the world consists of at least three ontologically distinct sub-worlds; or, as I shall say, there are three worlds; the first is the physical world or the world of physical states; the second is the mental world or the world of mental states; and the third is the world of intelligibles, or of *ideas in the objective sense*; it is the world of possible objects of thought: the world of theories in themselves; and of problem situations in themselves. (*Objective Knowledge*, 1972, p. 154, Popper's emphasis)

In a companion paper entitled 'Epistemology without a Knowing Subject' Popper's conception of the contents of this third world is amplified:

> Among the inmates of my 'third world' are, more especially, *theoretical systems*; but inmates just as important are *problems* and *problem situations*. And I will argue that the most important inmates of this world are *critical arguments*, and what may be called – in analogy to a physical state or to a state of consciousness – *the state of a discussion* or *the state of a critical argument*; and, of course, the contents of journals, books, and libraries. (*Ibid.*, 107, Popper's emphasis)

A specific illustration might help to clarify Popper's thesis. Newton's theory of universal gravitation was, initially, an inmate of world two, Newton's mind. Once the *Principia* had been published, however, it achieved an objective existence of its own. This is demonstrable by observing that (1) if no one living in, say, 1827, a century after Newton's death, knew the theory of gravitation, a reader of the *Principia* would learn of it; and (2) actions affecting the material world, including effects unintended by the actor, can result from knowledge of the theory of gravitation obtained in this fashion. The theory must have an objective existence if it can exogenously affect the content of consciousness and/or the material world. It is as existent as the material world that exogenously affects consciousness via sense data. But a theory does not have a material existence as a book does. Theories are inhabitants of another world. The same contention can be made of other things such as arguments concerning the existence of God, or the problem of economic justice. A person who is totally unaware of such things could become aware of them by going to the library, so they must exist there. But books and libraries are not the only sources. They may be embedded in the cultural milieu in which the individual lives, and he may become conscious of them even if he is illiterate.

Popper makes no reference to Durkheim and I doubt that he would be prepared to embrace the concept of a *conscience collective*. None the less, he sees the problem of understanding social phenomena in essentially Durkheimian terms. Speaking of 'the humanities', he says:

I will start from the assumption that it is *the understanding of objects belonging to the third world* which constitutes the central problem of the humanities. This, it appears, is a radical departure from the fundamental dogma accepted by almost all students of the humanities . . . . I mean of course the dogma that the objects of our understanding belong mainly to the second world, or that they are at any rate to be explained in psychological terms. (*Ibid.*, 162, Popper's emphasis)

This passage clearly constitutes a rejection of reductionism, and echoes Durkheim's insistence that social phenomena must be explained by other social phenomena, just as Popper's delineation of the contents of world three seems to echo Durkheim's notion that social facts are 'things'. Nevertheless, Popper repeatedly expresses a strong individualist position, not only in his political philosophy, but in his appraisal of the social sciences. Economics, in his view, is the only one of them that has attained scientific stature, and it has done so by practising methodological individualism. I leave this inconsistency unresolved, as Popper does. His conception of 'world three' is an interesting attempt to clarify the nature of the phenomenon of culture, but it has rendered no assistance in settling the debate between individualism and holism in the social sciences.

Note 2: Division of labour in economics, biology, and sociology

In the first chapter of this book I emphasized the importance of functional specialization to our understanding of the concept of 'society' and stressed the fact that the societies in which most humans live today are characterized by an extraordinary degree of specialization or 'division of labour'. In Chapter 7 we examined Adam Smith's famous discussion of the advantages of division of labour with which he begins the *Wealth of Nations*, and in the present chapter we have considered the reappearance of the concept, and the sociological importance of it, in the writings of Herbert Spencer and Émile Durkheim. So far as one can tell, these sociologists derived the notion from the continental biologists Henri Milne-Edwards and Karl E. von Baer rather than directly from Adam Smith or the other classical economists. It is impossible to determine whether the development of sociology would have been different if it had borrowed the notion of functional specialization from economics rather than biology but, at any rate, the use of it by Spencer and Durkheim was significantly different from Adam Smith's analysis and the extension of it by Ricardo.

Let us review Smith's and Ricardo's arguments. Smith pointed out that the significance of the division of labour is that it greatly increases productivity, by increasing the skill of workmen, by saving time that would be spent if workmen have to shift from one task to another, and by stimulating the invention of specialized tools or better procedures. Smith used this discussion to introduce his theoretical analysis of the market mechanism, pointing out that if the increased production is to be worth achieving, the commodities must be disposed of in an enlarged market. Smith deserves to be called the 'founder' of economics because, in this way, he focused attention on the market mechanism as a mode of social organization.

Ricardo's theory of international trade extended Smith's analysis by showing that, even in a model where human skill and technology are held constant, the output of commodities can be increased by specialization. Most strikingly, he showed that the opportunity for beneficial specialization, supported by trade, exists even when one country is more efficient than another in all lines of production. Ricardo's theory, though he apparently did not realize it, is not specific to national specialization and international trade. It applies to all economic activities.

There is no counterpart to these arguments of Smith and Ricardo, so far as I know, in von Baer's or Milne-Edwards's conception of organisms as composed of functionally specialized organs. The notion that the development of somatic heterogeneity is characteristic of 'higher' organisms might reflect Adam Smith's contention that the division of labour is a necessary condition of improvement, but one could not describe the efficiency of the kidney as a filter or that of the heart as a pump as due to the fact that these organs acquire skill in the performance of their specialized tasks, or that they save time, or invent tools or procedures to facilitate their functions. Unless one has a taste for bizarre metaphor, one would not say that this kind of specialization requires exchange and that the degree of it is, as Smith averred, 'limited by the extent of the market'. Nor could one claim, by analogy with Ricardo's theory, that the kidney specializes in filtering and the heart in pumping even though the kidney, say, is better at both than the heart is, because the kidney is *comparatively* more efficient in filtering. Milne-Edwards did indeed go very far in describing a parallelism between organ differentiation and the industrial division of labour, even comparing an organism to a workshop and saying that 'the diverse parts of the animal economy all compete towards the same goal' (Silvan S. Schweber, 'Darwin and the Political Economists: Divergence of Character', *Journal of the History of Biology*, 1980), but he apparently did not refer to Adam Smith's specific arguments concerning the division of labour or Ricardo's theory of comparative advantage.

What biologists borrowed from the economic analysis of the division of labour was much more restricted: it was no more than the general idea that functional specialization may increase efficiency and that, where it is adopted, the specialized parts become dependent upon one another. These simple notions are what, in turn, sociologists borrowed from biologists. They are not unimportant notions, but in economics they underwent a line of elaboration and development that has no parallel in either biology or sociology.

C. MAX WEBER (1864–1920)

Max Weber was brought up in Berlin, to which his family moved from Erfurt when he was five. On his father's side he was descended from successful businessmen and, by the time of his birth, the Webers occupied a position of solid standing in the German middle class. His mother's family was also comfortably situated, having inherited wealth originally derived from business, but her father, a schoolteacher, had intellectual interests which were prominent in her own upbringing and which she, in turn, brought to the Weber household. Weber's father was trained as a lawyer and was employed initially as a city official, but he spent most of his life in politics, becoming prominent in the National Liberal Party and winning elective office in the Berlin city council, the Prussian House of Deputies, and the German Reichstag. On both his father's and his mother's side, Weber was descended from strongly Protestant families which had suffered from Catholic repression. Weber's mother retained the strong Calvinist beliefs of her forebears; his father was less committed, a 'hedonist rather than a Protestant' (Lewis A. Coser, *Masters of Sociological Thought*, 1971, p. 235). Max was closer to his mother than to his father. In fact, strong conflicts developed between father and son and a breach eventually took place, which may have been a factor in causing a nervous breakdown that Weber suffered in 1897. He did not adopt his mother's religious piety, but his strong sense of duty and obsessive passion to be occupied in constructive work, which was a marked characteristic of his personality throughout adult life, reflected commitment to the moral values of his Calvinist mother and, correspondingly, repudiation of his father's personal philosophy. Without resorting to psychoanalytic interpretation, it is not difficult to connect these facts of Weber's family background with the thesis he advanced in his most famous work, *The Protestant Ethic and the Spirit of Capitalism* (1904–5).

Weber attended the universities of Heidelberg, Berlin, and Göttingen. His studies were in law, and he was admitted to the bar in 1886, but his main intellectual interest was in history and economics. He wrote a doctoral thesis on trading enterprises during the Middle Ages and a *habilitation* dissertation (necessary for anyone who aspired to an academic career) on the history of Roman agriculture. His teachers, who included some of the leading scholars in Germany, were greatly impressed by his abilities and, in 1894, he was appointed to the post of Professor of Political Economy at the University of Freiburg. Two years later, when Karl Knies retired from the University of Heidelberg, Weber was appointed to his Chair. Knies had been one of the founders of the German 'historical school' of economics which rejected the abstract modelling of classical economics and promoted the detailed study of economic history in a severely descriptive mode, without utilizing the theoretical concepts and propositions that had come to dominate English political economy. In 1896 Weber would have seemed the most promising young German to continue this line of scholarship. However, his interests, and his epistemological outlook, underwent a significant change. He continued to do research in history, but sociological rather than economic factors increasingly engaged his attention, and instead of rejecting economic theory he came to view it as exemplifying the appropriate methodology for all the social sciences.

Weber's illness, which began in 1897, forced him to resign his university post and for some four years he was unable to continue his work. He did not teach again until two years before his death. The period after recovery from his nervous breakdown, during which he worked as a private scholar in Heidelberg, was one of intense research on the subjects that, even today, are inseparably associated with the name of Max Weber as one of the seminal thinkers of the foundation era of modern sociology. During this period, though he had no university connection, Weber was a prominent figure in German social science circles. In 1903 he became one of the senior editors of the *Archiv für Sozialwissenschaft und Sozialpolitik*, which developed into the leading social science journal in Germany. In 1910 he joined Georg Simmel and Ferdinand Tönnies in founding the German Sociological Society and acted as its secretary for several years. He was also a prominent figure in German politics and wrote extensively on current political affairs. During the war he was severely critical of German political leadership. After Versailles, though motivated more by nationalist sentiment than by conviction of the merits of popular democracy, he allied himself with the liberals and played a role in the formation of the German Democratic Party, which aimed to transform the German political system along English lines. Weber never stood for political office, but one may speculate that increasing involvement in politics might have characterized his career if his life had not been cut short at the age of fifty-six by the great influenza epidemic. According to Raymond Aron, he 'always dreamed' of being a political leader and may be classed within 'the school of sociologists who were frustrated politicians, whose unsatisfied desire for action has been one of the motives, if not the motive, for their scientific effort' (*Main Currents in Sociological Thought*, 1967, II, pp. 182, 206). I do not know whether this is an accurate judgement of Weber's personality, but one should add that in the history of social science no one has been more insistent than he was in maintaining the thesis that facts and values are categorically distinct and in arguing that the study of social phenomena can be, and should be, pursued in an objective spirit, uncontaminated by the sociologist's own moral convictions and political commitments.

Weber did not put forward a general theory of human society as Spencer and Durkheim did. His research work on the history of modern economic development, the world's major religions, the structure of social organizations, and other topics, was not guided by a fundamental conception of the nature of society. One does not find, in his writings, the notion of society as an 'organism', or any other comprehensive paradigmatic idea that unites their various substantive contents into a coherent model. His recognition by modern sociologists as one of the major figures (some would say *the* major figure) in the creation of theoretical sociology rests upon the inspiration provided by his particular insights, substantive empirical arguments, and heuristic explanatory concepts, rather than by some synoptic view of society that can be recognizably denoted as 'Weberian'. Talcott Parsons, Weber's leading disciple in American sociology, interprets him as having the essentials of such a paradigm or model in his theory of 'action', and suggests that it implicitly guided his substantive work (*The Structure of Social Action*, 1937, Part III). Other commentators, however, view Weber as philosophically opposed to the construction of comprehensive sociological theories such as Comte's, or even ones with more content, such as Marx's, Spencer's, or Durkheim's (e.g. Raymond Aron, *Main Currents in Sociological Thought*, 1967, II, p. 183; *German Sociology*, 1957, p. 70; W. G. Runciman ed., *Max Weber, Selections in Translation*, 1978, p. 4).

Another difficulty that one encounters in attempting to come to grips with Weber is that most of his work was published as relatively short articles on specific topics. At the time of his death he was writing a large book under the title of *Wirtschaft und Gesellschaft* (Economy and Society), but it was left unfinished, and one is forced to rely upon more or less fragmentary materials. In addition, Weber wrote his scholarly papers in a complex and obscure style that makes his ideas difficult to grasp. Non-German readers, such as myself, must read translations and paraphrases that are frequently cast in what might be described as 'Teutonic English' or, when lucid, raise doubt as to their accuracy. Nevertheless, there now exists a large literature on Weber and, though differences of interpretation continue, considerable agreement prevails concerning most of the ideas that are associated with his name by historians of sociology. I say 'most of' in order to allow room for an important exception: much disagreement persists concerning what Weber intended to argue in his celebrated thesis concerning the role of Calvinism in the historical development of the modern economy.

1. The methodology of social science

When Weber recovered his capacity to work in 1902 his first efforts were devoted to two topics: the methodology of social science and the history of capitalism. Though he later wrote on various other subjects – the world's major religions, music, law, general economic history, authority and leadership, bureaucracy, etc. – he is best known today for his methodological writings and for his thesis that Calvinist theology played an important role in the development of the modern European economy. I begin this summary of Weber's ideas with a discussion of his methodological views, not only because they are important in themselves, but because they are inseparable from the rest of his thought. (Weber's papers on methodology have been collected and reprinted under the title of *Gesammelte Aufsätze zur Wissenschaftslehre*. Three of these, which contain the essentials of his methodological position, have been translated into English: *The Methodology of the Social Sciences*, 1949.)

In considering the nature of 'social laws' in Chapter 3 we noted that there has been a continuing debate on the question whether the study of social phenomena must model itself upon the methodology of natural science if it aspires to arrive at general propositions that possess explanatory and predictive power. In Chapter 14 C we reviewed the recent literature of this debate in so far as it bears on the question of historical explanation, taking as our point of departure the argument advanced by Carl Hempel that the historian can claim to have explained a past event only if he explicitly delineates the 'covering laws' that govern the class of phenomena to which that particular event belongs. Max Weber would have agreed with Hempel's contention that causal explanation requires reference to such nomological propositions, but he explicitly rejected the notion that the explanatory mode of the social sciences is homologous to that of the natural sciences. Weber cannot be easily classified within either of the strong positions that have been adopted on this matter. On the one hand he insisted upon the need to use theoretical concepts and empirical evidence the way natural scientists do, but he viewed the social scientist as also engaged in a special process of *Verstehen*, which, as we have seen, is regarded by numerous historians and other social scientists as a mode of investigation categorically different from that of natural science and more akin to the procedures of creative literature and the other arts. W. G. Runciman remarks that 'Weber's position . . . should be construed as a self-conscious and deliberate attempt to have it both ways' (*A Critique of Max Weber's Philosophy of Social Science*, 1972, p. 19). Weber's stature as a methodologist is due in large measure to the fact that many social scientists share his view that there is merit in both polar positions and regard him as having formulated an acceptable synthesis of them.

The main methodological distinction between the natural and the social sciences, in Weber's view, derives from a fundamental difference in the relation of the scientist to the phenomena he investigates. The natural scientist is an external observer of his material, but the social scientist lives within a social system and has the status, along with other humans, of a participant in social events. Herbert Spencer devoted the greater part of his *Study of Sociology* (1873) to a discussion of the intellectual and emotional biases that result from this insider status of the sociologist, arguing that it requires the exercise of special effort if scientific detachment is to be attained (see above, Chapter 15 A 1). A century and a half earlier, Giambattista Vico had argued the contrary position. According to Vico, the student of social phenomena has a great advantage in being himself a participant in the production of them rather than a mere spectator and can, as a consequence, arrive at social laws that are even more certain than the laws of physics, which only God, who made the world, can really know (see above, Chapter 14 C). The romantic movement, which was prominent in German intellectual circles in Weber's time, followed Vico in denigrating the claims of natural science. This had no appeal for Weber, but he did embrace Vico's notion that the student of social phenomena is assisted rather than hampered by being a participant in social events. Scientific detachment is essential, and achieving it is not unproblematic, but it does not require the social scientist to restrict himself to observing his subject matter from the outside. Properly utilized, the social scientist's introspective knowledge of himself enables him to penetrate to a level of empathetic understanding that is not open to the natural scientist. Nomological propositions concerning social phenomena can be (and must be) defined in terms of processes that lie at the level of consciousness, such as deciding, choosing, valuing, etc. Explanations that resort to biological factors that lie below the level of mind, or to psychological factors construed in behaviouristic terms, are methodologically flawed. Similarly, explaining social phenomena by other social phenomena, which Durkheim advanced as a basic principle of sociological method, is inadequate. Scientific method, according to Weber, requires reduction of the phenomena to their components, but the reduction must be carried to the appropriate level and not further. In the study of social phenomena, reduction to the level of individual consciousness is required; nomological propositions in sociology must be formulated in terms of the rational and purposive actions of individual persons. Weber was one of the most insistent advocates of the doctrine of 'methodological individualism' in the history of social science.

In Weber's day this methodological stance was most strongly identified with classical economics and the philosophy of utilitarianism. Many continental social scientists, including the German historical school, strongly opposed the individualistic orientation of English social science. There was, however, an outstanding exception: the Austrian school of economists, led by Carl Menger, who set out to develop theoretical models that were even more severely individualistic than those of classical economics. The great debate over social science methodology, the *Methodenstreit*, between the Austrians and the historical school was at its height when Max Weber was beginning his scholarly work (see above, Chapter 9 F). He never said explicitly that he sided with the Austrians; he maintained his close personal association with the leaders of the historical school, but it is evident that, when he resumed work after recovering from his nervous breakdown, he had rejected their holistic view of social phenomena as well as their insistence that empirical research must be done without resort to theoretical concepts.

The doctrine of methodological individualism does not necessarily require that sociological analysis be couched in terms that belong to the realm of consciousness. A model of social processes rigorously restricted to propositions in the language of behavioural psychology, which pictures persons as passively responding to external conditions, can be as 'individualistic' in its nomological level as one that construes them as engaged in rational and judgemental conduct. In Weber's view, however, methodological individualism is intimately connected with the notion that sociological theory must adopt, to use Talcott Parsons' term, an 'action frame of reference'. As a result of Parsons's own work in sociology, and the use of a similar mode of analysis by modern microeconomic theory, this aspect of Weber's methodology is fairly clear, but the same cannot be said for the associated concept of *Verstehen*. This may be rendered into English as 'understanding', but many commentators on Weber retain the German word or add an adjective to the English one because there seems to be more involved in it than can be captured by simple translation. That Weber regarded the concept as important is indicated by his intention to subtitle the book he was writing at the time of his death as *Grundriss der verstehenden Soziologie*.

What Weber seems to have had in mind resembles the argument Adam Smith made in his *Theory of Moral Sentiments* (see above, Chapter 7 C 3). In undertaking to explain the foundations of ethical judgements Smith contended that it is not necessary to resort to anything more transcendental than the fact that men are similar to one another. Such judgements are simply a manifestation of 'fellow feeling', which derives from recognition of this similarity. In effect, Weber extended this argument to the whole field of human conduct and, therefore, to social phenomena. By adhering rigorously to the proposition that social events result from the actions of individual persons, the social scientist can explain such events in terms of factors that are immediately familiar to anyone. The individual knows that he himself engages in actions that are purposive, and it is reasonable to construe the actions of others in similar terms. Words like 'prefer', 'decide', 'intend', etc., which refer to mental processes, have no place in the explanation of physical phenomena, but they are legitimate, and necessary, in explaining social phenomena. By tracing the causes of social events to individual actions that reflect the operation of such mental processes, the social scientist can make such events 'understandable'. The historian, for example, would not simply record that, when approaching Paris in August 1914, the German First Army wheeled south, exposing its flank to the French Sixth Army. He would explain General von Kluck's 'reasons' for this fatal departure from the Schlieffen Plan, since even an event that from the standpoint of grand strategy was senseless can nevertheless be 'understood' if we examine it, not in terms of the movements of armies, but in terms of the decisions of particular persons in particular circumstances. One can 'know' the role played by the machine gun in the battle of the Marne on the plane of material phenomena, but in addition to 'knowing' what von Kluck did and how Joffre and Galliéni responded to it, one can 'understand' these actions because military commanders have minds that work much like those of other folk.

This interpretation of Weber's notion of *Verstehen* would not be universally accepted by other commentators, but it would serve no useful purpose to review the various treatments of it that are to be found in the literature, since many of them are as obscure as Weber's own writings on the subject and others are plainly incorrect. Karl Popper is, I think, off the mark in claiming that mathematicians and physicists can attain an intimacy with their material akin to that claimed by Weber as unique to the social scientist, and he is certainly wrong in rejecting *Verstehen* as an intuitionist or 'oracular' philosophy that proposes to explain empirical phenomena in terms of Aristotelian essences (*The Open Society and its Enemies*, 1952, II, p. 292). Weber was a strong supporter of the mode of explanation of the natural sciences and, unlike the romantics of his time, he viewed *Verstehen* as supplementing it, not replacing it.

This is the relevant epistemological issue. If *Verstehen* can supplement the processes of theory-formation and/or empirical testing, then it has an epistemic status that deserves recognition. Ernest Nagel, in his *The Structure of Science* (1961, pp. 473–85, reprinted in May Brodbeck, ed., *Readings in the Philosophy of the Social Sciences*, 1968), gives a trenchant critique of the argument that the social sciences must employ *Verstehen* but he admits that the capacity of the social scientist to project himself imaginatively into the minds of others can be heuristically important in the formation of testable explanatory hypotheses. If Nagel's view is valid – and I see no way that an observer of social science practice can deny that such projection is, in fact, constructively employed – then *Verstehen* cannot be dismissed as devoid of heuristic capacity in the study of social phenomena. The natural scientist who undertakes to imagine what it must be like to be a molecule or a ribosome or a black hole is unlikely to advance our comprehension of such phenomena, and would probably be viewed by his colleagues as a candidate for confinement, but the social scientist can proceed usefully in that fashion as a normal mode of work.

The connection between the notions of *Verstehen* and methodological individualism is not completely reciprocal. Social phenomena can be analysed in terms of individual behaviour without necessarily making use of *Verstehen* concepts; but such concepts can be employed only in an analysis that proceeds at the level of the individual. The social scientist who says that he has an empathetic understanding of, say, the state, or the feudal system, or the coal industry, pretends to knowledge that, so far as we have any evidence, is beyond the capacity of the human mind. In speaking of 'the spirit of capitalism' Weber may seem to have laid claim to knowledge of this holistic sort and, if he had, he would have departed in practice from his methodological insistence that social wholes cannot be the object of empathetic understanding. As we shall see, his book on capitalism advanced the very different claim that one can begin to explain the historical development of the modern European economy by understanding the modes of reasoning, and the role of religion in forming the values and motivations, of the types of persons who were important in its creation. I am not certain that Weber confined *Verstehen*, as Nagel would, to the hypothesis-formation stage of scientific investigation, and he may have entertained the view that there is a more profound difference than this between the natural and social sciences but, if so, it remains enigmatic in his writings.

In the opening section of Weber's *Theory of Social and Economic Organization* (the English translation of Part I of *Wirtschaft und Gesellschaft*) Weber explains that in endeavouring to understand the 'meaning' of a social phenomenon we may be operating in three different contexts:

(a) as in the historical approach, the actually intended meaning for concrete individual action; or (b) as in cases of sociological mass phenomena the average of, or an approximation to, the actually intended meaning; or (c) the meaning appropriate to a scientifically formulated pure type (an ideal type) of a common phenomenon.

The example given above (mine, not Weber's) of General von Kluck's decision to wheel the right wing of his army corresponds to the first of these and is fairly straightforward. The second involves a certain degree of abstraction. If the price of sugar falls, every individual consumer may purchase more with the same money, but it is not necessary to show that all of them do so in order to explain an increase in the aggregate quantity of sugar bought in terms of the purposive action of individuals; reference to the 'average' person is sufficient. The economist, however, operates at a still higher level of abstraction in dealing with such a phenomenon, analysing not the actions of particular persons, or a statistical average of them, but the rational decision of a hypothetical consumer who is construed as aiming at maximizing the 'utility' derivable from his income. This corresponds to the third of Weber's categories. Immediately following the passage quoted above he says: 'The concepts and "laws" of pure economic theory are examples of this kind of ideal type.'

Most of the discussion of Weber's methodology that has taken place in the literature on the philosophy of social science focuses upon his notion of 'ideal types'. Many commentators regard this as his most important or, at least, his most distinctive contribution to the subject. As the above quotation indicates, he regarded the ideal type procedure as one of the forms of the *Verstehen* mode of explanation, and considered it to be legitimate for this reason. Weber's most fundamental methodological thesis was that causal explanation in the social sciences must trace events to factors that operate at the level of consciousness. This is a property of the individual person, but it is extendable for scientific purposes to the 'average' person or even to a non-empirical hypothetical person. Analysis of social phenomena in terms of the action of hypothetical conscious entities, construed as more purely rational than real persons, is what Weber meant by the method of ideal types or, as he sometimes phrased it, 'pure types'. In Weber's argument, the terms *Verstehen* and 'ideal type' are not synonymous. Fritz Machlup avers that the latter term has been used since the late nineteenth century in Germany to differentiate the social from the natural sciences (*Methodology of Economics and other Social Sciences*, 1978, p. 214). If so, it represents a departure from Weber's argument. In his view, *Verstehen* methodology, which includes, but is not restricted to, the special procedure of ideal type analysis, is the distinguishing characteristic. If my rendition of what Weber meant by ideal type analysis is correct, it is evident that the natural sciences make extensive use of such a procedure. The entities in Newtonian mechanics, for example, which are treated as having mass but no extension in space, are 'ideal' entities. The 'ideal gas laws' describe the motions of hypothetical, not real, molecules. Weber's ideal entities differ from these in having consciousness, which enables the social scientist to construct theoretical models of their interaction in terms of the subjective motives and reasons that operate in the real world inhabited by real persons.

Weber frequently referred to 'Gresham's law' as an example of ideal type analysis. It may be worth taking a moment to explain it. This proposition is named after Elizabeth I's financial adviser, Sir Thomas Gresham, who used it to explain the consequences of the debasement of the English coinage under Henry VIII. It became prominent in the economic literature of the late nineteenth century as part of a protracted discussion of 'bimetallism' – a proposal to enlarge the base of the monetary system by making silver, as well as gold, the legal standard. Economists pointed out that gold and silver are commercial commodities as well as monetary ones and that there would be a market rate of exchange between them, set by supply and demand conditions, which could differ from the rate established by the monetary authority. If the central bank undertook to redeem paper currency for either gold or silver at a ratio of 16 oz. of silver for 1 oz. of gold, but the ratio pertaining in the market were lower, say 15:1, it would be profitable to buy silver from, and sell gold to, the central bank and do the reverse in the market. Gold would disappear from circulation. The opposite would occur if the market ratio were higher than 16:1. At any moment of time, gold *or* silver would be the monetary standard, but not both. The empirical validity of this analysis was indicated rather dramatically in the 1850's when, as a result of new gold discoveries which lowered its market price, legally bimetallic countries such as France shifted from silver to gold as their actual operative monetary standard. Weber, significantly, did not refer to such empirical evidence in support of Gresham's law. He construed it as a purely theoretical proposition, predicting what would, necessarily, occur in a world inhabited by 'economic man', an ideal type. In his view such abstract propositions are scientifically valid and sociology, as well as economics, can make use of them.

It is difficult to assimilate all the instances in which Weber used the concept of ideal types to abstract economic theory, but it is evident that he regarded economics as exemplifying the basic features of ideal type analysis. The following passage is one of Weber's clearest statements of the characteristics and purposes of the ideal type method:

> The kind of ideal-typical model of social action which is constructed, for example, for the purposes of economic theory is . . . 'unrealistic' insofar as it normally asks how men would act if they were being ideally rational in pursuit of purely economic goals. It does so in order (i) to be able to understand men's real actions, shaped as they are, at least *in part*, by traditional restraints, emotional impulses, errors and the influence of non-economic purposes and considerations, to the extent that they are also affected by the rational pursuit of economic goals . . . ; but also (ii) to facilitate knowledge of their real motives by making use of this very deviation of the actual course of events from the ideal type. An ideal-typical model of a consistently mystical and other-worldly attitude to life . . . would have to proceed in exactly the same way. The more sharply and clearly constructed the ideal types are – in other words the more *unrealistic* they are in this sense – the better they perform their function, which is terminological and classificatory as well as heuristic . . . .
>
> From the methodological point of view, the only choice is often between a terminology which is not clear at all and one which is clear but unrealistic and 'ideal-typical'. In this situation, however, the latter sort of terminology is scientifically preferable. (Max Weber, *Selections in Translation*, 1978, pp. 24 f., Weber's emphasis)

As a gloss on this quotation three points should be noted. First, Weber does not construe the task of the social scientist as explaining the whole of social reality. All social theories are, necessarily, limited in scope. In this respect he places himself in distinct opposition to the Grand Sociology of Comte, Marx, and Spencer. Secondly, in the classification of philosophical positions, Weber clearly belongs with the nominalists and cognitive instrumentalists. His 'ideal types' do not bear any affinity to Plato's 'pure forms', and the characteristics imputed to ideal-typical entities are not Aristotelian 'essences'. And thirdly, in accordance with his instrumentalist view, he does not regard correspondence to empirical data as the crucial test of a theory. Not only are good theories necessarily 'unrealistic' but, even when they fail to explain or predict a real-world phenomenon, they may serve a heuristic function by focusing attention on factors that may account for the failure.

In the modern literature of the philosophy of science there has been a continuing debate between 'descriptivists' and 'prescriptivists' – between those who regard the role of the philosopher as describing and analysing the procedures actually employed by scientists who are engaged in extending our knowledge of empirical phenomena, and those who undertake to prescribe how the work should be performed. As a philosopher of social science, Max Weber was a descriptivist with respect to economics and a prescriptivist with respect to sociology, political science, and history. Working scientists and scholars are not inclined to pay much heed to the prescriptions of philosophers and, except for the Parsonian sociologists in the United States, Weberian methodology made little impact on social science research, perhaps least of all in Germany, where even academic economics continued to be historical and descriptive, impervious to the abstract model constructions of the increasingly predominant neoclassical school.

Starting in the early 1960s, modelling of this sort began to be extended to subjects outside the field of economics, particularly to the analysis of the behaviour of governmental bodies such as legislatures, bureaus, and regulatory agencies. The creation of 'public choice theory', as this has come to be called, is one of the most important developments in twentieth-century social science. It provides a more effective means than has hitherto been available for the scientific study of the governmental and other non-market institutions that play important roles in social organization. This branch of social science could be described as 'Weberian', since it is based on the methodology of *Verstehen* and the technique of theoretical modelling in terms of ideal type entities: the behaviour of a 'public choice' institution in determining laws and rules through which the authority and coercive power of the state are effected is analysed in terms of the rational actions of its officials in pursuit of their own individual ends, rather than as the action of a collective entity that has a putative objective of serving the public welfare. Gordon Tullock, one of the pioneers of public choice theory, describes his early book *The Politics of Bureaucracy* (1965, pp. 14 f.) as based on Max Weber's notion of *Verstehen*, but this is a rare acknowledgement. Most of those who have worked in the area of public choice theory and empirical research were trained in neoclassical economics and it is evident that their inspiration derives directly from it, unmediated by Weber's methodological writings or his substantive work on subjects such as authority and bureaucracy.

2. Sociology and society

In Max Weber's view, the most momentous development in the history of modern Europe was the spread of what he called the 'rationalistic' attitude. By this he meant the metaphysical outlook and methodological practice of the natural sciences. It is the fundamental factor that distinguishes Western civilization from others, and from its own pre-modern past. Not only has Western thought become rationalistic, but Western social organization has been 'rationalized' through the development of social, political, and economic institutions that, like the practical applications of natural science, are oriented to the efficient achievement of utilitarian objectives. Long-standing customs and traditions, and even religion, have given way to rational organization, or have been accommodated to its requirements. Herbert Spencer argued that the fundamental change in modern European history had been the replacement of forms cf organization that depended upon hierarchical order and coercion by the spontaneous co-ordination of voluntary individual activity, as exemplified by the market economy. Weber did not deny the historical importance of this, but even more fundamental, in his view, was the rationalistic character of modern economic, and other, institutions. The development of the market mechanism is a central feature of capitalism but, to the eye of the sociologist, more significant is that its industrial and commercial institutions are examples of a larger development, the modification of all social institutions to conform to a cultural ethos of rationality.

This is the central preoccupation of all Weber's writings, methodological, substantive, and normative. Scientific sociology is rationalistic in two senses: the ideal type models of the sociologist are instrumental aids in the study of empirical phenomena, not metaphysical truths; and the phenomena themselves are construed as resulting from the goal-directed actions of individual persons. Like Adam Smith in economics, Weber regarded the sociologist as engaged in the rational study of man's rational activity. But he went further: the main problems of modern Western society, in his view, result from the remoulding of its social and political institutions that has taken place under the influence of rationalism. Weber was no anti-modernist; he did not hold a nostalgic view of the past. He did not follow the romantics in excoriating the rationalist ethos, but he did consider that it had led to some very serious difficulties and, in the final years of his life, during the disturbed period after Germany's defeat, he was not optimistic that the continued development of Western rationalism would be capable of resolving the problems it had generated. He did not live to see his country demonstrate that, whatever might be said for or against rationalism, the marriage of rationalistic science and social organization to romantic ethical and political philosophy produces monstrous progeny.

Social institutions are, of course, collectivities, and society as a whole is a collectivity. In accordance with his methodological individualism, Weber rejected the notion that any collectivity can be construed as engaging in 'action'. What he calls 'social action' is not the action of a social institution; it is the rational action of an individual which, within the organizational framework of a collectivity, is undertaken in cognizance of its impact on other individuals and their reactions to it.

> Sociology is a science which attempts the interpretive understanding of social action . . . . Action is social in so far as, by virtue of the subjective meaning attached to it by the acting individual (or individuals), it takes account of the behavior of others and is thereby oriented in its course.

> Not every kind of action, even of overt action, is 'social' in the sense of the present discussion . . . . For example, religious behavior is not social if it is simply a matter of contemplation or of solitary prayer. The economic activity of an individual is only social if, and then only in so far as, it takes account of the behavior of someone else (*Theory of Social and Economic Organization*, 1947, pp. 88, 112 f.).

These passages indicate that Weber's conception of 'social action' prescribes a severely restricted domain for the discipline of sociology, in contrast to Comte, Spencer, and Durkheim, who viewed it as a general science of social phenomena. The notion of 'action' confines sociology to the study of the rational, goal-directed activities of individuals; the adjective 'social' limits it further to the subset of activities in which the individual actor 'takes account of the behaviour of someone else'. The behaviour of a person engaged in solitary prayer, and the behaviour of one who attends a church service, are both understandable as rational and purposive, but the latter is of interest to the sociologist as social behaviour that takes place within the framework of a social institution. The economic activity of a solitary, self-sufficient hermit is not social, but if he moves to town, takes a job, marries and has children, he finds himself engaged in interaction with other persons as a member of a family, a business firm, and other institutions. So far so good; no serious objection can be raised to defining sociology in such a way as to exclude human activities that are solitary. But people engage in a great deal of non-solitary activity that, according to Weber's definition, would be excluded from the domain of the 'social'. For example, the transactions that take place in what the economist calls a 'perfectly competitive market', which is construed as composed of so many buyers and sellers that the individual does not affect, and is not affected by, the actions and purposes of others, would be excluded. The individual who participates in the activities of a political party is engaged in social action, but when he enters the polling booth and the curtains close behind him, he is not. This is a defensible definition of the term 'social action' but it does not define the domain of what most sociologists consider to be their field and, indeed, Weber did not restrict his own research to this degree.

Weber's narrow definition of the domain of sociology was motivated, to a considerable extent, by his commitment to methodological individualism as a fundamental canon of social science. In a letter written shortly before his death he said that his main object as a sociologist had been to combat the use of holistic concepts in social analysis (Wolfgang Mommsen, 'Max Weber's Political Sociology and his Philosophy of World History', *International Social Science Journal*, 1965, p. 44 n.). Collectivist notions, such as the view of society as a living 'organism', and the state as an entity with ultimate values and immediate purposes that transcend those of individual persons, were widespread in the German literature of Weber's time. Though he made no reference in his writings to Durkheim, there is reason to believe that he was familiar with his and his followers' work, but he had need to look to France for examples of such ideas. Weber was prepared to accept the argument that holistic concepts can be used heuristically in other social science disciplines such as law, but only with great reservation, since, in his view, there is a strong tendency to reify them, turning analytical instruments into supposed social facts. Sociology proper must adhere to the individual level of action, making use of holistic propositions only when it draws upon other social sciences or takes note of the fact that individual actors may employ collective concepts in their own thinking. (The reader may well remark at this point that my account of Weber's conception of the domain of sociology is becoming rather unclear. I can do no more than refer him to the first four sections of chapter I in *The Theory of Social and Economic Organization* in the hope that it may provide a less vertiginous view of Weber's ideas than I have been able to obtain.)

Given Weber's conception of sociology, it is not surprising that many of the subjects that were central concerns of Spencer and Durkheim are not prominent in his writings. He pays little attention to such things as the division of labour, the problem of social solidarity, the evolutionary character of social systems, the phenomenon of enculturation, or the role of what Durkheim called the *conscience collective* in forming the values of individuals and in governing their behaviour. Since sociology is concerned with the actions of individuals that are oriented to their perceived interactions with those of others, such global matters lie outside its domain. Weber does not focus upon 'society' or 'culture' in a general way. Weberian individuals belong to groups, but these are much smaller units of organization. The society at large is composed of groups, which Weber defines largely in terms of economic interest, and global events result from the interplay of their divergent interests. But, as a sociologist, Weber is more interested in the internal organization of such groups than in analysing their interaction. For a more comprehensive view, he was inclined to adopt the stance of the historian and, instead of developing a general theory of 'society', undertake to explain important developments in the concrete history of a specific region. In Weber's opinion, the most significant material fact in the modern history of Europe was the emergence of the capitalistic form of economic organization.

This brings us to his famous thesis about the causal connection between the Protestant Reformation and the economic ascendancy of the West. It is not evident that this belongs within the domain of sociology as Weber construed it but, wherever it belongs in the classification of scholarly disciplines, it has been the focus of more debate over the past eighty years than anything else that Weber wrote.

3. Capitalism and Calvinism

At its best Weber's scholarly writing was not lucid, and it was not at its best in *The Protestant Ethic and the Spirit of Capitalism*. Forty years after its initial publication, in surveying the already large literature on it and Weber's additional writings on the subject, Ephraim Fischoff declared that Weber had been fundamentally misinterpreted by almost all commentators ('The Protestant Ethic and the Spirit of Capitalism: The History of a Controversy', *Social Research*, 1944). Another forty years have since passed and the literature on Weber's thesis has continued to grow, but there is still much dispute as to what he intended to say, not only between the critics of the thesis and its defenders, but even among those who regard it as an outstanding contribution to modern social science. So the reader must be warned that the presentation of Weber's thesis in this section is not what indeed it cannot be, one that would command universal scholarly agreement. I have to say also that, even accepting Weber's conception of the fundamental characteristics of capitalism, I am not convinced that his historical contention is empirically valid or, if valid, of more than minor significance; so a certain element of critical intention may have crept into my account of his argument.

As we have seen, one of Weber's central methodological propositions is that the social sciences differ from the natural sciences in that the social scientist can explain the phenomena he examines in terms of the conscious, goal-oriented activity of the individual entities, while this level of 'understanding' is not open to the natural scientist, who must adhere to a 'materialist' view of phenomena. Many interpreters of Weber's *Protestant Ethic* contrast it with the Marxian 'materialist interpretation of history' and some suggest that it was written with the deliberate aim of refuting Marx and Engels. Whether this was an important part of Weber's intention is uncertain, but there is no doubt that his thesis is 'anti-materialist', at least in the sense that it denies that material factors are the only autonomous causes of social change. Ideas, values, beliefs, etc., which Marx and Engels construed as mere 'epiphenomena' of more fundamental factors (the 'forces of production' and the 'relations of production') are regarded by Weber as autonomous, sharing with material elements the status of basic causal factors in historical developments such as the evolution of capitalism. Though the individual person is the primary locus of social action, his value orientation is greatly influenced by his culture, and the culture of a whole society can be significantly altered by ideas, which are individualistic mental phenomena. The emergence of modern capitalism, in Weber's view, is due in part to certain religious ideas that, since the Protestant Reformation, have been especially important in creating the dominant values of Western culture. Weber discussed the parts played in this development by the various branches of Protestantism, but his main thesis was that the theological doctrine of John Calvin was an especially important source of what he called the *Geist* or 'spirit' of capitalism.

We might note in passing that Weber's argument could be described as 'anti-Durkheimian' as well as 'anti-Marxian'. Durkheim regarded the value imperatives of religion as merely reflecting those that are already embedded in the *conscience collective*. Weber argued that religion can, on occasion, be an independent causal factor that changes the generally accepted values of a society, and such an influence has in fact been evident in modern European history: Calvinism's effect on the Western mind has been, not crucial, but sufficiently important that no explanation of the most important feature of that history – the development of the capitalistic economy – can neglect it. In considering Weber's thesis we should keep in mind that his early essays on methodology and the essays that became *The Protestant Ethic* were written at the same period, and the linkage between them is more than temporal. His historical analysis was, in part, a concrete example of *Verstehen* methodology, since it undertook to explain an empirical phenomenon through a subjective understanding of the motivations and reasoning of the types of individuals whose actions created it.

Like most theologians, John Calvin considered God to be incomprehensible, and then set out to comprehend him. According to Calvin, God created the world for his own glory, and man has been placed in it to serve that end. Some men will join God in heaven after their earthly sojourn, but others will not. Some branches of Christian theology (and other religions) have contended that the determination of one's status in the after-life depends upon one's behaviour during the brief period of earthly existence. Calvin denied that this is God's rule of selection. Everyone is morally obligated to behave in accordance with God's wishes, but whether a person does so or not has nothing to do with his ultimate fate. This is not to any degree contingent: at the moment that a new soul comes into existence it is irrevocably classified as either 'elect' or 'damned'. This fanciful elucidation of God's incomprehensible will – the doctrine of 'predestination' – was the central and distinctive proposition in Calvin's theology.

Such a doctrine would seem to lead logically to a life of pleasure. The English poet Robert Herrick advised his readers to 'gather ye rosebuds while ye may', since life is brief and what comes after is unknown. To one who is confident that he does know – that there is an after-life, and that earthly behaviour is irrelevant to one's status in it – Herrick's advice would appear to be even more cogent. Why not enjoy the pleasures of this world to the full, since the fate of one's immortal soul is already irrevocably determined? But theology, unconstrained by any empirical test, can easily rotate its axis of argumentation, and in the case of Calvinism, it did so the full 180 degrees. Sincere Calvinists, instead of devoting themselves to pleasure, or even to a resigned quietism, became noted for their moralistic dedication to hard work, and their willingness to deny immediate gratification in order to invest effort and wealth in the long-term improvement of their worldly condition. These were the attitudes which, according to Weber, made Protestant Europe the locus for the development of the modern capitalistic economy. Weber explains this apparent inconsistency between theology and practice in terms that, despite his own methodological aversion to psychological explanations of social phenomena, appeal to psychological factors. It would be natural, he argues, that a person who believes in the predestination of souls would crave some empirical sign that might indicate the fate in store for his own. Such a sign, it came to be believed, was provided by one's worldly achievements and economic success. Hard and efficient work, and the devotion of income to investment rather than consumption, could not alter God's decision, but the progressive accumulation of wealth that they produced might be construed as signifying that one was predestined for salvation. Through this inversion of Calvin's theology, according to Weber, the 'capitalist' emerged as a prominent 'ideal type' in Christian Europe, reinforced rather than constrained by his religious faith in activities that undermined long-standing tradition and brought a new economic order into being.

In *The Structure of Social Action* (1937) Talcott Parsons begins his exposition of Max Weber with an examination of *The Protestant Ethic* (which he had previously translated for English publication), considering this to reveal the essential characteristics of Weber's theoretical sociology. Concerning the historical argument itself, Parsons declares in summarizing his discussion that 'Weber may be said to have "proved" his original thesis' (p. 575). This view is not shared by historians. Weber's analysis has been subjected to fierce attack, on matters of empirical detail, causal interpretation, and logic. Some critics have set out to demolish a thesis that Weber never advanced – that the inverted form of Calvinist theology was both necessary and sufficient of itself to produce a capitalistic economy – thus presenting an easy target for counter-attack. But serious criticisms have also been made by those who interpret Weber as only contending that Calvinism played an important part, along with other factors, in the history of European industrial capitalism. It is not possible to determine the relative influence of factors that cannot be quantitatively measured, so the contention that Calvinism was 'important' in this particular case of economic development, or more generally, cannot be proved or disproved, as Parsons seems to recognize by his punctuation of the passage quoted above. Historians regularly find themselves dealing with unquantifiable factors, yet do not shrink from offering causal explanations, but Weber's explanation has not found a place in the standard historiography on the economic history of modern Europe.

Calvinist theology is seldom included as a causal factor, and Weber's thesis, in those rare instances when it is mentioned at all, usually appears as a footnoted reference to a discarded curiosum. The article on 'Capitalism' in the *International Encyclopedia of the Social Sciences*, for example, makes no reference at all to Max Weber, or to religion as a factor in its historical development. Weber's thesis lives on, but in the more speculative literature of Grand Sociology, in philosophical discussion of cosmic theories of history, and in some religious writings whose authors, though generally viewing capitalism with moral distaste, seem cheered by the notion that religion may have some significant influence in the age of modernity.

I cannot here undertake to summarize the debate over Weber's thesis, or to do more than suggest why I believe that historians are justified in paying little attention to it. One need not adopt a rigorously materialistic epistemology, or embrace a dogmatic empirical secularism that arbitrarily excludes religion from an epistemology which allows causal status to ideas, to find serious flaws in Weber's argument. How, for example, does one account for the ancient trading economies of Minoan Crete, Phoenicia, and Carthage? If Catholicism provided no basis for the development of a 'capitalistic spirit', how is the industrial revolution of the high Middle Ages to be explained, or the economic ascendancy of Renaissance Florence and Venice, where devout Catholic merchants were the nobility? If Calvinism served to promote capitalism, how do we account for the Scottish Renaissance (including such luminaries as Adam Smith, the father of the economic analysis of a capitalistic economy, and James Watt, who revolutionized industry with his steam engine) which took place immediately *after* the power of the (Calvinist) Presbyterian Church had been broken? If the hallmark of capitalism is 'rationality' how much weight must be given to Calvin's scholastic reasoning as compared to the scientific rationalism of Galileo, Harvey, Newton, Boyle, *et al.*? Since the country that led the way in modern industrial development was England, how important was Calvinist theology (Puritanism) there as compared to other ideational elements such as utilitarianism, empiricism, constitutionalism, and a high regard for personal freedom? Even if it were historically true that devout Calvinists led the way in European economic development, is it necessary to explain the apparent inconsistency between their belief in predestination and their worldly activities by tortured theological reasoning? The simple observation that men of affairs are rarely troubled by conflict between religious faith and mundane interest will serve. That the successful Calvinist capitalist might construe his wealth as signifying that he was one of the elect is credible; the notion that he was motivated to amass it by the desire for such a sign must be treated with scepticism. Weber himself averred that the modern world, including the 'authentic modern bourgeoisie', is characterized by 'indifference to or rejection of religion' (*Selections in Translation*, 1978, p. 178). But enough; let us go on.

When Weber spoke of the development of 'capitalism' he was not referring primarily to the organization of an economy by means of the market mechanism, or competition, or the emergence of markets for such things as labour and land, or private ownership of the means of production. These are all features of 'capitalism' as that term is commonly used, but Weber focused on the *Geist* of capitalism, by which he meant the spirit of rationality which, in his view, was the central characteristic of modern society, not only in the economic sphere but in all its aspects. His work in economic history was construed by him as offering a window of observation into the most important characteristic of Western civilization and its most troubling problems. A year before his death Weber was appointed Professor of Sociology at the University of Munich and, as his first extended course, gave a series of lectures under the title of 'Outlines of Universal Social and Economic History'. (The text of this, compiled mainly from students' notes, has been translated by the distinguished American economist Frank Knight as *General Economic History*, 1927.) Most of the material in these lectures consists of a descriptive account of economic history. Weber did not undertake to defend or restate his, by then much criticized, thesis concerning the relation between Calvinism and capitalism. I do not suggest that he had abandoned it, but it is clear that his attention was now focused, not on explaining the genesis of the capitalist 'spirit', but on examining its essential nature and its, to him, momentous consequences. In the final lecture in this series he declared that while such things as cheap transport and high demand for goods were important elements in the development of capitalism, the crucial factor was the application of rationalist modes of thought and action:

> In the last resort the factor that produced capitalism is the rational permanent enterprise, rational accounting, rational technology and rational law, but again not these alone. Necessary complementary factors were the rational spirit, the rationalization of the conduct of life in general, and a rationalistic economic ethic. (p. 354)

Weber intended to examine the consequences of the pervasive application of rationalism with regard to the development of the modern state in his next course of lectures. He did not live to complete them, but he had written a great deal on this theme in his unfinished manuscript *Wirtschaft und Gesellschaft*. His discussions there, and in some earlier writings, on the subjects of authority, leadership, and bureaucracy constitute his most important and lasting contributions to substantive social science. Weber's Calvinism–capitalism thesis has virtually disappeared from contemporary historiography, but his studies of 'charismatic' leadership and bureaucracy are the acknowledged points of departure for most of the literature on these topics in sociology and political science.

4. Authority, charisma, and bureaucracy

In using words such as 'rational', 'rationality', and 'rationalization' Weber was not referring to the aims that motivate human action. He did not argue that, say, materialist or utilitarian objectives are more rational than religious ones. The values that men hold are not, in themselves, rational or otherwise, but these values, whatever they might be, may be serviced by rational or non-rational modes of behaviour. When human action is governed by tradition and custom it is non-rational. The significance of capitalism in the cultural history of the West is that, through it, the rational methods of science and industry have been introduced into all areas of life. Not only have business enterprises been 'rationalized' but all social institutions have been restructured to further their various objectives by technically efficient methods. In examining the modern state, says Weber, the key question is not 'What is it for?' but 'How does it work?' and the answer to the question is furnished by viewing the state as an institution that, like the business firm, is structured to work 'rationally'.

This does not mean that there are no important differences between the state and the economy. A competitive market economy is a pluralistic system of independent enterprises, but the state is a singular entity and, Weber emphasizes, possesses within the domain of its jurisdiction a monopoly over coercive force. The structure of the modern state is designed to facilitate the efficient exercise of this power. Weber did not share Spencer's view that social evolution tends towards the steady reduction of coercion by some men over others. In his judgement, the significant trend is the modernization of the state's exercise of coercive power by its adoption of rationalistic methods and the staffing of its departments with people who are skilled in the arts of efficient administration. Needless to say, on this matter Weber was far more perceptive. Spencer's cosmic evolutionism led into a metaphysical swamp; Weber's notion of 'rationality' opened one of the most important avenues of theoretical and empirical investigation in modern social science.

Weber did not conceive of the state as a simple repository of force. Citizens obey the orders of the state not only for fear of punishment, but because they regard the state as a *legitimate* authority. Every system of authority, says Weber, relies upon a considerable degree of voluntary obedience and, to this end, clothes itself with the mantle of legitimacy. Utilizing the methodology of 'ideal types', he distinguishes three pure forms of legitimacy: traditional, legal, and charismatic. The first type is the authority that claims that its powers are legitimate because they are a continuation of long-standing tradition, and that the persons who exercise those powers have acquired their positions in the traditional way. An arbitrary and tyrannical authority could claim legitimacy on such grounds. The legal type of authority is one that operates within a framework of laws, which establish the boundaries of legitimate power and the procedures that are permissible in exercising it. Weber sometimes calls this the 'rational' type of authority. The third type refers to the situation where the citizens voluntarily obey the commands of the state because they believe them to emanate from a person or persons of 'exceptional sanctity, heroism or exemplary character'. Authority of this type is legitimized by the charismatic qualities of those who exercise it. (*The Theory of Social and Economic Organization*, 1947, p. 328.) Weber points out that these categories are intended to be heuristic abstractions; in real-world politics all three criteria of legitimacy are normally present, with different weights in different nations, and in the same nation at different times. His main purpose in developing this typology was to analyse the characteristics of the charismatic and legal types of authority and to show that while the role of the former in human history has at times been momentous it is inherently unstable and tends to degenerate, while, at least in the modern West, the latter tends increasingly to prevail in the domain of politics as in all other areas of social organization.

Weber's term 'charisma' was taken from a Greek word meaning 'the gift of grace' which, he noted, was part of 'the vocabulary of early Christianity'. Christ was a charismatic leader whose authority derived from his special status as the son of God. In his studies of various religions, Weber was struck by the prevalence of the notion that one was duty-bound to obey the commandments of worldly persons because of their special status with regard to the divine person, the ultimate legitimate authority over all things. Like other religious ideas, this had become secularized in the modern West, generating the conception of the ruler whose legitimacy is transcendental, not because he has been anointed by God, but because of the qualities of character and personality that differentiate him from ordinary men. Adolf Hitler, who appeared on the German political scene for the first time in the year of Weber's death, has often been instanced as the prototypical example of a secular charismatic leader, but Weber did not lack historical examples to draw upon in delineating the characteristics of this ideal type and in demonstrating its historical importance.

The charismatic leader, according to Weber, is constrained neither by tradition nor by law. On the contrary, his appeal lies in the very fact that he undertakes to break the constraints imposed by established customs and rules in order to bring about revolutionary change. The charismatic leader is an innovator, and the political leader who is legitimized by the possession of charisma is empowered to innovate on a grand scale. Weber's theory of charismatic leadership might be compared to Gustave le Bon's famous study of crowd psychology (*Psychologie des foules*, 1895). The members of a crowd, Le Bon observed, throw off the constraints of custom, prudence, and reason that govern them in ordinary life, and allow themselves to be led by one who is recognized to possess the qualities of a 'Caesar'. The leader is adept at manipulating others and, under certain conditions, they desire nothing more intensely than to do his bidding. In an effort to construct a general theory of politics, Le Bon extended his analysis of crowd behaviour by arguing that the basic psychological features that one observes in a mob are also present in more orderly assemblies of persons such as parliaments, committees, juries, etc. He felt he had discovered, in crowd psychology, the most momentous fact of the modern age, which was transforming civilization. In effect, Le Bon argued that crowd-like phenomena had become a permanent feature of modern life, and the 'science' part of social science must be the science of psychology. Weber did not share this view. Social science cannot be reduced to psychology. He fully recognized the social-psychological aspects of charisma, but he regarded its influence as transitory, confined to unusual occasions. Like Le Bon he thought that he had identified a momentous fact of modern society, but it was a sociological, not a psychological fact: the social imperatives that always and necessarily undermine charismatic authority and replace it with one of the other ideal types.

Weber's argument on this point is straightforward and, it seems to me, theoretically sound, empirically correct, and important. The exercise of charismatic authority, he observes, is incompatible with the orderliness that is necessary to conduct the everyday activities of social life. Economic and other social processes cannot be carried on when the rules are constantly changing. The activities of government, no less than those of others, depend upon a high degree of stability. Even a tyrant will be pressed by his subordinates to limit the exercise of his transcendent capacity for imaginative innovation in order to allow them to enjoy secure tenure of office and to perform their administrative work effectively. The achievement of order may be accomplished by the restoration of traditional rules of conduct but, according to Weber, in the modern West it is more likely to take the form of the legal or rational type of authority. What he calls 'the routinization of charisma' refers to the tendency, especially in countries that have experienced the rationalizing impact of capitalism, for the apparatus of government to be cast in a bureaucratic mould. The legal form of authority is not only one in which the state operates through and within a framework of law. This provides it with legitimacy, but more important is that the law is administered by professional personnel who, like businessmen, are experts in the rational application of means to ends.

Bureaucracy, in Weber's view, is the concrete form of the rational-legal ideal type of legitimate authority that has emerged in the West. More than anything else, this distinguishes modern Western society from others and from its own past. After reviewing the differences between industrialized Europe and other societies in science, scholarship, and the arts, Weber declares:

> Above all, it is only in the West that we find the specialist official, the cornerstone of both the modern Western state and the modern Western economy. No more than the beginnings of such a body can be found elsewhere . . . . in no country and in no period in history has our whole

existence, the very political, technical and economic foundations of our life been confined in such an absolutely inescapable way inside the casing of a bureaucratic organisation of trained specialists as in the modern West . . . . The 'state' in general, in the sense of a political institution with a rationally formulated 'constitution', rationally formulated laws and administration by means of specialist officials obeying rationally formulated rules or principles, is known only in the West . . . notwithstanding suggestions of it elsewhere.

The same is also true of that force in modern life which has had most influence on our destinies: capitalism. (Max Weber, *Selections in Translation*, 1978, p. 333)

Weber viewed the main significance of capitalism, not as creating a system of social organization that works by the automatic processes of an 'invisible hand', but as having introduced a more 'rational', i.e. more efficient, mode of hierarchical organization. This is why, in discussing capitalism, he pays little attention to the market mechanism and concentrates instead on the internal administrative organization of business enterprises. These were the first fully formed bureaucracies. Nor does Weber lay much emphasis, as Marx did, upon the private ownership of the means of production. The bureaucratization of business enterprise, which has moved the centre of power from the owners of capital to its professional administrators, led the way for the shift of the authority to exercise the coercive power of the state from politicians to officials. Weber's focus on bureaucracy rather than ownership undermines the categorical distinction between capitalism and socialism, and illuminates an important characteristic that they share. In today's literature, A. A. Berle and G. C. Mcans arc usually credited with pointing out the bureaucratization of business (*The Modern Corporation and Private Property*, 1932), and Milovan Djilas with revealing that in the communist world, behind the rhetoric of 'the dictatorship of the proletariat', a bureaucracy had established itself in power (*The New Class*, 1957). Both of these theses were anticipated by Weber's analysis of the characteristics of rational authority as an ideal type.

The role of charismatic leadership and the conflict between it and the rational-legal type of authority occupies a prominent place in the modern literature of sociology and political science. Economics, emphasizing as it does the necessity of an orderly framework of laws concerning such things as property rights, is not inclined to see much merit in the disruption of this framework by the exercise of charismatic power. There is, however, one important exception to this that is worth noting: the thesis advanced by Joseph A. Schumpeter in his *Theory of Economic Development* (1934; first published in German, 1911). Schumpeter spent his youth and early career in Vienna, where he studied under the leading figures of the Austrian school. At the age of forty-eight, in 1931, he was appointed to the Economics Faculty at Harvard. The magnitude of his influence on the students who attended his classes there, and on others through his writings, is certified by the numerous articles and symposia on him, which continue to appear today, four decades after his death. Schumpeter makes only one passing reference to Weber in the *Theory of Economic Development*, but the book is characteristically Weberian in various respects. Through Pitrim A. Sorokin and Talcott Parsons at Harvard, Weber's ideas were explicitly transmitted to American sociology; through Schumpeter, also at Harvard, some of them were implicitly transmitted to American economics.

Classical economics and Marxian economics were centrally concerned with the question of economic evolution. As we shall see in Chapter 17, this virtually disappeared from neoclassical economics, which focused mainly on what Marshall called 'economic statics'. The revival of interest in the developmental dynamics of a capitalistic economy can be dated from Schumpeter's book. In his analysis of a market economy Schumpeter emphasized that business firms do not compete with one another only through the prices they charge but, much more significantly, by introducing new products or improved qualities of old ones. Entrepreneurial innovation in these and other respects is, according to Schumpeter, the key feature of a capitalistic economy. Innovation, however, is not easy. It must break with tradition to get started and, after the new practices have become established, they inevitably become transposed into conventional routine, which hinders further innovation. Schumpeter amplified this thesis in various ways, in the consideration of such diverse topics as monopoly, business cycles, and the comparative merits of capitalism and socialism as economic systems and their relation to democracy. Space cannot be devoted to these questions since we are concerned here with Weber's views, not Schumpeter's. The point I wish to make is that there are notable similarities between them: Schumpeter's entrepreneur is Weber's charismatic leader; and the dynamic force of innovation, in the theories of both, is braked by the tendency to routinization. Like Marx, Schumpeter predicted that capitalism is doomed, but he saw the endogenous forces working to bring this about as Weberian rather than Marxian. The Schumpeterian way of thinking about capitalism (that is, the Weberian way) has found much greater response among American economists than the Marxian.

Weber regarded the tendency towards bureaucratization in modern societies with considerable apprehension. Coser describes him as 'not a prophet of glad tidings to come, but a harbinger of doom and disaster' (Lewis A. Coser, *Masters of Sociological Thought*, 1971, p. 234). Dedicated though he was to reason, Weber's sociological analysis had revealed it to have a dark and menacing import. He was not a democrat in his political views, and he had little faith in the ability to control the power of the bureaucracy by means of constitutional structures such as the governmental systems of Britain or America. On occasion he referred to charismatic leadership in politics as the only means by which the established 'casing of bureaucratic organization' might be broken. Weber did not regard the consequences of rationalism as wholly good, and he did not view the upheavals produced by charismatic leadership as wholly bad. Charismatic leadership had played a constructive role in the modernization of the West by breaking the mould of tradition that had for so long constricted the social and economic life of Europe. Perhaps it might again be constructive in breaking the equally constrictive mould that rationalism had constructed. Lenin did not win Weber's approval as a charismatic leader of primitive Russia, where capitalism had not yet worked its transforming power of rationalization. We do not know how he might have reacted to the rise of Hitler in a rationalized Germany.

5. Science and values

The categorical distinction between matters of fact and matters of value was a notable feature of the reorientation of Western philosophy during the era of the Enlightenment. This distinction, stated most influentially by David Hume, provided support for the detachment of science from ethics, and fortified the conviction of natural scientists that their work was 'objective'. When the early economists and sociologists spoke of their desire to create a 'science' of social phenomena, the notion that was uppermost in mind was the achievement of objectivity. Max Weber, as we saw in the above discussion of his views on methodology, argued that the social scientist, unlike the natural scientist, is engaged in explaining phenomena by achieving a 'subjective understanding' of the motives and reasons of those whose actions produce them. Using the adjective 'subjective' in the English rendering of *Verstehen* is legitimate, but it does not mean that Weber opposed the notion that the study of social phenomena can be objective. On the contrary, he embraced the criterion of objectivity without reserve and advocated it more passionately and at greater length in his writings than any other major figure in the history of social science. Freedom from value judgements – *Wertfreiheit* – was, for Weber, not merely a possibility but a necessity in social science, and he considered the practitioner of any of its branches to be morally obligated to recognize this and behave accordingly. In consonance with this view, he embraced the fact–value dichotomy, enunciating it repeatedly in his writings as a cardinal philosophical principle that is especially important for social science. Weber's views on this matter have become a prominent reference point in the literature on the philosophy of social science. His name appears with great frequency as an outstanding upholder of the fact–value dichotomy in philosophy and advocate of *Wertfreiheit* in social science. In recent years, such views have come under heavy attack from a variety of quarters. Weber's arguments in support of his position must engage our attention, not only to complete a review of his thought, but to amplify one's understanding of an important issue in the philosophy of social science that continues to be debated with great energy and commitment.

The first point that should be made is that Weber did not intend to exclude values from the subject matter of sociology. As we have seen, he rejected psychological explanations of social phenomena because they construe persons as responding more or less passively to stimuli; whereas, in his view, the fundamental character of human behaviour is that it is consciously directed at the attainment of specific goals, and these goals reflect value judgements. The values that men hold are, therefore, facts which the sociologist must not disregard in his analysis of social phenomena. The economic theory of marginal utility, Weber notes, has provided a scientific analysis of the phenomenon of market prices by treating the subjective valuations of individuals as primary facts. The sociologist must go still further and analyse the values that people hold. Particular values are usually part of a value system, such as a religion, and the internal logic and inferences of such a system are important material for the sociologist. In his thesis concerning the origins of capitalism, Weber did not start from the proposition that at a particular time and place there were certain values that motivated men to act in certain ways; he undertook to explain these values as reflecting a general philosophical outlook. His extensive studies of the world's major religions were pursued in order to amplify our understanding of the valuational elements in human social behaviour. Ordinary people may hold their values with little thought, but the task of the sociologist is to analyse them. The natural scientist asks penetrating questions about physical phenomena that others regard as 'self-evident'; the sociologist, as a scientist, asks similar questions about conventional values, not, it should be noted, in order to debunk them, but as part of the *Verstehen* procedure of social science. Unlike the Vienna Circle philosophers, who argued that statements concerning such things as values are totally meaningless and must be excluded from scientific discourse, Weber contended that, on the contrary, the scientific study of social phenomena can make no headway without recognition of the role of values in the rational and purposive activity of human subjects.

What, then, is the nature of the distinction between facts and values? Weber held, as Hume had, that this is a logical dichotomy, not an ontological one. Reality is not divided into two domains that cannot interact. Values can affect facts and facts can affect values in the real world, but a statement in the subjunctive mood does not have the same semantic status as one in the indicative mood. To say that a person does, as a matter of fact, hold certain values is not equivalent to saying that he is morally correct (or incorrect) in holding them. In short, Weber insisted on maintaining a categorical semantic distinction between *is* statements and *ought* statements.

Weber does not go so far as to claim that the sociologist makes no value judgements of his own. On the contrary, he argues that in choosing topics for research, in determining causation, in considering the social significance of the results obtained, and in offering advice on social policy, the sociologist is unavoidably involved in making value judgements. How, then, is scientific objectivity attained? Not, says Weber, by attempting to reduce such judgements to the minimum, nor by adopting the view that the morally correct values must lie between the extremes embraced by contending parties. Minimal or modal value judgements do not necessarily have more moral merit than any others. The sociologist, like other men, must make value judgements that spring from his own moral sense. An attitude of moral indifference, Weber says, has no connection with scientific objectivity; it is likely to be a 'pseudo-neutrality' that serves only to disguise a partisan interest or commitment. True objectivity in sociology consists in making it plain when one is speaking about facts and when one is resorting to value judgements of one's own. The sociologist's factual statements can be empirically tested; his values can be critically debated, and, to assist the latter, he is obligated to maintain the fact–value distinction in his work. The only matter, so far as I know, on which Weber expressed direct criticism of the other members of the Verein für Sozialpolitik and of Gustav Schmoller ('our master') was their failure, in his view, to differentiate adequately between facts and values. Being himself a man of strong moral sense and, at the same time, a firm believer in scientific objectivity, he was especially sensitive on this issue. Some of his most passionate and most lucid writing concerns the obligation of the professor to adhere rigorously to the fact–value dichotomy and to avoid using his classroom as a vehicle for moral instruction under the guise of science.

Like all strict moral precepts, this injunction is difficult to follow. Differentiating between factual statements and moral statements is a great deal easier to accomplish when one is speaking abstractly or freely composing sentences to illustrate the point than when one is engaged in the practical work of social science. The most conscientious scientist will, indeed, find it impossible to differentiate between the facts and values in his work if values are introduced into its methodology rather than (or in addition to) the locations that Weber identified. If the instruments of empirical investigation themselves contain value judgements, the results they provide are, necessarily, a mixture of facts and values that cannot be disentangled. One would have no reason to suspect that, say, in measuring a length with a metre stick, value judgements might have affected the reading obtained. But there can be less confidence on this point when one uses complex concepts as instruments of research (such as, for example, the concept of 'fitness' in evolutionary biology) and, in the social sciences, the contamination of research methodology by the value judgements of the scientist is perhaps very likely. Weber did not discuss this problem directly, but he was at pains to defend his own methodological principles from any charge that might be levied against them on this score. The principle of methodological individualism, he says, has no normative implications; it does not involve any commitment to individualism as a moral value or a political philosophy. The concept of ideal types is totally devoid of any normative notion of 'ideal'.

Disclaimers of this sort are not wholly convincing, and the literature on the philosophy of social science since Weber's day shows little disposition to regard these central features of his methodology as wholly objective. Methodological individualism in particular has been severely attacked as an attempt to smuggle a particular species of moral judgement and political commitment into the analytical core of social science. But not only by critics: some defenders of methodological individualism have argued that one of its merits is that it is sanctioned by moral and political considerations as well as by scientific ones. A similar complex of views has been expressed by critics and defenders of methodological holism. The issue is cast further in doubt by the contention of some philosophers that Hume's fact–value dichotomy is untenable to begin with. At this stage in the development of the social sciences there is little reason to be confident that social scientists can fulfil Weber's prescription. The most that can be said for it is that it is a precept that scientists may be urged to accept as an archetypal norm, comparable, say, to the injunction that one should always be rigorously truthful. This is no small thing, to be sure, but it is much less than Weber hoped to extract from the fact–value dichotomy.

Some philosophers have recently attempted to show that value statements can be logically derived from factual statements. These efforts have not been successful but, so far as I know, no one has provided a counter-demonstration that goes beyond the initial proposition which asserts that *is* statements and *ought* statements belong to disjunct semantic categories, so we cannot say flatly that it is impossible to derive values from facts. Any rigorous demonstration that it can be done, no matter how artificial, would have momentous import for the future development of practical social policy as well as academic philosophy, but the lack of proof that it cannot has already played an important part in Western social thought, reflecting the view that the domain of empirical science has no boundaries. Adam Smith argued, in his *Theory of Moral Sentiments*, that value judgements derive from man's inherent capacity for fellow-feeling. The implication of this is that such judgements are necessarily subjective, and transcend a purely personal status only because, and to the degree that, individual persons are similar. This seems to be a rather weak foundation on which to erect an edifice of moral rules, and it is understandable that moral philosophers, and others, should search for a stronger, i.e. a more objective, one. The notion that such a foundation has been provided by God, whose will may be derived direct from divinely inspired texts or indirectly through the mediation of consecrated persons, has not disappeared from Western culture, but it lacks the force it once had. At least among intellectuals, the notion that science can provide an objective foundation for value judgements has a larger appeal. The moral *ought* is expected to be derived from the factual *is* through the mediation of the scientist. We have already noted various instances in which social scientists have claimed this majestic role for their own discipline.

Unlike Comte and Durkheim, Weber did not regard sociology as capable of furnishing a scientific system of morals. Nor did he consider that any science might be able to do so, now or ever. Value judgements, in Weber's view, are irredeemably subjective. Differences among conflicting values must be resolved by choice and compromise. No science can even instruct the individual person how to deal with the competing values he himself holds, let alone produce a universal code for a whole society. Sociology studies the values that men hold; it cannot tell them what values they ought to hold.

> I am most emphatically opposed to the view that a realistic 'science of ethics', i.e., the analysis of the influence which the ethical evaluations of a group of people have on their other conditions of life and of the influences which the latter, in their turn, exert on the former, can produce an 'ethics' which will be able to say anything about what should happen. (*The Methodology of the Social Sciences*, p. 13, Weber's emphasis)

> Even such simple questions as the extent to which an end should sanction unavoidable means, or the extent to which undesired repercussions should be taken into consideration, or how conflicts between several concretely conflicting ends are to be arbitrated, are entirely matters of choice or compromise. There is no (rational or empirical) scientific procedure of any kind whatsoever which can provide us with a decision here. (*Ibid.*, 18 f.)

Weber held his own moral views with strong conviction and he ardently desired to contribute, morally as well as scientifically, to the improvement of German society. He had a low opinion of anyone who did not have a strong moral sense or who was unprepared to devote himself to a cause, but he did not demand that his own values should be universally adopted. He was, in this sense, a pluralist. It would serve as a nice completion of this review of Weber's thought if we could record here his views as to how a society might be organized politically in order to accommodate a plurality of values and to resolve them in the formation of public policy. He apparently entertained the notion that a combination of strong (charismatic?) leadership and public opinion expressed through plebiscites would form a viable political system for Germany. At the political level his individualism was more akin to that of Nietzsche and the romantics than the utilitarians and liberals who promoted the development of pluralist constitutional democracy. But he amplified his political philosophy too little to enable one to give an account of his specific views on the vital questions of constitutional organization and function.

Chapter 16

Biology, social science, and social policy

In the preceding chapters we have had frequent occasion to note that the social sciences developed in an intellectual climate that had been profoundly affected by the natural sciences. The scientific revolution of the seventeenth century changed the European conception of reality and introduced new methods of investigation. Early social scientists, major and minor, conceived of themselves as examining social phenomena in the spirit of 'natural philosophy', as exemplified in the fields of astronomy, physics, biology, and chemistry. Until the nineteenth century, the natural sciences impacted on social thought mainly through their general metaphysical and epistemological canons rather than their substantive findings. Such things as Galileo's model of ballistic motion, or Newton's investigation of the composition of light, or Boyle's law of gases, had no application to social phenomena. William Harvey's discovery of the circulation of the blood may have been the original source of the conception of the economy as a circulation of money and commodities that the Physiocrats and some other eighteenth-century economists employed, but as we have seen, that notion played no role in classical economics or the other social sciences that came into existence in the nineteenth century. However, it is evident from our study of Herbert Spencer and Émile Durkheim (Chapter 15) that other features of biological science, theoretical and empirical, general and specific, had a profound influence on the social sciences. In this chapter we shall examine that influence further. But the focus of our attention will have to be widened beyond social *science* to consider also the influence of biology on social *policy*, since an outstanding feature of the role of biology in modern social thought has been its direct application to the analysis of social problems, accompanied by specific proposals for their solution.

The impact of biology on social thought was, and continues to be, inseparable from the theory of organic evolution. From the standpoint of man's conception of himself and his relation to the cosmos, the development of the theory of evolution in the nineteenth century was no less than a second scientific revolution, but in terms of the philosophy of science it was a continuation or extension of the first, applying to organic phenomena the same conception of the world as governed by laws that are essentially 'materialistic' in nature and thereby reducing still further the significance of spiritual, and indeed mental, factors in the explanation of reality. This extension of materialism to the organic world began with Harvey's discovery of the circulation of the blood in 1628. The human body was viewed as a mechanism; the heart was demoted from being the seat of the 'soul' or the repository of the 'vital spirit' to the mechanical role of a pump. The advance of physiology along such lines was celebrated by the French physician Julien Offray de la Mettrie in his *L'Homme machine* (Man a Machine, 1747) which argued, as the title indicated, that even the highest of all organisms is a machine, and nothing but a machine. But it was the theory of evolution, which explained in materialistic terms, not only what man is, but how he came to be what he is, that emphatically introduced biological science into modern social thought.

A. EVOLUTION

1. Evolutionary theory before Darwin

The first chapter of the Book of Genesis describes how God created all living things, each plant and animal 'after its own kind'. But God did not intend that the members of each 'kind' should be completely alike; he left room for differences in characteristics within kinds, and apparently for changes in the frequency of certain characteristics. In chapter 30 the story is told of how Jacob, having been tricked by Laban into serving him for fourteen years rather than the agreed seven for the hand of Rachel, finally bested his father-in-law. They had agreed that, in return for further service, Jacob should take for his own those animals of Laban's whose coats were of a certain sort. Jacob arranged for the animals to mate while seeing 'pilled rods' which he had devised to cause them when so exposed to bear young with coats that marked them as his. And so Jacob 'increased exceedingly, and had much cattle, and maidservants and menservants, and camels, and asses'. The theory of inheritance implied by this account (that the external environment of an organism has a direct effect upon the characteristics of its progeny) is common in today's folklore, and the discovery of the genetic effects of radiation and chemicals has given it a scientific status, but more interesting in the story of how Jacob came to be a man of wealth is that he is said to have used his device of the 'pilled rods' only on Laban's 'stronger cattle'. This suggests, albeit obliquely, what must have been common knowledge from almost the beginning of agriculture: that the characteristics of domesticated animals, and plants, can be modified by selective breeding.

It does not seem a giant step from this to the notion that even in the wild state some process may be at work through which organisms are modified. Nevertheless, historians have failed to find much trace of the idea of organic change under natural conditions prior to the eighteenth century and, if what we are looking for is a systematic theory, not merely remarks whose significance depends on the hindsight we can now bring to them, the award of priority must go to Jean Baptiste Pierre Antoine de Monet, Chevalier de Lamarck, whose *Philosophie Zoologique* was published in 1809, the same year that Charles Darwin was born. Though Lamarck was a respected biologist, his theory of organic evolution was rejected, indeed parodied and derided, by leading scientists and, today, the term 'Lamarckism' is frequently employed in the biological literature as automatic condemnation of an unsound thesis. But, between Lamarck's time and ours, his theory was prominent in the scientific and popular debate over evolution. It played an important role in the relation between biology and social thought, which was not confined to Herbert Spencer's endorsement of it.

Lamarck's theory is sometimes represented as arguing that the external environment of an organism has a direct effect upon its genetic constitution and, therefore, upon the characteristics of its progeny. This notion, which goes back to biblical times as we have observed, was advanced by Lamarck's contemporary fellow Frenchman Étienne Geoffroy Saint-Hilaire. The continuing debate over the respective roles of environmental and genetic factors in human behaviour has frequently been muddied by failure to distinguish between Lamarckian and Geoffroyan propositions. Lamarck argued that the role of the external environment in the process of organic transformation is purely passive. Changes in genetic constitution are endogenous, produced within the body of the organism by its own activities. To the extent that the actions of an organism are undertaken in response to environmental conditions, genetic changes will occur which make successive generations of the species better able to deal with those conditions. But it is the individual organism's 'use and disuse' of its bodily parts that cause anatomical and physiological changes to be embodied in its germ plasm, not the environment as such. The long legs and neck of the giraffe are due to the fact that successive generations of the species had engaged in a great deal of stretching in order to browse the foliage of trees but, presumably, similar bodily structures would have come into existence if a species had engaged in the same degree of stretching for other reasons. Arnold J. Toynbee's famous thesis (*A Study of History*, 12 vols 1934–63) that the progress of a 'civilization' is due to the improving effect upon itself of the responses it makes to the challenges that confront it is, in the domain of human social phenomena, an even closer analogue of Lamarckian theory than Spencer's sociology.

Another misinterpretation of Lamarck's theory that we should note here is that an organism was viewed by him as effecting changes in its genetic constitution by 'will'. According to this construal, it is not the stretching activity of the giraffe, as such, that impacts on the germ plasm, but its desire to reach higher. Lamarck did not argue in this fashion. Not only did he apply his theory to plants, where such an argument would clearly be inappropriate, but his philosophical stance as a scientist was rigorously materialist. Like most scientists of his day he believed that nature had been created by God and, indeed, he followed Leibniz's doctrine that the world had been made as a beneficent harmonious order, but he did not invoke either transcendental forces or vitalistic elements in advancing his thesis that the earth's population of organic species had evolved from earlier life forms.

As an explanation of organic evolution Lamarckian theory is almost universally rejected by modern biologists because it involves a notion of inheritance that is considered erroneous. The science of molecular genetics, which locates the genetic information in the DNA molecule, traces a path of transmission from that molecule to the proteins which make up the somatic constitution of the organism, but (at least at the present time of writing) it is not considered possible for the reverse process to take place; that is, to paraphrase what has become known as the 'central dogma' of molecular biology, information can pass from nucleic acid to protein but not from protein to nucleic acid. Nothing was known about this in Lamarck's day. The opposition to Lamarckian theory was then, and for a half-century after, based on the conviction that the organic population of the earth had *not* evolved. Some earlier writers (Buffon and Maupertuis are often mentioned by historians) had questioned the doctrine of the immutability of species, but this made no headway among the general body of scientists. We now recognize the fossil record as offering strong empirical evidence that the population of the earth's species has changed but, until Darwin, no leading scientist interpreted the evidence in this fashion. Georges Cuvier, the leading palaeontologist of Lamarck's era, was firmly convinced that species were immutable, and derided Lamarck's theory as a groundless speculation. Charles Lyell, whose *Principles of Geology* (1830–2) was the outstanding work on that subject, went out of his way to criticize Lamarck. According to Lyell, the fossil record showed only that some life forms had migrated and that some had become extinct, not that there had been changes in the original species. Lyell was a close friend of Darwin, and urged him to publish the *Origin*, but he never fully accepted the theory of evolution as an explanation of the diversity and geographic distribution of organic species.

After the idea of evolution had been embraced by most scientists, which was not until the 1870s, Darwin was vexed to find some writers contending that it had been 'in the air' for some time before the publication of the *Origin*. He was not a vainglorious man, but he knew that when he was a youth the idea that species had evolved was given short shrift by scientists and treated as a scandalous heresy by others. His own conviction that species had evolved had been painfully arrived at, requiring the shedding of early beliefs and the courage to face the possibility that, if he should be wrong, he would go down in history as one of the biggest fools in Christendom. Darwin is regarded by historians of biology as the first to put forward a scientifically plausible hypothesis concerning the mechanism of organic change rather than as the originator of the theory of evolution as such, but a reading of the *Origin* suffices to demonstrate that Darwin himself construed his main objective to be the replacement of the belief that all forms of life were the work of 'special creation' with the view that, however the earliest forms had come to be, the present diversity and distribution of organic species on the planet reflect the working of natural processes that are not metaphysically different or detached from the laws that govern other natural phenomena.

In the period while Darwin was working on the problem of the 'transmutation of species', the discussion of evolution in England centred not on Lamarck's theory but on a book published anonymously in 1844 under the title of *Vestiges of the Natural History of Creation*. The author, Robert Chambers, was the co-owner with his brother of a prominent Scottish publishing firm, but to help conceal his authorship, he gave the manuscript to a London publisher. The *Vestiges* was a striking success. Four editions of it were printed in the first seven months; by 1859, when Darwin's *Origin* appeared, it had gone through ten editions, with sales greatly in excess of any other book on a scientific subject.

Like Herbert Spencer later, Chambers's interest in evolution was initiated by reading, and being unconvinced by, Lyell's criticism of Lamarck. But he did not undertake to defend Lamarck's theory. He was not a scientist and could not argue technical matters with authorities such as Cuvier or Lyell. But as a well read layman it seemed to him that the historical evidence of organic forms embodied as fossils in geological strata showed that, not only had some species become extinct, but wholly new species had appeared at various times in the past. Moreover, the newer forms were 'higher' than older ones in that they displayed greater complexity. He drew also upon von Baer's discoveries in embryology (which, as we noted above, greatly impressed Spencer) to suggest an analogy between the embryological development of the individual organism and the evolution of species since the creation of the original inhabitants of the earth. The *Vestiges* did not advance a systematic theory of the mechanism by which evolution may have occurred, but it presented a sustained and powerful argument in support of the proposition that it had, in fact, occurred.

One of the noteworthy features of the *Vestiges* is that Chambers was anxious to point out to his readers that the idea of organic evolution can be embraced without abandoning one's faith in the existence of God as the creator of all that exists. The process of evolution is simply the method that God chose to populate the earth with living beings. God made the world as an orderly system and it is reasonable to suppose that his intention was that the same kinds of laws that he decreed for the governance of physical phenomena should also apply to the phenomena of life. Chambers's attempt to extend deist theology to the organic domain was, however, unavailing. The *Vestiges* was condemned by theologians, who reflected the almost universal opinion that it was outrageously heretical. Scientists were equally hostile to it, not as a theological argument, but because they considered it to be a work of such amateurish science that it deserved no serious consideration. T. H. Huxley, who later became the leading champion of Darwin's theory, wrote a scathing review of it that surpassed the normal boundaries of even his own broad conception of argumentative propriety. The large sales of the *Vestiges* do not indicate that the educated classes of the time were prepared to entertain the idea of evolution. It was a *succès de scandale*. If England and Scotland had not become by this time societies in which freedom of expression was allowed wide scope, Chambers would have had more to fear than verbal condemnation. Nevertheless, he considered it prudent to continue to conceal the authorship of the *Vestiges* and it was not revealed until 1885, after Chambers, his brother, and his wife, were deceased.

If nothing else, the reception of the *Vestiges* would have made Darwin fully aware that, in considering the mutability of organic species, he was treading on ground that endangered his repute as a Christian gentleman, and as a scientist. He delayed publishing anything on the subject for twenty years after he had become convinced in his own mind that species had evolved. He knew that the empirical evidence he could marshal, though extensive, was incomplete, and that his theory, though plausible, was not compelling; but he also knew that he would have to face a torrent of public denunciation, and from his fellow scientists the best he could hope for was respectful scepticism. He wrote a great deal on the species question, and confided his thoughts to a few of his closest friends, but he published nothing on it. In June 1858 there arrived in Darwin's mail a letter from Alfred Russel Wallace, a naturalist who was then working in New Guinea, asking his opinion of an enclosed brief manuscript, which turned out to contain the essential argument of his own theory of evolution. Fortunately for the history of science, this threat to Darwin's priority was sufficient to overcome his apprehensions and he set to work immediately to prepare for publication a book which appeared in the following year as *The Origin of Species by Means of Natural Selection*.

2. Darwin and Darwinism

John Murray, the London publisher who had contracted with Darwin to publish the manuscript of the *Origin*, was not pleased when it was placed in his hands. As an editor, he regarded its argument to be undeserving of serious consideration and, as a publisher, he judged its commercial prospects unpromising. He was wrong on both counts. The first edition sold out immediately and was followed by a second, with a larger printing, a month later. It was read carefully by biologists and, though few were at first convinced, all regarded it as having presented the thesis of evolution (a word that Darwin himself avoided) in a way that demanded serious consideration. Though Darwin argued that all the existing organic species that inhabit the earth are descended from one, or a few, primordial ones, he said nothing explicitly about the species *Homo sapiens*, but readers of the book were quick to note its implications for the status of man. Scientists focused mainly upon Darwin's theoretical arguments and the empirical evidence he used to support them, but the attention of other readers was riveted upon the implications of the thesis for the Christian conception of man as the special creation of God. Darwin did not participate personally in this debate; he left it to his champions such as T. H. Huxley to carry biology into the domain of theology. His private papers contain extensive comments on man in relation to evolution which date from his earliest thinking on the 'transmutation of species', but he did not publish his views on this subject until *The Descent of Man* in 1871, by which time he had good reason to believe that his evolution thesis was winning the support of his fellow scientists.

Ernst Mayr, a leading modern authority on the theory of evolution and the history of biology, points out that Darwin's argument contained a number of distinct propositions. He distinguishes five: (1) that the organic world had evolved over its history; (2) that the present populations of species descended from common ancestors; (3) that the process has been characterized by the divergence of forms, so that not only have old species been replaced by new ones, but the number of different species has increased; (4) that this process has been gradual or continuous, not characterized by any sharp jumps from one form to another; (5) that the main mechanism by which this has taken place is the process of natural selection (Ernst Mayr, *The Growth of Biological Thought*, 1982, pp. 505–10; see also Mayr's paper in David Kohn, ed., *The Darwinian Heritage*, 1985). Mayr contends that the initial debate over the *Origin* failed to distinguish these propositions adequately and that modern historiography on Darwinism is marred by a similar defect. Within the scope of this book (and the competence of the writer) it is not possible to review this literature, but it is necessary to discuss some of the technical aspects of Darwinian theory, since they have a bearing upon the subject of this chapter.

Though Darwinism is today considered to be synonymous with the theory of evolution *by natural selection*, and Darwin included this phrase in the extended title of the *Origin*, the proposition that natural selection is the main mechanism of evolutionary change was not immediately accepted by Darwin's scientific contemporaries. Even Huxley was cool towards it, and doubted that it was essential to the general argument. In accordance with the development of his own ideas, Darwin prepared the ground for his argument by devoting the first chapter of the *Origin* to the selection that had been practised since ancient times by plant and animal breeders before proceeding to contend that 'the struggle for existence' in nature could have worked in the same way as the breeders' deliberate attempts to modify the characteristics of their crops and herds. But others who had not travelled the same intellectual route that Darwin had were unimpressed by the analogy. By the early 1870's most scientists, and many others, were convinced that organic evolution had occurred, and that the existing populations of the planet were due to it, but they did not accept the notion of natural selection. Darwin had profoundly altered man's conception of organic nature, and his place in it, but not, as yet, by persuading others to embrace the line of reasoning that had affected his own thinking. It was not, in fact, until the 1920's, or later, that 'Darwinism' and 'natural selection' became virtually synonymous terms. Anticipating what I shall say below concerning the connection between biology and views on social policy, one might note at this point that Darwin was more important at an earlier date in amplifying the scientific understanding of the *artificial* selection practised by breeders.

If a plant or animal were exactly like either of its parents, or if each of its characteristics were an average of those of its parents, farmers could not develop improved varieties. The most that a skilled farmer could do would be to increase the proportion of his crop having characteristics as good as the best of those that were present in the wild state. 'Lamarckian' theory argues that a farmer can do better than this because an organism may change during its own lifetime and the acquired characteristics can be transmitted to its progeny. According to 'Darwinian' theory, some individuals are genetic 'sports', having been born by chance, or 'spontaneously', with aberrant inherent characteristics, and the farmer can select for reproduction those individuals with desirable ones. I use quotation marks in characterizing these theories because Darwin was not a 'Darwinian' if that term is meant to exclude the operation of the 'Lamarckian' mechanism of inheritance. In the first edition of the *Origin* he contended that inheritable characteristics which deviate from the initial ones may be due to the effects of the organism's behaviour as well as chance, and in the later editions the significance of the former factor was increased to the degree that a reader of the sixth edition who approaches it with the supposition that 'Darwinism' and 'Lamarckism' are categorically different theories will be surprised to find that it repeatedly appeals to 'use and disuse' as an explanation of the source of inheritable variations. Darwin used the term 'natural selection' to refer to selection among those variations that are due to chance and this, plus the fact that the full title of the book contained that term, led his early readers to believe that he had totally rejected Lamarck's argument about the source of variations. Darwin emphasized, in the later editions of the *Origin* and in other writings, that he had not meant to exclude the effects of use and disuse (or the direct effect of environmental conditions) but only to argue that 'natural selection' is more important. He complained repeatedly that he had been misunderstood by many commentators. During the 1890's the term 'neo-Darwinism' came into use to signify a theory of evolution that excludes Lamarckian elements, which gradually lost its prefix and became the 'Darwinism' of today.

In the thinking of Darwin's time the notion of 'chance' was equivalent to 'causal factors as yet unknown', which is an admission rather than an explanation. Darwin tried to develop a theory of inheritance, which he called 'pangenesis', in an effort to break through the veil implied by the contemporary concept of chance and to accommodate the operation of use and disuse, but he did not succeed well enough to incorporate this in new editions of the *Origin*. Gregor Mendel sent him a copy of his seminal paper on plant variations, but

Darwin apparently did not appreciate its significance. The absence of a satisfactory explanation of inheritance remained for a long time the principal deficiency of the theory of evolution. This was not only because 'chance' was considered to be an unsatisfactory explanation, but also because it seemed plausible to suppose that, in nature, the breeding of aberrant individuals with normal ones would simply dissipate their special characteristics in the large gene pool. This argument was advanced by numerous critics of the *Origin*. (We might note in passing that one of these was Fleeming Jenkin, a Scottish engineer, who occupies a place in the history of economics for his work on the market for labour and for being one of the first to construct a graphic model of supply and demand of the type that later became characteristic of neoclassical microeconomic theory.) Not until the 1920's, when the Mendelian laws of heredity were shown to be consistent with the normal probability distribution of chance phenomena, could the theory of evolution that Darwin advanced receive the unreserved approval of scientists.

Among the basic propositions that Darwin advanced, one that he held with exceptional tenacity was the principle of continuity. We have already encountered this in our discussion of the metaphysical conception of existence as a 'great chain of being' (Chapter 10 A). Darwin adopted Leibniz's motto *Natura non facit saltum* (Nature does not make leaps) as an expression of his own conception of the organic world. Leibniz's metaphysical speculations had no appeal for him but he felt that organic variations are characterized by very small gradations, and that the theory of evolution shows that the earth's population of discrete species came into existence by the steady accumulation of such small changes over the vast stretch of geologic time. The principle of continuity had earlier been applied to the physical changes of the planet by the Scottish geologist James Hutton, and Charles Lyell had adopted Hutton's 'uniformitarianism' (i.e. continuity) in his *Principles of Geology*, one of the first books that Darwin studied carefully when he embarked upon the career of a naturalist. Some of those who accepted the general argument of the *Origin* felt that the principle of continuity was questionable and that Darwin made too much of it (e.g. T. H. Huxley and Francis Galton), but he was unalterably convinced of its validity and importance. In the 'recapitulation' of his argument in the last chapter of the *Origin* he says:

> As natural selection acts solely by accumulating slight, successive, favourable variations, it can produce no great or sudden modifications; it can act only by short and slow steps. Hence the canon of 'Natura non facit saltum,' which every fresh addition to our knowledge tends to confirm, is on this theory intelligible.

This is an issue that is still under debate by biologists. One of the best modern defences of Darwinism, Richard Dawkins's *The Blind Watchmaker* (1986), strongly stresses the continuity of organic evolution; but other biologists, most prominently S. J. Gould, have insisted that the principle of continuity should be replaced by the notion of 'punctuated equilibrium', which construes organic evolution as marked by alternating periods of stability and rapid change. This conception would seem to be at least as germane to the process of social evolution. So far as I know, no one has tried to construct an explicit 'punctuated equilibrium' model of social development but it is perhaps latent in the Marxian notion that there are stable periods of history during which 'contradictions' accumulate, followed by revolutionary periods when, as Engels put it, society is 'more or less rapidly transformed'.

In the language of social thought, the use of the term 'evolution' to denote a steady change by small steps, and 'revolution' to denote a sudden and large transformation in the social order, antedates the *Origin* by more than two centuries, but Darwin's insistence on joining the notions of continuity and evolution played an important part in defining the modern political doctrines of 'social evolution' and 'social revolution'. As we have noted in discussing Herbert Spencer, in the later nineteenth century evolutionism became identified with the view that social development is best achieved by the continuous accumulation of small changes. This has been widely construed, ever since, as a 'conservative' doctrine. The 'radical' doctrine, associated in the early nineteenth century with the 'philosophic radicalism' of the Benthamite utilitarians, later became identified with the thesis advanced by Marx and Engels that true social change could come about only by a discrete transformation of the social order, that is, by revolution. (For a brief note on Marx's and Engels's own reactions to the *Origin* see above, Chapter 13 B.)

Darwin's argument that selection analogous to that practised by breeders takes place in the wild requires that organisms procreate greatly in excess of the capacity of the environment to support them. The large rate of premature death that takes place in such circumstances selects against those individuals that are less efficient in the 'struggle for existence' than others. Herbert Spencer suggested the term 'survival of the fittest' to denote this mechanism, and in later editions of the *Origin* Darwin accepted it as more accurate than 'natural selection'. The notion of 'fitness', however, is fraught with difficulties, not the least of which is that it seems to introduce value judgements into an analysis that purports to be a scientific explanation of natural phenomena. Spencer was not in the least averse to making such judgements; indeed, he was one of the first to argue, contrary to Hume, that the domains of ethics and science could be joined – if scientific knowledge were made the foundation of moral judgements. Darwin did not discuss such matters, but he had a very high regard for Spencer as a philosopher, which he expressed on numerous occasions in his published work.

Darwin's writings, including *The Descent of Man*, contain no extended discussion of issues in moral philosophy. There are, however, occasional passages indicating that he regarded the mechanism of natural selection as a dynamic of utilitarian progress. I quote three of these:

The foregoing remarks lead me to say a few words on the protest lately made by some naturalists, against the utilitarian doctrine that every detail of structure has been produced for the good of its possessor. They believe that many structures have been created for the sake of beauty, to delight man or the Creator ... or for the sake of mere variety .... Such doctrines, if true, would be absolutely fatal to my theory .... It is scarcely possible to decide how much allowance ought to be made for such causes of change as the definite action of external conditions, so-called spontaneous variations, and the complex laws of growth; but with these important exceptions, we may conclude that the structure of every living creature either now is, or was formerly, of some direct or indirect use to its possessor. (*Origin*, sixth ed., 1872, chapter VI)

Although we have no good evidence for the existence in organic beings of an innate tendency towards progressive development, yet this necessarily follows ... through the continued action of natural selection. For the best definition which has ever been given of a high standard of organisation, is the degree to which the parts have been specialised or differentiated; and natural selection tends towards this end, inasmuch as the parts are thus enabled to perform their functions more efficiently. (*Ibid.*, chapter VII)

Von Baer has defined advancement or progress in the organic scale better than anyone else, as resting on the amount of differentiation and specialization of the several parts of a being .... Now as organisms have become slowly adapted to diversified lines of life by means of natural selection, their parts will have become more and more differentiated and specialized for various functions, from the advantages gained by the physiological division of labour. (*Descent*, American ed. 1874, chapter VI)

The mark of Spencerian social philosophy in these (and other) passages is unmistakable. Darwin may not have derived his social philosophy from Spencer but they clearly held similar views. There is no evidence, so far as I am aware, that they differed in any respect beyond the fact that Spencer wrote a great deal on social questions and Darwin did not. T. H. Huxley, in arguing in his Romanes Lecture of 1893 that evolution does not necessarily, or even probably, lead to moral improvement, directed his criticism at Spencer, but Darwin was equally vulnerable on this point. Some historians have attempted to blame the excesses of 'Social Darwinism' on Spencer rather than Darwin, but this is unjustified and, indeed, the most important of the social policy proposals that claimed the authority of evolutionary science, 'eugenics', derived from Darwin's theory of natural selection rather than from Spencer's Lamarckian evolutionism.

These and other aspects of the impact of Darwin on modern social thought will be discussed in section B below. In the following subsection we examine the opposite connection – the argument that Darwin's theory reflects the social science and social environment of nineteenth-century England.

3. Darwinism, classical economics, and capitalism

In his autobiography Darwin recounts the course of his thinking that led to the *Origin*. He describes how his observations of plant and animal life in South America and the Galapagos archipelago had impressed him with the possibility that the fine adaptation of each species and variety to its environment had come about by modification of the original forms, and that, when he had nearly completed his part of the report of the voyage of the *Beagle*, he began to collect material on organic transformation:

My first notebook was opened in July 1837. I worked on true Baconian principles, and without any theory collected facts on a wholesale scale, more especially with respect to domesticated productions . . . . I soon perceived that selection was the keystone of man's success in making useful races of animals and plants. But how selection could be applied to organisms living in a state of nature remained for some time a mystery to me.

In October 1838 . . . I happened to read for amusement Malthus on *Population*, and being well prepared to appreciate the struggle for existence which everywhere goes on from long-continued observation of the habits of animals and plants, it at once struck me that under these circumstances favourable variations would tend to be preserved and unfavourable ones to be destroyed. The result of this would be the formation of new species. Here, then, I had at last got a theory by which to work . . . . (*The Autobiography of Charles Darwin*, ed. Nora Barlow, 1958, pp. 119–20).

This statement, plus Darwin's references to Malthus in the *Origin*, the *Descent*, and other publications, plus the fact that A. R. Wallace specifically attributed his own independent discovery of the principle of natural selection to Malthus, plus the fact that Spencer's near-anticipation of the principle bears clear marks of Malthus in its wording, would seem to add up to the conclusion that the construction of the theory of evolution in biology is indebted to the earlier development of population theory in economics. But historians of biology have mixed views on the matter. Some argue that Malthus did indeed provide an essential idea, without which Darwin could not have proceeded to do more than collect data. Others argue that though the idea of a population pressure against the 'means of subsistence' was essential, it could have been obtained from many other sources and, at best, it served only as the accidental catalyst that brought together lines of thinking that Darwin, and others, were engaged in. Other historians have widened the focus, arguing that Darwin's indebtedness was due, not just to Malthus's population theory, but to the whole world-view of classical political economy. Still others claim that classical political economy, and Darwin's theory of evolution, reflect alike a still broader influence: the environment of Victorian capitalism. In order to make a path through this thicket of interpretations, we must begin by clarifying what it was in Malthus's *Essay on Population* that struck Darwin so forcefully.

In other places than the *Autobiography* Darwin is more explicit in stating what he found so significant in the 'ever memorable "Essay on the Principle of Population" by the Rev. T. R. Malthus'. It was the statement that the procreational capacity of human (and other) organisms is such that their numbers tend to grow at a 'geometric' rate. This provided Darwin with the clue he needed to perceive that there is a force working upon organisms in the natural state analogous to that which breeders produce artificially when they undertake to alter the characteristics of domesticated plants and animals. The cattle breeder, for example, selects the few members of his herd that have the desired characteristics, and breeds only them. Thus, successive generations of his herd are the result of severely restricted procreation. Darwin's central idea was that a similar degree of selection occurs in the wild state if animals procreate 'geometrically'. Many more young are constantly produced than can be sustained, and a large proportion of the young must therefore fail to survive to reproductive age. Since those who do survive must be the ones who are best adapted to their environmental conditions, the procreational stock is constantly and strongly being culled to weed out those individuals that are less well adapted. The 'survival of the fittest' in the 'struggle for existence' over many generations will result in altered varieties and, indeed, the eventual emergence of entirely new species. Darwin observes in his notebook that the common opinion among contemporary biologists is that animals in the wild state produce young only in such numbers as are able to survive, but 'the one sentence of Malthus' shows that the natural tendency is to produce many more than that and, therefore, the population is kept stable by a high rate of premature death. This operates, like the decisions of the cattle breeder, to select for procreation only the small number of individuals that possess certain characteristics.

If the reader will refer back to Chapter 9 C he will note that Malthus's *Essay* was initially aimed at attacking the utopian philosophers by pointing out that the tendency of population to grow beyond the means of subsistence would defeat any attempt to create a perfect social order. In making this contention he argued that population naturally grows at a 'geometric ratio' while the supply of food increases only at an 'arithmetic ratio'. But this was not the *theory* of population he advanced, and which became a central element in the classical model of economic development. The population theory in that model is based on the 'law of diminishing returns'. This law expresses the proposition that, with a fixed supply of land and a given agricultural technology, additional quantities of labour will result in diminishing increments of increased output, which, in due course, must result in a reduction in the *per capita* supply of food if population continues to increase. David Ricardo, who constructed the development model, acknowledged his indebtedness to Malthus on the matter of population growth, but he did not even so much as mention the 'ratios' in his *Principles of Political Economy* (1817). What is more, Malthus himself did not mention the ratios in the discussion of population in his own *Principles of*

Political Economy (1820). In John Stuart Mill's *Principles of Political Economy* (1848), which was the dominant text for the next forty years or more, Malthus's ratios are mentioned only in order to describe them as 'an unlucky attempt to give numerical precision to things which do not admit of it', and to point out that 'every person capable of reasoning must see that it is wholly superfluous to his argument' (1965 edn, p. 353). Historians of biology who have discussed the indebtedness of Darwin to Malthus almost universally depict the comparison of geometrical and arithmetic ratios as Malthus's 'theory' of population, but it was no more than a dramatic expression in a book that was originally written as a polemical tract on a subject of contemporary philosophical debate. Darwin found the clue he needed, not in the classical economists' theory of population, nor indeed even in Malthus's juxtaposition of two ratios, but only in one of them, the 'single sentence' which said that 'population, when unchecked, increases in a geometrical ratio'.

There is no evidence in Darwin's published work, or in his private papers, that he was familiar with the classical theory of population, or any of the other important elements of classical economics. He was accustomed to listing in his notebooks the books he was currently reading and taking notes from and commenting upon those he found useful. The only books on economics recorded there are J. R. McCulloch's *Principles of Political Economy*, a popularization of Ricardo, and J. C. L. de Sismondi's *New Principles of Political Economy*, which attacked the materialistic orientation, methodology, and policy proposals of the English classical school. He made no notes or comments on McCulloch and recorded only one word after listing Sismondi's book: 'poor'. Darwin was extraordinarily thorough in investigating all sources of information that might be useful to him. Clearly, he did not regard political economy as warranting his attention. In July 1881, nine months before his demise, Darwin received a letter from A. R. Wallace urging him to read Henry George's *Progress and Poverty*, which he judged comparable to Adam Smith's *Wealth of Nations* in 'making an advance in political and social science'. Darwin replied:

> I will certainly order 'Progress and Poverty' for the subject is a most interesting one. But I read many years ago some books on political economy, and they produced a disastrous effect on my mind, viz. utterly to distrust my own judgement on the subject and to doubt much everyone else's judgement!' (James Marchant, *Alfred Russel Wallace, Letters and Reminiscences*, 1916, I, p. 318)

None the less, numerous commentators have claimed that Darwin's theory of evolution by natural selection was inspired by the classical analysis of a competitive market economy, even indeed that Darwinian theory was nothing more that the transference of classical economics to the domain of nature. Stephen Jay Gould, a prominent evolutionary biologist and historian of biology, says: 'Darwin's theory of natural selection . . . was essentially Adam Smith's economics read into nature. Without Adam Smith and the whole school of

Scottish economics, I doubt that Darwin would ever have thought of it' (*U.S. News and World Report*, 1 March 1982). Such assertions cannot be supported with documentation, but they cannot be dismissed, either, since they are inherently unfalsifiable. In Darwin's day there was much condemnation of economists as having depicted, and approved of, a cruel economic order in which the only law is 'everyone for himself and the devil take the hindmost'. Darwin may have been influenced by such popular renditions of classical political economy – we do not know whether he was or not – but it deserves to be noted that they were caricatures, promoted by fiction writers such as Charles Dickens who found them useful for dramatic effect, by romantic social philosophers like Thomas Carlyle who regarded mechanistic science, political economy, and utilitarian ethics as only the more obvious symptoms of a civilization whose soul had been sold for dross, and by commentators on public policy who, for various reasons, opposed the Ricardian stance on the corn laws and other hot political issues of the day. As we noted above in considering the ideology of *laissez-faire* (Chapter 10 B), none of the major classical economists held the extreme and doctrinaire individualism that was, and still is, popularly attributed to them.

More specifically germane to our present topic is the notion of 'competition'. This concept in classical (and modern) economics is frequently construed as analogous to the competition between organisms engaged in what Darwin called 'the struggle for existence'. The common word, however, obscures a fundamental difference. In Darwinian theory each organismal group is pictured as operating in an environment that offers, so far as it is concerned, a fixed supply of food. The natural economy is, therefore, a zero-sum game. If some members of the group get more, others must necessarily get less. One of the important distinctions between man and other species is that man *produces* the food (and other things) he requires rather than merely foraging an exogenously given supply. The human economy is a positive-sum game. The emphasis of economists on the division of labour and the role of markets in bringing about the co-ordination that this requires devolves from the conception of the human condition as one in which man changes the environment in which he lives. Competition is viewed as contributing to productive efficiency, increasing the sum of a positive-sum game. Michael T. Ghiselin, a biologist who has strongly advocated the use of economic models in his own discipline, is far off the mark when he says (apparently with approval) that 'The classical economists had assumed that competition was a good thing, because God had ordained laws of nature such that right would triumph if they were obeyed' (*Current Anthropology*, September, 1974, p. 224). This qualifies for Bentham's characterization, 'nonsense on stilts'. Competition for the classical economists was not a metaphysical property, and certainly not a deistic one. It was an aspect of a practical mechanism of economic organization whose merits were much more modest than the triumph of right.

In introducing his theory of value, Ricardo says that it applies to 'such commodities only as can be increased in quantity by the exercise of human industry, and on the production of which competition operates without restraint'. He did not intend to exclude the restraints imposed by laws against theft, sabotaging a competitor's enterprise, adulterating products, etc. He was referring to restraints that limit entry to a market by means of such things as tariffs or other discriminatory taxation, restrictive licences, or monopoly privileges, all common in his day. When, later in the century, industrial giants battled against one another for the prize of *de facto* monopolization of a market, they were not engaged in what Ricardo meant by competition. In modern economics the terms 'imperfect competition' and 'monopolistic competition' are used to describe situations characterized by rivalry, and the orthodox analysis contends that under such conditions the 'sum' of the economic game is reduced and may even become zero.

Finally, there is the view that whether or not Darwin was influenced specifically by the theories of the classical economists is irrelevant. He lived in a capitalistic society which celebrated as virtues the very features of behaviour that lay at the foundation of his theory of evolution. In the article on evolution in the *International Encyclopedia of the Social Sciences* (1968) R. C. Lewontin, a prominent geneticist, says that the initial emergence of evolution, as a general concept, 'was deeply embedded in the social and economic conditions of the industrial West'. Darwin's specific theory was a product of the 'bourgeois revolution', like all of 'bourgeois science'. To be more specific, Lewontin notes that Darwin came from a family of prominent industrialists, which he pointedly calls, in relation to evolution theory, 'no accident'. Numerous statements by other commentators, not all embroidered with Marxist rhetoric, assert the thesis that the real credit (or debit) for the theory of organic evolution belongs not to Darwin but to capitalism.

Again we encounter a proposition that is inherently untestable. But I might note a few *caveats*. If the theory of evolution was so much in tune with the times, why was Chambers's *Vestiges* condemned by middle-class theologians and scientists? Why did Darwin's *Origin* receive a similar reception, even from scientists, for a decade or more after its first publication? If the Victorian virtues were those that Samuel Smiles celebrated in his famous books on personal improvement (*Self-help, Character, Thrift,* and *Duty*) why did bourgeois England not embrace Lamarckism, which argued that one can improve not only oneself but also one's progeny by engaging in the appropriate behaviour? Why did Francis Galton, Darwin's cousin, exclude businessmen from the sample of eminent men he constructed to study the hereditary transmission of superior human abilities? If Margaret Jacob is correct in contending that Newton's physics was quickly accepted because it was in tune with the contemporary capitalist ideology (*The Newtonians and the English Revolution, 1689–1720,* 1976), then that ideology was more widely embraced in the seventeenth than in the nineteenth century!

Poor Darwin. Vilified by the religious, rejected for a long time by scientists, an embarrassment to his family and friends; now that his work is recognized as one of the most significant achievements in the history of science, he is judged to have had no ideas of his own, but merely reflected the intellectual and social ambience of his time. He could not have discovered the theory of natural selection without that ambience; and with it, anyone could have done so. According to such a mode of investigating the history of ideas, the genius of Shakespeare's plays belongs to the audience, not the author, and the true inventor of the steam engine was not James Watt but the miners who were hampered by flooding.

4. Evolution and man

Darwin's notebooks that date from before the publication of the *Origin* contain numerous comments on man's origin and evolution, but he avoided discussing these matters in public until *The Descent of Man* in 1871. At the end of that book he describes its 'main conclusion' to be that 'man is descended from some less highly organized form'. If this were the substance of the book it would be of little historical interest, since that implication of the *Origin* was perceived as soon as it was published, and Darwin himself says that 'many naturalists who are competent to form a sound judgement' now regard man as the product of an evolutionary process. But, in fact, the *Descent* deals with a different, though closely related topic: the development of different 'races' or 'sub-species' of humans (and other animals). For at least half a century, the comparative study of the physical characteristics of groups of humans had been the central concern of anthropologists and, if a modern reader of the *Descent* did not know the name of its author, he would reasonably surmise that he must have been an early anthropologist or ethnologist who had a remarkably extensive knowledge of biology.

The central thesis of the *Descent* is that the various races of *Homo sapiens* that now occupy the globe have diverged from one another in physical characteristics owing to the operation of 'sexual selection'. There is clear evidence that mating does not take place at random in populations of the higher animals. Procreation is regulated by preferences and choices, females in particular accepting some candidates for union and rejecting others. This means that different, branching, lines of evolutionary development will be established, reflecting the operation of different aesthetic and other criteria. This is not the same as the process of 'natural selection'. It operates by discriminating not among individuals according to their ability to survive to reproductive age but among those who, as adults, differ in those characteristics that are relevant to the competition for mating partners. Through this process of sexual selection *Homo sapiens*, like many other species, has been split into population groups that differ from one another in physical characteristics. From his early interest in domestic breeding to the *Descent of Man*, the central motif in Darwin's thinking was *non-random genetic selection*. The artificial selection practised by breeders, the natural selection of the struggle for life, and the sexual selection of mating behaviour are essentially alike in that they alter the genome of a population by discriminating among its members as candidates for reproduction. This notion, which is the fundamental proposition of modern evolutionary theory, was Darwin's essential contribution to the science of analytical biology.

The Lamarckian notion that the composition of the genome can be altered by the transmission of acquired characters appears in the *Origin* as an important but secondary factor in evolutionary change. In the *Descent* the weight given to the inheritance of acquired characters is considerably increased and, for civilized societies, its importance appears to be greater than that of natural selection. For the social scientist the most interesting part of the *Descent* is the discussion in chapter five of the development of man's 'social and moral faculties'. This is thoroughly Lamarckian in argument. Darwin quotes 'our great philosopher Herbert Spencer' on the development of codes of moral conduct by the steady accumulation over successive generations of particular notions of right and wrong, and adds that 'there is no inherent improbability, as it seems to me, in virtuous tendencies being more or less strongly inherited'. The development of man's 'social sense' is seen by Darwin to be dependent on the development of moral sense, which he construes as a disposition to benefit one's fellows, not for a reciprocal material gain of one's own, but in order to obtain the praise and avoid the blame of other men. The wording and substance of the argument recall Adam Smith's *Theory of Moral Sentiments*, which Darwin refers to in discussing 'sympathy' as an emotional feeling. He does not note that, in the *Wealth of Nations*, Smith had emphasized the role of self-interested actions in a system of market exchange, rather than benevolent or altruistic behaviour, in explaining human social organization, nor does he note the even stronger emphasis on this in Spencer's sociological works.

In Darwin's day the study of racial differences by anthropologists had resulted in two schools, the 'monogenists' who argued that all human races are descended from the same (human) ancestors, and 'polygenists' who believed otherwise. In Darwin's view, monogenesis is supported not only by the general theory of organic evolution but by the empirical fact that the different races of man resemble one another greatly in 'tastes, dispositions and habits' and seem to have similar 'incentives and mental powers'. Darwin lived on the threshold of an era in which biological science and anthropology were joined with nationalistic political theory in creating the 'racism' that fully deserves the odious import of that term in present-day discourse (see section B below). Darwin's theory of evolution played an important part in the development of racist thought, but Darwin himself bears no responsibility for that. Judging by the views expressed in the *Descent*, he would have been appalled at the use that racists have made of his work.

An issue that will occupy our attention below (section C) is whether man has transcended the process of natural selection. Darwin had never argued that natural selection is the sole mechanism of evolutionary development, in man or in other species. A. R. Wallace, who had independently hit on the concept of natural selection, held fast to it more rigorously than Darwin did in that he rejected altogether the Lamarckian notion that acquired characteristics can be inherited. But he regarded the emergence of *Homo sapiens* as marking a distinct new era in evolutionary history. Man's large brain cannot be accounted for by natural selection, since its capacities could not have been of survival value to the early members of the species. This anatomical structure, in Wallace's view, is clear evidence that man must have been created by a higher intelligence which, by doing so, inaugurated a new era in which further development is governed by mental and supernatural factors rather than the material ones that had been hitherto in complete control. Wallace's spiritualism alienated his scientific colleagues, including Darwin, but his argument about the brain not being explainable by the principle of natural selection still troubles evolutionary biologists, and his notion that the introduction of *Homo sapiens* to the world scene has given rise to a new and fundamentally different mode of evolutionary development is one that, with the excision of its spiritualist referents, most social scientists would accept. This is the notion of 'cultural evolution' as it has come to be called.

When used to distinguish between the roles of social and biological factors in human experience, the term 'culture' is frequently used in a very broad way. It embraces knowledge, beliefs, values, and other ideational elements; the whole range of social, economic and political institutions; and also the physical environment that man has produced by replacing forests with farmland, erecting buildings, making roads, etc. 'Cultural evolution' refers to the changes that have taken place, and are currently taking place, in man's ideas, institutions, and artefacts. The feature of such changes that most obviously distinguishes them from the anatomical and physiological changes of biological evolution is that cultural evolution is, or at least can be, much more rapid. Less than two hundred years ago Lewis and Clark travelled from the Mississippi to the Pacific through a vast territory thinly occupied by population of humans that had made only small changes in their physical environment. The scientific revolution occurred only three hundred years ago. Little more than a hundred years ago, the place of slavery in the culture of America was the object of a civil war; and less than fifty years ago southerners considered their culture to be threatened by the demand that blacks share the same schools, waiting rooms, and bus seats as whites. Many human cultures have been stable over long periods of time but cultural evolution can take place at speeds that are far beyond the capacities of biological evolution, which is restricted to the slow processes of genomic alteration.

It has become common in the literature to refer to biological evolution as 'Darwinian' and cultural evolution as 'Lamarckian'. The justification for this is that, in a certain sense, the innovations made by one generation in its artefacts, ideas, institutions, etc., are transmitted to successor generations. But cultural evolution and the Lamarckian process differ in very important respects. Lamarckian theory, like Darwinian theory (in its modern form), depicts a regime in which the individual organism responds to an environment which is constant or, at least, is negligibly affected by the organism's activities, or even by the aggregate activities of the population group to which it belongs. A significant aspect of cultural evolution, by contrast, is that human populations may make large changes in their physical environment and, in addition, create elaborate social environments into which the young are enculturated and within which most human activities are carried on.

By the 1870's, Darwin's *Origin* had convinced most scientists that organic evolution is an indisputable fact, but the theory of natural selection was not generally accepted. August Weismann's 'neo-Darwinism', which purified Darwin's account by rigorously excluding Lamarckian elements, was accompanied by the rise, especially in the United States, of 'neo-Lamarckism' among biologists who remained unconvinced that environmental selection of chance variations is the sole mechanism of evolution. The debate over the mechanism of inheritance eventually ended with the victory of the Darwinians in the 1920's. Only in the Soviet Union, where, during the Stalin regime, Mendelian inheritance and chromosomal genetics were declared to be 'bourgeois idealizations' incompatible with Marxist 'materialism', did Lamarckism survive, until the fall of Khrushchev in 1964. The history of biology in the U.S.S.R. during this period does not convince one that it is desirable to subordinate biological science to social theory, but one might be equally sceptical of the contention, recently made in the West, that the social sciences should be subordinated to Darwinian biology. In his *Sociobiology: The New Synthesis* (1975) E. O. Wilson, a biologist, argues that social scientists are all on the wrong track, that social phenomena and the evolution of societies can be better explained in terms of the genetic factors that have created structures such as the hypothalamus and limbic system which control our emotions and ideas. We will examine the contentions of 'sociobiology' briefly in section C below, but first we must extend our historical survey by discussing the relation between biology and social thought in the period between the publication of the *Origin* and the second World War.

B. THE REDUCTION OF SOCIOLOGY TO BIOLOGY

In the intellectual historiography of the later nineteenth and early twentieth centuries no theme is more prominent than the influence of Darwin's theory of evolution. On the subject we are considering here, this influence was immense, but in order to understand it properly we must note that the *Origin* also had a profound impact on the way in which biologists viewed their science and their role in society. Before Darwin, biologists (or 'naturalists', as they were then customarily called) regarded themselves as strict empiricists, their task being largely confined to making detailed descriptions of the earth's flora and fauna and classifying them according to the scheme that the great Swedish naturalist

Carolus Linnaeus had constructed in the mid-eighteenth century. One of the criticisms that was levelled at Lamarck's theory of evolution was that it was a 'theory', a term that the naturalists of the era considered to be equivalent to 'speculation'. The role of theoretical modelling in science had long been accepted by physicists and chemists, but geologists and biologists firmly held that their sciences must be pursued in a strict 'Baconian' mode. In the great debate that was initiated by the *Origin*, biologists found themselves discussing not only the theory of species evolution that Darwin had advanced but questions of broad philosophical and religious import: the metaphysical foundations of biological science, the nature of man, his relation to the cosmos, to his fellow creatures, and to God. From this emerged a new conception of biology as a science, a greatly enlarged view of its scope, and the view that biologists had special knowledge which gave them the authority, and imposed on them the obligation, to speak on social issues.

The introduction of biology into the field of social debate brought it into conflict over territory that was occupied, in Darwin's time, not by the social sciences but by philosophy and religion. The only social science that enjoyed any recognition at all was political economy, and its authority was much disputed even on narrow technical questions like the determination of relative prices and the effects of tariffs. The sociology of Henri Saint-Simon and Auguste Comte, though it had a considerable following in England, had not established itself as a scientific approach to the large metaphysical and social questions it addressed. These questions remained where they had been from time immemorial, in the domains of philosophy and religion.

Much has been written on the conflict between science and religion and more specifically on the conflict between biology and religion. There was indeed such a conflict, and it was of great importance in creating the modern Western world-view, but it was not one in which all scientists supported one side and all believers in God the other. The metaphor of 'warfare', once popular among historians, has now been abandoned in recognition that the relation of science to religion was much more complex. Indeed, even the term 'conflict' does less than justice to that relation, because it tends to obscure the fact that there was a long period during which Christian theology was characterized by a mode of reasoning which, rather than placing religion and science in opposition, made them allies in man's search for the understanding of existence. This was 'deism' or 'natural theology', which dominated orthodox theology, especially in England, from the end of the seventeenth century until Darwin's day. Some comprehension of the nature of this alliance is germane to our subject, so I will begin here with a brief discussion of it.

1. Deism and the mechanistic world-view

The central tenet of deist theology was that nature reveals, in all its aspects, the property of coherent *design*, which stands as undeniable evidence of the existence of a *designer*. To use an analogy much favoured in the deist literature, if one knew nothing about watchmakers and came upon a watch, one would infer that it must have been made, as a deliberate and purposive act, by an intelligent being. Ordinary reason is sufficient to convince one that such a thing could not have come into existence by the unmanaged confluence of phenomena. So it is also with natural things. The investigations of scientists show that nature is even more remarkable in its design than a watch is, thus demonstrating that there must be a cosmic watchmaker of transcendent power and intelligence. One does not have to rely solely upon the Bible as authoritative documentary evidence of the existence of God, for nature displays on every hand that the account of the creation in the first two chapters of the Book of Genesis must be true. In medieval Europe, the primary focus of religious thought was upon Christ the Saviour, whose divine mission was the redemption of man. The scientific revolution of the seventeenth century shifted that focus to God the Creator of all things. This is evident in the religious thought of the leading figures of that revolution (Richard S. Wesfall, 'The Rise of Science and the Decline of Orthodox Christianity: a Study of Kepler, Descartes, and Newton', in David C. Lindberg and Ronald L. Numbers, eds, *God and Nature*, 1986). By the end of the seventeenth century this mode of reasoning was well established in theological discourse. In Darwin's youth the classic restatement of it was William Paley's *Natural Theology* (1802), which was well known to all educated people and was obligatorily studied by university students, including Darwin. In the 1830s it was expressed again in the eight 'Bridgewater Treatises', written by respected scientists with the object, as their patron the Earl of Bridgewater had instructed, to show 'the Power, Wisdom, and Goodness of God, as manifested in the Creation'.

The Bridgewater Treatises carried an authority that theology could no longer command on its own. But they marked almost the end of the harmonious relations between science and religion that deism had sustained. Theologians found it very difficult to accept the notion of organic evolution and, especially, its implications for the origin of man. When the debate over Darwin's theory among scientists came to an end, religion and science were again no longer in conflict, but only because theologians had abandoned completely the domain of natural phenomena and had accepted the restriction of their profession to spiritual and ethical concerns. Galileo's defence against his Inquisitors that no proposition can be heretical if it is empirically true led, through deism, to the modern conception of natural science as authoritative because it investigates material phenomena by methods that are appropriate to the acquisition of knowledge in that domain.

The seeds of this transformation in Western thought were implicit in deism itself. The analogy of the watch that deist theologians were so fond of implied recognition of the natural world as a *mechanism*. By arguing that the world must have been made by a transcendent mind, deist theology inadvertently supported the view that there is no property of mind *within* the domain of nature, and that organisms, including man, are no more than complex mechanisms. This metaphysical conception had been adopted by William Harvey in his investigation of human physiology at about the same time that Galileo was applying it to physical phenomena, but the notion that organisms are fundamentally different from mechanisms remained for a long time, and indeed is still prominent, in Western thought. Francisco J. Ayala, a leading modern biologist, describes Darwin's *Origin* as having produced a 'conceptual revolution' which 'opened a new era in the intellectual history of mankind' by extending the 'conception of the universe as a system of matter in motion governed by natural laws' to organic phenomena (Theodosius Dobzhansky *et al.*, *Evolution*, 1977, p. 495). Revolution it was, but it had long preparatory antecedents in theology as well as science, and its victory was far from complete, even in secular philosophical thought.

The notion that organisms are mechanisms and that the laws of matter and motion govern life phenomena is difficult to accept by anyone who cannot go the whole hog, as Laplace and La Mettrie or the Vienna Circle philosophers did, in embracing the doctrine of physicalist determinism. The great debate over the *Origin* banished God from scientific discourse, but it did not banish the idea that (some) organisms are endowed with qualities that non-living entities do not possess. One of those who participated in the debate was James Martineau (brother of Harriet Martineau, whom we encountered as a doctrinaire advocate of *laissez-faire* in Chapter 10 B), the leading Unitarian theologian of the period. Writing on 'The Place of Mind in Nature and Intuition in Man' (*Contemporary Review*, 1872), Martineau said that while he was prepared to grant that organic species might have evolved, he could not accept the theory of natural selection, because its mechanistic ontology left no room for properties that manifestly do exist. After elaborating upon this theme, Martineau concluded:

> These considerations appear to me to break the back of this formidable argument in the middle; and to show the impossibility of dispensing with the presence of Mind in any scene of ascending being, where the little is becoming great, and the dead alive, and the shapeless beautiful, and the sentient moral, and the moral spiritual.

This theme has been repeated, in various ways, and in various genres of expression, until the present. The philosopher Henri Bergson, who won the Nobel Prize for his *Creative Evolution* (1907) and other books, opposed the metaphysical conception of monistic materialism, arguing that there exists an *élan vital* in the organic domain which is the true cause of evolutionary development. George Bernard Shaw celebrated the Bergsonian 'life force' in his philosophical drama *Man and Superman*. Samuel Butler, in a number of novels and essays, fiercely attacked Darwinism as denying the existence of the phenomena of consciousness and will. D. G. Ritchie, in his *Darwinism and Politics* (1892), rejected the application of biological concepts to social problems for similar reasons. In sociology, as we have seen, Herbert Spencer's social organicism was controlled by the conception of the individual as the locus of consciousness, and Émile Durkheim's concept of a *conscience collective* construed society as an ontological entity endowed with qualities akin to mind. In biology itself, Hans Driesch rejected Darwinism as having tried to show that organic structures arose from the 'throwing together of stones' and argued for a reconstitution of the discipline in terms of 'dynamic teleology' as a 'vitalist' science, distinct from physics and chemistry, which recognizes the autonomous capacities for purposive action possessed by living things.

Such responses to the doctrine of mechanism failed to replace it by an alternative metaphysical conception that could serve heuristically in the natural sciences but, elsewhere, the doctrine continues to be denied general acceptance. This would be a matter of minor interest to the subject of this book if it were not for the fact that the most striking proposals for social policy that derived from biology were inspired, not so much by the notion that *Homo sapiens* is the product of evolution from other organic forms through the process of natural selection, as by the materialist conception of human nature which it implied.

2. Biology and social policy

In this section we will examine the connections between evolutionary biology and programmatic proposals for the improvement of human nature, or 'eugenics' as they were generally called, and the connections between these and the development of political ideologies that were oriented around the notion that the differentiation of the world's people according to race and/or nationality is the most fundamental social fact, and the most important concern of social policy. A generation ago it was customary to discuss such matters as aspects of 'Social Darwinism', but recent historical research has shown that that term has been employed to cover such a wide spectrum of political postures, embracing every notion that someone has supported (or attacked) on the ground that it is 'Darwinian', that it defines nothing in social thought that can be distinguished from anything else. Even the biological content of the notion is too broad, since it lumps under the one term the theory of evolution by the natural selection of chance genetic variations, the theory that acquired traits are transmitted, and the theory that the genome of a population is modified directly by environmental conditions. As a descriptive term 'Social Darwinism' was originally derived from a criticism of Herbert Spencer by the Belgian economist Émile de Laveleye, who apparently did not see any significance in the fact that Spencer was one of the most prominent defenders of the Lamarckian theory of evolution. A recent survey of the literature on the concept of 'Social Darwinism' as a vehicle for the appraisal of Darwin's impact beyond the field of biology comes to the conclusion that historians would do well to abandon it (Antonello La Vergata, 'Images of Darwin: a Historiographic Overview', in David Kohn, ed., *The Darwinian Heritage*, 1985).

In Chapter 10 B above we examined the more restricted use of 'Social Darwinism' to refer to the economic ideology of *laissez-faire* so there is no need to consider here the thesis popularized by Richard Hofstadter that, especially in the United States, late nineteenth and early twentieth-century economic thought and policy were dominated by ideas drawn from, and rationalized by appeal to, evolutionary biology. Like others who have written on this theme, Hofstadter takes as an epitome of this the report of an address by John D. Rockefeller to a Sunday school class in which he praised the theory of natural selection as an embodiment of economic as well as biological wisdom, and compared the development of great business firms like his own to the evolution of a superior variety of rose. If Rockefeller intended by this homily to celebrate the virtues of uncontrolled competition (which one may doubt, since he was one of the leading creators of monopolies in his era) he was on treacherous ground. Even one of the children he addressed could have pointed out that if a garden were left to the regime of *laissez-faire*, it would be quickly populated by pigweed, crabgrass, mouse's ear, and creeping charlie, rather than magnificent roses. In order to make and sustain a garden one must practise *artificial* selection; the survival of the fittest will not do at all. The eugenics movement, which I will now proceed to discuss without further preliminaries, may have had its immediate inspiration in Darwin's theory of evolution, but it sought to apply to man the policy of organic modification by deliberate interference with natural processes, using principles that had been known since the dawn of agriculture.

Anticipation of the central thesis of eugenics is to be found, like so much else in Western thought, in Plato. The discussion of the 'guardians' in the *Republic* stresses the regimen of education and testing that is necessary to obtain men with qualities appropriate to the exercise of absolute power, but Plato also argues that restrictive breeding must be practised. Just as plants and animals must be carefully bred in order to produce superior types, so must the guardians breed only with women of like metal. In the utopian literature of later times, a prominent motif is the need to improve humankind in order to create a perfect society, but the main emphasis is placed upon education, other social arrangements, and the physical environment, as factors that effect the required transformation in human character. Undoubtedly there were utopian writers who suggested that the programme of improvement should be pushed back to the level at which the biological substrate of human behaviour is generated, but it was not until the later nineteenth century that this became a prominent feature in Western social thought, supported (its proponents claimed) by scientific knowledge based upon quantitative empirical evidence.

The originator of eugenics was Charles Darwin's cousin Francis Galton. His first publications were in the fields of exploration, geography, and meteorology, for which he was awarded the Gold Medal of the Royal Geographical Society at the age of thirty-one, in 1853. His extensive travels had generated an interest in ethnology, and reading Darwin's *Origin* induced him to shift his attention from physical phenomena to the study of human heredity. Darwin had been inspired by the work of plant and animal breeders to develop a theory postulating a selective force operating in nature that produces organic modifications. Galton could have been similarly motivated by the work of breeders to consider whether the same deliberate process might be applied to man, but it was the *Origin* that influenced him in this direction, perhaps because he thought that his cousin had provided, by his theory of *natural* selection, a scientific understanding of the art of *artificial* selection in agriculture. In his writings on human heredity he insisted that selective breeding, and only selective breeding, can achieve the changes in human behaviour that are necessary to the improvement of society.

Galton's first publication on his new interest was a two-part essay on 'Hereditary Talent and Character' (*Macmillan's Magazine*, 1865). The opening paragraph states the thesis that guided his work:

> The power of man over animal life, in producing whatever varieties of form he pleases, is enormously great. It would seem as though the physical structure of future generations was almost as plastic as clay, under the control of the breeder's will. It is my desire to show more pointedly than – so far as I am aware – has been attempted before, that mental qualities are equally under control.

He went on to describe an imaginary society in which young men and women had been selected for 'every important quality of mind and body' and were encouraged to marry one another by a wedding gift of £5,000 paid by the state. This would cost little and yield much, he declared:

> If a twentieth part of the costs and pains were spent in [such] measures for the improvement of the human race that is spent on the improvement of the breed of horses and cattle, what a galaxy of genius might we not create!

In Galton's day, nothing was known about the mechanism of heredity. Chromosomes were first observed in 1841 but it was not until the twentieth century that their role in hereditary transmission began to be understood. From his youth, Galton had been an ardent quantifier. On any subject that interested him he collected numerical data and drew general inferences from them. He proceeded in this fashion, a novel mode of investigating biological phenomena, when his attention turned to human heredity. He constructed a sample of eminent men (scientists, statesmen, judges, artists, and clerics) and calculated the proportion of them that were blood relatives. Finding this proportion to be very high, he inferred that the mental and behavioural traits that had made these men eminent run in families and are transmitted genetically from one generation to another. This convinced him that further study of human heredity was a priority subject for scientific investigation, and that policies of selective human breeding, guided by the findings of such investigation, deserved serious consideration. Galton followed up his 1865 essay with a much larger statistical study in book form entitled *Hereditary Genius: an Inquiry into its Laws and*

Consequences (1869). The immediate reception of it by the scientific community was cool. Darwin was not happy with it, and avoided mention of Galton's thesis in the *Descent of Man*, which he was in the course of writing at the time. But *Hereditary Genius* became the foundation book of the scientific discipline and social policy for which Galton, in 1883, coined the name 'eugenics'. Its initial development was slow, but by the first quarter of the twentieth century it was well established in Britain, the United States, Germany, Russia, Japan, and elsewhere. It is sometimes referred to as the 'eugenics movement' because it was more than a programme of scientific research. It was enthusiastically supported by many non-scientists, its disciples embarked on a well financed campaign of public education in order to promote the voluntary adoption of eugenic principles in marriage and procreation, and they urged their governments to exercise the power of the state in the interest of compulsory genetic improvement.

Galton had inherited considerable wealth, which he used to finance his own work and to promote eugenic research by others. Conventional biologists were not accustomed to statistical and mathematical methods and were reluctant to accept work that employed them. Galton therefore financed the creation of a new journal, *Biometrika*, in 1902, and founded a research fellowship in eugenics at the University of London in 1904. This fellowship developed into the 'Galton Laboratory of National Eugenics', which was directed by Karl Pearson until 1933, when he was succeeded by R. A. Fisher. In any history of biology, or of mathematical statistics, the names of Pearson and Fisher appear prominently as pioneers in the development of fundamental statistical theory and the techniques of data analysis that now play such a large part in all branches of the natural and the social sciences. In other countries, equally distinguished scientific authorities supported the movement. In Germany, Ernst Haeckel, an eminent zoologist, founded the Monist League in 1906 to promote a strong programme of artificial selection in human procreation. In Russia, within five years after the revolution of 1917, a Eugenics Department was created at the Institute of Experimental Biology in Moscow, a *Journal of Eugenics* was started, and organizations for the promotion of eugenics were established in Leningrad and other large cities, under the direction of leading biologists such as J. A. Philiptschenko, who, in a book on eugenics published in 1924, declared eugenics to be an instrument which would assist the victory of the proletariat over the bourgeoisie. In the United States Mrs E. H. Harriman provided funds and property for the establishment, in 1904, of a 'Eugenics Record Office' at Cold Spring Harbor on Long Island which developed, in time, into the world-renowned centre of biological research that exists there today. Under the direction of Charles B. Davenport, who was convinced that virtually all human traits, from alcoholism to 'thalassophilia' (love of the sea) are hereditary, Cold Spring Harbor became the centre of eugenic research and programme promotion. By the 1920s, according to the American Eugenics Society, instruction in eugenics was available at 350 colleges and universities. The favourite text, by W. E. Castle, a Harvard professor of biology, traced social problems to genetic factors and advocated, as their solution, more procreation by university graduates, the avoidance of interracial marriage, sterilization of the 'feebleminded', and other voluntary and enforced policies. Today, the eugenics movement is recognized as flawed in its theoretical reasoning and grossly deficient in the empirical evidence that had been used to support its contentions, but in its heyday the movement could claim the authority of many distinguished scientists who, within the domains in which they applied the caution and scepticism of scientific method, deserved the high repute in which they were held.

In addition to biologists, the eugenics programme was supported by an extraordinary list of prominent persons. To mention some English and American names that will be familiar to the reader: George Bernard Shaw, Sidney and Beatrice Webb, Alfred Marshall, John Maynard Keynes, Harold Laski, Havelock Ellis, H. G. Wells, Winston Churchill, Theodore Roosevelt, Alexander Graham Bell, Oliver Wendell Holmes. Membership of eugenic societies covered the whole range of political viewpoints, from the brightest red to the deepest blue. Its appeal was one that we have encountered on numerous occasions in this history: the vision of a world in which man has, at last, conquered the problems that beset him as a social being through knowledge of 'natural laws', not as Aquinas had conceived them, or Comte, or Harriet Martineau, Marx, Spencer, or others, who had found them, variously, in God's will, or in history, economics, or sociology, but in the place where Galileo and Newton had looked, the material world of matter and energy. Many of the eugenists struck a pessimistic stance, warning that our civilization would decay if the findings of biology were not heeded; but others construed the new knowledge as a message of hope. Charles Van Hise, president of the University of Wisconsin, declared that the promised land was at hand; it was only necessary to apply what we already know:

> We know enough about agriculture so that the agricultural production of the country could be doubled if the knowledge were applied; we know enough about disease so that if the knowledge were utilized, infectious and contagious diseases would be substantially destroyed within a score of years; we know enough about eugenics so that if the knowledge were applied, the defective classes would disappear within a generation. (Quoted in Daniel J. Kevles, *In the Name of Eugenics*, 1986, p. 68)

It is doubtful that many persons followed the dictates of eugenics in their own procreational behaviour, but the programme did find expression in some areas of public policy, especially in the United States. In Britain the Mental Deficiency Act of 1913, which ordered the sexual segregation of mental patients in order to prevent their procreation, was, according to one historian, the only legislative success of the eugenists. British politicians 'failed to be drawn into the eugenics movement' (Nancy Stepan, *The Idea of Race in Science: Great*

Britain, 1800–1960, 1982, p. 121). Even this Act, though, does not serve as clear evidence of new-found enthusiasm for compulsory eugenics, since the same segregation had been part of the Poor Law Amendment Act of 1834, designed at that time to limit the procreation of paupers. In the United States the story was different. State laws regulating marriage by eugenic criteria began in Connecticut in 1896 and were adopted in many states during the first two decades of this century. A physician at the Indiana State Reformatory in Jeffersonville pioneered the procedure of male sterilization by vasectomy in 1899 and in subsequent years performed the operation on hundreds of inmates, not, one may assume, with their uncoerced consent. Indiana passed a compulsory sterilization statute in 1917, which fifteen other states copied during the next decade, mandating the sterilization of habitual criminals, rapists, epileptics, and insane or feebleminded persons. A test of such statutes went to the Supreme Court in 1924, which declared them to be constitutional, with only one dissent, by a practising Catholic. Oliver Wendell Holmes, who wrote the court's judgement, argued that science had demonstrated the social necessity for such an interference with individual liberty (D. J. Kevles, *In the Name of Eugenics*, 1986, Chapter VIII; p. 168).

Such uses of state power, though deplorable on both scientific and ethical grounds, were mild compared to the policy of *Rassenhygiene* ('racial hygiene') adopted by Nazi Germany. This eugenic programme was directed at genetic 'improvement' by the wholesale elimination of racial groups who were supposed to harbour undesirable genes. British and American eugenic thought was not free of racist elements, and the connection between biology and racial social theories deserves specific discussion, but I defer this briefly in order to consider further the focus of eugenics upon traits that, whether endemic in large groups or not, were construed as biological characteristics of individual persons. Enthusiasm for eugenics as a social policy was brought to an end by abhorrence of the racial policy of Nazi Germany, but before the barbarity of this was fully realized, biologists themselves began to doubt the scientific validity of eugenic postulates concerning the transmittal of traits between parent and child.

Francis Galton's initial work was aimed at revealing the genetic foundations of *intelligence*. The eminent men he studied were, in his opinion, possessors of 'genius'. A side-effect of the eugenics movement, which turned out to be more important and more enduring than the programme of selective breeding, was the notion that everyone is born with a definite level of 'general' intelligence, which is unalterable. Attempts to devise procedures for measuring this date from 1904, when Alfred Binet, in France, constructed the first intelligence tests. Such tests, though much criticized, are today used by research and clinical psychologists, and figure prominently in certain areas of social policy. In England, the educational system was based upon the division of students according to their inherent mental capacities, which were assumed to be ascertainable at an early age, by the Education Act of 1944. The leading figure in this development was Cyril Burt, a psychologist associated with the London County Council, which was responsible for educational policy in the London region. Burt had been inspired by Galton's work and was firmly convinced that intelligence is hereditary. His own work appeared to provide conclusive confirmation of this, showing that identical twins who had been separated at birth and reared in different family environments achieve similar scores on intelligence tests. In the 1970's Burt's data were revealed to be fraudulent but, by this time, the educational system based on his convictions was too well entrenched to be easily reordered.

The debate on the inheritability of intelligence still continues; not in terms of whether intelligence is wholly genetic or not genetic at all, but whether the notion of *general* intelligence is sound and applicable to educational policy and, if it is, *how much* of such intelligence is due to the individual's unalterable genetic constitution. The idea of raising the average level of intelligence in society by selective breeding has been abandoned so far as public policy is concerned, but the conviction that it is scientifically valid and socially desirable persists as a remnant of the eugenics movement. H. J. Muller, a professor of biology at Indiana University who won the Nobel Prize for his pioneering work in the investigation of radiation-induced genetic mutations, was a strong advocate of selective breeding and, in the 1960's, campaigned for what he called 'genetic progress by voluntary germinal choice'. This was to be effected by storing sperm donated by selected outstanding men, which women could use for artificial insemination. Such a sperm bank now exists in the United States, but it does not seem that the demands made upon it have been sufficient to achieve the improvement in American intelligence that Muller considered to be urgent.

High intelligence is not the same thing as good *behaviour*. In the second part of his 1865 paper, Galton stated that the eminent men he studied must be presumed to have inherited qualities of good character as well as intelligence. He, and later eugenists, assumed that such things as criminal behaviour, selfishness, disregard of the future, laziness, and overindulgence in strong drink are behaviour traits rooted in genetic factors, just as are a person's intelligence and physical constitution. In fact a great deal of the research that was conducted by eugenists was aimed at investigating the inheritance of character traits that result in socially undesirable behaviour, and most of the propaganda of eugenics promotion societies focused upon this, rather than intelligence. Galton excluded from his list of eminent men those who had been successful in industry and commerce, as later eugenists also did, reflecting the doubt held by scientists, intellectuals, artists, and social philosophers, that business acumen is correlated with good social behaviour but, this interesting exception aside, the eugenists were confident that social problems could be greatly ameliorated by selective breeding.

The contention that behavioural traits are genetic is a much larger claim than that intelligence is. One can accept the notion of the brain as a genetically determined computational instrument and the IQ score as an index of its power without embracing the view that human behaviour is similarly determined. Just as a computer must be furnished with 'software', so the comparable apparatus in a human organism must be furnished with comparable programmes. The contention that human behaviour is genetic, as an unqualified proposition, not only eliminates the operation of all autonomous elements of individual valuation and choice; it eliminates all cultural elements as well. The reduction of behaviour to genetics is the ultimate step in the application of mechanistic materialism. It reduces sociology, and the other social sciences, to biology, which in turn, is reduced to chemistry and physics. In the heyday of eugenics a few social scientists attacked it for neglecting the aspects of human culture and behaviour that they were accustomed to focus upon, but the main assault on eugenics emerged as a criticism, by biologists, of its biological foundations. This criticism developed as knowledge of the mechanism of inheritance was beginning to be obtained through work in chromosomal genetics.

The decline of eugenics as a result of these advances in biology is a story that would take us far afield and involves difficult technical matters. But some consideration of the relevant scientific issues is essential to an historical account of the relation between biology and social thought, so I will discuss this briefly. For convenience, I shall focus upon the criticism of eugenics by H. S. Jennings, a highly regarded professor of biology at Johns Hopkins University, in his essay 'What Can we Hope from Eugenics?' published in *Plain Talk* in 1928.

The early eugenists not only assumed that intelligence and behaviour traits are inherited but they took it for granted that, if persons with desirable traits were to procreate more and those with undesirable ones less, there would be a significant decrease in the relative frequency of undesirable traits within a few generations. Plant and animal breeders could have told them that practical eugenics is not so simple: that some traits cannot be modified by selective breeding and that, even when breeding is rigidly restricted to individuals with the desired traits, the undesired ones reappear in later generations none the less. Jennings pointed out that even if human behaviour traits are modifiable by selective breeding, an effective eugenic programme would have to resort to carefully controlled breeding in order to reveal the hidden deleterious genetic factors. A mere decrease in the relative procreation of individuals actually displaying the undesirable trait would 'leave untouched the great reservoir of defective genes present in normal individuals'. If criminals, for example, were prevented from breeding, the effect on the incidence of criminal behaviour, said Jennings, would hardly be detectable even if such a programme were rigorously maintained for a thousand years. But accelerating the process by controlled breeding to reveal the presence of such deleterious genetic factors, he pointed out, would require placing an authority in control of human procreation that had as much power over humans as a breeder of domesticated species has over his plants and animals. Jennings was doubtful that 'mental characteristics shown in behaviour' are significantly due to genetic factors, but he did not engage the eugenists in a 'nature versus nurture' debate; he attacked them on their own ground, showing that their biology was faulty. The publications of the American Eugenics Society, said Jennings, contained 'glib statements' which promised solutions for a wide range of social evils, but the programme would have worse than negligible results if it effected a 'disastrous' diversion of attention from the non-genetic causes of those evils.

The basis of Jennings's biological argument lies in the fact that humans (indeed, all but a small number of species) carry two complete sets of chromosomes in their cells, derived from the two parents of each individual. In the simplest case, where a trait is controlled by one gene only, there are two forms of it, called 'alleles', which may not be identical. For example, eye colour is a one-gene trait. If an embryo has inherited blue-eye alleles from both parents, the person's eyes will be blue; if it has inherited two brown-eye alleles, the eyes will be brown; but if it has inherited one blue and one brown allele, the eyes will be brown, because the brown allele is 'dominant' and the blue 'recessive'. Thus a brown-eyed person may harbour a hidden blue-eye allele, which may be transmitted to offspring. Blue-eye alleles could be eliminated from the genome of a population by preventing mating between adults with blue eyes, but it would take a long time. In 1917 the mathematician G. H. Hardy calculated that a one-gene recessive-allele trait initially evident in as few as three persons in a thousand could be totally eliminated only if no persons manifesting that trait mated for 250 successive generations, that is, several thousand years.

Jennings also pointed out that many traits are in fact controlled by more than one gene, which renders the eugenic programme even more problematic. Since Jennings's day, genetic research has revealed, and continues to reveal, additional complications. (Even the eye colour case is not as simple as I have represented it above.) The eugenics movement is now generally recognized to have been based on biological propositions that were simplistic and, indeed, fundamentally erroneous. The early eugenists did not support these propositions by faking empirical data, as Cyril Burt did, and though their empirical work would not now receive a passing grade in a class in elementary statistics, they did tackle the investigation of the heritability of intelligence and behaviour with the knowledge and tools that were available to them. Galton, Pearson, Weldon, and the other initiators of eugenic research cannot be criticized for not knowing what scientists discovered only later. But they deserve to be reproached on another, and more serious, ground. In claiming, and allowing others to claim without demur, that the social policy proposals of the eugenics movement were soundly grounded in science, they went far beyond what the knowledge of the time supported. They were not the first, nor the last, to make such improper extensions of science. Economists, sociologists, anthropologists, and physicists, as well as biologists, have at times deviated from scientific research, which requires the constant exercise of doubt, to lend their authority to propaganda, which demands certitude. Fortunately, the eugenics movement in itself had little impact on social policy and it is remembered today only by historians. But the relation between biology and social thought, more broadly viewed, went well beyond the specific policies that eugenists favored. Though they often spoke of superior and inferior 'classes', the focus of their argumentation and proposals was upon the character traits of *individuals*. The application of biology to *groups* of humans, races and nations in particular, though not unconnected with eugenics, deserves separate discussion.

We have not had much occasion in this book to refer to racial differences. From time immemorial these have been prominent in popular social thought and politics, but the social sciences made almost no use of them in constructing general models of social processes or explanations of specific social phenomena. In fact, the leading figures in the development of the social sciences assumed that biological differences between persons are of negligible significance. Hobbes assumed that the state of nature would be the same no matter what race of humans were in it, and that in all cases the same solution to its evils would be found: the creation of a sovereign with absolute power. In Locke's political analysis, all persons are presumed to have the right to judge the exercise of that power. Montesquieu argued that the English had established a governmental system of checks and balances, not because they were biologically different from other peoples, but because their culture placed great weight on freedom. Adam Smith did not trace the division of labour, as Plato had, to biological differences, but to its productive advantages in a world where all men are alike, and Ricardo's theory of exchange between countries was based on their different natural resources and levels of technology, not their genetic endowments. Comte's 'law of the three stages' applied to all societies. Durkheim's *conscience collective* was a cultural, not a biological phenomenon. Marx's categorical distinction between worker and capitalist was based on ownership of the means of production, not biological differences. One finds very little reference to biological differences in the early history of the social sciences, with one exception, anthropology. This discipline first emerged as *physical* anthropology, with a close connection to biological work in comparative anatomy, and racial differences as its main interest. Nancy Stepan's book *The Idea of Race in Science* gives anthropology a prominent place in the development of the racial orientation in modern scientific thought.

In his great *Systema Naturae* (1735) Linnaeus took the bold step of including man in the classification of animals. He named him *Homo sapiens*, focusing upon the large brain of the species. But in his subclassification of the species into varieties Linnaeus included behavioural and social characteristics as well as anatomical ones. Native Americans are 'choleric' and 'obstinate', and are 'regulated by customs'. Africans are 'phlegmatic', 'relaxed', 'crafty', 'indolent', and 'negligent', and are 'governed by caprice'. Asiatics are 'melancholy', 'severe', 'haughty', and 'covetous', and are 'governed by opinions'. Europeans are 'sanguine', 'gentle', 'acute', and 'inventive' and are 'governed by laws' (Daniel J. Boorstin, *The Discoverers*, 1983, p. 464).

The anthropologists who began to work on racial differences towards the end of the eighteenth century did not attempt to make such fine differentiations, but they focused upon the brain, the material locus of behavioural phenomena. Long before other social scientists began to compile quantitative data, anthropologists were measuring the size and shape of the human cranium as an indicator of what lay within it. This mode of investigation was well established before Darwin's *Origin* was published. As early as 1795, Johann Franz Gall introduced the notion that a person's mental characteristics, determined by his brain structure, could be ascertained by examining the irregularities of his skull. The 'reading' of heads enjoyed some popularity for a time, and not merely as parlour entertainment, since it appeared to be based on the sound scientific principle that all phenomena have material foundations.

Other forms of cranial study proved more lasting. In particular, the 'cephalic index' (the ratio of skull width to length) was regarded by anthropologists as a highly significant indicator of fundamental differences in mental traits between races. Such views were widely accepted as scientifically sound for a long time, and supported the notion that the incessant conflicts between the peoples of Europe are explicable in terms of fundamental biological differences rather than the economic and political interests that historians were accustomed to focus upon. The use of cranial measurements as indicators of genetic racial differences was based on the assumption that they are independent of nutritional and environmental factors. In the early twentieth century Franz Boas undermined this fundamental supposition by showing that the cephalic indexes of American-born children differed from those of their foreign-born parents. Even so, it was a while before anthropologists abandoned 'craniometry' as a method of differentiating and classifying the races of man. As an approach to the comparative study of cultures and other sociological questions these early approaches in anthropology are now recalled with embarrassment or scorn, but it is well to note that those who pursued such lines of investigation were good scientists, conscientiously trying to increase our understanding of social problems by applying methods that, at the time, appeared to permit the reduction of sociology to the harder science of biology.

The notion that there are racial differences is not the same as 'racism'. That term denotes the belief that some human groups are categorically superior to others and, therefore, the race to which an individual belongs is the paramount factor in determining his unalterable rank in a hierarchy of merit that nature has created. Darwin shared many of the racial and national prejudices of his fellow Englishmen (and, *mutatis mutandis*, others), but there is very little in his writings that suggests racism. The main object of the *Descent of Man* was to show how the various races that now populate the earth, which Darwin assumed to have had common ancestors, might have become differentiated. He does not suggest that 'sexual selection', the process that had created racial differentiation, operated in such a fashion that some races became superior to others in their intellectual, cultural, and moral qualities. Nevertheless, a convinced Darwinian was at liberty to adopt the view, if he chose, that some human groups are more highly evolved than others, not merely in their possession of superior cultural artefacts, but in their biological constitutions. By this route, Darwinism was pressed into service as 'scientific' support for racist theories and racist policies. Such theories were widely promulgated in all countries where the Darwinian explanation of organic evolution gained acceptance. They were prominent in the literature of the eugenics movement, and they were influential in specific areas of governmental legislation such as that which ended the 'open door' immigration policy of the United States. But it was in Germany, during the Nazi era, that racism became a central pillar of state policy, leading to the second World War and the holocaust. It is impossible to estimate how much of the responsibility for this can be attributed to racist biology but Daniel Gasman's study of *The Scientific Origins of National Socialism* (1971) shows that it was not negligible. Nazi ideology was a bizarre compound of romanticism, utopianism, mystic nationalism, nature worship, and 'political biology'. Alfred Rosenberg, the official 'philosopher' of the Nazi party, drew upon extreme racist ideas expressed earlier by Ernst Haeckel, who was an internationally renowned biologist and the leading advocate of Darwinism in Germany. The Monist League, which Haeckel founded in 1906 to give political expression to his interpretation of Darwinian theory, advanced a programme for state action that bears close resemblances to the policies of *Rassenhygiene* and territorial aggrandizement that were adopted by Germany in the 1930's.

The connection between biology and *nationalism* is a different story. There is little evidence that nationalistic sentiment, abstracted from racism, derived any significant inspiration from biology, but a twist was given to Darwinian theory that played a role in, at least, the rationalization of the extreme nationalism that developed in the period between the Franco-Prussian War and the first World War. This 'twist' consists of shifting the locus of Darwin's 'struggle for existence' from competition among the members of a group to competition among the groups themselves. In Darwin's model of natural selection, the 'geometric' capacity of procreation produces a situation in which the number of individuals of a particular species in a habitat exceeds the capacity of that habitat to sustain them. The individuals are in severe competition *with one another*. Darwin neglected the fact that different species might compete for the same habitat, but it was precisely this form of competition for survival that came to be stressed in the political literature, with 'nations' as the entities that were presumed to be locked in inescapable conflict. The Nazis, who identified race with nation, reflected this idea in claiming that the need for *Lebensraum* (living space) justified their conquest of other countries, and depopulating them.

The notion that science had demonstrated the inevitability of inter-national conflict is prominent in the political literature of the period leading up to the first World War. The eugenics movement played a significant role in this. From its inception, it had emphasized the biological improvement of the *nation* as the entity of central concern. Galton and Pearson consistently referred to their work as 'National Eugenics'. Eugenic biological theory focused on the individual as the carrier of the genetic material, but a motif that recurs over and over again in the eugenic literature is that selective breeding is an urgent necessity, not only because internal social problems are pressing, but also because the improvement of the nation's biological stock is vital in preparing it for the inevitable clash with other nations in a world of fixed size and limited resources. By this route Darwinian evolutionism was drawn into the ultra-nationalist, militarist, and imperialist ideologies of the period. It is a testament to the scientific value of Darwin's theory that it has survived the many perversions of it that were made for political purposes.

C. BIOLOGY AND THE SOCIAL SCIENCES

The impact of biology on social thought that engaged our attention in the preceding section is now an almost forgotten episode in Western intellectual history. The idea of human improvement through selective breeding is not entirely dead, racism is, at best, dormant or on the defensive, and xenophobic nationalism is as strong as ever it was; but they have been deprived of the claims to scientific support that were once made on their behalf. This is, however, not the whole story: we have not yet examined the relation between biology and social *science* in the restricted sense of the analysis of social phenomena in a 'positive' fashion, abstracted from the promotion of programmes of social policy. In this section I shall undertake to sketch the role of biology in forging the methods of *quantitative* research that are now so prominent in the social science disciplines, and to evaluate the role of biology in the development of the *theoretical* models that these disciplines employ. As a coda to the latter topic I shall briefly consider in the third section the recent re-emergence, under the name of 'sociobiology', of the view that social phenomena can be effectively investigated only if human behaviour is traced to the genetic factors that are its subliminal foundations.

1. Statistics and statistical methodology

We have had frequent occasion to note in this book that the early social scientists worked on the assumption, which they sometimes explicitly expressed, that social phenomena are law-governed. This is the most fundamental proposition in the philosophy of social science, for, without it, there can be no discipline that is both *social* in its substance and *scientific* in its method. Many of the early social scientists boldly compared themselves to the great figures of the scientific revolution such as Galileo, Harvey, and Newton. Adam Smith was not so immodest, but he wrote an essay on astronomy in which he argued that the conceptions and procedures used in that discipline furnished the proper methodological paradigm for all others. Nevertheless, very few students of social phenomena were prepared to embrace the full-blown mechanistic determinism that was adopted by physicists and astronomers; most insisted that human entities are fundamentally different from physical ones, endowed with the properties of mind, if not soul. But how can one argue that social phenomena are governed by general laws, which dictate consistent regularities, while regarding individual persons, whose behaviour *en masse* constitute the social phenomena, as possessing powers of autonomous 'free' action? This problem was eventually resolved (to the degree that it *has* been resolved) by construing social phenomena as 'statistical' in nature, and their governing laws as 'probabilistic'. The first expressions of such views are to be found in the French philosophical literature of the Revolution period, and continental physical scientists and mathematicians were the earliest to begin the development of techniques for dealing with statistical phenomena, but it was not until the subject was taken up in England by biologists, as an adjunct of the eugenics movement, that statistical regularities were widely appreciated by scientists as having the character of 'laws'. (In a more comprehensive book on the history and philosophy of social science than this one is, a substantial chapter would have to be devoted exclusively to the development of statistical theory and its applications. I present here only a brief discussion as part of a chapter on biology and the social sciences, in order to highlight the most important points without becoming too involved in technical matters.)

The outstanding pioneer of social statistics was Adolphe Quetelet, the Astronomer Royal of Belgium. Trained initially as a mathematician, Quetelet studied astronomy in Paris in the early 1820's, and was greatly impressed by the Saint-Simonians at the École Polytechnique who argued that the study of social phenomena could be made as scientific as the physical sciences (see Chapter 12 A above). He also became acquainted at this time with work done by Fourier and Laplace (who taught at the École) in the analysis of data on social phenomena. As a mathematician and astronomer Quetelet was familiar with the 'normal curve of error' which Karl Friedrich Gauss had devised to deal with the fact that repeated measurements of an astronomical phenomenon do not yield precisely the same value. Gauss's famous bell-shaped curve depicted how these measurements would be distributed, owing to 'chance', around the true value. When Quetelet turned his attention to human and social phenomena he applied the Gaussian distribution in a striking way. His first book on this subject was published in 1835 under the title *Sur l'homme et le développement de ses facultés, ou essai de physique sociale* ('On Man and the Development of his Faculties, or, An Essay on Social Physics' – the last two words show the influence of the French positivists). This was translated, and published in England in 1842 under the title of *A Treatise on Man and the Development of his Faculties*. Quetelet presented data not only on human anatomical character-istics such as height, but also on intellectual capacities, 'moral' traits, and the incidence of social phenomena such as crime. He arranged the data on each subject in the form of a frequency distribution, and showed that all displayed the general characteristics of a Gaussian curve. The impact of this was profound. Henry Buckle, in his widely read *History of Civilization in England*

(1857), hailed Quetelet as having demonstrated that no matter how 'arbitrary and irregular' or dependent on 'the peculiarities of the individual' an act (such as murder) may seem to be, the incidence of such acts reveals the operation of a general law. John Stuart Mill, in his discussion of the methods of social science in his magisterial *System of Logic* (8th edn, 1872) described such demonstrations as 'very startling to persons not accustomed to regard moral actions as subject to uniform laws'.

Quetelet indeed went even further. He interpreted the bell-shaped distribution of human properties as being *exactly* like the error curve in astronomical observations. Thus, for example, he treated the distribution of the heights of a group of men as exactly the same as the distribution of readings that would be obtained if one made a number of measurements of one man, or a statue. Reasoning in this fashion, he construed the 'average man' derived from his statistics as *the* man, the entity that the science of 'social physics' deals with (see Victor L. Hills, 'Statistics and Social Science', in Ronald N. Giere and Richard S. Westfall, eds, *Foundations of Scientific Method: the Nineteenth Century*, 1973). This notion, which reminds one more of Plato's 'pure forms' than Max Weber's 'ideal types', did not prove useful, and was disregarded by subsequent workers who applied statistical methods to social phenomena, but it was Quetelet who first showed that mathematical concepts and analysis could be effectively employed in social research.

Let us divert our attention for a moment from the mathematical analysis of numerical data to the task that must precede it, the collection of such data. Inundated as we are today with statistics on every aspect of life, we have to remind ourselves that before the second quarter of the nineteenth century people had very little quantitative information about the societies in which they lived. Even basic demographic statistics were scanty when Malthus wrote his *Essay on Population*. The array of statistics on various countries that he introduced into the second edition of the *Essay* (1803) required a great deal of work in searching for data and compiling it, not just the copying of figures from standard sources available in a good library. In the 1830's there occurred in England a remarkable wave of interest in the collection of social statistics, almost amounting to a craze. Data of all sorts were collected by both governmental and private institutions, focusing on the social problems of a society that was experiencing the effects of rapid industrialization and urbanization. 'Statistical Societies' were formed, composed of concerned citizens who felt that these problems could be understood and dealt with only if they were reduced to the precision and objectivity of numbers. In 1835 the British Association for the Advancement of Science added a section on 'Statistics' (changed to 'Economics and Statistics' in 1856), thus officially recognizing the scientific importance of this work.

This 'statistical movement', as historians have called it, was a notable part of the campaign for social reform that was becoming an increasingly important element in English politics. The reformers of this period, like their successors who created the modern 'welfare state', assumed that problems such as crime, poverty, and unemployment were due primarily to social conditions, rather than defects in human character, and that they could be solved by education and changes in environmental conditions. This period of the 1830's and 1840's brought an enormous increase in factual information and its introduction into political debate, but there were no significant developments in the methods of analysis. Little more was done with the flood of data than to tabulate it and draw the simple inferences that could be done with common arithmetic. The development of sophisticated methods of statistical analysis using more advanced mathematics did not commence until the study of social problems was undertaken by those who regarded them as due, not to environmental factors, but to hereditary deficiencies.

Francis Galton was the initiator of this. He was a compulsive quantifier, numbering practically everything that captured his attention, but when his interest turned to human and social phenomena he realized that a compilation of raw data yields little useful information. He was not a good mathematician himself, but he could formulate problems in ways that enabled him to obtain assistance from others who were more skilled. Proceeding in this fashion, he solved the problem of measuring the relationship between different phenomena, creating the methods of correlation and regression analysis that are still today, though much refined, the basic tools of quantitative empirical research in the social sciences. Karl Pearson and R. A. Fisher were the two most important figures in the further development of statistical analysis in the period after Galton. All three were mainly interested in the genetic foundations of human behaviour and were convinced that social problems could be solved only by changing the incidence of good and bad traits in the human genome. Though the historian of statistics cannot neglect earlier work (e.g. by Jacques Bernoulli, Laplace, and Legendre, as well as Gauss and Quetelet) the period from the 1860s when Galton realized that the Gaussian curve could be used to describe the natural variation of a property in a population as well as measurement error, to the publication of Fisher's work on the mathematical foundations of statistical analysis in the 1920's, was the founding era of modern statistical methods. During this period, most of the creative work in the subject was inspired by the same social theory and social philosophy that the eugenics movement represented. The social policy promoted by the movement was devoid of scientific support, but the attempt to supply it created a discipline that today is indispensable to the scientific study of social phenomena.

2. Biology and theoretical social science

In the social science literature of the late nineteenth and early twentieth centuries there are prominent figures, such as Herbert Spencer and Walter Bagehot, who explicitly referred to biology (and especially to the theory of evolution) as the foundational paradigm of their own explanatory models of social phenomena; and there are numerous others who argued that the social sciences must strive to become more 'biological' or 'evolutionary'. Alfred Marshall, for example, spoke modestly of his own work in economic theory as constituting only the first part of a three-stage process that would progress from 'static' models to the construction of 'dynamic' ones, and eventually arrive at the much-to-be-desired 'Mecca' where economics would be a comprehensive 'biological science'. Thorstein Veblen, the first major figure in the development of American 'institutional economics', severely criticized the work of his contemporaries who were happily engaged upon the elaboration of Marshall's 'statics' for failing to push forward to the development of an 'evolutionary science'. Taken at face value, such remarks and the many similar ones that punctuate the social science literature of the period suggest that biology had a strong impact on the social sciences. But from the vantage point of the present, it is evident that the effects were small. Veblen could repeat his criticism of economics today, and extend it to the other social sciences, without much amendment. The modern literature of the various social disciplines (including *social* psychology and *social* anthropology) reveals little influence of biological theory or resort to biological factors. Spencer's contention that the aspiring sociologist must prepare himself by the study of biology is not reflected in the list of required courses that are typically prescribed for students majoring in sociology, and the same is true of the other social disciplines.

In order to amplify this point, even as briefly as I shall do here, it is necessary to distinguish between (1) the reductionist view that social phenomena are explainable only by reference to the biological factors that are the causal determinants of human behaviour; (2) the notion that in the domain of social phenomena there is a process at work that corresponds to the principle of 'natural selection'; and (3) the view that social change is *gradual* – 'nature does not make leaps' as Marshall, no less than Darwin, was fond of saying. The older social science literature reveals very little evidence supporting the view that the prominent theorists may be classified under the first two of these categories. None attempted to reduce social phenomena to biological factors, and none adopted Darwin's theory of evolution by natural selection as the paradigmatic model for the study of human social and cultural history. When this literature speaks of investigating social phenomena in a 'biological' and/or 'evolutionary' mode, the reference is almost entirely to the notion that socio-cultural development is characterized by the continuous accumulation of small changes rather than discrete 'leaps' from one social state to another.

This perception was regarded by many as novel and deserving explicit methodological note, because the traditional focus of historiography had been upon *political* history, typically divided into discrete eras separated by particular occurrences such as wars, dynastic changes, or other climacteric events marking large and rapid transformations in the social order. By a decade or two after the publication of Darwin's *Origin*, the words 'biology' and 'evolution' were linked closely together in common discourse, and the words 'evolutionary' and 'revolutionary' were used as general oppositional terms to refer, respectively, to continuous and discrete phenomena. When social scientists of this era referred to their work as 'biological' or 'evolutionary' in character they commonly meant only that they focused upon the small and steady changes that transform human society rather than the 'great events' that were the stock-in-trade of traditional historians.

Walter Bagehot is a case in point. His *Physics and Politics* (by which he meant the application of science to the study of society), published in 1872, was subtitled *Thoughts on the Application of the Principles of 'Natural Selection' and 'Inheritance' to Political Society*. Darwin thought highly of it, but it contains very little 'application' of his theory of evolution beyond the notion of gradual change. There is no use made in it of the ideas of competition and the 'survival of the fittest'. The same is true of Bagehot's two books that have won a permanent place in the literature of social science. In *The English Constitution* (1867), which has had a large influence on political theory on both sides of the Atlantic, he undertook to show that the central constitutional principle of the English system is the supremacy of Parliament, and argued that this was not clearly recognized because the changes that brought it about had been so small and gradual that they had passed unnoticed by political scientists. In *Lombard Street* (1873) he described how the Bank of England, a private corporation, had changed into an agency of the state, a central bank, so gradually that bankers, politicians, and economists were not aware of the transformation. In Bagehot's treatments, the development of England's political and financial institutions was 'evolutionary' only in the sense that it had taken place by the accumulation of small steps. If one goes to Bagehot's writings for evidence of some more specific impact of biology on theoretical social science, the trip is without yield.

The same is true of Herbert Spencer. Unlike the other social scientists who spoke of the need for evolutionary and biological approaches to social phenomena, Spencer actually studied biology with some care. But as we have seen above (Chapter 15 A 4), his evolutionism was a metaphysical principle that embraced all reality, not a specific or differentiating characteristic of biological and social phenomena, and he did not undertake to explain human social behaviour in terms of biological factors. His analogies between the organic and social domains served mainly to focus attention on functional specialization or the 'division of labour,' which, as a social phenomenon, derives more directly from Adam Smith and the classical economists than from von Baer's and Milne-Edwards's adaptation of it to biology. The notion that a system of competitive markets serves as a vehicle of social organization in what Spencer called an 'industrial' society, in contrast to the hierarchical organization of a 'militant' one, is not easily traceable to anything in the field of biology, but its indebtedness to Smith's 'invisible hand' and the analytical model of Ricardian economics is obvious. Spencer's individualism has a biological element, since it rests upon the proposition that central nervous systems are properties of individual organisms, not groups, but he does not construe mind as reducible to brain. Leonard T. Hobhouse, Spencer's most prominent successor in English sociology, wrote a great trilogy on social evolution (*Mind in Evolution*, 1901; *Morals in Evolution*, 1906; *Development and Purpose* 1913) in which he focused upon the autonomous capacity of the individual for original thought and innovative behaviour rather than on biological factors or the process of competition in a Darwinian mode of natural selection.

In the more recent social science literature, one continues to encounter frequent characterizations of this or that phenomenon as 'Darwinian', such as, for example, the notion that financial bankruptcy, which alters the population of business firms, is analogous to the mechanism by which 'unfit' organisms are destroyed in what Darwin called the 'struggle for life'. A. A. Alchian's essay on 'Uncertainty, Evolution, and Economic Theory' (*Journal of Political Economy*, 1950) has spawned a mini-literature that has attempted to replace the notion of the 'entrepreneur' as a conscious decision-making agent who 'optimizes' with firms that are 'adapted' to changes in the environment in a populational fashion by selection. Somewhat earlier, the first economist to attempt to graft a theory of economic development on to the trunk of neoclassical economics, J. A. Schumpeter, proceeded in a similar fashion by postulating the existence of a Gaussian-type natural distribution of 'innovative' capacities (see Scott Gordon, 'Alfred Marshall and the Development of Economics as a Science', in Ronald N. Giere and Richard S. Westfall, eds, *Foundations of Scientific Method: The Nineteenth Century*, 1973). Some recent writers rival Spencer in suggesting analogies that reveal isomorphisms between the biological and social domains. At the 1977 meeting of the American Economic Association, Jack Hirshleifer, an economist, claimed isomorphisms to exist between a 'species' and an 'industry', 'mutation' and 'innovation', 'mutualism' and 'exchange', and 'evolution' and 'progress', while Michael T. Ghiselin, a biologist, suggested that 'firms' are analogous to 'species' and 'employees' to 'organisms' (*American Economic Review: Papers and Proceedings*, 1978). More generally, Kenneth E. Boulding, in a series of books beginning with *A Reconstruction of Economics* (1950), has attempted to biologize economics, while Ghiselin, since the publication of his *The Economy of Nature and the Evolution of Sex* (1974), has campaigned steadily for the transformation of biology by the adoption of neoclassical economic models and the emulation of its methodological individualism. I think it is fair to say, though, that, as yet, neither discipline has been much affected by the other. Most notable are some striking recent cases in which biologists have been able to make constructive use of specific economic theories and, if we add these to older ones such as the adoption of Adam Smith's division of labour by von Baer in his work on embryology, the current, such as it is, seems to run from social science to biology rather than the other way round.

3. Sociobiology

The study of sociality in non-human species is well established in biology as part of the general study of 'ethology', or animal behaviour. Edward O. Wilson coined the term 'sociobiology' for this sub-discipline and used it for the title of his monumental work that surveyed in close detail virtually all that was known on the subject (*Sociobiology: the New Synthesis*, 1975). The body of this book contains only occasional general references to behaviour in *Homo sapiens*, and makes no use of the social science literature, but the first and final chapters constitute a virtual manifesto, demanding that the study of human social phenomena should be taken over by biologists. Wilson contends that evolutionary biology, and allied sciences such as neurophysiology, are now capable of tackling the subject of human sociality and investigating the causes of social problems which, in his view, have eluded the efforts of the established social science disciplines. Wilson's title phrase 'The New Synthesis' was not intended to refer to what had already been accomplished by biologists in the field of animal behaviour, but to the proposal that their modes of investigation should be extended to embrace man. 'Sociobiology' was proposed as the appropriate title for this more comprehensive science. Wilson amplified this thesis in *On Human Nature* (1978) and, in co-authorship with a physicist, Charles J. Lumsden, published *Genes, Mind, and Culture* (1981), which presented mathematical models showing how human behaviour might be incorporated within the theoretical framework of evolutionary biology.

Since Wilson's initial declaration in 1975 a large literature has appeared, supporting and criticizing the thesis that the study of human social phenomena should be reoriented to focus upon the genetic constituents of human nature. Reviewing this literature in detail would be a large task but, for the purposes of this book, it would also be premature, since the status of sociobiology as a science of human sociality is, as yet, undetermined. Twenty years hence it may be possible to write confidently about it as initiating a significant scientific advance, or as an unproductive diversion in the history of man's efforts to understand his social condition. For now, I restrict myself to a brief discussion of the main issues that have emerged in the sociobiology literature since 1975.

The notion that human behaviour and social problems are rooted in genetic factors is not new, as we have seen above in the discussion of eugenics. The contention that the social science disciplines have failed to provide answers to pressing social problems, and should give way to a new approach based on biology, is not new either. Alexis Carrel, a Nobel Prize winner in biology, argued so forty years before Wilson in his popular book *Man the Unknown* (1935). What is new is that there have been, during the past quarter of a century particularly, such enormous and fundamental advances in genetics, neurophysiology, biochemistry, and other related disciplines, with rapid development of scientific investigation in areas hitherto closed, that it would be dogmatic to claim that human social behaviour lies beyond the reach of modern biology.

I do not undertake here to predict the future, or to prescribe what social scientists or biologists should or should not attempt to do. The reader will quickly perceive, if he has not already done so, that I do not view the sociobiological approach to human social phenomena as a promising scientific research programme, but this is, necessarily, a tentative judgement, based on the fact that the debate over sociobiology has disclosed serious difficulties in such a programme, and that the substantive application of it has, so far, yielded no significant new knowledge.

In his initial enthusiasm for the potentialities of a synthesis of biology and the social sciences Wilson made unguarded statements which led some critics to infer that he embraced an unqualified biological determinism. The almost simultaneous publication of another widely discussed book, Richard Dawkins's *The Selfish Gene* (1976), seemed to support this view, since Dawkins argued that the behaviour of an organism reflects the manipulative power of its genes, which operate in a wholly 'selfish' way, that is, to reproduce *themselves*. But neither Wilson, nor Dawkins, nor most others who have emphasized the biological foundations of human behaviour, argue that it is totally determined by specific imperative instructions contained in the genome. The socio-biological research programme recognizes human social organization and cultural evolution as phenomena that differ significantly in their modes from those which govern the morphological structure and physiological processes of individual organisms and the modification of these over time by the mechanism of natural selection. Obscured at first by the polemical (and ideological) debate that followed the publication of Wilson's *Sociobiology*, the basic issues involved in pursuing the research programme he advocated can now be seen to focus on the following problems: (a) *What traits* of human behaviour can be identified as genetically controlled? (b) What is the *degree* of that control? (c) How can human *social organization* be explained in terms of genetic factors? (d) How are the different processes of organic and sociocultural *evolution* related? The reason why sociobiology has not been widely accepted as a promising scientific research programme is that satisfactory answers to these questions have not yet been provided. During the past two decades or so, biologists have demonstrated that a great deal of animal behaviour, including social behaviour, is tightly controlled by genetic factors, and there is good reason to believe that the role of such factors will be increased by further research, but the extension of the sociobiological research programme to human sociality remains problematic.

No reflective critic of sociobiology would argue, as A. R. Wallace did, that the human brain marks the creation of an organism that totally transcends its biological constituents, much less follow him in evoking spiritual or spiritualist explanations of human behaviour. But Wallace was correct in claiming that man's distinction from the other animals rests upon a brain capacity that is capable of supporting such uniquely human activities as abstract thought and languages capable of recording and transmitting complex ideas. Some defenders of sociobiology accept man's distinction from other animals in these respects but argue that since such things as human language depend upon anatomical structures that were produced by the Darwinian process of natural selection, therefore all human properties, including the development of elaborate sociocultural systems, must be rooted in biological factors and explainable in Darwinian terms (see Michael Ruse, *Taking Darwin Seriously*, 1986, chapter 4). This is a simplistic argument, which rests upon the uncontradictable proposition that everything an organism does in fact do evidences the existence of a biological capacity to do it. Birds fly but rabbits do not, and this may be explained by noting that the process of evolution was such that some organisms developed biological structures giving them the capacity to fly while others did not. But in order to explain how it is that man can fly, one has to refer to his acquisition of scientific and technical knowledge and his production of artefacts. The proposition that the modern system of air transport is due to the human brain is true, but uninformative. Such a statement fails to provide an explanation of specific features of man's culture. Similar propositions about culture in general are equally devoid of explanatory content.

The basic flaw in this kind of argument can be more clearly seen if we distinguish between biological capacity and *changes* in biological capacity. Rabbits could fly if, and only if, specific changes in their bodily structure took place which, in turn, could occur only through changes in the rabbit genome. The development of air transport by man was indeed dependent upon his possession of appropriate brain capacity but it required no *change* in that capacity, or any other alteration in his biological constitution. The humans who design, build, operate, and ride in aircraft today are not genetically different from our ancestors who had not even invented the wheelbarrow. Measured in terms of its size (or the number of 'bytes' of information that it can store), the human brain is no larger today than it was 100,000 years ago.

The rapid development of the brain from the 450 cc of man's immediate ancestors to the 1,650 cc of *Homo sapiens* continues to perplex evolutionary biologists, since it cannot simply be explained by the theory of natural selection. A recent appraisal of the scientific status of evolutionary theory by Elliot Sober, a philosopher (*The Nature of Selection*, 1984), makes the important point that there is a difference between selection *of* a property or trait and selection *for* it. Consider, say, a sieve with holes that are 3 cm in diameter. Put into the sieve a mixed collection of balls, white ones that are 2 cm in diameter and black ones that are 4 cm. After shaking, all the white balls will have fallen through and the black ones will remain. This mechanism selects *for* size, but selection *of* colour also takes place. With such linkages between properties as in this illustration, it is plain that one must not assume that every organic phenomenon is, in principle, traceable to an evolutionary process that selected *for* it. Whether this throws light on the development of the human brain I cannot say, but it does mean that human traits, and changes in such traits, are not necessarily due to a process that selects for them, as described by Darwinian theory. Critics of sociobiology who deny that human behaviour is significantly explainable in terms of genetic factors need not place themselves in general opposition to evolutionary biology; they are on secure enough ground in rejecting the proposition that the principle of natural selection is capable of explaining all organic phenomena. Not all selection is selection for traits that contribute to survival and reproductive success, and modes of evolutionary development are possible that are not Darwinian. This does not mean that the sociobiological approach to human sociality is fatally flawed, only that it is not necessarily the best way of investigating it. The sociobiology programme derives no support from the fact that the social sciences are unable to explain (or predict) phenomena such as crime, war, unemployment, and poverty as well as we might like; the test is whether sociobiology can do better.

The first step in the development of a sociobiological approach to human sociality is the precise identification of genetically controlled traits. The main difficulty here is that social phenomena are not linked to individual traits in an obvious way. Is war as a social phenomenon linked to the presence in human nature of 'aggression', or 'greed', or a 'territorial imperative', 'xenophobia', 'religiosity', or some other trait that is more fundamental than these? What should we be looking for when searching through the human chromosomes for the genetic factor that is a causal agent in war? Biologists who are now actively engaged in chromosomal mapping do not have to worry about this. For example, the genetic cause of the Rh negative factor that afflicts about 15 per cent of the human population was discovered by an investigation in search of the gene that codes for a specific protein which was known to be the immediate casual agent in the disease. Even if the social phenomenon of war has its root in a human trait, it is not obvious *what* trait is at work and, therefore, it is unclear what it is that the molecular biologist should be looking for at the level of the chromosome. We would have to know a great deal more than we do now about the causes of war before such work could commence. Sociobiological investigation of other social phenomena faces similar problems. Until we can identify their proximate causes in human traits we cannot proceed to discover their deeper causes in the human genome. At the present time all that can be said is that the role of genetic factors in human sociality is greater than zero. Describing that role even by such imprecise terms as 'large' or 'small' goes beyond the evidence that is available.

On the other hand, there would seem to be good empirical evidence that individual human traits are strongly affected by cultural factors – the process of 'enculturation' that we have frequently referred to in this book – and that significant changes can take place in those cultural factors themselves in ways that apparently do not depend upon changes in the genome of the population. The main evidence is the rapidity with which changes may occur in the traits of individuals and in their ambient culture. If, say, a child born in Japan of Japanese parents and ancestry that extends back undiluted for centuries is brought up in a community of Icelandic-Canadians in Manitoba, his ways of thinking and behaving at maturity resemble those of the other members of that community far more than those of his close genetic kin in Japan. The general culture of a community – its mores, values, customs, knowledge, and artefacts – may remain constant for centuries, but it is common experience that societies can undergo large cultural changes within the time-span of a generation or two. By contrast, scores of generations are necessary to produce even small changes in the morphology or physiology of an organic species by the process of natural selection. Herbert Spencer, despite his penchant for parallels between biological and social phenomena, pointed out that social evolution can take place much more rapidly than biological evolution, and argued that the former cannot therefore be construed as a manifestation of the biological process of natural selection. The different speeds of social and biological evolution remain, today, one of the main obstacles to efforts to tie social and biological phenomena firmly together.

Nevertheless, there is no warrant for regarding individual behaviour traits and the cultural characteristics of groups as totally independent of the human genome. If, as Wallace believed, the process of natural selection ceased to operate in the genus *Homo* when the species *Homo sapiens* emerged, the sociobiological approach to human sociality would be fatally flawed in its biological foundations. Some critics of sociobiology have argued along such lines, referring to the great plasticity of human behaviour and the rapidity of cultural change in support, but such evidence, though strong, is not conclusive. Cultural factors may act upon the human genome in a selectionist fashion, in the same general way that environmental factors operate in Darwinian theory, thus fixing in the genes coding instructions for certain adaptive behavioural traits. Responding to the criticisms that were advanced against Wilson's initial theories, some sociobiologists suggested that the appropriate way of tackling the problem of human sociality is by construing it as reflecting a 'co-evolutionary' process, that is, a mode of evolution in which cultural and genetic factors interact. The most ambitious attempt, to date, to sustain sociobiology in this way as a valid research programme for the scientific investigation of human sociality has been presented by Charles J. Lumsden and Edward O. Wilson in their *Genes, Mind, and Culture: the Coevolutionary Process* (1981; a popular version has been published as *Promethean Fire: Reflections on the Origin of Mind*, 1983).

Though somewhat muted, the original programme proposed by Wilson in *Sociobiology* inspires *Genes, Mind, and Culture*. Lumsden and Wilson construe 'co-evolution' as a process by which behaviour-controlling instructions are embodied in the human genome. The idea that the mechanism of organic evolution may operate in such a fashion that behavioural changes become fixed in the genome is not new. In the late nineteenth-century controversy over evolution it was strongly argued by the prominent novelist and essayist Samuel Butler (see, for example, part III of his 'The Deadlock in Darwinism', *Universal Review*, June 1890) as evidence in support of the Lamarckian notion that acquired characteristics may be transmitted from parent to progeny. Lumsden and Wilson do not follow this line of argument. Their intention is to construct a model that shows how behaviour-controlling instructions may be embodied in the genome by a strictly Darwinian mechanism. In earlier publications Wilson spoke of the genes as 'holding culture on a leash'; the object of *Genes, Mind, and Culture* is to present a theoretical model describing how that leash is formed (and modified) by the process of natural selection. The model is complex and is presented in a form that demands mathematical skills beyond my capacity, but numerous appraisals of it have been published (favourable and critical), and it is possible to obtain from these, and from the less technical summaries written by Lumsden and Wilson themselves, a fairly clear idea of the central argument. The model is built upon two conceptual pillars, called 'culturgens' and 'epigenetic rules'. The validity of the sociobiological research programme, as Lumsden and Wilson conceive it, depends upon the heuristic value of these concepts in the empirical study of social phenomena.

In order to understand these concepts it is useful to refer to their antecedents in traditional biology. A 'gene' (simply put) is a segment of a chromosome that codes for the assembly of chemical elements into a specific protein which governs a specific organic trait, such as hairy ears, eye colour, or the Rh negative factor noted above. (This disregards complications, such as the fact that chromosomes come in pairs and the two codes, or 'alleles', may differ; some traits require the joint participation of more than one chromosomal segment; and some segments participate in the control of more than one trait). There is no reason why genes cannot code for behavioural traits as well as for anatomical ones and, indeed, there is clear evidence from animal studies that they do. 'Culturgens' are conceived by Lumsden and Wilson as genes coding for human behaviour traits that constitute the culture of a group. Like other genes, these culturgens have been embodied in the human genome by a selective mechanism that is no different in principle from that by which our bodies (and the diversity in these among human groups) have come to be as they are. The concept of 'epigenetic rules' is derived from the notion of 'epigenesis' in embryology. Before the development of empirical embryology, many biologists viewed the egg (or the sperm) as containing within itself a complete organism, which only grows in size during its sojourn in the womb. Evidence that the organism begins with a single undifferentiated cell destroyed this notion of 'pre-formation', as it was called, which was replaced by the conception of embryological development as a process of guided construction which takes place after the egg and sperm have united to form a 'zygote' cell – that is, an 'epigenetic' process. (*Epi* is a Greek word sometimes used as a prefix in English meaning 'after'.) In the terminology used by Lumsden and Wilson, human cultural development is guided by 'epigenetic rules', which function in an analogous fashion to the process by which genes control the step-by-step development of bodily structure in the individual organism. The distinction between a 'culturgen' and an 'epigenetic rule' is rather unclear, but the heart of the argument is that the human genome contains behaviour-controlling instructions which, like the other elements there, are the product of an adaptive evolutionary process. Since culture plays a selective role in that process and is, in turn, the product of behaviour, genetic and cultural evolution 'proceed as a coupled system'.

The mathematical model presented by Lumsden and Wilson undertakes not only to specify how such a complex system works, but to estimate the speed with which culturgens and/or epigenetic rules can be embodied in the human genome. They arrive at the conclusion that fifty generations are sufficient to accomplish this, which they call the 'thousand-year rule'. This being so, the many thousands of years that have elapsed since the dawn of human sociality are enough time for a great many behaviour-controlling genes to have developed by way of the co-evolutionary process. In terms of the phenomena that social scientists are interested in, however, a thousand years is a very long time. Even if this demonstration were valid (which critics have contested) it is not obvious that it calls for a reorientation of the traditional modes of explanation in the social sciences in the direction of genetic factors. In Lumsden's and Wilson's view, however, such a reorientation is essential because, without it, the explanation of social phenomena is superficial, paying attention only to the range of behaviour that is permitted by the leash that constrains it instead of the more fundamental factors that determine the leash itself.

The co-evolutionary model presented by Lumsden and Wilson does not, it seems to me, succeed in supporting the claims for a sociobiological approach to human sociality. The criticisms of Wilson's earlier statements noted above remain unanswered. The proposition that human culture is held on a leash that is *short* and that, therefore, the weight of genetic factors is *large*, still has the status of an assumption; no empirical evidence has been furnished in support of it by Lumsden and Wilson, or by anyone else thus far. No specific 'culturgen' of 'epigenetic rule' has yet been identified. The central problem of the social sciences, the investigation of the processes through which individual behaviour is co-ordinated to form a co-operative social system, is not addressed by the Lumsden–Wilson model. It does suggest a possible scenario of human evolution in which genes and culture interact, but its central concepts do not appear to have heuristic value in the empirical study of social phenomena.

One of these points of criticism deserves some further note. The theory presented in *Genes, Mind, and Culture* is exclusively focused on factors that are presumed to govern *individual* behaviour. The co-evolutionary process describes how human culture may act in a selectionist fashion to embody behaviour-controlling factors in the genome, but no attempt is made to explain how humans are able to co-operate with one another in organized groups to achieve goals that are far beyond the capacity of the individual members. This is rather surprising in view of the fact that the initial inspiration for sociobiology was provided by a theory that was the first to offer a plausible explanation of the sociality that characterizes various non-human species such as bees and ants. In these species some phenomena are evident that are difficult to explain with the Darwinian theory of natural selection. Individual insects, for example, may be specialized in their behaviour and even in their anatomical structure to perform particular tasks for the colony. Many of these specialized castes are sterile, taking no part in the procreation of new generations. How is it possible for the genetic instructions that govern such specialization to be transmitted from one generation to another? How indeed is it possible for such properties to have arisen in the course of organic evolution? Darwin himself noted this difficulty and remarked that the existence of sterile castes and behaviour traits that are 'altruistic' (benefiting the colony at the expense of the individual) could be a fatal flaw in the theory of natural selection. For a century after the publication of the *Origin of Species* this problem was neglected by evolutionary biologists but, in 1964, W. D. Hamilton published a remarkable paper which appeared to solve it ('The Genetical Theory of Social Behaviour', *Journal of Theoretical Biology*).

Hamilton observed that the chromosomal structure of insects such as bees and ants is peculiar. Some individuals have the two sets of chromosomes that characterize almost all organic species, but others are generated from unfertilized eggs and have only one set. Hamilton showed that, because of this, the individual members of an ant or bee colony share more common genes than the members of other species do. The individual who performs an act of self-sacrifice eliminates his own chromosomes from the gene pool of the group, but if his act preserves the lives of others who have the same genes in their chromosomes, it may result in a net increase in terms of common genes. Such a net increase is possible for all organic species but, because of their chromosomal structure, it is more easily attained by species like ants and bees, and therefore, it is claimed, accounts for their extraordinary degree of sociality. The genes that programme the individual insects to perform altruistic acts would not be eliminated by natural selection; indeed, by improving the colony's ability to compete in the struggle for existence, they can replicate themselves more effectively. Man is not like the social insects in chromosomal structure, so no one would undertake to argue that human sociality is explainable by reference to this factor, but Hamilton's theory has general implications, since the degree of gene-sharing among human individuals, while not as great as among the members of an ant colony, is, nevertheless, large. E. O. Wilson, whose own field of research was the social insects, was struck by the possibility that human sociality could be explained in a similar fashion, by focusing on the selectionist viability of genes that programme individuals to perform altruistic acts for the benefit of the group.

This notion articulates with a theme that is prominent in the history of social thought. In the utopian literature, for example, the ideal society is commonly depicted as one in which individual self-interest has been suppressed and the members' behaviour is oriented to the general welfare of the group. The notion that altruistic or group-centred behaviour is meritorious and constructive while self-centred behaviour is sordid, wicked, and baneful to social life is conspicuous in almost all genres of social philosophy. The long history of the organism–society metaphor reflects the notion that the good society is one in which specialized individuals contribute to the collective life, and derive their own material (and psychological) sustenance from it, just as the individual organs of the body serve, and are served by, the organism as a whole. Such views are common in modern political thought, with the nation-state usually construed as the proper collective entity.

Whatever might be the ethical merits of such ideas, the mainstream social sciences have not proceeded along these lines in their efforts to explain the dynamics of social organization. Hobbes, Locke, and Montesquieu established a tradition of political analysis based upon the view that self-interest is the dominant characteristic of human nature. Since their times, political science has focused upon the control and channelling of self-interest by organized co-ercive power, a complex problem, since those who wield such power are not less self-interested than other men. Constitutional theory, as we have seen (Chapter 4), has persistently concerned itself with controlling state power by institutional artefacts rather than by following Plato's notion that the key to good government is the selection of persons who can be relied upon to work for the general welfare. Orthodox economic theory has, similarly, been centrally concerned to elucidate the co-ordinating dynamics of a market system in a functionally differentiated economy whose individual producers and consumers are presumed to be primarily motivated to serve their own interests. Sociologists have focused their attention on the process of enculturation and the control of individual behaviour by social institutions, with more emphasis than other social scientists on the customs and mores that orient individual behaviour to collective ends, but not even Durkheim undertook to show that man is a social animal because he is an altruistic one. No social scientist who has not surrendered to a deeply blinkered individualist ideology would deny that man can entertain altruistic sentiments or that he does in fact behave from time to time in ways that subordinate the interests of self to those of others or to the collectivity but, so far, the conception of human nature as dominated by self-interest has been of more heuristic value in constructing models of social organization.

The genome of a species may contain codes that, through the chemistry of protein synthesis, control behaviour. Empirical evidence seems to show beyond doubt that the behaviour of the individual ant is genetically directed, and that the co-ordination of functions in an ant colony is accomplished by such codes. It cannot be denied, therefore, that the DNA molecule has the capacity to serve as a vehicle for the construction and operation of a complex social organization. But this does not mean that it is the only mode through which such phenomena can be mediated. In addition to the genetic mode, the co-ordination of individual behaviour in a social system may be achieved by the process of learning and enculturation, by a hierarchical status structure in which the co-ordinating commands (and sanctions against disobedience) are initiated at the top and transmitted downward, and by the mechanism modelled in economic theory as a system of voluntary exchange. These non-genetic modes of co-ordination are not capable of forming 'perfect societies', if that term is construed, as it is by E. O. Wilson, to refer to social systems in which the individuals are 'fully subordinated to the colony as a whole' (*Sociobiology*, 1975, p. 379), but they obviously play important roles in the less perfect societies that humans inhabit.

From the ecological point of view, the most striking feature of the modern world is the extent to which it is dominated by the species *Homo sapiens*. Compared to many other animals, man is a clumsy and defenceless weakling, badly equipped to compete in a primal struggle for existence. His paramount position in the ecology of the planet is due to an extraordinary capacity to acquire, store, and transmit knowledge, and to construct artefacts that modify and control his environment. Even casual observation is sufficient to demonstrate that these capacities are more social than individual, reflecting the development of modes of social organization more significantly than anatomical and physiological properties. Social organization by means of complex political and economic systems is unknown in any other species – and they do not require the kind of subordination of the individual to the group that Wilson regards as ideal. The social sciences have had some modest success in modelling these modes of organization and in identifying their limitations and weaknesses. If sociobiology is to become a research programme that can replace the social sciences it will have to show that it is able to explain the structure and dynamics of human social organization more effectively than economics, political science, and sociology are able to do. This is not in principle undemonstrable, but it has not yet been demonstrated.

Note: Parts of section A 3 are drawn from my paper 'Darwin and Political Economy', *Journal of the History of Biology*, 1989.

Chapter 17

The development of economic theory

In Chapter 5 we began our study of the history of economics with the French Physiocrats who, in the 1760's, constructed the first systematic and comprehensive economic model. François Quesnay and his disciples failed to initiate a continuing school of economic thought but they deserve a prominent place in the history of social science for a number of reasons. Their classification of the members of society as 'agriculturalists', 'artisans', and 'landowners' introduced the notion that the fundamental structure of the social order consists of classes that are defined in terms of their *economic* roles and status. This became, with modifications, a central feature of orthodox classical economics and the grand social theories of Karl Marx and Friedrich Engels. The Physiocratic notion that the agricultural sector of the economy produces a 'surplus' introduced an idea that, again with modifications, played a prominent role in the Ricardian and Marxian models and, as we shall see in this chapter, the 'neoclassical' economic analysis which, in the later nineteenth and early twentieth centuries, replaced the Ricardian model. Though they did not advocate *'laissez-faire'* as a general policy, the Physiocrats viewed economic processes as governed by general 'laws', analogous to those that control natural phenomena, thus introducing the nomological conception of economics, which has dominated the methodological stance of the discipline down to the present day. The most prominent feature of the Physiocratic model, the conception of the economy as a circular flow of expenditures and incomes, was not used by the classical economists. It lurked in the background of the nineteenth-century literature that focused on the functioning of the monetary system, but it re-emerged prominently as an analytical paradigm in the 1930s when the sub-discipline of 'macroeconomics' began to be developed in a systematic fashion.

The main deficiency of the Physiocratic model was its failure to address the problem of economic *organization*. In a scientific analysis of a system that is composed of specialized parts, it is necessary to explain how the activities of these parts are co-ordinated. One of the reasons why Adam Smith, rather than François Quesnay, is usually regarded as the founder of scientific economics is that the discussion of the division of labour in the first three chapters of the

Wealth of Nations is followed by an analysis of markets, which recognizes the role of prices in the co-ordination mechanism. In the Physiocratic model, prices serve only as a numeraire, a counting device that enables one to aggregate the diverse products of the economy into an omnibus magnitude. In the *Wealth of Nations* prices serve this function in Smith's examination of the national income and its distribution among the socioeconomic classes but, in addition, his 'theory of value' is used to describe how the specialized activities of the various parts of the economy mesh together. Classical economics is a mixture of these focuses, which today are differentiated as two distinct branches: 'macro-economics' and 'microeconomics'.

This distinction is as important in the history of economics as it is today in the standard academic curriculum. Modern microeconomic analysis reflects a line of development that began in the 1870's. The diligent historian can identify precursors, some of whom clearly formulated problems and analytical concepts that economists generally did not take up until decades later. But our chief concern in this book is with the main lines of historical development in the social sciences, so in this chapter we shall use the dates noted above as our starting points in tracing the development of modern economic theory. Some historians emphasize the differences between modern economics and classical 'political economy' to the extent of using the term 'revolution' to refer to the innovations of the 1870's and the 1930's. Others have argued the contrary, that modern economics has been a continuous 'evolutionary' development of the Ricardian model. The reader will perceive that I lean to the former view, treating the literature of the 1870's and the 1930's as initiating concepts and modes of economic analysis that differ, in very important respects, from classical political economy.

A. THE NEOCLASSICAL THEORY OF ECONOMIC ORGANIZATION

Webster's dictionary defines a 'classic' as a work 'of the highest class; being a model of its kind; excellent; standard; authoritative; established'. Historians of economics refer to David Ricardo's *Principles of Political Economy and Taxation* (1817) as the foundation book of 'classical economics', since, for a long time thereafter, it met the requirements of this definition. All the leading economists of the mid-nineteenth century employed the concepts and mode of analysis of Ricardo and accepted, without significant alteration, his central theories of value, income distribution, and economic development. Karl Marx departed from Ricardo to a greater extent than others but he also worked with an analytical structure that was essentially Ricardian, and modern historians (including Marxists) usually characterize him as a 'classical economist'.

The use of the term 'neoclassical' to refer to the body of economic theory that was constructed in the later nineteenth and early twentieth centuries is somewhat misleading, since it may seem to imply that no fundamental change occurred, the new model differing in detail and refinement but preserving the essential features of the Ricardian one. The term is justified, however, if we read it in terms of the dictionary definition quoted above to mean the economic analysis that came to be accepted by the great majority of professional economists as 'standard, authoritative, established', replacing the Ricardian analysis which had previously enjoyed that status. This is what is taught today in university courses in microeconomics, so we are here examining the historical origins of that branch of modern economics.

Though Ricardian economics was 'classical', it was subjected to a great deal of criticism. The literature of the mid-nineteenth century contains such strong attacks on the various elements of the Ricardian model that a leading historian of economics speaks of 'the bankruptcy and disintegration of classical economics in the 1850s and 1860s' (Mark Blaug, *Economic Theory in Retrospect*, 1985, p. 299). But scientists, unlike business firms, do not shut up shop when bankrupt. J. S. Mill's *Principles of Economics* (1848), which reiterated all the essential propositions of Ricardo's model, was accepted by economists for a long time as an authoritative statement of the best that economists had to offer. In dealing with complex phenomena, theories are indispensable tools of scientific thought. A basic theory is never abandoned because it is shown to be deficient; old tools are discarded only when better ones become available. In this respect economists are not different from physicists or other practitioners of natural science. But in the study of social phenomena, lacking the ability to experiment or otherwise to test theories definitively, it may take longer for the superiority of a new model to be recognized. At any rate, neoclassical concepts and modes of analysis were not embraced by economists quickly. The basic innovations took place in the 1870's. Alfred Marshall's *Principles of Economics* was published in 1890, but Mill's book continued to be used as a text in American university courses for another ten years or more, and most other textbooks up to the first World War were more classical than neoclassical in content. If by the word 'revolution' one means *rapid* change, the developments recounted in this section were not revolutionary.

I shall be emphasizing here the differences between classical and neoclassical economics, but we should note at the outset that in their fundamental conceptions of the economy the two are the same. The object of analysis is a world characterized by division of labour, private property in the means of production, and markets. No attention is paid to activities by which individuals or small groups satisfy their economic wants by direct production for themselves. Everyone sells his personal services and the services of his property, or uses them to produce commodities for sale. The income so obtained is used to purchase consumer goods or to invest in further acquisitions of property. It is an economy in which the specialized activities of individuals are organized systematically by the market mechanism. The role of the state in providing a general framework of law is recognized, but the state makes no explicit appearance in the basic models, either as an agent engaged in the production of goods and services or as a participant in the mechanism by which economic activities are co-ordinated. The markets that constitute the organizational mechanism are construed by both classical and neoclassical economics as characterized by competition. Classical and neoclassical economists did not deny that the state acts as an important agent in the production of what we now call 'public goods', that state policy typically goes far beyond the provision of a legal system to serve the needs of private enterprise, and that many markets in a typical capitalistic economy are not fully competitive. But these features of the real economy were not incorporated into the classical model, nor into the neoclassical one in its initial form.

These similarities, though important, should not be overstressed, since the analytical structures that were built upon such common simplifying assumptions were dissimilar and, what is more important, proved to have different capacities to be modified and extended to deal with the complexities of the real world. The modern theory of non-competitive markets and the analysis of the diverse roles of the state in the economy that one finds in standard textbooks are extensions of the neoclassical model. The followers of Ricardo did not achieve much in these areas, not for lack of interest and effort, but because the model with which they worked was severely limited as a heuristic instrument. The main reason for this was that the classical economists did not in fact construct an explanation of how markets function as an organizational mechanism in an economy composed of functionally specialized elements. They knew, intuitively, that the system works through the information contained in the prices of commodities and factors of production, but they did not succeed in translating this intuition into an explicit account of the market mechanism.

The central defect in the classical model was its theory of value. As we saw in Chapter 9, Ricardo attempted to sustain the proposition that the relative prices of commodities in competitive markets are determined by the relative quantities of labour required to produce them. Even if the role of inputs other than labour is given more quantitative weight than Ricardo was willing to grant, a theory of value that construes market prices as determined solely by the conditions of production suffers from a fundamental defect in that it focuses only upon the sellers and disregards the role of the buyers in market transactions. As Alfred Marshall remarked, this is like trying to cut a piece of paper with one blade of a pair of scissors. Unable to resolve Adam Smith's paradox that some commodities, like water, are very useful but sell at a low price while others, like diamonds, command a high price though not being of much use, the classical economists were locked into a framework of market analysis that neglects the demand side of the process. They knew that the wants of consumers are transmitted, through the market mechanism, to those who produce commodities for sale, but they could not give an explanation of the transmission process.

Adam Smith made some suggestive remarks on this matter but Ricardo did not follow them up. He sometimes resorted to heroic assumptions such as, for example, construing the working class as spending all its income on 'corn' and treating the quantity of corn each person consumes as a given amount, independent of the price at which it can be bought in comparison to the prices of other goods. Even in Ricardo's day, the English labourer spent a good deal of his income on non-food items and his food basket contained many things besides bread and other grain products. All scientific theories must make use of simplifying assumptions, but there may be a great difference between simplifications that the theorist finds convenient and ones that have heuristic power in examining the phenomena of the real world. The classical theory of value was unable to explain how the tastes of consumers, and changes in those tastes, provide producers, through market prices, with information as to what commodities, and what quantities of them, it is profitable to produce.

The most important element lacking in the Ricardian model was an analysis of the demand side of the market in terms of the actions of economic agents as *consumers*. In his essay 'On the Definition of Political Economy' (1836), John Stuart Mill objected strenuously to the tendency of contemporary writers to describe the science as dealing with 'production, distribution, and *consumption*'. Political economy, he said, 'has nothing to do with the consumption of wealth' and went on to point out that 'We know not of any *laws* of the *consumption* of wealth as the subject of a distinct science: they can be no other than the laws of human enjoyment,' which require no special attention from the economist. Many of the early critics of Ricardo focused their attacks on his theory of value, and some of them made contentions that anticipated the neoclassical analysis of consumption, but they were not followed up, and it was not until the 1870's, a full century after Adam Smith's statement of the water–diamonds paradox, that the construction of an alternative model began as a continuous historical development.

Here we encounter another of those curious 'multiples' in the history of science: occasions when two or more persons, independently of one another, make an important innovation. In this case three economists, William Stanley Jevons in England, Carl Menger in Austria, and Léon Walras in Switzerland, put forward the notions now called the concept of 'marginal utility' and the 'law of diminishing utility'. Jevons's *Theory of Political Economy* and Menger's *Grundsätze der Volkswirtschaftslehre* were both published in 1871, Walras's *Eléments d'économie politique pure* in 1874. With the aid of these analytical tools, Adam Smith's paradox is easily resolved. The high utility of water and the low utility of diamonds that he noted refer to their general usefulness as commodities. If a consumer had to consider his state of affairs if he were deprived of these commodities altogether he would assuredly rank water much higher than diamonds. But this is economically irrelevant, since the transactions that take place in markets deal in small unit quantities of commodities. Consider an economy in which water is bought and sold in litre units. The consumer who is considering the purchase of a litre of water pays no attention to the general usefulness of water: the relevant question for him is the *marginal* utility of a litre of water, that is, the contribution that an *additional* litre can make to his well-being. This depends on the amount he is already consuming, per day, let us say. If he is consuming very little and is exceedingly thirsty, an additional litre of water will yield a high marginal utility; if he is consuming a great deal and the use to which he would put an additional litre were, say, watering house plants, its marginal utility would be very much less. As the amount of water used (in a time period) increases, the marginal utility of water declines: this is the 'law of diminishing (marginal) utility'. It is misleading, therefore, to speak of the 'usefulness' of water without reference to the quantity of it that is consumed. If water is sold at a uniform price per litre (without differentiating between buyers or the various uses that they make of it) then that price will be low if the quantity is large, since only a low price will induce consumers to purchase a commodity whose marginal utility is low. Speaking generally, water is very useful and diamonds are not, as Adam Smith observed, but water is plentiful and diamonds are scarce, and it is their marginal utilities that operate in the markets where relative prices are determined.

Through the concept of marginal utility and the law of diminishing utility, a new theory of value was constructed that recognized the active role of demand. In their initial enthusiasm for the new approach, some of the early neoclassical economists argued that values are determined *solely* by utility, thus attempting to construct an explanation that focused exclusively upon the demand side of the market mechanism, just as their predecessors had focused exclusively on supply. Remnants of this approach remain today in the writings of economists who regard themselves as descendants of the 'Austrian school' initiated by Carl Menger, but the 'Cambridge school' founded by Alfred Marshall, which dominated the profession of economics during the first half of the twentieth century, modelled the market process as a conjunction of demand-side and supply-side factors. The modern student of economics, who has learned to use the apparatus of demand and supply curves in the analysis of market processes, can read Marshall's *Principles* with the sense of being in familiar territory. Microeconomic theory has been greatly refined during the past century, but it remains, in it essentials, 'Marshallian economics'.

The economists who followed Marshall's lead did not simply join the new theory of consumer demand, based on marginal utility, to the existing classical theory of supply. The analysis of the production side of the economy was reconstructed, using the concept of the 'margin' more generally than its initiators of the 1870's had envisaged. We will examine this feature of neoclassical theory in a moment. Here I want to note that the word 'margin' is the neoclassical economist's term for a concept that had been already established for a long time in mathematics and had been used, since Newton, in the analysis of physical phenomena. If we express two factors, A and X, as functionally related, i.e. $A = f(X)$, the economist's marginal magnitude is simply the first derivative of this function. If A is the total utility derived from consuming a quantity of a commodity designated by X, the marginal utility, at that level of X, is dA/dX. The law of diminishing utility is the assertion that the second derivative of the function is negative. In view of the power of the differential calculus as an analytical device in the natural sciences, it is not surprising that economic theory was tremendously influenced by the development of a concept that permitted the formulation of models in calculus terms. As it turned out, the part of the theory of marginal utility that had the most profound and extensive impact on economics was the margin concept as an analytical device, rather than the substantive proposition that utility is a determinant of value in a market economy. Modern economics is highly mathematical. Prior to Jevons and Walras (who were both convinced that effective economic analysis requires the use of mathematics) there had been some attempts to formulate economic theory in mathematical terms, but it was the concept of the margin that began the continuous line of development that led, though slowly at first, to modern mathematical economics.

According to Ricardo's theory of value, the market price of a commodity reflects its production history. In order to produce a commodity, certain costs are incurred: the compensation that must be paid to labourers for their work (i.e. wages), and the compensation that must be paid to investors to induce them to allow their wealth to be used in production instead of consuming it (i.e. interest). Labourers must be paid wages, not only because they must have income in order to live, but because 'work' is, by definition, an unpleasant activity that will not be performed gratuitously. Capitalists must be paid interest because production processes take time, and those who invest wealth must wait for their income, another activity that will not be performed without reward. The money costs of production therefore reflect 'real' costs: the dislike of work and waiting. Rent, according to Ricardo, is not an element in a commodity's cost of production because the services of land require no compensation. The rent income of landlords is a surplus of value that landlords obtain, not because of any personal sacrifice in contributing to production, but because they are the legally designated owners of a factor that is scarce, and fixed in quantity.

The neoclassical economists regarded this conception of cost as fundamentally wrong. By focusing on the compensation that must be paid to individuals to induce them to work and invest, it adopted a concept which, while meaningful from the point of view of the commercial enterprise, failed to identify the essential nature of cost when viewed in terms of the economy as a whole. From the social point of view, the crucial fact is that the act of producing any particular commodity uses up productive resources that could have been used to produce something else. In a Robinson Crusoe economy, the true economic cost incurred by Crusoe in producing fish with a net is not that he must wait for the fish while he is engaged in making the net and that he finds casting the net (and making it) onerous, but derives from the fact that he could have devoted his time and effort to harvesting coconuts, or to other activities. So the economic cost of fish is the coconuts, and/or other things, that could have been obtained. The same is true of a complex economy of many persons. Everything that is produced involves using productive resources that have alternative uses. From the standpoint of the economy as a whole, the unpleasantness of work and the undesirability of waiting are irrelevant. In any economy that has 'scarce' (i.e. limited) resources, the true sacrifice involved in producing something is the other things that could have been produced. This is the notion of 'alternative cost' or 'opportunity cost' that plays a central role in the theory of value taught today in introductory courses in microeconomics. An important implication of this conception of cost is that all factors of production are alike from the economic point of view. The classical distinction between 'labour' as the human factor, 'capital' as the non-human but man-made factor, and 'land' as the natural resource factor has no economic significance. All factors are scarce in supply (relative to the demand for them) and the cost of using a unit of any of them in the production of a commodity is the marginal utility of the other commodities that are sacrificed by so doing.

Any model of the market mechanism as a system of economic organization must explain the determinants of the prices of factors of production as well as the prices of consumer goods, and it must show how the markets in which production factors are bought and sold are linked to the markets for consumer goods. These tasks were poorly performed by the classical model. In the 1890's, the neoclassical economists applied the concept of the margin to the production side of the economy and developed a different theory to explain the determinants of wage rates and the prices of other production factors. The central pillar of this part of neoclassical theory is the concept of 'marginal productivity'. It was, in fact, an extension of Ricardo's analysis of agricultural production to all industries. Ricardo had argued that when increased quantities of labour are applied to a given plot of land, production increases, but at a diminishing rate: the celebrated 'law of diminishing returns'. Formulated in marginal terms, i.e. focusing explicitly on the *additional* quantities of output obtained when successive units of labour are applied to the land, the argument is that this 'marginal product' of labour declines. Ricardo viewed this as a special property of agriculture; manufacturing does not display diminishing (marginal) returns. The neoclassical economists argued that the phenomenon occurs in all industries, and every factor of production yields a distinct marginal product, which depends (in part) on the quantity of other factors with which it is combined. Accordingly, one can notionally specify the marginal product of labour, the marginal product of capital, and the marginal product of land, in every line of commodity production. In mathematical terms, the equation $A = f(X, Y, Z)$ is a 'production function' in which the output of a commodity, A, is expressed as a function of the quantities X, Y, and Z of three factors. The marginal product of labour (X, say) is the first partial derivative of A with regard to X; and so on for the other factors. The law of diminishing returns states that, beyond a certain point, the second partial derivative of each of these factors becomes negative.

These notions provide a theory of the demand for labour and other factors which links together the prices of the production factors and the prices of the consumer goods they produce. The marginal product of labour, multiplied by the price of the product, tells the entrepreneur what revenue he will obtain if he hires an additional unit of labour, uses it in production, and sells the resulting product. The wage rate tells him what costs he will incur by doing so. These magnitudes determine the quantity of labour that the entrepreneur will employ. He will hire additional units if the value of labour's marginal product is greater than the wage rate, and he will reduce his labour force if that value is less than the wage rate. In the ideal world of perfect competition, where individual buyers and sellers have no power to affect the wage rate or the prices of commodities, the wage rate will be equal to the value of the marginal product of labour in all industries. The same argument is made for the other factors of production. The demand for capital and the demand for land are determined by the values of their respective marginal products and, with perfect competition, at equilibrium, will be equal, respectively, to the interest rate and rent rate.

Some of the early neoclassical economists interpreted the concept of alternative cost to mean that the classical distinction between labour, capital, and land as categorically different factors of production is invalid, since the notion of marginal productivity and the law of diminishing returns applies to all production factors without exception or distinction. But Marshall, and others who were less inclined to stress the 'revolutionary' character of marginal analysis, recognized that the theory of marginal productivity explains only the demand side of the market for factors of production. On the supply side, the markets for labour, capital and natural resources differ significantly from one another. The distinctions between them have been retained in modern economic theory, not as ontologically 'essential' differences, but as empirical differences in their conditions of supply. Ricardo's theory of rent, for example, is retained in modern economic analysis, but not as a phenomenon that applies only to agriculture because of the unique properties of land. Ricardo himself recognized that his theory of rent depended upon the empirical proposition that the total quantity of land is fixed, as a natural fact. Neoclassical theory extends this by recognizing that there are also other factors of production which are naturally fixed in quantity; that some factors may be artificially fixed in quantity by the actions of the state or those of private persons in special circumstances; and that even factors whose amount can be increased are fixed in the short run because it takes time to increase an economy's stock of them. In all such cases Ricardo's theory of rent applies. Thus we find modern economists referring to the income yielded by the unique talent of a famous musician, or that derived from a monopoly or the possession of a patent, or that obtained temporarily by the suppliers of goods or services for which demand has increased but the supply has not yet responded, as 'rent'. To the layman's ear this is a peculiar way of speaking, but it is a very important proposition in economic analysis.

In another respect the neoclassical theory of production constitutes a more fundamental departure. The classical economists not only thought of wages, interest (or profit), and rent as reflecting the categorical differences between the basic factors of production, but they construed them as the incomes of three distinct social classes: labourers, capitalists, and landlords. Ricardo's theory of the prices of production factors was therefore also a theory of the distribution of the national income in a society composed of three social classes. This class-focused analysis played a central role in Ricardo's model of economic development and, with amendment, in Karl Marx's economic, social, and historical theories.

One of the deficiencies of classical theory is that it treats the factor categories as if they are internally homogeneous, paying little attention to the fact that, for example, there are many different kinds of labour, differentiated by skill and other important considerations, and many different types and grades of land. This presents no serious difficulty for neoclassical theory, since its mode of analysis does not involve the specification of three or any other fixed number of production factors. One may distinguish as many kinds of labour as one wishes and notionally ascribe to each its own marginal productivity schedule. In principle, one could have a separate schedule for every person. The grouping of factors into categories, in the mode of neoclassical theory, may be determined freely by the economist, on heuristic grounds, to suit the needs of theoretical analysis and the technical capacity of empirical research; they are not presumed to be determined by objective social facts that the economist is bound to accommodate.

As a result of this, the social class orientation of economic theory that the Physiocrats initiated, and the classical economists adopted, plays no significant role in the neoclassical model. Some Marxist critics of neoclassical theory have claimed that it is a mere exercise in capitalistic apologetics, deliberately constructed in order to suppress the focus on class relations and class conflict that Marx had revealed to be the fundamental characteristic of the capitalist system. The historical record fails to support this charge. Among the initiators of marginal utility theory, only Menger paid any attention to Marx, and the subsequent literature in which the marginal apparatus was developed does not indicate that other marginalist economists were much interested in confounding Marxian theory. Whether the lack of a social class orientation in neoclassical economics is a defect or not is another question, the answer to which depends upon what it is that one takes to be the purpose of economic theory.

For the orthodox classical economists, the main task of economic theory was the construction of a model of economic development and the use of that model to identify the kinds of governmental policies that promote development and those that retard it. For Marx and his followers, economic theories are constructed in order to reveal the mechanism by which capitalism operates as a system of exploitation and to demonstrate that capitalism, like all economic systems preceding it, necessarily generates forces that lead to its destruction and replacement. The neoclassical economists eschewed such attempts at historical dynamics and focused instead on the construction of a model of an economy that would provide a positive analysis of the market mechanism as a system of economic organization, and the derivation of general normative criteria by which the market mechanism, or any other system of economic organization, could be evaluated. The neoclassical model is 'static' in the sense that it deals with an economy in which certain basic elements are regarded as constant: the size of the population, the tastes of consumers, the stock of capital and natural resources, and the technology of production. In such a restricted hypothetical world, the central economic problem is the allocation of productive resources among the various uses to which they can be put. Robinson Crusoe, all alone on his island, must determine what to produce day by day, i.e. how to allocate the productive resources he possesses. His well-being depends upon this. In an economy of many persons, with extensive division of labour, the same task must, somehow, be performed, and the general economic welfare of the society will depend upon the effectiveness of the mechanism that performs it. The objectives of neoclassical microeconomics are (1) to establish criteria of maximum efficiency, that is, normative criteria which, if met, would maximize the general economic welfare; and (2) to construct a positive model of the market mechanism that permits it to be evaluated according to such criteria.

The leading neoclassical economists did not contend that the allocation of resources in a static economy is all-important and that the factors held constant in their model are of negligible significance. We noted earlier in discussing the technique of *ceteris paribus* as a scientific procedure (Chapter 9 F), that it is sometimes used to refer to a situation, such as in a laboratory experiment, where the factors assumed to be constant are indeed constant; sometimes to refer to factors that are considered to be quantitatively negligible; and sometimes it is used to establish a simple model as a first step in an extended analysis that will progressively incorporate more and more of the factors initially neglected. Most of the neoclassical economists viewed themselves as engaged in the third of these exercises in model-building. Alfred Marshall spoke of the 'Mecca' of the economist as consisting of the construction of a grand model of 'economic biology' which would incorporate changes in population, technology, the stock of productive resources, and even changes in people's tastes and preferences. The journey to this Mecca must, however, be taken in stages, beginning with the construction of 'economic statics' and proceeding from there to 'economic dynamics'. Only after long and careful work in these two modes could the shrine of 'economic biology' be approached. Marshall, modestly but correctly, regarded his own work as restricted to the first of these stages.

Since the second World War, with the increased application of sophisticated mathematical techniques, a large literature has been produced in the fields of economic dynamics and the theory of economic growth, and these subjects now occupy prominent places in the standard curriculum of graduate training. In terms of practical application, however, the yield of these branches of economics has, so far, been disappointingly small. By contrast, and perhaps surprisingly, the simple model of resource allocation in a static framework has proved to be exceedingly fruitful in supplying tools of analysis that are applicable to a large range of important practical problems. This branch of neoclassical theory is called 'welfare economics'. Before passing on to that topic, however, we must extend our examination of the neoclassical theory of economic organization a bit further.

Let us consider the problem of defining the criteria of optimum resource allocation in a static economy. How do we know whether or not the productive resources of the economy are allocated to their various uses in the best possible way? The neoclassical economists took the view that the object of an economy is to serve the wants of consumers. Productive resources are therefore allocated with maximum efficiency when the total utility that consumers derive from the resulting consumer goods is maximized. In this respect neoclassical economics does not differ from classical economics. Both adopted utilitarianism as a normative philosophical principle. Both also adopted psychological utilitarianism as a scientific principle, embracing the positive proposition that people will, in fact, act in such a way as to maximize their utility. The difference between them is a technical one: the neoclassical economists succeeded in translating these utilitarian propositions into a specific theory of economic organization while the classical economists provided only suggestive generalities.

Marshall's procedure was to approach the theory of resource allocation by first applying the marginal analysis to an ultra-simple case. Consider a boy picking and eating blackberries. The problem is to establish how much time he will spend at this activity. The marginal utility of blackberries (MU_b) declines as he consumes more of them, while the marginal disutility of picking activity rises as he does more of it. In speaking of 'disutility' Marshall retained some remnants of the classical notion of cost, but the arguments can easily be restated in terms of the neoclassical concept of alternative cost: we can say that as the boy spends more and more of his time picking blackberries the marginal utility of the things he could obtain by other activities rises, since he has less time available to spend on them. Call the marginal utility of the alternatives sacrificed the 'marginal cost' of blackberries (MC_b) to him. The boy will continue picking as long as MU_b is greater than MC_b and he will stop picking when they are equal, since additional picking would involve the sacrifice of more utility than is gained. The equation

$$MU_b = MC_b$$

not only states a positive equilibrium but also defines a normative optimum, since, if this equality is satisfied, the net or surplus utility obtainable from blackberry picking is maximized. We encounter here another concept of *surplus*, a notion that, with varying definitions, plays a prominent role in the economic models of the Physiocrats, Ricardo, and Marx. The Marshallian concept of surplus plays a different, but equally important, role in the neoclassical model and, as we shall see in section B, its application to practical problems.

In the neoclassical model of a complex economy, all commodities are presumed to be produced for sale, and consumers satisfy all their wants by buying commodities in markets. The allocation of productive resources in such an economy is achieved by the adaptation of consumers and producers to commodity prices. Let the symbol P_i stand for the price of any commodity, and MU_i and MC_i respectively for that commodity's marginal utility and marginal cost. If every consumer purchases commodities in those quantities that equate the marginal utility of each of them with its price, i.e.:

$$MU_i = P_i$$

and all producers produce commodities in quantities that equate the marginal cost of each of them with its price, i.e.:

$$MC_i = P_i$$

then it necessarily follows that the factors of production are being allocated in such an economy so that:

$$MU_i = MC_i$$

which is the same equation, generalized, that we obtained previously for optimum allocation in the blackberry illustration. Standard theorems in neoclassical theory demonstrate that, under ideal conditions, consumers who aim to get the most utility they can from a limited budget will indeed buy a mixture of commodities that satisfies the equation $MU_i = P_i$, and that producers who aim to maximize their profits will produce quantities of commodities that satisfy the equation $MC_i = P_i$. (The reader must forgive me for not giving these theorems here, since it would involve reproducing large sections of a standard textbook in elementary microeconomic theory.) It follows from this – again, we should note, *under ideal conditions* – that the market mechanism can function as a perfectly efficient system for allocating the productive resources of the economy. Its deficiencies, as we shall see, are due to the fact that the real world fails to correspond, in many important respects, to the ideal conditions.

Neoclassical theory does not demonstrate that *only* the market mechanism can achieve the efficient allocation of resources. An economy organized by means of a central planning board could accomplish the same task if the board were able to allocate resources so that the marginal cost of production equalled the marginal utility for all commodities. This criterion applies to all economies, so long as it is granted that the objective of an economic system is to accommodate the wants that consumers actually have (rather than those that, say, a moral authority decrees). Some prominent advocates of socialist planning have argued that, in an economy where the means of production are state-owned, consumers should be allowed to spend their incomes as they please in markets where prices are set by the planning board to achieve an equilibrium of supply and demand, and the managers of state enterprises should be instructed to produce commodities in such quantities that their marginal costs are equal to those prices. In view of the fact that Marxists emerged as the leading advocates of central planning, it is curious, and perhaps ironic, that the technical criteria defining the efficient operation of a planned economy derive from the marginal analysis of neoclassical economics rather than the analytical apparatus constructed by Marx and developed by his followers.

In the above account of the market model I emphasized that it refers to 'ideal conditions'. In the next section we shall see that the neoclassical economists construed the role of the state in the economy as deriving from the fact that in the real world the market system fails to correspond to the ideal model. But this is not the whole story. The ideal model specifies the optimum allocation of resources only for a specific distribution of income. The prices of commodities that appear in the above equations might well be different if the distribution of income were different. For example, an increase in the degree of equality in the income distribution might increase the demand for beefsteak and decrease the demand for caviare, producing a higher price for the former and a lower price for the latter. The import of this is that the allocation of productive resources, even in an economy where marginal utilities and marginal costs are equal to prices, is 'ideal' only in a limited sense. In order to give full approval to such an economy the distribution of income would also have to be 'ideal' in some acceptable sense of the term. At this point, economic theory becomes deeply entangled with sociological, political, and ethical considerations. The subject of income distribution has generated a huge literature, which continues to grow. In section C we shall examine the main themes in this literature that were associated with the development of neoclassical economics. The application of neoclassical theory to the role of the state, which I now go on immediately to discuss, will be restricted, for the sake of convenience, to the analysis of defects in the market mechanism that reduce the efficiency with which the productive resources of the community are allocated. In accordance with the 'static' mode of this analysis, the discussion will not only assume that consumers' preferences and the community's stock of productive resources are given, but that the distribution of income-yielding personal and material assets among the members of the community is also. These restrictions on the model, as the neoclassical economists recognized, are severe; they are adopted in order to make some headway in the scientific analysis of a reality that is exceedingly complex.

B. NEOCLASSICAL ECONOMICS AND THE ROLE OF THE STATE

In Chapter 10 above we examined the 'ideology of *laissez-faire*' in the field of economics in relation to the philosophical theory that all domains of existence, whether physical, organic, or social, are parts of an all-embracing system of harmonious order. It is important to distinguish this general view of the world from the specific proposition that the market mechanism can function, under certain conditions, as an automatic process that achieves an efficient allocation of productive resources. The latter is an empirical contention which can be scientifically investigated; the former is a metaphysical doctrine, beyond the reach of scientific method. Some advocates of *laissez-faire* in the domain of economics employed a mode of argument in which it served, not as an empirical conclusion, but as a metaphysical premise. In the London *Economist* of the 1840's, under the editorship of James Wilson, contemporary state policies were condemned, not because they were shown to have deleterious effects, but because they offended the fundamental principle of *laissez-faire*. In its support of the campaign to repeal the corn laws, for example, the *Economist* of this period made no reference to Ricardo's theory of international trade; free trade was advocated solely on the ground that in this area of economics, as in all others, the harmonious order of nature must not be blemished. In the popular literature of the period one will find a number of writers who used *laissez-faire* in this way, as a primary principle or ideology. But none of the leading economists of the classical school took such a stance. Their view of the role of the state in economic affairs was essentially pragmatic. In this respect, mainstream economics did not change when the classical model was replaced by the neoclassical one. Neoclassical theory provided new techniques that could be applied to the analysis and evaluation of governmental economic policy, and one could argue that this was indeed its most significant contribution to the history of modern social thought, but it did not represent a shift in political philosophy. The pragmatic utilitarianism of the classical economists was continued by their neoclassical successors.

Adam Smith was severely critical of the 'mercantilist' writers on numerous specific points of economic analysis, but also because he perceived them as harbouring the presumption that the economic prosperity of a nation could not be preserved and promoted without widespread and detailed intervention by the state. They had, in his view, underestimated the capacity of the market mechanism and, as a result, had promoted economic policies that did more harm than good. But, contrary to the image of Adam Smith that persists in the popular literature down to the present day, he did not view the market mechanism as a universal and flawless mode of economic organization. Smith had high regard for the capacity of the market mechanism, and he was deeply suspicious of government, but there are many passages in the *Wealth of Nations* where the necessity of state intervention in the economy is acknowledged and, indeed, some where the state is urged to undertake responsibilities that it had not yet adopted.

Laissez-faire does not emerge in the writings of Adam Smith as a meta-physical or ideological principle, but another principle concerning the role of the state is evident in his thinking that was subsequently adopted almost universally by economists. This is the principle that state action in economic matters must be justified by prior specific demonstration that the market mechanism is faulty. The import of this is that the burden of proof lies upon those who support existing state policies or advocate new ones. It is not sufficient to argue that the state can accomplish a desired economic objective; one must also show that the market system is incapable of achieving it. The analysis of cases of 'market failure' by the techniques of neoclassical economics, which we shall examine below, derives from this principle which, though not explicitly stated by Adam Smith, is implicit in his thinking. Some critics of capitalism, and not only those who followed Marx, have argued that the market system is so deeply and pervasively flawed that it must be replaced altogether by another mechanism of economic organization, but most of the mainstream economists adopted the less radical stance that the market system should be retained as the basic mode of economic organization, the power of the state being used to modify and to supplement it where necessary. This was, for example, the view taken by John Stuart Mill, despite his dislike of the commercial character of his own society and his profound conviction that it contained much unnecessary evil and intolerable injustice. Similar views were held by the major early neoclassical economists, such as Jevons and Marshall, and remains today the predominant outlook of professional economists.

We might note before we proceed that economic analysis, as such, cannot furnish support for the proposition that the best way of organizing an economy is a compound system of markets and government in which the former has the primary role while the latter is supplementary. The Soviet Union, until very recently, adopted the opposite principle of policy: the central planning authority was established as the primary mode of economic organization, with the market mechanism playing a secondary role. Why must the advocates of state intervention be obliged to show that the market is faulty, rather than the advocates of markets being obliged to show that the state is a flawed instrument? It is impossible to demonstrate scientifically that the burden of proof lies necessarily on the one side or the other. Adam Smith said nothing specific to support his contention, but it is possible to infer from his writings that he viewed government, not only as inefficient, but as dangerous, threatening the liberties of the people as well as their material welfare. This view of the state is plainer in J. S. Mill's writings. Though attracted to socialist arguments and other proposals for social reconstitution, Mill abhorred the tyranny of an unconstrained state more than the injustices and other defects of a market economy. This political judgement, widely held in the England of Mill's day, was considerably abated in the later nineteenth and early twentieth centuries by the extension of the franchise and the development of other features of modern consitutional democracy. Meanwhile, reforms in the bureaucratic apparatus of the state had made it more efficient, less corrupt, and more subject to the control of Parliament, public opinion, and the other institutions of a democratic polity. In the writings of Marshall and other economists of the period one finds less concern for the political dangers of an expanded role of the state. Nevertheless, the view continued to be maintained by most economists that state intervention must be justified by prior demonstration that the market system had failed in some specific way to perform the functions that were required of it.

This view of the case was considerably sharpened and strengthened by the development of the neoclassical theory of optimum resource allocation, since it provided a means by which the efficiency of the market system could be evaluated. Smith, Mill, and others who required the advocates of state intervention to prove that the market was flawed had in fact demanded what was, at that time, impossible. No economic model then existed that could enable one to identify defects in the market system in a scientific fashion. The classical economists held that the primary criterion of any well-functioning system of economic organization is that it should serve the wants of consumers (Adam Smith criticized the mercantilists for focusing on the welfare of producers and failing to appreciate that, as he put it, 'consumption is the sole end and purpose of production'); they appreciated the fact that, in a division-of-labour economy, the satisfaction of this criterion requires a method of economic organization which adjusts the allocation of resources to the production of commodities that consumers want; and they regarded competitive markets as such a co-ordinating mechanism. But, working as they did with a theory of value that excluded the role of demand, they were unable to describe how that mechanism works. In his *Theory of Pure Economics*, Léon Walras severely criticized the classical economists for making favourable judgements about the market system without providing a scientific analysis of it. Alfred Marshall was less critical of his predecessors than Walras, or Jevons, but he was obviously also dissatisfied with what he had found in the classical literature, since he devoted more than twenty years of his life to constructing a theoretical model of the market mechanism as a system of resource allocation. With the publication of Marshall's *Principles of Economics* in 1890 the consideration of the role of the state in the economy began to develop the shape it now has in professional economics. The model it contained provided not only an effective theoretical foundation for a positive analysis of the market mechanism but, as Marshall intended, the means for a systematic investigation, guided by explicit normative criteria, of its limitations and defects.

The fundamentals of Marshall's model have been outlined in the preceding section. To review briefly: using the notions of diminishing utility and diminishing returns (or increasing marginal cost), an optimum allocation theorem is constructed which says that the total surplus of utility over cost will be maximized if the economy's productive resources are so distributed that each commodity is produced in an amount that makes its marginal utility equal to its marginal cost. Translated into market processes, this maximum is attained if consumers spend their incomes so that the marginal utility of each commodity bought is equal to its price and producers set their production schedules so that the marginal cost of each commodity produced is equal to its price. Any system of economic organization fails to achieve an optimally efficient allocation of productive resources if the several marginal costs of production are not equal to the respective marginal utilities. The market mechanism therefore fails if the $MC_i = P_i$ and $MU_i = P_i$ equations are not satisfied. A large part of the economic literature since Marshall has been concerned with the investigation of such 'market failures'. I cannot undertake here to survey the history of this investigation in detail, but a brief discussion of its main features is necessary to an understanding of modern economics and the views that mainstream economists now hold concerning the economic role of the state.

To begin with we should note again that the underlying ethical philosophy of neoclassical economics was, like that of classical economics, individualistic utilitarianism. Only sentient individuals are regarded as capable of experiencing 'pleasure' and 'pain', so the well-being of a social community is the aggregate of the 'happiness' of its individual members, not a quality of a collective entity as such. The social institutions of a community, according to this view, are instrumental artefacts that must be evaluated in terms of their capacity to serve, as Adam Smith put it, 'the desire of every man to better his condition'. The fierce attacks that were levelled at this philosophy continuously from the early nineteenth century did not persuade the classical economists to abandon it. Even John Stuart Mill, who was strongly attracted to romanticism and to collective notions of community, retained utilitarianism as the philosophic foundation of his work in economics. The neoclassical economists were equally impervious to the philosophical criticisms of utilitarianism but their own success in developing a superior economic model revealed technical difficulties that they were unable to brush aside.

The most fundamental of these difficulties derives from the fact that individual entities can be meaningfully aggregated only in terms of some specific comparable quality. Apples and candlesticks are very different things, but because they are comparable in terms of physical mass it is possible to weigh an apple and a candlestick, sum the quantities, and arrive at a magnitude that can be meaningfully described as their combined weight. If the force of the earth's gravitational attraction on apples were different from that on candlesticks, we could not do this unless we were able, somehow, to render the different forces quantitatively comparable. In the neoclassical economic model all consumers are construed as alike in that they derive 'utility' from using commodities, but is the utility of one person comparable to that of another? The central issue is not whether the utilities can actually be measured but whether the utilities of different persons are comparable *in principle*. F. Y. Edgeworth, a major figure in the early development of mathematical economics, contended that such interpersonal comparisons of utility were theoretically valid and that, in due course, techniques would be developed which would permit empirical economists to measure them in quantitative units. He had no doubt that, when this day arrived, it would be found that the consumption of a given commodity yields different amounts of utility to different persons but, since the amounts are measurable, it would be possible to calculate the aggregate utility, and to ascertain whether a change in the distribution of commodities among consumers would increase or decrease this aggregate. Vilfredo Pareto, who succeeded Walras in the Chair of economics at Lausanne, was equally certain that utilities are *not* comparable between persons. From him derives the 'Pareto criterion' which states that a governmental policy, or any other economic event, can be declared good only if it benefits someone and harms no one, and bad if it harms someone and benefits no one. The Pareto criterion occupies a prominent place in the modern literature of economic theory, testifying to the fact that neoclassical economists have generally held the view that interpersonal comparisons of utility are not theoretically permissible. But that criterion is too hard a test for practical economists to accept, since there are few economic events, and probably no state policies, that can satisfy it. Rigorous avoidance of interpersonal comparisons of utility would render economics a purely scholastic exercise in logical and semantic refinement, with no practical applications. The analysis of market failures adopts a more pragmatic stance.

The most obvious case is where markets are not competitive. Adam Smith and the other classical economists regarded monopolies as the main defect of the market system, but they were unable to describe how they function. The marginal analysis of neoclassical economics provided a means of doing this, without attributing motivations to monopolists that differentiate them from other folk. Extension of that analysis to the behaviour of business firms shows that while a firm in a competitive industry will find that profit is maximized if a production level is adopted that equates marginal cost with the market price of the commodity, a monopolist will find that profit is maximized at a lower level of production. Thus the profit motive induces the adoption of behaviour that optimizes resource use in a competitive industry, but the same motive does not induce the same behaviour in a monopolized industry. Adam Smith complained that monopolists were able to levy 'an absurd tax' on consumers by raising prices. Neoclassical theory showed that, in addition to such a transfer of income, monopoly wastes productive resources by allocating them inefficiently. The development of legislation to regulate industries that, for some reason, are 'natural' monopolies, and legislation to prevent 'artificial' monopolies from being constructed in other industries, owed a great deal to this analysis. In the 1930's neoclassical theory was broadened to embrace cases of 'oligopoly' – industries with more than one producer, but too few of them to generate the 'perfect competition' of the ideal model. This led to the development of a branch of modern economics under the title of 'industrial organization', which is today one of the most important areas in which the question of government intervention is studied. The remaining cases of market failure that we shall consider are ones in which even perfectly competitive markets may not be sufficient to achieve the efficient allocation of productive resources.

In his *Principles of Political Economy* (1883), Henry Sidgwick devoted the final section to 'The Art of Political Economy', which contained a remarkably perceptive discussion of the defects in the market mechanism that, in his view, called for the intervention of the state. But the earlier parts of the book, which dealt with the pure 'science' of economics, were classical, and Sidgwick was unable to show that his claims for intervention were logically derived from his theory. Alfred Marshall's model supplied the required focus on the conditions of optimum resource allocation and it was Marshall's successor in the Chair of economics at Cambridge, Arthur Cecil Pigou, who first used it systematically to develop a coherent analysis of state intervention. Pigou's seminal book *Wealth and Welfare* was published in 1912; an expanded version, entitled *The Economics of Welfare*, in 1920. The theoretical treatment of market failures and state intervention is today called 'welfare economics' because of Pigou's role in the early development of this subject. Sidgwick's *Principles* had anticipated most of the important propositions in Pigou's books, but Sidgwick's arguments were largely intuitive while Pigou's were analytical. In common speech, when one refers to a practical activity, such as for example medicine or farming, as an 'art', it is usually an acknowledgement that success in the activity involves a large component of intuitive understanding which cannot be reduced to the hard reasoning and explicit demonstration of 'science'. Pigou's work suggested a prospect that the modern Western mind found immensely attractive: that the day was at hand when government (at least in the economic sphere) would cease to be an art practised by statesmen and become a true science, thus ending at last the discord and contention that had heretofore characterized all societies and had not been ended even by the development in some of them of democratic forms of political organization. Enthusiasm for the scientific potentialities of 'welfare economics' has cooled considerably since Pigou's day, but it still remains a vital part of the corpus of mainstream economic theory.

A. C. Pigou is most frequently noted in today's economic literature for his analysis of a class of market failures that derive from what are now called 'externalities'. To use Pigou's most famous illustration, an 'external cost' exists if a firm producing steel emits smoke into the air, because this causes more resources to be devoted to clothes washing, house cleaning, etc., than would otherwise be required. The cost of these resources, however, is not borne by the steel producer, it is 'external' to his accounting calculations, so the 'private' marginal cost of steel production (i.e. the cost of an additional ton of steel *to the producer*) is less than the true, or 'social', marginal cost of steel production. If steel is a perfectly competitive industry, the firms in it do not obtain higher profit as a result, but the productive resources of the economy are misallocated between steel and other industries, producing what economists call a 'deadweight loss'. This demonstrable misallocation, and other similar forms of pollution externality, are at least *prima facie* cases for corrective state action. There may also be externalities that *benefit* others. For example, if a householder plants an attractive garden in front of his home, part of the utility it yields accrues to others, so the private marginal utility of gardening is less than its social marginal utility, leading again to resource misallocation.

Obviously, the class of cases embraced by the concept of externalities is very large, but this is only the beginning of the catalogue of failures that even a perfectly competitive market system is subject to. If consumers are to equate the marginal utilities of the things they use with their prices they must know what those utilities are. Irving Fisher, one of the leading American economists of the early twentieth century, argued that consumers are not well informed and, moreover, frequently lack the will power to do what is in their long-run interest even when they are. He was prominent in the campaign for the legal prohibition of alcohol consumption which, in 1919, culminated in the eighteenth amendment to the U.S. constitution (repealed in 1933 after a decade of unsuccessful attempts to enforce it). Most economists took the view, and still do, that individuals are better judges of their personal welfare than others are, and it is unwise, if not improper, for the state to attempt to modify individual preferences, but there still remains the question whether consumers are adequately informed about the commodities that are offered for sale (the presence of carcinogens, for example) and whether the state should play a role in the provision of such information. Special problems arise in the case of technically complex commodities or services where the information that consumers need is provided by the producers of them, who, of course, do not have the same interests as consumers. Commercial advertising, for example, contributes to the functioning of the market system when it is informative, but since there is reason to believe that the interests of producers may lead them to make false claims for their products, government regulation of advertising can be justified by the neoclassical economic model.

In addition, there is a large class of cases where the commodity or service cannot be purchased in different quantities by different individuals in accordance with their diverse preferences. Each consumer may purchase shirts and refrigerators of whatever quality and in whatever quantity he pleases (within his income), thus equating their marginal utility *for him* to their price, but it is not possible for each member of a community to obtain different quantities and qualities of roads, or weather reporting, or national defence, in accordance with his individual preferences. In the case of such 'public goods' the criteria of optimum resource allocation cannot be met, even where it is possible to charge prices for them. The provision of such goods has long been regarded as the responsibility of the state.

This review of market failures could be greatly extended, but it is perhaps sufficient to indicate that, within the framework of the neoclassical model, the theoretical potentiality for state intervention is very large, more extensive indeed than one finds in practice in any modern economy. We have so far, however, neglected an important aspect of the subject. Just as the market mechanism is not a perfect system of economic organization, neither is the state political mechanism; there may be 'government failures' as well as 'market failures'. If the apparatus through which public policy is determined and administered operated flawlessly, every case of market failure would call for state intervention. Since this is clearly not so, state intervention may do more harm than good. Henry Sidgwick, with his uncommon ability to see both sides of any question, noted the deficiencies of government, and did not depreciate their importance, but he drew no conclusions from this concerning the proper role of the state in the economy. Vilfredo Pareto, who had been an enthusiastic supporter of the new Italian Republic, became so disgusted with the ensuing efforts to establish a constitutional democracy that he welcomed Mussolini as a charismatic leader who would restore state authority and social order, but the long history of governmental incompetence and corruption also convinced him that the market mechanism should be regarded as off limits to state power, however it might be constituted. A. C. Pigou took a simpler stance: except for a very brief reference, he ignored the issue of governmental defects and construed his analysis of market failures as a sufficient warrant for state intervention. Up to the second World War, and for a decade or so thereafter, the literature of welfare economics followed Pigou's lead. Much refinement of the analysis took place and, though concern for the problem of interpersonal comparisons of utility persisted, the domain of potential state intervention was enlarged by the steady discovery of additional market failures.

A fully scientific determination of the proper role of the state in a market economy requires more than a theoretical identification of market failures; the capacity of a real (not an ideal) government to deal with them must be assessed and, moreover, the two must be subjected to quantitative comparison. A necessary preliminary to this is the development of a general theory of public policy formation and administration. In recent years, a branch of economics has emerged that is concerned with this. The theory of 'public choice', as it has come to be called, deals with matters that appear to belong to the discipline of political science, but it has developed mainly within economics, partly (if not largely) in reaction to the market failure analysis of welfare economics. A notable feature of the theory of public choice is that it assumes that government personnel, whether elected or employed, are motivated by self-interest, just as consumers and producers are presumed to be in the main corpus of economic theory. For this reason it has sometimes been described as 'the economic approach to politics'. Public choice theory is now an established sub-discipline in the social sciences.

In the above discussion of market failures we have so far focused upon those that can be identified within the framework of the neoclassical model and analysed in terms of its normative criterion. There is another, and a major one, that cannot be assimilated to the microeconomic orientation of neoclassical economics: unemployment. The neoclassical model focuses upon the allocation of productive resources in a world where the wants of consumers exceed the capacity to satisfy them. The market mechanism is depicted as a process by which decisions are made as to what wants are satisfied (and to what degree) where resources are, in this sense, 'scarce'. But if there is unemployment of labour and other factors of production, it is evident that the economy is more correctly construed as *wasting* productive resources rather than being constrained by their scarcity. The classical economists argued that unemployment cannot exist, except as a transitory condition, in a market economy. Some economists still hold this view, but the predominant opinion, since the Great Depression of the 1930's, is that unemployment represents an important market failure that calls for corrective action by the state. The neoclassical model was a great improvement over the classical one as a heuristic instrument for the analysis of the market failures discussed above, but it did not provide a means for the theoretical and empirical investigation of the phenomenon of unemployment. In response to the problem of persistent unemployment in Great Britain, John Maynard Keynes constructed a new model to deal specifically with this particular market failure. The 'macroeconomic' analysis that developed from this has not yet been integrated with neoclassical theory, so this part of the history of economics requires separate treatment.

Before we pass on to that subject, however, we must complete our survey of neoclassical economics by reviewing its relation to the issue of the distribution of income. The neoclassical model focuses solely on the *efficiency* with which an economy's productive resources are used. As we have already noted, its efficiency theorem is not independent of the prior distribution of income-yielding personal qualities and material property: different distributions of these may yield different results so far as the allocation of resources is concerned. The question of the ethical quality of the economic system, which was prominently raised by the old economics, was equally pronounced in the literature that accompanied the development of the new. In the modern tradition of Western social philosophy, reflection on the human condition is not satisfied by scientific demonstration that we live in an economically efficient society that services the desire of its citizens for material welfare, or even by the conviction that it allows a high degree of personal freedom and wide participation in the formation of public policy; in addition to these, *justice* is demanded, and the main focus of this has been, and continues to be, on the distribution of income.

C. THE DISTRIBUTION OF INCOME

Neoclassical economics was developed in an era in which the subject of the distribution of income, and particularly the inequality of that distribution, engaged the attention not only of economists and other professional scholars, but of journalists and other writers on political subjects, practising politicians, clergymen, businessmen, labour leaders, and indeed all sorts of people who were concerned with public affairs. No subject is more prominent in the English-language literature of the period from, say, 1880 to 1914, on both sides of the Atlantic, than the distribution of income. The extension of 'marginal' analysis to provide a new theory of income distribution is an important part of the history of economics as a scientific discipline, but it also articulates with the concurrent widespread discussion of income distribution as a major social problem and the demand for state action or other modes of social reform. In this section I shall first give a review of the main features of the discussion of distribution in the general literature of the period before going on to discuss the theory developed by the neoclassical economists and the application of it to issues of contemporary concern.

Much of the criticism of capitalism that punctuated the literature of the early nineteenth century focused upon the erosion of traditional values that was perceived to be the consequence of the growth of industrialism and the extension of the market sector of the economy. Thomas Carlyle spoke scathingly of the 'cash nexus' as having become the only connection between the members of society, bringing with it competition in place of co-operation, self-interest instead of devotion to communal goals, the replacement of noble and heroic values by the 'pig philosophy' of utilitarianism and, generally, the decline of civilization. Across the Atlantic, Thomas Jefferson, though not frenetic like Carlyle, contended that the new and better civilization that was being built in America required the continuation of an agricultural economy of small communities which met their simple wants directly, without much need of cash markets. The utopian literature of the period, without exception, presented a similar conception of the ideal society as sufficiently small to promote communal values and resist the corrupting effects of materialism, individualism, production for sale instead of use, money, and the other evils that were evident in societies that had allowed their economy to become dominated by private property and the market mechanism. These views continue to find expression in the utopian literature of our own time, but by the end of the nineteenth century it was evident that, for good or ill, the Western world was unalterably embarked upon a road that led to industrialization, urbanization, increased division of labour, and the market system as the main mode of economic organization. Objection to capitalism was not overwhelmed by these events, indeed it increased, but its main focus shifted from the sociological and philosophical considerations that had energized its early critics to a more strictly economic question, the distribution of income and wealth.

The American literature of the last quarter of the nineteenth century was dominated by deep concern over this issue. The popular media of the period contained incessant reference to 'trusts' and 'robber barons', claiming that the great tycoons had amassed their wealth by unfair practices, subverting the market mechanism by monopolies and other devices that restricted free competition. But even among those who might have granted John D. Rockefeller's contention that he was merely a superior competitor in a fair contest there was much concern about the concentration of income and wealth that was widely perceived to be taking place. Many writers regarded the very foundations of American democracy to be threatened. A different political society was, they feared, in the making: a plutocracy, in which the industrial and financial tycoons would control not only the economy but the organs of government as well. A century before, John Adams had spoken of America's need of an aristocracy, in order to complete the model of 'mixed government' that he favoured. Now that an aristocracy of wealth appeared to be rapidly in the making, only the tycoons themselves viewed the development with approval.

In England, of course, the existence of an aristocratic class was a matter of long standing. Some political writers regarded the replacement of the old aristocracy of lineage and landed property by a new aristocracy of commercial wealth with great misgivings, but the literature of the period focused much less upon this than upon the dangers of increased concentration of wealth and income. The classical economists had argued that the share of the national income going to the landed class would continue to grow with economic development, and the share of the owners of industrial capital would shrink because of the fall in the rate of profit. But the rate of profit did not fall. Writing in 1905, the prominent English economist Edwin Cannan pointed out that since the stock of industrial capital was increasing much faster than the population, without the rate of profit decreasing, the capitalists' share of the national income must grow larger, with no limit short of the impoverishment of the rest of society.

Laid against the growing egalitarian sentiment in the social philosophy of the period, the concentration of income and wealth was perceived to be a serious problem in itself. But this was not all. Some economists regarded the maldistribution of income as the source of other problems as well. John A. Hobson anticipated J. M. Keynes's theory of unemployment by ascribing it to a deficiency of demand for goods and services which, in turn, he traced to the inequality of income. A strong opponent of the Boer War, Hobson extended his argument to contend that the contemporary resurgence of imperialism was due to the same basic cause: the powerful European nations were establishing colonial dependencies in Africa and elsewhere in order to secure markets abroad for the commodities that could not be sold at home on account of the maldistribution of income.

Arguments such as Hobson's are reported here merely for illustration. The popular and professional literature from about 1880 to 1914, on both sides of the Atlantic, was filled with multiple anxieties about the distribution of income too varied to be surveyed briefly. The writers of the period had access to very little factual information, since statistical compilations and techniques for measuring the degree of inequality in the income distribution were still in their infancy, but such data as did exist suggested that the distribution of income was shockingly unequal, and most writers had no doubt that it was becoming more so. 'The rich are getting richer and the poor poorer' was a common slogan of the age and reflected the main focus of social movements of every complexion, from Marxists who argued that the whole capitalist system must be overthrown in a revolutionary upheaval to those who were inspired by Henry George's contention that a single specific defect accounted for all its evils, easily correctable by using the taxing power of the state to transfer the 'unearned increment' in land values from private hands to the public purse. Economists of the period did not accept J. S. Mill's broad contention that the distribution of income 'is a matter of human institution solely' and therefore can be altered at will, but many believed that it could be altered considerably, and should be. During this period a great deal of the effort of professional economists was devoted to considering how the inequality of income might be reduced without seriously impairing incentives to work and invest or the capacity of the market mechanism to allocate productive resources efficiently.

The economic theory of Ricardo, and indeed Marx, did not focus directly on the question of income inequality. That issue has to do with how individuals (or families) compare with respect to the *size* of the income they receive, irrespective of the *source* of that income. Ricardo's theory of distribution was aimed at explaining how the national income is divided among three social classes, each of which is construed as deriving its income from a distinct source: labourers from the sale of labour, capitalists from investment in capital, and landlords from the ownership of land. Marx's only amendment to Ricardo in this respect was the reduction of the number of social classes to two: labourers, who receive wages for their work, and the owners of the means of production, who receive 'surplus value'. Despite the great concern for the size distribution of income in the neoclassical era, the economists who developed a new theory of distribution with the use of marginal analysis did not undertake to show how that size distribution is determined in a market economy. The new theory was, as we noted above, designed to explain how the mechanism of competitive markets determines the prices of the various factors of production. It was, in fact, more restricted than the classical theory, since it did not attempt to demonstrate – in its analysis of the labour market, for example – the determinants of the share of national income that is paid out in wages to the whole labour class, or even the *average* rate of wages (per hour or per day) of the whole labouring class, but the *particular* wage rate paid for labour of a specific sort. The concept of 'marginal productivity' cannot properly be applied to a heterogeneous category such as 'labour' or, for that matter, 'capital' or 'land'. These generic terms were retained by the neoclassical economists, but the theory they constructed was not tied to any intention to explain the class distribution (or the size distribution) of the national income.

A basic requirement of any theory of income distribution is that it should be consistent with the theory of production in the sense that the various distributional components of the former should add up to no more, and no less, than the total value of the aggregate production of the latter. Measuring in some standard unit, if the annual production of an economy is 185 million units, then the various annual incomes must add up to the same sum. This is not merely an accounting requirement; the *theories* of production and distribution must satisfy it in principle. The simplest way of achieving this is to make one of the distributive categories residual, that is, it is construed as receiving what is left over after the other incomes have been determined. Ricardo provided specific theories of rent and wages, with profit being residual. Marx had only two categories and provided a theory of wages with 'surplus value' residual. In the neoclassical analysis, there is no residual category; all recipients of income are placed on the same plane, as providers of productive services that receive rates of return equal to the value of their marginal products. An important step in the development of neoclassical theory was a rigorous mathematical demonstration that (under certain conditions) the various incomes determined by these rates would add up to the national income. The provision of such a demonstration was undertaken by Philip Henry Wicksteed, a prominent figure in the Unitarian Church and one of the leading English authorities of his day on Italian Renaissance literature. His interest in economics derived from the ethical issues punctuating the widespread discussion of income distribution that we noted above. He became a strong supporter of the marginal utility approach to value theory, studied mathematics in order to improve his comprehension of it, and published, in 1894, his *Essay on the Co-ordination of the Laws of Distribution*, which historians now refer to as one of the great landmarks in the development of neoclassical economics. Wicksteed's proof was in fact incomplete, but a reviewer of the book pointed out that a standard proposition in mathematics, 'Euler's theorem', could supply what was wanting in it. The marginal productivity theory of distribution was thereby shown not only to satisfy the accounting requirement that any theory of distribution must meet, but it did so in a way that was much more elegant than the classical method of construing one of the shares as residual. The new theory of distribution was not immediately embraced by economists but, after intense discussion, it was generally accepted and, without significant alteration, that theory is what one finds today in microeconomics textbooks.

We should note once again that the neoclassical model is static. Ricardo's theory of distribution was used by the classical economists as the foundation for a dynamic theory of economic development. In Marx's model the analysis of distribution was part of an attempt to describe the 'laws of motion' of capitalism. The neoclassical economists were not uninterested in such larger questions, but their theoretical efforts were devoted almost entirely to the elaboration of the static model of production and distribution. Economic development continued to be the primary concern of Marxist economists and economic historians, but the mainstream of orthodox economics did not attempt to construct a theoretical model of that important phenomenon until after the second World War.

There was, however, another matter of great consequence and concern that some of the early neoclassical economists did undertake to address: the ethical evaluation of the distribution of income. The popular social literature of the period focused mainly on this weighty issue. In their own professional literature, economists entered the debate, utilizing the new concept of marginal productivity. This generated another of those occasions in the intellectual history of the West when the claim has been made that science was now ready to break out of its confinement to the domain of empirical phenomena and invade the territory of moral philosophy. David Hume's contention that ethical propositions concerning what *ought* to be cannot be derived from scientific propositions about how the world *is*, though almost universally embraced by scientists as a general rule, has rarely acted as a constraint upon any social or natural scientist who, in the flush of enthusiasm that accompanies a new development in his field, persuades himself that it can be applied to ethics. Efforts to realize this invariably demonstrate, upon calm reflection, that Hume was correct, but the failure of previous attempts does not appear to dampen the hope that scientists might be able to do what philosophers and theologians have not: solve the agonizing problem of determining right and wrong. On this occasion an appreciable number of economists, of great and small distinction, entered the contemporary debate with confidence that the new theory of distribution would, at long last, resolve the dilemma. John Bates Clark, the premier American economist of the period, led the way, proclaiming that everyone has a right to take from the communal harvest an amount equivalent to what he has contributed to it, neither more nor less, and that the proper measure of that contribution is his *marginal product*. Economic analysis had shown that, in a perfectly functioning market economy, every factor's income would equal its marginal product and, since the sum of the incomes so determined would equal the national income, all rightful claims could be satisfied. The import of this is that a market economy is prevented from being a regime of perfect justice only by imperfections, such as monopolies and other restraints on competition, which enable some members of the community to reap more than they have sown, at the expense of others. This argument seems bizarre today, and only the most doctrinaire worshippers of the market mechanism espouse it, but in the early neoclassical period, in the excess of enthusiasm that frequently accompanies a new scientific development, it was supported by many otherwise judicious and able economists.

As always in such cases, the scientific jargon and mathematical form of the argument disguised the fact that an ethical proposition was embedded in it as a primary premise. The notion that one ought to receive as income an amount equivalent to one's contribution to production is an ethical proposition, not a scientific one. Introducing the adjective 'marginal' did not change the character of the proposition in this fundamental respect. Nor did it in fact constitute a significant departure from earlier notions of distributional ethics. Ricardo's labour theory of value and his theory of rent had been used by numerous writers to demonstrate that the market system was unjust because it did not distribute income in accordance with the contributions to production. Marx's theory of exploitation was based on the ethical proposition that the producers of value ought to receive all of it. This criterion of distributive justice, which the neo-classical economists accepted with only a technical modification, is gravely flawed in itself, since it rigidly excludes other criteria that can be strongly supported by rational argument and command widespread intuitive assent. Take, for example, the criterion of 'need'. Does a disabled person, or an elderly person no longer capable of work, have no moral claim to even a small share of the national income? Hardly anyone would reject such a claim and even those who contend that such persons should be supported solely by private charity do not deny that it is their *need* which gives moral force to the contention that others are obligated to provide for them. Only a seriously warped moral philosophy would lead one to argue that there is no such obligation. Another example is the criterion of 'equality'. If a social system existed in which everyone received an amount equivalent to his contribution but the resulting distribution of income was grossly unequal, not many would be prepared to regard such a society as an exemplar of flawless justice. Need and the reduction of inequality are not the only criteria of distributive justice that must be added to the contribution principle (for a fuller discussion see my *Welfare, Justice, and Freedom*, 1980, chapter 3). I note them explicitly for historical rather than philosophical reasons: because they were especially prominent in the distribution debate of the period we are reviewing. Most of the early neo-classical economists, to their credit, accepted these criteria as philosophically valid and viewed the state, as well as private persons, as morally obligated to support the needy and to reduce the inequality of income, with little concern that such a stance was not derived rigorously from economic analysis.

In addition to its exclusion of important ethical criteria, the marginal productivity theory of distributive justice suffers from numerous other defects which, as they were revealed by critics, rapidly cooled the initial enthusiasm for the invasion of the domain of moral philosophy by economic analysis. Some of these are technical in nature and it would be excessively tedious to review them here, but one characteristic of marginal productivity theory as a scientific approach to the study of distribution, which is sufficient by itself to destroy its moral pretensions, should be noted. The marginal productivity analysis made no distinction between the services rendered by persons and by property. Labour, capital, and land, and the various subcategories of these, were all placed on the same plane as 'factors of production'. But the marginal products of capital and land are not paid to them as such; they accrue to the persons who own them as private property. Their marginal products are determined by market forces, but the laws of property determine who shall receive them as income. If the laws of inheritance, contract, etc., were different, the marginal products of the factors of production might be the same, but the distribution of income would assuredly be different. In order to claim, therefore, that a perfect market system generates a just distribution of income, one would have to show that the distribution of private property is just. This is difficult to do, and especially so in a society where a great deal of property has come into the hands of its current owners through inheritance, reflecting the accidents of heredity which, even at best, can provide only weak support to any moral claim. By considering only the flow of *income*, neoclassical theory disregarded the distribution of the stock of *wealth*, which acts powerfully in determining the direction of that income flow to persons. In the popular literature of the period a great deal of attention was paid to the distribution of wealth, and some of the prominent proposals for social reform were aimed at altering it rather than (or as well as) the distribution of income.

During the first half of the nineteenth century, much of the interest of economists in developing a theoretical model was focused upon the determinants of the welfare of the labouring class. As Adam Smith had earlier pointed out, in discussing 'The Wages of Labour' in the *Wealth of Nations*: 'No society can surely be flourishing and happy, of which the far greater part of the members [the labourers] are poor and miserable.' The two great public policy debates of Ricardo's era, concerning the Poor Law and the Corn Laws, engaged the interests of economists and provided additional motive for them to preserve in their theoretical work the economic class orientation that Smith had established, since it was the labouring class that drew upon Poor Law assistance, and the tariff on imported food grains impacted most heavily on families of low income. With the advent of the marginal analysis, economic classes as primary analytical categories disappeared from the theoretical model, but 'the labour question', as it came to be called in the popular literature of the late nineteenth century, continued to be prominent in the ancillary writings of economists. The new marginal productivity theory of distribution was invoked by some to contend that nothing *can* be done by social action to increase the wages of the labouring class and that nothing *ought* to be done, since the mechanism of competitive markets assures that labourers get what they morally deserve. But other adherents of marginal productivity theory argued the contrary, that wage rates are not so rigidly determined, and that the efforts of institutions such as trade unions to raise them deserve the support of economic science. Enough has been said above to show how marginal productivity theory was used to support the first contention; the reasoning that supported the second was based on an interesting and important twist in marginal productivity theory called the 'high-wage economy' argument.

The essentials of this argument were clearly stated by Alfred Marshall. In an economy where wages are low, the level of consumption that labourers can enjoy may be insufficient to enable them to apply as much physical and mental energy to work as they could if their incomes were higher. Higher wages would increase the productivity of labour and thus, so to speak, 'earn themselves'. A similar contention was reflected in the 'Eight Hour movement' that was prominent in the social reform agitation of the period, the argument being that a labourer would produce as much, or more, in a work regime that allowed adequate time for rest and recreation than under one that did not. In addition,

Marshall and others pointed out, there is more incentive for firms to invest in labour-saving machinery when wage rates are high than when they are low, so a high-wage economy stimulates the invention and introduction of devices that increase the productivity of labour. For this reason, too, high wages can be said to 'earn themselves'. No one, of course, argued that wage rates could be increased without limit, but many economists of the time took the view that they could be raised considerably above their current levels without entrenching upon the incomes of other members of society. The notion, prevalent in much of the radical literature, that the only way the economic condition of the working class could be improved was by a redistribution of the national income was thereby confronted with a strong argument that there was an alternative way. Many of the economists favoured redistribution in the interests of greater equality, but few took the stance that no improvement in working-class incomes was possible without it.

The formal structure of the high-wage economy argument should be noted, since it illustrates the general methodological principle that a demonstration that two things are equal to one another does not establish the direction of causality that might exist between them. The neoclassical proposition that the equilibrium wage rate of a certain class of labour is *equal to* its marginal productivity does not necessarily mean that the former is *determined by* the latter. The high-wage argument contended that the causal connection may, under certain circumstances, be the reverse, with a change in wages affecting the marginal productivity of labour sufficiently to preserve the equality required by the theory. In their purely theoretical analysis the neoclassical economists treated the marginal productivity theory as a simple one-way explanation of wage determination, but those who supported the high-wage argument in effect recognized that the forces operating in the labour markets of a competitive economy are more complex.

The high-wage argument can be traced back to some minor eighteenth-century writers on economics; there is a hint of it in Adam Smith's *Wealth of Nations*, and more than a hint in J. S. Mill's *Principles*, but the classical model could not be used to accommodate it. Ricardo's theory of wage determination in the short run construed wages as being paid from a 'fund' that was generated by the savings of capitalists. An inescapable implication of this is that any increase in the wages paid to a particular class of labour – for example, owing to the action of a trade union – can only result in a reduction in the wages of other labourers. In the long run, according to Ricardo, the general level of wage rates is determined by the supply of labour, which, according to Malthusian population theory, is at equilibrium only when the wages paid to the working class are sufficient to provide a 'subsistence' standard of living and no more. As we noted in Chapter 9 C above, the conception of 'subsistence' as a sociological datum rather than a physiological one opened the way for the classical economists to argue that an improvement in the income of the labouring class, if maintained for sufficient time, would raise the subsistence standard and thus make the higher income permanently sustainable. This resembles the later high-wage economy argument, but most of the classical economists did not consider that trade unions could play a constructive role by representing their members as collective bargaining agents on the supply side of the labour market. Working men's associations, in their view, should restrict themselves to providing insurance, education, and the other services of voluntary 'benefit societies', and not attempt to raise wages. Marx and Engels on the contrary urged workers to organize and to demand higher wages and other concessions from employers, and to strike if they were not granted. But the economic model presented in *Capital* treated the rate of wages as unalterably determined, like all market prices, by the 'law of value'. In the view of Marx and Engels the real significance of militant trade unionism was not that it raised working men's incomes but that it increased their class consciousness and solidarity, thus preparing the proletariat to play its destined historical role in the overthrow of capitalism.

In the last quarter of the nineteenth century a view of trade unions that differed significantly from both Ricardian and Marxian conceptions was widely adopted by many professional economists. The growth of the union movement came to be regarded by them with general favour. The industrial disputes of the period were not interpreted, except by a few, as the work of dangerous agitators who wished to overthrow the social order, or as exemplifying the evils that ensue from failure to understand the scientific laws of economics, but as indicating the need for seriously considered social reform. Article 3 of the newly formed American Economic Association (1885) expressed a view that was prevalent in professional circles on both sides of the Atlantic: 'We hold that the conflict of labor and capital has brought into prominence a vast number of social problems whose solution requires the united effort, each in its own sphere, of the church, of the state, and of science.' By 'science' the framers of this article meant to refer to the contribution that economics could make to the understanding of these problems.

In reviewing the history of the neoclassical theory of income distribution and its application to contemporary issues in this section we have so far focused upon the neoclassical theory of production and the use that was made of the concept of 'marginal productivity'. The other side of the neoclassical model, the theory of consumption and its central concept of 'marginal utility', also had important implications for income distribution which we have already noted. If individuals are alike in their capacity to derive utility from the goods they consume, and if the 'law of diminishing marginal utility' can be extended from the particular commodities a person consumes to the general level of his consumption, then it would appear that the utilitarian criterion of maximum aggregate utility requires a regime in which everyone is able to consume the same amount, i.e. (neglecting savings) when there is complete equality in the distribution of income. The neoclassical economists refrained from driving the argument to this extreme, but there was a widespread view among them that

the new economic analysis provided support for the contention that the degree
of inequality in the distribution of income should be reduced. In the domain of
public policy, the most important impact of this view during the late nineteenth
and early twentieth centuries was that it induced economists to lend their
professional support to political movements that were aimed at the reform of
the system of taxation.

A new view of the taxing power of the state came into existence during this
period. Previously, taxation had been regarded solely as a means of financing
state functions. Economists had for a long time been interested in the economic
effects of different kinds of taxes, in determining the conditions under which a
tax might be shifted from its immediate payers to others, and the criteria of
fairness that might be used to evaluate the ethical merits of different ways in
which the activities of the state could be financed. Long before the theory of
marginal utility was developed, many economists supported the contention that
taxes should be levied according to 'ability to pay', as indicated by income
and/or wealth. The inference derived from this was that property taxes, taxes
on large inheritances, and taxes levied proportionately (or at progressively
increasing rates) on incomes above a certain amount, are the fairest forms of
taxation. The notion that the state should tax the rich and not the poor was not
a novel idea in the late nineteenth century, but the proposals that were then
being made for greater use of property, inheritance, and income taxes had an
additional perspective. In addition to making the tax system fairer, the proponents of these proposals aimed at using taxation as a means of making the
distribution of income in the economy fairer, that is, more equal.

In England this view of the fiscal role of the state was evident in Joseph
Chamberlain's proposal in 1885 that the Conservative Party should adopt a
'Radical Programme' and in the discussion of Sir William Harcourt's budget of
1894, which historians now regard as marking a crucial point in the emergence
of the modern interventionist state. In the same period in the United States the
public debate over the attempt of the federal government to introduce a
progressively graduated income tax (declared unconstitutional by the Supreme
Court) brought out the same argument.

Many of the neoclassical economists, most prominently F. Y. Edgeworth
and A. C. Pigou, supported the notion that the fiscal power of the state should
be used in the interest of greater income equality. Some explicitly referred to
the doctrine of diminishing marginal utility as providing a 'scientific' foundation
for this, and many others who were more cautious in what they wrote and
published nevertheless appeared to regard the new economic theory as
supporting it to an important degree. Economists today are more cautious still
in drawing a direct line of inference from the theory of marginal utility to the
proposition that income distribution should be more equal but, none the less,
the great majority of orthodox economists accept greater income equality as a
desirable social goal, and specialists in the sub-discipline of 'public finance', as
a matter of standard practice, use equality as a reference point in evaluating a

particular tax, the whole taxation system, or the omnibus fiscal system that embraces the spending as well as the taxing activities of the state.

In the 1930's the fiscal responsibilities of the state were again expanded, and economic theory again played an important, but here more explicit, role in the development of new principles of public finance. The taxing and spending activities of governments were perceived to have important effects on the community's general level of economic activity. State fiscal policy could therefore be used as an instrument to combat the deep economic slump into which the industrial world had sunk. The economic theory that supported this additional role of the state was developed, initially by J. M. Keynes, in response to the Great Depression.

D. KEYNESIAN MACROECONOMICS

John Maynard Keynes was the son of John Neville Keynes, a distinguished Cambridge philosopher, who was a close friend of Alfred Marshall. We encountered J. N. Keynes above in Chapter 9 F as the author of *The Scope and Method of Political Economy* (1890), which played an important role in countering the attacks of the historical school and in assuring economists that the use of abstract theoretical models in the investigation of economic phenomena is a sound, and indeed essential, methodological procedure. J. N. Keynes's philosophical defence of theoretical economics is germane to our story here. Prior to his son Maynard's *General Theory of Employment, Interest and Money* (1936) there was no theoretical model of a market economy that could embrace the phenomenon of unemployment. Even before the onset of the Great Depression numerous economists had advocated anti-unemployment policies of the sort that were later to be called 'Keynesian', but they could support their proposals only with commonsense arguments. The object of the *General Theory*, as the title implies, was to supply a *theory* of unemployment. It contained very little explicit discussion of economic policy, but it provided analytical support for policy proposals that were common at the time of its publication.

As a student at Cambridge, Maynard Keynes specialized in mathematics. He achieved honours standing in the subject but not sufficiently high to result in the immediate offer of an academic appointment. Marshall urged him to study economics and he did so, but with the aim of writing the examinations for the civil service. He was appointed to the India Office, where he quickly distinguished himself as an expert on Indian public finance and monetary problems. In his spare time he continued to work on the theory of probability, which had engaged his interest while a student of mathematics at Cambridge. His book on the subject, *A Treatise on Probability* (1921), is still regarded as an important work on the philosophical foundations of probability theory. By the time it was published Keynes had already become well known among professional economists (he was appointed editor of the Royal Economic

Society's *Economic Journal* in 1911, succeeding F. Y. Edgeworth), and more widely as a severe critic of the economic terms of the Versailles peace treaty. During the first World War Keynes had been a senior official in the Treasury and he accompanied the British delegation to the Versailles conference as its senior economic adviser. He became convinced that the terms that Germany was being forced to accept were extremely bad, not only for Germany, but for the whole European economy. He resigned and wrote a book, *The Economic Consequences of the Peace* (1919), which was an immediate and worldwide sensation. During the 1920's he devoted himself to economic journalism, business affairs, and to lecturing on current economic events at Cambridge while administering the finances of King's College. He had also become interested in the arts and was a member of the famous Bloomsbury Group of artists and writers who were convinced that the somewhat unorthodox aesthetic and ethical principles they held provided important guidance for the future development of English society.

Like many other English intellectuals of the period, Keynes was a rebel, but not a revolutionary. He viewed many aspects of contemporary society with great distaste, but Marxism and other ideologies of total transformation had no appeal for him. Indications of his own brand of heterodoxy in economic theory can be seen in his writings of the 1920's but his first full-scale attempt to construct a comprehensive model of the economy did not appear until 1930, when his two-volume *Treatise on Money* was published. While it was in press the American stock market crash occurred and the plunge of the industrial world into the Great Depression began. Keynes felt that the *Treatise* had been rendered irrelevant by events and set to work immediately to construct a theory that was aimed directly at the problem of unemployment.

It will be useful if we take a brief look here at the views of Keynes's predecessors on the subject of unemployment. The word 'unemployment' did not come into general use until the 1880s, but the phenomenon was not unknown previously and, in fact, it was the subject of one of the sharpest controversies among the classical economists, with T. R. Malthus and David Ricardo as the leading protagonists of two distinctly opposed views. Ricardo argued that general unemployment could not occur in a market economy except, possibly, as a transitory condition that would be speedily eliminated by the automatic operation of the market mechanism. The basis of this was an argument that Ricardo, following his mentor James Mill, attributed to the prominent French economist, Jean-Baptiste Say. The proposition that became known as 'Say's law' contends that the aggregate demand for commodities is determined by the aggregate supply of them and therefore there can never be a general deficiency of demand or, in the language of the period, a 'general glut' of commodities, except as a temporary result of events such as financial panics which, for a brief period, disturb the working of the market mechanism. In this respect, so went the argument, a complex market economy is no different from a simple one. In the one-man economy of Robinson Crusoe, it is evident that, since Crusoe produces in order to consume, there is no supply of commodities without corresponding demand. In a complex money-exchange economy, supply and demand similarly correspond in the aggregate, since, though commodities are produced for sale rather than direct use, the income generated on the production side of the economy is used to buy commodities of equivalent value. If a person does not use all his income for consumption, the rest is devoted to investment, or it is loaned, directly or through financial intermediaries, to others who make investment expenditures. In any case, aggregate demand will always match aggregate supply.

Malthus rejected Say's law, contending that there could be a large and lasting deficiency of aggregate demand and, as a result, unemployment, since some labourers who were willing to work at the going wage rate would be unable to find work because of the deficient demand for commodities. Malthus was on the right track (Keynes recognized him in the *General Theory* as a precursor), but he did not construct a coherent theory to support his view, and the victory went to Ricardo, whose authority on theoretical matters was, at the time of this debate (the 1820's) unchallengeable. For a long time thereafter, in fact until Keynes, Say's law was generally accepted as indisputable economic truth.

Quite apart from Say's law, which, in effect, denied the existence of unemployment, the theoretical apparatus of classical economics was quite incapable of dealing with the problem. One reason for this was that, according to classical wage fund theory, the demand for labour is determined by the savings of capitalists, not by the demand for commodities. As J. S. Mill put it, 'demand for commodities is not demand for labour'. Until the wage fund theory was rejected and the demand for labour was recognized as derived from the demand for the commodities that labour produces, it was not possible to take the first step in developing a theory of unemployment. Another defect of classical economics in this context was that the theory of value it contained implicitly ruled out the possibility of unemployment. A common feature of all variants of classical value theory is that the cost of production of a (non-agricultural) commodity is independent of the quantity of it produced. If this were true, the scale of production would be irrelevant and one man, by himself, could produce hats, say, at the same per-unit cost as a large hat factory could. Anyone who could not find an employer to hire him could simply produce hats, or anything else, on his own, so there could be no such thing as involuntary unemployment.

The neoclassical model did not suffer from these specific defects. Its recognition of the significance of fixed costs, and its extension of the law of diminishing returns beyond the domain of agriculture, destroyed the classical notion that manufactured goods are produced at a constant cost, independent of the quantity. Also, the notion of 'marginal productivity' became the foundation of a new conception of the demand for labour as derived from the demand for commodities, which replaced the classical wage fund theory. But the neoclassical economists did not reject Say's law and, with only a few notable exceptions, the dominant view was that general and persistent unemployment is impossible. John A. Hobson was denied appointment to university teaching posts because his views on unemployment were regarded as demonstrating that he was 'unsound'. As we noted above, Hobson regarded unemployment as occurring in a capitalistic market economy because the grossly unequal distribution of income resulted in a deficiency of aggregate demand for the commodities that can be produced. But beyond this he could not go, because the neoclassical theory, which he accepted, could not be used to tackle macroeconomic phenomena such as general unemployment.

Within the framework of the neoclassical model, with its focus on the operation of specific markets, the existence of unemployment can only be due to something that prevents the labour market from functioning according to the canons of perfect competition. Like other things traded in markets, the quantity of labour that workers wish to supply will always be equal to the quantity that employers demand unless the price of labour, i.e. the wage rate, is prevented from performing its equilibrating function. According to this reasoning, unemployment is due to the actions of trade unions, or the state, in maintaining the wage rate at too high a level.

Embedded in this argument is a flaw of the sort that logicians call the 'fallacy of composition', the attribution of a proposition that is true of the parts of a whole, to the whole itself. In a particular labour market (the market for a specific class of labour in a specific location), the inability of some of the suppliers of that labour to find employment must be attributed to a specific wage rate above the equilibrium level, since it would speedily be corrected if the wage rate were to fall. In the *General Theory* Keynes pointed out that this proposition cannot be applied generally to the labour markets of a whole economy. A general fall of wage rates will result in a contraction of the aggregate income of the working class and, therefore, will cause a reduction in their demand for commodities. Since wage earners are a large part of the population and their demand for commodities is, therefore, a large part of the aggregate demand, one cannot argue with any assurance that a fall in wage rates will increase employment. In a perfectly competitive economy a fall in wage rates will lead to a reduction in prices, and this will increase the quantity of commodities purchased by those whose incomes have not fallen, but since the income of the labouring class is now lower, the aggregate demand for commodities may in fact be reduced rather than increased.

Some economists have interpreted Keynes as arguing that unemployment is due to 'sticky' wage rates, but this is incorrect. His model was based upon the assumption of perfect competition, where all prices, including wage rates, are free to move in response to the forces of supply and demand. Like his predecessors who investigated the 'market failures' of a competitive economy, Keynes's theoretical approach to unemployment was guided by the notion that it reflected a basic flaw in such a system of economic organization rather than the consequence of interference with its mode of operation. But he departed from his predecessors in market failure analysis in a significant way. The phenomenon of widespread and persistent unemployment, he realized, could not be analysed by means of the neoclassical model; it required the construction of a new model in which the level of analysis is shifted from particular markets to the behaviour of the economy as a whole.

Before I go on to sketch the essentials of Keynes's theory, we should note that it is not quite true to say that the classical and neoclassical economists construed unemployment to be literally 'impossible'. The repeated occurrence of economic depressions in the nineteenth century would have been sufficient, of itself, to falsify such a bold proposition. Empirical investigation of such events seemed to indicate periodic regularity in them, which suggested that a market economy is characterized by recurrent cycles of alternating prosperity and depression. Clément Juglar, a French physician who became interested in economics, pioneered the study of what was later called 'business cycles' in his *Les Crises commerciales et leur retour périodique en France, en Angleterre et aux Etats-Unis* (1862), in which he not only described the phenomenon but attempted to construct a theoretical model to explain it. Numerous economists followed Juglar's lead and, by Keynes's time, the literature contained many models of the business cycle and many empirical studies of what had become generally recognized as an important economic phenomenon. So far as the problem of unemployment is concerned, the significance of these studies is that unemployment was construed as due fundamentally to the business cycle, something that occurs during the cycle's depression phase. In order, therefore, to understand why people sometimes cannot find jobs one must explain why business cycles occur, and in order to prevent unemployment one must make changes in the structure of the economy that will dampen down its cyclical behaviour.

When Keynes began to work on the problem of unemployment he adopted this stance. The cyclical pattern of economic activity was prominent in the first drafts of the *General Theory* but, as his work proceeded, he gradually suppressed this orientation, and when the book was sent to the publisher the notion of cycles had disappeared from the main text and was confined to a brief appendix at the end. Keynes attempted to explain, not why the level of unemployment goes up and down, but why high levels of unemployment can persist for a long time. Britain had not enjoyed the prosperity of the 1920's that the United States and other countries experienced. The depression of the early 1930's meant, for Britain, a further increase in unemployment that had been high continuously since the end of the first World War. In Keynes's view, the problem that demanded the attention of economists was to explain why unemployment could exist as a state of 'equilibrium' in a market economy. According to the business cycle approach, if there were no cycles the economy would experience a steady state of full employment with no significant interruptions. The model of the *General Theory* depicts an economy in which a high level of unemployment can persist as a steady state, the normal operation of the market mechanism being insufficient, by itself, to correct the situation. The notion of cycles still perseveres in the popular and professional discussion of macroeconomic problems, but none of the theoretical models of the business cycle has been generally adopted by economists, and little effort is now being devoted to constructing new ones. Many economists do not accept Keynes's view that an economy may be construed as being in a state of 'equilibrium' when it has a high level of involuntary unemployment, but the basic framework of macroeconomic analysis that students of economics are taught today is derived from the non-cyclical model of the *General Theory*.

John Maynard Keynes was an outstanding master of English prose. Many of his works, even those dealing with technical matters, are models of lucidity and style. But even economists, who are accustomed to reading bad prose, unanimously regard the *General Theory* as one of the most obscurely written books in the history of the discipline. It was composed in haste, and the manuscript was sent to the publisher before Keynes had succeeded in working out a coherent analysis. It was severely criticized, and some prominent economists dismissed it altogether as not meriting serious consideration. But there were others who perceived the book to contain a promising new approach to the problem of unemployment, and two of them, most notably A. P. Lerner and J. R. Hicks, published brief and lucid accounts of what they conceived to be the essential argument of the *General Theory* which powerfully influenced the views of professional economists. Within a few years, Keynes's basic ideas were widely accepted and his way of explaining the causes of unemployment replaced the cycle models and other modes of analysis. If methodological novelty and rapidity of professional acceptance are the criteria of a 'scientific revolution', then the late 1930's were an era in which a revolution took place in the field of economics. It was a partial revolution, however. Keynes did not undertake to replace the orthodox neoclassical theory of resource allocation or its analysis of market failures. His aim was to supplement that theory by providing an analysis of unemployment which, though it was the most conspicuous and most important of those failures, was beyond the analytical capacity of neoclassical microeconomics. For the purposes of this chapter it is, fortunately, unnecessary for us to examine the *General Theory* in detail, or to study the various interpretations of it that have been advanced over the past fifty years. I will outline, very briefly, the essential features of Keynesian macroeconomics in the form that modern students are introduced to it in standard elementary courses in economics.

The first point we should note is that, though the analysis of unemployment was Keynes's central objective and remains one of the main concerns of modern macroeconomics, unemployment as such does not appear as a variable in the Keynesian model. The reason for this is that a direct measurement of unemployment must run in terms such as the number of persons who cannot find work or the number of man-hours wasted, which cannot be rendered commensurate with the other variables of the model, such as the magnitude of consumption expenditures or the foreign trade of an economy, which are expressed in monetary terms. Keynes's solution for this mensuration difficulty was to use the size of the 'national income' as a proxy for the volume of employment. For a given level of technology, the stock of capital, etc., the national income will vary directly with the volume of employment. In such a static economic model there is, therefore, a certain level of the national income that corresponds to full employment. The analytical object of Keynesian theory is to explain why an economy may have, persistently, a national income less than this full employment level.

The fundamental structure of Keynesian theory was described above in Chapter 6, where some examples of theoretical models were given to illustrate the methodology of modelling in the social sciences. The central analytical idea of the model, as we there observed, is the depiction of the economy as a circular flow of income and expenditure. We encountered the circular flow paradigm earlier, in our study of the eighteenth-century French Physiocrats (Chapter 5). Keynes made no reference to the Physiocrats in the *General Theory* and, though he had a keen interest in the history of economics, he may not have recognized any affinity between their work and his. But, at any rate, the differences between the Keynesian model and the Physiocratic one are more important than the similarities.

In the standard rendition of the Keynesian model, two omnibus categories, 'individuals' (or sometimes 'households') and 'firms' are depicted as the primary economic entities. All property is considered to be owned by individuals, who sell its services, and their own personal services, to firms. The firms use the productive services they have bought to produce commodities which they sell to individuals, who buy them with the income they have obtained by selling productive services. Thus a circular flow of incomes and expenditures is occurring.

As so far described, the model cannot be construed as causal in nature. The magnitudes of aggregate income and aggregate expenditure are equal to each other, but no inference as to which determines which is implied. The crucial step in making this model 'Keynesian' is the contention that aggregate expenditure is the driving force of the economy, determining the national income and, therefore, the level of employment. Keynesian economics stresses the primary importance of the demand side of the economy; in effect, it reverses the causal direction of Say's law. Keynes agreed with the classical notion that aggregate demand equals aggregate supply, but while the classical economists had argued that supply creates demand, Keynes's view was that, on the contrary, demand creates supply.

The basic Keynesian model can be easily extended by dividing the economy into three sectors: the private sector, the public (or government) sector, and the international sector. In each of these sectors activities can be identified that constitute income-generating expenditures on the nation's goods and services, and activities that do not. In the private sector, expenditure on consumer goods and capital goods generates sales receipts for firms which translate into income for the individuals who supply firms with the services of factors of production. But if individuals save some of their income, the circular flow is reduced, income receipts fall, and unemployment ensues, unless the individuals who save (i.e. refrain from consuming) use their savings to purchase capital goods or lend them to firms which make such investment expenditures. Any difference between the aggregate savings of individuals and firms and the aggregate volume of their investment expenditures will drive the national income up or down. In the government sector, taxes absorb some of the private income, while government expenditures are income-generating. In the international sector, expenditures on imported goods divert some of the nation's income flow to foreign channels, thus reducing the volume of one country's circular flow and increasing that of another. Exports, of course, do the reverse. Summarizing, we can say the circular flow of income and expenditure is contracted if saving exceeds investment in the private sector, if tax collection exceeds expenditure in the government sector, and if imports exceed exports in the international sector. The flow is enlarged if these relationships are reversed.

The import of this construction is that the national income will move up and down in response to these variables. Its equilibrium value, which is the net result of the expanding and contracting factors, need not necessarily be at the level that corresponds to full employment, and the market mechanism, which operates through prices, cannot be relied upon to drive the national income towards the full employment level when it is below it. A state of unemployment in a market economy can therefore persist for a long time unless the government intervenes. Keynesian theory does not specify that the government should intervene in its own sector, since the state can in various ways affect the behaviour of the private and international sectors, but the implication of the theory with regard to the fiscal operations of the state was its most striking and controversial feature in the domain of economic policy. According to the Keynesian model, if the contributions of the private and international sectors to the circular flow are insufficient to generate full employment, the state can compensate for the deficiency by modifying its tax revenues and/or its expenditures in order to generate a budgetary deficit in the public sector.

Prior to the publication of the *General Theory*, many economists, in both Britain and America, had been urging their governments to take action against the depression by increasing public expenditures, and some had also recommended that tax rates should be reduced. But others had argued strongly against such policies on the ground that they would impact upon the private sector in ways that would negate the beneficial effects and, indeed, probably make the situation worse. Neither of these opposed policy positions could be supported by systematic theoretical reasoning. In several earlier writings Keynes had attacked the notion (which he perceived to dominate the views of the senior economic advisers of the British government) that the state was powerless to combat the depression by means of its fiscal policy. One of the main aims of the *General Theory* was to demonstrate that the 'Treasury view', as he called it, was invalid, by constructing a theoretical model showing how the various sectors of the economy articulate together in the determination of the national income. The acceptance of this model by economists meant that the weight of professional opinion was mobilized in support of the contention that the fiscal policy of the state could be, and should be, oriented to the aim of full employment. The passage of the Employment Act of 1946 in the United States, and similar official actions in other countries, is indicative of the fact that, by the end of the second World War, the Keynesian view of public-sector policy had become the dominant one. The larger import of this is that the modern state was charged with another major responsibility in the economic domain. In addition to supplying collective goods and services, correcting the market failures that distort the allocation of resources, and redistributing income, which had derived from classical and neoclassical economics, the Keynesian model led to the view that the state bears a primary responsibility for combating unemployment and, more broadly, for maintaining a high and stable level of economic activity.

In addition to its impact upon economic theory and the economic role of the state, Keynesian macroeconomics also played an important role in the development of empirical economics. While Keynes and his colleagues at Cambridge were struggling with ideas and concepts that might be used to construct a theory of persistent unemployment, work was in progress elsewhere (particularly by Simon Kuznets in the United States) aimed at devising a method of macroeconomic accounting that would present a systematic and comprehensive overview of the economy in terms of quantitative magnitudes. The successful completion of this work was greatly assisted by the conceptual framework of the *General Theory*. And, in turn, one of the reasons for the rapid acceptance of the Keynesian model was that the parallel development of national income accounting showed how the model could be invested with empirical quantities. A mastery of the structure of the 'national income accounts' is now an indispensable part of any economist's academic training. On a different level, the Keynesian model also played an important role in the use of mathematics to devise more powerful techniques for the analysis of statistical data. The development of 'econometrics,' like national income accounting, was well in train before the *General Theory* was published, but the Keynesian model supplied a practical focus for it that engaged the interest of many more economists and led to the rapid maturation of its methodology and its adoption, in all branches of economics, as the dominant mode of empirical research.

Keynesian macroeconomics was, as I have repeatedly emphasized, oriented to the understanding of a particular economic problem and its practical solution, but the prefix 'macro' has some broader philosophical implications that we should note before we leave the subject. In Chapter 3 B above we observed that though the principle of reduction has frequently been advocated as the appropriate methodology for all scientific investigation, even in the natural sciences it has not been rigorously adopted. If it were, all scientific explanations would run in terms of laws that operate at the level of particle physics. But biologists and geologists, for example, consider that their work is satisfactorily complete when they are able to supply nomological statements which apply to much higher levels of organization. In fact all sciences, and their branches, operate at distinctive 'nomological levels'. Within the general field of biology, for example, modern genetics operates at the molecular level, while ecology deals with the interaction of whole organisms in a habitat.

The doctrine of 'methodological individualism' that many social scientists have supported does not contend that social phenomena should be explained in terms of physical, or chemical, or even biological laws; the thrust of the argument is that these phenomena result from the actions of individual persons and must, therefore, be traced to laws that operate at the level of individual decision-making. As we have frequently observed in this history of the social sciences, economists have generally adopted this epistemic principle, while sociologists, on the whole, have not. But within economics, macroeconomics employs synthetic variables such as national income, aggregate savings, imports, etc., while in microeconomics, the prefix indicates that the phenomena are explained in terms of propositions – such as the law of diminishing utility and the law of diminishing returns – that operate at the level of the individual consumer and producer. Keynesian macroeconomics represents a significant breach in the principle of methodological individualism. Some critics of Keynesian theory contend that this breach is impermissible, and that the arguments of macroeconomics cannot be accepted as scientifically valid unless they can be rigorously derived from nomological propositions that pertain to the level of individual behaviour. The linkage of macroeconomics to microeconomics that this view demands has, so far, eluded the efforts of economic theorists. In the meantime, reflecting the fact that most economists value heuristic effectiveness and practicality more than the principle of methodological individualism, macroeconomics remains an established, even though much troubled, branch of the discipline. We cannot usefully examine any further here the philosophical issues that are involved. They will engage our attention in the next, and final, chapter, in which I will undertake a general assessment of the philosophical status of the social sciences.

Chapter 18

The foundations of science

A famous remark by Immanuel Kant about the complementarity of 'concepts' and 'percepts' has been paraphrased by Imre Lakatos to contend that 'philosophy of science without history of science is empty; history of science without philosophy of science is blind'. In the preceding chapters of this book I have tried to follow Kant's advice that philosophy and intellectual history should be blended by discussing philosophical questions as occasion has offered within the framework of a (more or less) chronological account of the development of the social sciences. This procedure, convenient for the writer, has, I hope, also served the needs of the reader; but we have not yet confronted directly the central issues that are addressed by the philosophy of science in general and the particular philosophical problems that are encountered in attempting to apply 'scientific methods' to the study of social phenomena. These matters have received a great deal of attention, especially during the past half-century or so, from professional philosophers and social scientists. This literature, however, has settled few, if any, of the epistemic problems of natural or social science. On the contrary, we live in an era in which, while scientists claim to be making progress at a faster pace than ever before, philosophers have thrown a cloud of doubt upon their enterprise by raising fundamental issues concerning the basic foundations of knowledge which, though largely disregarded by practising scientists, cannot be ignored if one is to avoid the blindness that Kant spoke of. In this chapter I will sketch and appraise the recent developments in the philosophy of science that have raised these doubts, discuss the main suggestions that have been advanced by those who contend that some radical new approach to the understanding of the scientist's beliefs about the world is required, and discuss the special problems that are encountered when the object of the scientific enterprise is to advance our knowledge of human society.

The reader of the preceding pages will know already that I have a high regard for science and for its contributions to Western civilization. Criticism of the logical foundations of science, and warranted concern about the effects of some of its applications, do not negate the fact that science has furnished us with reliable knowledge about the world we inhabit and has enabled us to conquer many of the ills that, until just yesterday on the time-scale of man's existence, ubiquitously beset the human condition. In saying this I am referring not only to the progress of pure science in revealing the structure and organization of nature, nor only to technological progress in the form of such things as eyeglasses, electric motors, antibiotics, and hybrid corn. Equally, or more, significant is the role that science has played in emancipating us from certain metaphysical beliefs that made the social lives of our ancestors fearful, servile, and miserable. We no longer throw women, bound hand and foot, into a pond to ascertain whether or not they are witches, not because scientists have devised a better test, but because the scientific way of thinking has undermined belief in occult powers. The four primary forces that physicists tell us are the bases of our universe are incomprehensible to the layman, but they are quite unlike the forces that mystics of old invoked to bully, maim, and murder the powerless members of their communities.

In Chapter 8 above we examined, in the context of political theory and social philosophy, the notions of 'progress' and 'perfection'. We found there that, while some social philosophers have been content with the assurance that man can improve his social life, others will settle for no less than a perfect social order. For the latter, any flaw in the social order is sufficient to condemn it altogether. The literature of the philosophy of science is punctuated by a similar opposition. Some regard the philosophy of science as undertaking to explain how our knowledge of the world has been able to grow more reliable and more extensive; others view it as an exercise in apodictics – the search for principles that guarantee the absolute certainty of knowledge. Just as utopian social philosophers are unable to find any functioning society that meets their demand for perfection, apodictic philosophers of science find that the practices of working scientists must be denounced, because they cannot guarantee certainty. In section A of this chapter I will begin by examining the historical background of the demand for certainty and its modern embodiment in the philosophy of 'positivism'. Then I will discuss various philosophies that have sought to occupy the domain that became vacant when it was finally realized that certainty is impossible. Finally, I shall present a brief account of an 'instrumentalist' philosophy of science, which takes the stance that objectivity and progress in our search for knowledge are possible, even though certainty is not.

A. THE PHILOSOPHY OF SCIENCE

1. The rise and fall of positivism

The philosophy we shall be examining here is the theory of the foundations of knowledge promulgated in the 1920's by the Vienna Circle philosophers as 'logical positivism'. It was later renamed 'logical empiricism' but it is still referred to in the literature of epistemology as 'positivism'. The term was coined

by Auguste Comte but, as we noted above in Chapter 12 D, there is little affinity
between the positivism that Comte and Saint-Simon and their disciples
espoused and the epistemological doctrine that, following the work of the
Vienna Circle, was widely accepted by philosophers of science and by most
practising scientists who explicitly considered the epistemic foundations of
their craft. Rudolph Carnap, one of the members of the Circle, suggested the
term 'logical empiricism' in order to avoid the association with the ideas of
Comte that 'positivism' conveyed. There was, however, one important point on
which their views were the same. Comte had adopted the term to signify that
science can furnish knowledge of which one can say that one is not the least bit
doubtful. The Vienna Circle and their successors had very different ideas as to
how such knowledge could be obtained, but they were inspired by the same
notion that absolute certainty was possible.

Comte invented the term, but not the idea. As a mathematician he was heir
to a tradition that went back to the development, in ancient Greece, of
knowledge derived by logical deduction from propositions that were construed
to be self-evident 'axioms' and, therefore, indubitably true. The corpus of
Euclidian geometry, which contained many propositions concerning the
properties of space that were not self-evident in themselves, was viewed as
beyond dispute because it was derived from axioms. In the era that we call the
'scientific revolution', Euclidian geometry was widely regarded as the ideal
which all seekers of truth should aspire to emulate. Descartes, in his *Discourse
on Method* (1637), undertook to deduce, from a single indubitable axiom, not
only new mathematical propositions, but the orbits of the planets, the existence
of God, and the location of the human soul. Newton's physical mechanics was
more empirically constrained, but his great *Principia* (1687) was laid out in
Euclidian form. Spinoza tried to do likewise in his *Ethics* (1677), and Hobbes
wrote his *Leviathan* (1651) in the conviction that a science of politics as
demonstrative as Euclid's geometry could be constructed. These are just a few
of those whose work reflected the sway of Euclidian certainty over the
seventeenth-century mind. The influence of this way of thinking was undermined by the steady advance of empirical science, which, especially in fields
outside physics, had to deal with materials that did not lend themselves to
axiomatization. Euclidian geometry itself was dethroned from its pinnacle,
during the first half of the nineteenth century, by Lobachevsky, Bolyai, and
Riemann, who demonstrated that if one of Euclid's axioms (that parallel lines,
when extended, cannot cross) were abandoned, other geometries could be
devised which represent different spatial worlds. In physics, the bastion of
mathematical certainty, the properties of the material universe were similarly
rendered more contingent by the development, in the early twentieth century,
of Einstein's relativity theory, Heisenberg's uncertainty principle, and the
replacement of Newtonian physics by quantum mechanics.

None the less, philosophers of science did not abandon the quest for
certainty. Biologists, geologists, and even physicists might have had to regard

their explanations of natural phenomena as tentative, subject to modification, but the *methodology* of scientific investigation need not itself be construed as unavoidably contingent. The Vienna Circle positivists and their followers took the view that though we may be unable to arrive at apodictic truths about the world for practical reasons, we can establish, once and for all, the ideal epistemic principles that must be followed by those engaged in the search for truth. Epistemology was not construed by them as an empirical science; it was a metascience that undertook to establish the 'higher-level' rules of scientific investigation. At this level, certainty is not only possible, they argued, but essential to the furtherance of proper science and the rejection of 'pseudo-science'.

Before we embark on an examination of how positivism undertook to realize its epistemic goals, we must note another trend in thought which, during the nineteenth century especially, claimed to have discovered a method of cognitive certainty. This was romanticism, and its method was intuition. According to the romantics, man's capacity for obtaining knowledge by intuition is not restricted to the propositions about space that provide the foundational axioms of Euclidian geometry. The power of intuition can enable us (or, at least, some of us) to apprehend infallibly the real nature of the world and its fundamental properties, its metaphysics that lies beneath its physics, the transcendental entities and forces that are more fundamental than the immediate appearances of things and events. This line of thought, a revival of Platonism, had more influence in the arts than in the sciences, but, especially through Hegel, it had a considerable impact upon European philosophy. In stating their principles of epistemology, the positivists aimed to destroy the metaphysical pretensions of romanticism. In this they were successful, but they went too far, claiming that science has no need of any metaphysical assumptions about the world and that the presence of such assumptions in a theory is sufficient warrant to reject it as pseudo-science. But we are getting ahead of the story. Let us turn now to examine the principles that the positivists sought to establish as the proper philosophy of science.

In dealing with the ideas of any group of people in general terms, one unavoidably does less than justice to the individual members. The Vienna Circle was a close-knit group of thinkers. They met frequently to discuss their philosophic views and issued a manifesto expressing their common opinion. Nevertheless, even the three or four leading members of the Circle held somewhat different views. I shall not discuss these differences, but concentrate here on the epistemological doctrines that are today usually identified as the central theses of their shared philosophy.

Vienna Circle positivism derived from three traditions in the philosophy of science: one, exemplified by Euclidian geometry, emphasized the power of *a priori* reasoning in obtaining knowledge about the world; another was the tradition of empiricism as established mainly by English writers such as Francis Bacon, Locke, Hume, Whewell, John Herschel, and J. S. Mill; and a third which stemmed from the efforts of various philosophers, following Kant, to treat his novel notion that there are concepts, such as space and time, that are both *a priori* and 'synthetic' (i.e. empirical) as posing a semantic problem, and the insistence on close examination of the language in which thought is expressed by philosophers such as G. E. Moore. The Vienna Circle undertook to blend these diverse traditions into a unified philosophy that would state the foundations of human knowledge. In calling their manifesto 'The Scientific Conception of the World' they did not mean that they intended to delineate the particular world-view of natural scientists, or to restrict their principles to the domain of material phenomena. Though they often seemed to have physics in mind when speaking of 'science', and matter and energy in mind when speaking of 'phenomena', they felt that they had arrived at foundational epistemic principles that apply to all properly conducted attempts to obtain knowledge, not excluding those that deal with psychological and social phenomena. Indeed, the manifesto of the Circle, issued in 1929, ended with the confident statement that 'We witness the spirit of the scientific world-conception penetrating in growing measure the forms of personal and public life, in education, upbringing, architecture, and the shaping of economic and social life according to rational principles.'

Social scientists paid little attention to the Vienna Circle philosophers, but we should keep in mind, as we consider their doctrines, that the members of the Circle, and most of their successors, regarded positivist principles as applying, without amendment, to the social sciences. These principles were viewed as mandatory normative rules for the investigation of *all* phenomena. The Vienna Circle philosophers, despite holding the view that physics is the archetypical science, did not undertake merely to *describe* the methods that physicists and other successful scientists employ; their aim was canonical, to *prescribe* methodological maxims for all rational procedures of inquiry.

Euclidian geometry, as we have seen, undertook to establish indubitable propositions about reality by logical analysis, using premises that were considered as factually true by 'self-evidence'. The positivists had no objection to the use of deductive logic but they were wary of the notion of self-evidently true factual propositions. In their view, the only reliable source of factual information about the real world is the empirical data we obtain by our senses. Euclidian geometry claimed that the world *cannot* be otherwise, a contention that had been cast down by the construction of non-Euclidian geometries. The positivists took the stance that the task of science is to tell us how the world *is* and, in this enterprise, *a priori* axioms, or metaphysical assumptions, or any other notions that do not represent observable entities are not permissible. The positivists were ultra-empiricist in insisting that the concepts of science must refer only to sensory-world things and events and that the language of scientific discourse must be strictly representational. They were greatly influenced in this by Ludwig Wittgenstein's *Tractatus Logico-philosophicus* (1921). This advanced the view (which Wittgenstein later abandoned) that a language of communication consists of terms that directly correspond to sensory-world entities. One may, as an individual, have thoughts that do not consist of 'pictures' of the real world outside one's mind, but such thoughts cannot be expressed in language, for language cannot be private; it is a social phenomenon. The positivists took the same view and, going further than Wittgenstein, declared that statements that do not represent observable entities are simply meaningless noises or unintelligible marks on paper, and applied this severe judgement not only to professional scientific discourse but to all domains of human communication.

According to the initial positivist view, the task of the scientist is to describe the world, not to explain it. Any purported explanation of a phenomenon, the *why* of its occurrence, is an effort to delineate its causes, and causation is not a legitimate concept. In this the positivists followed David Hume's view that causation is not an observable property. We may observe that one event regularly precedes another, for example, but we are not justified in calling one the cause and the other the effect. Our senses inform us only that they are empirically associated; causal connection is a theoretical inference that neither factual observation nor deductive logic can support. The later 'logical empiricists' did not take such an abstemious stance. The 'covering law' model of science advanced by Carl Hempel, as we have seen in our examination of 'The Methodology of History' (Chapter 14), advanced the view that the central task of human inquiry is to explain phenomena, and indeed, that non-observable entities – causal connections – play an essential role in explanation. Hempel and other 'logical empiricists' viewed science as proceeding by making theoretical 'hypotheses' which need not necessarily refer to observable entities as long as inferences can logically be deduced from them that are verifiable by direct observation. This revision of positivism, though more defensible than the epistemological stance of the Vienna Circle, was subjected to strong criticism, beginning in the 1950's. What historians now refer to as the 'downfall of positivism' resulted more from inadequacies that were discovered in logical empiricism than from the doctrines of the Vienna Circle and their hard-line disciples. Before we examine these criticisms a few more remarks on the original positivist stance are necessary in order to prepare the ground for consideration of the 'downfall' and its effects on the philosophy of science.

We might note first that the rules prescribed by the Vienna Circle philosophers for the conduct of human inquiry were not applied by them to their own investigation of the philosophy of science. They did not base their epistemological propositions on empirical evidence and did not eschew the use of concepts that refer to non-observable entities in advancing their prescriptive doctrines. Nevertheless, they obviously did not regard their own statements as meaningless; in effect, they claimed that the philosophy of science is exempt from the rules of inquiry that must govern all other disciplines. Many philosophers, including critics of the Vienna Circle doctrines, have contended that epistemology, being a 'meta-science', is not required to adhere to the rules it prescribes for scientific inquiry. This contention is defensible but, nevertheless, the test of 'self-reference' (that no epistemic proposition may demand criteria of validity that it itself cannot meet) would seem to be legitimate, if not crucial. Recently a number of writers have argued that the philosophy of science must itself be an empirical science, using as its primary data the history of science and the practices of contemporary scientists. This extension of positivist descriptivism is prominent in the work of Thomas Kuhn, Imre Lakatos, and a number of writers on the 'sociology of science'. These approaches are of special interest to the social scientist because they emphasize the point that knowledge is a social fact and that scientific investigation is a social phenomenon. We will examine these views anon.

One of the main objectives of the Vienna Circle was to banish what they called 'metaphysics' from the domain of rational discourse. The opening paragraph of their manifesto refers to 'metaphysical and theologising thought' and 'speculation' as being 'on the increase' but expresses confidence that 'the opposite spirit of enlightenment and *anti-metaphysical factual research* is growing stronger' (italics in original). The word 'metaphysics' was used as an omnibus term for all forms of discourse that employed non-observational concepts. A. J. Ayer, whose *Language, Truth and Logic* (1936) represented the high-water mark of positivist semantics, in an essay entitled 'Demonstration of the Impossibility of Metaphysics' (*Mind*, 1934) declared that

> any attempt to describe the nature or even to assert the existence of something lying beyond the reach of empirical observation must consist in the enunciation of pseudo-propositions, a pseudo-proposition being a series of words that may seem to have the structure of a sentence but is in fact meaningless.

The positivists may have intended to attack the notion, still prevalent in the modern world, that there are invisible spirits, occult forces, and divine powers, beyond the reach of human cognition, that exercise influence on worldly events. In doing so, however, they denied not only scientific status but even unsophisticated intelligibility, or 'meaning', to a large domain of human thought: poetry and the other fine arts, ethics and other disciplines engaged in the study of values, and all forms of religious belief. It is one thing to point out that there is a difference between beliefs that are supported by empirical science and those that are not; it is quite another to claim that the latter are necessarily nonsensical. According to the canonical demands of positivism, the social science disciplines that employ non-observational concepts such as 'motives', 'preferences', and other states of mind, even though they make use of empirical data, would have to be reconstructed so as to eliminate such concepts if they were not to be dismissed as worthless.

Quite apart from their failure to apply the canons of positivism to their philosophy of science, the early positivists did not rigorously adhere to them in their own scientific work. The most striking example was Otto Neurath.

Neurath and Rudolf Carnap were the members of the Vienna Circle who insisted on the most extreme interpretation of the view that science deals only with observable entities. They embraced Ernst Mach's doctrine of 'physicalism' – that only physical entities have a real and observable existence and that the language of science must, therefore, consist of quantitatively precise descriptions of space–time points. If we examine Neurath's writings in his own field of sociology, however, a very different stance appears. (The following remarks are based upon a collection of his papers published in English under the title of *Empiricism and Sociology*, 1973). Neurath asserts that sociology has attained the full status of a science in that 'one can today formulate purely scientific sociological statements . . . in the sense of natural science' (p. 329), but he does not explicitly identify any such statements, much less show how they can be construed as 'physicalist'. On the contrary, he makes innumerable statements about social phenomena that could not meet even the least demanding request for supporting empirical evidence and are, in fact, clearly derived from his personal political ideology. Neurath was a Marxist and most of his sociological views were extensions of what he construed (not very accurately) to be Marxian theory. He did no empirical research in sociology and was evidently not well read in the social science literature of his day. He interpreted Marxian 'materialism' as epistemically equivalent to his own 'physicalism', and lauded Marx and Engels as having provided the foundations for a truly scientific study of society. In the future, he confidently declared, the proletariat will become 'the bearer of science without metaphysics' (p. 297). In the communist society that will inevitable come to pass, says Neurath, the economy will dispense with markets and the use of money, and will be administered perfectly without employing any numeraire for measuring and comparing the economic values of commodities. Foundationless declarations of this sort comprise the bulk of his contributions to 'empiricism and sociology'.

Neurath's views have some special interest for us because he was a professional sociologist, and they may perhaps be taken as providing some information of historic interest concerning the Vienna Circle view of the social sciences or, at least, help to explain the occasional remarks about them in the manifesto. But Neurath's role as chief publicity agent for the Circle raises an issue that goes well beyond its attempt to establish the canons of scientific inquiry. Words like 'scientific' and 'meaningful' are not merely descriptive terms; they carry evaluative connotations, designating something as worthy, deserving admiration and emulation. But people do not have to obtain a licence from some transcendent authority to use such words, so they *can* use them, if they have a mind to, for ideological propaganda, seeking to persuade by means of declarative labelling, without the use of reasoned argument or empirical evidence. We cannot avoid making evaluations, in scientific work as in other facets of life, but the cognitive enterprise is not furthered when words are used as flags to afford immediate identification of the contending parties in a dispute that is construed as a Manichaean struggle between the forces of good and evil for the governance of the world. It is noteworthy that the early positivists, while insisting that a meaningful language must not employ valuational and emotive terms, did not forgo the use of such terms in advancing the hegemonic claims of their philosophy.

The linguistic orientation of the Vienna Circle led to a dead end, not because of failure to abide by its own canons of meaningful language, but because the positivist programme shifted the focus of concern from the methods of scientific inquiry to the verbal statements used in scientific discourse. Epistemology was collapsed into the linguistic study of syntax and semantics. The linguistic analysts who were inspired by positivism made significant contributions, but statements about real-world entities are not the entities in themselves. In pursuing the linguistic implications of their doctrines the positivists abandoned their empiricism, and positivist philosophy degenerated into attenuated scholastic discourses on how scientists should *talk* about what they do. Neurath and Carnap even rejected the view that linguistic scientific propositions are verifiable by experience, contending that a complex of such propositions is self-verifying if the members of the complex support one another. The 'truth' of a single proposition is, according to this view, simply its 'meaning' in the complex. Such a stance, in effect, makes the verbal coherence of linguistic discourse the dominant epistemic criterion of science, asserts the primacy of *definitions*, and demotes sense data to, at best, a minor role. The aim of the Vienna Circle, to blend the three traditions of Euclidian deductivism, empiricism, and linguistics into a complete, universal, and indisputable philosophy of science was not realized.

One of the most serious weaknesses of early positivism was that it appeared to reject the use of any criteria to enable one to establish the domain of a scientific investigation by demarcating relevant from irrelevant factors. Without using a causal theory, how can one decide, say, that it is not necessary to take the density of Mars into account when investigating the shape of the DNA molecule? Astrology, which the positivists derided, employs concepts that refer to observable phenomena. How can its claims be dismissed without using an *a priori* metaphysical conception of reality that allows one to regard the positions of the planets as irrelevant to human events? According to the Vienna Circle canons, one would have to describe everything that is observable in order to describe anything. Such a demand would spell the end of rational inquiry, not its advancement.

Recognition of the necessary role of theory in scientific investigation led to the reformulation of positivism as an epistemic doctrine that focuses upon the explanation of a delimited class of phenomena by means of procedures in which empirical evidence is used to test the validity of theoretical propositions concerning causal linkages. As we noted in considering the INUS model of causation (Chapter 3 A 3 above) no real-world phenomenon can be explained by reference to a single causal factor, since all phenomena result from a *set* of factors. Lightning may be called the cause of a forest fire in an abbreviated account but a full statement would have to list the other factors that are necessary, such as dryness, the presence of combustible material, etc. In a famous paper published in 1948 ('The Logic of Explanation', *Philosophy of Science*) Carl Hempel and Paul Oppenheim argued that a full account of such a phenomenon would also have to include a statement of the relevant 'governing laws', such as, for example, that when the temperature of dry wood is raised beyond 400°C it commences to oxidize rapidly. Universal statements or 'laws' are necessary components of causal explanation, even of singular phenomena such as a particular forest fire. But how do we come by such general governing laws? They are not generalizations derived from immediate observation. They are theoretical hypotheses which, together with other postulated conditions, enable one to deduce certain conclusions that refer to observable phenomena. So, the argument goes, in this way the laws can be verified by sense data. Thus, for example, the occurrence of a forest fire, and many other singular events, including ones produced in laboratory experiments, certify the truth of the general law that wood begins to oxidize rapidly when its temperature is raised above 400°C. A reformulation of positivism that became widely accepted construed scientific explanation to be a form of argument using general covering laws which, though 'hypothetical', are legitimate because they have been verified, indirectly, by empirical experience.

This philosophy of science was not new. Its essentials had been stated a century earlier by (among others) John Stuart Mill in his *System of Logic* (1843). Moreover, many practising scientists explicitly stated equivalent epistemic doctrines or were implicitly guided by them. This takes nothing away from the importance of Hempel's argument. In view of the contentions of the Vienna Circle and the insistence of their claim to have set epistemology on the right track, a restatement of what was, in effect, a long-standing orthodox view was necessary. When the Hempelian formulation of positivist epistemology came under attack in the 1950's the effects on the philosophy of science were profound. The Vienna Circle doctrine was a self-destructing eccentric fad in the history of epistemology, but the Hempelian 'deductive–nomological model' had longer, and stronger, credentials. Its downfall ushered in an era that has witnessed an exploding volume of literature in the philosophy of science, in which numerous novel approaches have been proposed but, so far, no generally accepted statement of the foundations of scientific knowledge has emerged.

The basic form of the deductive–nomological model is equivalent to that of the Aristotelian syllogism, which we examined above in Chapter 3 A 2. It has three parts: (1) a proposition that is asserted to be universally true of a class of phenomena, i.e. a general law that covers all members of the class; (2) a proposition asserting that a particular phenomenon is a member of this class; (3) a proposition that is derived from (1) and (2) as a matter of logical deduction. If, for example, we say that (1) all swans are white; that (2) a particular entity is a swan; then it follows (3) that the entity is white. The formal logic of this procedure is impeccable, but the *empirical* truth of (3) rests upon the empirical truth of (1) and (2). Both these premises are problematic. Particular entities do not naturally arrange themselves neatly into classes; a classification system is a human artefact that is imposed upon the observation data. So, therefore, propositions such as (2) are not *purely* empirical, they contain a 'theoretical' component, or, as some philosophers say, empirical observations are 'theory-laden'. It will be convenient if we defer discussion of this problem until a later point, and focus here upon propositions such as (1) above which assert the existence of universal laws.

In order to maintain the empirical certainty of inferences obtained by the deductive–nomological procedure, the universal law premise must be empirically certain. To say that 'many' or even 'most' swans are white will not serve. It is not even formally sufficient to note that all swans that have ever been observed have been white, since there are, and have been, many unobserved swans in the world, and of course, future swans are not observable. In fact, this particular universal proposition had to be abandoned when black swans were found in Australia. We have no assurance that any universal empirical proposition is safer than the above proposition about the whiteness of swans. The 'problem of induction', as this came to be called, demonstrates that the law premise in the deductive–nomological model is not secure. Karl Popper, arguing that this problem is insurmountable, contended that if science is to be empirical, its so-called 'laws' must be treated as tentative hypotheses. Popper grossly exaggerated his differences from the Vienna Circle in his early writings, perhaps in part because of his fierce hostility to the Marxism that Neurath had brought to the group. His similarities to the positivists, however, were greater than the differences (see Ian Hacking's comparison of Carnap and Popper in *Representing and Intervening*, 1983, pp. 5 f.). But one point of difference deserves emphasis: the positivists aimed to specify methods that would generate certain knowledge while, in Popper's view, we can only hope to improve what must always remain imperfect.

In developing his own philosophy of science Popper seized upon the limitation of the *modus ponens* mode of logic that we noted when discussing it above (Chapter 3 A 2). If the premises of a syllogism are true, the conclusion must also be true. But this theorem is not reversible, that is, it does not permit one to say that if the conclusion is true the premises must be true. Such an assertion would commit the logical fallacy of 'affirming the consequent'. True conclusions can be logically derived from false premises. For example, the propositions that (1) all professional physicists are Marxists, and (2) Otto Neurath was a professional physicist, lead logically to the conclusion that (3) Neurath was a Marxist. If (1) is a theoretical hypothesis, then (3) is empirical evidence that helps to confirm it, since (3) is true. But (1) is not true. In order to avoid arguments that allow true empirical evidence to confirm false theories, Popper contended that scientific reasoning must use the *modus tollens* mode of deduction, which draws inferences about the premises from the observed *falsity* of the conclusion. The empirical truth of a conclusion tells us nothing for certain about the premises from which it is logically derived; but the empirical falsity of a conclusion is a certain indicator that at least one of the premises must be false. The famous Michelson–Morley experiment, for example, was conducted in order to test the proposition that there is a medium, called 'ether', through which light travels. The procedure was to deduce certain observable consequences that must logically follow if this proposition were true. The experiment was set up to test one of these consequences by means of a measuring apparatus. The data did not conform to the predicted value, thereby falsifying the currently accepted theory of light and casting doubt upon the concept of an ether. This 'negative experiment' played a significant role in sub-sequent work in theoretical physics which, according to some historians, led to Einstein's theory of relativity. Popper took this procedure as an archetypical exemplification of scientific method. Scientific knowledge, he maintained, is acquired by means of successive *Conjectures and Refutations* (the title of one of his books). Theories are tentative 'conjectures'. They cannot be verified by empirical evidence, but they can be refuted. We build up our knowledge of the world by ascertaining what is *not* true.

This ingenious 'solution' to the problem of induction appeared to place the enterprise of science on a solid epistemic footing. Popper's central thesis had been, apparently unbeknownst to him, clearly stated previously by William Stanley Jevons (*Principles of Science*, 1874), whom we encountered in Chapter 17 as one of the founders of 'marginal utility' theory in economics. But the context of Popper's statement was that, at the time that it was made, the philosophy of the Vienna Circle was rapidly rising to hegemonic status. Popper's *Logik der Forschung*, published in 1934 (translated into English as *The Logic of Scientific Discovery*, 1959), was as much an attack on the Vienna Circle as it was the presentation of an alternative epistemology. Popper's views made little headway initially, but as the difficulties of positivism became apparent his epistemology came to be widely embraced by philosophers and scientists. It was introduced to English-speaking economists by T. W. Hutchison's *The Significance and Basic Postulates of Economic Theory* in 1938 and, by 1980, Mark Blaug was able to argue with considerable plausibility in *The Methodology of Economics* that Popperian falsificationism was the philosophy of science that most economists accepted, though he noted that they failed to practise its precepts. In the natural sciences, too, Popperian epistemology was embraced (e.g. see Francisco J. Ayala's discussion of the philosophy of biology in chapter 16 of Theodosius J. Dobzhansky *et al.*, *Evolution*, 1977).

Popper's thesis that science proceeds by falsifying theories proved, however, to be as flawed as the claim that it proceeds by setting up empirical tests that can verify them. Again, the fact that a causal analysis involves attributing a phenomenal observation to a *set* of conditions is the heart of the problem. The universal law that wood burns when its temperature rises above 400°C is a necessary element in such a set, but it is not logically sufficient, in itself, to predict a forest fire. If a lightning strike, or a discarded match, or an unattended camp fire, or even the deliberate action of an arsonist, fails to start a forest fire, it does not demonstrate conclusively that the law must be wrong, since the failure may be due to the absence of other necessary factors. This point had been made, a generation before Popper's *Logik*, by Pierre Duhem, in 1906, and was restated by Willard van Orman Quine in 1951. The 'Duhem–Quine' thesis, as it is now called, does not say that falsifying observations are worthless in evaluating a theory, but it is a compelling argument against the contention that such observations are unambiguous evidence that the theory is wrong. In his *Logik* Popper rejected this thesis, but later he admitted that empirical evidence can only test a set of propositions and modified his falsification argument, most significantly by asserting that a theory cannot be rejected unless another theory is available that is better, according to certain criteria which he tried to establish. This was an important concession, since it, in effect, involved the notion that scientific knowledge grows by means of a contest between alternative theories, not simply through a confrontation between theory and empirical evidence.

So far we have considered only the *logic* of scientific explanation and confirmation. Another attack came from a different angle, questioning the reliability of sense data themselves. No one would argue that empirical observations are completely free of error. Science can contend with that, by better instrumentation, multiple observations, refined methods of statistical collection, etc. But what if the observations, however made, are guided by an *a priori* theory? In such a circumstance the theory can be neither verified nor falsified by the factual data, because so-called 'facts' are commingled with the theory that is to be tested. Some philosophers, most prominently Norwood Russell Hanson (*Patterns of Discovery*, 1958), contended that this problem is ubiquitous, and insurmountable. No factual data are free of theory, and none can be made free, since a theory of some sort is necessary in order to make any factual observation. The notion that theories can be tested by *independent* empirical evidence must be abandoned. This argument, which appeared to be supported by psychological findings as well as philosophical considerations, gave the *coup de grâce* to all versions of positivist epistemology, including Popper's, and indeed called into doubt the very possibility of constructing an objective body of scientific knowledge.

This problem would appear to be serious enough when one construes the enterprise of science as the construction of theories that are verified by, or at least not falsified by, empirical tests. It becomes more serious still if one takes the view that the role of empirical evidence is not to test a single theory, but to enable one to choose among alternative theories. Louis Althusser, for example, contends that one cannot choose between the economic theories of David Ricardo and Karl Marx because they are incommensurable, each having its own standards of validity (*Reading Capital*, 1970). According to this view, treating Ricardian and Marxian value theory as both having been falsified by the same empirical evidence (that the capital–labour ratio is not uniform across industries – see Chapters 9 A and 13 D 1 above) represents a failure to understand the nature of scientific inquiry. W. V. O. Quine formulated this problem more concretely in the terms of standard epistemology, without resort to the notion that observations are theory-laden, as the 'underdetermination thesis'. Stated briefly, this maintains that if more than one set of causal factors is sufficient to account for a phenomenon, then the empirical observation of it cannot tell us which set is operative, even if the observation is totally objective and not theory-laden.

Let us consider for example a problem in medical diagnostics. According to physiological theory, a painful swelling in the ankle joint might be due to (a) an injury, (b) a bacterial or viral infection, (c) an auto-immune disease such as arthritis, or (d) blood cancer (leukemia). These are quite different biological processes. The observation data (the swelling) are insufficient to determine which of them is the cause of the swelling. Modern medicine is not stumped by this sort of ambiguity, for other observations can be made to narrow the possibilities and, in many cases, reduce them to one. But Quine's point is that the central problem is not an empirical one but epistemic, since it is always possible to postulate additional theories that may account for the phenomenon. With a little theoretical inventiveness we may add to the above list such things as (e) environmental contamination, (f) childhood sexual trauma, (g) the conjunction of the planets, and (h) witchcraft. How do we then choose between the contending theories? Some theories, for example ones like (f) and (g), might be rejected on the grounds that they rest upon unacceptable meta-physical presumptions. However much one might be persuaded that this was so, it could not be proved; but even the adoption of a severely constrained mechanistic ontology would not do away with the problem of under-determination, since an unlimited number of mechanistic explanations can be postulated. Popper tried to solve the problem of theory choice by establishing criteria that would compare competing theories in terms of their 'truth-value.' The attempt failed, and it now seems clear that other types of criteria must be employed.

A criterion of theory choice that has a long lineage in the philosophy of science, going back at least to the heretical William of Ockham in the fourteenth century, says that, among equally explanatory theories, the simplest is the best. But we have no warrant for believing that the world is simple, or, as Newton put it, that 'nature is pleased with simplicity', so, as a representation of reality, a simple theory is not necessarily better than a complex one. Some philosophers have suggested that simplicity is a valid *aesthetic* criterion of theory choice, but what do aesthetic value judgements have to do with veridical accuracy? The romantic poet John Keats wrote that 'Beauty is truth, truth beauty – that is all Ye know on earth, and all ye need to know' – a good lyric, but bad philosophy. Simplicity, however, can be defended on other grounds if one adopts the view, which Ockham may have had in mind, that theories are not necessarily required to be representational models of reality, but are constructs that serve to render reality intelligible to the human mind. Given our limited intellectual powers, simple theories are better on pragmatic grounds than equally explanatory complex ones. Indeed, a perfect representational model, if it could be constructed, would necessarily be as incomprehensible as reality itself. Some modern macroeconomic models, consisting of hundreds of equations, while still far from capturing the complexity of the economy, seem already to have reached the limit of intelligibility. The computer prints out the solutions to the equations but its masters have difficulty explaining the *why* of these results in economic (as opposed to mathematical) terms. The criterion of simplicity, which accepts with equanimity that theories will be 'unrealistic', is based on the notion that theories are human creations designed to serve utilitarian purposes. We shall return to this point below.

So far we have focused on the flaws in the ultra-empiricist epistemology put forward by the Vienna Circle philosophers, in its reformulation by Hempel and others into the 'deductive–nomological' model of scientific explanation, and in Popper's thesis that a body of secure knowledge can be progressively developed by using the information provided by the empirical refutation of conjectural hypotheses. But the presence of a flaw in an epistemic thesis is not fatal, unless one takes the perfectionist view that the beliefs one holds about the world constitute scientific knowledge only if there are objective empirical grounds for regarding them as altogether beyond doubt. For the non-perfectionist the issue is: how important are these epistemic flaws for the enterprise of science? In considering this question I shall concentrate upon the 'problem of induction' and the notion that all observations are 'theory-laden'.

So far as scientists themselves are concerned, it seems that the problem of induction is not recognized even as a caution, much less as an impassable barrier to progress. When necessary, a scientist will, without a qualm, use 'Avogadro's number', which, though it has been computed from a limited set of specific cases, asserts that *all* gases, at equal temperature and pressure, contain 6.023×10^{23} molecules per gram molecular weight. In the *Handbook of Chemistry and Physics* there are literally hundreds of thousands of such universal numerical statements for particular elements and compounds: boiling points, melting points, solubilities, densities, X-ray diffraction angles, etc., most of which are not even given with ± qualifiers. Biologists have studied intensively the genetics of only a small number of organic species, yet they make universal statements about the general laws of genetic transmission with only slightly less confidence than physicists do when referring to all copper as having the same thermal conductivity. For the working scientist, the problem of induction is, clearly, not perceived as a problem. Are scientists wrong to behave in this way? A moment's reflection is sufficient to tell us that if scientists were to heed the injunction against universal empirical statements, the work of scientific investigation would not be improved, but would come to a halt altogether. If a philosopher were to tell a scientist that he had no warrant for asserting that the melting point of gold was 1,064.43 °C because he had not melted all the gold in the universe, the scientist would be well justified in curtly bidding him to be gone.

It is not reason, but the abuse of reason, to insist that no universal statement should be made about a class of phenomena unless all members of the class have been examined. The most that the philosophical empiricist can reasonably demand is that we regard such statements as inferences drawn from limited experience that may be generalized as *probably* true universally, and recognize that different general statements may be embraced with different degrees of confidence, excluding only the probability extremes of 0 and 1. This was recognized more than a century ago by W. S. Jevons, who declared that 'the theory of probability is an essential part of logical method' because 'no inductive conclusions are more than probable' (*Principles of Science*, 1874, p. vi) and, implicitly, by J. S. Mill in contending that all general laws, such as those used in economics, are statements of 'tendency' ('On the Definition of Political Economy and on the Method of Investigation Proper to It', *Essays on some Unsettled Questions in Political Economy*, 1844). Carl Hempel extended his covering law model of scientific explanation to include explanations based upon law-statements that are statistical ('The Logic of Functional Analysis', in Llewellyn Gross, ed., *Symposium on Sociological Theory*, 1959), thus greatly reducing the weight of the 'problem of induction'. In a widely used textbook on scientific method Ronald N. Giere says, concerning Galileo's law of the pendulum, 'the generalization, "All real pendulums satisfy Galileo's law," is surely false. But the hypothesis that most real pendulums approximately satisfy the law might be true. This is really all that science requires.' This view, which replaces the utopian demand for certainty with the utilitarian one of explanatory adequacy, has been advanced by philosophers such as Abraham Kaplan and Bas C. Van Fraassen. It raises some special problems for any science whose findings are used as a guide to action, since probability theory, as such, does not tell us how much risk we should be willing to take of accepting a false theory or rejecting a true one (this point will be discussed further in section B 3 below). But so far as the celebrated problem of induction is concerned, working scientists are right to be unconcerned, and not to worry much over whether theoretical hypotheses should be verified or falsified. Neither can furnish certain knowledge, but imperfect confirming and falsifying procedures can both supply empirical evidence that may be used in building up our cognition of the world.

The notion that observations are 'theory-laden', is a more serious and more far-reaching attack on scientific method because it says, in effect, that we cannot rely upon the information supplied by sense data. David Hume initiated the long debate over induction by pointing out that observation of particular entities does not warrant the making of universal statements about all members of the class to which they belong; Russell Hanson and others say that we cannot even claim that the particular observations are valid, because observations are necessarily controlled by prior theories. Empirical data are subject not only to the randomly distributed errors that arise from imperfect precision in measurement, but to unavoidable *systematic bias*. Upon examination, however, this problem too diminishes greatly in significance. (For trenchant critiques of the Hansonian thesis see Israel Scheffler, *Science and Subjectivity*, 1982, especially chapter 2, and Ian Hacking, *Representing and Intervening*, 1983, chapter 10.) The nub of the issue is that the word 'theory' in the phrase 'theory-laden' is used imprecisely, failing to differentiate between a number of quite different types of controls that may impose themselves upon factual observations. In the discussion of this issue that has taken place in recent years five distinct contentions have been advanced, though often confounded.

(1) *Observations are concept-laden.* In order to make an empirical observation we must make use of generic concepts that enable us to order the sensations we receive. As I look about me at this moment I see such things as a computer, books, files, windows; I hear the furnace fan and a car passing by; I smell coffee; and so on. The sensations are classified by means of concepts such as 'furnace fan' and 'window' that I have learned to apply. In scientific research we also use such ordering concepts. A chemist can observe 'benzene rings', an economist 'imports' and 'exports', and a sociologist 'crime' only because each already knows how to identify what he observes. In science, such concepts are 'theoretical' because they are derived from a theory about the world. Thus, for example, the concept of 'phlogiston' was part of an explanatory theory about the mechanism of combustion. It is no longer used; instead scientists speak of 'oxidation', which derives from a different theory. But the concepts used by an explanatory theory are not the same as the theory. Concepts are like the nouns in a sentence; they assert nothing in themselves. Theoretical sentences assert something about how the world works. That observations are concept-laden cannot be denied, but it does not mean that explanatory theories cannot be subjected to empirical test. On the contrary, without such concepts scientific tests, as well as ordinary life, would be impossible. In so far as the claim that observations are 'theory-laden' refers to the fact that observations are concept-laden it is true but, in itself, this does not cast doubt upon the possibility of using empirical evidence to evaluate a theory. The crucial contention is the one we examine next.

(2) *Observations are hypothesis-laden.* Empiricism demands that theoretical hypotheses be subject to test by observational data. If the observations are so controlled by the hypothesis itself that contradictory observations are not possible, then indeed this demand cannot be met. But a procedure in which a control of this sort is exercised is simply *bad* science; it is not an inherent characteristic of science, as Hanson and others have claimed. The point can be shown by an illustration. In the *Statistical Abstract of the United States* we find, for example, data on U.S. 'interest rates' and the 'trade balance', the latter computed by subtracting 'imports' from 'exports'. To compile these data, theoretical *concepts* must be employed. Now let us take a theoretical *hypothesis* such as, say, that the level of interest rates acts as an important causal factor in

determining the trade balance. The data are clearly independent of this hypothesis and can therefore serve, by the use of appropriate econometric techniques, as an objective test of it. Economists, like other scientists, are perfectly aware of the fact that data can be massaged to support a theoretical hypothesis. This is a practical problem in maintaining the honesty of scientific work. It is not a fundamental epistemic difficulty, as Hanson claimed.

(3) *Observations are value-laden*. This is the contention that aesthetic, moral, religious, political, or ideological values contaminate the empirical process. That they *may* do so and in fact sometimes *do* is incontrovertible but, as with (2) above, the claim that this presents an insurmountable epistemic difficulty is incorrect. In the social sciences, and indeed in all scientific work that has social policy implications, the contamination of empirical evidence by value judgements is a danger that one must guard against. It is not so deeply embedded in the methodology of scientific investigation as Hanson and others have claimed, but it raises an issue of special importance for the social sciences, since they are more oriented to social problems and social policy than are the natural sciences. We shall return to this matter below in section B 3.

(4) *Observations are interest-laden*. This is the notion that scientists have personal interests or interests that derive from their membership of a social or economic class, or a national group, etc. This thesis, which has been especially prominent in the radical literature of the social sciences, can be disposed of by simply repeating the arguments advanced under (2) and (3) above. But one additional point is worth making: the thesis fails the test of self-reference. When Joseph Stalin declared that Mendelian genetics was 'bourgeois', reflecting the class interests of Western biologists, did he not expose himself to the parallel contention that his acceptance of Lysenko's views on genetics reflected the interests of the ruling class of a communist state? Fortunately, such a game of epistemic tit-for-tat is not all that can be done to contradict such claims. Lysenkoism was undermined by its inability to serve as the foundation of a successful empirical research programme in biology and by its failure to produce the predicted practical results when applied to Soviet agriculture.

(5) *Observations are laden with culture-specific ontologies*. This is a more general contention than the other four. It recognizes that every mature human is the product of an enculturation process, and that cultures may differ from one another in their fundamental conceptions of the nature of the world. The individual who is raised from infancy to maturity in a twentieth-century Western society is programmed, so to say, to view the world in a different way from one who is enculturated into a Buddhist society, or one brought up in a social environment where belief in magical powers is part of the pervading culture. According to this view, what we call 'scientific knowledge' reflects the metaphysical beliefs of only a part of humankind, and perhaps indeed the smaller part. The empirical observations made by scientists are laden with the particular ontological outlook of their culture. Science is therefore culture-relative, not objective in any general sense.

That humans are the products of enculturation, and that cultures differ, cannot be denied. Indeed, I have stressed these points repeatedly in this book. But this does not force one to the conclusion that the findings of science are so culture-bound that no claim to objective validity can be certified. Let us take, for example, the view that rain can be caused to fall by the performance of certain prescribed ceremonies such as, say, a ritual dance. This view is held in some societies and not in others, reflecting different ontological conceptions. That such different views are held is clear, but it does not mean that a rain-dance does indeed cause rain to fall when it is performed by believers. If this were so the world would be even stranger than physicists tell us it is; it would be whatever one believed it to be. According to such a view, matter is the creation of mind, and by an act of mentation one could create any kind of world one wished, not only different for different cultures but, in principle, different for every individual. The world is *perceived* differently by different cultures and even by different individuals, but this does not mean that in fact there *are* many worlds. The aim of science is to transcend the subjectivity of individual per-ceptions and the control of cultural conceptions, and come to know a world that is external to ourselves. We have ample evidence, if from nothing else than the practical success of science, that this aim is not incapable of realization. This is perhaps more difficult for the social sciences, since in those disciplines we are trying to transcend the control of culturally embedded conceptions in the study of culture itself. But there is no warrant for the view that the social sciences are irredeemably subjective, or culture-relative to a degree that prevents them from arriving at reasonably objective inferences about social phenomena.

Where do we emerge, then, from this examination of the 'problem of induction' and the contention that empirical observations are 'theory-laden'? If these and allied criticisms of the methodology of science had to be taken seriously the consequences would be profound. As Israel Scheffler puts it:

> The overall tendency of such criticism has been to call into question the very conception of scientific thought as a responsible enterprise of reasonable men. The extreme alternative that threatens is the view that theory is not controlled by data, but that data are manufactured by theory; that rival hypotheses cannot be rationally evaluated, there being no neutral court of observational appeal nor any shared stock of meanings; that scientific change is a product not of evidential appraisal and logical judgment, but of intuition, persuasion, and conversation; that reality does not constrain the thought of the scientist but is rather itself a projection of that thought. (*Science and Subjectivity*, 1982, p. xi)

However, as Scheffler recognizes, we are not forced to this conclusion. The criticisms of the positivist epistemic programme did not succeed in demonstrating that it, and all other claims that science can furnish objective knowledge, are fatally flawed. Like the positivists themselves, their critics went too far, claiming in effect that if scientific theories cannot be certain they cannot be objective, and that objectivity must therefore be abandoned, even as an ideal. During the past twenty years or so the literature of the philosophy of science has been punctuated by the contention that positivism has been utterly discredited, root and branch, and that some radically different approach to the philosophy of science is required. We go on now to review this literature or, at least, those parts of it that are of interest for the philosophy of social science.

2. Current epistemological theories

The philosophy of science is at present in a state of disarray. Numerous epistemic doctrines have been proposed and debated but none, as yet, has won a degree of acceptance comparable to that which positivism achieved. A full examination of the currently competing theories would require a large book in itself, so I must here be selective, and very brief. The theories noted in this section have some features of interest for the social scientist but, for various reasons, must be rejected as inadequate. In section 3 we will consider a theory that seems to me to be more satisfactory as a philosophy of social science, and perhaps defensible also in respect of the natural sciences.

In evaluating these epistemological theories we should keep in mind the basic agenda of the philosophy of science: (1) It should give a reasonably accurate generic account of the methodology that has been practised by sciences that may be considered to have achieved some measure of success in providing rational explanations of empirical phenomena. (2) It should, however, be able to accommodate the conception of scientific knowledge as tentative rather than final; that is, it should not demand that scientific pro- positions be judged as 'true' or 'false' in the absolute or dichotomous sense of these terms. (3) It should be able to explicate the relationship between theoretical hypotheses, which are imaginative mental constructs, and empirical data. (4) It should account for scientific progress in terms of the replacement of one explanatory hypothesis by a better one and by improvement in the tech- niques for obtaining empirical data. (5) It should provide a satisfactory account of the relationship between pure science and its practical applications. (6) It should explain the difference between scientific propositions and other beliefs.

(a) Predictive instrumentalism

We noted above that the Vienna Circle philosophers embraced the view that a scientific theory should only describe observable phenomena and not endeavour to explain them. To 'explain' means to assert a causal connection between phenomena and, in the view of the Circle, causality is a 'metaphysical' notion that must be rigorously excluded from scientific discourse. Predictive instrumentalism (often simply called 'instrumentalism' in the literature) takes the view that theories need not explain, nor indeed even describe, phenomena. All that is required of a theory is that it should be able to *predict* future events in the domain to which it is deemed to apply. According to this view, a theoretical hypothesis is a device for making forecasts. Neither its correspondence to the real world nor its explanatory power has anything necessarily to do with its scientific status. Science must be empirical, but the empirical tests must be applied to the conclusions generated by the theory, not to the premises upon which those conclusions are based. As we noted above, in it is logically possible to generate empirically true conclusions from empirically false premises. For the predictive instrumentalist this is of no concern whatever.

Causality is a difficult concept, still under debate, but most philosophers of science hold that causal explanation is a fundamental task of science. Predictive instrumentalism in effect construes science as a mysterious black box of propositions. They work, but we do not know why they work and we do not need to know. Predicting the onset of bad weather from a pain in one's toe joint has the same scientific status *a priori* as the models used by meteorologists. Explaining that toe joint pain frequently precedes bad weather because people who suffer from osteoarthritis may experience such pain owing to a drop in ambient air pressure is totally irrelevant. According to predictive instrumentalism, science does not furnish knowledge about the way of the world, just a set of devices which, shrouded in a mystery which we have no need to penetrate, satisfies our desire to foretell the future. The predictive capacity of a theory is of course an essential consideration in all branches of applied science, but forecasting is intellectually unsatisfactory unless one has rational grounds for expecting the predicted event to occur.

In one of the social sciences – economics – this epistemic doctrine was, for a time, the centrepiece of methodological debate. Milton Friedman, the leading member of the Chicago school of economics, which emphasized empirical research as the foundation of the discipline's claim to scientific status and the use of sophisticated statistical techniques, published an essay in 1953 entitled 'The Methodology of Positive Economics' (*Essays in Positive Economics*), which became the most widely read, discussed, translated, and reprinted paper on epistemological foundations in the history of economics. Friedman adopted the term 'positive' to represent the empirical orientation of what he regarded as scientific economics and to emphasize the distinction between this and the consideration of 'normative' issues. He was, apparently, unfamiliar with the philosophical literature and did not intend to state a position derived from the epistemological views of the Vienna Circle or its successors. In fact he advanced a strict predictive instrumentalism, arguing that the sole empirical test of an economic theory is the correctness of its forecasts. The assumptions employed by a theory to generate these forecasts are, he contended, of no account. They need not be supported by empirical evidence; they are necessarily unrealistic and, indeed, the more unrealistic the better. It took a while for economists to identify Friedman's epistemology as 'instrumentalist' rather than 'positivist' (See Lawrence A. Boland, 'A Critique of Friedman's Critics', *Journal of Economic Literature*, 1979), and to recognize its inadequacies, but the brief period of enthusiasm for it is now only an historical footnote in the debate over the philosophy of the social sciences.

(b) Conventionalism

This doctrine contends that a scientific theory is, like a descriptive language, a device for ordering and communicating information which works because the members of a community know the rules and obey them. Thus, for example, in a telephone book all names are arranged in order according to the rules of the alphabet. This is purely a matter of convention. Any other ordering system could work equally well if it were generally accepted. The concepts of science, according to this view, are, similarly, only conventions that scientists have created. They are used to order empirical data but they cannot be construed to satisfy the positivist insistence that concepts should be representations of the real world.

This view of science has some merits. It emphasizes that science is a human creation and a *social* phenomenon, and it focuses on the utility of scientific concepts rather than their brute descriptive realism. But its defects greatly exceed its virtues. Like the contention that empirical observations are 'theory-laden', it considers only the nature of *concepts*, and neglects the role of *explanatory hypotheses* in scientific investigation. Moreover, according to the conventionalist view, the properties of the real world exercise no control over scientific concepts; they are purely arbitrary constructions, just as the alphabet is. In effect, science is simply the language that scientists have adopted in conversing with one another. Scientific propositions cannot be construed as even tentatively 'true'. Scientific laws are like legislative laws, decreed by established authorities as normative rules of human behaviour. The philosophy of science undertakes to explain why scientists hold certain beliefs and why they change their beliefs. Conventionalism cannot address these questions satisfactorily.

(c) Rhetorical analysis

This resembles conventionalism in focusing on the language used in scientific discourse, but takes a different and even more extreme tack. Scientific language does not consist of neutral terms that are designed to arrange sense data and communicate information; its fundamental purpose is to *persuade*. The philosopher of science who truly wishes to understand what scientists do, so goes this argument, must devote his attention to the examination of the techniques of persuasion. He must therefore acquaint himself with 'rhetoric', that is, the analysis of the art of persuasive speech that the Greeks initiated centuries ago. Rhetorical analysis has been revived in modern times by disciplines that study speech and other media of communication and has become an important focus of interest in the academic, as well as the more immediately practical, aspects of journalism, political science, sociology, and business administration. (For a good discussion of this see the article on 'Persuasion' by Irving L. Janis in the *International Encyclopedia of the Social Sciences*.)

The proposition that rhetorical analysis is an epistemic doctrine and not merely an aspect of social science has recently been strongly argued by Donald N. McCloskey in his book *The Rhetoric of Economics* (1985). McCloskey develops and illustrates this thesis by reference to the literature of economics, but he makes it plain that he construes it to apply to all disciplines that claim to be objective empirical sciences. In essence, McCloskey contends that the claim is a sham; when one examines the literature closely one finds little empiricism and no objectivity. The typical scientific publication consists of the use of the various devices of rhetoric, such as metaphor, analogy, metonymy, etc., mobilized to persuade the reader to adopt the writer's personal opinion. According to McCloskey, the methodological examination of scientific publications must take the form of literary criticism, for they are, essentially, exercises in imaginative literature.

This much may be granted: economists, and others, do try to persuade their colleagues, and they do use rhetorical devices in doing so. But this is not *all* they do. Scientists spend a great deal of time and effort in collecting data by surveys and experiments; they apply complex statistical and other computational procedures; and they take pains to see that their theoretical arguments conform to the canons of logical reasoning. At least sometimes, rhetorical devices such as metaphors and analogies are used by scientists, not simply to persuade, but to clarify and simplify a complex notion or argument in an effort to assist the reader to understand it. If McCloskey were right, all these efforts would have to be regarded as fakery, designed to dull the reader's critical sense and enable the protagonist to insinuate his own views. The methodology of science would have to be regarded as a sophisticated form of the art of propaganda, which only the trained literary critic could unmask.

Admittedly, scientists sometimes behave in this fashion, especially when issues of public policy are at stake which engage ideological, religious, or other passionately held beliefs. There is bad science, and some of it is deliberate and subtly camouflaged. But scientists, including economists, have succeeded in discovering something about the world that can be construed as objective knowledge. McCloskey gives one no indication of the means by which this knowledge has been acquired. In effect, he contends that the only hard knowledge we have is knowledge of the techniques of persuasion. This, according to him, can be methodically investigated by means of rhetorical theory and the examination of texts, but it is, it would seem, exempt from the flaws it attributes to other disciplines. In effect, rhetorical practice is construed to be a unique empirical phenomenon in that it, and it alone, can be studied objectively! This is, of course, an insupportable contention.

(d) Phenomenology

This approach to the philosophy of science is mainly associated with Edmund Husserl, a German philosopher who was strongly opposed to positivism, though he shared its view that the task of science is to produce apodictic propositions about the world. The early positivists felt that certainty is guaranteed by a methodology of investigation that relies solely upon empirical data. Phenomenology contends that what we know for certain consists of our internal mental impressions; it is as radical in its subjective view of knowledge as Vienna Circle positivism was in its objectivism. According to phenomenology, knowledge of the external world can be achieved because one can, through intense reflection upon one's mental impressions, grasp the fundamental nature of worldly phenomena. Positivism restricted itself to the mere appearances of things; phenomenology focuses on their 'essences'.

Phenomenology reflects a long tradition in philosophy that emphasizes the power of intuition. It has made no impact, so far as I can tell, on the natural sciences, and it is rarely discussed in the literature on the philosophy of science. I note it here mainly because, according to some commentators on the philosophy of social science, the doctrine of 'methodological individualism' which contends that social phenomena must be explained in terms of the intentional actions of individual persons, and Max Weber's methodology of *Verstehen*, reflect a phenomenological epistemology. This seems to me rather far-fetched. The notion that one may obtain useful information about human behaviour by introspection, and that the social scientist should pay attention to mental entities such as purposes and preferences, is not the same as the claim that apodictic knowledge of the world may be obtained by intuition and by it alone.

There is, however, a feature of phenomenology that merits more serious consideration. Immanuel Kant made a celebrated distinction between 'phenomena' and 'noumena', that is, between the information about external things that emerges from the interaction between sensations and our cognitive apparatus, and the things 'in themselves'. Phenomenology emphasizes this distinction. Sensations do not provide direct knowledge of noumena; they only generate electrical impulses in our nerve fibres, which must be processed by the brain before one has an intelligible perception. What we call 'empirical information' is therefore not immediate, but some steps removed from the object it is taken to represent. This is especially so in science, where most empirical data are yielded by indirect observational procedures. For example, the physician who is looking at an X-ray plate is not perceiving a fractured bone. Photons impact upon the retinas of his eyes, generating electrical impulses in nerve fibres which are delivered to certain centres of his brain, where, together with stored information from previous experience, they create his mental impression of a fractured bone. The import of this is that it is naive to treat empirical data as unproblematic equivalents of real things. This does not mean that empiricism must be abandoned, as phenomenologists claim; it calls rather for an appraisal of the role that empirical 'facts' play in scientific inquiry which is more sophisticated than the notion that facts sit in judgement on theoretical hypotheses. We shall return to this point below.

(e) Evolutionary epistemology

Some philosophers take the view that epistemology is a 'meta-science', that is, the object of its investigation is science, but it is not itself an empirical science on the same plane as physics, biology, economics, etc. The propositions of epistemology refer to empirical phenomena, but they lie on a different plane of discourse, which constitutes a higher level of abstraction than that of the sciences. Others reject this view, contending that the task of epistemology is to explain science and its development in the same way that scientists explain other phenomena. Philosophers must descend from their transcendent height and give a 'naturalistic' account of science. We now go on to examine four theories that adopt this stance, starting with the notion that the development of science can be explained in terms of the operation of a mechanism analogous to Darwin's theory of natural selection.

Herbert Spencer, as we noted above (Chapter 15 A 4) held the view that evolution is not merely the process by which the earth has been populated by a medley of organic species; it is a cosmic principle that pervades the whole realm of existence. Following this metaphysical conception, we ought to be able to account for the development of scientific knowledge, like all other phenomena, in terms of the operation of the laws of evolution. Spencer suggested such a notion, but it was more explicitly advanced by Georg Simmel, one of the founders of German sociology, in a paper published in 1895 ('On a Relationship between the Theory of Selection and Epistemology', reprinted in H. C. Plotkin, ed., *Learning, Development, and Culture: Essays in Evolutionary Epistemology*, 1982). According to Simmel, organisms use 'concepts' in dealing with the problems they confront and 'a true concept for an animal is that which makes it behave in a way most fitting its circumstances'. In the process of selecting among variations in organic structures, including the organs of 'knowing,' the mechanism of evolution selects progressively more efficient 'psychogenic concepts'. The survival of the fittest organisms means also the survival of the most 'life-promoting' concepts. Man's knowledge, according to Simmel, results from this selection process. Accordingly, the relation between the truth of man's knowledge and its practical utility is that 'knowing is not first true and then useful, rather it is first useful and then referred to as true'.

Karl Popper espoused an evolutionary view in his theory of the development of knowledge, but shifted the focus significantly, construing human knowledge as growing by means of cultural, not organic, evolution. According to Popper, the entities that compete for survival, at least in civilized societies, are not people but scientific theories. When a conflict of beliefs is decided by physical combat, there is no guarantee that the victors entertain beliefs that are more objectively true than those of the vanquished but, in Popper's view, progressive growth in objective knowledge is assured if the beliefs themselves compete in a contest of verisimilitude where nature is the judge.

There are numerous variants on the theme of evolutionary epistemology (see Michael Bradie, 'Assessing Evolutionary Epistemology', *Biology and Philosophy*, 1986). Some follow Simmel in treating the philosophy of science as a branch of biology, that is, 'sociobiology'. Others maintain, as Popper does, that epistemology is an autonomous discipline and contend that the evolutionary process at work in the development of science is not literally Darwinian, but only analogous to it. Stephen E. Toulmin does not advocate the reduction of the philosophy of science to biology, but he maintains that a Darwinian theory of the development of science is not merely a suggestive metaphor or analogy, but provides an explanation of the phenomenon ('The Evolutionary Development of Natural Science', *American Scientist*, 1967; Toulmin maintains the same view in his *Human Understanding*, 1972). Michael Ruse, on the other hand, is a strong supporter of the sociobiological research programme in general and, in respect of epistemology, he claims that the Darwinian mechanism solves such fundamental problems as the nature of induction and causality, but he regards evolutionary epistemology as proceeding by analogical argument and points out important respects in which the theory of organic evolution by natural selection fails to have counterparts in the evolution of science (*Taking Darwin Seriously: a Naturalistic Approach to Philosophy*, 1986). I note Toulmin and Ruse here in order to illustrate briefly the wide variety of views held by advocates of evolutionary biology. The matter is still under debate and no systematic doctrine has so far emerged as the consentient view.

Nevertheless, it is not premature to note that the basic approach of evolutionary epistemology has defects which would seem to render it ineligible for general acceptance. The most conspicuous of these is that it treats the notion of 'progress' as inapplicable to the history of science or, if it is, as equivalent to survival. Even Darwin pointed out that the survival of an organism is merely indicative of its adaptation to the environment, not a certificate of merit. In the domain of ideas one perhaps has little reason to be more sanguine. Astrology, for example, has not been driven from the field of competition. It flourishes, along with belief in magic, folklore medicine, and a score of old and new mysticisms, even on university campuses in 'enlightened' societies. For a quarter of a century in the Soviet Union, belief in the Lamarckian theory of inheritance had much more survival value than Mendelian genetics, yet one would hardly say that it constituted a step in the progress of scientific knowledge. In the domain of economics, neoclassical theory demonstrates that competition generates progress – in certain limited respects and under certain specific conditions. But evolutionary epistemologists have advanced no comparable theory to sustain their contentions. They have a naive faith in competition, assuming that, whatever the conditions, the surviving beliefs are better than the failing ones.

Some evolutionary epistemologists reject the notion that beliefs can be compared in such terms, contending that all we can say about surviving beliefs is that they have survived. This is either an empty truism or makes evolutionary epistemology into a biologicized version of the epistemological theory examined above under the heading of 'conventionalism'. Karl Popper avoided this by insisting that a *scientific* belief about the way of the world must be compatible with empirical data. It is not a question of the popularity of a belief, or its acceptability to established authorities; it is the warrant one has for holding it that distinguishes science from non-science. Evolutionary epistemology does not seem capable of addressing the issue of the warrantability of belief. It either construes survival as equivalent to progress, or it contends that the notion of progress is inapplicable to our knowledge of the world. Nevertheless, the emphasis of evolutionary epistemology on the competition of ideas is salutary. Though not an adequate epistemology, it calls attention to another important, but quite different, subject, the social organization of scientific research.

(f) Kuhn's paradigm model

One of the notable features of evolutionary epistemology is that, when viewed in terms of cultural rather than biological evolution, it directs attention to the fact that science is a social enterprise. In recent years, historians and philosophers of science have paid increased and growing attention to the social context of science, a field previously cultivated only by a few sociologists. (A pioneering scholar in this field was Robert K. Merton; a collection of his papers has been reprinted as *The Sociology of Science: Theoretical and Empirical Investigations*, 1973.) This line of thought was greatly stimulated by Thomas S. Kuhn's *The Structure of Scientific Revolutions* (1962), which, interestingly, and perhaps ironically, was published as a volume in the 'International Encyclopedia of Unified Science' series, which Otto Neurath had initiated in order to promote the positivist philosophy. During the past twenty years or so no theory of the nature of science has received more attention than Kuhn's, by natural and social scientists as well as by professional historians and philosophers of science.

Kuhn takes the view that the philosophy of science must be empirical, drawing its conclusions from an examination of the historical record of science. One must also pay attention to the fact that scientists working in a particular field constitute a cultural community whose members, like those of other social groups, share certain enculturated ideas, since the fate of any new scientific theory depends critically upon the response of the established peer group of scientists. Kuhn's *Structure* was a bold attempt to unite the history of science, the philosophy of science, and the sociology of science into a comprehensive theory of scientific development. It is comparable in its aim to Comte's 'law of the three stages' as a theory of mental evolution, and Marx's 'dialectical' view of historical change.

Kuhn's basic thesis is that the history of any science reveals two alternating phases, a period of 'normal science' and a period of 'revolution'. During the first of these scientists proceed with their work within the frame of the established basic conceptions or 'paradigm' of the peer group. But, as scientific investigation proceeds, bits of empirical information come forward that are not consistent with the accepted paradigm. Initially, scientists do not worry about such apparent falsifications of the basic conceptual framework with which they are working, but as the 'anomalies' accumulate the established paradigm becomes increasingly untenable. Eventually, it is cast out by a 'revolution' in scientific thinking, a new paradigm is adopted, and the 'normal' work of science resumes. Though Kuhn does not note the point, his theory closely resembles Karl Marx's thesis that each stage in man's socioeconomic history is characterized by the accumulation of endogenously generated 'contradictions' which, eventually, can no longer be contained, and the 'social integument' 'bursts asunder' in a revolutionary transformation.

Kuhn's scenario of scientific development is appealing, especially since we have become accustomed to identifying certain prominent events in the history of science as 'revolutionary'. The literature freely refers to the 'Copernican revolution', the 'Einsteinian revolution', the 'Keynesian revolution', and so on. But this locution, though sometimes convenient, raises more problems than it solves. For example, the reader of I. Bernard Cohen's recent book, *Revolution in Science* (1985) is introduced to so many revolutions identified by the author that there would seem to be hardly any domain left for 'normal science' to occupy. Kuhn himself, in a postscript to the second edition of *Structure* (1970), accommodated his critics by loosening his notion of revolution to such an extent that it cannot serve effectively as a differentiating concept. Historians of science have on the whole been very critical of the empirical value of Kuhn's central notions of paradigm and revolution, and are disinclined to accept his model as a satisfactory depiction of the actual history of science. In effect, Kuhn was attempting to state a universal 'law of history', and his thesis, like other similar general propositions about history, is more speculative than empirical. Philosophers of science have been equally critical of Kuhn (see, for example, Stephen Toulmin, *Human Understanding*, 1982, pp. 98–130; Israel Scheffler, *Science and Subjectivity*, 1982; and Ian Hacking, *Representing and Intervening*, 1983).

In the initial formulation of his thesis Kuhn construed the paradigm of a science to be a primary metaphysical postulate. It is the ontological conception shared by the peer group of established scientists which guides their work. A paradigm shift is like a mass religious conversion; the scientists, so to say, are 'born again' and look at the world through new eyes. Different paradigms are incommensurable. There are no general criteria that can be used to determine whether one paradigm is better than another and, therefore, there can be no question of progress in scientific knowledge, or indeed of differentiating scientific from non-scientific propositions. Kuhn's argument, like evolutionary epistemology, is really an extension of conventionalism. Good science is simply that which is in accord with the paradigm convention of the peer group; when that convention changes, it becomes bad science.

Kuhn, apparently, did not anticipate the storm of protest that this brought down upon him from philosophers, who pointed out that his conception would deprive science of any claim to be an empirically controlled method of objective inquiry, or even one that is rational. In subsequent statements Kuhn significantly modified his original position, saying that he did not intend to argue that a scientific paradigm is such an autonomous ontological conception that it is totally immune from empirical and other tests of the sort that scientists routinely apply to lesser propositions. Paradigms are not absolutely incommensurable and the usual epistemic criteria of theory choice (such as degree of observable verisimilitude, scope, simplicity, fruitfulness, etc.) come into play in persuading scientists to shift from one paradigm to another. With such admissions, however, Kuhn's theory of science falls to the ground. A 'paradigm' becomes merely a theoretical hypothesis, perhaps one that is more central to a field of science than others, but not differing from them in any fundamental way. A 'revolution' in science becomes simply a period of exceptionally rapid advance, initiated by discoveries that prove to be unusually fruitful in the investigation of old problems or in opening up new lines of scientific inquiry.

The extraordinary enthusiasm that some social scientists have shown for Kuhn's model partly reflects the power of language. For a decade or so it was avant-garde to talk in terms of 'paradigms' and 'revolutions'. But there is more to it than that: first, though Kuhn did not succeed in sustaining his ontological view of paradigmatic propositions, there are, in some fields of science, certain 'core' propositions that are more important to the whole field than others, and scientists are loath to abandon them when there is contradicting evidence. In economics, for example, the conception of consumers and producers as rational agents has been maintained despite conflicting empirical experience and the psychological theories of Freud and others which deal with the non-rational substrate of human mentation. Secondly, while Kuhn did not do anything that can properly be described as sociological analysis, he did call attention to the social nature of science, and especially to the role of peer groups as established authorities. The first of these issues was addressed by Imre Lakatos in advancing his 'methodology of scientific research programmes' (MSRP); the second by the Edinburgh school's 'strong programme in the sociology of science'.

(g) Lakatos's methodology of scientific research programmes

By the late 1960's a great deal of the debate on the philosophy of science had come to focus on the difference between Kuhn's approach and Karl Popper's revision of positivism. Imre Lakatos, whose earlier work on the philosophical foundations of mathematics was highly regarded, entered this debate with the intention of combating Kuhn and supporting Popper. I mention this point because the reader of this literature will find that, though Lakatos's theory resembles Kuhn's much more than it does Popper's, he expresses his opposition to Kuhn in strong, sometimes indeed abusive, terms, and is by contrast civil and even deferential to Popper. Lakatos died young, without developing a book-length treatment of his philosophy of science. His MSRP approach is contained in a few papers published between 1968 and 1971.

Lakatos defends Popper against the charge of 'naive falsificationism', that is, the notion that a theoretical hypothesis is immediately shown to be false if there is any evidence that is inconsistent with it. He makes two main points in this connection: first, that specific scientific hypotheses are part of a general complex or 'series' of theories which together constitute a coherent 'research programme'; and secondly, that such a programme is not abandoned when specific empirical anomalies are disclosed unless another, superior, programme is available. Popper is correct in stressing that empirical evidence can only falsify a theory, not verify it, but science, says Lakatos, progresses by means of 'sophisticated falsification', which focuses on the comparative evaluation of whole research programmes. ('Falsification and Methodology of Scientific Research Programs', Imre Lakatos and Alan Musgrave, eds, *Criticism and the Growth of Knowledge*, 1970). So far, Lakatos's epistemic theory appears to be equivalent to Kuhn's in substance, if not in terminology. The difference between them appears when one examines his explication of the notion of a 'research programme'.

According to Lakatos, every scientific research programme has a 'hard core', a set of propositions that are immune from empirical test because it is surrounded by a 'protective belt' of assumptions, conditions, etc., which can be invoked to deflect the impact of any contradictory evidence. Outside the hard core lie theoretical hypotheses that can be tested, and abandoned if the evidence so indicates, without calling the hard core of the programme into question. Some commentators interpret Lakatos's 'hard core' as equivalent to Kuhn's 'paradigm', that is, an ontological postulate. But Lakatos rejects the notion that it consists of such metaphysical-level assumptions. For example, he identifies the hard core of the Newtonian programme as Newton's three laws of motion and his principle of universal gravitation. Even with such an example, however, it is not easy to understand what Lakatos means by the hard core of a programme, and to apply the notion to other fields of science. It is more definite than Kuhn's paradigm, but not a great deal more. Nevertheless, one may agree that in every science there are some propositions that play a more fundamental role than others, and that the scientists working in the field are more inclined to employ stratagems that save them when contradictory evidence appears than to abandon them forthwith.

The history of science, says Lakatos, shows that scientific knowledge progresses, most notably when one research programme is replaced by another. This is not, as Kuhn implied, a 'mystical conversion' to a new ontology, but results from a rational appraisal of the relative capacities of the two programmes as general frameworks of scientific inquiry. A new programme will be adopted when it is shown that it can explain everything that the previous programme could, and more besides. With the adoption of a new programme, not only are many of the empirical anomalies of the old one eliminated but a 'problem-shift' often occurs, that is, new areas of inquiry are opened that were hitherto unrecognized by scientists or beyond their reach. The history of science is basically an account of how research programmes gradually 'degenerate' and finally give way to 'progressive' ones. In Kuhn's view, says Lakatos, the choice between competing paradigms is a matter of 'mob psychology', while in his own epistemic theory the preference of scientists for one programme over another is rational. Lakatos, in effect, postulates that the scientist has what economists call a 'utility function', in which his scientific goals are the arguments. His behaviour in choosing between programmes is rational action to maximize this function, subject to the constraints which are imposed on it by the state of development of his science (see Richard J. Hall, 'Can we use the History of Science to Decide between Competing Methodologies?' in Roger C. Buck and Robert S. Cohen, eds, *Boston Studies in the Philosophy of Science*, VII, 1971). In Lakatos's view we should not regard scientists who in former times held theories now discarded as irrational or even misguided. The adherents of the phlogiston theory of combustion, for example, were as sensible as modern scientists are; they chose the best research programme that was available to them at the time (Lakatos, 'History of Science and its Rational Reconstructions', *ibid.*). This is, in my view, a significant point of merit in Lakatos's epistemic stance. The MSRP model allows the possibility of gaining knowledge by using theories that are subsequently regarded as, in the absolute sense, false. The history of science is largely a record of progress made with such 'false' theories. If one takes the view that a theory is either categorically true or false it is impossible to explain how progress can have occurred. But Lakatos's epistemic model does not explain it, either, it only allows that it is possible.

We might pursue this issue a bit further, since it reveals a serious weakness, not only in Lakatos's MSRP but in all epistemological theories that claim to be empirical in the same way that physics, biology, and the other scientific disciplines are. According to this conception the empirical data that can be used to test an epistemological theory are provided by the history of science. Such a contention rests upon a false analogy: that these historical data are homologous to the data the scientist obtains by observation of the real world. This is clearly incorrect. The real world provides the chemist, say, with data about the process of combustion; the history of chemistry provides data about *theories* of combustion. It is indeed a fact that Joseph Priestley believed combustion to be a process in which a substance, 'phlogiston', is given off by the burning material. But his belief was wrong; the existence of phlogiston is a non-fact. The history of science is largely a record of erroneous theories. The non-facts postulated by erroneous theories cannot serve to test an epistemic proposition empirically, any more than erroneous laboratory observations can test a scientific proposition. Unlike the scientist, the philosopher has no reliable data. If indeed he did have access to 'correct' data, he would have no work to do but record them. There would be no problem for him to address. The problem he does address has to do, not with the beliefs of scientists, but with the warrantability of their beliefs. The philosophy of science is a normative enterprise, not an empirical one.

Lakatos's MSRP has not survived criticism better than Kuhn's paradigm model of science. Like most philosophers of science, Lakatos seems to have physics exclusively in mind when speaking of 'science'. Other natural sciences cannot as easily be accommodated to the Procrustean bed of the MSRP. In the social sciences only economics appears to offer the possibility of an easy fit, and there have been a number of efforts to reconstruct the history of economics in Lakatosian terms, but they have not been convincing (see Douglas W. Hands, 'Second Thoughts on Lakatos', *History of Political Economy*, 1985). This does not mean, as some have strongly argued, that the philosophy of social science must be fundamentally different from that of the natural sciences; its import is that, as a model for the *history* of science, the Lakatosian MSRP fails to meet the empirical test of general applicability.

Philosophers too have found the MSRP wanting. Lakatos observes that scientists do make comparative evaluations of alternative research programmes, and he insists that these are based on 'rational' considerations, but he fails to elucidate the criteria that are employed. The justification of programme choice is not addressed. Like Kuhn, Lakatos attempts to deduce the methodology of science from empirical evidence offered by the history of science instead of evaluating scientific practice in terms of normative philosophic principles. If the MSRP is a law of scientific development it is, at best, an empirical generalization, an example of the 'inductivism' that Lakatos himself rejects. We may take it for granted that science is an effective cognitive enterprise. The MSRP undertakes to describe *how* science works, but it fails to provide an explanation of *why* it works. Responding to his critics at a symposium on the MSRP ('Replies to Critics', in Buck and Cohen, eds, *Boston Studies*), Lakatos admitted that some normative epistemic principle is required to save his theory from degenerating into inductivism on the one hand or conventionalism on the other. In defending his theory, however, he shifted ground significantly:

> My critics . . . seem to have missed my thoroughgoing *methodological instrumentalism*. In my view all hard cores of scientific research programs are likely to be false and therefore serve only as powerful imaginative devices to increase our knowledge of the universe. This brand of instrumentalism is . . . consistent with realism . . . .' (Lakatos's emphasis)

This remark, however, points to a different line of epistemological theory, which has little resemblance to the MSRP model.

(h) The 'strong programme' in the sociology of science

When Lakatos speaks of abandoning one research programme for another on the basis of an evaluation of their relative merits he assumes that the factors entering into the 'rational' choice between them are only those that are relevant to the goal of obtaining objective knowledge of the world. He rejects the notion that external factors such as the political, social, or economic environment have anything to do with the fate of particular scientific theories or the choice of general research programmes. The 'externalist thesis', which argues the contrary – that such factors do indeed play a significant role in science – has a long history, especially with respect to the social sciences. The 'Edinburgh school', whose leading figures are David Bloor and Barry Barnes, carry it a giant step further. They take the stance that all scientists are dominated by their cultural ambience in all aspects of their work and thought; it determines not only their choices of problems to investigate, but their so-called philosophical conception of the nature of science and the criteria of warrantability that they use in evaluating beliefs. All beliefs, according to this view, are epistemically 'symmetrical', whether they are beliefs about observable phenomena, or beliefs about philosophical principles, or beliefs about the efficacy of witchcraft or the power of deities. Science, and the philosophy of science, which are just sets of beliefs like any other, should be deprived of their pretensions to rational detachment and construed purely as empirical social phenomena. Some evolutionary epistemologists wish to make the philosophy of science a branch of biology; the Edinburgh school argues that it is properly a branch of sociology, which they describe as the 'strong programme' in the sociology of science. (The central theses of the strong programme were first clearly formulated by David Bloor in his *Knowledge and Social Imagery*, 1976. For a good discussion of the programme the reader is referred to a series of papers on it in *Philosophy of the Social Sciences*, 1981. Chapters 7 and 8 of Paul A. Roth, *Meaning and Method in the Social Sciences*, 1987, also contain a good exposition and critique.)

The strong programme view of science has some close affinities to two notions we have already encountered: the argument advanced by Russell Hanson and others that science cannot be objective because empirical observations are 'theory-laden' (see the discussion above of the version of this that construes observations as laden with 'culture-specific ontologies'); and W. V. O. Quine's 'underdetermination thesis', which contends that, even if objective empirical observations could be made, ambiguity concerning their causes would persist because it is always possible to postulate more than one theory to account for observed phenomena. We have already considered the reasons why these are not compelling arguments against scientific objectivity and need not repeat the considerations here, but it is worth taking a moment to note the inference that the advocates of the strong programme draw from the underdetermination thesis.

If observation facts do not enable us to choose between alternative theories, how do we choose? The strong programme contends that the choices of scientists in this ubiquitous state of affairs are determined by sociological factors. Critics of the programme point out that this is itself a theoretical hypothesis, not a hard fact (see Larry Laudan, 'The Pseudo-science of Science?' *Philosophy of the Social Sciences*, 1981). There are other criteria of theory choice, such as simplicity, scope, practical applicability, etc. The defender of the strong programme might reply that all these criteria are no more than social conventions that scientists have been enculturated to accept, but this reduces the programme to little more than the assertion, which no one would want to quarrel with, that scientists are human beings who belong to a social community. It does not demonstrate that the Newtonian theory of the planetary system is merely a social convention of Western-educated astronomers. As Laudan points out, the contention that beliefs have causes does not mean that all beliefs have the same causes, much less that 'social factors' are the only causes that operate in the domain of human mentation.

David Bloor refers to case studies conducted by adherents of the strong programme, citing one that, according to him, conclusively showed that Pasteur's famous experiment demonstrating that life forms could not arise from non-living matter was accepted by the scientific establishment because it harmonized with the political and social conditions and the theological beliefs of nineteenth-century France ('The Strengths of the Strong Programme', *ibid.*). He does not note that scientists in other countries then, and since, have accepted Pasteur's theory, and does not consider that they have done so because they regard the empirical evidence as warranting its acceptance as a true proposition about the world. Reference to external reality does not enter the ambit of the strong programme. According to Barry Barnes, some 'over-enthusiastic' devotees of it may have given the impression 'that reality has *nothing* to do with what is socially constructed' but, nevertheless, he comes within a hair's breadth of this contention himself: the notion of 'truth', he declares, is like 'good' – 'an institutionalized label used in sifting belief or action according to socially established criteria' (*Scientific Knowledge and Sociological Theory*, 1974, pp. vii, 22; Barnes's emphasis).

As epistemology the strong programme fails, but we might note before we leave it that it does not stand up well as sociology, either. The assertion that undefined 'social factors' account for our scientific beliefs is not a sociological theory. These factors must be specified, and the way in which they operate must be indicated, in order to make even a beginning at the construction of a sociological theory of science. The adherents of the strong programme do not do this. When pressed, they resort to the 'interests' of scientists, thus throwing the issue into the domain of the economist. In principle, the analytical apparatus of microeconomic theory could be applied to this matter, since scientists may be construed as making choices between alternative theories on the basis of their 'utility functions', just as consumers are construed as choosing what commodities to buy in order to maximize their satisfaction. Recently, economists have devoted some attention to the 'knowledge industries', but have not attempted to argue that this line of investigation can replace the philosophy of science. Lawrence A. Boland has, indeed, convincingly shown that there are technical reasons why the economic analysis of rational choice cannot be extended to provide an acceptable account of theory choice by scientists ('Methodology as an Exercise in Economic Analysis', *Philosophy of Science*, 1971). One may glibly say that scientists, like other humans, are motivated by their 'interests', but translating this into an epistemological theory, as the Edinburgh school seeks to do, does not appear to offer much prospect of success.

The sociology of science is an important subject, especially in a world where science has become professionalized and so much scientific work is conducted within the administrative and policy framework of social institutions such as business firms and governmental agencies, and where university science must be financed by grants derived from public funds and foundations. But the sociology of science is not the philosophy of science, and unsupported sociological assertions will not assist us to understand the place of science in the modern world.

We have now almost finished our survey of the epistemological theories that have emerged as successors to positivism. Since none of them appears to be a winning candidate, the philosophy of science is said to be 'in crisis', a state of affairs that does not seem to concern scientists, who pursue their craft with undiminished enthusiasm and confidence. Some commentators on the current state of epistemology suggest that, since no epistemological theory has won general acceptance, we should adopt a 'pluralist' stance (e.g. Bruce Caldwell, *Beyond Positivism: Economic Methodology in the Twentieth Century*, 1982, chapter 13, and Paul A. Roth, *Meaning and Method in the Social Sciences: the Case for Methodological Pluralism*, 1987). But it is not clear what this means. Is a particular science, such as economics, to be epistemically construed as being a compound of predictive instrumentalism, Lakatosian MSRP, and other items from our smorgasbord? Or is one science to be regarded as wholly Kuhnian and another wholly conventionalist? Paul Feyerabend advocates the ultimate pluralism: since no epistemological theory is acceptable, then all methods of obtaining knowledge that human ingenuity can imagine are equally meritorious, and none should be condemned as invalid; philosophers of science should shut up shop and seek other, more productive, occupations (*Against Method: Outline of an Anarchistic Theory of Knowledge*, 1975). This distressing counsel is unlikely to be heeded, and it need not be. The so-called 'crisis' in epistemology is greatly overblown; it stems from the original positivist notion that scientific theories must be demonstrated to be 'true' in the sense of isomorphic correspondence to reality, and the reactions against this which, in effect, declare that science is simply what scientists do, and truth is what scientists believe, without any reference to the rationality of their actions and the warrantability of their beliefs. It is not necessary to adopt either of these positions. Scientists themselves do not, nor do the standard textbooks that are used in university courses to introduce students to the nature of modern science. The dominant view one finds at these levels is that scientific theories are instruments of inquiry which are employed in the discovery of truth, not true or false in themselves. The controversy between the 'instrumentalist' and 'realist' view of theories is an old one. 'It is a matter of historical record,' says Ernest Nagel:

> that, while many distinguished figures in both science and philosophy have adopted as uniquely adequate the characterization of theories as true or false statements, a no less distinguished group of other scientists and philosophers has made a similar claim for the description of theories as instruments of inquiry. (*The Structure of Science*, 1961, p. 141)

This controversy is not merely semantic, as Nagel believes. It revolves around the central issue of how we can be said to 'know' something about the world when our theories are incomplete and provisional and, moreover, will most likely be shown in the future to be false. This issue is important for all the sciences, but especially so for the social sciences, which deal with a world that is itself in flux. We go on now to examine the epistemology of instrumentalism or, in order to distinguish it from the 'predictive instrumentalism' discussed above, 'cognitive instrumentalism'.

3. Cognitive instrumentalism

We often speak of 'scientific knowledge' in ways that imply that it is different from other kinds of knowledge. This is a useful and justifiable locution, but it can also be misleading. Science is best viewed, not as a body of knowledge, but as an activity – the search for truth, not the possession of it. If apodictic truth were discovered, science would come to an end. Cognitive instrumentalism takes the view that the task of the philosopher of science is to examine the nature of this search activity with the object of explaining its capacity to yield reliable (but not certain) knowledge of the world.

(a) Science, intelligibility, and public knowledge

We have two basic tools at our command in investigating the world: logic, and factual data. A theory concerning a real-world phenomenon is particularized logic. Instead of saying, for example, 'If all A is B, and if X is an A, then X is B,' we replace these letters, which stand for anything and everything, by particular terms that refer to the phenomena of current interest such as: 'If all swans are white, and if the large birds on the river Avon at Stratford, Ontario, are swans, then those birds are white.' When we take this a step further and say that 'In fact, all swans are white, and, in fact, the birds in question are swans,' we may infer that this compels us to conclude that the birds are white. But this is too strong. The combination of logic and facts tells us only that it is *rational to believe* that the birds are white. This amendment seems like nitpicking in the given illustration, but most of the information we have about the world is much more complex and uncertain, and when we make logical inferences based on such facts it is important to regard them as rational judgements. Cognitive instrumentalism does not attempt to avoid this; it regards logic and factual data as instruments that may be used to arrive at beliefs that are, in the circumstances, rational to hold.

One of the legacies of positivism that has been especially difficult to shake off is that we have knowledge of the world when we have constructed a literal picture-model of it. This has been especially tenacious because physics, the archetypical science, seems to construct such models. Upon reflection however, this is clearly not the case. Even Bohr's model of the atom, or the Newtonian model of the planetary system, depicts only certain aspects of the phenomena it addresses; and modern particle physics can hardly be described in terms of picture-models at all. When we say that Bohr's model enables one to 'see' how the atom is structured, or to 'grasp' its structure, we are speaking metaphorically. What we mean is that the model renders this aspect of the real world rationally intelligible. There are many non-picture models in science, such as, for example, Darwin's theory of organic species, the economist's market model of price determination, and the political scientist's checks-and-balances model of constitutional organization. These too enable us to 'see' or 'grasp' certain aspects of reality in the sense of rational intelligibility. Science is an activity that uses logic and factual data to understand the way of the world in rational terms. The understanding so obtained is 'public knowledge' because it can be communicated to others with minimal ambiguity, and shared by an indefinite number of people without any depreciation of cognitive value.

The positivistic picture-model of knowledge led philosophers of science to neglect the fact that scientists not only try to depict the world but they actively engage in manipulating it. Ian Hacking points this out in noting the role that experimentation has played in the search for knowledge, since the 'scientific revolution' of the seventeenth century; science consists of both 'representing' the world and 'intervening' in its processes (*Representing and Intervening*, 1983). But, long before the rise of experimental science, men were manipulating the world in their everyday practical activities of agriculture, metallurgy, cooking, etc., which did not simply accept the world as it was, but modified it for utilitarian purposes. Science did not begin in the seventeenth century. Its roots lie with those of our far-off ancestors who viewed man's capacity to manipulate the world as intelligible in logical and empirical terms, and tried to communicate their understanding to others. The seventeenth century was revolutionary, not in creating something entirely new, but in greatly extending the domain of rational intelligibility. 'Science,' says Gellner, is 'a type of cognition which has radically, qualitatively transformed man's relation to things: nature has ceased to be a datum and become eligible for genuine comprehension and manipulation' (*Relativism and the Social Sciences*, p. 120).

Practical arts such as agriculture and metallurgy can be pursued simply on the basis of observed sequences of phenomena, relying upon the experienced but uncomprehended stability of nature. Such 'recipe' procedures work, but they are not science. Failure to appreciate this point is the basic error of 'predictive instrumentalism' as a theory of scientific epistemology. Science undertakes to explain why such procedures work by explicating the causal connections between phenomena. What is communicated to others and is added to the accumulating corpus of public knowledge as 'science' are not the recipes for practical action, however successful they may be, but the rational understanding of nature that renders the *why* of their working intelligible. 'Cognitive instrumentalism' is an epistemological theory that views the logical constructs called 'theories' and the sense data called 'facts' as instruments that are used in the process of cognition. We cannot obtain immediate and irrefragable knowledge of the way of the world, but we can make it intelligible by the use of such tools. The concepts that science uses are much more complex than the artless ones employed in simple propositions about the whiteness of swans. As one philosopher puts it:

> the concepts of science are the working tools of scientific thought. They are the ways in which the scientist has learned to understand complex phenomena, to realize their relations to each other, and to represent these in communicable form. Among the most wonderful of those things we consider inventions of science are the concepts of science. They are, in effect, the sophisticated instrumentation, the high technology of scientific thought and discourse. (Marx W. Wartofsky, *Conceptual Foundations of Scientific Thought*, 1968, pp. 4 f.)

Empirical data too are far removed from the brute facts that our unaided senses can supply. The biologist grinds up some organic material, whirls it about in a centrifuge, and then places it in a spectrophotometer, which delivers electrical signals to a computer that prints out a graph of the light absorbance of the specimen at different wavelengths. Then he records as 'data' that the material he started with contains a certain type of chlorophyll. Like theories, such data should also be regarded as instruments employed in a cognitive enterprise.

(b) Theories, facts, and empirical adequacy

Karl Popper forcefully argued that theories are 'conjectures' about the world, which can be accepted as having scientific status only if they are so framed that it is possible for empirical data to falsify them. Popper's objective was to establish a criterion that enables one to distinguish between 'scientific' and 'non-scientific' propositions. Anyone may make conjectures about the world; the scientist is obligated to make falsifiable ones. Popper's falsification criterion has not proved to be sustainable; nor has the positivist criterion that theories should be capable of empirical verification. None the less it seems reasonable to demand that theories should, somehow, be submitted to empirical test. Ernest Nagel phrases the matter very broadly:

> It is the desire for explanations which are at once systematic and controllable by factual evidence that generates science. . . . [It is] the deliberate policy of science to expose its cognitive claims to the repeated challenge of critically probative observational data . . . . (*The Structure of Science*, 1961, pp. 4, 12)

Cognitive instrumentalism takes the view that this places the wrong construction on the relation between theories and observation facts. It treats scientific inquiry as if there is a court of nature, so to speak, where the theorist advocate pleads a case and the empiricist jury renders a verdict, with the philosopher of science acting as a presiding judge who sees to it that proper rules of scientific procedure are obeyed. The instrumentalist view of science is quite different. It is more like a workshop, where theories and factual data are used as complementary tools employed in a co-operative process of cognition. Or, to modify one of Alfred Marshall's metaphors, theories and facts are like the two jaws of a pair of pliers which 'grasp' some part of reality between them. A theory, by itself, can do no cognitive work. But neither can data alone. Contrary to Nagel's notion, facts do not control theories any more than theories control facts. They work together. The empirical quality of a theory, therefore, is a matter not of the testability of one by the other, but of their functional articulation as instruments of inquiry aimed at a specific scientific problem. Scientific progress takes place when new theories are developed that articulate with a wider range of known facts, and when new facts are obtained that articulate well with existing theories.

In the philosophic literature a contrast is sometimes drawn between 'instrumentalism' and 'realism' on the ground that realists construe theories as representations of reality, while instrumentalists do not. This is overdrawn. Instrumentalists can accept a picture-model of an aspect of reality, such as Bohr's model of the atom, as an effective instrument of investigation if it proves to have cognitive value in practice. That such models are representational is beside the point. In fact, only a few branches of science employ models that have literal representational qualities, and even in these domains the models are often highly *un*realistic. Edmund Halley used a planetary model consisting of only two bodies; yet he was able to calculate the date of return of the comet that bears his name with impressive accuracy. The 'ideal gas laws' describe a model that applies only to non-existent gases whose molecules have no volume; the theories of levers and pendulums apply to no real levers or pendulums; yet no 'realist' rejects these models as unscientific, or even as wrong. Moreover, there are some branches of science where alternative incompatible theoretical conceptions of the same subject matter are employed. Physicists sometimes treat light as a wave and sometimes as a stream of particles; chemists sometimes regard a liquid as composed of discrete particles and sometimes as a continuous medium; economists sometimes apply the 'cartel model' to an organization of producers attempting to exercise market control and sometimes the 'price-leadership model', or the 'basing-point model'. Such diverse conceptions cannot all be 'true', but each is usable as a cognitive device in appropriate circumstances. A well developed science has a rich repertoire of such devices, which gives it versatility and scope.

Instrumentalism is sometimes rejected by realist philosophers as an epistemology that has no concern for truth. This is incorrect; what divides these two philosophies of science are different views about the relation between theories and facts in inquiries that are aimed at finding out what is true. In the instrumentalist view, it is not disembodied 'science' that explains phenomena; human scientists do, using the cognitive instruments of logical theory construction and observation. One could say, for example, that the Mendelian laws of genetics explain the incidence of sickle-cell anaemia, but the instrumentalist would insist that this should be interpreted as meaning that biologists *use* the Mendelian laws to explain the phenomenon. Scientific explanation is a human activity.

The main difficulty with the notion that theories must be empirically 'true' is that it leaves no middle ground between 'true' and 'false'; they are treated as logical contradictories, 'false' being construed as 'not true' and vice versa. May Brodbeck asserts that 'knowledge is the body of true belief; we cannot know that which is false' (*Readings in the Philosophy of the Social Sciences*, 1968, p. 81). If this were so we would have very little knowledge at all, since most current beliefs, including scientific ones, are in the absolute sense false, and we do not know which ones will be discarded tomorrow and which may last for a century. The philosophy of science must provide room for beliefs that do not meet such a hard truth criterion. Bas C. Van Fraassen, as part of an extended defence of instrumentalism (*The Scientific Image*, 1980), advances the weaker criterion of 'empirical adequacy'. Whereas the realist insists that a theory must be a literally true description of the subject domain in all its details, and the concepts of a theory must refer to entities that actually exist, Van Fraassen's 'constructive empiricism' demands only that a theory should be adequate to deal with the specific problem that the scientist undertakes to solve. We are not called upon to believe that a scientific theory is empirically true; only that it is empirically adequate. In deciding between competing theories, the operative criterion is not their relative degrees of truth-likeness, but their comparative usefulness as instruments of investigation. Scientific explanation is essentially an exercise in pragmatics. Some problems cannot be successfully tackled because we lack a theory that is adequate to the task, or because adequate factual data are not available, but there are many others that can be investigated with, admittedly imperfect, theories and data. As Peter Medawar puts it, 'science is the art of the soluble' (*Pluto's Republic*, 1982). As science progresses, more and more of the world can be rendered intelligible, but completeness and perfection remain beyond reach.

Except for the empiricist approaches to epistemology such as those of Thomas Kuhn, Imre Lakatos, and the Edinburgh school, and Paul Feyerabend's philosophical anarchism, which declares that 'anything goes', the philosophy of science undertakes to prescribe normative rules for the conduct of science. The early positivists demanded that all theoretical concepts should refer to observable entities. Karl Popper demanded that theoretical propositions should be empirically falsifiable, at least in principle. Carl Hempel demanded that all explanations of specific phenomena should show them to be instances of empirically true general 'covering laws'. Does cognitive instrumentalism, which regards theories and observation facts as instruments of inquiry, advance prescriptive rules? It seems to me that, implicitly, it makes two kinds of demands. First, theories should be coherent, and not offend against any of the standard rules of formal logic. The fallacy of *ignoratio elenchi* is perhaps one that the instrumentalist would be especially anxious to warn against. This is the fallacy of contending that one has answered one question when one has in fact answered a different one. Secondly, empirical data should be derived and used according to principles of sound practice. These range all the way from the rule that data should not be manufactured to serve the scientist's personal interests or beliefs to the insistence that data should be processed according to the best available techniques of mathematical statistics. These are the criteria that scientists themselves employ in reviewing one another's work. As a prescriber of good scientific conduct the philosopher is unlikely to be able to go further.

(c) The problem orientation of science

When speaking in general terms one might say that science consists of the investigation of the way of the world. But no science takes 'the world' as its province. Even the most comprehensive of them focus upon much more restricted and specific domains. A particular science can be defined in terms of the problems that it addresses but, except in broad terms, it is not possible to give a perdurable and timeless statement of them because the interests of scientists change and the boundaries between the sciences shift. Defining a science therefore consists of stating its problems at a particular time. The solutions to these problems do not constitute eternal truths; they are explanations that scientists, for the time, consider to be serviceable in making some limited aspect of reality intelligible. Even with respect to a given problem, a theory that is subsequently discarded as untrue may, in its time, render such service. The Ptolemaic model of the planetary motions is now regarded as false, but before the Copernican model was developed by Kepler and Newton it provided a rational account of the universe that articulated with empirical observations. If theories and facts are regarded as cognitive instruments, it is easy to understand why the Ptolemaic model solved a certain scientific problem and why Newtonian mechanics solved it better. It would not be rational, today, to view the heavens in Ptolemaic terms, but it was the most rational way of doing so a few centuries ago.

When a science undertakes to address a new problem, the theoretical and empirical instruments appropriate to the task may be different from those applied to the older problem. In Chapter 17 above we saw that the development of neoclassical microeconomics not only replaced the classical theory of value with a better one but shifted the focus of attention from the problem of economic development to the static efficiency of resource allocation. Keynesian theory undertook to replace classical (and neoclassical) monetary theory, but it also involved a shift of focus, from both economic development and allocative efficiency to the problem of the general underutilization of a society's productive resources. In some respects classical, neoclassical, and Keynesian theories offered alternative explanations; in other respects they were complementary, addressing different problems. If one insists that an economic theory must be a true representation of 'the economy' we must choose between them. But if theories are regarded as instruments for tackling particular problems, all of them can be comfortably included in the economist's repertoire.

On the plane of pure science the choice between competing theories rests upon their instrumental usefulness in providing rational explanations of phenomena. On the applied plane an additional criterion must be adduced: the concepts of a theory must be translatable into terms that permit one to modify the world. In choosing between two theories, one may be superior in its explanatory capacities, but the other may offer better opportunities for application. In economics, for example, the theory of general equilibrium is superior to all others as a rational explanation of how a market economy functions, but it is of very little use in tackling practical problems. This tension between the pure and the applied may be present in all sciences, but it is especially important in the social sciences. The difference between predictive instrumentalism and cognitive instrumentalism as social science epistemologies is that the former says that we need only be able to predict events, while the latter says that we need to understand their causes or, rather, we need to understand them sufficiently to act rationally, and in terms of concepts that enable one to engage in such action. The reason why Keynesian theory made such a dramatic impact upon the economists of the 1930s is that it explained the phenomenon of mass unemployment in terms that supported the desire to combat it by means of practical public policy devices.

One often encounters comments expressing a general appraisal of the comparative worth of the various sciences; for example that physics is the premier science or that economics is superior to sociology, or that all the social sciences are inferior to all the natural sciences. Such appraisals are based on a failure to recognize the problem orientation of science and the epistemic implications of this with regard to comparative evaluation. Physicists and chemists are very good at addressing problems that belong to their professional domains. Their record in analysing social problems is negligible (see, for example, the various writings of Frederick Soddy, Nobel Prize-winning chemist, on monetary theory and other economic issues). An implication of instrumentalist epistemology is that scientific procedures can be comparatively appraised only with reference to the same, or similar, problems. To compare the effectiveness of physics in respect to physical problems with the effectiveness of economics in respect to economic problems is to commit an *ignoratio elenchi* of a gross sort. It follows also that there is no warrant for believing that the social sciences could necessarily be improved by adopting specific models and concepts that have been successful in the natural sciences. Numerous attempts have been made to model social phenomena as analogous to Newtonian celestial mechanics or evolutionary biology, or to apply concepts such as entropy or metabolism, but these have been more noteworthy as displays of scholastic ingenuity than as contributions to our understanding of social processes. Cognitive instrumentalism requires that theoretical models should be applicable to the problem one wishes to solve. That a model or concept is useful in one domain provides no assurance that it will have cognitive value in another.

So much for comparisons of disciplines that are called 'sciences'. What about the more general distinction between 'scientific' and 'non-scientific' modes of cognition? Demarcating them from one another was a main objective of Vienna Circle positivism, Hempel's deductive–nomological model of science, and Popper's falsificationism; while Feyerabend and the Edinburgh school set out to show that no such demarcation is valid. What can one say on this issue from the standpoint of cognitive instrumentalism?

(d) Science and non-science

Some philosophers regard the establishment of a criterion that distinguishes scientific propositions from non-scientific ones as a matter of the highest importance. For Karl Popper a satisfactory criterion of demarcation is essential to protect the edifice of modern Western thought from the attacks of relativists and sceptics who question the possibility of objective knowledge, and refuse to grant science a cognitive status different from that of religious revelation, political ideology, or personal intuition. Israel Sheffler speaks of 'the moral import of science' as springing from its insistence on *'responsible* belief', that is, beliefs justified by logic and evidence, in contradistinction from beliefs that are not, in this sense, 'responsibly' held (*Science and Subjectivity*, 1982, *passim*). Ernest Gellner says that 'epistemological principles are basically normative and ethical: they are prescriptions for the conduct of cognitive life' (*Relativism and the Social Sciences*, 1985, p. 34), the kind of life he regards as morally worthy. If such grave issues hinged on the establishment of a demarcation criterion, Western civilization would be in a parlous state, since no defensible criterion has so far been defined. Nevertheless, even without it science has been a powerful force in our cognitive life and scientists have effectively challenged those who claim to have come, by non-scientific means, into possession of knowledge about the world. Even 'creationists' now feel obliged to show that their rejection of Darwinian theory in favour of the Book of Genesis is founded upon 'scientific' considerations.

In viewing this matter, social scientists have more reason for concern than natural scientists. With the prominent exception of the theory of organic evolution, few of the propositions of natural science are now attacked on theological or ideological grounds. The day is long past when Galileo had to submit to the superior authority of the Church on matters of nature. There is, however, a continuous open season on the propositions of the social sciences, which, for various reasons, cannot as readily be defended as having 'scientific' status. Moreover, social scientists often have to ward off attacks from natural scientists, sometimes as naive and prejudiced as ones derived from strong political ideologies and other idealist fancies. More often than not, the natural scientist who becomes interested in a social question will rush into print without consulting the literature on it and, moreover, without bringing to the subject the same constraints of logic and empiricism that he regards as obligatory in his own domain of expertise (see, for example, Gary Werskey's history of the 'science and society movement' in England during the 1930's, *The Visible College*, 1978).

As a philosophy of science, cognitive instrumentalism cannot supply the cleanly defined criterion of demarcation between science and non-science that some regard as essential. But in certain respects it can do better than other philosophies. Positivism and its successors tried to establish the notion that a scientific proposition is one that can be tested empirically. A non-scientific proposition is not testable. According to this criterion, if a fourteenth-century dervish had declared in a trance that the sun is stationary and the earth is a revolving sphere, it would be a scientific proposition because it could be tested empirically. Yet something seems amiss here. It cannot be that the theory was advanced by a dervish, for, according to positivist canons, the scientific quality of a proposition depends on what the proposition states, not its source. Cognitive instrumentalism agrees that the source is irrelevant, but it rejects the view that a proposition can be scientific or non-scientific in itself. If scientific concepts and theories are construed as tools of cognition, then the central issue is whether the dervish's statement was usable in this fashion. In the fourteenth century the notion that the sun is stationary and the earth revolves was incapable of employment as a cognitive instrument. If a carpenter, living in a remote place without electricity, comes into possession of a power saw, it would not be, for him, a tool of carpentry. So also with the tools of scientific inquiry.

This epistemological view explains why some notions which are worthless speculations in one era achieve scientific status in a later one. When Democritus (fifth century B.C.) asserted that solid matter really consists of very small particles in motion, it was not a scientific proposition. It could not, then, be 'responsibly' held, as Scheffler would say. Today's physicists universally accept it. Cognitive instrumentalism is a kind of relativism, to be sure, but not the sort that Popper and others decry as denying the possibility of objective knowledge. A concept or a theory is objectively tested by its heuristic capacity, the assistance it renders to the work of scientific inquiry in a particular field and in the context of the existing state of knowledge. The innovator in science is 'ahead of his time', but if he is very much ahead his ideas are worthless.

In anticipation of an issue that will engage our attention in the next section we might note at this point that, from the instrumentalist standpoint, concepts referring to human mental entities such as motives, preferences, and beliefs are not inherently non-scientific. That they are properties of consciousness rather than material things does not mean that they lack explanatory capacity. On the contrary, in dealing with social phenomena, which result from the behaviour of individual persons, they can be, and have been, effectively employed by the social sciences.

Where do we stand, then, on the issue of demarcation? Assuredly there is a difference between astronomy and astrology, between Darwinian theory and creationism, between macroeconomic theory and the notion that changes in the pace of economic activity reflect the operation of transcendental 'cycles' or supposed 'natural rhythms'. But what *is* the difference between scientific and non-scientific modes of thought? To come to grips with this, let us examine a specific case that philosophers and scientists (Feyerabend excepted) would assign to the non-scientific category, a case of witchcraft and 'demonic possession'. (The following illustration is taken, with some changes, from my *Social Science and Modern Man*, 1970, pp. 7 f.)

In his *The Devils of Loudon* (1952) Aldous Huxley gives an account of the trial of one Urbain Grandier, who was burnt at the stake for witchcraft in the early seventeenth century. The events that led to this event took place in the small French town of Loudon, near Tours. The nuns of the Carmelite monastery there suddenly began to act rather strangely. It was suspected that they had become 'possessed'. The Church authorities were called in to investigate; and Grandier, a local priest, was accused of having entered into a pact with the devil to torment the nuns. The important part of the story is the care with which the charge was examined. The authorities did not move to quick judgement; they approached the contention that a demonic possession had occurred with commendable scepticism. They demanded supporting factual evidence and, indeed, they got it. In addition to what was extracted from Grandier by torture (which wasn't much), the ecclesiastical investigators compiled an impressive bill of hard data: while 'possessed' the nuns were observed to 'speak in tongues'; the characteristic marks of 'stigmata' appeared on their bodies; in their tormented writhings they performed feats of extraordinary strength and endurance, and so on. In modern courts of law less empirical evidence would be regarded as sufficient to show that a crime had been committed. But no present-day Western court would consider a charge of witchcraft, no matter how much empirical evidence of demonic possession was adduced. Nor would any modern philosopher or scientist give such a proposition even hypothetical status. We simply do not believe in demons or witches.

With this illustration before us we can see that any *epistemic* demarcation between science and non-science is extremely difficult, perhaps indeed impossible. The Church authorities at Loudon had a well formed theory to work with; they insisted on logical argument; they demanded empirical evidence. Neither positivist nor instrumentalist epistemology can produce a criterion of demarcation that will permit one to consign the notion of witchcraft to 'non-science'. The difference between the modern scientist and the seventeenth-century theologian is essentially *metaphysical*; it is based upon different ontological conceptions of reality. The 'revolution' in science that was under way at the time of Grandier's trial generated new views concerning the methodology of scientific investigation, but its more significant impact upon the culture of the West, which even the great Newton failed to appreciate, was in creating a metaphysical outlook that rejects preternatural forces. Demons have been cast out of our world, not by burning witches and performing rituals of 'exorcism', but by the success of science as a cognitive and pragmatic enterprise. The metaphysical presumption of science may be wrong but, so far, the burden of secure evidence indicates that it is rational to believe otherwise.

B. THE STUDY OF SOCIAL PHENOMENA

According to Harry Elmer Barnes, the social sciences were created by the industrial revolution, which he describes as 'the greatest transformation in the history of humanity'. This revolution 'broke down the foundations of the previous social system' and 'out of the confusion, as an aid in solving the newly created social problems, . . . to reconstruct the disintegrating social order' sociology and the other social sciences came into being (*An Introduction to the History of Sociology*, 1948, pp. 47 f.). There is much to be said for this view, emphasizing as it does the relation of the social sciences to the social problems that attended the development of a much more complex system of economic and social organization. Nevertheless, the social sciences remained for a long time almost purely academic disciplines. Economic theory made some tentative appearance in the eighteenth-century discussion by businessmen of international trade and the monetary system, and political theory in the English constitutional debates of the seventeenth century, but, as we have seen, systematic social theory was largely a nineteenth-century creation and, though it was clearly oriented to the discussion of contemporary social problems, its main venue was the academy rather than the domain of practical affairs.

Indeed, up to the middle of the present century, professional economists, political scientists, and sociologists found employment almost entirely in academic institutions. Since then, the nature of the social science professions has undergone a profound change. There are far more economists today in governmental agencies and business firms than in the universities and, to only a lesser degree, professional sociology and political science have experienced a similar transformation. If we take the view that the willingness of practical men of affairs to spend good money for a service certifies its value, the social sciences are today generously certified. One of them, economics, has since 1969 even been endorsed by the highest court of science itself, the Nobel Prize Committee.

Nevertheless, considerable doubt remains concerning the scientific credentials of the social disciplines. Philosophers of science, and practitioners of the disciplines themselves, continue to question their epistemic foundations, some castigating social scientists for failing to adopt the proven methodology of science, others complaining that they have been led to pursue incorrect methods by attempting to imitate the natural sciences, still others contending that the very idea of a 'scientific' study of social phenomena is a delusion, or an abomination. Moreover, some writers on this question have radically altered their views. Alexander Rosenberg, a philosopher whose initial work was on the epistemological foundations of economics (*Microeconomic Laws a Philosophical Analysis*, 1976) declared the discipline to be truly scientific in its methodology, even by comparison with physics, and strongly defended the economist's use of mental entities, such as preferences and purposes, as causal factors. But more recently he has declared that such entities do not have causal status (*Sociobiology and the Presumption of Social Science*, 1980); that economics is not really an empirical science but just a branch of mathematics ('If Economics isn't Science, What is it?' *Philosophical Forum*, 1983); and that the social sciences in general are not yet sufficiently developed to permit a philosopher to subject them to epistemic analysis ('Philosophy of Science and the Potentials for Knowledge in the Social Sciences', in Donald W. Fiske and Richard A. Schweder, eds., *Metatheory in Social Science*, 1986).

I cannot undertake here to review the literature on the philosophy of the social sciences, or even to do so comprehensively for one of them. In any case, many of the issues that have been addressed, and the positions taken, parallel those examined in the preceding section. I shall concentrate on three matters that seem to me to require special attention: the relation between the social and natural sciences; the epistemic status of mental states and the debate between individualism and holism; and the problem of objectivity.

1. Social science and natural science

The notion that the social sciences must be judged by reference to the natural sciences has been, and continues to be, the most prominent theme in the literature of the philosophy of social science. It not only reflects the general view that there is a 'unity of scientific method' but, more specifically, that the practices of the natural sciences constitute the standards to which the social sciences are obliged to conform. This notion has survived the controversies among philosophers concerning the philosophy of science. As we have seen, there is, today, no consensual view of this. Presumably, the social sciences are to be judged by reference to the natural sciences even though there is no agreement concerning the epistemic foundations of the natural sciences themselves.

Isaac Newton said, in reference to the methodology he practised: 'if natural Philosophy in all its Parts, by pursuing this Method, shall at length be perfected, the Bounds of Moral Philosophy will also be enlarged' (quoted from the *Opticks* in S. A. Grave, *The Scottish Philosophy of Common Sense*, 1960, p. 7). In the terminology of his day Newton meant 'moral philosophy' to include not only ethics but the study of human and social phenomena. By the eighteenth century Newton was revered as the greatest scientist of all time, not only on account of his specific discoveries in mechanics, but for having established the true method of scientific investigation. Giambattista Vico and J. G. von Herder were the most prominent of the eighteenth-century writers who argued that the study of social phenomena must be methodologically different from the natural sciences (see above, Chapter 14 C), but their view did not carry the day. David Hume, despite having thrown a cloud of scepticism upon the methodology of science that has not been dissipated by the past two centuries of philosophical discourse, nevertheless embraced the unity of science thesis. Adam Smith, when destroying his unpublished papers shortly before his death, saved from the flames an early essay on the 'History of Astronomy' in which he argued that Newtonian celestial mechanics was the prototype of the method of investigation appropriate for all subjects. In the nineteenth century, leading philosophers (and social scientists) such as William Whewell, J. S. Mill, and W. S. Jevons held that all the sciences are united by a common philosophy of knowledge. Henry C. Carey, the most prominent American social scientist of the pre-Civil War period, contended in his *Principles of Social Science* (1858) that the study of social phenomena should parallel Newtonian mechanics, arguing (among other things) that Malthus's theory of population was shown to be false by the law of the conservation of matter.

In 1878 Francis Galton proposed to the British Association that economics should be removed from its roster because it was not properly a 'science', but he was rebuffed on the grounds that economics was not inherently unscientific, just more difficult than the natural sciences. Economics, or 'political economy' as it was then called, was accorded scientific status, not so much because of its specific findings as on account of its method, which even at that stage resembled physics in its use of abstract modelling. Indeed, many of the strong mid-nineteenth-century opponents of political economy, such as the romantics, objected to it *because* it was scientific, applying Newtonian methods to phenomena which, in their view, belonged to a fundamentally different ontological category.

The view that the sciences, or at least those disciplines that are truly sciences, are united by the adoption of a common philosophy of knowledge and the use of similar methods of investigation was a central principle of the Vienna Circle positivists, a notion that Otto Neurath, the social scientist of the group, promoted with uncompromising vigour. Carl Hempel, in his influential revision of early positivism, firmly sustained the unity of science thesis. This was the philosophical foundation of his attack on narrative historians that initiated the debate on the methodology of history which that we examined in Chapter 14. That the social sciences deal with unique, non-recurring, phenomena (as historians claim) or with statistical or populational phenomena which must be treated in probabilistic terms (as other social scientists contend) does not, according to Hempel, indicate any epistemic difference between the natural and social sciences. The positivist theory of science, and the revisions of it such as Hempel's and Popper's, have been abandoned, but the unity of science thesis still has considerable support among social scientists and philosophers. 'The possibility of a social science in principle as perfect as physics,' says Brodbeck, 'remains the unexamined premise of the vast majority of present-day social scientists' (*Readings in the Philosophy of the Social Sciences*, 1968, p. 1).

None the less, serious objections to the unity of science thesis have been expressed by a variety of writers. In our examination above of the ideas of Max Weber (Chapter 15 C) we encountered a theme that continues to punctuate the literature on the philosophy of social science. Weber argued that the study of social phenomena must be pursued in a fundamentally different way from the natural sciences. Social phenomena result from the rational, evaluative, and purposeful actions of individuals. The natural scientist cannot go beyond the construction of a body of knowledge based upon external observation; but the social scientist, who shares the property of consciousness with those entities whose actions make social phenomena, can, and must, present a more intimate, empathetic *understanding* of these phenomena. Weber's concept of *Verstehen* has been variously interpreted by philosophers and social scientists but, in one way or another, it lies at the root of most of the claims that there are fundamental epistemic differences between the social and the natural sciences, as advanced, for example, by Frank Knight, Friedrich Hayek, Ludwig von Mises, and the modern 'Austrian school' in economics, and by Talcott Parsons and his followers in sociology. The word 'scientism' was coined by Hayek as a derogatory term for the view that social phenomena should be studied by the methods of the natural sciences (*The Counter-revolution of Science: Studies in the Abuse of Reason*, 1955). On the whole, philosophers have been hostile to the Weberian thesis, but Karl Popper seems to go a considerable distance towards it in contending that social scientists should pursue 'situational analysis', investigating the decisions of human agents in the situations in which they find themselves (see Douglas W. Hands, 'Karl Popper and Economic Methodology: a New Look', *Economics and Philosophy*, 1985).

Weber did not argue that the study of social phenomena is not scientific; on the contrary, he contended that the method of *Verstehen* is essential to making it so. But others have taken the view that the nature of the subject matter of the social disciplines, and the relationship between the investigator and his subject matter, are so fundamentally different from those of the natural sciences that the term 'social science' is an oxymoron, combining two notions that are inherently contradictory. Weber's rejection of the unity of science doctrine is regarded by them as insufficient; the study of social phenomena is not, cannot be, and ought not to be regarded as in any way akin to the study of natural phenomena. In a widely discussed book (*The Idea of a Social Science, and its Relation to Philosophy*, 1958), Peter Winch argues that the study of social phenomena must be 'philosophical' rather than 'scientific', by which he means that the proper way to comprehend such phenomena is by conceptual analysis rather than by means of empirical research. The notion of 'cause', says Winch, does not belong to the domain of social phenomena; what is needed instead is a penetrating analysis of the concept of man as a 'rule-following' being. According to Winch, the relations between the individual members of a society are, at bottom, the relations between *ideas*. Economists, sociologists, and others should abandon their attempts to discover the causal determinants of social phenomena and try to make society 'philosophically intelligible', or else give way to philosophers, who are trained in conceptual analysis and understand the social (i.e. 'rule-governed') nature of language. A. R. Louch (*Explanation and Human Action*, 1966) agrees with Winch but criticizes him for failing to see that, since social phenomena are the result of deliberate individual actions, they are irredeemably moral in character. These moral judgements are directly ascertainable and they should form the basic material of social analysis. In effect, Louch tries to overturn two Humean doctrines – the non-observability of causation, and the distinction between facts and values – and to argue that because the social scientist, an inside observer of social events, can escape Hume's restrictions, his epistemic foundations are fundamentally different from those of the natural scientist.

Winch and Louch do not supply their readers with concrete examples of how the social sciences could be improved by following their prescriptions. Lacking such demonstration, one is reasonably justified in taking the view that what they propose is unlikely to give us a better understanding of our social world or enable us to deal with its problems through social policy. Most philosophers continue to insist that empirical phenomena, of whatever sort, must be investigated by procedures in which empirical methods play a vital role. The views expressed by Winch and Louch may perhaps receive a sympathetic response from some modern Marxist social scientists, and some orthodox ones such as the disciples of Ludwig von Mises in economics and those of Leo Strauss in political science but, generally speaking, social scientists are now firmly committed to the view that the investigation of social phenomena should strive to be objective and empirical, limited in this only by technical feasibility.

Max Weber did not intend to drive his notion of *Verstehen* in the direction taken by Winch and Louch. He insisted upon the firm separation of facts and values, the need for scientific detachment and objectivity in social investigation, and the indispensable role of empirical evidence. The philosophical issue that is raised by Weberian *Verstehen* is the epistemic status of mental entities such as motives and preferences. Is it permissible to construe such factors as causal variables in explaining social phenomena? This is an important question which deserves specific attention. I defer discussion of it to the next section.

The arguments put forward by defenders of the unity of science leave something to be desired. A great deal of the literature on this proceeds as if the only natural science were physics. But large areas of biology, geology, and other natural sciences are very different from physics, more so perhaps than some areas of the social sciences are. If one sets up physics as the standard there is no unity of science within the domain of natural science itself. The early positivists adopted such a standard but, as we have seen, philosophers of science have abandoned positivism, and it has been succeeded by a large number of epistemological theories, none of which has achieved general acceptance. Since there is no unity in epistemological theory, how can it be claimed that there is epistemological unity in science? However, if the reader is prepared to accept the argument advanced above that 'cognitive instrument-alism' is a more acceptable epistemology than the other candidates, he will have no difficulty in embracing the unity of science thesis. This epistemology sets up no specific science as representing the ideal, and makes limited prescriptive demands that can, in principle, be satisfied by scientific investigation in all domains. According to cognitive instrumentalism, theories and empirical data function as complementary implements of investigation, and the only rules that must be followed are that theories should be coherent and logically sound, and articulate with observation data that are objectively obtained and properly processed. Except for those who reject empiricism, these are the rules that are, in fact, accepted as binding by social as well as natural scientists.

None the less, there *are* important differences between the natural and social sciences. Epistemological unity does not mean homogeneity of substantive content, or homology of research procedures in all domains of scientific inves-tigation. In understanding a scientific discipline it is necessary to comprehend not only what it shares with other disciplines but also wherein it is dissimilar. There are important differences among the social sciences themselves (as there are among the natural sciences), but to examine these in detail would extend the length of this book beyond reason, so I will confine the discussion to the more general differences between the natural and social sciences. This issue has been extensively discussed in the literature, some writers claiming that there are good grounds for regarding the natural and social sciences as categorically distinct, others saying that the differences are only matters of degree (see, for example, an excellent paper by Michael Scriven, 'The Frontiers of Psychology: Psychoanalysis and Parapsychology', in Robert G. Colodny, ed., *Frontiers of*

Science and Philosophy, 1962). In the 'Preliminary Remarks' on this matter in Chapter 3 C above we noted that social phenomena are not as uniform, or as constant over time, as natural phenomena are; that social scientists cannot carry out the kinds of experiments that natural scientists can, and test their 'hunches' in that way; that value judgements are more involved in the social than the natural sciences; that social phenomena reflect the operation of psychic entities while natural phenomena (or, at least, non-organic phenomena) do not; and that social scientists are less able to isolate particular causal factors from their general context than natural scientists. Further discussion of these and related matters will occupy our attention in the remainder of this chapter. They will not be discussed in terms of comparison between the natural and social sciences, for these issues must be addressed by the philosophy of social science quite apart from that comparison. But before we leave the subject of this section, we should consider a difference between natural and social phenomena which is an ontological difference, a categorical distinction of kind, not merely one of degree. Here and there in the preceding chapters we have had occasion to note the importance of social *organization* and the distinctiveness of the modes and mechanisms of organization in human societies. Now I want to reiterate this and emphasize its philosophical significance.

The Vienna Circle philosophers declared metaphysical propositions to be meaningless, but this only served to disguise from themselves and their followers that the positivist philosophy of science was based on the ontological postulate that all real existence consists only of material objects. They were on the right track in insisting on the epistemic unity of science, but not in presuming that it derives from the ontological homogeneity of the world. In order to sustain the unity of science thesis, one must show that the same basic principles of epistemology apply to the investigation of very different kinds of phenomena.

If one rejects the notion that there are non-material transcendental entities of the sort that idealist philosophers and theologians talk about, the positivist doctrine of metaphysical monism appears to be inescapable. All things, including organisms and their brains, are composed of molecules, and these in turn are composed of more elementary physical particles; all events, including social events, involve the operation of the primary physical forces. The metaphysical monism of the modern positivists reflects a theme that has a long history, going back at least as far as the pre-Socratic philosophers of ancient Greece. Parmenides, the leader of the Eleatic school, contended that all reality is composed of one substance. Phenomenal diversity belongs only to the appearances of things; their true reality is homogeneous: the Many are, at bottom, One. But this assertion failed to satisfy other philosophers, who advanced the notion of a plurality of primary substances. This line of thought developed, in Greek philosophy, into the view that all reality is composed of four things: earth, water, air, and fire – a notion that was embraced by Aristotle and remained prominent in Western philosophy until the rise of empirical science.

One may tackle this issue by invoking the notion of emergent properties (see above, Chapter 3 B). According to this view, the existential diversity we observe empirically does not (necessarily) reflect differences in the fundamental constituents of things, but properties that become manifest at different levels of organization. With a new level of organization, new properties appear, which may be taken to reflect the coming into existence of new real things. Water, for example, is a different thing from the oxygen and hydrogen which compose it and we may speak of it without impropriety as having a real existence of its own. So also we may regard mountains, solar systems, organic cells, and termite colonies as real things, having properties that distinguish them from other things. Scientific investigation would get nowhere if it were to cling firmly to the notion that all things are made up of whirling particles and insist that all explanations be in terms of them. For every science, the 'laws' that it postulates are propositions that pertain to a particular level of organization, and causal explanation is, primarily, elucidation of how a particular type of organization works. Newtonian celestial mechanics, for example, describes the planetary motions in terms of the organization of the solar system, and explains that organization in terms of the operation of gravitational attraction, which is taken to be the dominant force at that level. Every science focuses upon a specific level of organization and the phenomena it investigates are the properties that pertain to at that level.

Existential phenomena are exceedingly diverse, reflecting the many different levels of organization that have evolved since the primordial beginning of the universe. But, in addition to the emergence of novel properties, on one planet at least among the billions that exist there have also evolved two novel forms of organization: organic systems and social systems have come into existence. Living organisms do not differ from non-living matter only in the emergence of new properties when the requisite chemicals are combined; a fundamentally different mode of organization is involved. And human societies do not merely have properties that come into existence when individuals live together in a co-operating fashion; their organization involves the operation of unique co-ordinating mechanisms. There are, one might say, three ontological categories of existence: the domain of matter and energy; the domain of life; and the social domain. Karl Popper attempted to make such a distinction in his proposition that there are 'three worlds' (see above, Chapter 15 B, Note 1), but he did not succeed in identifying the fundamental differences. He focused upon certain properties of life and society instead of considering their special modes of organization.

The difference between living and non-living phenomena has exercised the attention of philosophers since the dawn of philosophy in ancient Greece. A modern biologist would stress the capacity of some organisms to utilize the energy of sunlight to build up complex organic molecules from chemical elements, and the ability of others to do likewise by feeding on those that can perform photosynthesis. By this means organic structures are built, and energy is stored. This energy is released by the disassembly of organic molecules, and may be utilized to power the processes of growth, movement, and reproduction, which phenomenally differentiate living from non-living things. The distinction between them does not appear to be categorical, however, since metabolism (the building up and breaking down of organic molecules) can be explained as chemical processes that are not fundamentally different from those of the non-organic domain. Dissatisfaction with what appeared to be a 'mechanistic' view led some late nineteenth and early twentieth-century writers to postulate the existence of a special entity that is uniquely present in living phenomena. Most prominent in taking this stance were the French philosopher Henri Bergson (in a series of books, the most popular being *Matter and Memory*, 1896, and *Creative Evolution*, 1907), and the German biologist-philosopher Hans Driesch (*The History and Theory of Vitalism*, 1905). But Bergson, Driesch, and other writers who followed this line of thought were unable to explicate the nature of the special entity (Bergson called it the *élan vital*) that differentiates the living from the non-living world in a fashion that would satisfy an empiricist. The notion was embraced by some prominent literary figures of the period (e.g. Samuel Butler and George Bernard Shaw), but scientists and philosophers of science firmly rejected it. Understanding of the fundamental difference between the organic and the inorganic world, in non-mystical terms, had to await the development of modern genetics.

The DNA molecule, in chemical terms, is just a molecule. But its philosophical significance is momentous. It has the capacity to encode information, which controls the embryological development of an organism from a single cell into a complex system of functionally specialized parts. After birth, the DNA-encoded information controls the internal physiological processes of the organism and, for most species, it totally controls the organism's responses to the external environment. This information is transmissible from one organism to another when reproduction takes place and, at this point, changes in the information content of the DNA can occur, making the progeny different from its parents. An organism is not merely a distinct level of organization with emergent properties that are different from its chemical constituents; it represents a different *mode* of organization, one in which certain chemical constituents carry encoded information which creates and governs the structure and function of an integrated and co-ordinated system.

To explain the organization of a mountain we need not resort to anything other than the laws of matter and energy. To explain a living organism we have to recognize the addition of a fundamentally different mode of organization that is mediated by encoded information. This point has recently been strongly emphasized by Ernst Mayr in some of the essays collected in his *Toward a New Philosophy of Biology* (1988; see especially chapter 1). Mayr is right in rejecting 'vitalistic' explanations of organic phenomena and also in chiding philosophers for their preoccupation with physics, but he also contends that biology requires a fundamentally different epistemology from other natural sciences, and this is not sustainable. What is required is the delineation of an ontological difference between living and non-living phenomena, based not only upon the emergence of unique properties in the domain of life but, more fundamentally, on the emergence of a unique mode of organization, one that is mediated by instructions encoded in a form that permits their transmission from entities whose existence is limited to a short time-span to their, similarly limited, successor entities. By this means, *populations* of organisms may persist indefinitely while the individuals who compose them have only a brief span of existence as organized entities. One should stress, in this connection, that genetically encoded instructions control organic *processes* as well as somatic structure, and these processes are understandable as performing *functions*. In describing an inorganic natural entity such as, say, the solar system, it would not be meaningful to speak of a planet as performing a function that is necessary to the dynamic equilibrium of the system, but the status of an organ such as the liver in a living organism cannot be understood without reference to its functional role in maintaining the organization of the organism.

A similar ontological distinction can be claimed for societies composed of organisms. Whether this applies to social systems other than those of the species *Homo sapiens* is problematic, and I will consider here only human societies. In addition to controls that are exercised by information encoded in the human genome, the behaviour of individuals is channelled in ways that permit the emergence, maintenance, and orderly development of social systems by instructions that are mediated by three other modes: established customs, traditions, and values; the exercise of coercive power by some individuals over others through hierarchically structured institutions; and the co-ordination of voluntary actions in the economic domain through the information carried by market prices. The oft-made assertion that 'the whole is more than the sum of its parts' does not refer only to the fact that the parts interact with one another and thus generate new properties. If that were so, the assertion would be little more than a cliché, or a way of stating what is obvious. The scientific analysis of wholes would require only that the 'composition laws' that govern the assemblage of parts into wholes be elucidated. But, in some cases, fundamentally new modes of organization, which are not obvious to casual observation or captured by composition laws, come into existence. These have special scientific and philosophical significance, which can be appreciated only by resorting, again, to the concept of *function*. The significance of customs, governments, and markets derives from the functions they perform in maintaining the organizational integrity of a social system. Because of the presence of such modes of organization, societies deserve to be recognized as distinctive ontological existents, significantly different from both material and organic entities. Like populations of organisms, societies persist beyond the life-span of their member individuals but, unlike populations, their persistence is not explicable solely in terms of genetic factors.

Adam Smith initiated the scientific study of social systems as ontologically distinct phenomena by pointing out that the division of labour which increases productivity can be practised only if, and to the degree that, there are trading markets in existence. Herbert Spencer's distinction between the 'militant' and 'industrial' types of societies focused upon the difference between co-ordinating mechanisms that operate through the exercise of coercive power and those that utilize market exchange. Émile Durkheim regarded the *conscience collective* as a co-ordinating mechanism that controls behaviour through enculturation and by placing social pressure upon individuals to conform to established norms. However, the philosophical significance of such modes of organization was not recognized by these writers or, so far as I am aware, by subsequent ones. The doctrine of the unity of science is still widely held by philosophers and social scientists. I emphasize again, though, that recognition of the ontological distinctiveness of social systems does not mean that there is an epistemic difference between the social and natural sciences. Scientific explanation, in all domains, must utilize coherent and logically valid theories that model empirical phenomena, and treat relevant empirical evidence carefully and objectively. The social, biological, and physical sciences differ from one another mainly because they address phenomena that emerge in differently organized systems. (This point is amplified in my 'Why does *Homo sapiens* Differ?' *Journal of Social and Biological Structures*, 1988, and my lecture *How many Kinds of Things are there in the World?* Indiana University Press, 1990.)

2. Mentation, individualism, and holism

Max Weber contended that the methodology of the social sciences is fundamentally different from that of the natural sciences, and necessarily so, because the explanation of social phenomena requires an analysis of what individual persons do, not in terms of their physiological processes or their passive responses to changes in ambient conditions, but as active agents with the rational capacity to choose the means of achieving their objectives. It is easy to see why Weber thought that the social and natural sciences differ. Physical entities such as atoms and planets cannot be regarded as active agents in this sense; and, while non-human animals can be, the biologist is too far removed from other species to achieve an empathetic understanding of their behaviour. Weber was wrong in regarding these factors as calling for a distinctive epistemology of social science, and he failed to perceive that the existence of different modes of organization is what most significantly differentiates physical, biological, and social systems. But his insistence that the social scientist should regard social phenomena as resulting from the rational acts of individuals is less easy to dismiss. In Weber's day, one of the social sciences, economics, was already dominated by theoretical models in which the central role was played by rational individuals. During his lifetime, this type of theory was entrenched still further by the development of neoclassical economics.

More recently, 'methodological individualism', as this has come to be called, has been extended beyond the specialized domain of economics to political science, sociology, and law. These developments have been accompanied by intense debate, among philosophers and social scientists, concerning the epistemic foundations, and the ethical and political implications, of this conception of social phenomena, with 'methodological holists' contending that it seriously misdirects social research and social philosophy. I cannot review this debate in detail here (see section 4 of May Brodbeck, ed., *Readings in the Philosophy of the Social Sciences*, 1968, for a small, but good, selection of representative papers), but the main issues involved warrant more discussion than has been devoted to them thus far. As a first step we must consider the epistemic status of the mental entities that occupy a central place in the individualist methodology.

A wide variety of terms is available for reference to mental phenomena. We speak of a person as having 'desires', 'preferences', 'purposes', or 'intentions', and as being 'lonely', 'irrational', 'happy', or 'apprehensive', to name only a few of the words that the English language supplies. For our purposes we may collapse this dictionary of mentation into three terms; 'motives', 'tastes', and 'beliefs'. The first of these refers to that which is valued by the actor, the end or ends he hopes to attain by his actions. Two individuals may have the same general motives but differ considerably in their 'tastes' for specifics. One may rank brandy higher than beer and ballet higher than basketball, while the other may have the opposite schedule of preferences. Under the heading of 'beliefs' we include the individual's views concerning the probability that an action will, in fact, serve to realize his motives; that is to say, the knowledge he considers himself to possess with respect to the relevant relations of cause and effect. The individual may also have moral beliefs, and these may affect his motives, but I will not take these into account in the immediate discussion here. A person may consider more than one thing to be worthy and there may be more than one way of attaining any particular end, so a fourth mentational concept is useful: 'choice'. Economic analysis tries to cut through the complexity of multiple ends and multiple means of attaining them by postulating that the individual seeks to maximize his 'utility'. Thus economic theory has been described as 'the logic of rational choice', an explication of the choices that a rational utility-maximizing person would make in a given situation. This way of looking at human behaviour, which has characterized economics from its earliest beginnings as a systematic discipline, has been subject to unremitting attack by other social scientists, psychologists, and occasionally by economists themselves when engaged in methodological meditation, but this will not concern us here. The immediate problem before us is not the particular ways in which mental entities are used in explaining social phenomenon but the justification for using such entities at all.

What is the source of our knowledge about mental entities? They are not observable in the way that chairs, rivers, and other things are. They are objects of perception, but the type of perception involved is what psychologists call 'proprioception', the perception that one has of one's own physical body and other aspects of oneself. Knowledge of one's own *mental* state is a form of proprioception usually called 'introspection'. The argument has been made that this knowledge is 'subjective' and, therefore, cannot be used in a scientific analysis of social phenomena. One may perhaps explain the action of a particular individual in terms of his own motives and beliefs, but such mental entities cannot be used to explain things like crime rates and inflation. The central issue here is whether information about mental states derived by introspection can be generalized. In explaining the foundations of government Thomas Hobbes argued that *everyone* desires security and believes that it can be obtained by the centralization of coercive power. Max Weber's concept of 'ideal types' rests upon the view that, while it is not true that all people at all times have the same motives and beliefs, the social scientist can employ the conception of an idealized person for analytical purposes just as the physicist uses the concept of an idealized mass.

The use of such idealizations as heuristic generalizations about human agents has played a large role in the development of social theory, but not without considerable concern over its methodological validity. In economics, the development, in the 1870's, of the concept of 'marginal utility' to explain the market values of commodities initiated a debate that has persisted down to the present. The notion of 'utility', it has been argued, is irremediably subjective. One cannot compare the utility of one person with that of another, and one cannot apply the concept of utility to groups of individuals, for this would be equivalent to ascribing properties of mind to populational categories such as classes, clubs, communities, or nations. This argument has been accepted by most orthodox economists. Many textbooks in elementary microeconomics and virtually all in more advanced 'welfare economics' tell the student that it is impermissible to make interpersonal comparisons of utility. Nevertheless, economic theory continues to make heavy use of ideal type analysis in which the postulated agent is represented as a utility-maximizing individual; the recent extensions of economic theory to the analysis of political and legal phenomena proceeds as if interpersonal comparisons of utility are permissible; and much applied economics assumes that such comparisons can be made, and even estimated quantitatively. In order to make the concept of utility instrumentally effective in social analysis some relaxation of the ban on generalizing it is necessary. Pragmatics overwhelms scholastics in social science as in other areas of scientific inquiry.

This does not mean, however, that the door is open to whatever mental entities one may care to postulate *a priori*, or to the varied and complex mental states that psychologists and psychiatrists deal with. In order to render social phenomena intelligible, social theory must restrict itself to mental entities that are very simple, and understandable in commonsense terms. The notion that human agents seek to maximize their utility and pursue actions they believe to be effective in promoting this end is such a simple and commonsense notion. So is, it seems to me, the 'law of diminishing marginal utility', which states that the satisfaction one derives from consuming additional units of a commodity declines as one's rate of consumption of it increases. Mentational concepts such as, for example, those of Freudian psychology, may be more sophisticated, but they are unlikely to be serviceable in explaining market prices, or other social phenomena, in terms of mental entities. A Weberian 'ideal type' of human agent is one whose mentation is construed as consisting of simple motives, tastes, and beliefs that are immediately understandable by other humans. Economics and the other social sciences have demonstrated that reference to mental entities, if severely constrained, can be effectively used in constructing cognitively instrumental theories. Weber, and many of his followers, claimed that social phenomena cannot be analysed without the use of mentational concepts. This is too strong, since it makes the use of mentational concepts *obligatory* in all branches of social science. Showing that such concepts are required in tackling some problems does not demonstrate that they are required in all. But Weber's contention was quite unnecessary. From the standpoint of epistemology, the issue is not whether reference to mental states is obligatory but whether it is permissible in scientific explanation.

Some philosophers of science (e.g. Ernest Nagel, Karl Popper, A. F. MacKay, Daniel Hausman) accept references to mental states in scientific explanation; others (e.g. May Brodbeck) regard such references as dubious; while still others (e.g. Gustav Bergmann, Alexander Rosenberg in some of his more recent writings) firmly reject them. The central point at issue is whether social phenomena may be explained by construing motives and beliefs as their causes. The early positivists, as we have seen, attempted to eject the concept of causality from the domain of scientific inquiry. They were unsuccessful, but the restoration of causality leaves open the issue of what sorts of things may properly be accorded causal status in a scientific explanation. Resolution of this question would seem to rest upon the solution of a prior problem: the nature of causality. But philosophers have come to no agreement about this as a general issue in epistemology, so firm statements that motives and beliefs may be construed as causes, or that they may not, would seem to be at least premature. But we may have to wait a long time for philosophers to reach a satisfactory definition of the nature of causality. Meanwhile, science proceeds. If one is prepared to adopt cognitive instrumentalism as an epistemological theory, the question can be reformulated: does reference to mental states enable one to render an observed phenomenon more intelligible than it would be without it? Some primitive peoples resort to mentational concepts in explaining everything; 'animism' is the notion that all existence is characterized by the operation of entities of the sort that one knows by introspection. In more advanced communities the use of concepts like the Hegelian *Geist* or 'divine will' is not dissimilar, but the application of such concepts to physical phenomena has been generally rejected by philosophers.

The question is, are simple, commonsense, *human* mental states instrumentally useful in explaining human social phenomena?

Let us take a simple illustration. John Smith enters a shop carrying a loaded revolver, has a verbal exchange with Henry Jones, a clerk, whom he shoots and kills, and then departs with the contents of the cash register. One could expand this account by furnishing more details, such as the type of revolver, what organs of Jones's body were injured, etc., but we cannot make the events more intelligible as a social phenomenon without referring to the motives and beliefs of Smith and Jones. The INUS model of causation has not been generally accepted by philosophers, but one of its merits is that it enables one to clarify the causal role of mental entities in such situations. According to this model (see above, Chapter 3 A 3) the requirements of necessity and sufficiency can be met by only defining a set of causal factors, since no single factor by itself is sufficient, and sometimes is not necessary, to cause an event. Applying it to the above illustration, it is evident that the motives and beliefs of both Smith and Jones were both necessary to cause Jones's death, since no sufficient set can be complete without them. If Jones had not chosen to resist Smith's demand, he would not have been shot, so he was a partial agent in his own demise. On the other hand, if Smith had intended to leave no witnesses, Jones would have been shot even if he had not resisted, so reference to *his* mental state is not necessary to the completion of a causal set.

Let us alter the story: when Jones refuses his demand, Smith does not shoot and flees empty-handed. In this case no murder, or robbery, takes place. But this does not mean that an explanation is not required. A satisfactory explanation can be reached by noting that the mental states of Smith and Jones were, in this case, incapable of completing any causal set sufficient to produce a murder or a robbery. For the strict behaviourist, who eschews reference to mental states, non-events are difficult to handle without resort to linguistic rephrasing that construes them as events. But in social phenomena, non-action can be as significant as action. For example, if the President of the United States refrains from signing a statute passed by Congress before the deadline prescribed by law, it is described as having been 'pocket vetoed' by him. But in fact we do not observe the President as doing anything with respect to the statute, and this is what requires explanation. It is difficult to see how such cases can be handled without reference to mental states. If Rosenberg were right in claiming that mentational concepts cannot be used in scientific explanation because they do not represent entities that are 'natural kinds', then it would be equally improper to use such concepts in considering everyday phenomena. But we do persistently use them in vernacular speech to make sense of our normal experiences. It is Rosenberg, not common folk, who is in epistemic error (see A. F. MacKay, 'The Incredibility of Rejecting Belief–Desire–Action Explanations', Philosophy of Science Association, *Proceedings*, 1982, Vol. II).

The physical sciences have no warrant for referring to motives, tastes, and beliefs, because such things do not operate within the phenomenal domain of their concern. In communicating with one another, however, scientists are engaged in a social activity. Alfred Schutz, a strong advocate of Weberian epistemology, points out that when one scientist considers the work of another he must know not only what the other did, but what his purpose was in doing it ('Concept and Theory Formation in the Social Sciences', *Journal of Philosophy*, 1954). Scientific papers are written as reports of observable events, using the passive voice, but if the reader wishes to understand what is going on he must reconstrue the text in terms of motives and beliefs. The text may say something like 'the sample was centrifuged at 30,000 G and the supernatant fluid decanted' but the reader must know what the scientist was hoping to achieve by this in order to make scientific sense of it. Despite his strong insistence that there is no place for mental entities in science, Alexander Rosenberg nevertheless refers to them without restraint in evaluating the work of other philosophers. Is philosophical discourse exempt from the rules it prescribes for other social phenomena? If one does not, and cannot, practise what one preaches, the normative prescription becomes dubious; as Hume succinctly put it, 'ought' implies 'can'. The communication of ideas cannot be conducted without reference to mental entities.

This view has recently been aggressively attacked by a school of literary criticism called 'deconstructionism'. The adherents of this view claim that the proper way to read a text is to take it as it is, without reference to the author's thoughts, just as if it had been written by an inanimate being. Deconstructionists are manifestly unable to follow this rule when quarrelling among themselves, or with literary critics of other schools. The contention that no reference to mental entities should be made by the reader of a text seems to be clearly untenable (even if it were possible) when the matter in hand is as personal and subjective as are poems, novels, and other forms of art, but it is equally untenable with respect to scientific texts.

The above illustrations show, conclusively it seems to me, that reference to introspectively known mental states is serviceable in rendering social phenomena intelligible. That is to say, the epistemological theory of cognitive instrumentalism permits the use of mental entities. But other epistemologies may not be able to accommodate them, or to do so easily. We should note especially Carl Hempel's 'covering law' model of scientific explanation in this regard. Many philosophers who examined the scientific status of mental entities in the 1960s did so in terms of Hempel's model (see Paul M. Churchland, 'The Logical Character of Action – Explanations', *Philosophical Review*, 1970). As we saw in discussing the debate over historical explanation in Chapter 14 A, Hempel argued that the use of mental entities is permissible if, and only if, they can be formulated as general laws, and chided historians for failing to do this. According to Hempel, when an historian explains, for example, why Henry IV of France rejected his Protestant upbringing and embraced Catholicism in 1593, he is obligated to state the operative covering law, such as 'whenever anyone is faced with a choice between his religion and a crown, he will choose the crown'. Naturally enough, historians regard Hempel's demand as placing an obligation upon them that they cannot meet, and any attempt to do so would only expose themselves to justified ridicule. A strict Hempelian would say that this simply shows that the work of historians is not 'scientific', and he might go on to extend this judgement to a wide range of social science, since it is not possible to state many empirically true general covering laws of human behaviour in terms of mental states. The difficulty, however, lies more with Hempel's epistemology than with the practices of historians and other social scientists. Covering laws are explanatory, but they are not the only form of scientific explanation. In fact, physics and economics are the only sciences that persistently employ such laws. Economic propositions such as the 'law of demand' show that mental entities *can* sometimes be embodied in general law statements but this does not demonstrate that this is the only way in which they may be used in scientific explanation.

Social scientists who accept the causal status of motives, tastes, and beliefs frequently treat explanations in terms of them as complete. This can be defended in terms of the division of labour among scientists. The economist, for example, might say that he has reached the boundaries of his disciplinary domain of investigation when he has traced phenomena to the utility-maximizing motives of the actors. As Joseph Schumpeter put it, 'the task of the economist is finished when his vessel grounds upon a non-economic bottom'. Further investigation may be undertaken by psychologists, or sociologists, or biologists, but so far as economics is concerned the explanation is complete. A stronger view is that the mental entities that the economist uses are not scientifically explicable, by economics or by any other discipline. Neither of these positions is easy to accept. The first appears to construe the disciplinary boundaries as if they were properties of the phenomenal world rather than as conventions, which they clearly are. The second appears to regard motives, tastes, and beliefs as belonging to an ontological domain that is categorically distinct from all other phenomena.

If we reject the notion that mental entities are ontologically distinct it does not follow that social scientists are obligated to furnish complete explanations of social phenomena. The contention that complete explanations are required is implicit in the argument of some philosophers and social scientists that, while motives, tastes, and beliefs may be construed as causes, they are only links in a causal chain, being themselves the effects of other causes, which must be elucidated. This seems to be the root of the view adopted by sociobiologists that social phenomena should be analysed in terms of genetic factors; mental entities may be referred to, but only in the course of passage to the genes. But why stop there? Scientific investigation is not truly grounded on bottom until it has reached quantum mechanics or the Big Bang. The demand for such a radical reductionism is clearly not helpful in advancing the enterprise of science. The boundaries between the disciplines may be conventional, but they are also useful to the furtherance of scientific inquiry. The contention that the present boundaries should be redrawn can be certified only by concrete demonstration of the improvements in scientific inquiry that would ensue. That mental entities are unobservable is no argument for insistence that we go beyond them. There are lots of unobservable entities in science, including 'genes'.

Émile Durkheim took a different tack on this issue. He opposed the notion that social phenomena should be explained by reference to mental states, but he also rejected the view that human behaviour is explained by reduction to biological factors. 'Social life,' he said, 'should be explained, not by the notions of those who participate in it, but by more profound causes which are unperceived by consciousness' (quoted by Antony Flew, *Thinking about Social Thinking*, 1985, p. 46). These 'more profound causes', in Durkheim's view, are the social factors that mould and govern the ideas of the individual members of a society. I defer discussion of this for a moment, until we come to consider the deficiencies of methodological individualism that some regard as calling for a holistic approach to social phenomena.

The term 'methodological individualism' was coined originally by Joseph Schumpeter to refer to what he viewed as the dominant methodological precept of orthodox economics. It has come since to be used more generally for the doctrine that social phenomena must be explained in terms of the behaviour of individuals. This contention is not based merely upon the view that societies are composed of individual persons; similarly banal composition propositions can be made about everything in existence. The proponents of methodological individualism favour reduction in scientific analysis but insist that this be carried to the appropriate level and no further. The appropriate level is construed to be the human individual, because it is at this level that mentation occurs and choices are made among alternative behaviour possibilities. As Herbert Spencer argued, the notion of consciousness can be applied to individual organisms but not to social groups as such. If social phenomena are to be explained in terms of mental states, it follows that the appropriate unit of analysis is the individual. There is a close connection between the debate over the causal status of mental entities and the debate over methodological individualism. But, as we shall see, it does not follow that anyone who grants causal status to mental entities is thereby committed to a rigorous methodological individualism in social science, and certainly not to the extreme form of it that some have advocated.

Methodological individualism has been strongly advocated by some sociologists and political scientists, but most notably by economists, and in the interest of brevity I shall confine the discussion here to the debate in that venue (see R. P. Dore, 'Function and Cause', in Alan Ryan, ed., *The Philosophy of Social Explanation*, 1973, for an excellent defence of methodological individualism in sociology). The standard treatment of microeconomic phenomena in the current economic literature is individualist. In explaining the determinants of market prices, for example, the market demand functions for particular goods and services are derived by simple aggregation of the demand functions of the individual consumers. On the other side of the market, the supply functions of the several producing firms is similarly aggregated. The producing 'firm' is treated as if it were an individual person, neglecting the complexities of large corporate organization (or deferring them to subsidiary examination). Consumers and firms are construed to be the appropriate units of study because it is at these levels that 'decisions' or 'choices' are made on the basis of motives, tastes, and beliefs. Economists are, generally speaking, strongly committed to such an approach to the explanation of the phenomena in their domain and feel it necessary to construct models that rigorously adhere to the canons of methodological individualism. Macroeconomic phenomena such as unemployment and inflation have not been satisfactorily modelled in this way, and many economists have expressed the view that macroeconomic theory remains insecure until it has been furnished with 'microeconomic foundations'.

The central thesis of methodological individualism was stated by John Stuart Mill in his *System of Logic*. Speaking 'Of the Chemical, or Experimental, Method in the Social Sciences', Mill declared:

> The laws of the phenomena of society are, and can be, nothing but the laws of the actions and passions of human beings united together in the social state. Men, however, in a state of society, are still men; their actions and passions are obedient to the laws of individual human nature. Men are not, when brought together, converted into another kind of substance, with different properties; as hydrogen and oxygen are different from water . . . . Human beings in society have no properties but those which are derived from, and may be resolved into, the laws of the nature of individual man. (Book VI, chapter VII)

The most influential formulation of this thesis in modern economics was contained in Lionel Robbins's *Essay on the Nature and Significance of Economic Science* (1932), which, frequently reprinted, became almost a manifesto of orthodox economic methodology. Economics, said Robbins, develops its theorems by rigorous deduction from premises that state propositions concerning human nature. These premises are so simple and plain that, though they are derived by personal introspection, their universal truth is undeniable. *Modus ponens* logic therefore guarantees that the conclusions deduced must also be true. One cannot use introspection, or any other means, to obtain similarly 'self-evident' truths about social groups, so economic theory must analyse social phenomena in terms of the rational actions of individuals. Robbins did not, I think, intend to claim that the construction of such deductive models is all that economists are called upon to do. He was not, at least in principle, averse to empirical work in economics, though some critics (especially T. W. Hutchison) criticized him severely on this ground. Robbins never clarified his position on this matter satisfactorily, but he was, it seems, talking not about the methodology of 'economic science' but about that part of it which is economic *theory*. None the less, so far as our present subject is concerned, he adopted a clear individualist stance, and it was largely this that was responsible for the widespread favourable reception of his book even in an era when empirical work in economics was rapidly developing.

Robbins and the 'Austrian school' of economists have often been treated as having similar methodological views, but this is incorrect. Ludwig von Mises and his followers argue that deducing conclusions from propositions about mental states is the whole of economics. Moreover, they regard such propositions as *a priori* truths; they are not furnished by an empirical procedure such as introspection. Robbins spoke of the mentational postulates of economic theory as 'indisputable facts of experience'. The Austrians regard 'experience' as having nothing to do with economics. They reject empiricism altogether and contend that economics, when properly conducted, differs from the natural sciences in being purely deductive. Economics is methodologically akin to Euclidian geometry and, like it, furnishes a body of apodictic truth. A small school that sometimes refers to itself as practising 'subjectivist economics' has developed under the inspiration of this methodological thesis. The main effect so far has been to bring into disrepute the notion that mental entities can be accorded causal status in a scientific explanation. But any idea can be made nonsensical by exaggeration, as the medieval scholastics, the philosophical ancestors of the Austrian school, amply showed. There is a great deal of difference between claiming that mental entities *may* be employed as causal factors in a scientific analysis of social phenomena; claiming, as Weber did, that they are *necessary* in scientific social inquiry; and contending that they, and *modus ponens* logic, are *sufficient* to enable one to discover the indubitable way of the social world.

If the only criticisms that could be mounted against methodological individualism were aimed at its extreme forms, the precept would remain undamaged. But there are others that must be more seriously considered. The most important of these is Émile Durkheim's. David Braybrooke notes that the fundamental position adopted by methodological individualism is that 'the only ultimately satisfactory strategy of explanation in the social sciences is one that moves from person facts to explain group facts and not the other way round' (*Philosophy of Social Science*, 1987, p. 33). Durkheim's contention was that the 'other way round' is the most significant feature of human sociality:

> Individual minds, forming groups by mingling and fusing, give birth to a being, psychological if you will, but constituting a psychic individuality of a new sort. It is, then, in the nature of this collective individuality, not in that of the associated units, that we must seek the immediate and determining causes of the facts appearing therein. The group thinks, feels, and acts quite differently from the way in which its members would were they isolated. If, then, we begin with the individual, we shall be able to understand nothing of what takes place in the group. (*The Rules of Sociological Method*, 1938, pp. 103–4)

This passage stands in sharp contrast to the one quoted above from J. S. Mill. In its wording Durkheim's position here is indefensible, since it seems to say that social groups possess the property of mind. Whether Durkheim did or did not embrace this highly suspect notion is debatable, but he did emphasize the methodological implications of something that cannot be empirically denied, or disregarded, in social inquiry: that the social group(s) to which an individual belongs play a strong role in determining his motives, tastes, and beliefs. This point has been highlighted repeatedly in this book, starting with the first chapter, where we noted that humans are exceptionally altricial animals who undergo a long period of enculturation. The biologist can disregard the properties of humans that are derived from enculturation, but the social scientist cannot, since the object of his inquiry is social phenomena. The causal connections between the mental states of the individual and social phenomena are reciprocal. The individualist and the holist argue for unidirectionality of causation, but in opposite directions. When moderately expressed as empirical statements, both positions are right; when expressed as hard methodological principles, both are wrong.

The methodological individualist construes the action of an individual as explicable in terms of mental states, but it is evident that reference to these is frequently meaningless without at least implicit reference also to the relevant social context of the act. If we observe that a person writes his name on a piece of paper 'in order to obtain currency from a bank', a social context is implied. But different social contexts are relevant if the same act of writing is intended to identify the agent as confessing to a crime, or as the official authorized to conclude a treaty, or is an exercise in calligraphy by a student in a course on drafting. Within each of such social contexts we may generalize about what individuals do when they write their names, but any generalization about an act of 'signing' as such would be meaningless. Similarly, words such as 'buy' and 'sell' do not simply signify that money and goods change hands in opposite directions. Pieces of paper and metal that play a role in such exchanges in Sri Lanka may not do so in Hungary, or in the Amazon jungle. Most of the terms used in social science are replete with reference to a social context, and many of them are meaningful only within a particular context. Even leaving aside the fact that the mental states of individuals are the products of enculturation, the actions of individuals cannot be divorced from the relevant social institutions and cultural ambience. In speaking of the necessity for a social scientist to understand the 'meaning' of an act, Weber was referring to such factors.

The multisociality that characterizes many human societies makes recognition of the context of an action even more imperative. The individual may be described as seeking to maximize his utility in all his actions, but his specific acts may have different meanings in relation to his membership of a church, a professional association, a political party, or a tennis club, which cannot be disregarded in the analysis of social phenomena. If we focus upon the most fundamental problem in social science, the operation of the modes and mechanisms of social organization, we encounter again the fact that these function within particular institutional and cultural contexts. Even the market mode, in which the voluntary self-interested acts of individuals play the primary role, functions within a context of legal, business, and other social institutions, and is constrained by cultural norms. Human individuals are ontological entities, but this does not mean, as methodological individualists contend, that the scientific explanation of social phenomena must run exclusively in terms of mental states. Social wholes are ontological entities as well.

Among the many institutions that compose the general social ambience within which individuals are raised to maturity and live out their adult lives, those that generate and disseminate scientific knowledge are especially important. The social nature of knowledge poses no special problems for the natural scientist because the phenomena with which he deals are not affected by it. The orbits of the planets did not change as a consequence of the publication of Newton's *Principia*. But new knowledge about social phenomena may affect the phenomena, by influencing human action. Even if such knowledge fails to alter anyone's motives or tastes, it may well alter the beliefs that people hold concerning the actions that are most likely to attain the desired ends. A person who knows economic theory may act differently from one who does not. Some economists who adhere strongly to methodological individualism have recently postulated that everyone acts as if he were in command of the best economic theories currently available; everyone, in this sense, is said to be 'rational' in the expectations he holds concerning the effects of his own actions and those of others, including the actions that may be taken by governmental authorities to affect events. The scientific value of 'rational expectations theory' in economics is, to my mind, doubtful, but this is not the issue that concerns us here. It points to a special problem that arises in domains where mental states operate as factors in the causal chain of events.

Philosophers have called this the problem of 'reflexive predictions.' In an excellent paper ('Reflexive Predictions', *Philosophy of Science*, 1963) Roger C. Buck argues that though it is in principle a serious problem for the social sciences it is of no great concern in practice because it requires wide dissemination of knowledge. If a prediction is secretly made, using a theory (which Buck takes to be the typical case, contrary to the assumption of 'rational expectations theory'), the phenomena will not be altered by the prediction. This is, I think, sometimes, but not universally, correct. If the few who are privy to the knowledge have substantial power, their actions may be sufficient to influence events. For example, if a central bank makes a prediction about the future state of the economy, and acts upon it, it may affect events even if the officers of the bank are the only ones who know about the prediction and the theory on which it is based.

A notable case of reflexivity is that of Girolamo Cardano, a sixteenth-century Italian physician and mathematician who was one of the founders of modern probability theory. He was also a strong believer in astrology and became famous for his medical horoscopes, casting one for Edward VI of England which accurately predicted that he had not long to live. Cardano is said to have constructed a horoscope for himself from which he predicted that he would die on a certain day and, when that day arrived, he committed suicide. Does his death serve as confirmatory evidence of his astrological theory? One would think not. But there are other cases that are more problematic. The announcement that a bank is insolvent and about to close its doors may cause a 'run on the bank' which forces it to close. Should we regard the announcement as true? If the economic advisers of a government predict an impending depression and the government, persuaded by them, undertakes actions that succeed in preventing it, were the economists wrong? Do the political events that took place in Russia in 1917, in which convinced Marxists played a crucial role, certify that Marx's theory of history is correct? It is difficult to answer these questions with assurance. Apart from the immediate difficulties that such cases pose for the social scientist, the problem of reflexivity throws additional doubt on the view espoused by methodological individualism that the only way to analyse social phenomena scientifically is in terms of the mental states of acting individuals.

Reflexivity, or the 'Oedipus effect', as Karl Popper called it, is a unique problem in human societies. It arises from the reciprocal connection between individual action and social phenomena – in this case the crucial linkage is the social nature of knowledge. The choice that an individual makes among alternative possible actions is based upon his beliefs as well as his motives and tastes, and even when the latter are stable, his beliefs concerning the relative efficacy of different courses of action may change rapidly. Under certain conditions, which are not rare, the beliefs of a large number of people may change at the same time and in the same way. In recent years economists have paid a great deal of attention to the role of 'expectations' as mentational causal factors in certain events. In macroeconomic theory this has been especially prominent – for example, the important role of 'inflationary expectations' in the dynamics of inflation is now universally recognized, and is not confined to rare events such as the German hyper-inflation of the 1920's. But dealing with public expectations within the epistemic rules of, as Braybrooke put it, a 'strategy of explanation . . . that moves from person facts to explain group facts and not the other way around' is obviously incapable of addressing such problems effectively.

Many of the strong proponents of methodological individualism appear to embrace it, at least in part, because of what they perceive to be the nefarious objectives of holists. The main objects of attack are Marxists who regard Marxian theory as not only scientifically true but as a potent political instrument that can be used to bring its predictions to pass. In effect, reflexivity is construed, not as an epistemic problem, but as a political opportunity. V. I. Lenin made this into Communist Party doctrine by declaring that a cadre of professional revolutionaries, convinced of the truth of Marx's theory of history, is necessary to bring about the predictions of that theory (*What is to be Done?* 1902). Not all holists can be accused of such a perversion of science, and it certainly is not an inherent property of a holistic methodology. The debate between individualism and holism as epistemic doctrines does not hinge upon which of them has been more abused and exaggerated by its adherents.

The main difficulties of methodological holism stem from the problems that are encountered in identifying the entities that are to serve as the 'wholes' in a social theory. In a complex society like that of the United States there is an almost limitless array of social entities to choose from. In Keynesian macro-economics, the entities are defined in terms of types of 'effective demand'; for example, 'consumers' and 'investors' are treated as operative aggregates. In orthodox Marxism, the entities are 'classes' that are defined in terms of the ownership of the means of production. Political scientists talk about the 'black vote' or the 'anti-abortion lobby' or the 'farm bloc'. Friedrich Hayek and other strong individualists have argued that such notions are permissible if they are construed as theoretical concepts and not as real things; they cannot be real things because they are not 'natural' entities (see, for example, Hayek, *The Counter-revolution of Science: Studies on the Abuse of Reason*, 1955, Part One, chapter VI on 'The Collectivism of the Scientistic Approach'). This argument seems to me to be untenable. Social phenomena are not any less 'natural' than physical phenomena are, and the 'farm bloc' is at least as observable as is the electron. It is not 'naive realism', as Hayek calls it, to regard social entities as real. It is, indeed, 'naive positivism' to regard the concepts of *any* science as necessarily referring to observable physical entities that occupy a definite position in space–time.

Some methodological holists, however, have been led into highly questionable contentions by treating social entities as natural. If societies are natural entities, what kind of natural entities are they? We have argued above that they are distinct entities of their own, owing to the fact that their organization makes use of special modes and mechanisms. However, a long tradition in the philosophy of metaphysics holds that there are only two kinds of natural existents, mechanisms and organisms. Holists appear to accept this, and regard societies as belonging to the latter category. Since Plato, the conception of society as an organism has appeared over and over again in the history of social thought. Just as Bergson and Driesch argued that the property that distinguishes living organisms from physical matter is the existence of a 'vital principle', so some holists seem to believe that a society possesses an equally mystical property of its own, a *Geist*, an animating spirit, a *vis vitae*, or a teleological mission that is its historical destiny. The notion of societies as organisms appears to be supported by the 'functionalist' approach in social science, which treats the various social institutions in terms of the functions they perform in the operations of the whole, analogous to the way in which the physiologist explains the functions of the heart, liver, kidney, etc., in an individual animal. This leads by a short step, or a stumble, to the contention that societies have purposes and objectives of their own, and to the accompanying judgement that the welfare of a 'society' is different from, and has moral priority over, that of the persons who compose it. Societies are, by such reasoning, not only reified, but reified as entities that possess mentational and moral properties. To avoid this error it is not necessary to embrace the epistemic and ontological canons of methodological individualism. Acceptance of the notion that societies belong to a distinct ontological category, being neither mechanisms nor organisms, will serve. From this triadic standpoint, mentation is a property that only organisms possess, but *organization*, operating through different modes, is a property of all three types of existents.

Part of the problem we encounter in the individualism–holism debate is semantic rather than philosophical or scientific. When Romeo exclaims, 'Juliet is the sun,' we know that he does not mean that she is a fiery ball 865,000 miles in diameter; and when a journalist writes that 'the White House consulted the Pentagon' we know that he does not mean that the two buildings talked with each other. But when we say things like 'the Catholic Church opposes abortion' or 'Hitler invaded the U.S.S.R.' it is more difficult, but just as important to clear thinking, to recognize that figures of speech are being employed. Narrative historians, especially those who regard their craft as belonging to the domain of literature rather than social science, tend to use figures of speech with little restraint, apparently preferring them to straightforward descriptive locution. For example, J. J. Scarisbrick in his widely acclaimed biography *Henry VIII* (1968) often says 'Henry' or 'England' when he is really referring to the group of persons responsible for the formation of the government's foreign policy; in the one case being excessively individualistic and in the other excessively holistic. It would be ridiculous to demand that history should be written like a scientific paper, without recourse to metaphors, metonymies, and other figures of speech. But some writers who adopt methodological holism use not only language but *arguments* in which collective entities are construed as having powers of autonomous action. In our day and age, the nation-state is the favoured collective entity for such endowment, but it is not at all uncommon to read popular, and academic, literature in which religions, cultures, socio-economic classes, language groups, or, with grand comprehensiveness, 'society' or 'history' are treated as if they possess such powers and have needs and aims different from, and superior to, those of individual humans.

The great debate between individualists and holists that was prominent in the literature of social science a quarter-century ago was largely initiated by Karl Popper's *The Open Society and its Enemies* (1945). Popper argued that there is a close connection between epistemology and political philosophy. He traced the development of modern totalitarianism as exemplified by fascism in Germany and communism in Russia to 'the spell of Plato', which had been transmitted to the modern West by Hegel and Marx. As a philosopher of science Popper viewed the central error of these political doctrines to be epistemological: fascism and communism were, in his judgement, based upon methodological holism, an epistemic error. Individualism is not only the proper methodology of scientific inquiry in the social domain, but provides a philosophical bulwark against the enemies of democracy and personal freedom. At the time, this seemed for some of Popper's readers to be a revelation of profound importance. The fundamental philosophical source of political totalitarianism had been identified; now it would be possible to recognize its nascent forms in social science, and extirpate them, by rational criticism, before they could undermine the fabric of a free society.

Popper was undoubtedly correct in perceiving an historical connection between the totalitarian philosophy of the state and the notion that a society or, rather, a nation, is a whole that is 'greater' than the sum of its members. One has only to pay attention to the language of modern romanticist political philosophy to become convinced that this connection persists. But Popper overstated his case. The rise of fascism and totalitarian communism in Germany and Russia cannot be ascribed solely, or 'fundamentally', to a holistic conception of society or the adoption of methodological holism in the analysis of social phenomena. Moreover, social scientists, especially historians and sociologists, have effectively used holistic concepts without slipping into the error of ascribing preternatural powers, teleological missions, and valuational capacities to social wholes.

In making a linkage between the political philosophy of democratic states and the epistemology of social science we have to recognize the role of utilitarianism. As a political philosophy utilitarianism developed a strong individualist orientation, especially in the hands of John Stuart Mill and Henry Sidgwick. This focused, not on the necessity of eschewing holistic entities in social science, but on recognition of the fact that only individuals have the power of choice and moral judgement. The companion of utilitarian political philosophy and ethics in the epistemology of the social sciences is cognitive instrumentalism. This does not consider scientific concepts in terms of their inherent nature but evaluates them in terms of their capacity to connect with empirical information in ways that render social phenomena intelligible, and manageable by individual and collective human action. How we *should* act does not come within the orbit of instrumentalist epistemology, because science and value judgements belong to different domains of rational discourse. One cannot derive moral values from the findings of social science any more than one can from physics or biology. But the social sciences have, unavoidably, a closer connection with values than do the natural sciences. Clarifying that connection is a major issue in the philosophy of social science, to which we now turn our attention.

3. The problem of objectivity

Among the many properties that have been described as unique to the species *Homo sapiens*, the possession of the mentational capacity for moral judgement has frequently been instanced. Sociobiologists have argued that the performance of altruistic acts (which they regard as the fundamental nature of moral behaviour) is no different in man than in other animals and is not, at bottom, a matter of mentation. It is governed by biological imperatives that reflect the degree of gene-sharing between the performer of the act and the beneficiary of it. But other biologists reject this as a satisfactory explanation of human morality. Ernst Mayr has recently argued (noting that other biologists have made similar contentions) that 'the emergence of genuine ethics' has come about only with the evolution of an organism that is capable of anticipating the consequences of alternative courses of action and choosing between them on the basis of moral principles. 'Human beings,' says Mayr, 'have the capacity to make such judgements because of the reasoning power provided by the evolving human brain,' and adds, in italics, *'The shift from an instinctive altruism based on inclusive fitness* [i.e. gene-sharing] *to an ethics based on decision making was perhaps the most important step in humanization'* (*Towards a New Philosophy of Biology*, 1988, p. 77). There can be no question that an organism can do only what it has the biological capacity to do, and humans do appear to make value judgements. The issue that concerns us here is not whether this is a mere appearance that masks the operation of genetic imperatives, as strict sociobiologists would claim. I will accept Mayr's view of the case, that humans make rational choices which are influenced by value judgements. The problem we must now consider is the connection, if any, between this and the other rational activity that is an outstanding property of mankind, our ability to obtain objective knowledge of the world in which we live.

If an empirical science of ethics could be constructed, the connection between these two activities would be very close. Some biologists and philosophers have recently argued that this is now possible, that we can explain not only the moral principles that men hold, but demonstrate what principles they *ought* to hold by construing such beliefs as having evolved, like the brain, by the process of natural selection (see Michael Ruse, *Taking Darwin Seriously*, 1986, chapters 3 and 6, for a good discussion of this). We have noted from time to time in this book the argument that ethical principles can be directly derived, not from biology, but from the social sciences (see, for example, the discussion above of David Ricardo's theories of value and rent, Chapter 9 A and B). Such contentions amount to saying that, contrary to David Hume's famous dictum, moral propositions *can* be derived from factual propositions. Though philosophers still debate this, no one has yet been able to provide even a hypothetical example of such a connection, and it seems to me that 'Hume's fork' remains untarnished.

But this does not mean that there is no connection at all between moral propositions and scientific ones. On the contrary, we rely upon our scientific knowledge to supply the specificity to general moral principles that is necessary for action. For example, if we accept the general moral principle that the members of a society should have greater equality of opportunity, we rely upon empirical sociology and economics to tell us whether we ought therefore to adopt specific social policies such as the special taxation of inherited wealth and the financing of education from state funds. This kind of connection between values and science creates no problems that need concern us here. The connection we have to examine raises the question whether it is possible to construct a social science that is objective or, put differently, if scientific knowledge is defined as having the property of objectivity, is it possible to have *scientific* knowledge of social phenomena? The main contention that this is not possible rests upon the view that in the study of social phenomena there is such an intimate and unavoidable entanglement between the values held by scientists and their research procedures that objective findings are unattainable.

If the members of a community believe that a bridge would be desirable in a certain place, engineers can be relied upon to construct it by using objective knowledge. If engineering knowledge were itself so deeply affected by value judgements that, for example, the stress data for bridge trusses were dependent upon the engineers' values, the community would be in great difficulty, even if its members were unanimous in regarding a bridge as desirable. Is this the case with the social sciences? Is the work of economists, sociologists, and others unavoidably entangled with value judgements to such a degree that there can be no reliable knowledge in this domain? In the discussion earlier in this chapter of the general epistemic argument advanced by Russell Hanson and others that empirical observations are 'theory-laden' (section A 1), this problem was dismissed rather summarily; now we must examine it more fully.

The examination of the sociological ideas of Herbert Spencer and Max Weber in Chapter 15 noted that, in their methodological writings, they regarded this problem as very important. The greater part of Spencer's *The Study of Sociology* (1875) is devoted to it. In Spencer's view the sociologist is likely to bring certain preconceptions to his study of social phenomena because he has been enculturated into, and remains a member of, a society with certain commonly held beliefs and values. He regarded this as a problem for scientific sociology, but not an insuperable one, since the conscientious sociologist can identify the biases he may possess and guard against them. It is perhaps significant that his book was frequently adopted as a text in introductory courses in sociology in American universities. Apparently American socio- logists, at this early period in the development of their discipline, regarded Spencer's warnings, and his advice on this matter, as salutary. In Germany, Max Weber expressed a similar view even more strongly. The social scientist, he repeatedly insisted, must adopt a meta-value, the obligation to keep his work free of value judgements. Gustav Schmoller and his followers in the then dominant school of German social science held a different view with equal pertinacity. The social scientist, they contended, is morally obligated to promote values in his teaching and writing. Needless to say, they took it for granted that values which they themselves held should be the ones promoted. The issue of what Weber called *Wertfreiheit* (value-freedom) became a matter of sharp controversy, which punctuated the meetings of the Verein für

Sozialpolitik, the leading association of German social scientists. The controversy spread to neoclassical economics with the almost simultaneous publication of Gunnar Myrdal's *The Political Element in the Development of Economic Theory* (1930) and Lionel Robbins's *Essay on the Nature and Significance of Economic Science* (1932), which took opposite positions. Myrdal argued that economics is inextricably entangled with value judgements; Robbins claimed that economic theory, as a pure logic of rational choice, achieves the *Wertfreiheit* that Weber demanded. Since then the controversy has continued unabated (for an excellent review of it see Mark Blaug, *The Methodology of Economics*, 1980, chapter 5). With the downfall of positivism the issue has also entered the domain of general epistemology. The 'rhetorical analysis' espoused by Donald McCloskey declares that all claims of scientific objectivity are a sham and that so-called scientific publications should be read as exercises in persuasion, which are strongly governed by the author's own value judgements. A similar view is contained in the writings of the Edinburgh school. Less bluntly recognized, the view that science and value judgements are interlaced is implicit in the epistemological theory of conventionalism, Thomas Kuhn's paradigm model, and Imre Lakatos's methodology of scientific research programmes. On the other side, realists and cognitive instrumentalists defend the view that value judgements can be detached from pure science (except, of course, for the meta-value that it is better to know the truth than to be ignorant or misinformed), and that these two domains need be intimately connected only at the level of application.

A companion issue that intersects with the debate over *Wertfreiheit* is the contention that the work of the scientist is influenced by his 'interests', that is to say, his desire to achieve objectives other than the advancement of knowledge. That scientists are not saints but, like common folk, are motivated by the desire for wealth, fame, power, respect, and admiration is scarcely to be doubted. That these motives, rather than the search for knowledge in itself, frequently dominate their activities, as scientists, is equally plausible, supported, for example, by James Watson's frank account in *The Double Helix* (1968) of how he and Francis Crick discovered the geometry of the DNA molecule, Nuel Pharr Davis's *Lawrence and Oppenheimer* (1969), David Hull's *Science as a Process* (1988), and numerous other books and articles recounting the 'inside story' of scientific discoveries, and by biographies of prominent scientists. The role of non-intellectual motives in scientific practice is, in fact, a matter of more interest to the social scientist than the issue of *Wertfreiheit*, since it raises the question of whether the institutional organization of science and the incentive structure it contains contributes to the advance of objective knowledge or retards it. But let us defer that issue for a moment.

Ernest Nagel has surveyed the question of objectivity, with specific attention to the social sciences, in his *The Structure of Science* (1961). Focusing on his discussion will serve our purposes, since he considers the main arguments that have been advanced against the notion of *Wertfreiheit* in social science and gives counter-arguments in defense of it. (In this summary, and the following discussion, I will draw upon material in my paper 'Social Science and Value Judgements', *Canadian Journal of Economics*, 1977.)

The first argument examined by Nagel is the contention that social scientists do not study all social phenomena with equal intensity; they select among the potential specific topics of study and, it is claimed, their selection is determined by value judgements. Nagel rejects this argument, on the ground that no scientist can study everything, even within the limited domain of his discipline, and that social scientists are no different from natural scientists in selecting among potential topics. This seems to me to be an inadequate defence of social science, for two reasons. First, one cannot acquit one branch of science from a charge of questionable procedure simply by showing that other branches are also culpable. Secondly, and more important, there is the question whether the social and natural sciences are *equally* culpable. One cannot measure this quantitatively, but there would seem to be good reason to believe that the selection of specific topics for investigation is governed by value judgements to a greater degree in the social sciences. Social research is strongly oriented towards social problems and social scientists may differ greatly in how they evaluate such problems. For example, one economist may regard the distribution of income between workers and property owners as important in assessing the quality of a society, another may think that this is better indicated by the size distribution of income regardless of its source, and a third might regard the number of people whose income is below the 'poverty line' as the relevant indicator. Natural scientists may select among lines of research on grounds of their comparative potentials for social betterment, but they are less strongly impelled to consider the practical applications of their research than social scientists are. In the area of pure science, topics are selected for research by considering the comparative potentials of different lines of research in yielding scientifically important results. In doing this scientists are making value judgements. But this is not the kind of value judgement that is relevant to the assessment of scientific objectivity, for either the social or the natural sciences. To claim that a scientist is not being objective when he chooses one line of research as more promising, scientifically, than another, would lead to the ludicrous contention that the claim to objectivity could be sustained only if scientists were to allow their research topics to be determined by a process of random selection!

Nagel makes a distinction between 'characterizing judgements' and 'appraising judgements' and contends that some of the arguments made against the notion of *Wertfreiheit* in social science rest upon a confusion of these. Every scientist must characterize the specific phenomena he observes and investigates as belonging to a certain generic class. The biologist, for example, uses a definition in order to determine whether a particular phenomenon belongs to the classification 'respiration' or 'photosynthesis'. In doing so he is making characterizing judgements, but he is not making any evaluative appraisal of the phenomena. In the social sciences, says Nagel, equally immaculate characterizing judgements may be made. In principle, this may be correct, but in practice there are great difficulties. If an attack is made on a village by a group of armed men, is it an act of 'terrorism', or 'liberation from tyranny', or a 'bandit raid'? Such characterizing judgements are obviously infused with values, and the implicit values govern the research undertaken to explain them. In the social sciences there are many concepts, such as, for example, 'money supply', 'voting', 'congressional committee', and 'professional association', that permit purely characterizing judgements to be made, but there are many that cannot be detached from valuational connotations: 'unemployment', 'crime', 'drug addiction', 'log-rolling', to cite just a few examples of the many that could be instanced. The value-loading of such concepts may be a matter of language, due to the fact that ordinary language is used for scientific purposes in economics, sociology, and the other social disciplines. But it is doubtful that any language, even an artificially contrived one, could be preserved from contamination by values, when used to examine social phenomena.

Nagel notes the contention that the social sciences cannot be objective because prior values govern not only the choice of specific topics for investigation and the concepts employed, but are injected into the analysis itself and effectively control the conclusions reached. This amounts to saying that social scientists are prone to employ warped logic and improper treatment of empirical data in order to support views they held prior to the investigation. I think that Nagel is right to dismiss this as a problem specific to the social sciences, since it is simply bad scientific practice *tout court*. Such practices may be easier to conceal in the social than in the natural sciences, but the contention that the possibility (or even the probability) of this destroys the claim of objectivity is not warranted.

There is, however, a problem in the treatment of empirical data that cannot be reduced to a matter of sound or unsound practice, which Nagel considers but, in my view, underrates. This problem was first noted by Jerzy Neyman in his early papers that led to the development of the Neyman–Pearson model of statistical inference in the 1930's and emerges clearly in Abraham Wald's formulation of statistical inference as a process of decision-making under conditions of uncertainty. The heart of the problem is concisely stated by Richard Rudner, a philosopher, in a paper unambiguously entitled 'The Scientist *qua* Scientist makes Value Judgements' (*Philosophy of Science*, 1953). When the data used in a scientific investigation are statistical, as is usually the case in the social sciences, one rarely finds that they provide categorical answers to the question at issue. Take, for example, the 'law of demand' in economics. This stipulates that people will purchase more of a commodity at a lower price than at a higher one, other factors affecting purchases held constant. If we wish to ascertain whether this is consistent with empirical evidence, we might collect the relevant data by means of a sample survey of households and compute the general mathematical relationship between quantities purchased and prices. Leaving aside the technical difficulties in doing this, suppose we find that the relationship between prices and quantities purchased is indeed negative as the law of demand states. Our data, however, are merely a sample, not the whole population of households in the community. What econometricians do in such a case is to calculate the probability that such a survey will yield the results it did by chance. Let us say that this tells us that such results could occur by chance four times in a hundred if we were to do the exercise over and over again. Should we conclude that the data support the postulated law? If we do so we risk some danger of accepting the law when in fact it is not true. If, however, we conclude that the law is not supported by the data, we risk rejecting it when in fact it is true. There is no objective way of determining when we should accept and when reject: is a 4 per cent chance of being wrong 'small' or 'large'? The economist might say that, in this particular case, he is prepared to accept such a chance of being wrong. But suppose the data yielded a *positive* relationship between prices and quantities purchased, not the negative one postulated by the law of demand. In this case the economist might well say that, since the law plays such a vital role in the general structure of microeconomic theory, he is unwilling to accept the result of the survey and reject the law even though there might be a 96 per cent chance that the law of demand is indeed false. What probability of being wrong would convince him? Mathematical statistics deserts one here. A value judgement must be made, and such judgements might well differ among scientifically conscientious economists.

The above illustrations indicate that a scientist might be unwilling to accept the results of an empirical study, even if the mathematics of inference indicated that there was only, say, a 4 per cent probability that the results were untrue, when such acceptance would do grave damage to a central pillar in the general structure of the science as presently constituted. One of the merits of the epistemological theory advanced by Imre Lakatos is in pointing out that certain propositions in a 'research programme' are more vital than others, being part of the 'hard core' of the programme. Scientists are reluctant to accept empirical evidence that is inconsistent with the hard core, for to do so would require the abandonment of the programme, and no viable alternative may be available. The judgement involved here concerns the scientific, not the moral consequences of regarding contradictory evidence as conclusive. That is, it is not the kind of judgement that involves values other than the scientist's general belief that the advancement of scientific knowledge is a worthy aim. Indeed, the insistence that one must eliminate *all* values from science would amount to the destruction of scientific inquiry. Mark Blaug points out that the acceptance of empirically true statements rests upon the view that they *ought* to be accepted (*The Methodology of Economics*, 1980, p. 131). If this were the only value judgement involved in science, its claim to objectivity would be secure against attack by all but the most determined scholastic pedant.

Social scientists have a heuristic interest in protecting their hard core propositions, just as natural scientists do, but choosing between the risk of accepting a false hypothesis and rejecting a true one also enters when statistical data are used to provide empirical foundations for decisions on matters of social policy. The judgements involved here are not devoid of valuational content. For example, if the data show that there is a positive correlation between the level of the legal minimum wage and the amount of unemployment, with, say, a 4 per cent chance of being due to chance, should one advise the governmental authorities to lower the minimum or repeal the law altogether? Undoubtedly, economists employed by labour unions and ones employed by business firms will differ on this; but even economists who are not interested parties may differ, for the decision hinges upon value judgements. This problem applies to all applied sciences. An engineer might, for example, accept a 90 per cent safety probability for a coal-fired generator but insist on a much higher one for a nuclear power plant. The social sciences, however, are more dependent upon non-experimental statistical data (some of which are quite soft) than the natural sciences are, and more of their work is directly oriented to making assessments of social policies.

These are the main arguments that one finds in the literature on the issue of *Wertfreiheit* in the social sciences. Nagel's general conclusion is that the contention that the study of social phenomena cannot be objective is not sustainable or, at least, that the problems one encounters in the social sciences are no more severe than those that face natural scientists. I have tried to show that, with respect to most of these issues, Nagel's view is questionable; value judgements do enter in significant ways into all domains of scientific inquiry but they do so to a greater degree in the study of social phenomena and the application to social policy. Does this mean the notion of objectivity must be abandoned? Not by any means. In our general review of the epistemology of science in the first section of this chapter we found that the notion of *absolute certainty*, which the early positivists embraced, must be abandoned in any realistic view of scientific knowledge and its potential for further development, but that does not mean that it is illusory to believe that we have some objective knowledge of the world and that we can improve that knowledge. Perfect insulation of science from value judgements is not possible, but this is merely one of the reasons why we must regard our knowledge as contingent. The instruments of scientific inquiry cannot furnish apodictic truths about the world, but they can enable us to obtain limited and tentative knowledge about it and, in some areas, that knowledge is sufficiently reliable to serve practical purposes.

Objectivity, then, like certainty, must be regarded as a philosophical ideal rather than a characterizing property of scientific knowledge. Most philosophers of science, including most of those who have abandoned positivism, hold that it is desirable to make our knowledge of the world more objective and more certain. This is, of course, a value judgement, but it is one that serves the process of scientific inquiry rather than rendering it problematic. That these ideals cannot be attained is not a reason for disregarding them. Perfect cleanliness is also impossible, but that does not serve as a warrant for not washing, much less for rolling in a manure pile. All knowledge is human knowledge and humans are imperfect beings, who can only cope with the problems they encounter as best they may. Scientists are human too. That they make value judgements in selecting problems for investigation, in framing theoretical concepts, and in drawing inferences from empirical data means only that science requires the use of informed judgement as well as the application of formal logic and the rules of empirical methodology.

If objectivity is regarded in this way, the important issue is the pragmatic one: by what means can the *degree* of objectivity in scientific work be raised, or prevented from declining? Herbert Spencer advocated that social scientists should be conscious of the biases they may harbor owing to family background, education, and the general norms of their culture, as well as their personal interests. Insisting that all aspiring social scientists should take a course in professional ethics modelled after Spencer's *The Study of Sociology* would probably do no harm, but one may be sceptical that this would suffice to assure that social research would be pursued with a degree of objectivity sufficient to preserve it from gross contamination by value judgements and other biases. Max Weber argued that *Wertfreiheit* requires consciousness of potential bias, and recommended honest and public admission by the social scientist of the values he embraces, but he also made the much more important point that the accumulation of reliable knowledge depends as well upon the social organization of science. Ernest Nagel echoes Weber's point in emphasizing 'the self-corrective mechanism of science as a social enterprise' that operates when scientists are free to criticize one another and pursue their activities in a regime of friendly competition.

The importance of the social organization of science with regard to the issue of objectivity can be illustrated by comparing two cases of extreme lack of objectivity: the outright fabrication of empirical data. Several years ago a scientist named Summerlin, at the Sloan-Kettering Institute in New York, claimed to be able to make successful skin and corneal transplants in mice. This would have been an important contribution to scientific knowledge, and possibly to the Institute's programme of cancer research, if it had been valid. But Summerlin's data were fabricated. Other scientists tried to reproduce his results, with lack of success, and the fraud was quickly discovered. The story is reported in Joseph Hixson, *The Patchwork Mouse* (1976). In reviewing this book, P. D. Medawar (*New York Review*, 15 April 1976) gave an excellent discussion of the problems posed by cases of data fabrication in science but came to the conclusion that 'no great truth about scientific behavior is to be learned from the Summerlin affair except perhaps that it takes all kinds to make a world'. On the contrary, there is an important lesson to be learned from it: that when free, independent inquiry is permissible, fraudulent practices may be quickly exposed, and negligible harm done to the body of scientific knowledge or its practical applications. By contrast, there is the case of Trofim Lysenko in the Soviet Union, who fabricated data on genetic transmission in plants in the 1930's. As president of the Lenin All-Union Academy of Agricultural Sciences Lysenko was in charge of Soviet agricultural research and its applications. He was also head of the Institute of Genetics of the Soviet Academy of Sciences, and a member of the Supreme Soviet, the highest legislative organ in the political system of the U.S.S.R. Other scientists were not free to dispute Lysenko's theories. Those suspected of harbouring other views lost their posts, some went to prison, and some were executed. The consequences were that Russian work in genetics, which had been in the forefront of world research before the rise of Lysenko to power, was utterly destroyed, and remained locked into the Lamarckian theory of inheritance that Lysenko embraced, until the fall of Khrushchev in 1964. During this period immense harm was also done to Soviet agriculture, which was obliged to follow Lysenskoist prescriptions. If science in the U.S.S.R. had been organized differently, been more pluralist, less subject to the control of political authorities, it would have undoubtedly been more objective. Political ideology, however, is not the only thing that can generate gross departures from the ideal of objectivity. Any form of organization that seriously constrains free competition in the domain of scientific research can have similar effects, including control by scientists themselves. Francis Bacon's notion that a 'Solomon's House' of science should be established, in which scientists would be brought together as a unified authoritative agency to speak with one voice, is a prescription for the destruction of science, not for the furtherance of scientific knowledge and its reliable application to practical problems.

The social sciences are more heavily involved with value judgements, political ideologies, and other contaminants of objectivity than are the natural sciences and, lacking the ability to make closed-system experiments, they are less able to contend with fabricated data and other abuses of empirical evidence. But mainstream social scientists are committed to an epistemology of empiricism, and where they work in a pluralist environment of intellectual independence, the ideal of objectivity can be approached, even though never attained. In his famous essay *On Liberty*, John Stuart Mill argued the case for intellectual freedom on utilitarian grounds, as a form of social organization that promotes the advance of knowledge. The thesis he advanced need not be defended as a matter of faith or liberal political ideology; it is certified by the historical experience of science in all its domains.

Name index

This is an index of individuals only: Acts of legislation, journals, organizations, etc. will be found in the subject index. Writings (books, essays, lectures, etc.) have been included where discussed in the text: they are arranged in alphabetical order at the end of the author's entry.

Adams, John 570
Alchian, A.A.: 'Uncertainty, Evolution and Economic Theory' 535
Alembert, Jean le Rond de 111; *Enclyclopaedia* (with Diderot) 89
Allen, Garland: *Life Sciences in the Twentieth Century* 378
Althusser, Louis 329, 601
Aquinas, St Thomas 25–6, 155–6; *Summa Theologica* 25
Argenson, Marquis de 223
Aristotle viii, 27, 61–3, 72, 640; and Catholic Church 19, 25; essentialism of 28, 384–5; and *ethos* 450; and property ownership 81; teleology of 46, 155, 322, 385, 395; and trade 195; as utopianist 154, 155, 215–16; writings: *Politics* 61–3, 448
Arnold, Thomas 296
Aron, Raymond 300; *Main Currents of Sociological Thought* 437; (quoted 336, 441, 467)
Augustine, St 18, 19, 150–1, 159, 217; *City of God* 30, 58, 150
Augustus, Caesar 182
Austen, Jane 336
Ayala, Francisco J.: quoted 516
Ayer, A.J.: quoted 212, 595; writings: *Language Truth and Logic* 595

Bacon, Francis 150, 166, 274, 592, 668; *New Atlantis* 166; *Novum Organum* 37, 69
Bacon, Roger 22
Bagehot, Walter 532–3, 534; *The English Constitution* 534; *Lombard Street* 534; *Physics and Politics* 534
Bakunin, Mikhail 221, 329, 370
Baran, Paul A., and Paul M. Sweezy: *Monopoly Capital* 340, 369
Barnes, Barry 621, 622
Barnes, Harry Elmer: quoted 634
Bastiat, Frédéric: *Harmonies économiques* 243
Bauer, Bruno 308, 372
Beard, Charles 395
Beccaria, Cesare Bonsana 137
Beethoven, Ludwig van 266; as deviant 15
Bell, Alexander Graham 521
Bentham, Jeremy 249–53, 260–1, 269; as deviant 15; influences on 117, 130; writings: *Introduction to the Principles of Morals and Legislation* 251, 253
Bergmann, Gustav 647
Bergson, Henri 516, 642; *Creative Evolution* 516, 642; *Matter and Memory* 642
Berkeley, George 224
Berle, A.A. 487
Berlin, Isaiah 401, 404, 406; quoted 405
Bernoulli, Jacques 532
Bernstein, Eduard 366

Bernstein, Leonard: *Candide* 218
Binet, Alfred 522
Black, Joseph 112
Blackstone, William 249; *Commentaries on the Laws of England* 250
Blaug, Mark: *The Methodology of Economics* 600, 665
Bloor, David 621, 622; *Knowledge and Social Imagery* 621
Boas, Franz 527
Bodin, Jean 65
Boisguillebert, Sieur de 223
Boland, Lawrence A. 623
Bolyai, János 591
Bonnet, Charles 426
Boorstin, Daniel J. viii
Bougainville, Louis Antoine de 160
Boulding, Kenneth E.: *A Reconstruction of Economics* 535
Bowen, Francis 244; *American Political Economy* 244; *Principles of Political Economy* 244
Boyle, Robert 27, 69, 76
Braybrooke, David 653, 656
Bridgewater, Earl of 515
Brinton, Crane: quoted 266
Brodbeck, May 647; quoted 628, 637
Bruno, Giordano 287
Buchanan, J.M., and Gordon Tullock: *The Calculus of Consent* 119
Buck, Roger C.: 'Reflexive Predictions' 655
Buckle, Henry T.: quoted 130–1; writings: *History of Civilization in England* 530–1
Bukharin, Nikolai 322
Burckhardt, Jacob C.: *The Civilization of the Renaissance in Italy* 21
Burn, W.L.: quoted 233, 234
Burt, Cyril 523
Butler, Samuel 516, 540–1, 642

Cairnes, John Elliot 300; *The Character and Logical Method of Political Economy* 203
Caius, John 18
Calvin, John *see* Calvinism
Campanella, Tommaso: *City of the Sun* 166
Cannan, Edwin 570
Cardano, Girolamo 655–6
Carey, Henry C. 241–3, 636; *Principles of Political Economy* 242; *Principles of Social Science* 636
Carey, Mathew 241
Carlyle, Thomas: and classical political economy 226–7, 235, 508; and positivism 285, 296; and utilitarianism 267, 268, 508, 569; writings: *Past and Present* 267, 325
Carnap, Rudolph 591, 596, 597
Carnegie, Andrew 434
Carneiro, Robert L. 58, 437
Carrel, Alexis: *Man the Unknown* 536
Carrithers, D.W. 84
Carver, Terrell 375
Castle, W.E. 521
Chamberlain, Joseph 578
Chambers, Robert: *Vestiges of the Natural History of Creation* 498–9, 509
Charles I, King (of Great Britain) 69, 71
Charles II, King (of Great Britain) 70
Churchill, Winston S. 521
Clark, John Bates 573
Cobden, Richard 241
Cohen, I. Bernard: *Revolution in Science* 616
Colbert, Jean Baptiste 89, 93, 223
Coleridge, Samuel Taylor 266, 267, 268, 269; *Constitution of Church and State* 285
Collingwood, R.C. 404, 406
Columbus, Christopher 159
Commons, John R. 266
Comte, Auguste 55, 153, 272, 273, 280, 286–95; and classical political economy 299; Durkheim and 440–1; English disciples of 296–7, 415, 441, 514; law of the three stages 279–80, 289–91, 450; and logical positivism 591; and Plato 59, 294–5; and Saint-Simon 276, 277, 288; Spencer and 415–16; writings: *Cours de philosophie positive* 287–92 *passim*, 296; *Le Systeme de politique positive* 288
Condillac, Étienne Bonnot de 111
Condorcet, Marquis de 111, 149; as sociologist 272; as utopianist 167, 184, 187, 274; writings: *Esquisse d'un tableau historique des progrès de l'esprit humain* 272
Congreve, Richard 296, 297, 415
Conkin, Paul K.: quoted 243

Contarini, Gasparo: *De Magistratibus et Republica Venetorum* 66–8
Cook, Captain James 160
Cooley, Charles H. 437
Copernicus, Nicolas 19–20, 21, 69; as deviant 14–15; economic theories of 141;
writings: *De Revolutionibus Orbium Coelestium* 19
Coser, Lewis A.: quoted 488
Cournot, Augustin: *Recherches sur les principes mathématiques de la theorie des richesses* 209
Coxe, Tench 241
Cozzi, Gaetano 65
Crick, F.H.C. 399, 662
Croce, Benedetto 404, 406
Cromwell, Oliver 69–70, 71
Cunningham, William 266
Cuvier, Georges 497

d'Alembert *see* Alembert
d'Argenson *see* Argenson
Darwin, Charles: and classical political economy 507; as deviant 15; as product of capitalism 31–2, 505, 509–10; social philosophy of 503–4;
writings: *Autobiography* 505; *The Descent of Man* 500, 503, 504, 505, 510–11, 520, 527; *The Origin of Species* 30, 326, 427–9, 454, 497–8, 499–504, 509; *see also under* evolution
Davenport, Charles B. 520
Davis, Nuel Pharr: *Lawrence and Oppenheimer* 662
Dawkins, Richard: *The Blind Watchmaker* 502; *The Selfish Gene* 537
Democritus 633
Descartes, René 52, 72, 211–12, 374, 451, 452; Cartesian co-ordinates 103–4; as deviant 15;
writings: *Discourse on Method* 52, 69, 78, 591
Dickens, Charles 190, 234, 235, 336, 508; *Hard Times* 235; *Little Dorrit* 234; *Oliver Twist* 190
Diderot, Denis 111, 137; *Encyclopaedia* 89
Djilas, Milovan 487
Donne, John 152
Dostoyevski, Fyodor: *The Brothers Karamazov* 454
Dray, William H. 396, 409
Driesch, Hans 517, 642
Duhem, Pierre 601
Dühring, Eugen Karl 243, 282
Dunbar, Charles 247
Du Pont, E.I. 91
Du Pont de Nemours, Pierre Samuel 91–1
Durkheim, Émile 291, 298, 411–12, 438–61, 464, 651, 653–4; and *conscience collective* 280–1, 449–52, 459–60, 461, 480, 517, 644; and organic theory of society 280–1, 442, 443–4, 446–52, 454–5, 457, 459–61; philosophy of science of 455–6; and Plato 59, 442, 448; political theory of 441–2, 448–9, 456–61; 'sociological point of view' of 273, 452–6;
writings: *The Division of Labour in Society* 439, 447, 448, 453, 454, 460; 'The Dualism of Human Nature and its Social Conditions' 451; *The Elementary Forms of the Religious Life* 439, 454–5; *The Rules of Sociological Method* 439, 442–6 *passim*, 453, 455, 653; 'Sociology and its Scientific Field' 461, *Suicide* 439, 453–4

Edgeworth, F.Y. 253–4, 258, 265, 563–4, 578, 580
Edward VI, King (of England) 656
Einstein, Albert 15; theory of relativity 591, 600
Eliot, George 296; *Felix Holt* 336
Elizabeth I, Queen (of England) 69, 189
Ellis, Havelock 521
Ely, Richard T. 247, 434
Enfantin, Prosper 277
Engels, Friedrich 310–12; collaboration with Marx 305–6, 308–10, 311, 312, 355;
writings of 314; *Anti-Dühring* 306, 312, 323, 373, 387; (on dialectic 375, 376–7, 379–80; on history 318, 321; on value 345, 348, 349); *Communist Manifesto see under* Marx, Karl; *The Condition of the Working Class in England* 306, 311, 325, 362; 'Dialectics of Nature' 327; 'Outlines of a Critique of Political Economy'

305, 308, 311, 361, 362, 364, 371; (on exploitation 325, 350); 'Principles of Communism' 305; *Socialism Utopian and Scientific* 282, 306; *see also* Marxian theory
Epicurus of Samos *see* Epicureanism
Espinas, Alfred 436, 440; *Des sociétés animales* 436
Euclid 591, 592, 593, 653

Ferguson, Adam 113, 137; *Essays on the History of Civil Society* 273
Feuer, Lewis S. 327
Feuerbach, Ludwig 381
Feyerabend, Paul 623, 629
Fichte, J.G. 375
Filmer, Sir Robert: *Patriarcha* 78–9
Fink, Zera S. 67
Fischoff, Ephraim 479
Fisher, Irving 566
Fisher, R.A. 520, 532
Fisher, R.S.: *Progress of the United States* 152
Fitzgerald, F.Scott: quoted 301
Fontenelle, Bernard de 149
Fourier, Charles 166
Franklin, Benjamin: *Observations Concerning the Increase of Mankind* 183
Frazer, James 273
Freud, Sigmund 133, 165, 451–2
Friedman, Milton: 'The Methodology of Positive Economics' 41, 609–10

Galen 17–18
Galiani, Abbé 94
Galileo, Galilei 19–21, 24, 27, 69, 72; as deviant 14–15, 31; Hobbes' meeting with 71, 72;
  writings: *Dialogue on the Two Chief Systems of the World* 20, 21; *Letter to the Grand Duchess Christina* 20, 24; *Letters on Sunspots* 20
Gall, Johann Franz 527
Galton, Francis 502, 509, 518–20, 522, 523, 525, 528; on economics 636; and statistics 519, 532;
  writings: *Hereditary Genius* 519–20; 'Hereditary Talent and Character' 519, 523
Gama, Vasco da 159
Gasman, Daniel: *The Scientific Origins*

of National Socialism 528
Gassendi, Pierre 382
Gauss, Karl Friedrich 530, 532
Gellner, Ernest: quoted 626, 631–2
Geoffroy Saint-Hillaire, Etienne 496
George, Henry 180–1, 571; *Progress and Poverty* 97–8, 180, 457, 507; *Protection or Free Trade* 98
Ghiselin, Michael T. 508, 535; *The Economy of Nature and the Evolution of Sex* 535
Giddens, Anthony 298
Giere, Ronald N.: quoted 604
Giffen, Robert: *Progress of the Working Class* 152
Ginsberg, Morris 445
Giotto 17
Godwin, William 164, 165, 184: *Inquiry Concerning Political Justice* 221–2
Gould, Stephen Jay 327–8, 502–3, 507–8
Gouldner, Alvin W.: quoted 298
Gournay, Vincent de 223
Gresham, Sir Thomas 473
Grosseteste, Robert 72
Grote, George 296; *History of Greece* 296

Hacking, Ian 625
Haeckel, Ernst 461, 520, 528
Halévy, Elie 202
Hall, Walter P.: quoted 225
Halley, Edmund 627
Hamilton, W.D.: 'The Genetical Theory of Social Behaviour' 543
Hanson, Norwood Russell 601, 604–5, 606, 621, 661; *Patterns of Discovery* 601
Harcourt, Sir William 578
Hardy, G.H. 525; quoted 39
Harriman, Mrs E.H. 520
Harrington, James 317; *Commonwealth of Oceana* 67
Harrison, Frederic 296, 300, 415
Hartley, David 129, 267; *Observations on Man* 129–30
Harvey, William 27, 97, 416, 494, 495, 516; *On the Movement of the Heart and Blood in Animals* 69
Hausman, Daniel 647
Hayek, F.A. 155–6, 303, 401, 637, 657; *The Counter-revolution of Science* 33; *Law Legislation and Liberty* trilogy 156

Hegel, G.W.F. 269–70, 402, 403, 450, 592; concept of 'dialectic' 373, 374–80; concept of *Geist* 321, 322, 383, 385, 402, 450; and Marxian theory 308, 317, 321, 322, 372, 381, 383, 385; writings: *Philosophy of Right* 340
Heisenberg, Werner Karl 591
Hemingway, Ernest: quoted 301
Hempel, Carl G. 404, 637; covering law model of 46–7, 391–400, 416, 594, 604, 629, 649–50; deductive–nomological model of 598–9, 603; writings: 'The Function of General Laws in History' 47, 391, 404; 'The Logic of Explanation' (with Paul Oppenheim) 598
Henderson, W.O.: quoted 311
Henry VIII, King (of England) 69, 160, 473; biography of 658
Henry, Prince (of Portugal)('The Navigator') 159
Heraclitus 154, 375
Herder, J.G. von 269, 280, 281, 403, 404, 405–6, 636; *Outlines of the Philosophy of the History of Man* 280
Herrick, Robert 480
Herschel, John 592
Hexter, J.H. 399
Hicks, J.R. 584
Hirshleifer, Jack 535
Hitler, Adolf 76, 269–70, 432, 485, 489
Hixson, Joseph: *The Patchwork Mouse* 667
Hobbes, Thomas 70–6, 110, 118–19, 446–7, 646; as materialist 382; as utilitarian 248, 255; writings: *Leviathan* 71–6, 145, 591
Hobhouse, John A. 340, 570, 582
Hofstadter, Richard 518
Hollander, Samuel 359
Hollis, Martin, and E.J. Nell: *Rational Economic Man* 39–40
Holmes, Oliver Wendell 521, 522
Home, Henry, (Lord Kames) 113, 116
Homer 28–9; *Iliad* 28; *Odyssey* 28
Hull, David: *Science as a Process* 662
Hume, David 120–30; on 'circulation' 97; economic theories of 124–6, 140–1, 178, 196, 342; epistemology of 114, 115, 116, 126–9, 592, 604, 636; and equilibrium 125–6, 191–2; and fact-value dichotomy 122–3, 425, 573, 649, 660; political theory of 123–6, 137; on Scottish Enlightenment 112; and Smith 131, 178; as utilitarian 265; writings: 'Of the Balance of Trade' 124–6, 191–2, 196; *Dialogues Concerning Natural Religion* 121; *Enquiry Concerning Human Understanding* 121; *Enquiry Concerning the Principles of Morals* 121; *History of Great Britain* 121; 'On the Populousness of Ancient Nations' 149, 182; 'That Politics may be Reduced to a Science' 124; *Treatise of Human Nature* 114, 118, 121, 122–4, 129
Husserl, Edmund 612
Hutcheson, Francis 113, 116, 117, 118, 130, 137, 249
Hutchison, T.W. 652; *The Significance and Basic Postulates of Economic Theory* 600
Hutton, James 113, 502
Huxley, Aldous: *Brave New World* 165, 294; *The Devils of Loudon* 633–4
Huxley, T.H. 423, 432, 498–9, 500, 502; 'Evolution and Ethics' 432–3, 504; 'The Struggle for Existence in Human Society' 432

Jacob, Margaret C. 31, 509
James I, King (of Great Britain) 69
James II, King (of Great Britain) 70, 77
Jefferson, Thomas 91, 569
Jenkin, Fleeming 502
Jennings, H.S.: 'What Can We Hope from Eugenics?' 524–5
Jevons, William Stanley 169–70, 265, 552, 561, 562, 636; *Principles of Science* 600, 604; *The Theory of Political Economy* 170, 550
Johnson, Samuel 114
Jones, Richard 203
Juglar, Clément: *Les Crises commerciales et leur retour périodique* 362, 583
Jung, Carl 133, 281, 291

Kames, Lord, (Henry Home) 113, 116
Kant, Immanuel ix, 121, 589, 593, 612; *Critique of Pure Reason* 374–5; 'The

Idea of a Universal History from a
Cosmopolitan Point of View' 219
Kaplan, Abraham 604
Kateb, George 161
Kautsky, Karl 322, 366–7; edition of
Marx 310
Keats, John 602
Kepler, Johannes 69, 629–30
Keynes, John Maynard 579–80; and
eugenics 521; on Locke 78; writings
of 584; *The Economic Consequences
of the Peace* 580; *The General Theory
of Employment Interest and Money*
96, 100–1, 579, 582–7 *passim*; *A
Treatise on Probability* 579; *see also*
Keynesian macroeconomics
Keynes, John Neville 579; *The Scope and
Method of Political Economy* 204, 579
Kingsley, Charles 230–2, 233; *Alton
Locke* 231–2
Knies, Karl 466
Knight, Frank 637
Knox, John, 111–12
Kuhn, Thomas S. 595, 615–17, 618, 619,
620, 629, 662; *The Structure of
Scientific Revolutions* 615–16
Kuznets, Simon 587

Lakatos, Imre ix, 589, 595; MSRP model
of 617–21, 629, 662, 665
Lamarck, Jean Baptiste de 427–9, 496–7,
509, 511, 512–13, 514; *Philosophie
Zoologique* 496
La Mettrie, Julien Offray de 516;
L'Homme machine 495
Laplace, Pierre Simon 111, 291, 516; and
statistics 530, 532
Laski, Harold 521
Laslett, Peter 78
Laudan, Larry 622
Laveleye, Émile de 517
Lavoisier, Antoine Laurent 111
Le Bon, Gustave: *Psychologies des foules*
450, 485–6
LeGendre (merchant) 223
Legendre, Adrien Marie 532
Leibniz, Gottfried Wilhelm 69, 213–18,
219
Lenin, V.I. 374, 387, 458, 656–7; as
charismatic leader 489; and 'econo-
mism' 320, 322; and French positivism
282, 297; and imperialism 340;

writings: *State and Revolution* 372;
What is to be Done? 297, 656–7
Leonardo da Vinci 15, 16–17, 21
le Play, Frédéric 439
Lerner, A.P. 584
Lewes, G.H. 296
Lewontin, R.C. 378, 509
Lichtheim, George 330
Lindberg, David C. 21
Linnaeus, Carolus 514; *Systema Naturae*
526
Lobachevsky, Nikolai Ivanovich 591
Locke, John viii, 76–82, 87, 94, 110,
118–19, 592; as utilitarian 80, 248,
263;
writings: *Essay Concerning Human
Understanding* 77–8, 126; *A Letter
Concerning Toleration* 77, 263; *Two
Treatises of Government* 77–82 *passim*
Louch, A.R. 638–9
Louis XIV, King (of France) 89, 93
Louis XV, King (of France) 89, 94
Lovejoy, Arthur O.: *The Great Chain of
Being* 215, 269, 401
Lucretius 249; *De Rerum Natura/On the
Nature of Things* 22–3, 381–2
Lukàcs, Gyorgy 387
Lumsden, Charles J., and E.O. Wilson:
Genes Mind and Culture 536, 540–2
Luxemburg, Rosa 340, 369
Lyell, Charles 497; *Principles of Geology*
30, 427, 497, 502
Lysenko, Trofim 378, 606, 668

McCloskey, Donald N. 662; *The Rhetoric
of Economics* 611
McCulloch, John Ramsay 226–8;
Discourse on Political Economy 227;
The Principles of Political Economy
226, 227, 507
Mach, Ernst 596
Machlup, Fritz 473
MacKay, A.F. 647
Mackie, J.L. 44
McMurtry, John 329
Maine, Sir Henry 419
Malthus, Daniel 183
Malthus, Thomas Robert 168, 183–4,
239; and unemployment 580, 581;
writings: *Essay on the Principle of
Population* 181–2, 183–9 *passim*, 219,
361, 427; (Darwin and 505–7;

mathematics in 209, 531); *Principles of Political Economy* 186, 209, 506–7
Mandeville, Bernard 137; *Fable of the Bees* 224
Manuel, F.E. and F.P. 158, 165
Marc-Wogau, Konrad 44
Marshall, Alfred 97, 170, 180, 365, 575–6; and biology 533, 556; and eugenics 521; as holist 281, 301; and Keynes *père et fils* 579; and metaphysics 216, 217; and resource allocation 557–8, 562; and utilitarianism 258, 265; writings: *Industry and Trade* 217; *Principles of Economics* 156–7, 170, 548, 551, 562; (geometry in 103, 209; Leibniz and 216, 217)
Martineau, Harriet 190, 240, 296; *Illustrations of Political Economy* 236–8, 245; *Poor Laws and Paupers* 238
Martineau, James: 'The Place of Mind in Nature and Intuition in Man' 516
Marx, Heinrich 307
Marx, Henrietta 307
Marx, Karl 307–10, 372–3; collaboration with Engels 305–6, 308–10, 311, 312, 355; and French positivism 273, 281, 282–3, 291, 297, 301; and 'Marxism' 63; and Physiocrats 95, 96, 97; and utilitarianism 265–6; writings of 313–15; *Capital* 309–10, 314, 339, 360, 384; (on communism 369–72, 376; Engels' role in 305–6, 309–10, 312, 355; interpretations of 339–41; on laws of motion of capitalism 364, 366, 367–8; mathematics in 209–10; on unemployment 361–2; on value 342–50; on surplus value 350–4; on wages 360, 361, 577); *Communist Manifesto* 305, 319, 323, 325, 329, 360, 364, 369; 'A Critique of the Gotha Programme' 324, 369–70, 371; *A Critique of Political Economy* 309, 317–18, 321, 330; *Grundrisse* 309, 314, 339; 'On the Jewish Question' 307; *Paris Manuscripts* 305, 313, 314, 322, 360, 364, 384; (on alienation 330, 332, 333; on capitalism 324, 325; on communism 369, 376; epistemology in 376, 379; on human

nature 328–9); *Theories of Surplus Value* 310; *Value Price and Profit* 361; *see also* Marxian theory
Mayr, Ernst 500; *Towards a New Philosophy of Biology* 642–3, 660
Means, G.C. 487
Medawar, Sir Peter: quoted 342, 629, 667
Meek, Ronald 223
Mencken, H.L. 114
Mendel, Gregor 501–2
Menger, Carl 204, 401–2, 470; *Grundsätze der Volkswirtschaftslehre* 550
Mercier de la Rivière, Pierre-Paul: *L'Ordre naturel et essentiel des sociétés politiques* 91, 223
Merton, Robert K. 615; quoted 273, 454
Michels, Robert 35–6; *Political Parties* 35
Mill, James 170, 180, 189, 255, 580; *Analysis of the Phenomena of the Human Mind* 129; *Essay on Government* 255, 257
Mill, John Stuart ix, 252, 256–7; on classes 96, 193; on Coleridge's economics 268; on consumption 363; on empirical laws 34, 36, 592, 604; and French positivism 293, 296, 300; on history 316–17, 403; on income distribution 205–6, 571, 576; on intellectual freedom 668; and land nationalization 180; and methodological individualism 652, 659; and population 188, 193, 507; on profit 365; on role of the state 561; on science 636; on trade 195; on unemployment 581; and utilitarianism 257, 563, 659; writings: 'On the Definition of Political Economy' 202, 363, 550, 604; *On Liberty* 256–7, 668; *Principles of Political Economy* 168–9, 300, 301, 507, 548; (on distribution 205–6, 576; on value 143–4, 176); *System of Logic* 34, 202–3, 296, 300, 531, 598, 652; *Utilitarianism* 257
Milne-Edwards, Henri 423, 424, 464–5
Milton, John 67
Mini, Piero V. 331
Mirabeau, Victor Riqueti Marquis de 90, 94; *The Friend of Mankind* 90, 182; *Theory of Taxation* 94
Mises, Ludwig von 637, 638, 653; *Human Action* 39–40

Monboddo, Lord, (James Burnett) 113, 116
Montesquieu, Baron de 83–7, 117, 182, 272; *De l'esprit des lois* 83–7, 89, 272
Moore, G.E. 430, 593
More, Sir Thomas 160, 162; *Utopia* 159–60, 162, 163
Morgan, C. Lloyd 429–30
Morgenstern, Oskar, and John von Neuman: *The Theory of Games and Economic Behaviour* 105
Morley, John 296
Muller, H.J. 523
Muntzer, Thomas 159
Murdock, G.P. 414
Murray, John 499
Mussolini, Benito 76, 459, 567
Myrdal, Gunnar: *The Political Element in the Development of Economic Theory* 662

Nagel, Ernest 471, 647; quoted 409, 624, 627;
    writings: *The Structure of Science* 662–4, 666, 667
Napoleon III, Emperor (of France) 277, 293
Nell, E.J., and Martin Hollis: *Rational Economic Man* 39–40
Neumann, John von, and Oskar Morgenstern: *The Theory of Games and Economic Behaviour* 105
Neurath, Otto 304, 595–6, 599, 615, 637; *Empiricism and Sociology* 596
Newcomb, Simon 245; *Principles of Political Economy* 245–6
Newman, John Henry: *Apologia pro Vita Sua* 230–1
Newton, Sir Isaac viii, 19, 27, 150, 629–30, 636; and capitalist ideology 31, 32, 509; and French positivists 280; law of gravitation of 34, 36, 48, 118; and Locke 76; and methodology of science 634; and Scottish Enlightenment 113–14, 132, 133; on simplicity 602; and theology 115; writings: *Mathematical Principles of Natural Philosophy* 69, 114, 115, 591; *Optics* 114, 129, 636
Neyman, Jerzy 664
Nicholas I, Czar (of Russia) 293
Nietzsche, Friedrich Wilhelm 493

Nisbet, Robert A.: quoted 151, 432, 451–2;
    writings: *History of the Idea of Progress* 151, 219, 432; *The Sociological Tradition* 437
Nozick, Robert: *Anarchy, State and Utopia* 58
Numbers, Ronald L. 21

Oakeshott, Michael 395
Ockham, William of 602
Oppenheim, Paul, and Carl Hempel: 'The Logic of Explanation' 598
Owen, Robert 161, 164, 165

Paley, William: *Natural Theology* 515
Pareto, Vilfredo ix, 34–5, 36, 265, 564, 567; *Cours d'économie politique* 34
Parmenides 640
Parsons, Talcott 436, 467, 470, 475, 488, 637; *The Structure of Social Action* 481
Pasteur, Louis 622
Peacock, Thomas Love: *Crotchet Castle* 227
Pearl, Raymond 36–7
Pearson, Karl 520, 525, 528, 532
Perrault, Charles 149
Perry, Arthur Latham 245; *Elements of Political Economy* 245
Philiptschenko, J.A. 520
Pigou, A.C. 565–6, 567, 578; *The Economics of Welfare* 565; *Wealth and Welfare* 565
Plato 59–61, 63, 81; and division of labour 59, 138, 139; French positivists and 59, 294–5; as perfectionist 154, 158, 162, 166, 215, 216; writings: *Laws* 63; *Republic* 59–61, 154, 158, 162, 448, 518; (and dialectic 374; quoted 295)
Plekhanov, G.V. 374
Pol Pot 76, 432
Polybius 59, 63–4
Pompadour, Madame de 90, 94
Pope, Alexander 62, 114, 266; *Essay on Man* 219, 242
Popper, Karl R. 377, 401, 631, 647, 656; and evolutionary epistemology 613–14, 615; and positivism 599–601, 602, 603, 617–18, 626–7, 629, 637; and totalitarianism 658–9; on Weber

471, 637; 'world three' conception of 462–3, 641;
writings: 'Epistemology without a Knowing Subject' 462; *Logik der Forschung* 600, 601; 'On the Theory of the Objective Mind' 462; *The Open Society and its Enemies* 658–9; *The Poverty of Historicism* 400

Porter, G.R.: *Progress of the Nation* 152
Prester John, legend of 159, 160
Priestley, Joseph 130, 619–20
Proudhon, Pierre 221, 370
Pryde, George S.: quoted 112
Ptolemy 23, 69, 382, 629–30; *Almagest* 23

Quesnay, François 89, 90, 94, 546; *Tableau Oeconomique* 90, 91, 92, 95, 96, 97
Quetelet, Adolphe 530–1, 532; *A Treatise on Man* 530
Quine, Willard van Orman 601, 602, 621

Rand, Ayn 165, 222
Rawls, John: *A Theory of Justice* 58, 119, 264
Reed, Lowell J. 36–7
Reid, Adam 113
Ricardo, David 168, 170–1; criticism of 548; and Malthus 184; methodology of 201–2, 208, 209;
writings: *Principles of Political Economy and Taxation* 168, 170–1, 201–2, 362, 547; (on subsistence 188, 189, 506; on trade 194, 195); *see also* classical political economy
Riemann, George Friedrich Bernhard 591
Ritchie, D.G.: *Darwinism and Politics* 516–17
Robbins, Lionel: *Essay on the Nature and Significance of Economic Science* 204, 652–3, 662
Rockefeller, John D. 518, 569–70
Roosevelt, Theodore 521
Rosenberg, Alexander 635, 647, 648, 649; *Microeconomic Laws* 33, 635
Rosenberg, Alfred 528
Rousseau, Jean-Jacques ix, 111, 117, 163–4, 165, 166; *Social Contract* 89
Rudner, Richard: 'The Scientist *qua* Scientist makes Value Judgements' 664
Runciman, W.G.: quoted 468

Ruse, Michael 614
Ruskin, John 268; *The Political Economy of Art* 268
Russell, Bertrand 213–14, 437; quoted 126

Saint-Simon, Henri 55, 273, 275–86, 299; and Comte 276, 277, 288; Durkheim and 440–1; and Plato 59; and work 163;
writings: *Lettres d'un habitant de Genève à ses contemporains* 278; *Mémoire sur la science de l'homme* 280; *Nouveau christianisme* 278; *Travail sur la gravitation universelle* 280
Say, Jean-Baptiste 292–3; *see also* Say's law
Scarisbrick, J.J.: *Henry VIII* 658
Scheffler, Israel: quoted 607, 631
Schenk, H.G.: quoted 266
Schmoller, Gustav 203–4, 266, 491, 661
Schneider, Louis: *The Scottish Moralists* 273
Schopenhauer, Arthur 267, 269–70
Schumpeter, Joseph A. 35, 487–8, 535, 650, 651; *Theory of Economic Development* 487, 488
Schutz, Alfred 649
Sciascia, Leonardo: *Candido* 218
Senior, Nassau W. 189, 202, 228–9
Shaftesbury, 1st Lord 76–7
Shaw, George Bernard 181, 521, 642; *Man and Superman* 516
Shelley, Percy Bysshe: *Prometheus Unbound* 221
Shinn, Terry 275
Sidgwick, Henry 258–64, 567, 659; *The Elements of Politics* 258; *The Methods of Ethics* 258–9; *The Principles of Political Economy* 258, 565; 'The Scope and Method of Economic Science' 204, 229
Simmel, Georg 466, 613, 614; 'On a Relationship between the Theory of Selection and Epistemology' 613
Sismondi, J.C.L. Simonde de: *Nouveaux principes d'économie politique* 299, 507
Skinner, B.F. 53; *Beyond Freedom and Dignity* 165; *Walden Two* 161–2, 164–5

Small, Albion W. 131, 298–9, 300
Smiles, Samuel 509; *Self-Help* 232; *Thrift* 232–3
Smith, Adam viii, 130–47; and Calvinism 482; and classes 96, 116–17, 193, 575; and competition 256–7; and consumption 562; cosmopolitan orientation of 240–1; and division of labour 7–8, 136–9, 448, 449, 464, 546–7, 643–4; epistemology of 131–3, 291; and Hume 131, 178; and *laissez-faire* 93, 146, 220, 225–6, 433, 560–1; and monopoly 179, 564; and Physiocrats 88, 89, 94–5, 130, 131; as precursor of Darwin 507–8; and progress 151–2, 158, 193; as utilitarian 117, 265; and value 95, 139–44, 171, 172, 342, 547, 549; and wages 193, 575, 576; writings: astronomy essay 132, 529, 636; *Theory of Moral Sentiments* 117–18, 130, 131, 134–6, 144, 447, 492; (and 'Adam Smith problem' 133); *Wealth of Nations* 130–1, 201–2, 546–7; (on division of labour 7–8, 136–9, 448, 449, 464; history in 146; on human nature 133–4, 151–2, 158, 511; on 'invisible hand' 144–6, 220, 225; mathematics in 209; on monopoly 179; 'nation' in title of 116–17; and 'political economy' 169; on rent 178; on spontaneous order 119; on trade 196, 560; on value 141, 142–3, 172; on wages 575, 576)
Sober, Elliot: *The Nature of Selection* 538
Soddy, Frederick 631
Sorokin, Pitrim A. 488
Spartacus 335
Spence, Thomas 180
Spencer, Herbert 412–38, 517, 534–5, 540, 651, 661, 667; and Darwin 414, 423, 427, 503, 504, 511; and Durkheim 440, 442; and evolutionary epistemology 613; as Grand Sociologist 273; and Malthus 505; and military-industrial dichotomy 419–20, 431, 435, 447–8, 534, 644; writings of 412–14; *Autobiography* 424, 427; *Descriptive Sociology* 414; 'The Development Hypothesis' 427; *First Principles* 414, 415; *The Man versus the State* 413; *Principles of Biology* 414, 423; *Principles of Ethics*
414, 433; *Principles of Sociology* 414, 416, 418–23 *passim*, 425–6, 431; 'Progress – its Law and Causes' 429–30, 431; *The Proper Sphere of Government* 412, 413; 'Prospectus of a System of Philosophy' 414, 415; 'Reasons for Dissenting from the Philosophy of M. Comte' 415–16, 431–2; 'The Social Organism' 421, 424–5; *Social Statics* 413, 415, 427, 431; *The Study of Sociology* 414, 416–17, 424, 432, 433, 436, 469, 661; 'A Theory of Population' 427
Spengler, Oswald 273
Spinoza, B. 214; *Ethics* 591
Stael, Madame de: *De la littérature considérée dans ses rapports avec les institutions sociales* 271
Stalin, Joseph 76, 270, 322, 387, 513, 606
Stepan, Nancy: *The Idea of Race in Science* 526
Steuart, Sir James 268; *An Inquiry into the Principles of Political Economy* 169, 224
Stewart, Dugald 113
Strauss, Leo 638
Summerlin (fraudulent scientist) 667
Sumner, William Graham 245
Sweezy, Paul M., and Paul A. Baran: *Monopoly Capital* 340, 369
Swift, Jonathan 149

Thierry, Augustin 276, 335
Thomas Aquinas, St *see* Aquinas
Tönnies, Ferdinand 466
Toulmin, Stephen E. 614
Toynbee, Arnold J. 273; *A Study of History* 49, 219, 496
Trollope, Anthony: 'Barsetshire' novels 336; *The Way We Live Now* 336
Trotsky, Leon 322
Tucker, George: *Progress of the United States* 152
Tullock, Gordon: *The Calculus of Consent* (with J.M. Buchanan) 119; *The Politics of Bureaucracy* 475
Turgot, A.R.J. 94, 111, 140, 149, 178
Turner, Jonathan 300
Twain, Mark: quoted 246
Twiss, Benjamin 246

Ureña, E.M. 327

Van Fraassen, Bas C. 604, 628
Van Hise, Charles 521
Veblen, Thorstein ix, 266, 533
Vesalius, Andreas 17–19, 21, 27; *De Humani Corporis Fabrica* 18
Vico, Giambattista 403, 404–5, 469, 636; *New Science* 405
Voltaire 111, 113, 185; *Candide* 89, 218
von Baer, Karl Ernst 416, 423–4, 464

Walker, Amasa 244–5; *Science of Wealth* 245
Wallace, A.R. 180, 427, 499, 505, 507, 512, 537
Wallace, Robert: *Numbers of Mankind* 182–3
Walras, Léon 265, 440, 552; *Eléments d'économie politique pure* 209, 550, 562
Ward, Lester F. 298–9
Wartofsky, Mark W.: quoted 626
Watson, J.D.: *The Double Helix* 399, 662
Watt, James 112–13, 482, 510
Wayland, Francis: *Elements of Political Economy* 243–4
Webb, Beatrice 521
Webb, Sidney 181, 521
Weber, Max 273, 404, 411–12, 465–93, 637–8, 639; on charisma and bureaucracy 484–9, 493; economic theory of 472–5, 479–83; on ideal types 472–5, 646, 647; on methodology of social science 468–75, 478, 479–80, 612, 644, 653; (and fact-value dichotomy 489–93, 661–8 *passim*); on sociology 476–8; writings of 467–8; *Gesammelte Aufsätze zur Wissenschaftslehre* 468; (*Theory of Social and Economic*

Organization 472, 477, 478, 485); 'Outlines of Universal Social and Economic History' 483; *The Protestant Ethic and the Spirit of Capitalism* 466, 468, 472, 479–83; *Wirtschaft und Gesellschaft* 467, 472, 483
Weismann, August 428, 429, 513
Weitling, Wilhelm 370
Wells, David A. 246
Wells, H.G. 521
Whewell, William 203, 592, 636
Whitehead, Alfred North viii
Wicksteed, Philip Henry 265, 572; *Essay on the Co-ordination of the Laws of Distribution* 572
Wilde, Oscar 457
William of Ockham 602
William of Orange 77
Wilson, Edward O. 304, 388, 536, 537, 541, 545; *Genes, Mind and Culture* (with C.J. Lumsden) 536, 540–2; *On Human Nature* 536; *Sociobiology: The New Synthesis* 513, 536, 537, 540
Wilson, James 240, 424, 560
Winch, Peter: *The Idea of a Social Science* 33, 638–9
Windelband, Wilhelm 409
Wittgenstein, Ludwig: *Tractatus Logico-philosophicus* 593–4
Wrong, Dennis 300
Wundt, Wilhelm 450

Xenophon 137, 449

Youmans, Edward L. 416

Zangwill, Israel 218
Zeno 374

Subject index

Writings (books, essays, lectures, etc.) will be found in the name index: they are arranged in alphabetical order at the end of the author's entry.

absolute advantage, principle of 197, 198–9, 200-1
accumulation of capital: in Calvinist doctrine 481, 482; in Marxian theory 362–3, 365, 368–9; *see also* saving(s)
Act of Union of 1707 (Great Britain) 112
action, social *see* social action
administration *see* bureaucracy
advantage, principles of absolute and comparative 195, 197–201
agriculture: in classical political economy 178–9, 186, 192–3; in Physiocratic model 91–4, 223, 546
alienation, concept of 163, 313, 314, 330–4
alternative cost, concept of 180, 552–3, 554, 557
alternativity, Saint-Simonian law of 277
altriciality 13–15, 272, 390; *see also* enculturation
altruism 10–12, 117–18 ; and natural selection 543–4; *see also* social distance
American Association for the Advancement of Science 33
American Economic Association 6, 247, 434, 535, 577
American Eugenics Society 520, 525
American Journal of Sociology 298
American Sociological Society 298
analogical argument 50–1; *see also* ignoratio elenchi
analytic laws 38–43
anarchism 221–2; in United States 247
anatomy, studies of 17–18
Année Sociologique 298, 439

anomie, notion of 453
anthropology 510, 511, 526–7
Anti-Corn Law League (Great Britain) 239, 241, 413
apodictics *see* positivism
Archiv für Sozialwissenschaft und Sozialpolitik 466
artificial selection *see* eugenics
association psychology 128–30, 267
Australian aborigines 9
Austrian school of economists 39–40, 204, 470, 551, 637, 653; *see also* Hayek, F.A.; Menger, Carl; Mises, Ludwig von

behaviour, human *see* human nature
behaviourism 53; *see also* Skinner, B.F.
best possible world, doctrine of 217–18
bimetallism 473–4
biological differentiation 6–9; *see also* evolution; functional specialization; labour, division of; racial differences
biology 494–545; and dialectic 377–8; and division of labour 6–10, 423–4, 463–5; (*see also* organic theory of society); and religion 514; and social policy 517–29; and sociology 417–18, 513–29; *see also* evolution; sociobiology
Biometrika 520
Bloomsbury Group 580
Boer War 570
bomm *see* cycles, economic
Bordeaux University, Durkheim at 439, 440, 441, 447

Bridgewater Treatises 515
British Association for the Advancement
    of Science 531, 636
Brook Farm (United States) 166
bureaucracy 484, 486–7, 488
business cycles see cycles

calculus, differential 216, 265, 552
Calvinism 465–6, 468, 479–83
Cambridge school of economists 551; see
    also Marshall, Alfred
Cambridge University, Keynes at 579, 580
capital: in Calvinist doctrine 481, 482; in
    classical political economy 172–4: in
    Marxian theory 323, 351–3;
    (accumulation 362–3, 365, 368–9;
    concentration 367–8; transformation
    problem 354–8); in neoclassical
    economics 553–4, 574; in Physiocratic
    model 98–9; see also capitalism;
    saving(s)
capitalism 319; and bureaucracy 486–7;
    and Calvinism 479–83; evolution of
    316, 319, 323–6, 364; and innovation
    488, 535; Marxian laws of motion of
    362, 364–9; and market mechanism
    323–4; and rationalism 476, 479–83,
    484, 486–7; and science 31–2,
    509–10; see also market(s)
categorical versus statistical differences
    8–9
causal laws 43–7, 53–4, 127–8; and
    historical explanation 395–400; see
    also covering laws; determinism;
    INUS model; teleology
central economic planning 260, 283,
    371–2, 420, 558–9, 561
certainty see positivism
ceteris paribus, technique of 207–8, 556
chain of being see continuity
charismatic leadership 485–6, 487,
    488–9, 493
checks and balances, theory of 63–4, 85–7
Chicago, University of 298
Chicago school of economics 609; see
    also Friedman, Milton
Christian Socialism 230
circular flow of expenditure 100–3, 107,
    109, 110, 546; in Keynesian
    macroeconomics 96, 100–3, 546,
    585–7; in Physiocratic model 91–4,
    96–7, 110, 546, 585

class(es), economic 96, 335–7; in classical
    political economy 175–6, 192–3, 337;
    in French positivism 282; in Marxian
    theory 96, 319, 324–5, 333, 334–8,
    341, 555, 571; (see also exploitation);
    in neoclassical economics 555, 575–7;
    in Physiocratic model 91–4, 96, 337,
    546; see also income distribution
classical political economy 168–71, 630;
    as 'dismal science' 152–3, 193; and
    economic development 190–4, 365,
    506, 555; education in 234–6; and
    French positivism 299–301; and
    harmony 211; and income
    distribution 205–6, 346, 570, 571,
    572, 573, 576–7; and international
    trade 194–201, 241, 464; and
    laissez-faire 220–1, 225–30;
    methodology of 201–10; nationalistic
    and cosmopolitan orientations of
    240–1; popular renditions of 236–8,
    508; and population 181–90, 192,
    229, 360; (and Darwinian evolution
    505, 506–9); and progress 153; and
    rent 97, 176–81, 554; and socialism
    175–6, 180–1; and unemployment
    362, 580–1; in United States 204,
    240–7, 266; and utilitarianism 170–1,
    265, 557; and value 141–2, 171–6,
    342–3, 344, 508–9, 549–50, 552; see
    also Malthus, Thomas Robert; Mill,
    John Stuart; Ricardo, David
'co-evolution' 540–2
cognitive instrumentalism 624–34, 639,
    659, 662; and mental states 647–9
Cold Spring Harbor, Eugenics Record
    Office at 520
communism 282, 314, 319; economic
    organization of 324, 369–72;
    epistemology and 658–9; see also
    central economic planning; Marxian
    theory; socialism; Soviet Union
comparative advantage, principle of 195,
    197–201
competition: economic see market(s);
    political and intellectual 256–7
concentration of capital: in Marxian
    theory 367–8; see also monopoly
conscience collective (Durkheim's)
    280–1, 449–52, 459–60, 461, 480,
    517, 644
consciousness see mental states

conspiracy theory of social phenomena 29
consumption: and availability of
   information 566; in circular flow
   model 101–2; in classical political
   economy 549–50, 562; in Marxian
   theory 363; in neoclassical economics
   550–1, 557–9, 562–4, 577–8
continuity of nature, concept of 215–16,
   219; and Darwinian evolution 502–3
contract theory see social contract
contradiction, law of 38
conventionalism 610, 662
corn laws (Great Britain), campaign for
   repeal of 179, 194, 199, 227, 238–40,
   560, 575
Cornhill Magazine 268
corporatism (syndicalism) 458–61
cost(s): alternative 180, 552–3, 554, 557;
   external 565–6; marginal 178, 557–8,
   562–3, 564; see also value
covering laws 46–7, 391–400, 416, 594,
   604, 629, 649–50
crime and punishment 251, 253, 453, 454
Crimean War 232
crowd psychology 485–6
culture: evolution of 219, 512–13, 537,
   539–42; see also enculturation;
   history, stages theory of
'culturgens' 541–2
cycles, economic 102, 362, 368–9, 583

Daily News (London) 312
Darwinism see Darwin, Charles; Social
   Darwinism; and also under evolution
deconstructionism 649
deductive-nomological model 598–9, 603
deism 27, 115–16, 514–17
demand see supply and demand
democracy 62–3, 64, 458; and hierachies
   35; pluralist, theory of 72, 86; and
   utilitarianism 253, 254–7, 263
demography see population
depression see cycles, economic
descriptivists versus prescriptivists 475
determinism: of Calvinism 480–1, 482;
   and historical methodology 395, 400;
   of Leibniz 214; of Marxian theory
   320–2, 382–3, 385–7; of Saint-Simon
   282
deviation 14–15, 31
Dial 245
dialectic 373, 374–80

diminishing returns, law of 41–3, 110,
   171, 177–9, 553–4; and agriculture
   178–9, 186, 192–3; and falling rate of
   profit 192–3, 365; and population
   186, 506
diminishing utility, law of 550–2, 577–8,
   647
distance, social see social distance
distribution see income distribution
division of labour see labour, division of
Dreyfus affair (France) 441, 456
dualism see mind-body problem
Duhem-Quine thesis 601

East India Company 180, 184
École de Médecine (France) 280
École Normale Supérieure (France) 438
École Polytechnique (France) 274–5,
   530; Comte and 286, 287, 296;
   Saint-Simon and 276, 277, 280
École des Ponts et Chaussées (France)
   274
econometrics 587, 665
Economic Journal 580
economics 88, 169–70; and charismatic
   power 487–8; and classification of
   societies 420; and division of labour
   463–5; and methodological
   individualism 72, 207, 300–1, 378–9,
   588, 651–3, 655; and natural selection
   508–9, 518, 535; and predictive
   instrumentalism 609–10; scientific
   status of 636–7; and sociology 281,
   291, 299–301; and spontaneous order
   119; see also individual models,
   schools, systems and theories
Economist, The 227, 240, 413, 424, 433,
   560
Edinburgh Review 113, 228
Edinburgh school 621–3, 629, 662
Edinburgh University 112; Hume at 120
Education Act of 1944 (Great Britain)
   522
Eight Hour Movement 575
élan vital 642
Eleatic school 640
emergent properties, doctrine of 47–50,
   422–3, 442–3, 641
empirical laws 34–7
empiricism, logical see logical positivism
Employment Act of 1946 (United
   States) 587

enculturation 13–15, 272, 654–5; and
    emergent properties 50; and
    happiness 254; and history 390–1,
    404–7; and perfection 164; of
    scientists 31–2, 509–10, 606–7,
    615–23, 661; see also *conscience
    collective*; organic theory of society
Encyclopaedia Britannica 113, 226, 227
England: biological science in 412–13;
    class system in 335–7; constitution of
    82–7; *laissez-faire* ideology in 225–40;
    legal system in 249–51; positivism in
    296–300 *passim*, 415, 441, 514;
    romanticism in 266–9; sociology in
    298, 415; utilitarianism in 249–64; *see
    also individual movements and writers*
Epicureanism 151, 249
'epigenetic rules' 541–2
essentialism, Aristotelian 28, 384–5
ethology *see* sociobiology
eugenics 504, 517–26; and nationalism
    517, 528–9; and racism 522, 528; and
    statistics 520, 530, 532
evil, status of 217–18
evolution(ary theory): Darwinian
    499–513; (and altruistic behaviour 543;
    and biologists 513–14; and economics
    508–9, 518, 535; and epistemology
    613–15; and eugenics 504, 517–26; and
    Huxley 432, 498–9, 500, 502, 504; and
    Marxian theory 326–8, 376, 503; and
    nationalism 511, 517, 528–9; and
    racism 511, 527–8; and religion 315,
    454, 498, 500, 515–17; and social
    science 532–4; and Spencer 414, 503,
    504, 511, *see also* Social Darwinism;
    sociobiology); of French positivists 272,
    281, 289–91; of Lamarck 427–9, 496–7,
    509, 511, 512–13, 514; of Spencer 414,
    416, 418–19, 423, 426–35, 437, 484
excluded middle, law of 38
exploitation, Marxian theory of 319, 325,
    341, 346, 349, 350–4, 573–4; degree
    of 347, 353–4; and interest rate
    discounting 260; and transformation
    problem 354–8
exports *see* trade
externalities 565–6

Fabian Society (Great Britain) 181, 457
fact-value dichotomy 135, 383; Hume on
    122–3, 425, 573, 649, 660; Weber on
    489–93
falsificationalism 599–601, 603, 618,
    626–7, 629
fascism: and charismatic leadership 485,
    489; and epistemology 658–9; and
    evolutionary theory 461, 520, 522,
    528; and nationalism 269–70, 528;
    and romanticism 269–70, 476, 528;
    and syndicalism 459, 460, 461
feudalism stage of history 319
fitness *see* natural selection
Fortnightly Review 296, 300
France 111; education system in 274–5,
    439; revolution in 89–90, 274, 275–6,
    288, 290, 316, 335, 459; *see also*
    French positivism; Physiocrats; *and
    also individual movements and writers*
Franco-Prussian War 438, 441
free trade *see* trade
freedom, Marxian concept of 329–30,
    332, 386–7
French positivism 271–304, 411; *see also*
    Comte, Auguste; Saint-Simon, Henri
functional specialization 9–10; and
    economics 88; *see also* labour,
    division of; market(s)

game theory 73–4; prisoners' dilemma
    model 105–6, 108, 109, 110
Geist, Hegelian concept of 321, 322, 383,
    385, 402, 450
genetic transmission *see* evolution
geometry, Euclidian 591, 592, 593, 653
German Democratic Party 466
Germany: economics in 203–4, 266, 466,
    469–70, 475; fascism in 269–70, 459,
    476, 528, 658–9; (charismatic
    leadership and 485, 489; evolutionary
    theory and 461, 520, 522, 528);
    hyper-inflation in 656; romanticism in
    267, 269–70, 469, 471, 476, 528; and
    Versailles Treaty 580; *see also
    individual movements and writers*
Glasgow University 112; Smith at 130, 146
Globe (France) 283
'Glorious Revolution' of 1688 (Great
    Britain) 77, 82, 90
government(s) *see* political systems;
    taxation
Grand Sociology 273, 291, 299, 316, 411
gravitational attraction, Newton's law of
    34, 36, 48, 118

Great Britain *see* England; Scotland
gregariousness 5, 10, 418
Gresham's law 473–4

happiness, utilitarian concept of 251–4,
  259–60; and political system 254–6
Harmony (United States) 161
harmony 161, 211–20, 401; and
  bureaucracy 486; and 'invisible hand'
  144–6
Harvard University: David A. Wells
  essay prize at 246; economics at 487–8
'hedonometry', science of 253–4
Heidelberg University, Weber at 466
hierachy 5–6, 8, 10, 15, 643; of sciences
  291; *see also* bureaucracy; class(es);
  eugenics; political sytems
high-wage economy argument 575–7
historical school of economics 203, 266,
  281, 466, 469–70
historicism 285, 401
history: as art 404–7; Marxian theory of
  315–28, 364, 385–7, 388, 479, 656–7;
  metaphysical 400–4; methodology of
  390–410, 637, 649–50; philosophy of
  400–1; and social laws 190–1, 407–10;
  (covering law model 46–7, 391–400,
  416, 594, 604, 629, 649–50); stages
  concept of 146–7, 279–82 *passim*,
  289–91, 319–20, 325–6, 364, 450
holism, methodological 49, 378, 645, 654,
  656–9; of Comte 292; of Durkheim
  443; and economics 207, 281; of Marx
  49, 281; and political systems 62,
  658–9; and sociology 300–1; and
  value judgements 492; *see also*
  organic theory of society
human nature: in Marxian theory
  328–30; and perfection 164–5;
  Scottish Enlightenment view of
  114–15; 116, 128, 132, 133–4; *see also*
  culture; enculturation; mental states

ideal types, notion of 472–5, 646, 647
idealism, Platonic 27, 28
ideology *versus* theory 99, 108, 120, 190,
  257
ignoratio elenchi 50, 108, 426, 629, 631
immiseration, Marxian law of 366–7
imperialism: and Marxian theory 340, 369
imports *see* trade
income distribution: in classical political

economy 205–6, 346, 570, 571, 572,
  573, 576–7; in Marxian theory
  358–63, 368–9, 370, 571, 572, 573–4;
  in neoclassical economics 559,
  568–79; Pareto's law of 34–5, 36; in
  utilitarian theory 260–4
India, caste system in 7
India Office, Keynes at 579
Indiana (United States), eugenics in 522,
  523
individualism, methodological 49, 72,
  378–9, 644–5, 651–9; and economics
  72, 207, 300–1, 378–9, 588, 651–3,
  655; and phenomenology 612; of
  Spencer 421, 424–5; and value
  judgements 492; of Weber 469–75,
  478, 479–80, 489–93, 644–5
induction, problem of 121, 127, 599,
  603–4, 607–8
industrial organization, study of 564
industrial society *see* militant–industrial
  dichotomy
inflationary expectations 656
innovation: and capitalism 488, 535; and
  deviation 15
Institut de France 274
institutional school of economics 203,
  204, 266, 281
instrumentalism: cognitive 624–34, 639,
  647–9, 659, 662; predictive 608–10,
  626, 630
international trade *see* trade
introspection, concept of 134, 135, 291,
  612, 646; Hobbes and 73, 132, 206–7,
  405
intuition: and phenomenology 612; and
  romanticism 267, 592; and
  utilitarianism 258–9
INUS model of causation 44–5, 47, 128,
  199, 396–7, 597–8, 648
investment *see* saving(s)
'invisible hand', concept of 144–6, 220
isomorphism 107–8, 193
'is-ought' dichotomy *see* fact-value
  dichotomy
Italy, fascism in 76, 459, 567

Japan, Spencer's influence in 435

Keynesian macroeconomics 49, 547,
  579–88, 630; and circular flow model
  96, 100–3, 546, 585–7; and

equilibrium 155, 583–4; and Malthus 184, 581; and profit 193–4, 365; and unemployment 184, 361, 568, 582–7; *see also* Keynes, John Maynard

labour: marginal product of 553–4, 574; in Physiocratic model 92–3; *see also* work
labour, division of 6–7, 8, 9–10; and altruism 10–11; and biological specialization 423–4, 463–5; (*see also* organic theory of society); evils of 138–9; and political organization 59, 61–2; and productivity 198–9, 200–1, 370; *see also* market(s)
Labour Party (Great Britain) 181
labour theory of value *see* value
laissez-faire, ideology of 93, 220–47, 433, 560; and free trade 199, 223–4, 239–40, 413, 560; in United States 240–7, 434–5, 518
Lamarckian evolution 427–9, 496–7, 509, 511, 512–13, 514
land: marginal product of 553–4, 574; nationalization of 180; ownership of 81, 180, 324; in Physiocratic model 92–3; supply of 179–80, 186; *see also* agriculture; ownership; rent
Latin America, positivism in 295
Lausanne University, economics at 564
leader(s), charismatic 485–6, 487, 488–9, 493
Lebensraum 528
Leningrad, eugenics in 520
liberalism, democratic: and utilitarianism 254–7, 263; *see also* democracy
logical positivism 304, 590–608, 612, 625, 632–4, 637, 640
London Positivist Society 297
London University, eugenics at 520
loyalty 15

macroeconomics 169, 546–7; circular flow model in 96–7, 100–3; *see also* Keynesian macroeconomics
Malthusian population theory 181–2, 183–9, 219, 361, 427, 505–7
Manchester school of free traders 239
Manichaeism 217
margin(al): cost 178, 557–8, 562–3, 564; productivity 553–4, 572–7, 581; utility 141, 550–2, 553, 557–8, 562–3,

577–8, 646–7; (and consumers' knowledge 566; and utilitarianism 262, 265)
market(s) 13, 144–6, 256–7; and capitalism 323–4; cyclical behaviour of 102, 362, 368–9, 583; failure 561–8, 582–3; imperfect competition in 156, 339–40, 367; (monopoly and oligopoly 179, 228, 564); model 103–5, 108, 109, 110; and natural selection 508–9, 518; see also *laissez-faire*; price; rent; value
Marxian theory 305–89; of class 96, 319, 324–5, 333, 334–8, 341, 555, 571; of economics 338–72, 384, 555; and evolutionary theory 326–7, 376, 503; of exploitation 319, 325, 341, 346, 349, 350–4, 573–4; (degreee of 347, 353–4; and transformation problem 354–8); of history 315–28, 364, 385–7, 388, 479, 656–7; of income distribution 358–63, 368–9, 571, 572, 573–4; interpretation of 306–7, 312–15, 331, 339; ('Marxists' and 63, 306, 314–15); of philosophy 297, 372–89; and revolution 320, 386, 503, 616; of sociology 273, 291, 301, 325, 328–38; of trade unions 361, 577; and utopianism 282–3; of work 163, 333–4, 366; *see also* Engels, Friedrich; Marx, Karl
materialism and Marxian theory 381–5; and conception of history 317–22, 364, 479; dialectical materialism 282, 374
mathematics: in economics 209–10, 552, 587; in social sciences 303; *see also* statistics
mechanistic world-view 514–17; *see also* deism
Mental Deficiency Act of 1913 (Great Britain) 521–2
mental states 46, 52–4, 633, 644–51; *see also* determinism; holism; individualism; mind-body problem
mercantilism 125, 145, 195–6, 224, 241, 264, 560
methodological holism and individualism *see* holism; individualism
methodology of scientific research programmes (MSRP) model 617–21, 629, 662, 665

Michelson-Morley experiment 600
microeconomics 169–70, 547; *see also*
    market(s); neoclassical economics
militant–industrial dichotomy (Spencer)
    419–20, 431, 447–8, 534, 644; in
    Japan 435
mind-body problem 52–3, 212, 382, 402,
    451–2, 462–3
minimax rule: and utilitarianism 262–4
misery, Marxian law of increasing 366–7
model(s) 100, 106–10, 132–3, 380; *see
    also individual systems and theories*
modus ponens 40–1, 599, 652, 653
modus tollens 40–3, 599–601
monism, social 460–1, 520, 528, 640; *see
    also* positivism
Monist League (Germany) 461, 520, 528
monopoly 179, 228, 564
moral issues *see* value judgements
Moscow Institute of Experimental
    Biology, Eugenics Department at 520
multiculturality 14, 272, 460–1
multisociality 13, 272, 654–5
Munich University, Weber at 483

Napoleonic wars 230, 267
national income accounting 587; in
    Keynesian macroeconomics 585–7
nationalism: and classical political
    economy 240–1; and evolutionary
    theory 511, 517, 528–9; and fascism
    269–70, 528; and free trade 240–1;
    and Marxism 332, 340; and
    romanticism 269–70, 403, 528; and
    socialism 442; and syndicalism 458–61
Natural Religion *see* deism
natural selection, concept of 500–1, 503,
    505–6; and classical political economy
    506–9; and competition 508–9, 518,
    535; and man 511–13; *see also* evolution
naturalism, ethical 388–9
Nazi Party *see* Germany, fascism in
neoclassical economics 547–59, 630;
    development of 169–70, 440; and
    income distribution 559, 568–79; and
    profit 193–4; and role of the state
    548–9, 559, 560–8, 574; (in taxation
    578–9); and unemployment 567–8,
    581–3; and utilitarianism 171, 265,
    557, 560, 563–4
New American Encyclopaedia 309
New Harmony (United States) 161, 165

New York Daily Tribune 309
Neyman-Pearson model 664
nomological propositions 34–47; and
    nomological levels 47–51
Nonconformist 412
non-contradiction, law of 377
normative and positive propositions
    54–6, 208; *see also* value judgements
North American Review 244, 245

occult 21–2, 28, 590, 633–4
occupational roles *see* functional
    specialization; labour, division of
oligarchy, iron law of 35–6
oligopoly 564
organic theory of society 269, 280–2, 291,
    292, 657–8; of Durkheim 280–1, 442,
    443–4, 446–52, 454–5, 457, 459–61;
    of Spencer 421–6, 517
ownership: of land 81, 180, 324; of means
    of production 319, 324–5, 333–4, 351,
    487, 574–5; *see also* capitalism
Oxford University: legal studies at 249;
    political economy at 189, 228, 229;
    positivism at 296, 297; Smith at 130,
    132

Padua, University of 17
paradigm model of Kuhn 615–17, 618,
    619, 620, 629, 662
Pareto criterion 564
Pareto's law 34–5, 36
Paris Commune 438
perfect competition model 156
perfection, social *see* utopianism
phenomenology 612–13
Philadelphia Society for the Promotion
    of National Industry 241
physicalism, doctrine of 596
Physiocrats 88–99; economic model of
    91–4, 96–7, 110, 546–7, 585; (and
    laissez-faire 222–4, 546); Smith and
    88, 89, 94–5, 130, 131; and
    utilitarianism 265–5
Platonism 133, 592
plenitude of existence, concept of
    214–16, 217, 219, 269
pluralist democracy, theory of 72, 86
political economy, concept of 169–70; *see
    also* classical political economy
political systems and philosophies: of
    classical age 59–64; of Durkheim

441–2, 448–9, 456–61; of England
during seventeenth century 68–87; of
French positivists 278–9, 283–4, 285,
292–5; of Keynesian macroeconomics
585–7; of neoclassical economics
548–9, 559, 560–8, 574; of
Physiocrats 92, 93–4, 95, 97–8; of
Scottish Enlightenment 118–19,
123–4; of Spencer 413–14, 431–2,
433–5, 442; of United States 66, 68,
75, 81, 86–7; of utilitarians 254–6,
263; of Venice during the
Renaissance 65–8; of Weber 484–9,
493; *see also* communism; fascism;
socialism; *and also individual
movements and writers*
Poor Law Amendment Act of 1834
(Great Britain) 189–90, 194, 228–9,
238, 522, 575
population 181–90, 192, 194, 229, 360,
505, 506–9
positive and normative propositions
54–6, 208; *see also* value judgements
positivism 271; French 271–304, 411;
logical 304; 590–608, 612, 625, 632–4,
637, 640
predestination 480–1, 482
predictive instrumentalism 608–10, 626,
630
prescriptivists *versus* descriptivists 475
price(s) 643; in classical model 549;
determination of 549, 551; and
income distribution 140, 559; in
market model 103–5; in neoclassical
economics 551, 553–4, 559; and rent
178; transformation problem 356–8;
see also value
prisoners' dilemma model 105–6, 108,
109, 110
probability theory 604; *see also* statistics
productivity: and division of labour
198–9, 200–1, 370; marginal 553–4,
572–7; and profit 366; and trade
198–9, 200; and wage rate 575–6
profit 192–4, 365, 564; falling rate of
364–6; and transformation problem
354–8; *see also* income distribution
progress, concept of 29–31, 148–53,
190–1, 590; and evolution 430–5,
503–4; and history of science 614–15,
619–20; and metaphysics 218–20; and
perfection 155–7, 218

prohibition of alcohol (United States)
566
property *see* ownership
protectionism *see* trade
psychology: association 128–30, 267;
crowd 485–6; and utilitarianism
251–4; and utopianism 164–5; *see
also* alienation; human nature;
mental states
public choice theory 475, 567
punctuated equilibrium 328, 503
punishment, utilitarian concept of 251, 253

quantum mechanics 216, 591
Quarterly Journal of Economics 247

racial differences 5, 7–8, 9, 510–11, 517,
526–7; and racism 511, 522, 527–8
Rassenhygiene 522, 528
rationality, situational 399–400
realization, notion of 368–9
recession *see* cycles, economic
reflexivity 655–6
Reform Act of 1867 (Great Britain) 82,
297, 315
relativity, theory of 591, 600
religion *see* theology
rent, Ricardo's theory of 97, 176–81, 554
resolutive–compositive method of
scientific investigation 72–3
resource allocation 557–9, 562–8
Revenue Commission of 1865 (United
States) 246
revolution(s): in American colonies 335;
and charismatic leaders 485; in
France 89–90, 274, 275–6, 288, 290,
316, 335, 459; in Great Britain 77, 82,
90; in Marxian theory of history 320,
386, 503, 616; in Russia 316, 320,
322, 656
rhetorical analysis 610–11, 662
romanticism 248, 266–70, 285–6, 592,
636–7; and cultural superiority 257,
269–70; and fascism 269–70, 476,
528; and history 403, 405; and Marx
308, 310, 330, 334; and nationalism
269–70, 403, 528; and science 267,
285–6, 469, 471
Royal Economic Society (Great Britain)
579–80
Royal Society (Great Britain) 76, 90;
foundation of 69, 166, 274

Rugby School 296
Russian Revolution 316, 320, 322, 656

Salem witch trials 21–2
saving(s): in circular flow model 102,
   586; in classical political economy
   192; and unemployment 581, 586; *see
   also* accumulation
Say's law 361, 362, 580–2, 585
science(s): hierarchy of 291; and
   non-science 25–7, 631–4; philosophy
   of 589–634; problem orientation of
   629–31; and progress 614–15,
   619–20; social context of 615–23; and
   social sciences 33–4, 51–4, 107–8,
   302–4, 635–44; sociology of 455–6,
   621–3; and utopianism 165–7; *see
   also individual movements and writers*
scientism 285, 303, 637
Scotland: during Age of Enlightenment
   111–20; *see also* Hume, David;
   Smith, Adam
selective breeding *see* eugenics
self-help, doctrine of 232–3, 509
self-interest: of governments 567; and
   happiness 252, 255; and natural
   selection 543–4
Sherman Antitrust Act of 1890 (United
   States) 435
simplicity: in theory choice 602–3
slavery stage of history 319
Sloan-Kettering Institute (New York) 667
social action, Weber's theory of 467,
   477–8
social contract, concept of 57–8, 74–6,
   80–1, 118–19, 123
Social Darwinism 245, 434–5, 504,
   517–18; *see also* eugenics
social distance 118, 122, 134, 135–6,
   259–60
social facts, Durkheim's conception of
   442–6, 448–9
socialism 282–3, 341; and bureaucracy
   487; and classical political economy
   175–6, 180–1; economics of 457–8;
   and nationalism 442; and
   romanticism 403; in United States
   245–6; *see also* central economic
   planning; communism; Marxian
   theory
socialization *see* enculturation
Society for the Diffusion of Useful

Knowledge (Great Britain) 190, 238
sociobiology 304, 388, 513, 536–45, 614,
   650, 659–60
sociology 271–2, 291, 411–12; *see also
   individual movements and writers*
solidarity of society 446–52, 454–5, 457,
   459–61
Sorbonne, Durkheim at 439
Soviet Union: biology in 513, 520, 606,
   614, 668; economic planning in 260,
   372, 561; Marxian theory of value in
   347–8, 349; revolution inaugurating
   316, 320, 322, 656; sociology in 273,
   299; totalitarianism in 658–9
Spain, fascism in 459
spontaneous order, concept of 95–6, 119
state, role of *see* political systems; taxation
stationary state 192–3, 365
statistics 152, 664–6; and biology 8–9,
   520, 529–32; and categorical
   differences 8–9
'strong programme' view of science
   621–3, 629, 662
subjectivist economics 653
subsistence, concept of 188, 192;
   Darwinian evolution and 505–6;
   high-wage economy argument and
   576–7; Malthus' use of 184, 185, 188;
   Marxian theory and 360–1, 366–7
sufficient reason, principle of 214, 217
suicide, Durkheim's theory of 453–4
supply and demand 103–5; and labour
   360; (*see also* unemployment); and
   rent 179–80; and value 140–1, 171
Supreme Court of the United States 246,
   522, 578
surplus value 346, 347, 350–4; and
   capital accumulation 362–3; and
   transformation problem 354–8; and
   wages 359–60; *see also* exploitation;
   income distribution
sympathy, Smith's concept of 133, 135–6,
   144
syndicalism 458–61

taxation 102–3; in classical political
   economy 180–1; in Keynesian
   macroeconomics 586; in neoclassical
   economics 578–9; in Physiocratic
   model 92, 93–4, 97–8
teleology, doctrine of 46, 155, 322, 385,
   388, 395

theology: and capitalism 479–83; Durkheim's analysis of 454–5, 457, 480; and evolutionary theory 454, 498, 500, 514–17; and science 18, 19–21, 25–7, 514–17; (*see also* deism)

theory-laden, observations as 599, 601–2, 604–8, 610, 621, 661

three stages, law of 279–80, 289–91, 450

Times, The 190

totalitarianism: epistemology and 658–9; French positivists' blueprint for 283–4, 293–4; *see also* Hitler, Adolf; Stalin, Joseph

trade, international: in circular flow model 103; and classical political economy 194–201, 241; Hume's view of 124–6; and *laissez-faire* 199, 223–4, 239–40, 241, 413, 560; *see also* mercantilism

trade unions 361, 575, 576, 577

transformation problem 341, 344, 354–8

transivity, law of 38

uncertainty principle 591

underdetermination thesis 602, 621–2

unemployment 579, 580–3; and Keynesian macroeconomics 184, 361, 568, 582–7; in Marxian theory 361–2; and neoclassical economics 567–8, 581–3; and wages 361–2, 581, 582

unions, labour: and income distribution 575, 576, 577; in Marxian theory 361, 577

United States: classical political economy in 204, 240–7, 266; eugenics in 520–1, 522, 523, 525, 528; (*see also* Social Darwinism); income distribution in 569–70; *laissez-faire* ideology in 240–7, 434–5, 518; neo-Lamarckism in 513; political system of 66, 68, 75, 81, 86–7; population growth in 36–7, 183; prohibition of alcohol in 566; Saint-Simon in 275; sociology in 298–9, 416, 437, 661; (modern 273, 291, 300, 411, 488); taxation in 180–1, 578; utopianism in 161, 165, 166; work in 163; *see also individual movements and writers*

universalism, utilitarian principle of 259–61

USSR *see* Soviet Union

utilitarianism 58, 248–66, 659; and classical political economy 170–1, 265, 557; economic theories of 170–1, 253, 264–6; influences on 117, 123, 130, 248–9; and neoclassical economics 171, 265, 557, 560, 563–4; romantics' view of 268, 269

utopianism and social perfection 153–67, 590; and economics 161–2, 206, 222, 569; (see also *laissez-faire*); and eugenics 518; and French positivists 271; and Marxian theory 282–3; and Nazi ideology 528; and progress 155–7, 218; *see also* harmony

value: in classical political economy 141–2, 171–6, 342–3, 344, 508–9, 549–50, 552; determination of 172–4, 347–8, 349–50; in Marxian theory 341, 342–50; (*see also* surplus value); measurement of 142–4, 173–4, 348; in neoclassical economics 551–5; Smith's theory of 95, 139–44, 171, 172, 342, 547, 549

value judgements 29, 52, 54–6, 136, 606, 659–68; *see also* fact-value dichotomy

Venice, fourteenth-century political constitution of 65–8, 82

Verein für Sozialpolitik 491, 661–2

Versailles Conference (1919) 580

Verstehen, concept of 468, 470–3, 475, 480, 489, 637–8, 639; and phenomenology 612

Vienna Circle philosophers 304, 490, 516, 590–7, 637, 640; 'The Scientific Conception of the World' (manifesto) 593, 595

wages: in classical political economy 188, 192–3, 576–7, 581; in Marxian theory 345, 358–63, 366, 571; in neoclassical economics 553–4, 575–7; and unemployment 361–2, 581, 582

welfare economics 191, 557, 565; *see also* market failure

Wertfreiheit 489, 661–8 *passim*

Westminster Review 421, 431

Wisconsin University, eugenists at 521

witchcraft 21–2, 28, 590, 633–4

work: in Calvinist doctrine 481; in Marxian theory 163, 333–4, 366; in utopianist literature 162–3 *see also* labour

'world three', Popper's conception of
462–3, 641

Yale University: 'Human Relations Area
Files' 414